Frederick Jackson Turner

Frederick Jackson Turner in 1910 as president of the American Historical Association. Reprinted with permission of the State Historical Society of Wisconsin, Madison, Wisconsin. (X3) 48588.

Frederick Jackson Turner

Strange
Roads
Going
Down

By
Allan G. Bogue

University of Oklahoma Press : Norman

Also by Allan G. Bogue

Money at Interest: The Farm Mortgage on the Middle Border (Ithaca, 1955)
From Prairie to Corn Belt: Farming on the Illinois and Iowa Prairies in the Nineteenth Century (Chicago, 1963)
The Earnest Men: Republicans of the Civil War Senate (Ithaca, 1981)
Clio and the Bitch Goddess: Quantification in American Political History (Beverly Hills, 1983)
The Congressman's Civil War (New York, 1989)

Bogue, Allan G.
    Frederick Jackson Turner: strange roads going down / by Allan G. Bogue
        p.   cm.
    Includes bibliographical references (p.   ) and index.
    ISBN 0-8061-3039-3 (cloth: alk. paper)
    1. Turner, Frederick Jackson, 1861–1932.   2. Historians—United States—Biography.   3. Frontier and pioneer life—United States—Historiography.   4. United States—Territorial expansion—Historiography.   5. Frontier thesis.   I. Title.
    E175.5.T83B64   1998
    973.91'092—dc21   97–43149
    [B]   CIP

Text is set in Trump Medieval with displays in Avant Garde.
Text design by Alicia Hembekides.

The paper in this book meets the guidelines for permanence and durability of the Committee on Production Guidelines for Book Longevity of the Council on Library Resources, Inc. ∞

1 2 3 4 5 6 7 8 9 10

To the graduate students in my seminars and reading
groups who so conscientiously supervised my
education at the University of Iowa and
the University of Wisconsin during
the years 1952–1991

Contents

Illustrations

Preface

My mentor in doctoral studies was a forthright man, who pursued his research in the history of western economic development with intimidating intensity. By the time I entered his seminar, Paul W. Gates had become the leading historical authority on the history of the public lands, a subject that Frederick Jackson Turner urged fellow historians to study throughout his career. Gates dealt with the controversies raging over Turner's ideas by ignoring them. He cautioned his graduate students against wasting their time and substance by involving themselves in such fruitless activity. Far better, he believed, to identify and develop substantive themes than to chop logic with the Turnerians. By and large I followed Gates's advice. However, an early search for illustrative lecture material on claim club activity in Iowa broadened into a research paper in which I pointed out that close scrutiny of squatters' associations revealed undemocratic patterns of activity that Turner's readers would not have expected. On the other hand, when I immersed myself in the sociological literature bearing upon the development of new communities, I discovered current social theory that seemed to predict the kind of human behavior believed by Turner to have been fostered by the frontier experience. Ambivalent, I left Turner and his friends and critics to simmer for many years; I introduced a topical organization in my course on the history of the American West, rather than continuing the frontier-by-frontier examination preferred by most of Turner's followers.

By the late 1980s academic entrepreneurs had realized that the centennial of Turner's delivery of his famous proclamation on the significance of the frontier was nearing, and several inquired as to whether I would participate in celebration of the event. Over the years I had become intrigued by various puzzling questions about Turner and his ideas, and so, in response to such queries, I planned to prepare a small book of complementary essays on a number of such problems. Completion of another project in 1989 opened the way for full-time concentration on Turner, and, subsequently, Richard W. Etulain suggested that I revise my plans and incorporate my work in a biography of Turner. Despite Gates's admonitions, the invitation was a challenge to someone who has always believed that one measure of the ability of historians is found in the degree of versatility they display.

Historians marked the centennial of Frederick Jackson Turner's essay "The Significance of the Frontier in American History" by scheduling panels on the programs at historical association meetings, organizing symposiums, and presenting independent lectures appropriate to the occasion. These proceedings attracted additional attention because of the controversial emergence of the "new western historians," some of whom utterly scorned Turner. Others conceded Turner's good intentions and perceptive insights but joined the critics in calling for approaches to the history of western America that emphasized subjects disregarded or underemphasized by Turner and his followers, and in urging a more critical analysis of western development that had been offered by their predecessors. Emphasis on the successive unfolding of frontiers of place, economy, and society, they suggested, should be replaced by the study of the members of interacting cultural groups within a west viewed primarily as region. The usual territorial boundaries of preference for this entity usually encloses an American west stretching from beyond the Missouri to the Pacific coast—a predilection emphasized by the decision of the Western History Association to hold its annual meeting of 1993 not, as invited, in Madison, Wisconsin, close by Turner's early academic haunts, but rather in the redevelopment wasteland of downtown Tulsa, Oklahoma.

Whether in the outpouring of reflections upon Turner in 1993 participants considered themselves to be new western historians or just western historians, few of them found it necessary to study intensively Turner's intellectual and professional development. A very small number of the speakers in the centennial proceedings had rigorously used the massive collection of Turner materials in the Henry E. Huntington Library. Insofar as they cited Turner's writings, few showed evidence that they had read all of Turner's published works or tried to trace his development as a historian and thinker. The standard formula—and it yielded some very provocative and useful work—identified Turner's position on a particular topic, sketched its inadequacies, and prescribed a research agenda designed to remedy omissions or shortcomings in Turnerian history. Others played the niche game, showing where Turner fitted in American intellectual development or his role in propagating some aspect of American myth.

These are valid intellectual exercises—much more useful certainly than an uncritical singing of praises.

In this book I try to return to Turner at first hand, or as near to that perspective as his papers and writings will allow. I try to recapture the individual who emerged from a midwestern county-seat town to become one of America's leading historians—with Francis Parkman one of its two most outstanding, according to the Council of the American Historical Association during the late 1940s. Turner's success rested upon his articulation of several major ideas that explained, he believed, a great deal about the institutions and national character of the United States. His was to be one of the most widely accepted explanations of American development. How he came to his understanding of the historical processes he emphasized is a story that intrigued a good many later scholars. But his ideas and their impact represent only part of his contribution. During the first twenty years of his career he built a leading department of history, and to the year of his retirement in 1924 he inspired legions of followers in both the classroom and the research library. Turner's graduate seminar—he referred to it as a "seminary"—became in his words a "workshop" where innovative methods of historical analysis were developed. Graduates of the seminar and other followers worked to fulfill the agenda of research that he outlined for the profession and to defend the validity of his interpretations of American history. To understand Turner is, obviously, to understand a good deal more as well.

There are other reasons for studying Turner and his career. To study Turner's career is also to study fundamental developments in American higher education. He rose to eminence in a period when higher education was changing significantly as college and university enrollments grew rapidly, faculties were enlarged, and graduate education became an important part of the university obligation. Now scholars could specialize in their teaching as never before in America; disciplinary focus was refined and lines drawn by placing academic disciplines in separate departments.

Within this changing environment history teaching became increasingly professionalized. The essence of being a professional involved mastery of a body of knowledge, commitment to its usefulness, command of learned skills related to it, adherence to general standards of practice in furthering that knowledge and imparting it to others, and construction of institutions designed to further these objectives. For professional historians the body of knowledge was humankind's history. The training of practitioners was to be completed in graduate school; the methods were to be scientific and to be imparted above all in seminars, modeled on what was believed to be German example. Organized in 1884 to further the study of history, the American Historical Association served as a professional forum for the discipline, and its members sought ways in which to foster communication, facilitate historical studies, and, more informally, to set standards of quality and professional behavior. To deliver papers at the organization's annual meeting or to serve on its governing council or its various committees became marks of distinction. Seminar directors enthusiastically developed cadres of neophytes — graduate students — and leading programs developed bulletin series in which their work was published Turner's career as a historian began in the yeasty early days of professional academic history, and to trace his life course is to enhance our understanding of that era as well.

The relation of academic scholars to the broader intellectual and cultural currents of their time is also a subject of interest. Although efforts to define progressive thought, motivation, and achievement have produced much disagreement, most agree that certain attitudes and values were common among the intellectuals of the late nineteenth and early twentieth centuries, although there was much diversity as well. Turner's values and behavior tell us something of these matters, in addition to helping us in our efforts to understand his developing career.

Turner's contemporaries in the historical profession considered him to be a great success, and Americans have always been intrigued by stories of success. How, we wonder, was it achieved? In Turner's case the interest of such inquiry is enhanced by the fact that there are unsolved mysteries in his career. Where did his ideas come from? How, precisely, were those special techniques that have been attributed to him developed? Why did he leave the University of Wisconsin? Did he come to regret that decision? What was his role in producing and subduing the uprising in the American Historical Association of 1914 and 1915? What was there about his teaching that so enthused the doctoral candidates who worked under his direction? Why did he fail to complete that great work of substantive research upon which he reputedly labored for more than half of his career? Why did his writings continue to serve as the fuel of controversy among American historians for generations after his death, in contrast to the forgotten contributions of many of his leading contemporaries? In some cases my answers differ from those of predecessors or provide what I hope is useful elaboration.

As we all know, there has been a great accumulation of writing about Frederick Jackson Turner. Several scholars have provided us with biographies. But most of the biographical work was completed before the mid-1970s, and perspectives change. Yet I owe a great debt to predecessors, particularly to Ray A. Billington and Wilbur R. Jacobs, who were the first to study the collection of Turner manuscripts in the Henry E. Huntington Library after it was opened to scholars in general in 1960. The two scholars worked to expand its dimensions still further and made scholarly access still easier by publishing particularly useful correspondence and hitherto unpublished selections from Turner's writings. I never knew Ray A. Billington well, and when our paths crossed, my research interests were fixed on very different issues than were his. But in the years I have been working on this study, I have come to know Wil Jacobs and have immensely enjoyed my relations with him. I regret that our friendship could not have begun earlier in our careers.

Over the years I have reread Billington's fine biography of Turner several times as well as various articles that he published during the course of preparation; the same is true of Jacobs's careful research. These men have influenced me, but my reading of Turner deviates from theirs in various respects. Billington explained that initial work in the Turner Papers at the Huntington Library made him "Turner's slave." Only an impervious curmudgeon could completely resist the personal charm, enthusiasm, intuition, and knowledge that Turner's correspondence reveals. But I found salutary Jacobs's tendency to question the Turner contribution in some respects, and I have extended that critical analysis. I place more emphasis upon the gritty mechanics of ambition and profession than have others.

My training and research background has led me to interpret some of Turner's contributions differently than have other authors. Revisionist criticisms of the Turnerian heritage since the 1960s have also caused me to assess various parts of it differently as well. In this respect I value Turner's studies of sectionalism more highly than do his major biographer or many who have chosen to write about Turner's contributions. The biographer has an obligation, I believe, to allow his subject his best shot. If part of that individual's impact reflects unique characteristics of personality, we should allow these elements full play. For this reason and also because much evaluation of Turner rests upon interpretation of his ideas, I have tried to let Turner speak for himself as much as I possibly could. In terms of Turner's ideas, the technique may sometimes seem repetitious, but it also brings out both the recurrent themes and the fine-tuning that characterized his work.

A word of explanation is in order concerning my use of Turner family names. Within the family circle Turner was Fred, as he was also to professional associates and in the signatures affixed to his early letters. He signed much of his professional correspondence, Frederick J., reserving Frederick Jackson Turner for Turner the author. I have sometimes used Fred when the context suggested some social intimacy but restricted myself to Turner in his professional persona. To Turner, his wife Caroline was Mae and daughter Dorothy was Peggy. I have normally used the less familiar Caroline, or Caroline Mae, and Dorothy in reference to these family members. In the correspondence of the Turner family, Alice Perkins Hooper usually appears as Mrs. Hooper; here, I call her simply Hooper, just as I call Turner's other professional intimates by their last names only.

The subtitle of this book points to the links in sentiment and attitude between an American historian of national expansion and a poet of empire. Years after his death, Dorothy recalled evenings when her father read poetry to the family, showing particular fondness for the verses of Rudyard Kipling. Turner believed that Kipling caught the spirit of the frontiersman or pioneer in his poems "The Explorer," "The Voortrekker," and "The Song of the Dead." He particularly loved the line from the last of these that runs, "We yearned beyond the skyline, where the strange roads go down." Dorothy believed that such a restless, exploring spirit typified her father's intellect.

During the preparation of this study I benefited from the advice or assistance of many individuals and institutions. It is impossible to mention all who helped me, but some I must acknowledge. I was the recipient of two fellowships at the Henry E. Huntington Library, and during my residence there, while on fellowship and during other extended visits, I became indebted to the librarians beyond all hope of adequate thanks. Martin Ridge was particularly supportive, and Robert C. Ritchie, Peter Blodgett, and Virginia Renner and her colleagues of the reader's services department met my every need and more. The staff members of the State Historical Society of Wisconsin continued to demonstrate that they ably serve one of the great research libraries of the country. Frank Cook, Bernard Schermetzler, and Cathy Jacob were always helpful. The staff of the Libby Collection at the University of North Dakota was very accomodating.

I must particularly thank various descendants of Frederick Jackson Turner. Despite well-founded skepticism about those who write about Turner, Jackson Turner Main was kindly supportive and provided me with a copy of "The Book That Turner Never Wrote," the one paper he has written about his grandfather. Turner's granddaughter, Lois Main Templeton, graciously loaned me a small collection of family correspondence that her mother had retained in family possession. Of the next generations, John Templeton, his son William, and their Labrador Allegra, interrupted a perfect Saturday morning in August 1996 to show us through the Moorings and help my wife Margaret and me to sense the magic that Turner found in the family's Maine retreat.

Wilbur R. Jacobs was unfailingly hospitable and knowledgeable when I visited San Marino. At a late stage in my research and writing, Wil kindly loaned me the notes that he had earlier made on Turner and his career. Although we had covered much common ground, these notes helped me to fill in chinks in my own record as well as to reconsider the emphases in parts of my narrative. My work benefited as well from my conversations with other members of the Huntington Library circle, notably, Gordon Bakken, Hal Seth Baron, Paul Zall, John Hardacre, Michael Steiner, and David M. Wrobel. Old friends Joel Silbey and Rodney O. Davis conducted searches for me in the libraries of their institutions. Neil Basen kindly gave me a number of nuggets that he uncovered in the course of his research. At Cornell University, Joshua D. Rothman supervised further copying of materials for me from the George Lincoln Burr Papers. Anne Barnes and Brian Cannon rendered inspired service to the Turner cause during the early stages of the research, and Carol Blanton performed secretarial duties impeccably prior to my retirement from the teaching faculty at the University of Wisconsin, Madison.

During the centennial year of the Turner hypothesis or shortly thereafter, I presented papers on aspects of the Turner theme before the research conference entitled "A New Significance: Re-Envisioning the History of the American West," at Logan, Utah, and at the annual meetings of the Organization of American Historians, the Western History Association, and the State Historical Society of Wisconsin. I also spoke at meetings of the Syracuse University Graduate Workshop and the Huntington Library brown baggers. I am grateful to the organizers of those presentations and to the members of the audiences

whose questions and suggestions extended my understanding of
Turner and his times. Two of these papers have appeared in print: "The
Significance of the History of the American West: Postscripts and
Prospects," *Western Historical Quarterly* 24 (February 1993), pp.
45–68, and "Frederick Jackson Turner Reconsidered," *American
Teacher* 27 (February 1994), pp. 195–221. I have not reproduced these
papers in this book, but I have included a number of revised passages
from them.

Richard W. Etulain's continuing encouragement and advice and his
editorial reading of a draft of the final product were invaluable. To him
I owe a special debt. Pamela Riney-Kehrberg read the same draft under
admonition that she look especially for instances of generational or
gender bias on the part of the author. I benefited greatly from her
comments. Paul Glad and Earl Pomeroy provided helpful further
readings and contributed in generous measure to any stylistic merit
that this work has. An indirect but major obligation is acknowledged
in the book's dedication. Although he might not today approve of a
work such as this, it was Lee Benson who first alerted me to some of
the interpretive challenges inherent in Turner's career and who was a
constant source of stimulation to me during years when we sought to
"reform" the profession. As always during the last half century,
Margaret Beattie Bogue contributed much appreciated counsel, and not
least, patience. I am grateful. Also, as ever, the errors or weaknesses
in the work are my responsibility alone.

Frederick Jackson Turner

1   Beginnings

"If I supposed you were going to learn to be a loafer"

In early 1862, Mary Olivia Turner described her son Fred, now almost three months old, as having a "good nice-shaped *head*, round face and blue eyes bright as 'sixpences.'" He could, she added, already "shake the rattle box considerable."[1] She was writing to her sister from Portage, Wisconsin, a little county seat located where the historic route of the fur trade from Green Bay on Lake Michigan had left the watershed of the Fox River and joined the downward flow of the Wisconsin to the Mississippi. Fred's father, Andrew Jackson Turner, spent his boyhood on the family farm near Schuyler Falls, New York, where the Turners had been part of the westward-moving tide of Yankee emigration. "With a capital of just ten cents" and a printer's skills, Jack Turner arrived in frontier Portage in 1855 and found employment as a compositor in the office of the *Portage Independent*, whose eccentric proprietor, Julius C. "Shanghai" Chandler, became the editorial voice of the emerging Republican party in Columbia County during the following year.[2]

Young Turner was twenty-two when he reached Portage, and during the next few years he worked for a number of newspapers, including the *Wisconsin State Journal* in Madison. Chandler moved from Columbia County to establish a paper at Friendship in adjacent Adams County where Turner joined him during parts of the years 1857–59. At a social gathering one evening in Friendship, Turner met the daughter of another Yankee family, the Hanfords, and, so he reported, announced to friends on the spot that she was to be his wife. Five years Turner's junior, oval of face, regular of feature, her hair a rich auburn in color, sufficiently educated to be the local school teacher, Mary Hanford eventually gave her consent. In 1860 the young couple established themselves in Portage, where Andrew Jackson Turner had once more entered the newspaper business.[3] There he became the leading voice in the management of the *Wisconsin State Register*.

Unfortunately, no rich store of Turner family correspondence reveals the family life of Mary and Andrew Jackson Turner during the 1860s and 1870s. The federal census taker of 1870 recorded a household of six members. Fred J. and his younger brother, Rockwell L. (Will), were reported as being eight and five years of age, respectively. Anna E. Turner, Andrew Jackson's younger sister, a store clerk, and eighteen-year-old Mary Bochm, a domestic of German parentage, completed the family circle. Ten years later the family also included a young daughter, Ellen Breese Turner. Now the domestic was Helen Edson, a Norwegian girl.[4]

The Turners lived in the fifth ward of Portage, but Andrew Jackson did not buy or build a house until his later years. Despite their energetic efforts, local historians have failed to agree upon the house or lot where young Fred lived during his years in Portage. This circumstance highlights the problems of the historian who wishes to study Turner's boyhood and to understand the shaping of a young intellect. We can learn about the institutions of Portage and the public concerns of its citizens from the records of city, county, and state, the columns of local newspapers, and the pages of several histories of Columbia County. We can sense the perspective of members of the Turner family as they viewed developing Portage during the 1860s and 1870s, because the head of the household was also the major editor of the city's surviving newspaper and was an active promoter of city development. He was particularly interested in the construction of railroads designed to enhance the economy of the city at the portage. At scattered intervals members of the family enter the surviving public record, but only a few family letters survive from young Fred's precollege years. Although he later accumulated some notes on family genealogy and history and included a few passages of reminiscence about his childhood and youth at the portage in speeches or in letters to friends and to his earliest biographers, the record of Fred Turner's early life is fragmentary.[5]

Fred Turner's family and its fellow residents in Portage lived where Euro-American passage and occupation had occurred well before the beginnings of settlement in most other areas of the young state. Proceeding westward from Lake Michigan, the traveler finds a parting of the surface waters about one third of the way across Wisconsin. Here, a divide, which separates streams destined for the Great Lakes from those flowing toward the Mississippi River, is traced from Wisconsin's northern highlands, southward through the central plains of the state, and thence to the southern border. Of the various rivers draining these watersheds, two particularly combined to provide navigable waters to the migrant or traveler seeking an east-west passage. Draining into Green Bay, the Fox River angles gently inland from that point and extends its lethargic and swampy upper course well into southern Wisconsin, arcing at one point within a mile or so of the Wisconsin River, as that stream, on a southerly course from its origin in Lac Vieux Desert on the state's northern border, fishhooks around to run westerly toward its destination in the Mississippi River. Where the north-bound waters of the Fox and the southward flow of the Wisconsin so nearly mingle, unknown generations of Indians portaged their canoes. Across this little strip of marshy ground, French fur traders, priests, and soldiers passed during the seventeenth century, probing the promise of the North American interior. At the portage, fur traders of French origin established themselves to exploit both the trade and the opportunity to charge for cartage across the portage. While the French contested the stakes of empire with other European invaders, the route from Green Bay to the Mississippi acquired strategic importance, as well understood by the Indians before them, and as acknowledged later by the English and the Americans.

French beginnings at the portage were engulfed in the expansive surge of the raw young American nation. By a long process of attrition and elimination among midwestern tribespeople, the Winnebago had become the primary native residents of the area, although the Menominees' claim to much of the region was also recognized by the United States government. Following a minor uprising of the Winnebago, a young West Point graduate, Lt. Jefferson Davis, directed the erection of Fort Winnebago at the Portage in 1828, one in a series of western fortifications marking what some for a time believed might be a permanent American Indian frontier. A few years later the United States located an Indian agency adjacent to the post. By the late 1830s American pioneers were establishing themselves near the portage. During the 1840s and 1850s a tide of settlement washed into the area as the federal government retired the Indian titles, its surveyors marked out the section lines, and its land office registers and receivers offered the lands for sale.

Several little clusters of industry, trade, and habitation developed in the area near Fort Winnebago. One lay close by the fort, another on the flats adjacent to the portage, and still another on the southward slope of land immediately to the north. From these beginnings the little city of Portage emerged during the mid-1850s, thriving on the needs and produce of its agricultural hinterland and the commerce generated by the pineries lying to the north. The lumbermen recruited workers in

Portage, purchased supplies for their camps there, and produced logs, which raftsmen floated down the Wisconsin during the late spring and early summer. The raftsmen often stopped to visit the taverns of Portage before continuing downriver to the mill towns of the Mississippi River. The years 1855 and 1856 brought boom times and heady expectation to the western country, and Portage residents shared fully in the exhilaration. In the first of these years Andrew Jackson Turner arrived at the portage. The young man was short, full-chested, and energetic, a "good talker" who loved a funny story or a droll turn of phrase. He was enthusiastic in his love of politics and shrewd in recognizing the personal opportunities that they offered. He was also an enthusiastic fisherman, hunter, and, ultimately, curler.

Throughout the Midwest and onward to the Pacific during the nineteenth century, hopeful town builders assessed the countryside in the early days of its American occupation, looking for those locations where combinations of geographical features seemed to promise that a new metropolis might rise under their wise and profitable guidance. Within this perspective the location at the portage seemed to promise much. It was well but not too far north of the state's potential and ultimate southern boundaries and centrally positioned between Lake Michigan and the Mississippi River. It lay on an east-west water route that could, residents hoped, be so improved by a simple canal at the portage and improvement of the channels of the Wisconsin and the Fox rivers that it would turn into a mighty artery of trade. In such a setting, thought some early dreamers, it was not too much to envision the glistening dome of a state capitol building. That was expecting too much; Portage became the county seat of prosperous, rural Columbia County.

The dream that Portage would sit astride a great artery of waterborne commerce did not materialize either. In early days shallow-draft steamers reached Portage from both directions. In 1856 the captain of one tiny craft capitalized on a year of high water in the West and audaciously piloted his craft from Pittsburgh westward in a circumnavigation via the Ohio, Mississippi, Wisconsin, and Fox rivers that carried it to Green Bay. A succession of agencies—private enterprise, the state of Wisconsin, utilizing income from a federal land grant, and ultimately the United States government—sought to construct a viable canal at the portage and improve the channels of the Wisconsin and Fox rivers to allow the passage of vessels of substantial draft. The fluctuating flow, migrating sandbars, intractable channels, and rocky constrictions of the lower Wisconsin, as well as the silty swamps along the Fox, frustrated proponents of the waterway for more than a generation. When the U.S. Army Engineers declared victory of a sort in the mid-1870s, the railroads had long since proved their superiority as long-distance carriers in central Wisconsin.[6] Portage residents first heard the whistle of the steam locomotive echoing in the Wisconsin valley in the mid-1850s. First to be completed were the city's east-west connections. At the beginning of the decade of the 1870s a railroad displaced the horse-drawn stages running to and from Madison, and in 1876 the town fathers rejoiced when they rode an inaugural special north through the remaining pineries to Lake Superior.

As elsewhere in the West, the depression of 1857 dampened economic development in Portage. Local historians portray a period of boom to that time and one of more sober but impressive development once the depression lifted. The emerging Chicago, Milwaukee, and St. Paul Railroad used Portage as a division point, and engineers, firemen, shop machinists, and depot workers were an important element in the population. Portage never became a great sawmilling center in the style of some Mississippi River and lake-front towns and cities, but millers thrived on the local demand for building materials, as did the proprietors of a planing mill. Local white clay provided a cream-colored brick of high quality, and several brick yards developed. There was a successful marble yard in Portage, and a grist and flour mill ran at full capacity from an early date. Several breweries prospered, and a foundry flourished for a time.

Stores handling staple foods, hardware, and dry goods thrived on local custom and on the traffic of passing businessmen and lumbermen. Hotel and tavern keepers were found in greater numbers—it was said—than in most midwestern county seats, benefiting from the transient's patronage as well as from local customers. The town had the usual complement of professionals—bankers, lawyers, teachers, doctors, dentists, and ministers. Milliners found their services in demand. Youthful Portage had its complement too of artisans and craftsmen—blacksmiths, carpenters, shoemakers, for example, and relatively large numbers, described by the federal census taker merely as laborers, who worked on the various canal projects, on the railroad, and in local construction. To its local historian of 1880 Portage had become and "remained the entrepôt of Central Wisconsin."[7]

Within this fabric of industry, trade, and occupation the newspaper editor and his family prospered, although the city's growth slowed perceptibly during the 1870s. Numbering 2,870 in 1860, the population of Portage stood at almost 4,000 in 1870 and 4,346 ten years later. The social environment was by no means homogeneous. To differences of class we must add differences in nationality and culture. Thirty-eight percent of the population of Portage in 1870 was foreign-born. Many of these residents were from the British Isles and British North America, but there were significant numbers from the German states as well. Since the census taker recorded children of the foreign-born as native-born, the Portage of the 1870s was a more potent cultural mixture than enumeration data might suggest. In 1870 the city marshall was born in New York state, a policeman in Prussia, and an aged constable in Scotland. The county sheriff was of Norwegian birth and his deputy Prussian. In jocular reaction to his German neighbors and friends, Andrew Jackson Turner called young Fred "Fritz" well into his college years, and Fritz heard at first hand in his home the accented speech of young German and Norwegian domestic helpers. The German element brought a commitment to music, to gymnastics, and to beer drinking that gave a distinctive cast to the local culture of Portage.

Fred Turner's adult memory reached back to the return of Civil War soldiers to Portage. But he left little record of his impressions and activities of the years intervening between those days and his days as an undergraduate student at the University of Wisconsin. Portage had its days of contested claims and claim jumping, the city won the county seat by firm rebuff of other aspirants, and there was intense rivalry among the hamlets adjacent to Fort Winnebago and the portage as to which should be the center of community growth. The rivalry was sufficiently bitter that the hillside cluster dominated by Yankee stock was dubbed "Gougeville."[8] If too young to experience or comprehend such developments, Turner knew of them through the recollections of his elders.

Many years later Turner recalled a few impressions of Portage during his boyhood for friends or prospective biographers. He remembered Indian ponies and dogs on the streets, their owners come to town to trade peltries for trinkets and paints and doubtless more substantial items as well. In the morning and evening he saw German women driving their cows to and from pasture on the city outskirts. He heard the shouts and laughter of red-shirted and pugnacious Irish raftsmen who had secured their rafts of pine logs at the river's edge before striding up to the taverns of the First Ward. Returning from school at the age of seven, he saw the body of a man left hanging in a tree by a lynch mob. Sometimes he and young friends crossed the marshy region to the east and played around the moldering remains of Fort Winnebago.

On the streets of Portage and in its stores and other places of business young Fritz mingled not only with the Yankees, Germans, and Irish residents but with Scots, English, Swiss, Norwegians, and a few Italians and southern Americans. The single black family drew the youngster's interest because its name was Turner. An Irish "keener" voiced his high plaint at the death of countrymen. There were in Portage men of university training among both the natives and the immigrants, and others who could not spell their names. In the Fifth Ward, where the Turners lived in 1870, the combined values of the personal and real estate of householders ranged from forty thousand dollars to zero. In school Turner mingled with children of the varied nationalities and levels of wealth. In retrospect, he reported, they got along together rather well. He also admitted, however, that he and friends stoned "Pomeranian" youths and were repaid in kind; they only ventured into the Irish district of Portage in strong company.[9]

Turner was perhaps too young to have watched the "extensive conflagration" on downtown Cook Street in 1866 when the women of the city formed a bucket chain and passed water from the canal to save Mrs. Wightman's millinery store, a "favorite temple of fashion," but there were a good many opportunities for youthful firewatchers thereafter.[10] Nearby Baraboo prided itself on being a center of the circus industry, and traveling shows delighted Portage as well. The local Schulze family band had played for royalty in its native Saxony and in Wisconsin enjoyed a reputation far beyond the boundaries of Columbia County. They were featured in Portage's centennial celebration of 1876. Touring theatrical troops, vocalists, and other performing artists included Portage in their tours. Nor was Portage devoid of local literary aspirations. Space is devoted in the county history of 1880 to the works of several local poets.

Young Turner would have been very conscious of the booming spirit that suffused the thought of the Portage elders and midwestern town builders in general. Local editors were expected to nurture and express the philosophy of development. We do not know whether Fred accompanied the party of Portage notables that made a celebratory voyage down the Fox in 1876 when the channel was declared complete; Andrew Jackson Turner, however, was aboard. We do know that young Turner was in the party of dignitaries and newspaper men who took an excursion north on the Wisconsin Central Railroad on its completion to Lake Superior in that year, rattling by the stumpy fields of logger-farmers on the northern fringe of Wisconsin's farm frontier and through the pineries and mixed hard- and softwoods still farther to the north. Hanging around the office of the *Register* in his teens, he must have absorbed the zeitgeist of a community emerging from its pioneer era. Now the rate of city development was slackening, its leaders groping for the strategies and resources that would keep the community growing.

Even so, frontier processes were not long past. From his home Fritz saw teamsters driving wagonloads of supplies northward up the "new pinery road," bound for logging camps where the great assault on the pineries of central Wisconsin was continuing. Provincial and raw Portage may have been, the more ambitious dreams of its leaders doomed, but it was no sleepy backwater. In his life there Fred Turner acquired knowledge of social, economic, and political processes upon which he later drew in much of his teaching and writing.

Of young Turner's boyhood companions, Jim Cole, also the son of a printer, William N. Cole, was a particular pal, and together they shared a boyhood adventure, which Turner recalled in a later letter to his betrothed. The boys had trudged a few miles west of Portage to fish in the Baraboo River, carrying an ample lunch in a bucket. This they left at the bridge when they descended to the bank of this tributary of the Wisconsin River. As they dodged rattlesnakes and picked choke cherries along the river, they passed a Winnebago encampment, ponies cropping the coarse grass of the bottoms and smoke rising from fires over which muskrats were being cooked in steaming pots. Returning to the bridge toward evening, Fred and Jim found no pail, and, frustrated, began the hungry walk back to Portage. Soon the Winnebago encampment, now en route, straggled past them—infants, youngsters, and adults—and, as one pony clopped by, its rider fixed them with a somber glance and said, "Heap good pail of grub!"[11] So much for fishing on the Baraboo! Other adventures of Fred Turner and Jim Cole went unrecorded.

In 1877 Andrew J. Turner organized a state militia company known as the Guppey Guards in honor of a local hero of the Civil War, and J. A. Cole and Fred J. Turner were recorded as privates in this organization, distinguished for the smartness that it displayed in drill competitions with other companies of the area. As a West Point graduate and young officer in the United States Army some years later, Jim Cole pursued Geronimo along the Apache Trail and returned to Wisconsin to head the military contingent at the University of Wisconsin, where he and Turner renewed their friendship. Turner's later relations with American Indians were never so dramatic as those of Cole, but in other recollections he told of a trip by dugout when he and his father floated down the Wisconsin from Grandfather Bull Falls (at Wausau). The Indian poleman in the stern fascinated the young Turner by carrying on a dialogue with his mate as they drifted by the Indian camp on the bank, his bass voice mingling in wilderness counterpoint with the fluting treble of his wife. Then they floated onward into silence and cool shadows along the shore, where they surprised an antlered buck that watched them in silent wonder and finally wheeled and plunged away with a splash, a flash of white tail, and a muffled thud of hooves.

Just as we are uncertain which of several houses was actually the Turner home during the 1870s, we know little of the human relationships within it that helped to shape the eldest son. Following the birth of his grandson, Frederick Jackson Turner wrote to his daughter that her son's "generation will have to live in a new age of rebuilding, and we must do what we can to prepare him for being useful. And that kind of an education begins in the mother's arms. How much of a child's life is woven out of his mother's love, and ambitions, and sacrifices, and self-repression, and guidance! It takes a life time to really know how much."[12] Platitudinous perhaps and intended to fortify a young mother against the exhausting months ahead, this passage hints at the debt that Turner believed was owed to Mary Turner. But details concerning her "ambitions, and sacrifices, and self-repression" we do not have, nor knowledge of the exact nature of the guidance. As a former school "marm," she undoubtedly encouraged Fritz in his aptitude for learning and in the exercise of his forensic abilities. She also, we know, kept a hospitable house where local community leaders and visiting politicians sometimes congregated—gatherings where Fred was allowed to mingle and express himself. These experiences perhaps helped generate the self-confidence and social poise that was a later hallmark of his personality.

Mary Turner had her own share of self-confidence. Stepping on young frogs escaping from her husband's bait pail did not ruffle her composure, and she waged a determined although unsuccessful battle to move the family to Madison when her daughter prepared to enroll in the university. Of young Fred's parents, Mary was the more religious of the two. But of her activities in the Presbyterian Church and other social relationships we as yet know little. We cannot identify her friends of Fred's boyhood years among the wives in the families who also lived in the "Society Hill" area of Portage. However, the ties of the Turners with the family of one of the little city's leading businessmen, Llewelyn Breese, were close; Fred's young sister was named Ellen Breese Turner. The Turners were part of the "county seataucracy."

Andrew Jackson Turner was a man of ability and intellectual force. During the 1860s he represented Columbia County in the state assembly on several occasions. He compiled the Wisconsin *Legislative Manual* during the early 1870s, setting the model of the state legislative *Blue Book*, and was later clerk of the Wisconsin Senate. During the 1870s he served repeatedly on the board of supervisors of Columbia County and became a member of the Wisconsin State Railroad Commission in 1878. In February of that year he sold his interest in the Portage *Wisconsin State Register*. Later he served as mayor of the city for many terms, and he supervised the taking of the federal census of 1890 and 1900 in the Portage area. Andrew Jackson Turner was also a delegate at various national political conventions and had strong claim to the title of Republican political "boss" of Columbia County. He managed the Republican Party's successful campaign against the Democrats' gerrymander of state legislative districts in the early 1890s. When he left the newspaper in 1878, he rendered public account: "We have, with unfailing regularity, paid our employees every Saturday. We have never suffered a . . . bill to go past due; we have held tax receipt No. 1 for many years; we generally stand recorded as No. 1 on the poll list at each election, and we have paid our pew rent promptly and cheerfully, and have most unselfishly permitted other people to occupy that pew more than we have ourselves, if we are not mistaken."[13] There was a similar strain of understated mischief or fun in many letters written years later by Frederick Jackson Turner to students or professional peers.

Whatever Fred Turner's relations with his mother, those with his father were close. Reflecting on their relationship after his father had narrowly escaped serious injury in 1887, Turner wrote, "He has always been the best of fathers to me; undemonstrative, often taciturn, but always kind and full of that deep affection that does not show itself at the surface so much—but which abides."[14] The streams and woods of the Portage area provided good fishing and hunting, and opportunities for sport farther north were even more tempting. Andrew Jackson Turner loved the outdoors and was an avid fisherman and hunter. In his eldest son he found an easy convert to these pleasures, particularly those of fishing. To use a word that was to recur in description of Frederick Jackson Turner's relations with his graduate students, father and son were "comrades" and in more than recreational activity. Fritz absorbed his father's consuming interest in politics; at the newspaper office he came to understand that private initiative and planning underlay public outcomes and that these might have deeper implications than appearances first revealed.

Young Turner learned the skills of the printer sufficiently well to set up the local news for the *Register,* and in his last year's residence in Portage contributed a "Scissors and Paste" column in which he presented favorite passages from literary and historical works. At this time he probably thought himself destined for a career in journalism, or perhaps journalism and politics. But there was another aspect of Jack Turner's interests to which his son was exposed. The editor and politician liked to reminisce about the Portage past and to write columns of local history. He was more serious about his facts than many journalists who were content to pass on a good story to their readers. He happily corrected the errors of predecessors, the more eminent the better.[15] He may indeed have written much of the local county history that was published in 1880. Neither his interest nor his skepticism would have escaped his son.

In the lives of some of the midwestern boys of the late nineteenth and early twentieth centuries who became scholars, writers, or other types of intellectual there was a pattern of intellectual emergence. At school, at the local library, or in the study of some local lawyer or judge, they found someone willing to guide them into the world of great literature and scholarship. We cannot identify any such person in the young Turner's life, aside from his father or mother. However, by the mid 1870s the Portage public high school was a respected institution and its principal W. G. Clough did take an interest in him. When Turner returned to Portage after 1900 and delivered an address on "The Settlement of the Mississippi Valley" to assist the Daughters of the American Revolution in purchasing books for the public library, he paid homage to Clough, who had become a Portage educational institution during the years intervening since he had taught Fred Turner. Clough, he recounted, had taught him the importance of thoroughness in preparation—a somewhat ironic encomium, coming from a man who typically was still in the throes of composition when he approached the podium and who was no great devotee of the scholarly footnote. None of his other high school teachers or older friends so fired his mind that he identified them in later years as opening the doors of an exciting realm of ideas and books. Young Fred, however, impressed the teachers. Despite the occasional lapse in deportment, he invariably ranked at the top of his class or very close to it.

Jim Cole and Fred Turner were part of a graduating class of nineteen at the Portage High School in 1878. Graduation exercises in the Portage of those days required each member of the senior class to give an oration. At the ceremony held in the Columbia County courthouse on June 28, 1878, Fred spoke on "The Power of the Press," before his classmates, the local superintendent of schools, and an assemblage of the friends and relatives of the members of the graduating class.[16] Gutenberg's printing press, he told his listeners, was "one of the greatest of all human inventions" rising "from the long night of the Medieval Ages. . . . like the sun from the mists of morning" and shedding "the blessed light of education upon the world." Earlier civilizations had lost their preeminence because they had failed to preserve and disseminate adequately their intellectual contributions. But now "he who now gives a truth . . . to the world, knows that mankind will possess it forever." And then Turner listed dimensions of the power of the press—that of educating the masses so necessary in a country of democratic government as in the United States and of shaping "the morals and customs of a people." These objectives were not yet completely achieved, alas, as "the rise in our midst of Communism, that fell child of ignorance and crime" showed.[17]

"Of all political powers the Press is the most important," asserted young Turner, and within its various departments none had wider influence "than that of the Newspaper." "A disseminator of news, the daily press is [also] one of the greatest of civilizers and public teachers, and is a necessary adjunct of every free government." It was said, he explained, that the age of great orators had passed. Now their "former power and influence" rested in "a new power, which unites to all his greatness the ability to speak to an audience of such magnitude as the orator of the past never dreamed . . . and to place its utterances in a form that can last forever. This is the glorious province of the News-paper." In the nation's travail it had been the Press that had "fired the Northern heart." Today the "great papers" treated the nation's financial problems more ably than did the politician in the legislative chamber.[18]

In conclusion, Turner returned to his larger definition of the press, recalling the "awe and solemnity" of a great library and then, in terse sentences and with growing oratorical momentum, took his hearers scene by scene through the great turning points of western civilization recorded in the books there, culminating in the martyr's death of Abraham Lincoln. "Thus has the Press joined the Past and the Present and made them one," he said, but was that all? Nay, for in "the leaves of *one* book" the "Future is unveiled to our mortal gaze" and "the New Jerusalem rises in its divine beauty." "Books," Fred concluded, "are the true Elysian fields where spirits of the Dead converse, and into these fields a mortal may venture unappalled. — What king's court can boast such company? What school of philosophy such wisdom?"[19]

If others among the graduating class of 1878 at Portage High School aspired to the prize for the best oration, they realized that their cause was lost when young Fred Turner sat down. Mature choice of words, loftiness of sentiment, range of effects and images, skillful use of rhetorical device, and all superbly delivered by a clean-cut, earnest youth of melodious voice — the combination was unbeatable. The local superintendent of schools had pledged a copy of Macaulay's *History of England* to the senior delivering the best oration, and Fred carried off the prize before his beaming family and friends. In retrospect his speech is impressive — surprisingly mature. Yet one also notes that it was essentially conventional in tenor — learning, democracy, and Christian values were transcendent objectives, ignorance and communism their antonyms. It was a forecast of the rather conventional man that always lurked below the surface of the innovative scholar and progressive political observer.

In August 1878 Mary and Andrew Jackson Turner and his sister, Anna, journeyed east to visit relatives, and Andrew and Anna went back to the family farm near Schuyler Falls, New York, where their mother was celebrating her eightieth birthday. Here Jack Turner reminisced with several of his brothers, tramped over the familiar fields, once more enjoyed the view of the Green Mountains, and recalled the aching arms and bleeding fingers that he had endured as a boy of twelve in helping to build a brick house for the family in 1844. Writing from there in answer to a letter from Fred, he said he did not want his boys to work as hard as he had been required to do. On the other hand, he had "learned what it was to work, as men must do to be successful. . . . how hard it was for men to earn money, and . . .

some habits of prudence that all men . . . ought to observe . . . things" that he hoped his boys would learn "without going through the same severe experience, that I did."[20]

The homily, Jack assured Fred, was not the main purpose of his letter. Rather he was writing in assent to Fred's plan to enter the University of Wisconsin in the fall that the latter had explained in a letter which reached his father at the home farm. Andrew Jackson Turner's response is a fine example of a tactful parental admonition to a son about to go to college. He had expected that Fred would wish to go to college, he wrote, and he was prepared to support him in his desire because he knew that his son planned to benefit from the experience. "If I supposed," he continued, "you were going to learn to be a loafer, as some boys I know of have done, I should say to you that that *can* be learned at home, at less expense." This he understood was not Fred's intent, and he approved also of his choice of a roommate, a local lad named Charley Alverson, the son of a former county officer, currently in the abstracting, real estate, loan, and insurance business. The Alversons were also members of the Presbyterian Church, and later Mrs. Alverson was a charter member of the local chapter of the Daughters of the American Revolution to which Mary Turner also belonged.[21] Wisely, Jack Turner offered no advice to his son about his ultimate choice of occupation.

And so young Fred Turner made his appearance in the preparatory class at the University of Wisconsin in academic year 1878–79. Although called a university, the institution, with its few hundred students and its handful of teachers, was hardly greater in its physical and intellectual resources than a fair number of private or denominational colleges of the time. Its setting on a commanding hill overlooking Lake Mendota was magnificent, however, and its few buildings were handsome, bordered with elms and backed by oak trees. Within the small faculty there were some outstanding minds. Portagers prided themselves on the quality of their high school, and Fred had been able to take additional work in classical languages there in preparation for the "Ancient Classical Course" at Madison. Even so he spent his first period of residence in Madison in intense study of Greek and Latin as a "sub-freshman," enrolling, in addition, in classes in mathematics, botany, and rhetoric. His transcript suggests that Fred did well in algebra and geometry, although he was less successful in trigonometry, and he received his highest grade—a 97—in botany.

Many years later Turner reminisced that the formal record of his first year at the university concealed a near disaster. He had perhaps failed his algebra exam but was, he believed, credited with the grade of the adjacent student, an excellent young mathematician who initially received a failing grade. That worthy protested, and the instructor removed the failing grade but did not assign it to Turner. The latter dreaded the mathematical challenges to be expected in the required sophomore course in mechanics, but, when he reached that level of study, a change in requirements allowed him to substitute a course in the Anglo-Saxon language. Evidence suggests that in recollection Turner sometimes improved upon factual details, but he did not like mathematics. His overall average in that first year was 90.8, and he could return to Portage for his summer well satisfied with his accomplishments.[22]

Before he took his final exams in the spring of 1879, Turner was involved in the first eruption of school spirit that his classmates had thus far experienced. A senior, handsome young Bob La Follette, had become noted for his oratorical skills, and in April 1879 he won the oratorical contest at the university, an honor entitling him to compete in a statewide competition in early May at Beloit College. In one of a number of despatches to the *Portage Republican* that Turner filed during his undergraduate days, he described La Follette's welcome in Madison after he had triumphed at Beloit by delivering his oration "Iago," an interpretation of one of Shakespeare's most memorable characters.

A crowd of students, mostly members of the Athenian Literary Society but including Turner, adjourned their evening meeting to wait at the telegraph office to learn the outcome. Then, with the great news of Bob's victory received, they celebrated for a couple of hours on campus and paraded at one-thirty in the morning to the station to greet the conquering hero. Two drummers beat out the marching rhythm, and Jim Cole "presid[ed] over the piccolo with his usual grace and dignity" while a freshman in science played the coronet. La Follette and his entourage were engulfed in an enthusiastic crowd, which escorted the orator home to the "inspiring strains of 'Brannigan's Band,'" and there the musicians rendered "'When Johnnie Comes Marching Home Again' in a touching manner." There was a congratulatory speech, and Bob thanked the members of the crowd for their "splendid" welcome, his voice trembling. When the cavalcade disbanded

at the university, "not a *drop* of liquor" had been imbibed, but Turner
was so stimulated by the occasion that he did not fall asleep until 4:00
A.M. Should Bob win the upcoming interstate contest—as he would—
Fred promised that the Wisconsin students would "everlastingly make
things hum."[23]

The implications of this incident extend beyond its illustration of
college student values and behavior at the end of the 1870s. Here at
first hand the young man from Portage saw the honor that fellow
students were prepared to pay the forensic gladiator. Given his own
high school success as an orator, Turner may have seen a path ahead
that could lead him also to approbation and success. In his farewell
comments to the history graduate students at Harvard in the spring of
1924, Turner reminisced about his youth and training as a historian,
and in the notes for his talk he jotted "La Follette—Iago" in a section
in which he commented upon several leading figures in the Wisconsin
faculty of the time. One scholar has maintained that Turner modeled
his own rhetoric and writing upon La Follette's great speech and that
the persuasive impact of his later famous essay, "The Significance of
the Frontier in American History," was greatly enhanced by its
rhetorical elements.[24] The fact that "Iago" and La Follette emerged
some forty-five years later in the notes for a retirement speech shows
that Fred Turner was deeply impressed by La Follette's speech and
triumph. But many other influences also were to play upon him.

During the summer after his first year at the university, Turner
contracted spinal meningitis while visiting his sick Uncle Charles in
Omaha. For a time his family feared that he would not recover, but he
rallied and returned to Portage. Later in the fall, however, he suffered
a relapse and was again on the brink of death. Slow recuperation set
in during midwinter, and by summer he had in large measure regained
his health. He re-enrolled at the University of Wisconsin in the fall of
1881 and pursued his studies without further health problems during
the next three years, graduating in the spring of 1884.

In a sense Fred Turner's lost years, 1879–81, were not wasted.
Surviving a serious illness may affect the molding of character—
imparting an inner serenity and a sense that there are things in life that
must be borne, regardless of personal desire. Perhaps young Turner
benefited in this way, and we have his own testimony that he emerged
from this experience convinced that he must not overtax himself and
that he must take adequate daily exercise. These years also allowed
him to broaden his knowledge of literature beyond that possessed by

most college freshmen of his era. The list of thirty-six titles that he noted in his "Commonplace Book" as read during 1880 is impressive, dominated by English nineteenth-century novelists and essayists.[25] Dickens was his favorite author that year. Turner recorded eight of his works, but he also paid his respects to Jonathan Swift, Oliver Goldsmith, William M. Thackeray, and George Eliot. Of essayists he read both Thomas B. Macaulay and Thomas Carlyle. Among American authors he read less but recorded Cooper's *The Red Rover*, Irving, Hawthorne, and, rather strangely perhaps, A. W. Tourgee, novelist of the Reconstruction South.

In the months of recuperation Turner also read Sir Edwin Arnold's *Light of Asia*, a rendering in poetry of the life of the founder of Buddhism. Of the English poets he dipped into Milton and Byron. Meanwhile he read Greek and Roman classics in both the original and in translation. There was some lighter stuff mixed in Fred Turner's reading as well, notably, Samuel Lover's humorous tale of Irish life, *Handy Andy*, and the *Biography of Kit North*. Turner's reading of 1880 provides few clues to the fact that a great historian was in the making. Still, he did peruse his copy of Macaulay's *History of England* and waded extensively in Taine's *History of English Literature*.

Turner's 1881 reading list was shorter than that of 1880, reflecting his greater activity and his return to university in the fall. Macaulay and Carlyle now held a more prominent place in the list, and *Lear*, *Othello*, and the characters of *A Midsummer Night's Dream* took stage. "I read in Shakespeare nearly every day," Turner noted in the "Commonplace Book." There too we find his translations of Horace's poems carefully copied, as he burrowed still deeper in the classics. For 1882 Turner was able to record a formidable list of volumes read or authors tasted, particularly in English literature, and his eager appetite withstood the mixing of Edmund Spenser's *Faerie Queene* and Herbert Spencer's *Education: Intellectual, Moral, and Physical*.

When Turner returned to school in the fall of 1881 his status was that of a "special student," but his class became that of 1884, placing him with students who in general were somewhat younger than he. The gap was not a great one and did not impede his full participation in student activities. He was, however, excused from physical education classes, and he was never a class officer. He was a member of the Adelphian Literary Society and Phi Kappa Psi fraternity, faithfully recording the words of the latter's drinking song in the "Commonplace Book." This was a mundane invocation to "drink 'er down," sung to the tune of "Old Ben." But an incident occurred during the winter of 1882 that may suggest that Fred was already taking a more responsible approach to college life than were some of his class-mates. Irked by what they considered to be the inadequacy of their instructor in Greek, Alexander Kerr, the members of the sophomore class came to recitation one day wearing flowing ties of red and yellow calico in the manner of Oscar Wilde, waving large handkerchiefs of the same material and flourishing bottles labeled "California Whiskey." As bedlam threatened, Kerr dismissed the class. Next day three ring-leaders were barred from recitation while the president and faculty considered further punishment. That, it turned out, was to consist mainly of pledging that there would no repetition of similar behavior.

Fred Turner's "Scrapbook" contains despatches to the *Portage Republican* that he apparently submitted. The first two were factual accounts of the incident, but the third, after explaining the resolution of the affair, waxed sarcastic. The sophomores had displayed "a gratifying evidence of their advancement toward the higher education" and shown their generosity by not throwing Professor Kerr out the window. Obviously "the regents should consult the sophomores as to the employment of instructors in future. Let the sophomores have things to suit them, if every member of the faculty has to be dismissed."[26] Here Turner adopted a different tone, perhaps because of his prior study with Kerr, perhaps in respect for institutional norms, or perhaps in a countering spirit of mischief.

Turner's interest in journalism found additional expression that year. In the fall of 1881 he and several other students organized an association to publish a weekly college newspaper, the *Badger*. During its first year of operation, Turner was "exchange" editor. He was to serve as secretary and treasurer of the association and during his senior year held the office of president. Given its era, the *Badger* was an excellent college publication, and leading figures in the group became professional journalists after leaving the university.[27]

Early in the first volume of the "Commonplace Book" Turner recorded Macaulay's reaction to mathematics—"Oh for words to express my abomination of that science" and in his sophomore year Turner thankfully bade farewell to such study, except insofar as it appeared in the courses in astronomy and the sciences. In his junior year the academic gates of history and English literature swung open to him. Now he read essay after essay of Emerson, including "On History," from which he copied several excerpts. His list of books read in 1883 ended with the note "and oceans of history."

Both in intellectual contribution and material assistance, two teachers helped to shape the young Fred Turner above all others at the University of Wisconsin. As professor of rhetoric and oratory, David B. Frankenburger taught forensics at the university for some thirty years. Turner ultimately eulogized him as a teacher, who "taught . . . more than the formal art of expression." His "rare, questioning smile" was unforgettable; he invited "the best and the highest lying like the seed within our souls."[28] Although continuing to prove himself an excellent student in general, Turner excelled particularly in oratory, winning the prize in that pursuit in his class year both as a junior and a senior. He brought both proven talent and speaking skills to Madison, and La Follette's example inspired him. But he matured as a speaker under Frankenburger's guidance. So satisfied with his pupil was Frankenburger that he began to think of making Turner his assistant, as growing enrollments at Madison suggested the need to enlarge a number of departments of instruction.

Turner learned much from Frankenburger and came to count him a friend. But another instructor so captured Turner's interest and admiration that he considered himself to be forever indebted to him. William Francis Allen, a Harvard graduate of the late 1840s, had studied in Berlin and Göttingen and seen much of Italy and Greece for himself. He had already established himself as an able teacher and classicist before going south to St. Helena Island in 1863 as a teacher under the auspices of the Freedman's Aid Commission and working later for the Sanitary Commission in Arkansas. At war's end he was assistant superintendent of schools in Charleston, South Carolina. Joining the Madison faculty in 1867 as professor of ancient languages and history, Allen immediately proved himself to be an outstanding teacher and a productive scholar.

Professor Allen demonstrated an amazing breadth of knowledge and was fully abreast of the trends of the day in history. He helped to collect and publish a volume of the songs sung by the southern blacks at the time of emancipation, and he made scholarly contributions to the study of Roman literature and history, European medieval and modern history, as well as American history to a smaller degree. He wrote a prodigious number of book reviews and notes dealing with many areas of history, and even ornithology, that were published in various periodicals, but particularly by the *Nation*. As a scholar he was especially interested in the study of primitive institutions. Frankenburger found in him a teacher of "profound learning, great ability in classification and arrangement of facts and principles, a rare power of exact statement, a simple sincerity that stooped to no pretence, and a love of truth that inspired to lofty endeavor." In his favorite subject, history, he "urged the students to go to the sources; discarded text-book recitations and, so far as possible, regular lectures in favor of the topical system of study, and of the examination of original authorities."[29]

An invitation to deliver a series of twenty lectures on the history of the fourteenth century in 1878 at The Johns Hopkins University attested to Allen's high standing among his peers, given the latter institution's growing reputation as America's preeminent center for graduate study in the social sciences and history. The graduate program at Johns Hopkins symbolized "institutional history," but the great Sir Henry Maine found the original suggestion of "the continuity of the German village community in New England" in an article in the *Nation*, "communicated" by William Francis Allen to that publication. Allen believed that land forms, natural resources, and areal boundaries helped to shape human behavior, as did economic and social forces in general, and the last scholarly paper that he presented to a national audience emphasized the importance of western issues in national development. Allen's section on gradation, bibliography, and the topical approach to history in the Pedagogical Library's volume, entitled *Methods of Teaching History*, comprised almost a third of the first edition of that work as published in 1883.[30] The rich list of sources that Allen included must have been a revelation to Turner. Gentle and sympathetic by nature, approachable and supportive, a Unitarian by both family tradition and conviction, he provided the young Turner with exactly the combination of authoritative knowledge and personal example needed to fan an interest in history to white heat.

When Fred Turner appeared upon the scene, Allen was both one-half of the classical studies department and the university's only history teacher. Turner studied Latin grammar and literature under Allen, but it was particularly when he enrolled in the latter's history courses that the young man came, saw, and was conquered. Allen may also have influenced Fred's attitude toward religion. Although his father's approach to this engrossing nineteenth-century concern was casual, his son was exposed to Presbyterian doctrines from the pulpit and in

Sunday school. Both Frankenburger and Allen were Unitarians, and the "Commonplace Book" contains a lengthy excerpt from Allen's public lecture on "Free Religion" that may have helped Turner clarify his ideas about religion. At least by the beginning of his graduate career, Turner was committed to Unitarianism. Many before Turner had retreated from the doctrines of Presbyterianism or Congregationalism to the gentler and more hopeful principles of Unitarianism, so we cannot assume that Turner's religious migration stemmed from opportunism rather than conviction. He was "tired," he confided to his sweetheart in 1886, "of hearing of how all the other creeds are wrong. . . . If men would simply teach the beauty of right action—they would do some good. But they don't and so myself and a good part of the world, too, drift into paganism."[31] Still, association with the Unitarian Society did bring him into closer contact with his two favorite professors.

At this time Allen was at the height of his powers as a scholar. For some twenty-five years he had been studying "primitive institutions, their rise and development under all possible environments." So deeply immersed had he been in such study that he could move easily in his teaching from the customs and manners of ancient Rome to the cultures of ancient Greece, the Orient, or the Teutonic peoples, forward to the Middle Ages or back again.[32]

Turner's classroom notes for Allen's courses in ancient and medieval institutions and Allen's course notebooks reveal the teacher's approach. In his course on ancient institutions Allen posed the question, "Is society necessarily progressive?" and cited the views of Sir Henry Maine, John Stuart Mill, and Walter Bagehot as the basis for discussion.[33] He outlined stages of societal development for his students and stressed the relation between such stages and the development of institutions. The latter he grouped under such headings as those relating to wealth, science, art, religion, freedom, and order. Allen was abreast of current theories and controversies, related his lecture material to them, and was not afraid to challenge the authorities in his fields. But Allen also dispensed solid substance, and Turner's notes in "Ancient Institutions" were thick with definitions of Latin terms and references to illustrative documents in that language.

On November 14, 1882, Allen was describing various forms of Roman land titles, and Turner recorded the fact that the Roman public land system "gave rise to possessio . . . valid title against all but State." So in that year, Fred Turner was learning about public lands and the ways in which their administration might affect the development of institutions. During the years of Turner's undergraduate training Allen was preparing a paper on "The Primitive Democracy of the Germans," in which he paid much attention to the landholding system of the Germanic tribes and argued that it reflected the "structure of [tribal] society."[34] Today's college history students may sit in course after course and fail to hear any mention whatsoever of so mundane a subject as the possession of land. That was not Turner's experience, and this fact had its bearing on his future.

As an undergraduate Turner found only one course, a scant semester in actuality, available to him in American history. Allen's notes show what would later be regarded as a conventional outline, with the Revolutionary War campaigns serving in part as backbone for the treatment of the Revolutionary period and presidential administrations fulfilling the same purpose during the history of the American republic. But the outline also shows that Allen broke the colonies into sectional entities for treatment and did not ignore the West. Although he was by training and interest primarily a historian of Europe, he had studied the New England land system and published a note on a surviving example of community common lands and their use in Nantucket—"A Survival of Land Community in New England"—and was sufficiently interested in the history of the Northwest to submit a paper, "The Place of the Northwest in General History," at the annual meeting of the American Historical Association (AHA) in 1888. In it he argued that "more than once . . . in the Northwest . . . we have found the key to problems of a national character." The final sentence of his paper ran, "Our territorial system, our policy of creating new States, our national guaranty of personal freedom, universal education, and religious liberty, found their first expression in the great act which provided for the government of the Northwest." Here was a point of view concerning the importance of the West that Allen's eager young student from Portage was to make his own.[35]

Although a fellow student recalled him as having been rather bookish, Turner was no cloistered grind in his last three years as an undergraduate at Wisconsin. His illness had committed him to exercise. He loved Lake Mendota, and he spent time on its waters both in its open and frozen seasons. The "Commonplace Book" contains a poem on the pleasures of iceboating. Trips to Chicago or Milwaukee enabled him to see more than two dozen major stage productions during his undergraduate years, including three different performances of *Richard III*. He saw the great Edwin T. Booth in *Hamlet* and Fanny Davenport in *As You Like It*. His "Commonplace Book" lists comparable, although somewhat less impressive, lists of concert artists and lecturers.

Turner's greatest collegiate triumphs came when his orations won both the junior and senior class prizes. The first of these he entitled "The Poet of the Future." Here, he argued that a great poet had epitomized all the glorious ages of the past, "from the Iliad of Homer to the Faust of Goethe," but that the present lacked "such a poet." "The two great features of the present are science and democracy," he told his listeners, and both awaited their poets. In his ending he took the audience, as he had at Portage, into "a vast library." Here were the poets of the past—Homer, Dante, Shakespeare, and other greats: "With intent and waiting faces they seemed to peer into the mists of the future; for they feel the coming of the master to whose genius they shall bow; in whose rich organ tones shall sound the splendor of the present, the divinity of man and nature."[36]

Thirteen months later Turner marked his graduation from the University of Wisconsin by delivering the prize-winning senior oration, "Architecture Through Oppression," arguing that the societies of the past that had produced magnificent architectural achievements had oppressed the greater part of their citizenry. "Millions groaning," intoned Turner, "that one might laugh, servile tillers of the soil, sweating that others might dream; drinking the lopwood of life, while their masters quaffed its nectar." But now in a sweeping "wave of democratic utilitarianism," "the Nineteenth century" was "striving to build humanity into a glorious temple to its God,—his only fitting temple. When the greatest happiness of the greatest number shall have become something like a reality, when life's tragedy shall cease to clash with life's romance . . . then again may 'music freeze into marble,' and forests blossom into stone."[37]

Turner's orations in the springs of 1883 and 1884 show enhanced mastery of forensic art. The sentences are crisper, more sharply focused, and the rhetorical impact more pronounced than in the declamation of 1878. Taken with the latter presentation they in some degree forecast Turner's professional style as a historian. Good ideas were not to be abandoned. The device of taking his listeners into a great library had been effective in Portage. So was it in 1883 in Madison. And a fervid commitment to democratic institutions runs through all three addresses. The best orator speaks only what he believes, and if this was true of the young Turner, his orations reveal an earnest, high-minded young man.

In 1884 Professor Allen gave Fred Turner two grades of 98 and one of 95. Frankenburger found him worthy of a 98 in the rhetoricals class. President Bascom was less impressed; Turner received a 93 in mental and moral philosophy and only 89 in aesthetics. Turner's grades in history might in theory have reflected little but a good memory and a willingness to slog. Professor Allen, however, was too perceptive a teacher to be fooled in this way.

By the end of his undergraduate history training, young Turner had discovered the exhilaration of working with sources in the collections of books, manuscripts, and old records that Lyman C. Draper had brought together in the State Historical Society. When Professor Allen set Turner the task of working out the details of French land titles in Portage, Draper—in Turner's words that "little thin voiced and thin-bodied man"—showed him the kind of materials available in the society relating to the fur trade. At that point, Turner was invaded by the virus of historical research, although he perhaps did not realize it. The paper that he prepared in his junior year briefly identified the early fur traders who established themselves on the land between the Fox and Wisconsin rivers across which the portage trail ran and described the nature of the title that they obtained. Fulfilling Turner's understanding that literary productions might be put to several uses, the paper for Professor Allen also became a column in the *Wisconsin State Register*, headed "History of the 'Grignon Tract' on the Portage of the Fox and Wisconsin Rivers." The product of a college junior, it was a kind of chronicle, built around official documents that constituted the chain of title to the land at the portage claimed by Augustin Grignon. Authorship was identified by the subhead, "Compiled by Fred J. Turner." It was a modest beginning to a great historical career, but the trap had been sprung.[38]

The handwritten "Class Book of the Class of 1884" described the members of the graduating class as well as preserving their photographs. Turner, wrote the scribe, was twenty-two years of age. "His height is five feet, eight inches. His weight is one hundred and thirty pounds. He is Liberal in religion and Independent in politics. His future occupation is Journalism. He graduates in the Ancient Classical Course with honors. He won the Burrows Prize and the Lewis Prize. He is a member of Adelphian literary society and of the Phi Kappa Psi

Fred Turner in 1884, the year of his graduation from the University of Wisconsin. Reprinted with permission of the State Historical Society of Wisconsin, Madison, Wisconsin. (X3) 918.

fraternity." He appeared in the class prophecy as

> *Turner*, in cloisters immured and to painful study devoting
> Day and night, his patient innocent life exhausting—
> *Turner*, than whom no senior with loftier intellect gifted,
> Nor with a finer soul, nor in virtue more absolute ever.[39]

The classmate who described Turner as quiet and bookish also reported that none of his fellow students imagined he would become a famous historian. Nor for that matter was Turner firmly set in his career trajectory. Frankenburger had proposed that he stay on at the university as an instructor in forensics. Initially Turner found that prospect pleasing, but the university regents balked at the proposed salary. The young orator who loved history decided not to pursue one of the fields in which oratory would serve him best, as for example, law, nor one that would indulge his appetite for history. Fred joined the fourth estate, where his own experience and his father's many contacts ensured that he could find a place.

2 Apprentice

*"One of the most brilliant opportunities
for a young man in this country"*

Fred Turner's plans in 1884 to pursue a career in journalism are understandable. Jack Turner had been a successful newspaper man, and his son had been his companion at both the newspaper office and on the streams and lakes of central Wisconsin. In 1884 Fred possessed practical knowledge of the newspaper business, writing skills, and a pleasing personality. Journalism promised him a career no less satisfying than his father was experiencing. Other young men who shared in the early management of the *Badger* expected to become newspaper reporters or editors. One of them was the Madison correspondent of the *Milwaukee Sentinel* during Fred's senior year, and in April 1884 he resigned that position. Young Turner succeeded him, adding the reportorial duties to his work for the *Badger* and to his academic studies. Even before graduation from the university in June 1884, Fred Turner had entered the world of professional journalism.[1] His admission to full-time status in the fourth estate was, however, more complicated than the "Class Book" of 1884 suggests.

Turner's work as the *Sentinel's* correspondent impinged peculiarly upon his future at the university. As he went about his task of covering local events in Madison and developments in the various government departments, he learned that Elisha W. Keyes, local Republican party boss and a power on the board of regents, was perfecting charges designed to bring down the controversial but beloved president of the university, John Bascom, at the board's meeting in June. Turner found reliable sources willing to provide details of Keyes's accusations and plans, and the *Sentinel* published his dispatch outlining the impending attack on Bascom. One head ran, "Keyes after the Scalp of Dr. Bascom of the State University." Students and other admirers of Bascom rallied to the defense of this "gray haired, white-faced, old man with his cold manner" and his talent for inspiring students to work for a kinder world.[2]

During the course of the spring Bascom had approved Frankenburger's request for assistance and agreed to place the appointment of an instructor in rhetoric and oratory before the regents. That recommendation was to be also considered at the regent's meeting in June—the nominee, Fred J. Turner. Knowing that Bascom's supporters had been alerted by the *Sentinel's* accounts, Keyes's colleagues on the board of regents referred his charges against the president to a committee for later consideration. But Keyes obtained some satisfaction. Although the regents approved Turner's appointment, the stipend proposed for the audacious young reporter was reduced from eight hundred to six hundred dollars. In some indignation, Fred Turner decided that he preferred to continue as the *Sentinel's* Madison correspondent. His opinion of Keyes was sour thereafter and his view of the regents always tinged with distrust. No doubt he was pleased that the *Sentinel* supported him by publishing scathing editorial criticisms of Keyes, but he must have realized that Keyes might well harm him in the future. He had, however, helped the press fulfill its educational function in a good cause, and as the son of another Republican manager he knew that he was not without friends in Keyes's party.

Turner later recalled his year as a newspaper reporter as one of drifting and unfocused energies. But he fulfilled the duties of local correspondent conscientiously, and the number of his lines of copy accepted for publication increased. The young district attorney, La Follette, launched a campaign to win the Republican nomination in the local congressional district, and Turner enthusiastically reported his maneuvering. He wrote his second account of a triumphal La Follette homecoming after the latter achieved his goal over the opposition of Keyes and his friends. When the state fair took place at Madison in September 1884, the Democrats subverted the understanding that the speakers were to be nonpartisan and treated fairgoers to a serving of Democratic dogma. Turner's dispatch to the *Sentinel* noted this breach of etiquette, enraging the secretary of the fair. Some days later the latter angrily refused to provide Turner with the list of prize winners in the cattle judging. The high-spirited young reporter responded with a derisive description of the encounter in which he took the high ground by alleging "Bourbon censorship" and favoritism on the part of the fair secretary in making public records available to the press.[3] By December 1884 Turner was thoroughly indoctrinated in the newspaper culture of Madison. He had made friends in the fraternity and impressed Reuben Gold Thwaites, of the *Wisconsin State Journal* staff, who toyed with the idea that he and Turner should establish a newspaper on the southwestern frontier and grow up with the country.

The state legislature assembled for its session in early 1885, and the *Milwaukee Sentinel* sent a more seasoned member of its staff to Madison to cover the proceedings. With the assistance of his father, Fred obtained the position of transcribing clerk in the state senate, a position that he combined with serving as legislative correspondent for the *Chicago Inter-Ocean*, a post that gave him desks in the press row of the assembly and the senate. The Wisconsin legislature of 1885 selected a United States senator, thus giving Turner perspective on the complete range of legislative activities. The contest for the senate seat held additional interest for Turner because his father was one of the managers of Gen. Lucius Fairchild. In this case, however, Jack Turner's manipulative skills proved inadequate; John C. Spooner was the choice.

Turner's dispatches to the *Inter-Ocean* were capably done, and the first months of 1885 provided him with invaluable understanding of legislative processes. Years later an eminent geographer criticized Turner for lack of work in the field.[4] But political processes were always at the heart of Turner's history, and his months in the Wisconsin legislature provided him with rich field experience. In addition, he emerged from his short newspaper career with an enhanced understanding of the press and its uses. There were also periods of boredom in these months, and another young member of the press row later reminisced about time spent matching pennies with Turner during the lulls in legislative activity. Turner judged the literary product of a press reporter to be shallow and flippant and later characterized his newspaper career as an unproductive time. In that spring of 1885 Professor Allen gave him an opportunity to test another occupation.

Because many years had passed since Allen had been in Europe, the focus of his research interests, he decided to spend most of the spring and summer of 1885 in recreation and study in England and southern Europe. Given permission for a departure in April, he arranged that Turner teach his classes through the last weeks of the spring term. Turner enjoyed the experience, and when the offer of an instructorship in rhetoric and oratory was renewed, he accepted the position. He would not be teaching history, but enrollments were also increasing in that department. Perhaps his teaching arrangement might be changed in the future, and in the meantime his duties would not be so onerous that he could not pursue postgraduate studies in history. In mid-September 1885 he assumed his duties in rhetoric, beginning the round of recitations at 8 A.M. four mornings a week and continuing instruction into the afternoon on Mondays, Tuesdays, and Thursdays. We do not know how much history he studied during this academic year, but we do know it was at this time he was convinced that he preferred to work in that subject rather than in rhetoric and oratory.

When he returned to the university in 1885, Turner took up residence in a boarding house at 778 Langdon Street. Here at the foot of University Hill, Mrs. Bross provided room and board for a dozen boarders, mainly students, in a large house that was soon to become the president's residence. Perhaps because two of her nephews were residents, Lucinda Sherwood, wife of a Chicago businessman, stayed there for a few days at the time of commencement in June 1886. With Mrs. Sherwood was her daughter, Caroline Mae, a petite, pretty, and vivacious young woman, although a sufferer from hay fever and considered to be somewhat fragile in health. During the Sherwoods' brief stay in Madison, Fred and Mae laid the foundation of a personal relationship that endured and grew until his death. The correspondence that the two began after Caroline's departure continued until their marriage and contains many revealing glimpses of Turner's professional development as well as the details of a late-nineteenth-century courtship.

Turner quickly decided that Mae Sherwood was the woman with whom he wished to share his life. They became formally engaged in early 1887. Turner wrote that his beloved's father "spoke kindly . . . but I could see that he was not overjoyed." When Turner sent the news back to Portage, Andrew Jackson Turner heartily congratulated him in reply and pledged his support. He also allowed a note of melancholy to creep into his letter, recalling the pleasure with which he had shared his son's vacations: "Now the question looms before me, mountain high . . . who is going to paddle the boat? Who is going to carry the fish? Who is going to dig the bait?"[5] In various letters Turner confessed that he was ambitious. Now that ambition was to be fueled additionally by the desire to achieve a position and income that would allow him to marry Caroline Mae Sherwood.

Another important theme in Turner's development in these graduate student years was his continued commitment to the love of the outdoors and of natural beauty that he had developed in Portage. Turner liked Madison in part for the magnificence of the university's setting and the opportunities to enjoy nature that the city and its surroundings allowed. On weekends he sometimes tramped into the countryside. In the late afternoon he often rowed on Lake Mendota or, after the purchase of a birch canoe in 1886, paddled along the water front. Following his landlady's move to State Street in 1887, he trundled the canoe to the lake on a wheel barrow, sometimes accompanied by a bevy of small boys hoping to see him fall in at the launching.

In September 1887 Turner told Caroline of paddling his canoe into a marsh off the Yahara where he found wild rice, cattails, and yellow flowers. "It is one of the beauties of Madison," he wrote, "that without getting far from home one can drop into the most charmingly wild places." In another letter he discoursed, "There is a freedom about a canoe that is lacking in a formal prim row boat in which you swing back and forth in a see-saw or pendulum-like way, . . . breaking your neck by efforts to look over your shoulder . . . But a canoe! . . . the light birch jumps under your stroke, obeying the slightest summons of the blade. You must have an alertness moreover lest you lean too far and plunge shivering into the cold Mendota—One seems in closer contact with the water in a canoe. . . . I am finding pleasure," he continued, "in emulating Thoreau and watching the little things in Nature." This was a year in which he also discovered the nature writings of John Burroughs, who, he said, "seems to be Thoreau minus some of the latter's philosophy. He is in love with nature and has eyes to see her secrets."[6]

In each summer of his graduate work at Madison, Turner returned to Portage for some weeks, largely devoting himself to fishing expeditions with his father or other friends. For instance, in late June 1886 he reported to Caroline, "My satchel is packed, my fishing rods furbished, and my eyes are turned toward the water brooks that brawl through the forest primeval of northern Wisconsin."[7] In his letters of 1887 and 1888 there is mention of plans for ambitious canoe trips from the source of the Wisconsin to the Mississippi—and even west along the old vogageur's route from Lake Superior to Lake Winnipeg. Possible travel companions were Thwaites, now established as Draper's heir at the Historical Society, or Jim Cole. But these were fireside dreams amid the stubborn realities of hearing endless declamations from stammering undergraduates, work on the master's thesis, and involvements in other essential university activities.

Related also to Turner's love of the outdoors was a larger regional commitment. Men like Andrew Jackson Turner who had helped to develop the western America of their era emphasized its achievements. Western soldiers had played a major role in saving the union, and the economic transformation of the north-central region of the country had been phenomenal. The 438,000 farms there in 1850 had become almost two million by 1890. The region's agricultural products, lumber, and minerals supported thriving industry and urban populations and contributed to industries elsewhere in the United States. Westerners almost monopolized the presidency between 1860 and 1890, and during the 1890s the north-central census region provided more than a third of the nation's congressmen. As his father's son and as an ex-newspaper man, young Fred Turner knew these things and was proud of them.

Increasingly there emerged in Turner's mind in these years of graduate study a sense of the contrast between the eastern and western United States. In June 1887 he traveled east to Boston, where he explored that old city and fell "in love with [it]—its quaint streets, paved and clean and narrow and winding as the labyrinth" but recoiled at the sights, sounds, and smells of "Jewry," a reaction that most young men of similar background would probably have experienced. He attended the Harvard commencement under the guidance of Professor Allen, who had returned for the fiftieth reunion of his college class, and then holidayed on Cape Cod with Caroline and her family, returning via New Haven and New York City.

Turner was struck by the contrast between the midwestern and New England landscapes. "But the farms!" he wrote, "Bits of rock covered, daisy-decked, hillsides, hemmed in by stone walls. Not like our sweep of corn fields, and uninterrupted seas of wheat!"[8] The Harvard commencement exercises were also different from those to which he was accustomed: "The speakers were very finished, and used strong terse Anglo Saxon with none of the bombast that is found in our western college commencements. On the other hand they lost something in force and vigorous earnestness." His father responded, "Your trip seems to be a sort of revelation or the unfolding of a new world and a new life to you. Well, there is a vast difference between the East and West. Your observations have been almost wholly in the West. We are new here yet, and the ways of the people, as well as the appearance of the country are quite unlike. On your trip you will see the bright side of the East." And then he reminded him that John L. Sullivan and other brawlers were also "Men of Massachusetts." After passing through Chicago on his way home, Fred reported, "Chicago never seemed so *western* to me as it did then."[9]

Writing to Caroline in late August, Turner confided

I understand myself better since I went to new England in many ways. In the first place, I was getting very provincial. . . . This my trip has neutralized. Then I was growing somewhat ascetic . . . this I am losing a little. The scenery too, taught me something about myself. I have lived all my life in a comparatively monotonous country. Portage has, it is true, for a sky line, some fairly good sized bluffs, but aside from these distant hills—the whole surroundings of my childhood and youth were made up of sand slopes and marshes;—there were no wide sweeps of land or water horizontally, no lofty hills, no deep valleys—it was *commonplace*. Even in Madison there is something of this. . . . My life caught something from the landscape, and from the people, like the landscape, for I am sympathetic—I thank heaven that I have an imagination and a love of books—two things that have lifted me out of my surroundings at Portage. Life in any case, is more or less coarse, and requires imagination to idealize it a bit, but this is especially so in such environment as that in which my early life has been spent.[10]

The summer of 1887 was, Turner told Caroline, "the happiest summer" of his life thus far, and he capped it with some trout fishing near Montello, boarding with a tender-hearted but very profane farmer whose language he excused, adding, "Country life in the west is far more meager than in the east—less civilized." He returned to this theme in early September. Contrasting the cultural opportunities in the East and West, he wrote, "I am placed in a *new* society which is just beginning to realize that it has made a place for itself by mastering the wilderness and peopling the prairie, and is now ready to take its great course in universal history. It is something of a compensation to be among the advance guard of new social ideas and among a people whose destiny is all unknown. The west looks to the future, the east toward the past."[11]

As these various themes become apparent in the life and thought of the young university instructor, he was also committing himself to a particular kind of history. As early as Turner's junior year at Madison he had begun to develop a special interest in Wisconsin history. Encouraged by Professor Allen, and perhaps assisted a bit by his father, he compiled his little history of the Grignon tract. Settling again into university life in September 1885, he confided to his father, "I hope I can get time to work out the early Green Bay fur trade history. It would add a chapter of interest in Wisconsin history."[12]

Professor Allen approved the Wisconsin fur trade as an appropriate subject for Turner's master's thesis, and he worked on the topic intermittently, painfully acquiring sufficient lingual skill to translate the business documents of the French Canadian traders. Turner hoped to finish his thesis by the end of academic year 1886–87, but the translation of documents in the French language went slowly, and there were other demands on his time. He was enlisted in the preparations for his first class reunion, and various club and social commitments distracted him. Among them was a meeting of the Literary Club in May, where the doctrines of Henry George were discussed, and he derived "the conclusion that it would be pleasant to be a land owner on a shady part of Mendota's shore."[13] Commencement came in 1887 and went, and completion of the work was postponed until the next year.

That next year, 1887–88, was crucial in shaping the later course of Fred Turner's career. He plugged away on his thesis and became increasingly friendly with Thwaites. Sometimes they canoed together on Lake Mendota, and Thwaites provided Turner with a key that enabled him to study on Sundays in the Historical Society library in the state capitol. They discussed the possibility of "doing work together in Wisconsin history." Both participated in a lecture series on the history of the Northwest under the auspices of the Contemporary Club of the Unitarian Society, and Turner contributed a paper on the history of the Northwest Ordinance. Meanwhile, Regent Keyes and his allies on the board had succeeded in forcing President Bascom to resign. His farewell speech moved Turner to tell Caroline, "A grand man, and if I ever wept I would feel like doing so at that time."[14] Bascom's successor, Thomas C. Chamberlin, geologist and geographer, received an invitation from the *Encyclopaedia Britannica* to prepare an essay on Wisconsin and requested Turner to prepare the historical and contemporary sections in it.

Professor Allen passed along to Turner the assignment of preparing a syllabus on the history of the Northwest for an adult education course for the National Bureau of Unity Clubs. Also at Allen's instigation, the editors of periodicals began to invite Turner to review books. Turner's first contribution of this kind appeared in *The Dial* in May 1887, an extended review by modern standards of the documentary book *Franklin in France*, by Edward E. Hale and his son. Although resorting to that most irritating gambit of the reviewer—the quibble over a book's coverage—Turner's review promised good things to come from its author in its occasional turn of phrase, general fair-mindedness, and broad perspective. "It will do as a first attempt," he told Caroline. "I dared not say all I wanted to on the book, believing that it was well to be a little cautious at first, especially since Mr. Hale possibly knows more about the subject than I do."[15] As the academic year 1887–88 drew on, Turner agreed to address the Madison Literary Club in May on the subject of the fur trade. Thwaites also invited him to give one of his papers before the Wisconsin State Historical Society at its next annual meeting. Thus friends and colleagues were giving Turner opportunities to develop his interest in western history.

As he worked on his thesis, Turner began to appreciate the larger significance of western history and the part that it might play in his own career. In September 1887 he wrote,

The more I dip into American History the more I can see what a great field there is here for a life study. One must even specialize here. I think I shall spend my study chiefly upon the Northwest and more generally on the Mississippi Valley. The history of this great country remains to be written. I shall try to add my mite in the way of studying it. The more I read Francis Parkman the more am I fascinated by the skill with which he has delved among so great a mass of facts and out of them selected with the penetration of genius, the essential things, grouped them and with dramatic insight and power presented the story to the reader, whose interest is held to the last sentence of the last chapter. It is very discouraging to an ordinary man.

Turner returned to Parkman in another letter of that same year: "All this morning I have been reading Parkman's *Conspiracy of Pontiac*—he has a delightful style, abounding in metaphor—and smooth flowing, but best of all he tells his story with as much fascination for the reader as if it were a novel—No, with more fascination, for I never could feel the interest in a novel I do in real history well told."[16]

Parkman taught young Fred Turner a number of important lessons. In his epic volumes detailing the struggle between France and England for the control of a continent, Parkman showed Turner that great and compelling history could be drawn from the American West of the Indian, the trader, the soldier, and the frontiersman. Parkman also convinced Turner that it was important to write well—a skill that included the use of artifice comparable to that which Turner was teaching in his classes in oratory and rhetoric. Turner found also in Parkman the message that to make a name in history one needed to find an important area of history and concentrate on developing it.

Writing to Caroline in early September 1887, he confessed that he found the subject of Spanish exploration fascinating but lamented that it would take "a life time to be an expert on the subject. This is one of the discouraging things in history as well as one of its pleasures— there is no end to the subject—and one must resolutely put aside many fields of study and stick to his own little *mowing lot* if he would be successful." But sometimes Fred Turner doubted that success would come. When Caroline expressed her confidence in him at about this time, he wrote, "I am afraid you really half believe that I may at some time win a name of which you can be proud. This is the most impossible of prospects! I understand myself too well to look for fame such as you mention. . . . will you love me less if I live my life, as I certainly must, not among the few men who win the ear of the world, but among the plodding students who look up to them?" But when further advanced in his graduate career, he wrote to her, "I am possessed too thoroughly by the daemon of ambition to do anything but grind away like a mill wheel on the wheat of knowledge—and if that runs short, perchance upon my self."[17]

Many graduate students dream of future eminence and work hard at their studies. Turner was prepared to go further and move in a calculating way to attain his objectives. His real and growing love was history, and Professor Allen obtained one-third of Turner the teacher during the academic year 1886–87. Turner appeared in the description of the history program of this year as instructor of Course IV: American History. In the catalogue of the next year, however, he was formally identified as an instructor in both history and oratory. At an early point in his graduate program Turner decided that he wished to be a professor of history at the University of Wisconsin, sharing Professor Allen's load and teaching American history. Allen approved of Turner's hopes, but we do not know when Turner first moved openly to achieve them. However, in late June 1887, following the conclusion of his second year as an instructor, Turner wrote that he was beginning "to feel a little less keenly the disappointment involved in failing to make the regents do what I so much wished them to do — The trouble is you see I am having to create a new department against the policy of the board which is to restrict the instructional force, and so I am hampered. But with lots of hard work . . . I shall try very earnestly next year to bring things as they should be." Six weeks later he told Caroline of a high school teaching position for the following year that would be much more remunerative than his present position. "I do not propose," he wrote, "to be placed at the mercy of the regents next year. If I can say to them that I have an offer of twice their salary it may help me, you see — to make them do what I wish them to."[18]

At about this time another means of strengthening Turner's hand entered his calculations. He might perhaps improve his credentials by enrolling for further graduate work at The Johns Hopkins University. That institution had become the prototype of a university where major emphasis was placed on graduate training. Under the directorship of Herbert Baxter Adams, its program in political economy and history had already produced a number of eminent graduates, including Woodrow Wilson. Adams was on friendly terms with Professor Allen. In early September President Chamberlin held a faculty reception, and there Turner encountered an acquaintance who was studying psychology at Johns Hopkins. They adjourned to an ice-cream saloon and talked about the university in Baltimore. Turner wrote to Caroline, "He talks very well and gave me an excellent idea of what the institution is. It would be a grand place to go to — containing as it does the most eminent specialists in the separate branches. Our western institutions are mere schools by the side of it." Six weeks later Turner told her of a new acquaintance, William S. Bayley, of the United States Geological Survey, formerly located at Johns Hopkins, who had kept Turner "greatly interested for an hour . . . with an account of the institution."[19]

We do not know the details of Turner's maneuvering during the fall of 1887 — he may have invoked aid from his father, who knew

President Chamberlin—but Turner certainly realized that he must improve his bargaining position if his hopes for a bright future at Wisconsin were to materialize. Perhaps he or Allen communicated his interest in Johns Hopkins to President Chamberlin. In early December the president inquired about his plans for the following year. Turner responded that he did not wish to cut his ties with Wisconsin unless assured that he would be taken back at the end of the year. Acknowledging that Turner's work had been "quite satisfactory," the president preferred to evaluate Turner's success at Johns Hopkins before making a decision.

Turner wrote to Caroline, "Dr. Chamberlin appreciates the fact that here is a grand opportunity for original work in American history and as he says—the field must come to be filled by not only a good man, but by a remarkably good man.—He will demand therefore that if I go to J.H.U. I do something very good there—and as you know J.H.U. is the center where the brightest workers in the department meet. I confess that I am distrustful of my ability to achieve the results he will demand." "The question with me," he confided to Caroline, "is whether to try to make a reputation here next year, or whether I can make it better at J.H.U." Both Professor Allen and the president believed that the appointment of a temporary instructor could be better arranged in 1888–89 than in 1889–90. "I must," Turner wrote, "do something within the next two years to make Prest Chamberlin think me the proper man for this place or fail to secure the department when it is made a full instructorship. You see the importance of what historical work I do this year therefore, especially my thesis on the fur trade and a lecture which I am to give if I can find time in a course by other Madisonians upon Northwestern history. . . . I presume I shall go to J.H.U."[20]

Turner was all too aware that the necessity of doing further graduate work elsewhere might delay marriage to Caroline, his "little Maisie." Still, he did not sentence himself to unremitting study during this year. There was during the fall term the occasional evening of whist or billiards with other young men of the university community. The Shakespeare Reading Club met weekly—educational, broadening, and besides, "the company is a choice one." Turner was also a regular at the meetings of the Literary Society and the Canning and Contemporary Clubs. Allen was a leading figure in the Wisconsin Academy of Sciences, Arts, and Letters, and in December Turner was accepted as a member. He found time also during that month to support his friend

Jim Cole for the position of professor of military science and tactics at the university. He reported to Caroline that he had "stirred up a congressman [Robert M. La Follette], adjutant general, insurance company's secretary, ex-congressman, and business men over the state to write" on behalf of Cole and to provide President Chamberlin with enough endorsements "to overwhelm him."[21]

Second semester 1887–88 was a blur of work and indecision for Turner. Professor Allen became seriously ill with pneumonia, and Turner had to teach two of his classes in European history. He worked up a long paper on the Northwest Ordinance for the lecture series in northwestern history and delivered it successfully. He did not give out, he reported, although some of his maps did. His landlady's daughter congratulated him on the fact that his face did not turn red, and Thwaites called his performance a ten strike. But, Turner confessed, "one thing . . . 'breaks me up'—Chamberlin wasn't there and I wrote that lecture for his benefit." In the midst of Turner's work on the Ordinance, Chamberlin had passed along to him the *Encyclopaedia Britannica* assignment. Since the president had proposed a collaboration to Turner, the young man could hardly turn him down. At about this point Caroline detected a settling in their relations, and Turner found this "awful" but explained that "just now my vision embraces only one object—a *reputation* sufficient as a basis for demands upon the University. If I seem less loverlike in the amount of my letters,—more serious—it is because I am wrapped up in that desire."[22]

Turner persevered. In late March 1888 he reported, "I do not talk anything now but Western history. . . . I have taken a fever of enthusiasm over the possibilities of the study of the great west and of the magnificent scope of United States history in general. If I can get time and am not too lazy, I shall find much work to do in this field. It widens daily." Meanwhile he was "grinding like a mill stone" on the fur trade. "It *is* such a dry mixed up subject to try to make interesting in many respects," he wrote. May 1888 arrived and with the date for the delivery of his paper only a couple of weeks away, Turner was still grinding—"I am showing," he wrote, "that it was the plain prosaic dealer in peltries that enabled the French to unlock the river courses of the great west[,] that changed the Indian and made him dependent upon the white man thus paving the way for civilization. I am trying to tell how the forest which was to the Englishman a gloomy, repellant, witch haunted realm . . . not to be entered except with defiant conquering spirit—was to the Frenchman a gay, witching,

inviting thing." Five days later he reported a week of work in which he
had been "trying to get some style and spice and connection into a long
row of facts and figures which I am to inflict . . . upon the Literary
Society next week. Some figures I like—yours for instance. Furs, too,
I like when I see a little girl whom I know wrapped up in 'em. But when
I try to make the figures in a dusty and mouldy French account book
do duty as figures of speech for a literary paper—why I feel very much
like . . . simply making the fur *fly*." But the paper was finished and
delivered as agreed. Revised into thesis form, it was accepted as the
major requirement for the master of arts degree in the spring of 1888.[23]

Turner's plans for the next year remained unclear through much of
the spring semester 1888. Professor Allen and the minister of the
Unitarian Church, J. H. Crooker, apparently did their best to convince
President Chamberlin that he should give Turner some guarantee as
to the future. Turner explained to Caroline, "Prof. Allen you understand is a mighty good friend, but he is not a *pusher*,—and Mr. Crooker
is, and has been manipulating things for me."[24] Allen and Crooker
hoped to have Turner confirmed as a regular instructor at an enhanced
salary, serve the next year in that capacity, and then take leave for a
year at Hopkins. Turner hoped that this scheme might allow Caroline
and him to marry in the near future and to go as a married couple to
Baltimore in 1889. But Chamberlin held firm, and by mid-May 1888
Turner had decided to spend the next year in residence at Johns
Hopkins. He must depart for Baltimore in September 1888, unmarried,
and without guarantees for the future.

Turner spent much of July in Madison, in part because his sister
Breese in Portage was ill with the measles. He worked on his Northwest history outline, which was to include a topical presentation with
appended recommendations for reading. Selecting these required more
background work than he anticipated, but the effort broadened his
growing knowledge of the literature of western history. There were
also finishing touches to be placed upon his fur trade manuscript,
which Thwaites planned to publish in the *Proceedings* of the State
Historical Society, and upon his paper on the Northwest Ordinance.[25]
A pleasant six weeks followed at Portage, with its fishing diversions,
and included a visit with Caroline and her family, who had fled to
Marquette, Michigan, to avoid Chicago's hay fever season.

While at home in early September Turner provided Caroline with a vignette of local politics that reflects his understanding of the workings of American democracy. Jack Turner took the family riding among the Baraboo bluffs, then "gorgeous . . . in robes of red and purple and gold," sumac blazing at the roadside beside purple asters and yellow-orange goldenrod. Prairie chickens and partridges in the road bed skittered before the approaching democrat, and beside a congregation of standing horses and wagons, they found a Republican party caucus in session in a log-shanty blacksmith shop covered with circus posters showing elephants, horses, and "pretty girls in appalling attitudes." The smith was caucus chairman; his hammer, lying on the anvil, served as gavel. Jack Turner, the Portage "boss," was invited in to talk to the assemblage, where there was "not an American in the crowd," but rather "Scotch, Swiss, Welch, and German." His father, Turner wrote, leaned against the anvil and discussed the candidates and issues skillfully, being "careful for they are jealous of Portage interference, and besides they are shrewd, hard-headed, sometimes very able, men." Turner cherished the memory of this incident, he said, because it allowed him to understand his father's local political influence better and also because "it was so picturesque, and so characteristic of our institutions." He would have "give[n] much to have had a foreigner see the spectacle."[26] One suspects that the scene in the blacksmith shop always remained thereafter at the core of Turner's vision of American democracy.

By the last week of September Turner was in Baltimore, putting up at a hotel and tramping "the old narrow" streets in search of a satisfactory boarding place. After a disheartening round of "disagreeable people, bad smelling and vile looking rooms," he found accommodation in the boarding house maintained by Mary Jane Ashton and her sister Hannah.[27] In past years Woodrow Wilson and John Franklin Jameson had been part of a succession of students in the graduate program in political science and history at The Johns Hopkins University who had found highly satisfactory lodging here. Among the current boarders Turner found Charles Homer Haskins, staccato of speech and so bright that although he was only eighteen years of age, he was already well advanced in the doctoral program. Miss Ashton was to prove a most solicitous landlady, and at six dollars per week

Turner's room cost less than had his lodging in Madison. The meals proved excellent in the variety and quantities of food provided, although, in Turner's eyes, too often prepared in the frying pan. There was cake at bedtime, and Miss Ashton tolerated student noise, occasional high jinks, and the teasing at which Turner professed himself adept. That year one of her spinster boarders moved out in disgust at the liberties allowed the young men.

Johns Hopkins was an even greater revelation to Turner than his visit to New England in 1887 had been. Turner's advisor, Adams, had a remarkable ability to spur students to achievement. His mind bubbled with ideas for strengthening the history discipline at Hopkins and in the eyes of the public. He was attracting outstanding young scholars to his seminar and was successfully placing them in good positions, particularly in the South and West. In self-congratulation he had prepared a map of the United States showing the "institutions of learning" that had employed his students, as a "graphical illustration" of "the colonial system of the Johns Hopkins University."[28]

Himself unmarried, Adams regarded the graduate students as his "boys." "No one," wrote his colleague Richard T. Ely later, "will say that he ever felt repressed by him." Adams, said Turner, "gave to me . . . an added enthusiasm for historical research and a definite desire to relate history to the present. . . . His greatest power did not lie in keenness of scholarship nor in the critical character of his investigations; but I have never seen a man who could surpass him in inspiring men with enthusiasm for serious historical work and in bringing out the best that was in them." Woodrow Wilson called him "a great Captain of Industry, a captain in the field of systematic and organized scholarship."[29]

Under Adams's guidance, Turner worked out a program in which he planned to study ancient, church, and constitutional history with Adams and develop a minor in political economy with another dynamic instructor, Richard T. Ely. Turner's knowledge in the latter area was thin, and he spent much time on it as a result. Soon he was allowed to drop the church history. This workload allowed him to read more American history. Adams and Ely decided that Turner's studies under Allen were sufficiently broad to justify counting them as two years of graduate residence. Adams also accepted the Wisconsin fur trade as an appropriate dissertation topic, allowing Turner to recast the master's thesis. In early October 1888 Turner reported to Caroline that coming to Johns Hopkins was "one of the best things I ever did in my life . . . I am already a new man for it" and a few days later, "I am in in the full swing of university life and I *like* it! . . . I really wish to jump and shout aloud in the new freedom and happiness of having pleasant work and *only* pleasant work. I am growing like a plant in the sunshine—and if only I had you here with me I should be absolutely content." In April 1889 Turner reported that his stay at J.H.U. had "permitted" him "to enter into possession of [himself] more than . . . ever . . . before" and that he had "grown . . . fat . . . in knowledge."[30]

The young westerner was not completely bedazzled by the Johns Hopkins program, however. When he planned his study year, he had counted upon benefiting from John Franklin Jameson's instruction in American history, but, once arrived, Turner discovered that Jameson had now assumed duties at Brown University. Although he found that Adams's "power of getting men interested and at work, is certainly remarkable," he believed that "a little more cautious scholarship in the historical line" was needed. He found the linkage of the English Constitution, United States Constitution, and American history in one course commendable: "It is in short, the development of the American nation *politically* that is emphasized—The great lack of it all is in getting any proper conception of the Great West. Not a man here that I know of is either studying, or hardly aware of the country beyond the Alleghanies—except two." Allen sympathized with Turner's chagrin at Jameson's absence but reminded him that "the principle thing is the methods, and getting yourself in touch with men."[31]

In later years Turner maintained that Adams had demurred at his proposal to write his dissertation on the fur trade and suggested on another occasion that further work on the history of American institutions was unnecessary. Accounts of this byplay do not ring true. Adams may have suggested to Turner that national Indian policy might provide a better dissertation topic than a study of the fur trade as institution. Turner did not reject the idea out of hand. But we find no evidence in Turner's letters to Caroline or to Allen that Adams argued strongly against Turner's desire to develop further the subject of his master's thesis. This was, after all, the Adams who had written an important monograph emphasizing the importance of Revolutionary era differences among the American states concerning claims to the western country. In a passage in the first edition of G. Stanley Hall's *Methods of Teaching History*, written a few years before Turner's stay at Hopkins, Adams had asserted, "there await the student pioneer vast tracts of American institutional and economic history almost as untouched as were once the forests of America, her coal measures and prairies, her mines of iron, silver, and gold."[32] This statement was carried into the second edition of *Methods* and its reprinting of 1889, the very year in which, according to Turner legend, Adams decried the future of American institutional history.

Quite rightly Turner acknowledged that Allen contributed more to his understanding of history and the role of the historian than any other teacher, including his mentors at The Johns Hopkins University. Allen, Turner always maintained, was "one of the greatest history teachers of the country," a fact "never . . . generally appreciated."[33] He was abreast of the historical writing of his time, and his primary interest lay in the development of institutions, as did that of Adams. But Adams and Ely were social scientists in orientation to a greater degree than Allen, and this had its impact upon Turner, particularly in Ely's case. Under Ely's instruction Turner studied the works of John Stuart Mill, and Turner told Allen that other writings of political economists to be read that fall included, "Ely's published books, [Francis A.] Walker, Ingram's Hist. of Polit. Econ. Clarke's Capital, Adams' Relation of the State to Industrial Action, Thompson's Harvard Lecture on Protection, Henry George's Progress and Poverty—and some others."[34] Simon H. Patten's text in political economy provided the foundation for Ely's advanced work in that area. Ely's instruction and prescribed reading, as well as his comments in seminar, greatly heightened Turner's awareness of the importance of economic factors in American development.

At the apex of the graduate instruction at Johns Hopkins was the seminar over which Adams and Ely presided in sessions that began at eight o'clock on Friday evening in the Bluntschli Library. The setting has been preserved in a famous photograph showing the aphorism of the English historian, Edward A. Freeman, boldly traced upon one wall, "History is past Politics and Politics present History." Each of the seminar members was assigned a drawer for his books and papers in the seminar table, new students ranged on one side, old hands on the other. Occupying the seat by Turner was Albion W. Small, already a seasoned instructor, who provided instruction during that year in American history and who later become one of America's most distinguished sociologists. Of the members of the group, Turner, Haskins, and a young man named Charles M. Andrews—"strikingly handsome . . . and keen as a knife"—were all destined to influence their discipline significantly and to become presidents of the AHA.[35]

Another seminar participant, John R. Commons, shaped the field of labor economics.

Turner found his interaction with the other graduate students at Johns Hopkins to be highly stimulating, but he had some reservations about the conduct of the seminar. It was, he reported from a vantage point in March 1889, a forum where students "bring the fruits of their research." There was, he thought, "very little of the workshop about it. Not enough to suit me."[36] Following the European practice, a member of the seminar acted as recording secretary, summarizing the proceedings. The perspective of the seminar was actually broader than Turner suggested because Adams frequently discussed developments in history, and seminar members reviewed works of interest to the group. Thus Turner heard his fellow boarder, Haskins, roundly denounce chapters in Justin Winsor's *Narrative and Critical History of America* as perhaps "narrative, but . . . certainly not critical, and *hardly* history" and listened to John R. Commons's interesting review of James E. Thorold Rogers's *Economic Interpretation of History*.[37]

Turner's participation in the seminar was not sufficiently active during its early months as to cause the secretaries to note his contributions. During the fall he had told Professor Allen that he hoped to investigate source materials in the Indian Department in Washington, apparently in connection with his doctoral research, and in January he reviewed *The Indian Side of the Indian Question*, by William Barrows, for the seminar. In mid-February, however, Turner spoke to the group on "The Influence of the Fur Trade in the Northwest from the Particular Standpoint of Wisconsin." Unfortunately, the secretary of the evening did not record the discussion that he reported to have ensued on both Turner's paper and on one treating the use of the referendum and related devices in America. Turner was himself seminar secretary for the last session of the year, that of May 17, 1889, summarizing several presentations but particularly one dealing with the practical application of the single tax.

Adams and Ely were impressed by the young instructor from Wisconsin. At this time both were enthusiastic about developing university extension programs and also hoped that university faculty would be able to upgrade the programs of the Chautauqua movement. Adams was working to develop a home study program in history in conjunction with Chautauqua and promptly drafted Turner to help in preparing a home study outline for a course in history. Learning of Turner's paper on the Northwest Ordinance, he arranged that Turner should present it as one of a series of lectures to be given to teachers in Washington and Baltimore. At Christmas Turner accepted Ely's invitation to dinner, a pleasant occasion, and returned to his lodgings with his teacher's copy of Edward Bellamy's *Looking Backward*. This he found to be a "most fascinating" book, which took him into "another world." Ely also invited Turner to supervise discussion in his undergraduate courses while that "quiet, odd, and yet most excellent" professor was away, and he later offered his Wisconsin student an assistantship that would have involved supervision of Chautauqua correspondence study during the following year.[38] Adams also expressed interest in providing Turner with assistance that might enable him to stay on at Hopkins for another year and, as the year drew on, even suggested the possibility of having Turner write the section on the Northwest in a textbook that he proposed to coordinate.

Turner showed in his early months at Johns Hopkins that he was able to adapt well to his new environment. In the Christmas recess he demonstrated this skill still further. The members of the AHA had planned a late summer meeting in Ohio in 1888 but changed their plans to assemble in Washington, D.C., in late December. The program had been flavored to western tastes, and as a result, Jameson described the sessions as "extremely stupid. . . . We had much western history warmed-over. . . . Western history is stupid anyway, I think." No matter eastern disdain, Turner read the paper that Professor Allen had contributed to the program, "The Place of the Northwest in General History," his voice pleasantly melodic, pitched and nuanced with elocutionary skill.[39]

"'More than once,'" he read to his audience, "'in the Northwest . . . we have found the key to problems of a national character.'" And summing up, he noted the crucial importance of the northwestern region in the imperial contest for the continent and for the future development of the United States. Lastly, the ordinance that provided for organization of the Northwest was integral to the development of our national policy: "'Our territorial system, our policy of creating new States, our national guaranty of personal freedom, universal education, and religious liberty, found their first expression in the great act which provided for the government of the Northwest.'" The written words were those of Allen, the spoken those of his student. But that student had a most absorptive mind at this stage of his development. Returned to Baltimore, Turner reported to Allen that "in the matter of breadth and philosophical treatment" his Wisconsin teacher's paper had been "superior to all the others" and also revealed that he, himself, had succeeded in meeting many of the leading scholars in attendance, including Maj. John W. Powell.[40]

Woodrow Wilson—"one of the J.H.U. pantheon"—arrived during February to present a course of lectures on governmental adminis- tration and, as one of Miss Ashton's former boarders, again took up residence in her establishment. Initially, Turner thought him "homely, solemn, young, glum, but with that fire in his face and eye that means that its possessor is not of the common crowd." Soon the two were on the best of terms, chatting at length in the boarding house "on all sorts of subjects" and going for walks together. Beneath Wilson's reserve Turner found a man capable of "talking the most delightful stream of anecdote and epigram." He was "very much impressed with [the] value" of Wilson's lectures and even thought that he might enjoy developing the same area if required in the future to teach subjects additional to history.[41] Wilson listened to Turner present his seminar report on the Wisconsin fur trade and enthusiastically praised it.

At home in Wisconsin Thwaites read Turner's paper on the fur trade to the members of the State Historical Society of Wisconsin and super- vised its printing in the society's *Proceedings*.[42] This paper was Turner's first substantial scholarly contribution. He distributed copies liberally, including on his list various literary or scholarly eminences. Thwaites warned him that other publications seldom noticed such papers, but some of the individual recipients acknowledged the paper's arrival with thanks, and the great Parkman assured him that he had "examined [it] with much interest."[43]

Perhaps because of his complete immersion in the exciting intel- lectual world of Johns Hopkins, Turner's romance was threatened during his year in Baltimore. Fred's letters contained more shop and less ardor than before. Caroline worried about her suitability as a faculty wife and became ill. She was placed on a restorative daily regime that included oatmeal porridge, cod liver oil, and onion. There was apparently an agreement that future plans would be placed on hold, and in the spring Caroline departed as the companion of an older woman on a far-flung junket to Europe. The correspondence, however, continued; Turner's attachment did not waver.

For much of the year while he was at Johns Hopkins, Turner shadow-boxed with President Chamberlin about returning to Madison. During the fall he was disturbed to learn that his former instructor in political economy, Professor John B. Parkinson, might withdraw from the university to oppose Robert La Follette in the latter's next race for office. If that occurred, the resulting vacancy might perhaps be combined with the one in American history and compromise Turner's negotiations with President Chamberlin. Adams and Ely were prepared to support Turner if he desired to stay at Johns Hopkins for another year, and Adams also offered to recommend him for a temporary position at Ohio State University. At the close of 1888 Turner wrote to Professor Allen, "You know that it is my ambition to hold the chair of American history [in Madison], and you know how pleasant it would be to me to work under you as the head of the historical department. I see possibilities in a chair thus established in connection with the libraries there, which I should be slow to abandon. . . . Are the authorities, in your opinion, likely to give me anything else than the instructorship and an instructor's salary?" Turner asked Allen whether he should perhaps seek additional experience by taking the Ohio position. Was there any possibility, he wondered, of being named an associate professor at Wisconsin? He summed up, "I am willing to make *some* sacrifices to grow up with the American History department in my own institution, but I think I can fairly ask the President for some *tangible* statement of the prospects — do not you?"[44]

Allen's response, wrote Turner, made him "think that [he was] likely to have to make application for the Ohio place if [he was] to get the salary" he wanted. Two weeks later he reported that "they are offering inducements to me to return [to Madison], but I am thinking seriously of trying to get away from old associations into a new world and so I may go to Ohio if I can, or somewhere else. It depends on circumstances." Soon he explained to Caroline that he could have a professorship at Wisconsin if he would "teach part of the time in Elocution." But Turner had come to detest the teaching of that subject.[45]

In early February 1889 Chamberlin was still not "ready to make any definite arrangement," and Turner reported to Caroline that he had "the satisfaction of not caring very much whether he does or not for . . . it is not impossible that Dr. Adams may get me to teach here next year." In the previous year Turner had coordinated the successful lobbying effort to have his friend Jim Cole named professor of military science. Now he informed Caroline that "Cole has been doing great work in 'frightening the authorities' with the idea that I am going to refuse to come back." But several weeks later Turner told her that "it now looks as if I would go back. Pres Chamberlin . . . has written to me that he intends to nominate me as Assistant Professor, at about twice my prior salary and so, unless some thing new develops, I expect to go back to Madison and spend my life there working in my historical mine—Mr. Crooker wrote me a letter the other day that told me that Prof Allen expected me to be his successor before many years, as the professor of history there. . . . It is a quiet life, but one in which there is opportunity for intellectual and moral growth, and I am going to accept it if it comes."

Discussing the matter still further a week later, he assured Caroline that he had not been "sad when I spoke of going to M[adison]" even though "[i]n Madison I must make things for myself." He now had, he said, a goal and was "nearly ready to shoulder my knapsack. The position is not financially important yet," he continued, "but in its possibilities it is, as Prof Allen, a cautious man says: 'one of the most brilliant opportunities for a young man in this country.'"[46]

President Chamberlin and Turner reached accommodation. He was to be an assistant professor at fifteen hundred dollars per year, and he would not be required to teach elocution. He and Professor Allen discussed the history program and Turner's role in it in a satisfying exchange of letters that again demonstrated the young man's diplomatic skill. Mixed with the deference due his teacher was a tactful critique of the Wisconsin history curriculum. In his experience at the University of Wisconsin, he had, he told Allen, found the assignment of topics that students then reported upon in class did not work particularly well at the freshman level, although it was an excellent technique of instruction in more advanced classes. Nationally known as an advocate of the topical method of instruction, Allen took the criticism in stride.

As Turner's year at Hopkins drew to a close, Caroline asked him if he was not sorry that it was almost over. In response he said it had been the "best year of [his] life so far as mental growth [was] concerned." He would miss the music and his association with "men of 'Urbane' ideas." He added, "Yes, especially, because I am here in daily intimacy with eager, ambitious, energetic young men, and older men, who are interested in the things I am interested in; who understand me, and stimulate me—One is at the heart of university life in America here—and very close to German thought, too." Balancing this, said Turner, was the fact that he "expect[ed] to return to a position at Madison that any one of the men here would jump to accept. . . . It has . . . disadvantages in regard to theaters and music and companionship but it has that advantage that Woodrow Wilson mentioned to me the other day. It is in the country where men can think out their own thoughts and not fall into city conventionalism." Madison was much more pleasant than Baltimore except in winter. Were he to stay at Hopkins the salary would be "very *small*" because the "*reputation* of teaching" at Hopkins was considered to be worth a considerable amount to the young scholar involved. Nor did such considerations take into account, he continued, "the fact that I am suited to work in *Western* history . . . for which there is not material here." Finally, wrote Turner, "I am getting eager to be settled down to my life work and to have a home. This and my strongest desire to see you, make the most important considerations."[47]

Turner realized that the Hopkins year had changed him. Returning in June 1889 to Portage, he reported that "Portage is terrible. . . . I have grown away from my native place." Several days later he wrote that he was "stagnating in Portage—What an awful life." Madison, a university town, was different. He could "live there and be happy." He reported, however, that he did not like some of his old friends as well as he once thought. "Except Prof. Allen—He is a grand man. I like him and shall enjoy his companionship increasingly. Thwaites is pleasant too, and more like my Hopkins friends. I suspect that these men will be my most intimate acquaintances after a little." Cole, he admitted, was "the same good fellow and devoted friend he always was, but we are not interested in the same things."[48] Thus Turner visualized friendship and profession to go together.

When Turner returned to Madison, he could savor significant accomplishments. He had carried his doctoral studies to the point where he could obtain the Ph.D. in the spring of 1890 by passing exams in French and German and various areas of history and by defending his dissertation. But he also carried back to Madison a full sense of the exhilaration of being at the cutting edge of a scholarly discipline and of engaging on even terms in scholarly discourse with other bright and enthusiastic minds. Though he did not realize it, he had become one of the members of the young elite of scholars in the social sciences that was emerging particularly from Johns Hopkins during the 1880s and 1890s, a group which laid the foundations of modern academia in their specialties.

The Hopkins experience was important in another respect as well. On his return Turner was much more of a social scientist than he had been one or two years earlier when he had reveled in the pages of the great narrative historian Francis Parkman. Adams and Ely were essentially social scientists. Adams compared his seminar to a laboratory in the natural or physical sciences and emphasized the importance of social and economic factors in historical development; Ely studied the past for the lessons it provided about the present and was prepared to meld economic science and his reading of the past as the basis for prediction and social policy. Contemporary social theory was on the lips of both of them. And at this point Turner was soaking up ideas like a sponge. Turner also found in both Adams and Ely examples of academic empire builders. Growing up in the home of a western-county-seat politician, exposed daily to the frontier developmental ethos in which community builders constantly schemed to make their towns the leading urban centers of the region, Turner now knew that this kind of attitude also paid dividends in academia.

Thanks to Allen's earlier instruction and to the Johns Hopkins experience, Turner was at the beginning of his professional career fully conversant with the intellectual currents in the history discipline, both those that were flourishing and those that were declining in importance. The example of the antiquary Draper he would use in his writing only as an illustration of what not to do. He would find it more difficult to divest himself of the influence of Parkman, the epitome of romantic narrative. He was aware that the historian wishing acceptance from his peers could no longer moralize in the fashion of George Bancroft. Of ascendant trends, he was fully versed in the commitment of American academic historians to rigorous and systematic evaluation and classification of evidence, which they believed—perhaps mistakenly—mirrored Leopold von Ranke's method of analyzing evidence in an effort to portray the event "exactly as it was." Turner was prepared to draw upon Social Darwinism to provide analogy and framework in his interpretation of history.

Allen defined institutional history as concerned with the "organized action of mankind." It involved "the study of institutions . . . their organic relation to one another in constitutions of government, and of the political conflicts that have grown out of them."[49] Both he and Adams traced institutions of American government backward to Germanic and even Aryan antecedents in the dim past. Exposed as he was to such analysis, Turner was undoubtedly aware that both Jameson and Wilson had found this emphasis upon institutional origins at Hopkins to be frustrating. In Ely, Turner had found a teacher who sought the meaning of America's postbellum record of capital accumulation and labor unrest and who was not afraid to include socialist alternatives in his discussions of ameliorative programs. History must now find a role for economic and social factors in its explanations of the past. In parallel tendency literary figures were turning to realistic description and themes, and Turner read the literary journals of his time. In this swirl of intellectual options Turner sifted and selected eclectically, marshaling support for his commitment to the field of western history.

The Hopkins experience had allowed Turner to prove himself as a promising young historian. He returned to Madison afire with professional fervor. But what kind of a young man was he, apart from the discipline? Obviously one with the ability to make the right political moves, a skilled communicator, a man of personal charm who made friendships easily but was shrewdly selective in those he advanced. The Class Book of 1884 had identified him as "independent" in politics, and his status as student in a university headed by a president who was so intensely interested in social problems and their possible solutions, as was Bascom, insured his awareness of the social and political reform currents that were so much a part of the pre-Progressive Era. So too did his relations with Crooker and his activity in Unitarian-sponsored clubs. When he had prepared for his Baltimore year, he was intrigued that The Johns Hopkins University offered a political science course on the subject of scientific charities. Perhaps, he suggested to Caroline, he should attend those lectures and "take a mission class." He continued, "truly I do lead an extremely selfish unhelpful sort of life, outside of my school duties. There is a great deal of philosophy in the doctrine of thinking about other people. But the only way to help them is to do it scientifically."[50] Social concern, however, never propelled him into the real world of the settlement houses.

In his Portage days the young Turner had seen Indians both in their camps and trading in the town—the "gypsy" Winnebagos, he later called them, and he knew them also as guides and boatmen. Vacationing near Montello, Wisconsin, in the summer of 1888, he dug a skull from an Indian mound, took it to the state museum, and apparently made some effort to explore the archeological literature relevant to the midwestern mound builders. After becoming established in Baltimore, he informed Professor Allen that he planned soon to go to Washington and "look over the material for work on the Indian department with especial reference to its bearing on the development of the west." In seminar in January 1889 Turner reported on William Barrows's effort to predict the success of the Indian Allotment Act of 1887 within the perspective of the failures of past Indian policies in the United States.[51] But Turner never made either past or present Indian policy a particular concern, diverted in the first instance perhaps by Professor Adams's suggestion that he use the topic of his master's research for the doctoral dissertation.

During his years as instructor and graduate student in Madison, Turner had observed that immigrant groups were displacing the first American settlers in various areas of Wisconsin, and he noted the need for research on such matters in both his "Commonplace Book" and later in correspondence with Allen. He did not pass judgment on such processes as being either good or bad. Growing up in Portage he had lived among a population of diverse national origins and within a household finely tuned to the political realities of such existence. But his reaction to Boston's Jewish quarter had been initially one of repulsion. Responding in the following year to Caroline's mention of a Jewish gentleman, he maintained, "I have no prejudice against any man's nationality as such—but I feel that however you shatter the Jewish jar, the scent of the roses of Israel will cling to it still, and socially I can't say I ever found one I could be contented with."[52]

To Caroline he confessed that the doctrines of women's rights sounded quite reasonable when advanced by some of the attractive young women instructors of the Madison faculty. It was with more humor than anger that he described an incident in which a women's rights lecturer jumped his claim to the railroad car seat that he had tried to reserve by placing his luggage on it. At the meeting of the AHA in 1888 he met Professor Lucy Salmon, who was to have a distinguished career at Vassar College. "A lovely young woman—with a face that glows with intelligence and sympathy," he reported to Caroline and concluded a similar report to Professor Allen with the words "and withal a *woman*." Still, none of these incidents indicate a deep commitment to the advancement of women in American society, although he was obviously comfortable with the University of Wisconsin's coeducational environment. When he chose a life's partner he did not want her to be an intellectual nor a social reformer. He explained, "I like persons particularly who like the things in which I am interested for *friends*. But for some one to *love*, I do not wish to have one who knows over much about whether I am doing well or ill in the world of letters. I dream only of having some one who is another world to me to which I can turn from the every day world." He explained to Caroline that he had not sent a copy of his article on the Wisconsin fur trade to her in the spring of 1889 because he "knew that its subject would not interest you."[53]

In the last years of his teaching, the Turners entertained some of his Radcliffe students. One of them bubbled to Caroline that sharing Turner's ideas and discoveries in history must have been a wonderful experience. Caroline responded that she and Professor Turner never discussed such matters.

Early September 1889 found Fred Turner established in the northeast room of the boarding establishment run by Mrs. Bross on State Street in Madison. He reported 105 students in one course and 85 in another, but he noted that he was "likely to have to do considerable elementary teaching and abandon the work in higher history and political economy" that had been initially arranged. He had, he confessed, been "ambitious to do a higher grade of work."[54] But there was to be much else on his mind. In addition to his teaching he had to prepare for doctoral language and subject field exams and the defense of his dissertation at Johns Hopkins at the end of the academic year. But he had another high priority—soon he was negotiating with his landlady for the space needed to house a young married man and his bride.

Turner married Caroline Mae Sherwood in late November 1889. The ceremony took place in Chicago, where Turner's good friend of those years, Charles [Charlie] Gregory, of the university law school faculty, acted as best man. Prior to the Chicago fire, Caroline's father had been a businessman with fine prospects. Although he never recovered from his losses of that time, his family maintained some social pretensions and, fearing that they might be out of place in Chicago society, Andrew Jackson and Mary Turner did not attend the wedding. The newlyweds began married life in Madison rooms rented from Mrs. Bross. Their happiness was soon interrupted. Two summers earlier Fred had fled from Portage when sister Breese fell ill with measles. Now it was his turn to be ill with the virus, and his bride hastily departed for Chicago, to avoid becoming infected also. Early in the next year she returned to Madison to take up married life with Fred in a rented house at 21 West Gilman Street.

Meanwhile, a shocking event occurred. Returning to Madison, Turner visualized a future in which he developed the field of American history there under the benign supervision of Allen while the latter taught the courses in European history. Both he and Allen expected that, after some years of preparation, he would assume direction of the whole program. But in December 1889 Allen once more contracted pneumonia and this time died. Turner wrote to Adams, "The gentlest, justest, most scholarly man I ever knew, has gone."[55] His grief aside, what would this mean for Turner? Would President Chamberlin offer Turner the opportunity to build upon the foundation laid by his brilliant teacher, or would that young man be forced to accommodate to the ideas and ambitions of a new and perhaps unsympathetic leader?

3 Inheritance

*"Someone with a reputation such that he would lift
the institution into prominence"*

As tutor and graduate student Turner had come to believe that to be
a highly successful historian one must occupy an important area of the
field and make it one's own. When he went to The Johns Hopkins
University he had already decided that the history of the Great West
or, as he sometimes put it, the Northwest, would be his special area
of interest. He persevered in this intent while in Baltimore, enriching
his general store of knowledge and filing conceptual ideas for later use.
At the same time he established himself within a stimulating and
supportive network of professional scholars—the Hopkins alumni in
history and the social sciences. But was he prepared to assume the
major responsibility for the history program at Madison under a
president determined to make his university a leader in the field of
higher education?

After Allen's death in late 1889 there were weeks of uncertainty.
Who was to replace him, both as program head and instructor in
European history? President Chamberlin kept Turner in uneasy limbo
for a time—asking the latter's advice on appropriate replacements.
Could he suggest, asked Chamberlin, a man "of established reputation"
or "young men [who] had distinguished themselves?" But after a trip to
Washington and consultation with Adams, Chamberlin temporarily
reappointed an instructor who had helped with the Wisconsin history
program during Turner's absence at Johns Hopkins and asked Turner
to assume Allen's duties.[1]

The larger question remained. What was the permanent arrangement to be? Late January 1890 found Turner, as he told his friend
Wilson, "kept like Mohammed's coffin" and growing "weary of having
to keep one eye off my work in order to look out for my 'official head.'"[2]
Several weeks later Turner assessed the situation. Chamberlin had
delayed making a permanent appointment because he was cautious
and also because he hoped to find "someone with a *reputation* such
that he would lift the institution into prominence." Failing such
discovery, Turner believed the position would be his, and he doubted

that the president could find the sort of man whom he had in mind. But Chamberlin was a "psychological puzzle."[3]

Wilson had written to Turner in late August, explaining that he was to write the volume in the "Epochs of American History" series that would cover the years from 1829 to 1889 and inquiring whether his Wisconsin friend could provide him with material that revealed a sense of western regional identity comparable to that found at the time in the South. He also asked if Turner would like to be recommended for the history chair at Wesleyan University that Wilson was to vacate at the end of academic year 1889–90. In response, Turner described the advantages of his current position but also noted his heavy teaching load and expressed interest in learning more about the position in Middletown, Connecticut. Turner's local friends rallied to persuade Chamberlin and the regents to appoint Turner to Allen's post, and Thwaites wrote to Wilson suggesting that he should write to the president of the board of regents on Turner's behalf. Turner, he said, was "too modest to lift a hand to shape the result," a statement worthy of several grains of salt.[4] Wilson was only too glad to help, writing strongly on his friend's behalf both to Chamberlin and to the regent. Perhaps—even probably—rumor of the Wesleyan option floated into the presidential precincts. Chamberlin invited Turner to assume the mantle of his old professor and in 1891 promoted him to the rank of professor.

Despite his uncertainties and heavy duties during that first year of full-time teaching, Turner appeared in Baltimore to complete his doctoral requirements in the late spring of 1890. When he left, having lost his umbrella, his glasses, and Miss Ashton's house key, he could rejoice that he had, in favorite phrasing, "pulled through" but also because Haskins had agreed to join him in Madison at the beginning of the next academic year as Allen's replacement in European history. Although his dissertation dealt with the Yazoo land frauds, Haskins was destined to become the leading American medievalist of his time. Unknowingly, Chamberlin had placed history at Wisconsin in the hands of two future presidents of the AHA. Turner now had a colleague whom he found highly congenial, committed to the Hopkins institutional approach, and sharing his views on the proper objectives of the emerging history discipline. Both Turner and Haskins were ambitious, highly able, politically skilled, and spurred by the sense that they must justify their comparative youth by outstanding per-formance. Haskins's driving professionalism spurred Turner no less

Caroline Mae Sherwood Turner and her husband in the early years of their marriage. Reprinted with permission of the State Historical Society of Wisconsin, Madison, Wisconsin. (X3)50974.

than it did Haskins himself. For twelve years the two men occupied adjacent offices in University Hall, and during the latter two-thirds of the period Haskins roomed in the house at 629 Frances Street that Turner built in 1894. Regarding each other as "brothers" in all but blood, the two remained close friends and admirers of each other's professional talents even after Haskins departed for Harvard University in 1902.

In late January 1890 Turner reported to Wilson that Caroline and he had "just gone to housekeeping in a modest little house" at 21 West Gilman Street and that "'happiness and strength'" had "indeed been added to me."[5] In early 1892 he informed Richard T. Ely that he was paying a yearly rent of four hundred dollars and that the dwelling had nine rooms. In organizing their domestic economy, the Turners engaged a maid named Barbara. Thereafter until Turner retired, the household seldom lacked one or two domestics. Such arrangements were usual in a period when the new academic professionals took their cues from the gentleman scholars whom they were displacing and when families within the urban midwestern middle class commonly employed "hired girls." Both Turner and his mother-in-law, Lucinda Sherwood, were convinced that Caroline's health was delicate, and periodically during her lifetime Mrs. Sherwood, a woman of great energy and practicality, assisted in helping the Turner household meet major challenges.

Caroline Mae Turner did not aspire to be a scholar or a student of literature, although the Turner family library ultimately contained its share of poetry and novels. Her lack of major intellectual interests did not disappoint Turner. As we have seen, he did not want a wife who was an intellectual peer. "American domestic life," he maintained a few months before he and Caroline married, "is of far higher type than European. A woman is neither a doll nor a drudge, and I think we recognize that here more than they do there."[6] As the Turner marriage unfolded, Turner proved a most solicitous husband. Although he rejected the suggestion that American wives were treated as dolls, he was not perhaps free of the sin. From courtship onward his letters to Caroline emphasize her small stature, her sweetness, and her fragility. On one occasion he sent her the text of the poem "In Praise of Little Women." Fred and Mae wrote to each other frequently when separated, and he endured their separations during hay fever season with understanding and humor, advising her on hotel escape routes in case of fire. If sometimes overly sentimental, his letters were, in their way, impressive—almost never recriminative nor petty, laced with humor, to the end sustaining and affectionate. Something of an impulse shopper himself, he accepted her tendency to overdraw the bank account with no more than the occasional admonition to be careful.

Caroline Mae Turner took her social responsibilities seriously, serving as her husband's hostess, faithfully returning calls, and responding to proffers of friendship within the overlapping university and Madison communities. The young couple were delighted when Dorothy Kinsley Turner arrived in late 1890, to be followed over the next few years by Jackson Allen and Mae Sherwood Turner. The growing family experienced the usual childhood illnesses. At six months Dorothy almost died of respiratory problems, and a distraught Turner became ill himself after summoning the doctor on foot in severe weather. But the family was for years a happy one.

Turner was a firm believer in the sustaining and restorative powers of exercise. Returned to Madison, he took up tennis and ultimately golf and throughout his career reserved a part of almost every summer for fishing. Caroline was an interested but restrained hiker and developed an interest in bird watching in company with other faculty wives. She tolerated a fisherman husband. Unlike Jessie Thwaites, however, she did not glory in her ability to wield a paddle or play the part of wilderness cook.

Although Turner informed Wilson that he and Caroline were not much interested in an active "social life," the university community and its intermingling with the town generated a good deal of diversion. He spoke to student groups and, after the organization of the University of Wisconsin School of Economics, Political Science, and History, assisted in establishing a history and political science club. No musician, Turner enjoyed local concerts and plays presented under university or community sponsorship. He participated in the activities and programs of the Channing Club and the Contemporary Club, and the Turners were members of the Madison Literary Society and the Town and Gown Club. He continued to join in Judge Romanzo Bunn's Shakespearean evenings, a diversion that enhanced his ability to produce appropriate allusions and allowed him to discuss fishing flies with the judge.

Turner liked good food and attendant spirits, and Caroline liked to dress well and entertain with style. Their guests found them to be pleasant and caring hosts. Turner had warned Caroline that he could not promise her riches, but they lived comfortably. From youth Turner loved books and he began to build a considerable personal library, an enjoyable but not inexpensive task. Both Turners readily accepted the common view at the university that vacations should be spent away from the campus, the more easily because Madison's summer selection of dusts, pollens, and fungi aroused Caroline's hay fever. A doting father, Turner kept diaries of the early progress of two of the children and happily recounted their brilliant sayings to friends. Domestic assistance, the Turners assumed, was essential. Turner's university salary was always generous, given the era, his age, and faculty rank, but he had no inherited wealth with which to supplement it, as did some academics of the time. Typically the Turner family lived at the outer edge of its means while in Wisconsin—bills often deferred until the end of the payment period and understanding sometimes sought from a friendly bank officer.

Having assumed Professor Allen's duties in early 1890, Turner taught courses on the French Revolution, ancient society, general history, political and constitutional history of the United States, a seminar on the history of the Northwest, as well as an additional course on the nineteenth century during the winter or spring of 1890. With Haskins on board in the fall of 1890, Turner could renew his hope of specializing in American history. That area, however, involved much work in elementary courses. Turner's first efforts to develop upper level undergraduate work produced a course in American constitutional history. President Chamberlin also wished Turner to follow his inclination to develop an offering in economic history, and the latter also believed that a course in the history of colonization might be successful. Wisconsin's faculty members were for the first time offering extension courses during Turner's first years back in Madison. Turner developed the colonization theme in a local lecture and in one of several extension short courses that he offered—but he never added it to the undergraduate curriculum. Turner's course in "Economic and Social History of the United States" appeared first in the University *Catalogue* of 1891–92.[7]

A sophomore transfer student from a small Methodist college in Iowa, Guy Stanton Ford, took the economic history course in the fall of 1892. He described the instructor as a brisk young man who did not coordinate his lectures with the textbook, who poured out "stimulating suggestions and flashing insights while handling over the miscellany on his desk," and who neglected to instruct the class about the bibliographies and citations required in research papers. The examinations were "unpredictable." Turner was not, thought Ford, "a good undergraduate teacher" by usual standards, and few "appreciated him" in that class. He did not court the jock nor the seeker of the gentleman's C. But he inspired those willing to work for themselves.[8]

One such in this era was Carl L. Becker, who later described how "Old Freddie Turner" drew a shy country boy from Iowa into history—not, Becker admitted, with historical facts, but with "indefinable *charm*," the magnetism of flashing blue eyes, an unmatched resonance of voice, and an unspoken invitation to join in the search for undiscovered revelation.[9] Turner provided much solid information in his lower-level undergraduate history courses in the 1890s and thereafter.

But he excelled in working with serious-minded juniors or seniors and graduate students. Reminiscing about Turner's class in constitutional history in 1892 and 1893, the distinguished economist Matthew B. Hammond recalled a dozen or so students meeting around a table in a corner of the Historical Library in the Wisconsin Capitol in a course that Hammond believed to have been "the most helpful one" in his experience as a student: "The ability to distinguish between primary and secondary sources of information, the importance of accuracy in statement and the methods of working up and presenting historical material were impressed upon my mind with more force than in any other course." Louise Phelps Kellogg described Turner's history of the West classes, a few years later, as "inspirational." His first words provided the keynote for the period—"sometimes merely a bald statement to be taken up, turned about, proved or disproved, accepted or rejected. Sometimes he would open class with a good story, sometimes with a bit of poetry—Kipling's virile verse was the favorite of this period." At some point in the hour there was always "a clash of mind on mind."[10]

Turner particularly loved teaching his seminar. James A. James studied with Turner as an undergraduate and later attended Johns Hopkins on his advice. He described the Wisconsin seminar in 1891 as the "Hopkins S. on a small scale."[11] Turner himself called it a workshop where students saw the chips fly and might cut their fingers. Each selected a topic that fit within the broader topic or chronological framework that Turner announced. During the school year 1890–91 the topic was "The Old Northwest," but the emphasis was upon German immigration into Wisconsin, a topic in which both Allen and Turner had been interested. The focus was chronological in the following year; class members studied the 1830s with emphasis on relations between East and West. The topics again involved German migration as well as the processes of settlement in New York during the late eighteenth and early nineteenth centuries and the English background of New England town government. During 1892–93 seminary members examined aspects of the history of the Erie Canal, the national land system, the Ordinance of 1787, and of Iowa's relation to the federal government, as well as continuing scrutiny of German immigration to Wisconsin.

Turner's first two Ph.D.'s emerged from these early seminars. Kate Everest's research on German immigration into Wisconsin proved sufficiently worthy that both the Wisconsin Academy of Sciences,

Turner's seminar meeting in the State Capitol Building in June 1894.
Turner is seated second from right. Reprinted with permission of the
University Archives, University of Wisconsin, Madison, Wisconsin.
(X3)46720.

Arts, and Letters and the State Historical Society published papers
drawn from it. She completed doctoral work in academic year
1892–93. During that same year a tall, intense, former school teacher,
Orin G. Libby, presented a master's thesis on the economic impact of
the Erie Canal and so impressively developed research upon the geographic distribution of the vote on the federal constitution that Turner
recommended he be included in the program of the AHA's meeting in
Chicago that summer. Libby obtained the doctorate in 1895.

Education on the Madison campus was changing during the early
1890s as President Chamberlin guided his institution toward the
status of a full-scale university. Student enrollments were rising. In
academic year 1887–88 the number of students was 722. The student
body stood at almost 4,400 in Turner's last year on staff, 1909–10.
Despite internal disagreements over educational philosophies and
policies, regents and legislators willingly supported the state's major
institution of higher learning. A College of Letters and Sciences was
created and a dean authorized; departments began to number several
members. Six course tracks emerged, as well as a "group system" of

organizing study in related disciplines, providing greater "continuity, concentration and thoroughness" and allowing in effect disciplinary majors.[12] President Chamberlin's ideal of a university envisioned flourishing postgraduate programs. His exhilarating experience at Johns Hopkins fresh in mind, Turner enthusiastically supported this objective. Soon he took the lead in establishing a School of Economics, Political Science, and History at the University of Wisconsin.

In the early 1890s President William Rainey Harper sought to move Herbert Baxter Adams and Richard T. Ely to the University of Chicago. In response, Johns Hopkins University promoted Adams to full professor but declined to improve Ely's appointment. Frustrated, Ely informed Turner that he would be willing to consider moving else- where. The latter, in turn, alerted President Chamberlin, who had been recently authorized to fill a chair of finance and statistics. Alert to the possibility of a prestigious appointment, President Chamberlin opened negotiations with Ely and in January 1892 obtained the approval of the board of regents to create a school offering postgraduate instruction in economics, political science, and history. Turner worked assiduously to convince his old teacher to accept the position and thereafter to make the arrangements necessary before Ely moved to Madison for the fall term in 1892. "Now," exulted Turner, "we shall be able to build up a postgraduate department at home, and when you are on the ground I am sure that Chicago University will have her hands more than full in her effort to monopolize political science, which I am told is her intention." Haskins joined his colleague in expressing his pleasure at Ely's decision and in assuring him that he "look[ed] forward to a great development in the studies that make for citizenship" at the University of Wisconsin.[13]

Ely was demanding. He wished to bring a bevy of Hopkinsians with him and urged as well that an endowment be established to support graduate students and other essentials of the new school. In the end, four young scholars accompanied him. Thwaites pledged his best efforts in building the library collections needed. Despite initial high hopes, however, Chamberlin and Turner were unsuccessful in per- suading Wisconsin business leaders to contribute to a school endow- ment, despite assurances that such a development would greatly benefit Wisconsin's economic growth. Although initially optimistic, Turner's reports of his activities on this front were always tempered. "The West has not learned *giving* as well as *getting*," he wrote. Six weeks later he explained, "The great difficulty lies in the fact that public support deadens private generosity—and that Milwaukee is not Chicago!"[14]

Turner contacted members of the business community in Milwaukee and at his extension lecture sites and enlisted the aid of ex-senator John C. Spooner. He speculated on the possibility of a large gift from Senator Sawyer but discarded the idea as perhaps raising the issue of accepting money from donors who were unsound on the tariff. He also suggested that the coeducational programs of the University of Wisconsin might sufficiently impress eastern advocates of women's rights that they would support the school. But Turner's reports of individuals approached were replaced by explanations of failure and assurances that the regents believed that state funds would be adequate.

While at Johns Hopkins, Turner had benefited greatly from Ely's instruction and appreciated his hospitality and professional support. He apparently believed that Ely's coming would impede neither his prospects nor the future of the history program. Ely's acceptance, wrote Turner, would "make it certain that the University of Wisconsin will not content itself with giving undergraduate instruction and becoming a feeder to Chicago; but that it will be a center of postgraduate work for the Northwest. This," he continued, "is the desire of Pres. Chamberlin, and it has long been an ambition of mine to find an opportunity to develop this side of our work. . . . Such a school will be a new departure in the West, and I believe our earnest western boys will supply the best sort of material."[15]

Turner hoped that the history program would benefit directly from the new school. He urged Ely to emphasize the need for strengthening library resources, and he explained the current needs of the history program in detail:

Permit me to express the thanks of Professor Haskins and myself for your good word to the President in regard to furnishing us with assistance—As it is now we have to do a good deal of work that might be done by instructors. I am myself becoming anxious to open some of the many fields for original work in American History that lie about me. If we are to contend with Chicago we must adhere strongly to the maxim—quality rather than quantity.

He closed this letter by assuring Ely that he and Haskins wanted him to come to the university as "head of this school" and that they would provide "hearty cooperation" in assuring the school's "highest influence."[16]

Writing several days later, Turner amplified the needs of the Wisconsin historians still more:

I am anxious to be relieved of Extension work altogether, or nearly so, next year, and to do this a special Extension lecturer in history would be needed. . . . Chicago's funds enable her to carry things by a coup-de-main. . . . Ought we not to meet this policy by developing certain special features that will attract men. Your idea of urging the sociological side of economics, and of developing certain lines in finance etc will be in this direction.

In history our really great collection in American history has no rival on this side the mountains, and in the line of western, local, and newspaper & periodical material, as well as in Dr. Draper's ms. collections for Ky. Tenn. & N.W. history, we are *un*rivalled—unless it be in newspapers—by two or three eastern libraries—In English history also we have a rich documentary and local collection. . . . Does it not seem to you that our aim should be to cultivate *Political Science* (broadly interpreted) as a means of good citizenship and preparation for the public service—and "Sociological Science" including all the activities of society—as a means of fostering good public teaching by the preachers, the Extensionists, and the teachers generally—Of course history is one of the methods of reaching these goals.[17]

Later Turner took the opportunity afforded by his work on the draft of an announcement of the offerings of the new school to write to Ely

If an instructor could be gotten in elementary work, and Modern History the historical work would be relieved of its excessive amount of elementary instruction, which would look bad in a circular to graduates.—I would prefer to give two advanced courses in place of Modern history, viz. Social and Economic History of U.S. . . . (especial reference to progress of Western settlement, immigration, internal improvements, land legislation, labor, manufactures, literature etc. etc)—And a course on the general history of *Colonization,*—"*Kolonial Politik*" . . . This would be a new course in American colleges, so far as I know, and I think I have some new ideas in regard to the subject.[18]

In continuing this letter, Turner noted that the titles of the historians
were now to be changed; he to become professor of "American History"
rather than of "History" and Haskins to be specified as specializing in
"Institutional History."

At this time the extension program at Wisconsin was enjoying a
highly successful first year of operation, no less than seventy-three
courses having been requested, the historians participating in sixteen.
Such offerings involved meetings during the course of six weeks and
Turner explained that such obligations took him away from Madison
during Friday, Saturday and part of Sunday. Next year, wrote Turner,
"I desire to devote myself to '*Intension*,'" and he believed that extension
activity might support some of the graduate students enrolled in the
new school. "We need," he wrote later, "a good safe extensionist who
can be trusted not to involve the University in religious or political
controversies and at the same time prove an inspiring and successful
speaker."[19]

In his efforts to assure the future of the history program in the new
school, Turner was as solicitous of Haskins's interests as his own. He
explained that it was essential to keep his colleague in the program and
that other institutions were already displaying interest in his services.
Promotion to professor should come as soon as possible. As the winter
wore on, President David S. Jordan of Stanford University approached
Haskins, and Turner sought immediate improvement in his position.
Ely assented to Turner's requests in every respect. "The sooner
[Haskins] can be made full professor, the better pleased I shall be," he
wrote. He pledged that he would do everything possible to support the
"historical side" and added that he had told Chamberlin that he would
"be very glad if in a few years we would be strong enough to make
history a distinct and separate school."[20] Haskins received his promotion to professor in that year, but Turner disclaimed any interest in
heading a separate school of history.

Ely's move to Wisconsin had its awkward moments. Professor John
B. Parkinson, the university vice president, had provided the only
offerings in political economy at the university. He expressed willingness to be part of Ely's school. But when he learned of the number of
individuals involved in Ely's transfer, he asked that his son be made an
assistant professor to work in Parkinson's area of specialty. Turner
advised Ely against making an issue of the matter, and Chamberlin
sought regent approval for an unnamed assistant for Parkinson on a
one-year basis. Inexperienced regents approved an amendment to

Chamberlin's recommendation, making Parkinson's son an assistant professor. Turner assured Ely that this was only a minor setback in their plans. The latter, however, was shocked to learn in June that Chamberlin was leaving to join the faculty of the University of Chicago. Ely bitterly reproached Chamberlin for deserting him as well as for failing to honor their agreement in some respects. The president defended himself indignantly, writing to Ely, "your methods of treating your friends and those of whom you seek aid are the worst I have ever encountered in similar correspondence." A new president, he suggested, might have more success in perfecting the arrangements of the school than he, given his differences of opinion with some regents.[21]

When Ely suggested that Turner should provide a personal guarantee against a possible shortfall in the promised remuneration of his assistant, Turner refused, noting that his salary was "but $2000, upon which I cannot do more than live."[22] Although Ely's demands probably dismayed Turner, he kept his poise throughout, emphasizing the positive aspects of the situation and astutely staying in the good graces of the major parties. When the respected historian and former president of Cornell University, Charles Kendall Adams, soon agreed to succeed Chamberlin, some of Ely's concern was alleviated. Under the economist's leadership the Wisconsin School of Economics, Political Science, and History moved the university to the forefront of social science training in the United States. It provided a setting that encouraged both Turner and Haskins to emphasize social science elements in their historical thinking and research.

Turner saw the creation of the School of Economics, Political Science, and History as a means of developing a leading center of graduate studies at Madison. During the extended correspondence with Ely, Turner frequently used developments at the University of Chicago as reference points, viewing Chicago as Wisconsin's major rival in a contest for educational hegemony in the Midwest. Competition with Chicago continued to be an element in Turner's thinking long after Ely's school was safely launched, as was the case with other faculty leaders at Wisconsin as well. In 1895 Ely and Turner served on a university committee charged with making recommendations concerning the graduate program. A section of the report's preamble runs, "Already Michigan has organized a distinct graduate school. . . . Chicago builds its whole future on this foundation, and will reduce us to the rank of a mere feeder to her advanced work, if we remain passive."²³ Almost a decade later Turner eloquently defended the summer school on the same grounds.

As with most of Adams's graduates, Turner remained on good terms with his former doctoral advisor after completing his graduate program. They exchanged cordial letters, and Turner was delighted when Adams came to speak before the members of the State Historical Society of Wisconsin, honoring both Thwaites's request that he emphasize the utility of historical societies and Turner's suggestion that he explain the benefits of extension programs. Turner was shocked when Ely suggested that Adams would now be unfriendly to the programs at Wisconsin. Turner hoped that this would not be the case; Wisconsin had only acted to improve itself as The Johns Hopkins University might have done in similar circumstances. Writing to Adams about the application for admission of a Johns Hopkins student at Madison, Turner noted, "[W]hile we are of course very happy over the addition which Pres. Chamberlin has made to our faculty in securing Dr. Ely, we are also glad that the intellectual resources of the Johns Hopkins University are such that we can be confident that the work in Economics there will continue with vigor." Plans were afoot for a Johns Hopkins Alumni Association in the Northwest, concluded Turner with mild jocularity. He did not reveal that he had set Chamberlin on the scent and served as deputy negotiator. Adams continued to be the supportive friend of the young man whom Ely described as being, at the time, "of slight build, medium height, and with a great deal of personal magnetism."²⁴

Placement of the history program within the School of Economics, Political Science, and History did not damage its development. Turner's desire for an additional instructor in modern history was gratified by the appointment of Victor Coffin, a Cornellian, in 1893. Coffin was able and companionable, according to Turner, and a fine teacher even though never attaining the scholarly eminence of his two colleagues. Growth in the history teaching cadre was to continue. Ely *was* self-centered, jealous of his prerogatives, and contentious, but he was also an energetic and dedicated scholar and, in these years, an excellent judge of talent. As his former students, Haskins and Turner respected his abilities. They sometimes chafed under his leadership but initially welcomed the opportunity of being part of a school that rapidly established a major reputation and attracted able students. For his part, Ely valued history and respected the Wisconsin historians, even proclaiming Turner to be a good economist, but he also chided

The faculty of the School of Economics, Political Science, and History, 1893. *Top row*, Charles H. Haskins, David Kinley; *middle row*, Turner, Richard T. Ely, John B. Parkinson; *bottom row*, William A. Scott, John M. Parkinson. Reprinted with permission of the University Archives, University of Wisconsin, Madison, Wisconsin. (X25)3065.

him years later for having blocked some of Ely's plans for developing the school.

Even though one biographer disparaged the University of Wisconsin in Haskins's years there as a little western "cow college," careful consideration of Allen's career belies the implications of that description in the history discipline. With Ely's arrival the Madison campus moved to the forefront of developments in economics and political economy. Chamberlin's successor, Charles Kendall Adams, was one of the country's eminent historians, and in late December 1892, he presided over a small conference in Madison on the teaching of history, civil government, and political economy in the secondary schools under the auspices of the National Educational Association. The conference members invited Turner and Haskins to attend their sessions, and Fred and Caroline entertained the participants at lunch on the first day of deliberations. At the conference, the young Wisconsin historians renewed their friendship with Woodrow Wilson and forged ties with

Albert B. Hart and James Harvey Robinson among others. Western it might be, and, indeed, there were dairy cows on the campus, but the Wisconsin of Turner and Haskins was no backwater in history and the social sciences.

For Turner as professional, the early 1890s were a period of beginning and part of a process that required him to establish himself as a scholar whose work impressed others. Hard of hearing, unswervingly conscientious, but with a touch of the gamin as well, Louise Phelps Kellogg spent her professional career in the service of the State Historical Society of Wisconsin, writing and editing Wisconsin and midwestern history. She became the leading authority on the French and British periods of Wisconsin history, writing substantial books on both regimes. In neither did she cite "The Character and Influence of the Indian Trade in Wisconsin: A Study of the Trading Post as an Institution," the doctoral dissertation of her graduate director, Turner. She admired him as a person, a teacher, and a scholar, but in writing the preface to *The Early Writings of Frederick Jackson Turner* in 1938, she justified the reprinting of the dissertation on the grounds that Turner's early publications were "virtually inaccessible" and should "be studied and their place in American historiography restored" in order "to understand the development of Turner's thought."[25] The doctoral thesis, she implied, was not a major substantive contribution to American historiography.

If this implication was intentional, Kellogg was correct. But, as she also suggested, for those seeking to understand the unfolding of Turner's ideas and career, the importance of the dissertation extends beyond its contribution to the history of Wisconsin and the fur trade. Thwaites published Turner's paper, based on his research for the master's degree, in the Historical Society *Proceedings* under the title, "The Character and Influence of the Fur Trade in Wisconsin." This was the foundation on which Turner based his dissertation and, perhaps, essentially the version that he presented to the Adams seminar in 1889. In the evolving graduate programs of the 1880s and 1890s the original scholarship required for the master's and doctoral degrees was less rigorous than that expected from later generations of students. As a master's thesis, Turner's Historical Society paper is more impressive than was the dissertation as an illustration of doctoral performance.

Turner began the Historical Society paper by noting the long history of "the commercial mingling of primitive and enlightened peoples"— even back to the Phoenicians, the extended documentation in history of the fur trade, its importance, and the fact that much "primitive inter-tribal" trading activity had preceded that between Indian and European. He described the system of lakes and rivers that allowed the trade to thrust itself into the interior of North American and the tribal groups resident in Wisconsin during the seventeenth and eighteenth centuries. Then he examined "the character and significance of the Wisconsin fur trade at three distinctive periods. . . . 1. The French, 1634 to 1763. 2. The English, 1763 to 1816. 3. The American, 1816 to 1834."[26]

Turner's treatment of his subject in the three eras was sketchy and episodic, but the narrative was clear and the quotations were colorful. Discussing the French period, Turner emphasized the importance of the wars with the Fox Indians and stressed the role of the Northwest Company during the English regime. Turner briefly sketched the changes that occurred in corporate control of the American trade and the federal law of 1816 that barred British traders and capital from American soil. He then described the trade in Wisconsin, the kinds of furs and skins, the goods traded for them, and the value of the commerce. In conclusion he discussed the social legacy of the trade in Wisconsin, listing the various posts, briefly describing the settlements that the trade had fostered and the character of the people there—"gay, shiftless, often prone to the cup, but withal hearty and hospitable, and on the best of terms with their Indian friends and relatives." He summarized the lasting influence of the American trade: "In a word the fur trade closed its mission by becoming the path finder for agricultural and manufacturing civilization."[27]

As we know, Turner mailed reprints of the paper in the Society *Proceedings* to a number of publications and scholars in the spring of 1889. He obtained acknowledgements from some scholars, mingling praise and qualification, as when Lucien Carr, of the Peabody Museum of American Archeology and Ethnology, responded that he had read it with "great interest and profit" but also confessed that he felt Turner had "hardly do[ne] justice to the missionaries." Others, including Francis Parkman, were supportive, if brief in response. But the "returns," he told Caroline, were "very flattering." "The state papers," he continued, "make my little work quite a hit." He was "anxious to do some work that will justify praise."[28]

Turner inserted an initial note in his dissertation that described it as a "rewritten and enlarged" version of the Society address. In the revision he substituted the word "Indian" for "fur" and added a subtitle to emphasize the institutional nature of the work. *The Character and Influence of the Indian Trade in Wisconsin: A Study of the Trading Post as an Institution* was eighty-three pages in length as compared to the forty-seven of the Society *Proceedings*. But the additional pages reflected in part the ability of Wisconsin printers to place more lines of text on a page than did their Baltimore counterparts. However, in his revision, Turner more fully traced the development of the British trade and the evolution of early American policy regarding the West. He inserted a new section on the American factory system and reshaped his discussion of the French wars with the Fox Indians. He clarified and expanded transition passages and enlarged his introduction, introducing a small contingent of German authors to fortify his notes. In an expanded conclusion he noted the disintegrative impact of the trade upon the Indians, the traders' role in paving the way for settlement, their strategic importance in the international rivalries of the European powers and the emergent United States, and their identification in Wisconsin of water power sites and of national transportation routes along whose lines "agricultural and . . . manufacturing civilization" was to follow. He also denied Thomas Hart Benton's contention that the hunter pioneered Kentucky, arguing that it was the trader who had done so.[29]

Growing in the role of scientific historian, Turner deleted a burbling description of the fur trade canoe in the earlier paper, as "the New World Argo that, in search of another golden fleece . . . carried French and English exploration through the great water systems of the continent."[30] Banished more regrettably were the pages in which Turner had described Wisconsin's Métis population of the early nineteenth century and a listing of trading post locations, a more significant contribution to American history than the lines devoted to the Phoenicians.

Students of his work have emphasized Turner's efforts to place his ideas within the perspective of the institutional history taught at Johns Hopkins, and it is true that he made such efforts—his expanded title a case in point. But he had already proclaimed affiliation to institutional history in the Wisconsin paper.[31] Here too he had argued that commerce was the root of change and presented a rudimentary stage theory of social development that began with savagery and progressed through trader and hunter phases to agricultural and manufacturing civilization. Allen's class notes and publications suggest that Turner had been exposed to basic elements of the institutional approach before he arrived in Baltimore.

In the dissertation the stage theory would be more explicitly stated. The economic stages of development now were trader, hunter, cattle raiser, cultivator of the soil, and manufacturing era. Turner also accepted the stages of transportation development described by Thomas Hart Benton. But in his conclusion and apparently for the first time in his published work he joined the stage theory to organismic metaphor, writing, "a continuously higher life flowed into the old channels, knitting the United States together into a complex organism."[32] This analogy of society as organism joined the stage theory and the commitment to the shaping influence of physiography, carried through from his Wisconsin studies, as part of Turner's basic stock of social theory.

Turner's dissertation adequately fulfilled its purposes. It demonstrated his scholarly abilities and provided a useful sketch of the fur trade in the watershed of the St. Lawrence River and adjacent territory. In the process of preparation Turner mastered a body of useful fact and social theory and developed arguments legitimating the importance of the subject area that he hoped to make his particular province. In practical terms it gave him a union card and status within the Johns Hopkins network. In the dissertation Turner suggested that the interaction of "primitive" and "more advanced" peoples of differing attainments deserved further study. Some historians have argued that this prescription would have provided a more fruitful approach to historical research than did his later essay upon the significance of the frontier.[33]

With degree in hand, Turner prepared papers in which he explained his understanding of the meaning of history and the role of the historian, proclaimed the importance of *his* area of history, and began to outline an agenda for its study. Before an audience of state school teachers in 1891 he explained "The Significance of History." This paper represented one of the few times that Turner publicly addressed the philosophy, methods, and uses of history. He would, however, display his fondness for the word "significance," many times in the future.

Turner began his address by reviewing the numerous approaches of historians—history as pageant, "artistic prose narration of past events," the study of politics and political institutions, and increasingly the "aim to show that property, the distribution of wealth, the social conditions of the people, are the underlying and determining factors to be studied." In illustration of "this new historical method" he quoted at length from James E. Thorold Rogers's *Economic Interpretation of History*. "The focal point of modern history," Turner continued, "is the fourth estate, the great mass of the people." Some, continued Turner, viewed history as an opportunity to fight out "present partisan debates." Carlyle found in history a "stage on which a few great men play their parts." Still others used it to explain the growth of religious ideas, to draw moral lessons, or to engage in the metaphysical exercise of deducing "a few primary laws."[34]

Turner explained that each age produced a different kind of history. So the symbols of war and legends of gods and heroes yielded to "the artistic and critical faculty" of a Herodotus, and the annalist and chronicler described the medieval era. By the nineteenth century a method of critical analysis of contemporary documents had evolved, brought to its height by Leopold von Ranke, but still in his hands "history was primarily past politics," although it had become inductive and scientific. The newer emphases of Rogers and others reflected an "age of socialistic inquiry." Turner concluded that "there is much truth in all these conceptions of history: history is past literature . . . past politics . . . past religion, . . . past economics."[35]

There followed a key paragraph:

> Each age tries to form its own conception of the past. *Each age writes the history of the past anew with reference to the conditions uppermost in its own time.* Historians have accepted the doctrine of Herder. Society grows. They have accepted the doctrine of Comte. Society is an organism. History is the biography of society in all its departments. There is objective history and subjective history. Objective history applies to the events themselves; subjective history is man's conception of these events. "The whole mode and manner of looking at things alters with every age," but this does not mean that the real events of a given age change; it means that our comprehension of these facts change.

We understand the past better today than formerly, Turner continued, because we "know how to use the sources better but also because the significance of events develops with time. . . . The aim of history, then, is to know the elements of the present by understanding what came into the present from the past. . . . Droysen has put this true conception into the statement, 'History is the "Know Thyself" of humanity—the self-consciousness of mankind.'"[36]

It followed that the historian must consider all human activity—"all kinds of history are essential," Turner argued, *"History is all the remains that have come down to us from the past, studied with all the critical and interpretive power that the present can bring to the task."* Turner admitted that the problem of "interpret[ing] the significance of events" was even more difficult than the evaluation of evidence. "All must be told," he maintained, "with just selection, emphasis, perspective; with that historical imagination and sympathy that does not judge the past by the canons of the present, nor read into it the ideas of the present. Above all the historian must have a passion for truth above that for any party or idea." Adding to these problems was the fact that "each man is conditioned by the age in which he lives." "No historian," said Turner, "can say the ultimate word."[37]

As corollary to his definition of history, Turner argued for the essential unity and continuity of history; events must be viewed against the perspective of the past, and local history must be studied in the light of world history: "Society is an organism, ever growing. History is the self-consciousness of this organism."[38] He quoted his teacher, Adams, who wrote that "this country will yet be viewed and reviewed as an organism of historic growth, developing from minute germs. . . . And some day this country will be studied in its international relations, as an organic part of a larger organism now vaguely called the World-State, but as surely developing through the operations of economic, legal, social, and scientific forces as the American Union." We must understand "the cosmopolitan relations of modern local life, and its own wholesome conservative power in these days of growing centralization."[39]

Turner explained that history had "utility" in furthering understanding of society and social "progress," as well as mental discipline. Here, however, he was more particularly concerned with "the utility of history as affording a training for good citizenship." Leaders of the modern world needed historical knowledge if they were adequately to meet the challenge of their positions. In England and Germany historical study was accepted as a valued prerequisite for public service. Not so, unfortunately, in the United States. Yet recent American history showed that our leaders needed knowledge of developments elsewhere in the world. Settlement "of our vast Western domain" had been related in many respects to developments and incidents in European history. Recent history research showed the relation of our institutions to those of Europe. Moreover, the peoples of other nations had important lessons for Americans.[40]

Turner admitted that the task of the historian might be daunting, "discouraging. . . . impossible of attainment. He must select some field and till that thoroughly, be absolute master of it; for the rest he must seek the aid of others whose lives have been given in the true scientific spirit to the study of special fields." He ended this address on a note of exhortation. For those who entered "the temple of history," there should be "no looking at history as an idle tale, a compend of anecdotes; no servile devotion to a textbook; no carelessness of truth about the dead. . . . 'History,' says Droysen, 'is not the truth and the light; but a striving for it, a sermon on it, a consecration to it.'"[41]

Only a few American historians have explained the role of the historian in truly memorable terms. We think, for example, of Carl L. Becker's "Every Man His Own Historian," or Samuel Eliot Morison's "History as a Literary Art." Turner's essay in an obscure western journal shows similar power to interest, to entrance, and to convince. Even more notable, Becker and Morison wrote from years of experience and reflection, whereas Turner was but six years beyond his admission to graduate study.

Somewhat repetitive, lacking the tautness of the best exposition, "The Significance of History" nonetheless displays Turner's rich vocabulary, his talent for felicitous phrasing, his fine eye for a telling quotation, his ability to sound a call to arms on behalf of a great cause. Here Turner made his declaration of faith as a historian and exhorted others to accept his views. What degree of originality or intellectual dependency did the essay display? Although he quoted authorities to great effect in "The Significance of History," Turner included no specific page references. He began a bibliographical note by explaining that "free use has been made of the following sources," and the first entry was "notes on the lectures of Professor Herbert B. Adams."[42] Thereafter he listed works by seven English and American historians and five German historians, including Johann G. Droysen but not von Ranke.

Like beauty, the definition of "free use" is in the eye of the beholder. Are we to believe that Turner had carefully read the authors cited, including those whose native tongue was German? In the spring of 1890 he passed a doctoral sight-reading examination in that language, but he never had a fluent reading command of it. However, among his books, Turner preserved—apparently from the Johns Hopkins year—a number of short German texts on historical method, including Droysen's *Grundriss der Historik*. Among the German masters, Droysen was Adams's favorite. Turner's director demonstrated a continuing interest in defining history and developing methods of teaching it throughout the 1880s and 1890s. In "The Significance of History" Turner advanced some ideas that we also find in Adams's writings. From the quotation that he drew from Adams's contribution to the widely used *Methods of Teaching History*, Turner excised his teacher's apparent endorsement of the aphorism, "history is past politics and politics present history." But it may be incorrect to picture Turner as pushing beyond Adams in rejecting Freeman's famous pronouncement. Adams later maintained, "I have never taught that all history is past politics and that all politics are past history, but only that some history and some politics are thus defined. It must be fully recognized that history is past religion, past philosophy, past civilization, past sociology, and includes all man's recorded action and experience in organized society."[43] Passages in Turner's essay on the significance of history have a similar ring. Although he had already begun his professional career, Turner apparently did not circulate copies of "The Significance of History" within the profession, perhaps because he regarded it primarily as a synthesis of ideas from Adams's classes and seminar. But the essay exudes a verve and elegance that Turner's mentor never matched.

Although he acknowledged other reasons for studying history, Turner justified the pursuit especially as training for citizenship and as a means of acquiring knowledge that would allow Americans better to understand and solve the social, economic, and political problems confronting them. Accepting the evolutionary social thought of the day as expounded by Adams, he believed that society was an evolving organism—truthful, nonpartisan knowledge of past development would allow society's leaders to shape a better world, one that demonstrated social progress. Turner realized that the task was difficult, the historian influenced by his time and place, but he boldly put forth truth as the historian's objective. Although historians could never completely understand nor accurately describe past events, they were obligated to use scientific methods of analysis and to strive for truth.

But Turner believed that the modern historian's answers would be better than those of his predecessors. The province of the historian was imperial in scope—people, events, and institutions flowed in endless continuity, and all should be subject to the historian's scrutiny.

"The Significance of History" was Turner's declaration of faith as a historian. How derivative it was from his work with Allen and his experiences at Johns Hopkins and how much it reflected the synthetic qualities of his own mind we cannot say. It endorsed scientific method but qualified von Ranke's contribution, it acknowledged the problem of relativism, it approved a history that melded present and past and embraced the whole experience of mankind. It maintained that studying history was of practical benefit. In illustration of Turner's argument, it briefly drew attention to America's westering past. Thereafter, Turner returned to historical theory seriously only in his presidential address of 1910, although occasional passages elsewhere reveal some of his views, as does his reminiscent correspondence of the 1920s. Turner's personal program of research moved beyond the Indian trade in the years ahead, and he expanded his command of research methods beyond those learned under the direction of Allen and Adams. But "The Significance of History" stands as his historian's oath.

Turner had been committed since his years as an instructor to justifying the importance of his own province of history and explaining how it should be developed. As he wrote in 1891 he should become "absolute master of it." "Problems in American History," the second of Turner's published papers of the early 1890s, was his first attempt to define his field. It appeared in the student newspaper, the *Aegis*, in early November 1892. In length it was the equivalent of some twelve printed pages.

In viewing this paper as a stage in his thinking about the substance of American history, however, it is necessary first to touch upon a paper entitled "American Colonization" that he delivered in early February 1891 before a meeting of the Madison Literary Society. In this paper, which he never published, he sketched the process of colonization from the days of the Phoenicians through the peopling of America. "American history," he said, "is the account of how this environment was occupied by a new organization. It is the history of the application of men and ideas to these conditions." The physiography of the continent greatly influenced these processes. But Turner placed American colonization within the perspective of a centuries-long contest between the Roman and the Germanic systems of colonization. He noted general differences between the development and contributions of the southern, middle, and New England colonies. When the American Congress approved the Northwest Ordinance, it "settled the destiny of the Great West" and determined that the Roman type of colony would not be the model for settlement there. In that region there would be three great groups of colonists: the pioneers of the Middle States and upland South, whose great gateway was Cumberland Gap; the New England migrants into the Old Northwest; and the immigrants from Europe. He praised the latter group for bringing "deeply invoked customs and ideas" as well as bone, sinew, and money. They were "important factors in the political and economic life of the nation. The story of the peopling of America has not yet been written. We do not understand ourselves." East of the Alleghenies the colonists had developed "an organism capable of throwing out offshoots of its own." In this period "were produced many of the germs of our national institutions."

Only now, Turner explained, was the colonizing era "coming to a close." He continued,

> I do not hesitate to say that this fact is the key to American history. As the occupation of the New World transformed Europe, so the occupation of the Great West has determined the flow of American energies, been the underlying explanation of political history, and has had profound reactive effects upon the social and economic life of the East. What first the Mediterranean sea and later the New World was to the Aryan peoples, breaking the bond of custom, and creating new activities to meet new conditions, that the undeveloped West has been to the American descendants of these Aryans.

Turner then went on to speculate that the completed national organism might bud as had seaboard America and at the least attach South American economic life to its own, citing "the law of colonization" in support of his suggestion.[44]

Turner's essay on colonization was not to be published, but it was a foundation upon which the essay for the *Aegis* rested. He began by recounting a conversation with a state senator who doubted that there was "anything of importance in American history not already adequately treated." According to the Turner of the 1920s, Adams said something very similar to graduate student Turner—a disconcerting coincidence. The query, however, allowed Turner to assert in response that probably no "historical field need[ed] more workers or offer[ed] more inviting material than . . . the United States." "Older writers . . . coming, like all wise men, from the East" had focused on the Atlantic coast. They had ignored the West or else treated it as incidental to activity in the "north and south regions of the Atlantic coast."[45]

Professor Hermann E. von Holst—a favorite target of young Turner—had complained of constitutional history in which the Hamlet, slavery, was ignored. But, said Turner, in his treatment of American constitutional development, this historian had left out the Hamlet of westward expansion.

> The true point of view in the history of this nation is not the Atlantic coast; it is the Mississippi Valley. . . . the real lines of American development, the forces dominating our character, are to be studied in the history of westward expansion.
>
> In a sense, American history up to our own day has been colonial history, the colonization of the Great West. This ever retreating frontier of free land is the key to American development. . . . American history needs a connected and unified account of the progress of civilization across this continent with the attendant results.[46]

At this point, Turner interjected a listing of inadequately studied aspects of American constitutional development: extension of the suffrage in America, the development of the ballot, the committee system in Congress, party conventions, and so on. But to concentrate on needed research at this level, Turner suggested, was to ignore the fundamental nature of the American experience. America, he explained, was an organism, an organism whose institutions "are compelled to adapt themselves to the changes of a remarkably developing, expanding people." "Let the student survey this organism, the American commonwealth; let him select its essential features and then trace their development." In this conception the investigator would find "a life work, a work demanding the cooperative study of many students for generations."[47]

"Without attempting any systematic presentation," Turner enumerated "problems in our social and economic history" worthy of consideration. In scrutinizing American settlement "we have to observe how European life entered the continent, and how America modified that life and reacted on Europe." "Who," he asked, "shall measure the effect on Europe of free land in America?" Considering America itself, "the abundance of material unused is still more inviting. . . . The subject is at bottom the study of European germs developing in an American environment. But little has yet been done toward investigating the part played by the environment in determining the lines of our development." In this respect "thorough study of the physiographic basis of our history" was needed. Turner expanded this thought by discussion of the ways in which the census population maps illuminated the American settlement process and its relation to natural features. He noted the importance also of Indian tribes in shaping the flow of settlement, not only in their resistance to settlement but through their discovery of communication routes and settlement sites:

> Civilization in America has followed the arteries made by geology, pouring an ever richer tide through them, until at last the slender paths of aboriginal intercourse have been broadened and interwoven into the complex mazes of modern commercial lines. . . . It is like the steady growth of a complex nervous system for the originally simple inert continent. If one would understand why we are today a nation rather than a collection of isolated states, he must study this economic and social consolidation of the country. In this progress from savage conditions lie topics for the evolutionist.[48]

The impact of the Indian on American political institutions also should be studied, urged Turner. He quoted Edward J. Payne: "'American history cannot be treated as a simple expansion of European enterprise on the virgin soil of the transatlantic continent.'" Turner approvingly noted. "The peculiarly *American* influences offer many unstudied topics to the investigator."[49]

Turner explained that there had been four principal periods of activity in the "colonization of the continent": settlement of the Atlantic seaboard, of the regions stretching from the Allegheny Mountains to the Mississippi, of the region from the Great Salt Lake to the

Pacific coast, and from the Mississippi River to the Rockies. Historians had studied the first of these areas intensively and begun work on the second and third. The fourth remained virtually untouched. "Upon each . . . independent, original investigation is demanded," wrote Turner.[50]

As historians studied the colonization of the Atlantic Coast by the various European nationalities, they should, Turner believed, consider contemporary conditions in the home lands more carefully, not "isolat[ing] the migration from its European connection, as many of our historians do." He was persuaded also that the "sectionalization" process in the colonial period should be more "adequately" considered, particularly in the middle states. "The extension of these sections" westward also required examination, and interstate migration would reward study. "The spread of New England men meant the spread of New England culture. One should also study the effect of this west-ward movement in changing the character of the states from which the migration proceeds." Conversely, he suggested, "we shall not under-stand the contemporary United States without studying immigration historically. Another line of investigation in the same direction consists in the study of that interesting process whereby the people of a single county (or township at least) will in successive years be at one time preponderantly American, then Irish, or Scotch, then German, then Bohemian; or will represent some similar series of occupations."[51]

In his final paragraph Turner suggested that "no topic in American history so much demands investigation as does the history of the management of our public domain, with the associated topics, internal improvements and railroad building. Space forbids the enumeration of the problems . . . such as the democratization of the country—which have grown out of free land." He had, he continued, perhaps shown the importance of a western perspective in historical study: "What the Mediterranean Sea was to the Greeks, breaking the bond of custom, offering new experiences, calling out new institutions and activities, that the ever retreating Great West has been to the eastern United States directly, and to the nations of Europe more remotely."[52]

With the publication of "Problems in American History" in the fall of 1892, Turner had laid the foundation for the issuance of a great proclamation that would shape both his career and his discipline. But before examining that step another aspect of his formative years requires mention. During his graduate study with Allen, Turner had begun publishing book reviews. Although he did not write a large number of such publications then, or during his early years in professorial rank, reviewing sharpened his critical talents, broadened his knowledge, and gave him an opportunity to think about his field, as well as to proclaim its importance.

Extended reviews in *The Dial* of each volume of the two-part compilation of documents relating to Benjamin Franklin's diplomatic career in France, by Edward E. Hale and his son, gave Turner little opportunity for advertising his particular interests. However, these reviews enabled him to point out the importance of the young republic's western boundaries in the diplomacy of the peace settlement between the United States and Great Britain. In discussing James R. Gilmore's *John Sevier as a Commonwealth-Builder* in the *Nation* in 1887, Turner noted the West's commitment to local self-government and the importance of sentiment for independence in the Mississippi Valley. The book, he explained, took "a much-needed step in calling attention to the fact that the history of the valley of the Mississippi is a too much neglected branch of the history of this country."[53]

When the editors of the *Dial* sent him the first two volumes of Theodore Roosevelt's *The Winning of the West*, Turner used his introductory paragraph to urge the study of the "Mississippi basin," an area that had not yet "found its historian." "General United States history," he asserted, "should be built upon the fact that the centre of gravity of the nation has passed across the mountains into this great region." Here "a new composite nationality is being produced, a distinct American people. . . . American history needs a connected and unified account of the progress of civilization across the continent. Aside from the scientific importance of such a work, it would contribute to awakening a real national self-consciousness and patriotism." Roosevelt's volumes were an "important contribution" to the task, providing "the first really satisfactory history of the field they cover." Although Turner's tone was laudatory, he thought Roosevelt's "generalizations . . . bold, frequently novel, and not seldom open to criticism." He challenged Roosevelt's interpretation of the peace settlement after the Revolutionary War and also criticized him for underemphasizing the importance of the pioneers in the Northwest relative to those below the Ohio River. In conclusion he found "merit" in Roosevelt's "vivid portraiture of the backwoodsman's advance," his sensible and impartial treatment of relations between settlers and Indians, his use of "a scientific method of criticism" in evaluation of sources, and his ability to place events "in the light of the widest significance."[54]

A review of the *Journal of William Maclay*, one of Pennsylvania's first United States senators, allowed Turner to read a classic description of congressional legislative processes and to note the differences in commitment between this representative of Pennsylvania's "west" and his eastern counterparts. Reviewing the first volume of Edward J. Payne's *History of the New World Called America*, Turner hinted that this author did not have "exhaustive acquaintance" with the relevant "monographic literature," although granting the ambitiousness of his effort "to set in its right relations the development of this 'huge social and political creation'" and noting his argument that American history was not a "simple expansion of European enterprise on the virgin soil of the transatlantic continent." Turner criticized Payne's "unfortunate tendency to strain the facts in order to show filiations, a dependence on older writers, and an apparent ignorance of many valuable investigators of recent date." However, he noted the originality of Payne's effort to "[work] out the effect of the physiography and natural products of America upon the aborigines of Mexico and Peru, and [to show] the causes of the various stages of culture in America, the relation of the Indians to Spanish settlement, and to the character of Spanish colonial life."[55]

Occasionally Turner displayed some of the smug ferocity of the young reviewer. In writing his biography of John Sevier, Gilmore, Turner charged, sometimes "prefer[red] boldness of characterization and smooth narrative to the accuracy and cautiousness . . . that should mark historical composition." He ridiculed Payne's faith in the Norse sagas that also peopled New England with cave-dwelling dwarfs and zapped him for placing a medieval chronicler in the wrong century. But in each of Turner's early reviews he ground grist for later writing. He began his review of the early volumes of *The Winning of the West*, for example, with the pronouncement that "American's historians have for the most part, like the wise men of old, come from the East; and as a result our history has been written from the point of view of the Atlantic coast." Somewhat reworded, the jibe appears in the first paragraph of "Problems in American History." Turner's early reviews do not reveal a mind rich in historical background and perspective, but they were more than competent in quality and gave the young author the opportunity to promote the historical province that he wished to claim. The reviewing process also provided him with information that he drew upon while composing his initial essays and allowed him to formulate ideas and to test phrasing that he incorporated in these position statements.

4   Proclamation

*"The true point of view in the history of this nation is
not the Atlantic coast, it is the Great West"*

Well knowing that it paid to advertise, Turner sent a copy of his *Aegis*
paper, "Problems in American History," to Herbert Baxter Adams, who
praised it and brought it to the attention of the members of the Johns
Hopkins seminar. Then secretary of the AHA, Adams suggested that
further development of Turner's ideas would make a paper suitable for
the association's next meeting. This was to be held in Chicago, where
the members would share in the proceedings of the World's Columbian
Exhibition during the summer of 1893. Thus began the immediate
sequence of events that allowed Turner to present the most famous
address ever delivered by an American historian.

The University of Wisconsin's new president, Charles Kendall
Adams, was authorized to invite Turner to give a paper. He agreed to
do so, as any ambitious young scholar must under such circumstances,
sending a note of acceptance to Adams on February 23, 1893. Turner
also recommended to the AHA Program Committee that two Wisconsin graduate students should be placed on the program. When this
suggestion failed to win approval, Turner urged that one of them, Orin
G. Libby, should take his place. He was enthusiastic about Libby's
research, but the proposal may also have reflected the fact that Turner
was himself heavily burdened with obligations. Fatefully, the program
committee did not accept Turner's offer to withdraw. At the conclusion of a scorching Chicago summer day on July 12, Turner delivered
"The Significance of the Frontier in American History," the last of five
papers in the association's evening session at the Art Institute. As was
customary throughout his career, he was still tinkering with his text
a few hours before beginning his presentation.

On first reading, the paper of 1893 appears to be a forthright statement, referring in its first paragraph to the observation of the superintendent of the Eleventh Census that a continuous American frontier
line could no longer be mapped, a development that marked "the end

of a great historic movement." Then follows a terse explanation of that
finding's relevance: "The existence of an area of free land, its continuous recession, and the advance of American settlement westward,
explain American development." Turner next carried his listeners
through a discussion of the meaning of the term *frontier*, the chronology and physiographic details of frontier advance, the various social
and institutional processes involved, their influence upon the conduct
of national government, and their relation to the national character, or
in his words, their "noteworthy effects." These included development
of a composite nationality, and, of most importance, democracy, as
well as "intellectual traits of profound importance . . . coarseness and
strength . . . acuteness and inquisitiveness . . . practical, inventive
turn of mind . . . masterful grasp of material things . . . restless, nervous
energy . . . dominant individualism . . . buoyance and exuberance." In
conclusion Turner warned again that an era had ended—"the frontier
has gone, and with its going has closed the first period of American
history."[1]

"The Significance of the Frontier in American History" offered at
least three major ideas or propositions. First was the assertion that the
"free lands," or natural resources of the West, shaped American development. Here too was the concept of sectionalism. Over time and
reflecting the country's physiography, the residents of geographic
regions developed differing identities, needs, and political behavior.
Turner's opening assertion that the disappearance of a continuous
frontier line from the census population maps "mark[ed] the closing of
a great historic movement" implied a modern America without a
frontier, a depleted resource base, a closing of opportunity or space—an
observation repeated in his final sentence.[2]

Turner set his themes within a framework of contemporary social
thought, employing the social evolutionary theory and metaphors of
his time. Society was an organism. In the face of environmental
challenge, imported institutional germs grew and developed new or
different organs. Society progressed through stages, moving from a
state of wilderness or savagery to advanced civilization—in the case of
the American colonials and their descendants, from fur trader to
resident of an urban, manufacturing society. Frontier by frontier,
society reverted to the primitive, but in each new progression, or
recapitulation, institutional survivals remained. Even personality
changed in these processes. Most important, a unique American democracy emerged. Turner's essay of 1893 not only explained America

and Americans as they were, but it also proposed an agenda of study, called for interdisciplinary research in the comparative study of frontiers, and assured its audience that to study American frontiers was also to study "the record of social evolution" in general, laid out for examination as nowhere else in the civilized world.[3]

There were in Turner's text arresting assertions and speculative comments that stand as subtheses. "Economic power secures political power," he noted, in explanation of the democratizing impulses of the settlers on the cheap western lands. "Movement," he noted elsewhere, "has been [American life's] dominant fact, and, unless this training has no effect upon a people, the American energy will continually demand a wider field for its exercise"—suggesting that closed space in the United States might in the future affect foreign policy. The frontier, he wrote, had been "a gate of escape from the bondage of the past," or, as he would write elsewhere, a safety valve that might mitigate the effects of economic depressions or labor unrest.[4]

But Turner also qualified the message of his essay. His first paragraph included the ringing declaration of the importance of free land. But it was preceded by the statement, "Up to our own day American history has been *in a large degree* the history of the colonization of the Great West" Later the reader learns that the paper's "aim is simply to call attention to the frontier as a fertile field for investigation, and to suggest some of the problems which arise in connection with it." Turner noted that there were social continuities between the older and the newer regions. "But with all these similarities," he observed, "there are essential differences, due to the place element and time element." Here, indeed, we note a fundamental step forward in Turner's thinking from the heavy stress on continuity in "The Significance of History." Whether Turner was positing a history of discontinuities or merely one of changing emphases is unclear.[5]

In an explanatory note Turner identified his article in the *Aegis* as the "foundation" of "The Significance of the Frontier in American History." His Chicago paper more than tripled the length of the 1892 publication, and he documented it more heavily. He clarified and further developed his ideas and raised the rhetorical pitch of his writing. Some of the alterations were minor in nature. In 1892, for example, Turner had written, "The true point of view in the history of this nation is not the Atlantic coast; it is the Mississippi Valley." This sentence he altered by striking the last two words and substituting "Great West."[6]

Other changes were more important. In 1892 he wrote, "In a sense, American history up to our own day has been colonial history, the colonization of the Great West. This ever retreating frontier of free land is the key to American development." A year later he rephrased the first sentence somewhat but greatly strengthened the second so that it became, "The existence of an area of free land, its continuous recession, and the advance of American settlement westward, explain American development."[7]

In both papers Turner equated developing institutions with the substance of the biological organism, repeating his arresting statement, "behind institutions, behind constitutional forms and modifications, lie the vital forces that call these organs into life and shape them to meet changing conditions. The peculiarity of American institutions is, the fact that they have been compelled to adapt themselves to the changes of an expanding people. . . ." In 1893 he inserted the words "and modifications" and deleted the words "rapidly developing" before "expanding," as well as changing a verb tense.[8] In 1893 also he filled in illustrative details of American development and expanded the organismic metaphor by stressing the recurrent progress from the primitive to civilized conditions.

As in the essay of 1892, Turner joined physiographic influences to organic metaphor, incorporating in full this lengthy passage:

> Thus civilization in America has followed the arteries made by geology, pouring an ever richer tide through them. . . . It is like the steady growth of a complex nervous system for the originally simple, inert continent. If one would understand why we are to-day one nation, rather than a collection of isolated states, he must study this economic and social consolidation of the country. In this progress from savage conditions lie topics for the evolutionist.[9]

There are other sections of the lecture of 1893 in which the *Aegis* draft is highly obvious. A lengthy passage describing the Middle Atlantic region and its importance carried through with little change. In the final paragraph of each essay Turner inserted the same striking simile, adding "and more" in the later version, so that it read: "What the Mediterranean Sea was to the Greeks, breaking the bond of custom, offering new experiences, calling out new institutions and activities, that, and more, the ever retreating Great West has been to the eastern

United States directly, and to the nations of Europe more remotely."[10] Turner still criticized Professor von Holst and constitutional history as practiced, although giving the topic less attention. A call for inter-disciplinary research carried over to the presentation of 1893, as did other minor ideas, phrasing, and factual matter.

The second essay differed notably from the first, however, in its focus. The word *frontier* is used but once in the lecture of 1892; months later Turner repeated it more than 130 times. He devoted much of the additional narrative found in the 1893 version to explaining the meaning of the term, wedding it to a stage theory of American develop-ment: "Fur-trader, miner, cattle-raiser, and farmer . . . . each . . . on the march . . . . in successive waves across the continent." Among the farmers too there were successive waves, "men of capital and enter-prise" ultimately replacing the squatters and their successors. Turner's version of stage theory allowed him to abandon a clumsy division of American colonization into four periods. He devoted pages to explain-ing how the frontier had affected American development and shaped unique national institutions and character. As a result, the essay changed from one in which the primary focus was on the importance of doing particular historical research to one that explained a theory of national development. The objective of 1892 was not renounced. Well into his introduction, Turner explained that his aim was "simply to call attention to the frontier as a fertile field for investigation," and he suggested a few topics for research, including the comparative study of frontiers. But the essay had now become primarily an evaluation of the significance of the frontier.[11] From the definition of particular research problems he had moved to a general proclamation.

Why the change in terminology and emphasis? At some point after drafting his article for the *Aegis*, he had realized the great utility of the frontier as a research concept, one infinitely more flexible, more subject to theoretical development and carrying a much greater symbolic charge than terms such as *West*, *the Great West*, or *the Northwest*. The latter two terms, however, Turner retained in his research vocabulary, sometimes using them interchangeably with *frontier*. His decision to emphasize the word *frontier* came, one must assume, while, or shortly after, he read *Extra Census Bulletin, 2* in which the superintendent of the census announced the disappearance of a continuous frontier line from the population maps of the federal enumeration of 1890. That decision did not add to his store of basic ideas but did greatly change the character of his presentation. For

Turner, *frontier* denoted time, place, stage of development, or social process. In the opinion of later critics, such word use was confusing. But much of the power of his presentation rested on this flexibility, and much of the resonance of his argument reflected the fact that the Census Bureau had validated the long-standing importance of the frontier line.

Other changes of emphasis in Turner's thought are traceable in the essay of 1893. He had placed heavy stress upon the continuity of history in "The Significance of History." In his paper of 1892 he quoted Edward J. Payne's warning that "American history cannot be treated as a simple expansion of European enterprise on the virgin soil of the transatlantic continent" and added that "the peculiarly American influences offer many unstudied topics to the investigator." In Chicago in 1893 he acknowledged the presence of "European germs developing in an American environment," but he continued, "too exclusive attention has been paid by institutional students to the Germanic origins, too little to the American factors." Later he noted institutional continuities between frontiers and then asserted that "with all these similarities there are essential differences due to the place element and the time element."[12]

But would not the enhanced emphasis on American elements that Turner was urging make the study of American history parochial — make it in modern phrasing, an exercise in exceptionalism? In implicit answer, Turner introduced a new player — the Italian political economist, Achille Loria. He quoted approvingly the latter's contention that "America has the key to the historical enigma which Europe has sought for centuries in vain, and the land which has no history reveals luminously the course of universal history." To study the American "continental page from West to East," was to "find the record of social evolution" itself.[13] Both Professor Allen and Turner had argued for the importance of the West in national development, and Turner in 1892 had suggested that developments in America had profoundly affected Europe. But now the task of the historians of western America was even more glorious; study of American history could reveal the basic processes of general historical development.

Turner's emphasis on the concept of sectionalism in 1893 was less pronounced than in the essay of 1892, but it appeared recurrently in the Chicago paper, and Turner refined its application to the West. Once settlement was beyond the Alleghenies, Turner noted, "The 'West,' as a self conscious section, began to evolve," and he particularly emphasized the role of that region in shaping national legislation relative to the public lands and internal improvements.[14]

When Turner argued in 1893 that a "great historic movement" had ended, as in his first paragraph, or that "the first period in American history" had closed, as in his last, he introduced an idea that he had not used in the publications of 1891–92. The conception of a frontierless modern America with diminished opportunity and endangered institutions was highly important in Turner's thinking thereafter. If the presence of the frontier had significantly shaped American development and institutions to the end of the nineteenth century, what would happen to America and Americans henceforth? If frontier processes had fostered the development of American democracy, what was to be that democracy's future in a new and more industrialized age?

Turner had, however, expressed the idea of closed space in the paper on American colonization that he had presented before the Madison Literary Society in early 1891 as well as in a series of extension lectures on that topic. Before the Literary Society he had remarked that "the colonization of the United States is now coming to a close" and had gone on to state "a law of colonization" that suggested that the United States might now seek to "[attach] South American economic life to our own."[15] Here again is the idea of closed opportunity stated with the corollary that it might affect American foreign policy. Two and a half years later, with the testimony of the superintendent of the census in mind, Turner declared closed space an accomplished fact.

Although Turner apparently prepared "The Significance of the Frontier in American History" in a relatively few days prior to delivering it on July 12, 1893, it was not the product of a sudden flash of intuition. The serious thinking about the nature of history and particularly of American history that he had begun as a graduate student at Wisconsin came to climax in the essay of 1893. The reader of Turner's earlier writings sees him at work accumulating and testing ideas, vocabulary, and figures of speech that appear later in his presentation at the Columbian Exposition.

Turner's paper of 1893 has been studied admiringly not only as history but as rhetoric. The essay does derive part of its persuasive force from Turner's literary style. Major assertions stand bold and stark, albeit with the occasional qualification. The language is clear, forceful, well chosen, sometimes colorful. Pack trains do not plod across the Alleghenies; instead, their bells tinkle. The narrative is, rhetoricians point out, marked by frequent use of arresting, even epigrammatic, antithesis and parallel constructions: "The true point of view in the history of this nation is not the Atlantic coast, it is the Great West."[16] Point sometimes follows point in reinforcing series. Great figures of American history appear opportunely to give forceful testimony. When Turner places the settler on the frontier, the characterization is so tersely vivid that one sees him plowing with a sharp stick and hears him giving the war whoop. Both in beginning and ending, Turner arrests the reader by proclaiming the end of an American epoch—a turning point in the history of humankind.

In citing Turner's student orations as training ground for the essay of 1893, scholars are convincing. But the late- nineteenth-century student of rhetoric was debater as well as orator. The essay of 1893 was as much a masterful argument for the affirmative as oration. It also reflected Turner's shaping in the hands of Adams and Ely because it was social science discourse. Turner began by advancing a hypothesis, followed with appropriate definitions, a presentation of evidence, and concluded by listing and evaluating the results of the process described. Implicitly, Turner asked his listeners to ponder the nation's future social policy when the West's natural resources were no longer freely available.

The statement of the "frontier hypothesis" neither convinced Turner's peers immediately of its essential truth nor marked Turner as a historian destined for sure professional success. It was years before one historian who chose to go to Buffalo Bill's Wild West show that day instead of listening to Turner admitted that he had made the wrong decision. Within a week of Turner's presentation in Chicago, Charles Kendall Adams evaluated his qualifications for serving as coordinating editor of the American history contributions in the forthcoming *Johnson's Cyclopedia*, of which Adams was to be the general editor: "He is a young man, Ph.D. Johns Hopkins, a very successful teacher, precise in his methods, and comprehensive in his judgments. He has great popularity throughout this state, and indeed, wherever American history is taken as a leading study. Though he is at the head of a large and flourishing department, he is not so well known that his name would carry great weight in the Cyclopedia." Adams said nothing of the Chicago paper. A few weeks later Adams evaluated the historical congress at Chicago. He noted the slim attendance at the panels and thought the meeting of the association was less successful than earlier ones. Whether this had been "because the program was unfortunately full or because the members present were so generally desirous of spending the time at the Fair, or because of the successive contending noises of the railway trains," Adams could not say. Again, he passed over Turner's paper without comment.[17] Always an enthusiastic sightseer, Turner may have received the most stimulation at the exposition from guiding family members around the exhibits.

Turner's paper cited "the admirable monograph by Prof. H. B. Adams, 'Maryland's Influence on the Land Cessions,'" an appropriate reference but also a mark of Turner's professional savoir faire.[18] Adams, as secretary of the AHA, in turn extended a helping hand to his "boys." There were twenty-three papers read in the various history sessions in the Chicago meeting, and Adams summarized most of them in his report in a sentence or two. Among the seven to which he devoted more extensive comments, four had been prepared by men with Hopkins ties, including Turner and Haskins. So worked the gentle arts of reciprocity and advertising within the emerging history profession. Or perhaps Hopkins men better knew the advisability of leaving legible abstracts of their papers with association secretaries. Whatever the explanation, Turner could pride himself on the fact that Adams had devoted nineteen lines, a good half page, of an eight-and-a-half page account of the Chicago meeting to "The Significance of the Frontier in American History." Haskins, however, could boast that his discussion of the eleventh amendment of the federal constitution had been allotted twenty-four lines by their former mentor.

Why did Turner formulate the frontier hypothesis? In part it was an intellectual exercise—a scholar's effort to explain the development of his country in a manner appropriate to the age. Turner's great proclamation of 1893 becomes more intelligible if we also understand that it reflected family and environmental influences, friendly professional guidance, intellectual preparation, personal and institutional ambitions, and even his love for Caroline, whom he had chosen to cherish and to share his home and success. To understand the essay's place in Turner's career we must reconstruct its social background.

Turner's father was interested in local history and helped him in his first real foray into original research—the little history of the Grignon Tract. When in the east in the summer of 1887, Turner discerned great differences between eastern and western society in the United States. Andrew Jackson Turner affirmed that this was indeed the case. As editor and railroad promoter, Turner senior exemplified the competitive developmental mentality of western county-seat residents, and his life was an object lesson in political technique. Turner senior also imparted his love of the outdoors to his son, and together they saw the processes of settlement at work, people reacting to the challenges of what they considered to be a wilderness environment, north of the Wisconsin River during the 1860s and 1870s.

With the encouragement of a supportive professor who believed that the West had contributed greatly to American development, Turner felt his way into a field of history where he hoped that in some measure he could duplicate the feat of Parkman. As Parkman had told the story of the conflict between France and England in America, he would tell the story of the Great West. But after his year at Johns Hopkins University, Turner did not try to write a great narrative epic in the Parkman manner. Adams and Ely and his fellows in seminar had turned Turner, at least in part, into a social scientist—a question asker, a hypothesis poser. But he clothed this approach with the rhetorical skills that he had learned and taught.

On his return to Wisconsin in 1889 Turner found the opportunity to move his area of specialty into the classroom—working on western history was not just research, pursued in odd hours or the summer time. Preparation of lectures and the interaction with students in classes and seminars contributed to his growing understanding of western development and its place within American history. As he set himself to proving himself as teacher and scholar, he also assumed responsibility for the entire history program. Turner's reputation was now tied to that program's reputation. Given his ambition to do well for his family and himself and the promotional environment in which he was reared, it is no surprise that he tried to make that program preeminent in the West.

Turner used the negotiations that brought Ely to campus to strengthen his own position and that of Haskins and to promote his plans for making western history a favored research area in the University of Wisconsin. He visualized the subject also as a weapon of the university in its efforts to be recognized as the leading institution of higher learning in the Middle West. So we see revealed the son of the county-seat politician and town promoter. These aspects of Turner too would be reflected in the paper of 1893.

The personal and institutional imperatives that drove Turner in these years led him, one concludes, to put his argument for the importance of western history with all the forcefulness, skill, and artistry at his command. He brought to the task equipment far beyond the ordinary. Years of interest in rhetorical expression, first as a prize-winning orator and then as a teacher of rhetoric and oratory, had been tempered by his experience as a newspaper reporter where philosophic embellishment must give way to direct speech. His classical training and broad reading had given him a rich vocabulary.

Turner's student orations had all celebrated American democracy, using a formula all the more successful because it expressed his convictions. So too with the essay of 1893. But it also celebrated the importance of his region. And it reflected Turner's personal experiences and conditioning—his firsthand encounters with natural environment, his observations of the social processes north of the Wisconsin River, including those callous-palmed farmers gathered in political conclave around the blacksmith's anvil in Columbia County, and his own knowledge of the differences between western and eastern America. It was a defense of the area of history that Turner had been developing through research and teaching since 1885—the historical province to which he wished to make a life-long commitment, where he hoped to win personal fame. In various respects it was also a professional and institutional proclamation. It showed his colleagues at Wisconsin that young Fred Turner could mingle with the brightest of his profession and have something worthwhile to say. In the western promotional spirit it maintained that the history of the West provided unparalleled opportunities for study.

Institutionally the essay carried the message to scholars and prospective scholars that the place to pursue such study was the University of Wisconsin and not the new university in Chicago. Indeed, among the few historians whom Turner criticized specifically in his paper for failing to recognize the importance of the West in American history was the distinguished Professor von Holst of the University of Chicago. In effect Turner ran up the Wisconsin flag in the front yard of his institution's leading rival for the hegemony of midwestern higher education. In his way Turner was no less committed to development than the western town promoters who rallied community support by invoking the threat of rivals. Turner had observed Adams's empire building at Johns Hopkins, and development and progress were part of the yankee ethos in which Turner had been reared. The essay of 1893 may also have proclaimed an important history agenda within Professor Ely's school, where there was strong tendency for everything to be sucked into the wake of the dynamic director.

There was much in Turner's background, training, and early career that readied him for the task of preparing "The Significance of the Frontier in American History." That fact does not detract from Turner's achievement. His paper of 1893 was an intellectual contribution of the highest order. As a scholar he had charted his own course, and he succeeded brilliantly. But knowledge of these contextual elements and professional considerations allows us to comprehend Fred Turner's great proclamation more fully. We learn more as well when we consider the origins of the ideas that Turner used in "The Significance of the Frontier in American History."

From where did Turner derive the message that he gave his listeners in Chicago? Within the scholarly discussion of his work a body of literature emerged concerning the question of Turner's originality. Were his ideas new, or had he borrowed them from elsewhere, and if so from whom? Long before Turner's death scholars were pointing out that "precursors" had called attention to frontier processes or to the importance of the frontier in American development.[19]

Some of Turner's ideas were found to have long histories. Listen for example to J. Hector St. John de Crevecoeur. From a Revolutionary Era vantage point, he proclaimed, "The American is a new man, who acts upon new principles." After describing the changing character of American settlements as one moved farther inland, he wrote:

> He who would wish to see America in its proper light, and have a true idea of its feeble beginnings and barbarous rudiments, must visit our extended line of frontiers where the last settlers dwell, and where he may see the first labours of settlement, the mode of clearing the earth, in all their different appearances, where men are wholly left dependent on their native tempers, and on the spur of uncertain industry.... They are a kind of forlorn hope, preceding ... the most respectable army of veterans which come after them.... who will ... change ... that hitherto barbarous country into a fine fertile, well regulated district. Such is our

progress, such is the march of the Europeans toward the interior parts of this continent.[20]

Recording his impressions of early nineteenth-century New England and New York, Timothy Dwight maintained that "few of those human efforts which have excited the applause of mankind . . . merited equal approbation" to *"the conversion of a wilderness into a desirable residence for man."*[21]

In early 1865 Edwin L. Godkin responded in the *North American Review* to critics of American democracy, notably de Tocqueville and Mill, asserting that of the

> phenomena of American society which it is generally agreed distinguish it from that of older countries, we shall find . . . that by far the larger number of them may be attributed in a great measure to . . . "the frontier life" led by a large proportion of the inhabitants, and to the influence of this portion on manners and legislation, rather than to political institutions, or even to the equality of conditions. In fact . . . these phenomena . . . instead of being the effect of democracy, are partly its cause.

Of democracy Godkin wrote:

> the agency which . . . gave democracy its first great impulse in the United States, which has promoted its spread ever since, and which has contributed most powerfully to the production of those phenomena in American society which hostile critics set down as peculiarly democratic, was . . . the great change in the distribution of the population . . . which continues its operation up to the present time.[22]

Godkin went on to enumerate characteristics that he believed were fostered by "societies newly organized in a new country"—"strong individualism, contempt for experience . . . eagerness in pursuit of material gain . . . want of respect for training . . . profound faith in natural qualities, great indifference as to the future, the absence of a strong sense of social or national continuity, and of taste in art and literature and oratory." The "great mass of powerful, energetic rusticity" had come to dominate American politics, and indeed, "the West," wrote Godkin, "has succeeded to a certain extent in propagating in the East its ideas and manners both political and social."[23]

In conclusion Godkin admitted that probably "the enormous extent of unoccupied land at our disposal, which raises every man in the community above want, by affording a ready outlet for surplus population," did contribute "to the general happiness and comfort," thus making "the work of government easy." But it also made difficult "the settlement of a new society on a firm basis" and produced an "appearance of confusion and instability" that rendered suspect any conclusions about the possible defects of "equality of conditions or of democratic institutions."[24]

In 1879 Henry George completed his great tract entitled *Progress and Poverty*. In it was the following passage:

> This public domain—the vast extent of land yet to be reduced to private possession, the enormous common to which the faces of the energetic were always turned, has been the great fact that, since the days when the first settlements began to fringe the Atlantic Coast, has formed our national character and colored our national thought. . . . The general intelligence, the general comfort, the active invention, the power of adaptation and assimilation, the free, independent spirit, the energy and hopefulness that have marked our people are not causes, but results—they have sprung from unfenced land. . . . all that makes our conditions and institutions better than those of older countries, we may trace to the fact that land has been cheap in the United States, because new soil has been open to the emigrant.
>
> But our advance has reached the Pacific. Further west we cannot go.[25]

Thus, during the previous century writers had stressed the importance of the westward movement and cheap land in American development and had described personal characteristics attributable to the settlement process. They had also suggested that the building of western societies progressed by stages and that the processes affected the eastern as well as the western populations. Writing close in time to Turner, George even declared the land-taking process to be at an end. Two of the authors cited here used the word *frontier*. We have no evidence that Turner read the writings of Crevecoeur or Dwight. Apparently he was unaware of Godkin's essay until it came to his attention when that author included it in a collection of his essays published in 1896. When, in his later years, Turner described the origins of his ideas, he failed to mention George's writings. But he had listened to George speak in Madison during his graduate student years there, read from his writings in one of Ely's courses at Johns Hopkins, and even served as seminar secretary when another member of the group presented a report on George's ideas.

In the spring of 1888 Turner sent a copy of the current number of *Scribner's Magazine* to Caroline, suggesting that she might find pleasure in some of the offerings. He asked that she return it because he wished to keep one of the articles, "The Centre of the Republic," by James Baldwin. This, the first of a two-part contribution, explained the importance of the Northwest Ordinance and emphasized the growing national significance of the states that had developed within the boundaries of the Northwest Territory established by the act. Baldwin described the westward progression of the center of American population, predicting that in 1890 it would have reached the state of Indiana:

> In the great Northwest, pioneers [Baldwin wrote] had found room to grow, to expand, to feel and to know true freedom, to originate projects and to carry them to successful issues. . . . [T]he Western pioneer developed a kind of self-reliant patriotism. . . . New aspirations began to fill his breast, new ideas and opinions found lodgment in his brain. In the untrammelled freedom of the forest, and beneath the limitless skies of the Western plains, old traditions were forgotten; the conservatism bred of years of dependence upon the mother-country became a thing of the past; a new meaning was added to the idea of independence—the true American spirit of self-government had then and there its birth. . . . every man acquired a kind of hardy self-reliance and a faith in his own opinions and abilities. . . . the ordinary class distinctions were ignored, and the equality of men, not only before the law, but in the relationships of life, was generally not more a precept than a practical reality.[26]

After outlining the "wise provisions" of the Ordinance, Baldwin again summarized,

> Through such conditions and causes—and moulded by their environments, natural and political—the men of the West

became thinkers and doers of a type distinctively Western. The States of the Ohio Valley became the nursery of new and progressive ideas; the rallying point of radical movements in politics; the birthplace of innumerable absurd theories, wild projects, and impracticable "isms"; but withal, the great center of influence whence has issued a mighty leaven shaping public thought, directing public action, and lending robust strength to the national character.

Later Baldwin would define his assignment as "trac[ing] the social and intellectual phases of development through which the people of the West have advanced." Pioneer ideals, the shaping influence of environment, stages of development, originality, impact upon the nation—all these were to be components of Turner's message of 1893.[27]

We could cite other writers to show that most of the ideas that Turner used in 1893 had long been in play in one form or another. Indeed, in 1884 the American humorist Bill Nye discoursed upon the "rusty, neglected, and humiliated empty tin can[s]," strewn across the West, and concluded "There ain't no frontier any more."[28]

During the 1930s one of Turner's former undergraduate students, Fulmer Mood, began to study the sources of his teacher's ideas. Mood published a series of papers on the subject as well as later discussions of the frontier and sectional concepts and edited copies of some of Turner's unpublished writings. The Colonial Society of Massachusetts published a substantial paper that presents Mood's understanding by late 1939 of Turner's development as a historical thinker. Here, following discussion of the Portage and undergraduate background, particularly Professor Allen's influence, Mood focused on the intellectual sources of Turner's frontier thesis.[29]

Mood suggested that the young scholar probably became acquainted with the concept of stages of social evolution from the work of Richard T. Ely, or perhaps the writings of Francis A. Walker. He pointed out the importance of the acquisition by the State Historical Society of Wisconsin in 1887 of a copy of Scribner's Statistical Atlas of the United States, compiled by Fletcher Hewes and Henry Gannett. Turner, he suggested, was greatly influenced by the maps in this volume, which showed the spread of American population by federal census years, as well as the essay on "Progress of Settlement" and the concept of geographical provinces outlined here. Once impressed by such material, it would be natural, thought Mood, for Turner to use the publications of the Eleventh Census as soon as available and to be intrigued by the superintendent's report that the continuous frontier line had vanished from the bureau's maps. Mood believed that Turner's understanding of the importance of free land developed during the course of his work at The Johns Hopkins University. Adams and some of his students had been interested in the relation between landholding systems and community development, and Ely had discussed land as a factor of production and the concept of rent.

Turner bequeathed his papers to the Huntington Library, and Mood, alleging the threat of an unsympathetic biographer, later persuaded Caroline Turner to restrict access to him alone. The prohibition remained until Dorothy Turner Main terminated it in 1960.[30] Until that time researchers in general were forced to base their under-standing of Turner's sources on the clues in his 1893 essay, the relevant literature of the era, and conjecture. Although relatively restricted, Turner's documentation in 1893 was more detailed than that found in most of his articles. It shows that he drew evidence from a wide range of sources, including some that Mood had emphasized. Even before he began to prepare his little syllabus for a course on the history of the Northwest, Turner's mind had been attuned to materials that aptly described or summarized the processes by which the lands beyond the Alleghenies were settled. His reviews, particularly those of Roosevelt's first volumes, introduced him to relevant ideas and facts. He continued to expand his stock of knowledge in preparing survey courses in United States history, a course in constitutional and political history, another in American economic and social history, and extension lectures, as well as through his guidance of students in seminaries focused on western development. As he had explained in his letters to Caroline and in "The Significance of History," he was trying to become the master of a field of history: the development of the "Great West."

Between the publication of the *Aegis* article and delivery of his paper in Chicago lay the better part of a year in which Turner was teaching his course on economic and social history and studying "the spread of settlement across the continent." But "The Significance of the Frontier in American History" was the culmination of some eight years of study. It was an interpretation of American history that flowed logically from Turner's earlier interest and research in Wisconsin history, the fur trade and other aspects of western history, and his classroom teaching, extension and incidental lectures. He melded ideas, insights, and evidence derived from his teachers, the *Congressional Globe*, the American travel and emigrant guide literature of the nineteenth century, the contemporary literary and scholarly journals, and considerable numbers of other books and monographs. There are suggestive passages in much that Turner read or may have read in these formative years. Writers have suggested that he was particularly influenced by Richard T. Ely and by his reading of the works of Achille Loria, Walter Bagehot, Henry George, and Lord Bryce. One can point to relevant sections in the writings of James Baldwin, John A. Doyle, Edward J. Payne, William Barrows, and others. Turner took notes as students reported in his seminary and in the course of his own reading. Yet scholars seeking to identify the authors upon whom Turner drew in making his case for the frontier sometimes overshot their evidence. For example, W. Stull Holt detected Hegelian influence in Turner's essay and maintained that Turner *must* have read this great historical philosopher while at Johns Hopkins, lack of proof notwithstanding.[31]

Some investigators sought particularly to identify the point at which Turner realized that the varied pieces of intellectual capital he had been acquiring could be fitted into a coherent thesis in explanation of unique American institutions and character. This flash of insight, this "aha" moment came, Mood and others have believed, when Turner read *Extra Census Bulletin, 2* of the United States Census of 1890 and learned that the federal cartographers were no longer able to draw a single frontier line marking the edge of the settled regions of the country. That fact certainly interested Turner—in his paper of 1892 he had drawn particular attention to the pattern of the frontier line in earlier years. Did he therefore experience the shock of creative inspiration when he found it declared missing, as has been suggested? Actually Turner had, himself, predicted that outcome. In his paper on colonization, delivered in early 1891, he remarked, "the colonization of the United States is now coming to a close."[32]

The "frontier," however, was a crucial element in Turner's proclamation of 1893. Its passing provided that attention-getting "hook" for his first paragraph that many writers seek. More important, Turner pressed the word *frontier* into frequent service as a synonym for West and also used it to symbolize social processes and adaptation, as well as a dimension of space. His emphasis on the passing of the frontier line allowed him to sharpen the concept of closed space first articulated in his essay on colonization. Thus, Turner's use of the word *frontier* shaped the proclamation of 1893 in extremely important ways.

He used the term to clothe or sharpen ideas that he already had in hand. But it is doubtful that the *Census Bulletin* provided him with that moment of truth sometimes posited by students of creativity. He had command of the basic ideas found in the essay of 1893 before he opened that publication.

The central thesis of Turner's essay, posited in the first paragraph, told his hearers that free land and its attraction of "American settlement westward, explain American development." The scholar who dates this revelation has perhaps identified Turner's great moment. A decade before the Huntington Library was allowed to give scholars free access to Turner's papers, a graduate student at Cornell University, Lee Benson, argued persuasively that between the time when Turner wrote "The Significance of History" and the publication of "Problems in American History" in the fall of 1892, he discovered the ideas of Achille Loria. This Italian political economist and theorist of the development of social systems posited that societies passed through an initial stage of development characterized by the presence of free land. Knowledge of Loria's ideas was being widely disseminated in scholarly publications during the early 1890s, and Ely was greatly influenced by them. During academic year 1892–93 a graduate student studying with Ely and Turner translated portions of the Italian's book, *Analisi della Proprieta Capitalista*, for Ely. Therefore, Turner was in a position to learn of Loria's ideas.

Benson sought to reveal the major roots of Turner's essay by comparing its passages to those in the appropriate section of Loria's work. In addition to Loria's emphasis upon the importance of a free lands phase of social development, Turner also found there the ideas that American development recapitulated the stages of "man's social and economic development" and the suggestion that the American example would allow the scholar to understand such developments in other societies. Benson was able to show that Turner used various figures of speech and vocabulary that also appeared in Loria's work. Thus, argued Benson, Turner's most potent ideas traced directly back to a European source, the comprehensive social theory of Loria. The young professor from Wisconsin had followed the political economist in affirming that "American history was *literally* a record of historical evolution," that "free land" was truly that, and that its "presence or absence . . . *was* the fundamental determining factor in society." The closing of the frontier removed America's safety valve, "a new epoch in American history was dawning."[33]

Mood discovered notes on Loria's work in Turner's files and attached a sheet noting that, he believed, they verified Benson's suggestions. After the Huntington Library opened Turner's papers to all researchers, Ray A. Billington used them to develop a more elaborate analysis of the steps by which Turner had developed his thesis of 1893, adding other names to the roster of scholars and journalists to whom earlier writers had alleged that Turner was indebted. But Billington saw no climactic discovery or culminating flash of insight at some point between Turner's preparation of "The Significance of History" in 1891 and the summer of 1893. Rather, Billington wrote, "he had arrived at most of his basic conclusions by January 1891, when he prepared his talk on 'American Colonization' for the Madison Literary Club." His reading of Loria and other theorists, his immersion in the literature of western settlement during this period, simply provided corroboration of theories already formed, believed Billington. He was somewhat in error, however. Although Turner emphasized the importance of the West in "American Colonization," he did not in that essay identify "free land" as the major element in the West's contribution, a basic relationship in Turner's thesis.[34]

Although scholars pointing to some crucial point in the development of Turner's ideas are sometimes persuasive, no analysis of this kind can be definitive. We can, however, be certain that the absorptive and synthetic qualities of Turner's mind were at their peak during the years culminating in 1893. Mood showed that the concepts of both frontier and section had long prior histories in American writing. A growing concern about the exhaustion of natural resources traced back at least to George P. Marsh's book of the 1860s, *Man and Nature*. From the mid-1870s the press frequently apprised the American public of fraud in the disposal of the public domain and of the accumulation of great holdings of timber or agricultural lands by individuals or companies.

By the late 1880s drought and declining prices were wreaking havoc with the agriculture of the plains country, and writers had begun to define the basic problem as one of overproduction linked in turn to the rapid alienation of the public domain. Soon the orators of the People's Party were excoriating land monopolists, including the land grant railroads and loan companies, and demanding that the remainder of the public domain should be allocated only to homesteaders. Those who saw the Anglo Saxon as peculiarly suited to be the champions of

Christianity joined forces with intellectuals like Francis A. Walker in advocating restriction of immigration, emphasizing the imminent exhaustion of the public domain among their reasons. The immigration question was of particular interest to Turner's teacher and colleague Richard T. Ely. These currents of thought all flowed through the popular periodical literature of the late 1880s and early 1890s, carrying the message of depleted public lands and closing space to a wide circle of readers.

The scholar who is interested in identifying the origins of Turner's ideas can point to works that he cited, and to others with which he was certainly familiar, as germinal sources and can speculate about other publications that might have influenced him. Indeed, the major components of the essay of 1893 were so widely in circulation that Turner had perhaps encountered them many times in his reading. But some of the points made by investigators are questionable. Turner's class notes for the first semester of Allen's "History of Ancient Institutions," reveal that he had been exposed to stage theories of development long before he had any contact with Ely. Allen also emphasized the importance of the distribution of public lands in Rome.

With a brilliant textual analysis Benson supported his argument in behalf of Loria's influence, noting the similar words and figures in Turner's essay and the appropriate passages of Loria's work. Each, Benson pointed out, used the word *palimpsest*. But Turner had used that word in a letter to Allen during his Hopkins year in describing the succession of settler groups occupying districts in Wisconsin. This communication took place some years before Turner is thought to have become acquainted with Loria's ideas. It is doubtful also that Loria's use of the phrase "free land" was Turner's first exposure to that concept.

Since Professor Allen used Bagehot's *Physics and Politics* in his teaching, Billington's suggestion that Turner became acquainted with it during his stay at Johns Hopkins is probably in error. Turner's heavy use of the book may have related much more to his teaching obligations in European history than to his search for clues on American development. But, as Billington notes, the work did spark Turner's comparison of the lure of the American West with the impact of the Mediterranean Sea upon the Greeks. And Turner recurrently used the phrase "breaking the cake of custom," a favorite expression of Bagehot.

Most scholars have failed to pick up the reference to Baldwin's article in *Scribner's* that parallels Turner's later arguments in striking respects. Other investigators may well find new clues to Turner's reading during the years preparatory to the writing of "The Significance of the Frontier in American History." They will not change the general conclusion that Turner drew from many sources and that he had probably encountered his major themes in several—even perhaps—numerous places. And we should not picture a young Turner intent on piecing together a great new interpretation of American history. Rather we should see a harried but happy and enthusiastic young man, afire with professional ambition, seeking to legitimize and promote his field of history and his department. Turner tried to write the strongest defense of western history possible, only to succeed beyond his dreams.

Of the many elements in the essay of 1893, the young Wisconsin historian invented few if any. If the ideas of free lands, sectionalism, and closure of opportunity are accepted as the major concepts, we know that all were current in the intellectual atmosphere—in the quality magazines, the learned journals, the political forums and the pressure group activity of the 1880s and 1890s, as well as in bits and pieces scattered through the work of earlier intellectuals and writers. The ideas of social process—adaptive evolution in the face of environmental challenge, society as organism, recapitulation, and stage theory,—were common stock in the graduate program at Johns Hopkins and present to some degree surely in the intellectual intercourse in which Turner had engaged earlier as a student and tutor at Wisconsin.

But Turner possessed the sharpness of mind and synthetic abilities necessary to fit the disparate parts into a powerful statement of historical cause and effect. We can see antecedent pieces or seeds, words or phrases, even in the graduate school correspondence with Caroline, in the master's thesis as presented to the Historical Society, in the dissertation, in the book reviews, and in the published and unpublished papers of 1891 and 1892. Nor was the process one of strict sequence. Turner had proclaimed the end of the westward movement in his lecture on colonization in early 1891 but not used the idea in the article of 1892.

Stimulated through the years 1891 to the early summer of 1893 by the pressure of preparing papers and lectures, carrying some ideas and materials forward with little change, incorporating new supporting evidence, refining and recasting the prose to please his orator's ear, Turner thought himself to the positions of July 12, 1993. He later admitted that he worked best while at white heat in meeting a deadline. I believe that Turner did most of the preparation for his Chicago lecture during the days of late June and early July before his departure for Chicago. But one doubts that there was indeed one moment when revelation dawned and, *voila*, he realized that he had captured a great truth, or a time when he concluded that he had a theory in hand which must be supported with additional evidence. He had long been convinced of the importance of western history in American development; his future rode upon others sharing that understanding. His was a developing argument; no one piece could have been *the* revelation. He was still tinkering with his text hours before delivery, but in the end he had done far more than mark an important field of history with his claim stakes. Although only one of many to argue for the exceptional nature of the American experience, he had created a compelling theory of American uniqueness.

Turner later claimed that acceptance of his thesis was slow. Certainly the paper was not an instant success. Just as he had circulated the *Aegis* article among his Johns Hopkins friends, he now sent copies to eminent authors and writers who might, he believed, be interested in his work. The responses were not rapturous, but in fact they were what one might have expected from busy men intent on their own concerns. Francis A. Walker thought the subject "fascinating," "the mere title . . . a success"; he had not yet read the essay but promised that he would do so with "deepest interest." John Fiske termed the essay *"admirable,"* showing a *"perspective"* that he too had been working toward with "fruitful" results. It had arrived at the "right time," responded Theodore Roosevelt, because he would be able to use it in the course of preparing the third volume of *The Winning of the West*. "I think," he continued, "you have struck some first class ideas, and have put into definite shape a good deal of thought which has been floating around rather loosely."[35] This remark has been quoted to show Roosevelt's lack of perception. Actually it was a reasonable statement of fact, although he failed to grasp the impact that the frontier essay was destined to have.

But hearty approbation was not long denied. Some weeks after delivery of the paper in Chicago, Turner read it to his friend Woodrow Wilson, who had come to Madison to try and commit him to edit a volume in an Athenaeum Press series. Wilson was enthusiastic, and Turner incorporated his suggestion that the word "hither" be used in describing the side of the frontier region adjacent to older settled regions. Wilson promptly incorporated Turner's major arguments in a book review and an important monograph. He and other professional colleagues praised Turner when Thwaites read a paper for him at the meeting of the AHA in 1896. Soon the *Atlantic Monthly* published popular presentations of his ideas. By the end of the decade the National Herbart Society had reprinted the essay in an expanded format for the use of school teachers. Soon it appeared as well under socialist auspices.

Acceptance of the importance of Turner's ideas rested upon a variety of factors. His was a proclamation, vibrant with rhetorical force and seductive in its choice and use of language. Even generations later, graduate students reported themselves charmed and excited by their first reading of the essay of 1893. But there was much more here than sound and fury. Within Turner's generation the credibility of his thesis among scholars was enhanced by the skilful way in which he set a factual argument and evidence within a framework of contemporary social theory. The idea that environment was a major factor in inducing adaptation of species was widespread within the developing fields of geography and other social sciences. By this time there was keen scholarly argument as to the way in which evolutionary processes occurred. In effect, Turner's use of the organismic metaphor seems to be an endorsement of the Lamarckian position that acquired traits could be inherited, but in his hands the evolutionary process was described in terms so general that he created the aura of science without recourse to deniable detail. Turner accepted and promoted ideas of the time but without joining one of various hostile camps.

The stage theories that Turner used—moving from the primitive to urbanized civilization in the one case and again from the Indianized backwoodsman to the prosperous farmer—were exercises in categorization that smacked of social science but were not pressed into the rigidity of scientific recapitulation where the organism's stages of development in theory were always the same. But if adaptation was the rule, how to account for society's retention of those traits associated with frontier conditions? Here entered the idea of the survival, a concept for which Turner needed to turn no further than to Professor Allen, who had published an article entitled, "A Survival of Land Community in New England." Rigorous definition of the various elements in Turner's social science can expose contradiction, but Turner did not seek rigor. For his theoretical capstone Turner turned to Loria, who wrote: "America has the key to the historical enigma which Europe has sought for centuries in vain, and the land which has no history reveals luminously the course of universal history." In the history of the United States in which the frontier played so important a role, the scholar could find "the record of social evolution." The suggestion that study of American history provided a unique understanding of universal history is, we suspect, Loria's major contribution to the frontier hypothesis, the supreme legitimation of Turner's argument for studying the westward expansion of the American people.

I have argued that Turner's essay was social science discourse. His was not a deductive model, however, in the sense that he derived theses for testing from a general body of social theory. His method was essentially inductive, proclaiming theses derived from general observation, as recorded in his sources. He then used other factual evidence and social theory to justify his assertion of hypotheses. But he also protected himself by arguing that he was "simply [calling] attention to the frontier as a fertile field for investigation." However great the weaknesses in his approach, it provided an impression of scientific analysis that helped convince his contemporaries in history of the validity of his argument and also made it acceptable to scholars in related disciplines.

There were institutional elements at work in the acceptance of Turner's ideas as well. The fixation upon the Teutonic or Anglo-Saxon origins of American institutions shared by various of the older American historians was wearing thin by the early 1890s. The ideal of history as romantic narrative was also crumbling as a generation of younger historians won their professional union cards by presenting analytical monographs as dissertations and, in the expansion of graduate instruction of the time, began to teach their graduate students to do likewise. The trend was not unique to history—this era was one of emergent realism among America's creative writers. In their rejection of broader philosophical and abstract idealism and endorsement of scientific method, American historians faced the danger of becoming little more than dull fact grubbers. But Turner's essay offered an exciting theory of national development and character and in effect called for recruits to test it and to do so in ways that would incorporate social and economic factors, as well as the political and diplomatic sides of history. Turner too, as we have seen, proclaimed the importance and merit of American institutions and their study. The American historian need no longer be a second class citizen in the land of Clio.

There was a generational dividing line within the historical profession of the United States around the turn of the century. The original leaders in the AHA, for example, were giving way at this time to J. Franklin Jameson, Albert B. Hart, Andrew C. McLaughlin, Turner, and Haskins, among others, who played major roles in the association for most of the following twenty years. In general, these men did not win the presidency of the association until after 1905, but they were actively at work in its institutional structure from the mid-1890s onward. Many in this group were intellectual leaders in their own right, but they accepted Turner's ideas as part of the current wisdom of their generation. And these men in turn had their influence among less prominent members of the profession.

If the American West had been relatively ignored to this point by scholars, that had not been true within American public consciousness. Going west, starting over, creating new homes beyond the western horizon had long been a basic part of America's heritage. The West too was a place of adventure and romance, and various forms of literature had fostered this conception in the public mind, from the captivity narratives of the colonial period, through traveler accounts, to the dime novels of the late nineteenth century, as well as through the publications of more serious writers like James Fenimore Cooper. Turner and his colleagues competed for attention in Chicago, as we have seen with western style entertainment provided by the likes of Buffalo Bill Cody. Despite its scientific trappings, Turner's essay struck a favorite chord for the American reading public—romantic primitivism. Westering was a reality within the American experience, but over time "The West" and its related experiences served as the basis for symbolic elaboration among Americans generally. Thus, where the symbols of science helped Turner's ideas to gain credence in the expanding scholarly community of the time, a different public also believed that the West was important. One of Turner's contributions lay in taking a concept already thoroughly integrated in American popular culture and making it acceptable within the halls of academia. Now in the American mind no other processes so symbolized national development as did those of the frontier.

Turner's achievements during the early 1890s were truly remarkable. On the foundation of these years he fashioned one of the outstanding careers in the American historical profession. Cushing Strout would call him the "true father" of the New History. Richard Hofstadter credited Turner, Charles A. Beard, and Vernon L. Parrington with formulating "the pivotal ideas of the first half of the twentieth century" in the historical discipline. They were, in his view, the greatest of the Progressive historians. Hofstadter quoted Beard's evaluation of Turner's frontier essay approvingly—a publication with "more profound influence on thought about American history than any other essay or volume ever written on the subject." Turner was the "first of the great [history] professionals."

In more esoteric analysis, David W. Noble placed Turner with George Bancroft and Charles Beard in a succession of historians who served as political theorists and theologians for their generation in interpreting the status of the covenant between God and his chosen people in America. As historian, it was Turner's sad role to announce the end of conditions that had allowed Americans to retain God's favor as members of a pure, simple, and democratic society. Later, developing his argument further in terms of the metaphor of two worlds and an American jeremiad of "promise, declension, and prophecy," Noble again cast Turner as bearer of ill tidings. Turner had shown that the freehold republic must end and capitalism insure that "the undemocratic social and political patterns of Europe would spread across the Atlantic, and American uniqueness would end." In the first full-scale study of the Progressive historians during the 1990s, Ernst A. Briesach acknowledged Turner as a pioneer in introducing or emphasizing aspects of the new history. However, he refused to place him among Progressive historians, arguing that he did not accept progress as both proven by historical facts and as an objective to which his writings should contribute as did James Harvey Robinson and Beard.[36]

In 1893 Turner could not foresee the deference that his work would win in the future. Nor were his early papers free of flaws in presentation or logic. For example, Turner's theory merged elements from several different perspectives—Darwinian adaptation, the succession of developmental stages, and generalizations about the settlement or colonization process. These concepts Turner brought to bear upon Americans confronting uniquely receptive space—a space so capacious that sectional differentiation would occur during the settlement process. If pressed to their limit, none of the three lines of theory boded well for the future. Adaptation presumably would be continuous, thereby eliminating frontier influence. One stage was destined to be replaced by another, and a vigorous colonizing stock might degenerate to the level found in older regions or nations. Such weaknesses suggest indeed that Turner was not trying to build a logical system but eclectically buttress an argument on behalf of the importance of the West and its study with the most impressive evidence available. In 1893 Turner had laid a foundation. Would he continue to build, to develop his ideas further, to recognize and replace faulty materials? Would he build new structures? Or would he play the lottery winner who chooses to bank his winnings?

5   Acceptance

"A man . . . who has the courage to put American history
in its proper setting"

Borrowing money from his father, Turner built a roomy house in 1894
for Caroline and the children at 629 Frances Street. There they forged
lasting friendships with three neighboring families whose heads were
also to be important members of the Madison faculty—Charles R. Van
Hise, Moses S. Slaughter, and Charles S. Slichter, specialists in
geology, classics, and mathematics, respectively. Their dwelling at the
end of Frances Street gave the Turners a striking view of the changing
moods of Lake Mendota and its hilly western shore, particularly
splendid in autumn. Fred's canoe rested on the porch during the
months of open water. The cost of building the house at 629 Frances
far exceeded Turner's expectations and perhaps in response—but also
in friendship—Haskins took rooms there soon after its completion.
This arrangement continued until Haskins left Madison in 1902.

The Turners settled in happily on Frances Street. Another Johns
Hopkins alumnus, William P. Trent, lectured on southern history at
Wisconsin in early 1896 and was Turner's houseguest. Later Trent
enthusiastically recommended Turner as a potential author to a representative of the Macmillan Company but cautioned *"entre-nous"* that
Turner's involvements at the university and "the pleasantness of his
delightful family life" seemed to "interfere somewhat with his
concentrating his energies in some one piece of work."[1]

A talented writer, Gertrude Slaughter later described Madison life
as her family came to know it after their arrival in 1896. It was, she
wrote, "quite unusual," perhaps "unique." Madison was still a small
town where friends did much "visiting one another, dining and wining
and drinking tea together"—simple pleasures. But "the character of the
people," their diverse interests, visitors from abroad, the enticing
possibility of long walks and picnics, gave the days there a special
character. The foods offered, however, in Madison hospitality might be
anything but simple. Pervading all was "the hum of culture" or "the free
play of intellect." Small clubs abounded, "reading clubs, drama clubs,
poetry clubs, a science club, a classical club." For faculty wives the
relation of town and university society might provide some elements

of tension. In his autobiography Ely reported that during these years the university social arbiters led by the president's wife, Mary Mathews Adams, poetess and lady of means, and Anna A. Ely, tipped the balance from town to gown. The wives of Frances Street, however, had reservations about the leadership of Mrs. Adams and Mrs. Ely and went their own way sufficiently to become known as "the Frances Street set."[2]

During the 1890s Madison residents succumbed to cycling fever. Turner became an enthusiast and bought a tandem bicycle on which he and Caroline rode to Portage on at least one occasion. Late June 1898 found him cycling through southern Wisconsin in company with Slaughter and William A. Scott, from the economics department, looking "like Red Indians"; fit targets for young Jack's gun, he joked, or perhaps the younger Turner would run when he saw them.[3]

Haskins's arrival allowed Turner to return to his original plans for concentrating on American history. Such specialization involved much work in the introductory course in that subject, however. In his first efforts to develop an upper-level undergraduate course in American history, Turner organized one in constitutional history. But an offering in American economic and social history would provide more opportunity to study and lecture upon topics relating to western American development. This course first appeared in the University *Catalogue* of 1891–92.

The Wisconsin *Catalogue* of 1895–96, wrote Billington, "announced a completely new course: 'History 7. the History of the West.'" "Particular attention," explained Turner in the description, "is paid to the advance of settlement across the continent, and to the results of this movement." "Here," wrote Billington, "was innovation, indeed—this was the first course on the history of the frontier to be offered anywhere." Disregarding the strong possibility that Turner had himself written the blurb, Billington cited the pride of the local press in this departure. He absolved Turner of provincialism by noting the continental sweep of the course. Interest in regionalism was widespread, he added, making it reasonable for Turner to believe that the history of regions must be known before that of the nation could be understood. Billington noted also that Turner's "decision to explain the 'West' to his students coincided with" arrangements to have Trent offer a lecture series on southern history at Wisconsin during the academic year 1895–96.[4]

"History of the West" was a new catalogue entry, but not a "completely new course." When Turner introduced "Economic and Social History of the United States" in the 1891–92 *Catalogue*, he included "the process of American settlement across the continent" among the topics to be considered. By the next year Turner was promising that "particular attention will be paid to the spread of settlement across the continent, and to the economic and social causes of sectional and national sentiment." In the *Catalogue* of 1893–94, Turner dropped the second half of this description, substituting "and to the economic and social results of this movement." He used this same course description when he placed the "History of the West" in the catalogue.[5] For a time Turner alternated the course in western history with one in economic and social history. In the year 1902–3, for example, he promised that the latter would consider immigration, interstate migration, distribution of population, transportation, and internal improvements. During the 1890s Turner also taught the undergraduate survey of American history.

Neither Turner's course in the history of the American West nor the celebrated essay of 1893 was conceived in a sudden flash of revelation. Both represented important steps in the process by which Turner laid claim to his historical province, steps beginning as early as 1888 when he prepared the syllabus entitled "Outline Studies in the History of the Northwest" for the National Bureau of Unity Clubs.[6] In effect the course was the Turner thesis prepared for classroom use; as the thesis grew in popularity, so did the course.

The Wisconsin *Catalogue* of 1891–92 listed a "Historical Seminary" described as "a graduate course for training in original research." Students would choose their subject for investigation, subject to approval by the instructors (at this point both Haskins and Turner appear in that capacity). In the next year consultation with the instructor was to precede the choice of topic. We have seen, however, that seminar students during the early 1890s chose topics dealing with the West for the most part. Both seniors and graduates sat in the seminary in its first years, but by 1893–94 the two groups met separately on occasion. Further development occurred in 1895–96 when seminars became available in American, medieval, and modern European history, open in the American case to graduate students and approved seniors "of suitable preparation." During the early years of

Turner's seminars, the *Catalogue* did not designate its topical focus, but in 1895–96 his students investigated "the period 1815 to 1850." The description promised that the years between 1845 and 1875 would be examined in the following year. Emphasis, Turner explained in addition, was to be on political and constitutional history. In the next year Turner's seminarians studied "the period beginning with colonization, and closing with 1789."[7] Turner continued to designate time periods for study in his seminar through 1900–1901. Once in the new century, Turner announced topics in western history for several years but after 1903 focused seminary work on one of the presidential administrations of the early national period, except in the year 1904–5 when nullification was the central theme.

In 1891 Emory R. Johnson completed his work for the master's degree in history at Madison, presenting a thesis on "River and Harbor Bills." Through the year 1900 fifteen additional master's candidates obtained their degrees in American history under Turner's direction. During this same period three students completed master's degrees with Haskins, and four degree candidates from other departments listed history as a second area of specialization.

As might be expected, the graduate students in American history at Madison worked within the framework of Turner's interests. During the 1890s candidates for the master's degree examined colonial charters, land systems, and other aspects of government and politics in the late colonial and revolutionary periods as well as during the early national period. They also selected topics in the history of immigration, settlement, and internal improvements. More specifically, candidates studied the territorial development of Georgia, electoral systems in colonial Virginia and Massachusetts, the nominating convention in Pennsylvania, the early spoils system in that state and in New York, popular forces in colonial Maryland, and federalism in early national Massachusetts. One seminar member investigated the relations between the Five Nations and New York during the eighteenth century. Others examined the Erie Canal as state enterprise, the dispute over internal improvements during the Monroe administrations, the system of federal land grants, and the origins of the use of land grants in support of education. The federal compact of 1787, Jay's Treaty, diplomatic relations with Mexico during the twenty years prior to the war with that power, and James G. Blaine's Pan-American policy also attracted the attention of participants in Turner's seminar during his first decade of teaching.

By the conclusion of academic year 1898–99 three other doctoral candidates had joined Everest and Libby in Turner's group of Ph.D.'s in American history. George H. Alden studied efforts to form governments west of the Alleghenies prior to 1780 and their British background. John B. Sanborn prepared a doctoral thesis on federal land grant aid to railways. Paul S. Reinsch defended a dissertation dealing with colonial attitudes toward the English common law. Louise P. Kellogg and Charles McCarthy swelled the group still further in 1901. The dissertations were all useful studies, and Libby and Reinsch so impressed Turner and Haskins that they offered positions as instructors to them.

A much-reproduced photograph of June 1894 shows Turner and the members of his seminar grouped around the table in their meeting place in the Historical Society Library—still at that point located in the state capitol. Five men are grouped at the rear, Turner and eight young women sit at the table, and two female members of the society staff hover in attendance. As only sixteen of the forty-six successful master's candidates in American history between 1891 and 1910 were women, this picture conveys a somewhat misleading impression of the Wisconsin graduate program. Of the eight women students who flanked the beaming Turner in the photograph, only one received an M.A. from the University of Wisconsin, but her major study was literature, American history her minor. The others did not complete graduate programs in history at Wisconsin. Although Everest was the first recipient of a Ph.D. in history at the University of Wisconsin, it was not until 1898–99 that a woman became a teaching fellow or scholar in the department. Kellogg followed in the next year. Other such appointments would be made, but Turner also later admitted that it was his inclination to award a position to a man rather than to a woman in cases in which the two appeared to be of equal ability and scholarly promise.

It was an era when a woman with an advanced degree in history could look forward usually only to a teaching position in a women's college, to service as a college dean of women, or to work in the manuscript, editorial, or research programs of historical societies, archives, or other research institutions. This situation did not move Turner to protest, but he did welcome women into his classes and give them careful counsel. He did not joke about the satin quarter as did his later colleague, Dana C. Munro.

A few of Turner's students of the 1890s later commented on their experience in the seminar. Guy Stanton Ford found himself in 1898 responsible for reporting on one colony as his seminar mates tried to become experts on the development of others during the late colonial period. In less skilful hands this organization of work could have been disastrous, Ford believed. He found compensation in the perception that Turner was deeply interested in what he was doing and that he, Ford, was contributing to knowledge that Turner would some day place with due thanks in a masterwork. Turner took notes as the reports were given, and Becker once slyly asked him if he was "bluffing" interest, a query that provoked a strong denial. Kellogg believed that her teacher's great talent as a seminar director lay in his ability to create a sense of "comradeship" and an atmosphere of "intellectual democracy" in which all members of the seminar viewed themselves as fellow workers. Despite "absurd theories," crude opinions, "conclusions occasionally preposterous," recalled another, seminar members were "somehow made to feel that we were all prospectors together."[8] An impression of professional stature, personal charm, humane humor, attractive appearance, melodious voice—and above all, enthusiasm—made Turner a veritable pied piper to many young historians.

Herbert E. Bolton noted that Turner in this period was "indifferent to *formal* method." He gave "general talks" in the seminar "on kinds of evidence, reputation of witnesses for intelligence, veracity, opportunity to know, bias, self interest, and questioned students on these matters, but he had few formulas."[9] In discussion he guided students to the position that problems of evidence varied so widely that one could not be dogmatic about them. Adams had made sure that Turner knew about the ideas of leading European historians. Turner believed that he practiced and taught scientific method, but he discounted the elaborate kind of evaluation of evidence that was enshrined in the formidable manual of C. V. Langlois and Charles Seignobos. In 1904 Turner maintained that American "problems with respect to material" differed from those of "Old World history" and primarily involved the identification and collection of "scattered material" rather than those relating to "the technique of verification and criticism of scanty documents."[10]

Imitating practice at Johns Hopkins, the University of Wisconsin began to publish dissertations as bulletins. Libby's dissertation was the first to appear in this form. "The Anti-Masonic Party," submitted by McCarthy, and Kellogg's "The Colonial Charter: A Study of English Colonial Administration" won the Winsor Prize of the American

Historical Association in 1902 and 1903. Others among earlier winners had also studied at Wisconsin, or, as in the case of Ulrich B. Phillips, at the University of Chicago. By the turn of the century Turner had established a reputation in the profession as a successful director of graduate work.

Mention of Turner's supportiveness, his enthusiasm, his ability to criticize and suggest without being destructive was recurrent in the letters that former students wrote about him when he departed from Wisconsin in 1910. Turner's interest in the research of his students did not end at the seminar door. He was willingly accessible in conference and office hours — excessively so, some of his friends and former students later believed. Turner rapidly learned that the direction of graduate students involved related responsibilities. Letters must be written in support of undergraduate majors and graduate students who sought graduate admission elsewhere. At Harvard, for example, Albert B. Hart learned that a young graduate of the civics-historical course, an agreeable fellow named Carl L. Becker, had done "careful and intelligent" work, "as satisfactory as possible with our material," and would surely make the most of "whatever opportunities" that Hart might "be able to afford him."[11] Other students required recommendations in support of their job-seeking efforts. Prospective graduate students inquired about the possibilities of admission at Wisconsin and increasingly sought Turner's counsel about appropriate research topics. An inveterate advice giver, Turner often responded at considerable length.

The presentation of "The Significance of the Frontier in American History" was a climactic event in Turner's career. But initially Turner had little inkling of that fact. He continued to develop his teaching program and for several more years journeyed about southern Wisconsin on weekends to deliver extension lectures. Although time-consuming, this kind of university service supplemented his income, and he enjoyed the kind of dedicated students that enrolled in such classes. On the Madison campus he administered a history program in which both the number of students and the instructional staff were growing. The presidents of the university early recognized Turner's ability as a committee member, and he took an active part in the discussions at the meetings of the faculty.

The inclusion of the history program within Ely's School of Economics, Political Science, and History involved Turner and Haskins in another level of decision-making. But the close association of the departments within the school meant that Turner numbered graduate students in economics and political economy among his students, and his understanding of American political and economic development deepened because of such relationships. Turner defended Ely loyally in 1894 when the Wisconsin superintendent of public instruction, an ex-officio member of the board of regents, accused Ely of endorsing subversive doctrines in his books and participating in the boycott of a Madison employer whose workers were on strike. In the resulting investigation by the regents, Turner helped gather evidence for Ely and prepare other aspects of his defense, lobbied friends on the university's governing board, and testified at the formal hearing of the case. He joined in the general jubilation when the regents exonerated Ely and included in their statement the "bold and eloquent affirmation" that ran, "we believe the great state University of Wisconsin should ever encourage that continual and fearless sifting and winnowing by which alone the truth can be found."[12] But, as the years passed, it was natural for the historians to chafe at an arrangement that placed two administrators, Dean Edward A. Birge and Ely, between them and the higher levels of power represented by the president and the board of regents.

Turner believed that creation of the School of Economics, Political Science, and History would make Madison a leading center of graduate studies. During the extended negotiations with Ely, Turner frequently used developments at the University of Chicago as reference points. This was perhaps natural since President Harper's interest in Adams and Ely put the ball in play at Wisconsin. But Wisconsin faculty members viewed Chicago as Wisconsin's major rival in the Midwest. That rivalry with Chicago continued to be an element in Turner's thinking long after Ely's school was safely launched. In 1895 both Ely and Turner served on a university committee charged with making recommendations concerning the handbook of graduate study and graduate work in general. As we have seen, they and their colleagues used the successful efforts to develop graduate work at the University of Michigan and at Chicago to justify similar activity in Madison. Wisconsin must not, they maintained, become a "mere feeder" of the programs at the University of Chicago.[13] Town builder philosophy perhaps, but effective. Ely's school thrived.

In the mid-1890s Turner was busily at work with his classes both in Madison and in rooms of the high school or town hall in centers like Columbus Junction where extension classes met. He participated actively in university affairs and closely followed developments in the board of regents and in the legislature. Thwaites and President Adams were trying successfully during these years to convince the state legislators that they should provide the funds to build a capacious home for the State Historical Society and the university library to share, only one of the projects that reflected energy and physical growth on the Madison campus. But Turner was also advancing his research and national reputation.

As Jameson planned the early development of the *American Historical Review*, he informed Turner that he must have a contribution from the western scholars of the country and invited him to submit an article. In answer Turner prepared "Western State-making in the Revolutionary Era," which grew into a two-part article as he discovered several "hitherto unnoted attempts at state-making" in the Draper manuscripts.[14] Turner began by restating the fundamental importance of the western free lands. He posited three "phases of growth": the initial occupation of the tidewater when European influences prevented "the modifying influences of the new environment from having their full effect," the spread of settlement westward where "the wilderness had opportunity to modify men already partly dispossessed of their Old World traits," and finally, the current phase when "the free lands are gone." The Revolutionary era was of particular interest, Turner argued, because Americans were undertaking the formation of institutions of government on a new frontier, the trans-Allegheny region. "How would they go about this, and on what principles?"[15]

In "Western State-Making" Turner traced efforts during the Revolutionary era to create governments in three "natural areas,"—West Virginia-to-be, the region drained by the upper tributaries of the Tennessee River in Virginia and North Carolina, and the Kentucky area. His principal viewpoint, he informed readers, was to be that of the backwoodsmen. After describing the various proposals to establish independent colonies or state governments in these areas, Turner concluded that interest in the Northwest Ordinance had led historians to pay too little attention to settlement below the Ohio. Here the frontiersmen had "tried to shape their own civil destiny." Turner stressed the importance of physiographic features in establishing the boundaries of activity and argued that "the frontier did not proceed on the principle of tabula rasa; it modified older forms, and infused into them the spirit of democracy" evident in the American Revolution generally. He noted the similarities in the various proposals for establishing governments, notably the westerners' interest in controlling land distribution. He found national sentiment strengthening in the West, reflecting desire for Congress to control the process of state development and the mixing of individuals of diverse origins in the West. In these "early political efforts of the rude boisterous West" Turner discerned "promise of the day when, in the person of Andrew Jackson, its forces of democracy and nationalism should rule the republic."[16]

In 1896 the program organizers of the AHA gave Turner an opportunity to present a research agenda for western history when they arranged a session to be chaired by Justin Winsor and offering papers by Turner and Theodore Roosevelt. The latter, however, failed to appear, pleading his duties as New York police commissioner. Absent also, Turner sent his paper, "The West as a Field for Historical Study," which Thwaites read on his friend's behalf. As secretary of the State Historical Society of Wisconsin, Thwaites also made available a listing of materials relating to the institutional history of the Old Northwest, which had been compiled by the librarian of the society.

In his short paper Turner explained "why the West should be studied, what are some of the historical problems which it offers, where there are proper materials for the study, and how they may best be utilized." He quoted a resolution adopted at the second annual meeting of the AHA in 1885, calling for historical study of the newer territories and provinces. Turner rejected it as an antiquarian prescription. Rather than the study of aboriginal survivals, he proposed "a widely extended and earnest historical inquiry into the development of Western society."[17] Only then would Americans be able to comprehend the last political campaign or "estimate the significance" of western leaders who had recently "supported an aggressive program of finance and social action." But Turner already understood the situation. These leaders were "the products of a society that sprang from the eastern . . .middle West . . . when it was just passing from frontier conditions to conditions resembling those of the East. Having avoided the transformations . . . by migration, they reflect[ed] the struggle of this society to adjust the old Western ideals, based upon American isolation, upon the nonexistence of classes, and upon freedom of opportunity, to the changed conditions of a settled nation." Even so, Turner argued, the Mississippi Basin was "almost virgin soil for the historian."[18]

As earlier, Turner maintained that the "real significance of Western history is that it is national history." The historian must "enable the present age to understand itself by understanding its origin and growth." And Americans must understand the development of the Middle West if they were to understand the nation's history. He quoted from the 1893 edition of Friedrich Ratzel's geography of the United States in which the German scholar discussed "space as a factor in the United States" and suggested that "the breadth of land has furnished to the American spirit something of its own largeness." This fact, Turner suggested, explained "some of the most distinctive features of American character." As in 1893, he argued the importance of American history "as a field for the scientific study of social development." He quoted Henry Adams: "Should history ever become a true science, it must expect to establish its laws, not from the complicated story of European nationalities, but from the methodical evolution of a great democracy." In such a "sociological interpretation" of American history, he maintained, "the Western movement is fundamental." "The wilderness has been the melting pot and the mold for American institutions . . . a field for new species of social life."[19]

Turner devoted little more than a page to specific recommendations for research. Indian-white relations should be studied and also those between blacks and whites, as well as federal Indian policies, "and, in general, the process by which the savage gave way to civilization in the farther West." So also should be examined "the rise of the great industries of the West," the ensuing "social organization" and their historical geography, and the "transition from one economic status to another," as well as transportation developments, the financial history, and the history of land tenure in the "newer states." The political history of the West was equally inviting—the evolution of the territories and territorial system, the history of western political parties, the admission of western states, and the sources and development of their constitutions and political institutions generally. More important still, Turner concluded, was "the history of social development in the West. The rise of its cities and their evolution in response to physiography and economic influences; the types of life . . . thus created; the movement of immigration from the Old World, and the interstate migration into the West. . . . A new society, with a composite nationality still in the process of formation, is before us, and its history is almost untouched."[20]

Turner viewed the current state of research resources in the West negatively and urged western libraries to increase their collecting, cataloguing, and cooperative activity. The historical societies should emphasize institutional history more, he believed. "Interuniversity migration of graduate students" should be encouraged, and institutions should concentrate on their strengths—an implicit plug for western history at the University of Wisconsin.[21]

Andrew C. McLaughlin, of the University of Michigan, and Woodrow Wilson, of Princeton University, commented upon Turner's paper. Both agreed heartily with Turner's major arguments. McLaughlin did, however, note that E. L. Godkin had attributed American qualities to the influence of the frontier some thirty years earlier. Wilson identified his fellow Hopkins alumnus as "one of those men who gain the affection of every student of history by being able to do what very few men manage to do, to combine the large view with the small one; to combine the general plan and conception with the minute examination of particulars; who is not afraid of the horrid industry of his task, and who can yet illuminate that industry by knowing the goal to which it is leading him, and the general plan by which it should be done." Scholars such as Turner should be "loved and supported," even though in this case the paper presented was "a dethronement of the Eastern historian." McLaughlin had noted that the materials of western history were fresh and its students young. Wilson quipped that it was rather a case "of the materials being young and the students being fresh." But given eastern disregard, western assertiveness was understandable. "It is eminently fortunate," continued Wilson, "that a man should arise like Professor Turner," self-possessed, "not bumptious," displaying none "of the qualities we object to, and who yet knows the things which we want, unpalatable though they may be, and who has the courage to put American history in its proper setting." Concluding, Wilson suggested that southern history too should be considered in a fresh light.[22]

Thus in 1896 influential historians praised Turner before a distinguished audience, and he contributed to the journal designed to shape the study of history in America. Writing his magisterial colonial history during the 1930s, Curtis P. Nettels still regarded Turner's article of 1896 as appropriate reading.²³ There was much rational calculation involved in Turner's early career. Now having crossed the threshold of professional success, he wished to spread his ideas before a more popular audience than that provided by college history teachers. This accorded with his views on the purpose of history, his journalistic background, and his admiration for Wilson, whose work was already reaching a wide public. Turner found a sympathetic editor in Walter Hines Page, of the *Atlantic Monthly*, who published his articles "The Problem of the West" and "Dominant Forces in Western Life" in 1896 and 1897.

Written in the aftermath of the depression of 1893 and amid the tumultuous national politics of 1896, "The Problem of the West" was a lesson in contemporary civics, explaining western political disaffection to a national lay audience. It appeared in September of that year while William Jennings Bryan, the "Boy Orator of the Platte," was rallying the forces of disaffection in the American heartland. Turner began, "The problem of the West is nothing less than the problem of American development. . . . What is the West? What has it been in American life? To have the answers to these questions, is to understand the most significant features of the United States of to-day." Then he explained that the West "at bottom" was "a form of society, rather than an area" and proceeded to sketch in the social processes that he had described in 1893— precipitation to the primitive, progress back toward "the older social conditions of the East," but with a difference because of "enduring and distinguishing survivals of its frontier experience." "The history of our political institutions, our democracy, is not a history of imitation, of simple borrowing; it is a history of the evolution and adaptation of organs in response to changed environment, a history of the origin of new political species."²⁴

Thus launched, and discarding the trappings of scholarship of 1893, Turner sketched the social and political differences between East and West through American history and showed the influence of the latter upon the country's political development. Now it was "western" processes that were emphasized, rather than those of the "frontier," but the story line was that of 1893. Societies diverge as settlers move westward, the cake of custom is broken, the pioneers freed "in a large degree . . . from European precedents and forces," as they face "the fundamental fact," the new society's "relation to land."²⁵ In a final two and a half pages he related this story to the current "western problem."

"With the settlement of the Pacific coast and the occupation of the free lands," expansion, "the dominant fact in American life," "has come to a check. That these energies of expansion will no longer operate would be a rash prediction." The region beyond the Alleghenies, he noted, favored "a vigorous foreign policy." "In the remoter West, the restless, rushing wave of settlement has broken with a shock against the arid plains." The western problem was now "a social problem on a national scale." "The greater West . . . from the Alleghenies to the Pacific" was now subdivided by class and subregion; it lacked the sectional unity now evident in the East. If the Old West made common political cause with the New South the result would be not "a new sectionalism, but a new Americanism. It would not mean sectional disunion   but it might mean a drastic assertion of national government and imperial expansion under a popular hero." What was the current situation? "A people composed of heterogeneous materials, with diverse and conflicting ideals and social interests, having . . . fill[ed] up the vacant spaces of the continent, is now thrown back upon itself. . . . The forces of reorganization are turbulent."[26]

In conclusion, Turner assured easterners that all would come right in the end. The West also was a land of industrial life and advanced culture. Within it the Old Northwest held the "balance of power." "In the long run the 'Center of the Republic' may be trusted to strike a wise balance between the contending ideals. But . . . she knows that the problem of the West means nothing less than the problem of working out original social ideals and social adjustments for the American nation."[27]

The *Atlantic Monthly* allowed Turner to explore the character of the "Center of the Republic" again in April 1897, publishing his essay "Dominant Forces in Western Life." Here Turner described the settlement and the economic development of the five states of the Old Northwest and the prairie states adjacent to the west. Then he again explained the western radicals. We think, with considerable justification, of Turner mainly as a historian who emphasized differences, or perhaps discontinuities, rather than continuities. But in this essay his concluding pages stress the continuity of frontier radicalism:

> If the reader would see a picture of the representative Kansas Populist, let him examine the family portraits of the Ohio farmer in the middle of this century.

In a word, the Populist is the American farmer who has kept in advance of the economic and social transformations that have overtaken those who remained behind. . . .

I do not overlook the transforming influences of the wilderness on this stock . . . nor do I overlook the peculiar industrial conditions of the prairie States. But I desire to insist upon the other truth, also, that these westward immigrants . . . could not but preserve important aspects of the older farmer type. In the arid West these pioneers have halted and have turned to perceive an altered nation. . . . They see the sharp contrast between their traditional idea of America, as the land of opportunity, the land of the self-made man, free from class distinction and from the power of wealth, and the existing America, so unlike the earlier ideal.[28]

The Puritan farmer, argued Turner, had been "responsive to isms." The Populist orator, Mary Elizabeth Lease, stood squarely in the line of descent from the "frontier farmers in the days of the Revolution." Turner contrasted the behavior of American statesmen who had stayed at home as the nation moved westward with that of Jackson and Lincoln who shared in frontier development and reflected the ideals of that region. The eastern reaches of the "Northwest as a whole" were similar to the industrialized East. But in

the process of expansion, in the persistence of agricultural interests, in impulsiveness, in imperialistic ways of looking at the American destiny, in hero-worship, in the newness of its present social structure—the Old Northwest has much in common with the South and the Far West.

Behind her is the old pioneer past of simple democratic conditions, and freedom of opportunity for all men. Before her is a superb industrial development, the brilliancy of success as evinced in a vast population, aggregate wealth, and sectional power.[29]

These concluding passages may have puzzled Turner's readers. Populism, he had explained, was the natural outgrowth of forces and processes under way in American life since the colonial period. The Old Northwest, "child of the East and the mother of the Populistic

West," was to be the mediating force within the nation and all would come right.[30] But were Mary Lease and her cohorts—descendants of generations of frontier dissidents—simply to pass away without issue? If three centuries of expansion and access to free lands had come to check, what now would be the characterizing force in American development? Turner would address such questions in the future, although perhaps never to his complete satisfaction.

Turner emphasized the importance of physiography in shaping historical outcomes in America. It is an element in his thought that underwent progressive development. His teacher, Allen, used maps and charts constantly in his courses. But these were, we suspect, primarily to show boundary lines, locate places, and to illustrate the spatial relationships involved in historic events. Allen contributed a lengthy section to both the 1883 and 1884 editions of *Methods of Teaching History*, and both editions also included a short section on "Physical Geography and History," perhaps prepared by John W. Burgess or possibly G. Stanley Hall. Its author argued that "a knowledge of the structure of the earth on which we dwell should underlie and precede all our studies of history and political science." Given his relation with Allen, Turner was probably familiar with this contribution at an early date. And here he would have found explained "some of the things which a good physical map of the United States tells us," including the fact that the Mississippi basin "was predestined to become one of the greatest granaries of the world." "Thus," asserted the author, "the history of this country was largely written before man came here."[31]

This sketch also recommended the reading of the discussion of physical geography written by Nathaniel S. Shaler for the fourth volume of Justin Winsor's *Narrative and Critical History of America*, the prefatory chapter in John G. Palfrey's *History of New England*, M. Whitney's contribution to the *Guide-Book to the Yosemite*, and Francis A. Walker's *Atlas of the United States*. Further extending the message of physiographic influence was the arrival in the State Historical Society Library during 1887 of the massive *Scribner's Statistical Atlas*, edited by Fletcher Hewes and Henry Gannett. The physical features, which this work displayed, said the editors, "more or less determine [the country's] development."[32] Within this context maps were research tools that enabled users to discern causal links rather than merely illustrating political boundaries and spatial relationships.

In addition to Professor Allen, perhaps Thomas C. Chamberlin also encouraged Turner's interest in physiography and cartographic representation. During 1887 and 1888 he met William S. Bayley, of the United States Geological Survey, and their walks together were instructive. At The Johns Hopkins University, President Daniel Coit Gilman was an eminent geographer. Both Adams and Ely encouraged students to learn geographic concepts and methods, and Haskins arranged a course of lectures for undergraduates at Hopkins on geographic subjects of interest to young historians. Within the assemblage of bright and inquiring young minds that Adams and Ely had assembled in Baltimore there were surely discussions of the uses to which historians could put the materials and methods of other disciplines, including geography. Returned to Wisconsin, Turner became a close friend of Charles R. Van Hise and listened to him lecture upon American physiography as well as peppering him with questions about landforms and human adaptation to them.

In his dissertation Turner had discussed the impact of physiography upon the fur trade, in three and a half pages describing the great interlinking systems of waterways that the traders used. "So powerful," concluded Turner, "was the combined influence of these far-stretching rivers, and the 'hardy, adventurous, lawless, fascinating fur trade,' that the scanty population of Canada was irresistibly drawn from agricultural settlements into the interminable recesses of the continent." Of the sources relating to geographic influence that we have noted above, however, Turner cited only Winsor's history, as well as Parkman's treatment of such matters in *Montcalm and Wolfe*. However, he discussed physiography in company with the attractions of the trade rather than emphasizing it as the major influence in shaping historical outcomes.[33]

Through the 1890s Turner sharpened his emphasis upon the importance of geographical factors. By 1896 he was, as we have seen, citing the ideas of Ratzel, whose followers among geographers in the United States were to be stigmatized as geographic determinists. He was also deeply impressed by John Wesley Powell's monograph, *Physiographic Regions of the United States*, published in 1895, and he incorporated its system of physiographic provinces in his descriptions of westward expansion.

During 1897 Turner delivered a paper to the newly formed Chicago Geographical Society upon the relation between history and geography. He noted the tendency of historians to emphasize single themes in explanation of American development—the struggle between Puritan and Cavalier, the slavery controversy, institutional development on the basis of European germs or antecedents, or the struggle for national sovereignty. "All of these 'keys,'" Turner said, "have some value as explanations of American evolution, but they are inadequate and not fundamental." Although "by no means the all engrossing factor" and a relationship "to be taken in a large sense," Turner found "the master key to American history" in its relation to geography, more specifically in the "geographical fact of an expanding people occupying a vast and varied area of the New World." Here Turner was perilously close to simple determinism, but just as in the essay of 1893 he appended qualifications.[34]

While teaching, writing, and lecturing in the busy years of the mid- and late 1890s, did Turner further develop his ideas about the influence of the frontier on American development? The compilers of the *Early Writings of Frederick Jackson Turner* compared the printed versions of the frontier essay as Turner approved their appearance in the *Proceedings* of the State Historical Society of Wisconsin (1893), the *Report* of the American Historical Association (1894), a reprinting for teachers by the National Herbart Society (1899), and that in his collected frontier essays (1920).[35] Most changes, they discovered, were minor revisions of emphasis or factual amplification. The greatest number appeared in the 1899 reprinting and involved introductory material and suggestions for instructors.

Some of the changes involved qualification. In the 1893 version of the frontier essay Turner quoted Loria's passage, "America has the key to the historical enigma which Europe has sought for centuries in vain," and continued, "He is right." A year later and thereafter he used the less positive "there is much truth in this." In 1899 Turner also qualified his claims concerning political creativity in the West, writing, "It offered a wide opportunity for speculative creation and for adjustment of old institutions to new conditions." But he continued, admitting "how slight was the proportion of actual theoretic invention of institutions . . . there is abundance of opportunity for study of the sources of institutions actually chosen, the causes of the selection, the degree of transformation by the new conditions, and the new institutions actually produced by the new environment."[36]

The most comprehensive additions to the 1899 version reflected Turner's interest in the relation of physiography to American development. He discussed the population maps of the United States Census and the utility of comparing them to maps produced by the United States Geological Survey, showing "the geologic system" and contour intervals, remarking that it would "become plain that for an adequate comprehension of the course of American history it is necessary to study the process by which the advancing flood of settlement flowed into the successive physiographic areas." Attractive, limestone-based soils, he explained, had significantly shaped the course of settlement in the process of American expansion.[37]

Turner predicted that "the conquest of the arid West will be by different processes than that of the other areas of western advance, and a different social type may be looked for in the region." Elsewhere he referred to " the tragedy of the occupation of the arid tract, where the optimism of the pioneer farmer met its first rude rebuff." Amplification of his description of the farmer's frontier introduced references to publications of the United States Department of Agriculture containing the maps "Life Zones and Crop Zones of the United States" and "Geographic Distribution of Cereals in North America." Turner's final insert repeated in part the bow to Ratzel that he had inserted in his paper delivered at the AHA meeting in 1896.[38]

Turner was at his most active as a reviewer during the mid- and late 1890s. Some of the books that he reviewed were of particular interest to him as a western historian. While Turner advertised his claims to the province of western American history, Theodore Roosevelt was also working the same territory. We have noted Turner's review of the first two volumes of *The Winning of the West*. In 1895 he published an unsigned review of these plus the next in the series in *The Nation*. "Westward expansion" had not been described satisfactorily prior to Roosevelt's efforts, Turner explained, and he credited him with using great amounts of untapped source material—although slighting the Draper manuscripts. Roosevelt wrote "with the skill of a practiced historian" and "with appreciation of the fact that he [was] describing a phase in the general movement of civilization." Turner particularly commended volume 3 for its "analysis of society in the second stage of Western growth" and the discussion of "the rise of a Western gentry," explaining that Roosevelt was not usually "disposed . . . to devote as much attention to social and economic aspects of the movement as the student of the period would like to have him give." He noted without demurral Roosevelt's position that criticism of war waged upon the Indians reflected a "silly morality."

Roosevelt, Turner suggested, had not freed himself completely from earlier points of view. He "lean[ed] to the romantic side of the subject." He faulted Roosevelt particularly for failing to explain the full significance of various plans for developing new settlements west of the Alleghenies and of the activities of the land companies. He had, Turner believed, also underestimated the tendencies of westerners in this period to unite in their common interests. Nor had he shown the impact of western developments upon the East. But despite signs of hastiness, Roosevelt in sum had done "valuable work." However, Turner concluded that "the study of the early stages of the spread of a democracy over the virgin soil of this continent is far from being exhausted."[39]

Turner's review impressed Roosevelt as "interesting and suggestive," revealing one "thoroughly conversant with the time." He contacted him through the intermediary of the *Nation*. "Good old Dr. Draper," Roosevelt explained, had refused him access to the Draper collection. He discussed his differences with Turner on the subject of the western land companies. Turner responded pleasantly. Roosevelt soon wrote again to agree that much remained to be done in western history. Turner's two major interests, Roosevelt suggested, were the influence of the West upon the East and the history of institutions. Roosevelt did not plan to treat the first subject and proposed to consider the latter only briefly in his fourth volume. Initially he had disagreed strongly with Turner's contention that westerners were more united in their interests than he had believed. When he wrote a third letter to Turner two weeks later, Roosevelt had concluded that the two were not so far apart on this issue. He reported that he was drawing upon Turner's ideas in the course of writing volume 4 of *The Winning of the West*.[40] Turner noted with pride that he had changed Roosevelt's thinking.

If Roosevelt had hoped to soften up a knowledgeable reviewer, the effort was unsuccessful. Reviewing volume 4 in the *American Historical Review*, Turner summarized Roosevelt's approach throughout the series. Roosevelt was little concerned with the West's "reactive influences upon the East," nor with developing institutions, nor with "the later history of events" after "the waves of pioneer life passed." Rather he was interested in "dramatic and picturesque aspects." He handled these with "dash and lightness of touch" but often failed to look beyond the obvious. Proofreading and citations were carelessly done. Finally, Roosevelt suffused his narrative with his own view of parties and politics and read little lessons from history, tossing in the Latin tag *haec fabula docet*—"this story teaches."

Although Turner found volume 4 of *The Winning of the West* interesting, he found much to criticize, particularly Roosevelt's effort to implicate Jefferson in Citizen Genêt's schemes, his dislike of the Jeffersonian Republicans, his inadequate treatment of western institutions, his neglect of land company activity in western New York and Pennsylvania, and of the Whiskey Rebellion. Turner predicted that the volume would be a "revelation" to the general reader, but the specialist would regret that Roosevelt could not "regard history as a more jealous mistress, and . . . give more time, greater thoroughness of investigation, particularly in foreign archives, and more sobriety of judgment to his work."[41] Turner's reviews of *The Winning of the West* breathe reason, respect, and restraint, but he made it clear throughout that there was much to be done in western history that Theodore Roosevelt had left undone—that the field of western institutional history lay open.

Turner's other reviews in the field of western history of these years did not require assessment of rival suitors. Reporting on the revised edition of the 1814 account of the Lewis and Clark expedition, Turner found editor Elliott Coues to be a "careful bibliographer and a sympathetic and well qualified editor of the geographical and natural history material of the volumes," but less diligent in providing context than desirable and given to "remarkable lucubrations."[42] This review well illustrates Turner's tendency to recycle favorite material. The superintendent of the census once more reports the disappearance of the frontier line, the frontiersmen again traverse Cumberland Gap and South Pass, and, as in the essay of 1893, we meet Daniel Boone and the mother of Kit Carson.

A decade earlier Turner had been enraptured by Francis Parkman's volumes. In his review of the 1898 edition of Parkman's works Turner still found him "the greatest painter of historical pictures that . . . perhaps . . . any country has produced." "As a literary treatment of his theme [his work was] definitive," destined to "live because he was even greater as an artist than as a historian." But now Turner found Parkman, "not so skilful in exposition of the development of institutions, as he was in the delineation of men and events. All his historical tastes and methods were formed before institutional history became fixed in the United States."[43]

Eager to display their professionalism, some young historians have skewered hapless amateurs in writing reviews. Turner was not completely free from this failing. In preparing a collection of materials relating to George Rogers Clark, George H. English, he concluded, revealed himself to be "deficient in legitimate historical imagination and constructive power, and his editorial principles . . . too lax to permit his reprints to be regarded as authentic texts."[44] By contrast, he maintained that Justin Winsor's record of historical production, ending with the latter's *Westward Movement, 1763–1798*, entitled him to "a position among the first of American historians." The book displayed the author's "immense research . . . skill and fairness in dealing with a multiplicity of detail, and of the continental breadth of his view." Even so, Turner emphasized that Winsor, like Roosevelt, had not exhausted the possibilities of western history in the period. Winsor's approach was that of the librarian who loved facts and used the card catalogue extensively but lacked the "artistic instinct" and "historical imagination" to fuse "separate elements of historical knowledge into a . . . pleasing presentation." His book was a "thesaurus of events." Although deprecating his criticisms as minor in nature, Turner filled three pages of the *American Historical Review* with reservations.[45]

As Turner confided to Haskins, he did not "quite care to figure in leggins and a breech clout all the time," and he also reviewed works relating to regions other than the West and to American history in general during the mid- and late 1890s.[46] Although judicious in such reviews, Turner did not hesitate to instruct the authors. James Ford Rhodes had given economic and social factors a discrete chapter in his survey of the years 1860–62 and had unfortunately separated "some things that belong together." The slavery struggle reflected the country's rapid growth—"the tremendous increase in railroad building, interstate migrations, occupation of the prairies and plains, meant intercourse between sections, and a struggle for ascendancy between irreconcilable institutions." A fuller account of American social development would have clarified the development of the Free Soil and Republican parties, and discussion of the changing patterns of intersectional trade would have explained much about sectional attitudes.

Rhodes was at his best in discussing public sentiment and leading politicians, and Turner favorably contrasted his use of documentation and discussion of evidence with the approach of von Holst.[47]

In another review Turner commended the topical arrangement of Harry P. Judson's survey of American history for the Chautauqua movement. It represented "a successful invasion of the sanctity of the arrangement by presidential administrations," but Judson's volume fell short, Turner believed, because he did not adequately treat western development and other elements of national growth.[48] The revised edition of James Schouler's five-volume *History of the United States under the Constitution* was a "safe and useful pioneer survey" but never rose to "greatness," thought Turner. However, he commended him for giving "considerable attention to . . . economic and social life," despite failure to correlate it adequately with political development. In considering John B. McMaster's volume dealing with the early national years Turner found "a general gain in historical workmanship" over previous volumes. But McMaster also had failed to emphasize important topics, particularly those dealing with western expansion.[49]

Edward Channing's secondary school history of the United States allowed Turner to applaud the author's understanding that history should no longer be viewed as "pleasant literature" but rather a "discipline of the mind," useful as training for citizenship. But Channing had insufficiently emphasized the importance of southern and western development. Turner praised Channing's "sympathetic consideration" of the southern view of state sovereignty as one that allowed students to understand it as a "survival rather than as a wicked invention." But he faulted the book for "numerous inaccuracies . . . and some very doubtful judgments," listing examples.[50]

Turner enthusiastically greeted Philip A. Bruce's study of the economic development of Virginia during the eighteenth century. Despite excessive detail and emphasis on commodities rather than "the growth of economic society," the book showed "considerable power, abounds in interesting information, and compels us to await further studies in [the] field with impatience." Turner also wrote approvingly of William W. Weeden's examination of economic and social development in New England prior to 1789. These volumes, argued Turner, "will do more to make clear the later history of the United States than will many large histories." Here was evidence explaining political developments like the contest of tidewater and back country and illustrating "the way in which the American environment effected transformations of the English colonists." Turner, however, rejected Eben G. Scott's regional approach in *Reconstruction during the Civil War in the United States of America*. This prosouthern scholar assumed "that constitutional principles [were] the sources of political events," and Turner disagreed with his criticisms of Abraham Lincoln.[51]

Although unsympathetic to American history through Confederate spectacles, Turner was more tolerant of George Otto Trevelyan's English point of view in the first volume of *The American Revolution*. This author did not discriminate between the American sections, nor did he give adequate coverage to economic and social factors, nor to the earlier "legal, administrative, and political contentions" between the home and colonial authorities. But Trevelyan found the cause of the colonists just and his account was "delightful reading."[52]

Turner's reviews of the first book in a three-volume series on the growth of American political parties, by John P. Gordy, and of the American years 1817–58, by John W. Burgess, allowed Turner to contrast the roles of the historian and the political scientist. "A scientific history of political parties," he wrote, "must find its basis in demographic facts, and must include a study of the evolution of the organs of party action." Gordy, he suggested, had erred in assuming that party history and political history were identical and produced a compendium of political history. In this book the political scientist's "attitude" sometimes overwhelmed "that of the historian." Nor had Gordy understood that sectional interaction involved more than the North and the South. A "tendency to absoluteness of statement" characterized his work.[53]

In considering *The Middle Period, 1817–1858* by Burgess, Turner again contrasted disciplinary commitments. Burgess explained that he had limited his narrative to events "significant of our progress in political civilization." In Turner's opinion he had focused unduly on "the slavery struggle" and had ignored "vast social transformations by immigration, interstate migration, industrial development, revolution of the transportation system, and all the tremendous forces of change involved in Western expansion of settlement," as well as "many topics of political importance." In describing the Missouri question, Burgess had fitted "the facts of a complex historical development into the simple and logical system of the political scientist." Burgess, Turner suggests, had deduced "historical forces from a few catastrophic events," ignoring the fact that "the application of the logical process to history is always a dangerous one." Turner also found "too much stress upon the influence of natural physiographic boundaries." But the book was "most suggestive . . . provocative of thought and discussion." Burgess had "advanced popular knowledge of the period by his political analysis, his recognition of Eastern and Western divisions in Congress," and by his argument that the slavery issue did not dominate the foreign policy of the period. "It is," he concluded, "at once the strength and weakness of the book that it is written by a political scientist with exceptional logical and analytical powers."[54]

Turner's reviews of this period gave him the opportunity to consider the implications of historical works that were basic contributions to his particular field of interest and American history generally. They also allowed him to stake his claim to recognition as an authority on the history of the American West. His interests, readers learned, were not those of Roosevelt nor his approach that of Parkman. He was, he informed them, an institutional historian who believed that economic and social factors must be given due weight in historical accounts and that sectional interplay and westward expansion had thus far been inadequately treated. The historian's role differed, he explained, from that of the political scientist. There is a judicious quality to his work in general, but he also displayed a keen critical sense, typically raising perceptive questions as to approach and content and sometimes challenging the author's facts. In this respect he was occasionally picky.

Turner's reviewing activity helped him develop his own ideas of what the ideal survey or textbook of American history should contain. These appear in his correspondence with publishers and particularly in an extended review of von Holst's multivolume survey of American constitutional history, which remained unpublished during his lifetime. Here he listed the historical processes that he believed "an American history that should correctly interpret American political life—to say nothing of economic and social life—should" cover. These included "the evolution of a composite non-English nationality [including the race question] . . . the movement away from the European state system; the rise of an American system . . . the movement westward . . . the democratic movement . . . the industrial transformations . . . the slavery struggle . . . the struggle of particularism, and sectionalism with nationalism . . . the growth of the constitution by evolution of political institutions unprovided by constitution and by the transformation of institutions provided for, by construction of the various departments of government, and by the modifications of the State Constitutions."[55] These processes, Turner explained, were related to

each other and the list could be expanded. At other times he also
identified ideas, immigrant groups, and custom as elements worthy of
special attention.

Turner tried, his reviews show, to evaluate the books on which he
reported against his understanding of the changing emphases in
American history. He opened an 1896 review article in the *Atlantic
Monthly* with a description of current trends in writing history.
Politics had dominated the thinking of historians during the eighteenth and much of the nineteenth centuries. This approach was being
succeeded by "an interest in the study of economic life and of the
development of social institutions." Only by this means could political
history be rightfully understood, a development that also showed past
politics and history to be "far from being identical." Turner identified
the new approach as a "sociological interpretation of history." Now
American scholars were beginning "to recognize the vital forces in
American society whose interaction and transformation have called
political institutions into life and moulded them to suit changing
conditions." American history involved "the rise and expansion of a
huge democracy in an area unoccupied by civilization, and thus
affording free play to the factors of physiography, race, and custom."[56]

Recurrently in his reviews Turner criticized authors for failing to
emphasize economic and social factors adequately. Although Turner
saw himself as being involved in the new approach, he also believed,
as we have seen in his reviews of the works of Gordy and Burgess, that
the historian approached the past differently than did investigators in
the neighboring disciplines. He was suspicious of their abstract theorizing and their tendencies to ignore historical complexity. But if, as
reviewer, he warned against such practice, as historian he himself
sometimes indulged in sweeping generalizations and assumed a far
more analytical tone than did narrative historians.

6 Professionals

*"Perhaps Princeton would object to a job lot
of Wisconsin professors!"*

Some twenty years after he assumed control of the history program at the University of Wisconsin, Turner became president of the American Historical Association. He had reached the summit of his profession. Had he wished, he could have congratulated himself on having achieved success without benefit of family wealth or heritage of scholarship. But within the frontier state of Wisconsin he did have advantages—his father was a self-made member of the county-seat elite, and one who sensed the value of education. He was also a respected journalist and political figure, a man who knew the political leaders of his state on first-name basis at the same time his son was establishing himself at the university. Perhaps his father's influence made Turner's passage to professorial rank at Wisconsin easier, and the young man exploited his accomplishments shrewdly. But Turner's appointment rested primarily on solid achievement, and his success in the profession involved an unusual combination of opportunity, abilities, scholarly message, and traits of personality.

Turner had been fortunate in his teachers. At Wisconsin, Allen helped him prepare so well for further graduate work that he needed to spend only one year in doctoral residence at Johns Hopkins University. Never again would there be such shaping years in higher education as the period between 1880 and 1914. The old classical college curriculums were bent, stretched, modified, supplemented, and in great degree replaced as the process of disciplinary subdivision within the social sciences proceeded and as graduate and professional schools gained form and status under university aegis. It was a period of great expansion of student bodies and the faculties that taught them, a circumstance that facilitated the adoption of new ideas and practices and opened job opportunities. There was no better place for a young historian or social scientist to acquire understanding of these developments than The Johns Hopkins University graduate program.

His experience at Johns Hopkins did more than introduce Turner to the best of contemporary scholarship, provide him with a union card, and inculcate professional savvy. Adams was not a great research

scholar, but, in contrast to Allen, he was a "pusher." In The Johns
Hopkins University Studies in Historical and Political Science he had
provided Ph.D. candidates with a prestigious setting in which to
demonstrate their abilities. More important, as secretary and an
important voice in the councils of the AHA, he could put in a good
word for Hopkins men when the opportunity presented itself.

In Adams's commitment to his students-in-residence and in the field
while the professional culture of the discipline was emerging, we find
an example of professional nurturing that Turner and his peers also
adopted in their relations with students. The commitment of seminar
directors to placing their students satisfactorily in the profession and
ensuring their future was reflected in the latter's continuing loyalty to
the ideas and person of their mentor. Within the historical profession
it was a pattern of behavior that continued for generations.

His indebtedness to Adams aside, the Hopkins experience acquainted Turner with a circle of scholars who were also to enjoy
success beyond the ordinary and whose destinies were linked at times
with his. These men benefited in their association with Turner but
also furthered his career. In no small way the members of the group,
including Turner, imprinted their values and practices upon the
emerging modern community of academic historians. Among the
members of the Hopkins circle, Wilson, Haskins, and Jameson were
particularly important in the development of Turner's career.

Other historians of Turner's generation worked with him as well in
the broader activities of the profession. In this group were Albert
Bushnell Hart, of Harvard, Andrew C. McLaughlin, of the universities
of Michigan and Chicago, Max Farrand, of Wesleyan University and
later Stanford and Yale Universities, H. Morse Stephens, of the University of California, Berkeley, George L. Burr, of Cornell, Haskins's
successor, Dana C. Munro, at Wisconsin and Princeton, and others.
Some of them, like Wilson, were so impressed that they sought to
bring Turner to their institutions as colleague. If these men became
powerful allies of Turner in joint activities, the relationships were not
parasitic. They found in Turner an exciting intellect, a man who
combined professional vision with common sense, a congenial companion, and, in Turner's own phrasing, "a good fellow." He, in turn,
valued the abilities, qualities, and influence of the others.

In the professional and social interaction of these men there was
little of sycophancy. These were exciting days—academic disciplines
were being shaped—and doors unlocked by the key of scientific

method were opening fascinating historical vistas. But it was also a period when the machinery of academic professionalism was being perfected. The emerging professionals of the time asserted control over bodies of specialized knowledge. They used and devised unique methods, skills, and training, defined criteria of competence, and sought to enforce standards. To further their objectives they devised institutional structures—associations and publications. Turner and his friends were prepared to build the machinery of the history profession and also to direct it and accept the professional plaudits and rewards that were involved. At a meeting of the AHA during the late 1890s a group of these kindred spirits conferred informal organizational status upon themselves and became "the Nucleus." Turner and others mentioned here were members. Those present dined together at AHA meetings for close to a decade at least. They liked fellowship, a good meal, and lots of champagne but also illustrated the processes by which a discipline was being built. As professionals, historians have never achieved the sophistication, discipline, and rewards found in medicine, law, or some other professions, but Turner's generation created a historical discipline far different from that known in the United States to its time.

Turner regretted that he had been unable to study with Jameson at Johns Hopkins because of the latter's transfer to Brown University. When the AHA created a Historical Manuscripts Commission during the mid-1890s, however, Jameson became its chairman and suggested Frederick J. Turner as one of the five other members, he to serve until 1899. In planning the first issues of the *American Historical Review*, Jameson, as managing editor, sought both ability and regional balance among his authors. He turned immediately to Turner and, as we have seen, the young westerner contributed a two-part article to the first volume of the *Review*. Turner was a frequent contributor to this periodical in its early years, and Jameson valued him as both author and advisor on editorial matters and, increasingly, upon broader aspects of the history profession. A brilliant editor, an indefatigable and highly successful scholarly promoter, and a highly perceptive scholar, Jameson nurtured a satiric sense of humor beneath an outer mask of austere serenity. Turner became one of his trusted intimates. Jameson's attentions were not the only signs that Turner was a comer in the profession. Program chairs sought Turner's advice on the papers to be presented at the annual meetings of the AHA. In 1896 Turner took advantage of that fact to urge that Haskins be offered a place on the program, and in the next year he used the site of the meeting in Cleveland as reason for including a strong representation of western historians.

Meanwhile, by the mid-1890s the representatives of publishing companies had identified Turner as an author of great promise. He returned their interest. The size of his household had grown rapidly. The mortgage on his house was a burden. Income from publications would be most welcome. He put the ideas that he had been developing about frontier and sectional processes into more popular form for periodicals during the 1890s. But he decided that this kind of publication was not his forte. More prestigious and more remunerative would be the publication of books. Now Turner was caught up in the excitement of negotiating book contracts with publishing houses. His friend, fellow Hopkins alumnus and member of the Manuscripts Commission William P. Trent, opened the door of the Macmillan Company for him. Trent hoped to serve as general editor of a Macmillan series dealing with American sections. For George P. Brett of this firm, Turner outlined plans for the first volume. He explained that he had been studying an area that in "geological terms" embraced "the Piedmont, the Allegheny ridges and the western part of the Allegheny plateau." This region needed "study irrespective of state lines, as a natural economic and social unity." He proposed to call it the "Old West, and treat its history with a view to showing the evolution of the forces in American history to which the name Western is applied."

Roosevelt had "written admirably" of "some phases" of this area's history, particularly of the wars and diplomacy involved in establishing control of it. Turner, however, would emphasize "how the West came to be, what it was, and is, in American life." He was uncertain as to a proper ending date, perhaps the Jackson presidency when "the Old West really came to fruitage." He planned to write, he explained, not solely for the "special student" but "for the general public, after [he] had so far as possible gone to the bottom of [his] subject." Much research remained to be done, but he would "devote" himself "to the subject if there seems to be proper encouragement for undertaking the work."[1] The firm preferred that specific terms be deferred until some of the manuscript had been submitted and its probable length estimated. This was April 1896, and Turner noted on Brett's letter that he hoped to submit the manuscript a year from the coming fall, although probably not until the following winter. For a time Turner worked on a manuscript for *The Old West*, but it was destined to be the first of his unpublished books. In June 1897 another Macmillan employee raised the possibility of Turner doing "a volume of stories of the Lewis and Clark and other expeditions," and he expressed interest.[2]

In that same year representatives of the McClure publishing firm inquired whether Turner wished to prepare a portrait essay of Andrew Jackson, and he tried in response to interest them in an "extensive biographical study" of the president who, he believed, symbolized the national victory of western democracy.[3] In the following spring, George H. Putnam followed the advice of Albert B. Hart and invited Turner to prepare the volume on the United States in Putnam's series "The Story of the Nations." After dalliance, Turner responded that he was not free to undertake this assignment, and Putnam responded that the firm wished to compete for other projects that Turner might have under way.[4]

Meanwhile, the Macmillan Company had been dangling other lures before Turner. In mid-September 1897 Brett inquired about the status of Turner's manuscript "The Old West" and, with the optimism typical of the acquisitive minds of publishers, soon sounded out Turner on the possibility of preparing "an elementary history of the United States suited to use in the higher classes in the grammar schools." Given his "interest in advanced and original work," Brett believed that Turner might not consider this "a very flattering proposition." Turner did not reject the bait. Although noting that Channing was already doing such a book for Macmillan, he outlined plans for an elementary text. Brett found this proposal potentially more rewarding than the Lewis and Clark project already discussed with Turner. But on this subject Ginn and Company were more persuasive, and Turner agreed in these years to write a grammar school text for that house. Discussions with Macmillan also involved a college text. But at the end of October 1897 Turner wrote to inform Brett that he had signed a contract to write a college history for another publisher. Brett complained that his house had been "somewhat unfairly treated" on this score because Turner had allowed another publisher "to revise his offer for the publication of your book either with or without knowledge of our offer for its issue and without giving us a similar opportunity." Brett fumed, "The spirit which dictated this action on your part seems to us most unfortunate under the circumstances."[5]

Henry Holt and Company was the winner in this contest for the affections of Fred Turner. Early in 1895 Edward N. Bristol of that house contacted him. Turner's essay on the frontier in American history and some of his other writings suggested, wrote Bristol, that he might be the "coming man" who would write the college textbook in American history that was so direly needed. Did the idea interest him? Would he care to draw up a "general plan" of the book and develop part of it so that the people of Holt and Company could see whether the approach appealed to the "sordid soul" of the publisher? Thus began negotiations that extended for almost three years, as Turner in turn fanned Bristol's interest by suggesting that he ought first to produce more restricted works to solidify his position in the field and haggled over the details of the book's future format and the author's remuneration. He was determined also that he would be well paid for his labors. Finally in October 1896 he informed Bristol that he would prefer to write his text for Holt and Company but that a competitor was making a more attractive offer. This gambit brought him an extremely handsome contract from Holt in which he was to receive a royalty of 10 percent of sale price on the first fifteen hundred copies sold, 12.5 percent on the next and 15 percent thereafter.

Holt and Company modified other provisions of the contract to meet Turner's suggestions and agreed to pay fifteen hundred dollars on receipt of manuscript. In agreeing to Turner's demands Holt wrote that the firm had "never before risked as high terms on any educational work whatever, and unless there is a revolution in business methods" did not expect to do so again. But the publisher believed that there was a unique opportunity for a successful college text in American history and that Turner was the right author to provide it. If Turner delivered a manuscript within three and half years, as agreed, there would be handsome remuneration for both author and press. But Turner never completed this book nor others that he visualized at this time. Publishing houses, however, could not predict the future. With one signature in hand, the officers of Holt and Company convinced Turner in the summer of 1900 that he could also, given his other text commitments, easily produce a manuscript for a secondary school history text.[6]

Turner enjoyed the flattery involved in negotiations with publishers. But he was ambivalent, expressing deep interest in original scholarship while also dreaming of broad audiences that would allow him to profit from his writing. To realize the latter objective, he believed that he must write a text, but he struggled with this task. In his review of von Holst's history he had outlined a number of major factors that should be treated in an adequate survey of American development. But the introduction that he wrote for a college history at some point during these years sketched a simpler approach. American history was "the story of the occupation of a vast wilderness in a brief period." As its vast area and its various "geographic provinces" were successively colonized, America might well have evolved into independent nations comparable to those of Europe but did not: "The evolution, interaction and consolidation of these sections has made an American nation, with a composite people; with institutions derived mainly from Europe and deeply modified to meet American conditions; and with an American spirit and democratic ideals differing from Europe, and fundamentally due to the experience of the people in occupying a new continent." Turner would, he wrote, "show how this nation came to be what it is."[7] This, alas, he was never able to do.

University and college faculty members may teach their subjects well, faithfully perform their committee duties, be supportive colleagues, and write articles and books, but their contributions pass unnoted until word spreads that another institution is "interested." Turner understood this truth even while seeking to return from The Johns Hopkins University to the University of Wisconsin. As we have seen, he explored the possibility of obtaining a position at Wesleyan University while he impatiently waited President Chamberlin's decision as to Allen's successor. In 1891 he informed his father that Indiana University had queried his availability, and Andrew Jackson Turner responded that he hoped that the University of Wisconsin would "be disposed to offer . . . a reasonable salary the coming year."[8] With Turner's reputation steadily growing, vistas of professional advancement began to appear. He had received "feelers" from faculty in four "prominent Universities" in the previous year when he received an exciting letter from Wilson in early November 1896. Now one of the most respected members of the Princeton faculty, Wilson explained that Princeton's endowment had recently been enlarged, providing funds that would allow creation of a chair in American history with a salary of perhaps $3,400. Could Turner be interested? Wilson earnestly hoped so. He had long desired him as a colleague. Letters between the friends during the remainder of that year again reveal Turner's skill in handling such negotiations. Ingenious modern academicians have added little in the way of technique, other perhaps than seeking a position for spouse as well as principal. Turner was a master at displaying sufficient interest and flattering respect for the inquiring institution to encourage the academic suitor while describing his present position in ways designed to heighten ardor.

Turner's letter of November 8, 1896, in answer to Wilson's question is a model of its type.[9] The history program at Wisconsin had increased substantially in size, he explained, since his return from Johns Hopkins. Then conducted solely by Allen and himself, it numbered about fifty students in elective classes. Now there were three teachers of professorial rank plus an instructor and a teaching fellow serving some six hundred students. Turner himself taught approximately 175 elective students including eight or ten graduate students. His yearly salary was $2,500 plus $300 earned in the summer school. The signs were good for a general improvement of salaries. The library ranked among the four or five best in the country in his areas of interest. It would soon move into a magnificent new building in which history seminar rooms and teaching apparatus were to be provided with easy access to library materials. He had made western history his field and, if all went well, he would grow more influential in it and the profession. His personal library reflected his interests, and he would regret leaving an important field in which there were still too few workers.

Madison was beautiful, and he would be reluctant to abandon his pleasant new home. Haskins was "a colleague after my own heart"; parting from him would cause "real regret." His parents lived nearby, and those of his wife in Chicago. Finally, added Turner, he liked the West. Such "considerations," he wrote, "constitute the cake of custom, and the conservative tendencies in my problem." But, "on the other hand, Princeton is a noble old University, with evidences that her vigor is augmenting rather than declining." No doubt, said Turner, "contact with eastern men and ideals" and "a new sort of student" would benefit him. Literary activity centered in the East. Caroline had close friends in New York; it would be a joy to associate with Wilson and his associates. The middle region and the southern back country might be just as fertile research fields as the west, and the East might benefit from an instructor who could "infiltrate . . . western interpretations of our national development." Nor was all perfect in Madison. Turner confided that he was "not entirely contented with the policy of President Adams." He did "not look for much progress while he and some of the Regents pursue[d] their present policy. He is not likely to press any vigorous educational ideals; and there are not the most cordial relations existing between the faculty and him."

Turner asked for more information. What of the Princeton library and particularly of the American history holdings? Were the students "in earnest"? what were the prospects of graduate work, and how many hours did professors teach? Were there religious tests? "I am no radical, or propagandist, but my sympathies are in the Unitarian direction. I have never been accused of lack of sympathy with the other religious movements in my historical work," he assured Wilson. Would Princeton's climate allow him to avoid the catarrhal colds that plagued him in Wisconsin, as had that of Baltimore? Mrs. Turner suffered from hay fever. An eastern location might allow summers on the Maine coast or in the eastern mountains, an expedient that their current income did not allow. What of salary enhancement at Princeton?—his family was not an "*in*expensive joy," given the need for a nurse. What schools would be available for the children? Was society divisive in Princeton? Neither he nor Caroline was much interested in social life but understood that in some eastern communities "old comers" and "newcomers" were "still at odds as . . . in the primitive days."

Turner closed this letter with the wish that he could talk the matter over with Wilson. He suspected, he told him, that he must soon face the question of whether he would stay in Madison even if his friend's interest failed to mature in a specific invitation. Representatives of other major institutions had recently made similar if less specific inquiries. He concluded, "in any case, let me tell you again how much I value your friendship."

Wilson answered Turner's questions at length, explaining among other considerations that the full professor's "normal salary" at Princeton might well be soon raised from $3,400 to $4,000 and that there were no religious tests "applied" at Princeton. Turner then restated his position several weeks later. Ought he to exchange his "library advantages" in Madison for "the greater dignity of a professorship in Princeton," participation in a more active intellectual environment, and "companionship" with Wilson? Family, friends, and colleagues would be left behind. Here would be "increasing means, reputation and power in the University as it develops—not to mention the question of other calls." The West he believed would soon "turn its youthful and vigorous enthusiasm and initiative into University lines." The University of Wisconsin would be a leader in such developments. He understood that his salary was to be soon raised. Turner informed Wilson that he did not wish to trifle but felt obliged to inform the university authorities of Princeton's interest. He was, he concluded, "very doubtful of the advisability of agreeing to accept a call on the terms you suggest." He did not wish to make a final judgment as yet, but he was hesitant to accept a Princeton offer as thus far described. Caroline, he suspected, "would vote the other way, but she is in Chicago on a visit and is ruled out!"[10]

In this letter Turner also raised the question of whether William M. Sloane's decision to move from Princeton to Columbia might change the situation. Sloane's departure did indeed alter the picture somewhat. Now Wilson proposed to bring both Turner and Haskins to Princeton. The thought of leaving the Wisconsin libraries still bothered Turner, but he admitted that the possibility of both Haskins and himself making the move "adds to the attractiveness of your suggestion." Haskins was "hardly more than a boy" at Hopkins; he was now no longer nervous in speech but "an exceptionally good class lecturer." Enthused by his recent year in Europe, Haskins had been no less impressed by a great lecturer such as Lavisse as by the textual "criticism of men like Langlois." He was "one of the strongest reasoners and effective debaters in our faculty meetings." However, continued Turner, "I cannot let you have Haskins, unless we both depart! Perhaps Princeton would object to a job lot of Wisconsin professors! But in fact Haskins belongs to the *comitatus* of Jameson and yourself and I grew up under the teaching of Allen and yourself, with Adams to keep me stirred up! So it's a miscellaneous job lot." But what of salaries and rents? He was "not anxious for riches," he said, "but would be glad if he did not have to worry about his "modest household expenditures."[11]

But even as Turner contemplated the possibility of a "job lot" exodus, opposition to Wilson's plans were building in the East. Conservative trustees opposed the idea of appointing a Unitarian, and others feared that the hiring would alienate orthodox Presbyterians within the Princeton constituency. In mid-December Wilson explained to Turner that the trustees were delaying until March their decision on plans for expansion of the history program because some of the new monies were not yet in hand. But he also tried to answer more of Turner's questions, and Ellen Wilson sent along estimates of housekeeping expenses in Princeton. Turner wrote a reply immediately in which he expressed relief that an immediate decision was unnecessary. But he also reported himself to be still interested and pleased that Wilson planned to talk with Haskins at the next meeting of the AHA. Both he and Caroline, he added, had been "most grateful" to Mrs. Wilson for information about household expenses. "Like Mr. Gladstone," she could "make a budget interesting." He commented admiringly on Wilson's scholarly productivity and the "stirring" quality of his Princeton oration, a "university utterance . . . with real human ideals in it."[12]

Hard-pressed in preparing documents from the Draper collection for the AHA Historical Manuscripts Commission, Turner neglected to send this letter to Wilson until the end of December. For the same reason, he did not attend the annual meeting of the AHA in New York. Wilson, however, attended the meeting, commenting, as we have seen, upon Turner's paper, as read by Thwaites, and listening to Haskins's presentation, as well as discussing Princeton's needs with him. Afterward he wrote to Princeton's president Francis L. Patton, reaffirming his regard for Turner and his good impressions of Haskins's performance at the meeting. But by the end of January Wilson was conceding to his wife that Turner's appointment was a "practical impossibility." In late March 1897 he confessed to Turner that he was "probably . . . the most mortified and chagrined fellow on this continent" that his plans for bringing his friend to Princeton had to be suspended.[13]

Turner responded gracefully, assuring Wilson that he had no occasion for remorse "over the outcome of our migration correspondence." Wisconsin had not extended a counteroffer, and no point of decision had been reached. The offer had been attractive, but the library and the Madison lakes were "pretty strong grappling hooks." Perhaps the fates had been ladylike in settling the matter. He "value[d] the incident as a proof of [Wilson's] regard." Should Princeton still retain their interest in Haskins, he added, they would only "secure him" through the "fault" of President Adams, not that of Turner.[14] Later in the spring Princeton did offer a position to Haskins, raising the proposed salary from $3,000 to $3,400 when he rejected the initial proposal. But for the time being, Haskins elected to stay at Wisconsin.

Although perhaps relieved at the outcome, Turner probably found the Princeton negotiations both frustrating and gratifying. In the small world on University Hill they perhaps enhanced his prestige as much as would have a specific offer. The Princeton broth had hardly cooled when John B. McMaster, of the University of Pennsylvania, inquired as to whether Turner was "finally settled" at the University of Wisconsin. James H. Robinson echoed his colleague McMaster's interest and assured Turner that they also expected to approach Haskins in the near future, since their department needed both.[15] The exciting intercourse with Princeton and Pennsylvania produced local results. As Princeton continued to woo Haskins, President Adams informed Turner in April that he was recommending scholarships in American and European history for the program and a special appropriation of five hundred dollars for the purchase of books in European history, this to be extended over a term of years. The regents would acquiesce.[16] But suitors continued to present themselves at Turner's door. At the annual meeting of the AHA in Cleveland in December 1897, the president of Adelbert University sought to transplant him from the banks of Lake Mendota to the shores of Lake Erie.

While Turner's professional life abounded with opportunity, the happy domesticity of the Turner family was shattered in 1899. In February diphtheria carried off the family's youngest daughter, and in October young Jackson Allen Turner died from the complications of a ruptured appendix. This last tragedy was too much for Caroline. She suffered a nervous collapse and was forced to take a rest cure in Chicago. Turner, so proud of his children's promise, was devastated. "I grew to married manhood," he wrote to Wilson, "without meeting death in my family, or among my closest friends, and the loss of my little girl and little boy inside of a year has made havoc with my hopes and joys."[17] Family recollection portrays Turner as so afflicted in mind that he was unable to apply himself seriously for an extended period. But, desolate with grief and distracted by worry about Mae's welfare as he was, he made during this period one of the most important decisions of his life and one that deeply affected the history program at the University of Wisconsin as well.

We have seen the mixture of envy, fear, and professional rivalry with which Wisconsin faculty viewed the University of Chicago, William Rainey Harper, and the Rockefeller-blessed endowment that, in Madison eyes, he was using with the prodigality of the nouveau riche. Caroline Sherwood was Chicago-reared. When Albion W. Small introduced Fred to President Harper at a luncheon in Chicago in early 1894, the latter remarked that a mutual friend often spoke of Caroline and her husband. "So it is as I suspected," reported Fred to her. "If any-one is called to Chicago Univ. it is likely to be my little wife!" So at this point the possibility that the University of Chicago might call Fred was sufficiently in the family consciousness for him to joke about it.[18] Chicago's initial move in building an American history program had been to hire the distinguished Professor von Holst. Turner noted in his essay of 1893 that this gentleman misunderstood the true currents of American history. Going further, he prepared a critical review of von Holst's *Constitutional and Political History of the United States*, which he may have presented locally during the fall of 1893. Although Trent wished to publish this manuscript in the journal that he was then editing, Turner did not release it, perhaps because Small had warned him in early 1894 that the sensitive von Holst might take offense.

President Harper hired a succession of Wisconsin faculty members during the 1890s, including Chamberlin, but he did not invade the history precinct in University Hall until 1898, and then only to invite Turner to teach a unit of the forthcoming summer school. Never averse to new experience and hard-pressed financially as always, Turner accepted the invitation and was well received by the Chicago students. By this time von Holst's deteriorating health had rendered him incap-able of instructing during the autumn quarter of 1899. As a result, President Harper suggested that Turner teach a weekend graduate course in the Chicago department during the fall, urging that he would thus meet numerous graduate students, provide an appropriate example of interuniversity cooperation, and render service to a neighbor in need. Equally telling, no doubt, was the salary of five hundred dollars.

Turner's arrangement with the University of Chicago was extended through the winter and spring terms. Thus when the decision to replace von Holst was made, Turner was a familiar figure on the Chicago campus, where his enthusiasm, his success with students, and his pleasant personality impressed many. In March 1900, follow-ing earlier discussions, President Harper invited Turner to head the history department at the University of Chicago, offering him an annual salary of four thousand dollars. Turner usually enjoyed the give-and-take of academic courtship, but he had enjoyed little during the year 1899. The family tragedies must have left him drained of both emotion and ambition but also, perhaps, suggested that a fresh start might benefit both of the Turners. He negotiated with his usual skill and carefully weighed the advantages of Madison against the potential rewards of the Chicago position.

It was his impression, wrote Wilson to Turner at this time, that the University of Chicago "Lacked academic steadiness, certainty of aim, dignity, the patience that does not pant for 'results'; that it was infected with the hurry."[19] Highly familiar with the situation in Chicago, Van Hise counseled Turner in a series of letters, contrasting the difference in library resources between the two universities and reminding him that "in some cases, vague general promises have not fully materialized in Chicago." He pledged his influence in having the university administration in Madison adjust Turner's teaching duties and fortify the history program as he might desire.[20]

Writing a week later, Van Hise assured Turner that opposition to the extension of graduate studies at the University of Wisconsin was less important than Turner believed. He could also be sure that more graduate students would come to work with him in Madison than if he were at the University of Chicago. Nor should their bereavement influence the Turners. "My dear Turner, there is more left behind than you and Mrs. Turner now dream. . . . the process of adjustment to a new environment will be one which can be accomplished by years of time only and much loneliness." Harper had pressed for an answer within weeks. This, wrote Van Hise, was "not fair play." Turner must ask for more time.[21]

Turner laid the Chicago offer before his superior in the School of Economics, Political Science, and History, Richard T. Ely. Well aware of Turner's worth and constitutionally combative, Ely was prepared to battle to retain Turner. The university, he suggested, should pledge commitment to the history program and to the development of advanced work under Turner and Haskins. Turner's salary should be raised to thirty-five hundred dollars per year, and he should receive a recuperative year's leave of absence with pay. Since regents might balk at the salary level without greater administrative responsibilities, Ely proposed that history should be made a separate school of which Turner should become director.

At this time Haskins was a visiting professor at Harvard, and Turner sought his advice "as a *man and a brother.*" He explained that he had not been initially enthusiastic about the idea of a separate school but, on consideration, such a reorganization might advance the history program beyond its current potential. Although the Chicago position might allow scheduling to avoid midwestern winters, "we have undoubtedly built up a department with a reputation here, and we can push it still further... *if the test shows popular and influential interest in it. . . .* unless our work is appreciated *here, outside* reputation will not help." He assured Haskins, "we ought to stick together on this thing . . . for I realize thoroughly that our union has been our strength, and I have no desire to follow a policy of one sided development any more than I have in the past.[22]

"Your letter has quite knocked me off my pins," replied Haskins, but he shrewdly discussed the elements required to improve Turner's position and that of the program. He understood the advantages that might accrue if the department became a school. His only question on that score, he confessed, was the nature of his own situation if Turner should later decide to leave Madison. He concluded, "I want to do anything and everything I can to make things at Madison as attractive to you as possible." President Adams was of like mind. Turner, he told the regents, was "perhaps more than any other, a child of the University, of whom the University has great reason to be proud."[23] In the dialogue with Harper, Turner went, as with Wilson earlier, to the point of suggesting that Haskins should be approached. Chamberlin, Wisconsin's former president, was now one of the most eminent of the University of Chicago's scientists. He urged Turner to join the Chicago faculty, as did Turner's former seminar colleague, Small. Another Hopkins man, John Dewey, wrote to describe the advantages of working in the graduate program at Chicago, in contrast with his earlier experience in a state university.

When he described Turner's offer to the board of regents, President Adams informed the members that he had assured Turner that none wished to check the development of graduate work in history. He further affirmed that "no university can flourish, as no university ever has flourished, which discourages graduate work." He did not understand that Turner wished "formal assurance" on such matters, but he urged "going as far as possible in order to keep him, and [to] make him happy and contented in being here."[24] Adams forwarded to Turner the individual replies of regents to his communication, and he, analytical scholar that he was, recorded their positions on a voting chart. Turner's distrust of the regents was of long standing, and both he and Haskins feared that members of the governing board too little understood the differing needs of introductory and advanced training in the university and unduly emphasized the practical side of education. But the response to the offer from Chicago was gratifying, acceptance in fact of provisions that Turner himself specified in a letter to Dean Edward A. Birge, and a landmark in the development of the Wisconsin history program.

Now the history program was to become a school of history, Turner serving as director at a salary of thirty-five hundred dollars per annum. In consideration of long and continuous service and recent family travails he was to receive a year of leave during academic year 1900–1901. The history staff was to be enlarged—an assistant professor added in American history and an instructor in the European field. The history program's allocation of graduate scholarships was to be maintained and two fellowships specifically assigned to the program. A new fund would support "special lectures" in the department of history. The university would provide additional monies for the purchase of library materials in European history. A history bulletin series would be established for the publication of doctoral dissertations in history. Turner refused the Chicago offer, and so was born the School of History at the University of Wisconsin. Members of later generations of history faculty at the University of Wisconsin sometimes criticized colleagues who received handsome raises on the basis of outside offers and thereby diminished the funds available for others. But the history program at the University of Wisconsin emerged as a separate school in the College of Letters and Sciences as the result of such an incident.

Turner's course in these negotiations has been portrayed as one dedicated primarily to the improvement of the history program at Wisconsin. There is truth in this view. Under his leadership the university's history program was winning national recognition. The negotiations with the University of Chicago allowed Turner to build for the future. But he had been long intrigued by the possibility of a Chicago offer. He withheld a manuscript from print because it might create animosity on the Chicago campus. He had good friends there, and his wife had been reared in Chicago. The resources in the hands of President Harper, the university's emphasis upon graduate training, and the charismatic president himself, would have intrigued any ambitious academic. In a year when so loving a family man as Turner had experienced the deaths of two of his children and the emotional breakdown of his wife, the prospect of reestablishing the family in Chicago perhaps demanded reserves of emotional energy that he simply lacked. But if Harper had had the resources to move Haskins as well, the outcome might have been different.

By early August 1900 the Turner family had perfected plans to spend most of the next academic year in Europe. They were to sail, Turner informed Haskins by letter, on the transport *Mesaba* on August 18. Among other arrangements, he gave a personal power of attorney to Haskins and a written request for him to "take care lest the Republic of history suffer harm," making his authority clear to "Coffin, Libby and the 'kids.'" The summer school, featuring Moses Coit Tyler, H. Morse Stephens, Franklin H. Giddings, and Jesse Macy had been successful in every respect but "numerical *gain*." Other university prospects were pleasing. But as to Europe, Turner had trepidations, asking Haskins: "Do you think I can do this on $250 per month? I am getting *skeered*."[25]

Turner reported to Van Hise during the crossing that he was enjoying the passage, and neither Caroline nor ten-year-old Dorothy complained that some of their fellow passengers were cattle. This trip was not a pilgrimage to the great scholarly centers of northern Europe where Turner sought out leading historians and learned their views on the state of the discipline. Rather the intent was recuperative for himself and particularly for Caroline. He hoped to see the countryside surrounding their various headquarters from the seat of his bicycle. The Turners spent much of September in Switzerland and then moved on to northern Italy.

In letters to family back home, he described European landscapes graphically, including the cows of the Gruyère country, traveling "in long processions, with cowbells that sound like church bells, & are as big," and the succession of agricultural zones as one journeyed upward to higher altitudes. He noted family reactions to the architectural wonders, galleries, plays, and the music of northern Italy, their sight-seeing sometimes marked by a certain doggedness. Preparatory to visiting Venice, Turner reported that they did not "expect to find the weather right for canal navigation, but we can't risk not seeing the place."[26] At Caroline's insistence, they confronted the Italian language, and Turner sometimes thought about an article that he was committed to writing for the *Atlantic Monthly*. The church bells of Florence rang in the year 1901 for them, and after an extended stay in the north, which had belied the name of "sunny Italy," they moved south to Rome and Naples.

A historian who found differences more interesting than continuities, Turner tried to describe the essential contrast between Europe and America. "It is the vast variety of Europe, in so limited areas that

Impresses me, and what makes it more interesting to the traveller from America than America. . . . I don't mean that I would wish to live and to do my work here. . . . America is full of the interest of the present and future and is in the process of making; but for a *pageant* to entertain and to amuse curiosity and to instruct as well, you must believe that Europe is superior for an American at least, who knows somewhat of his own land."[27]

Andrew Jackson Turner responded to Fred that his letters were of too "great interest" to match. But the son learned in late September that the frogs in his father's bait pail were "languishing for a more active life."[28] A month later his father sent a newspaper account in which he challenged the contention of Charles Francis Adams, Jr., at the dedication of the new Historical Society building that Madison had once been part of the Massachusetts Bay Colony. Jack Turner also tried to keep Fred abreast of politics in Bob La Follette's Wisconsin. In early spring he also learned that Fred and family had not indeed managed to subsist on $250 per month. Could father help? If not, Fred believed that he could probably arrange to obtain what he needed in Madison.

Preceding Caroline and Dorothy back from New York, Turner returned in mid-April to Madison, where he was rapidly absorbed into departmental activity. Slaughter and Thwaites opened their houses to him, as 629 Frances Street was leased for the duration of the term. Turner soon also visited a plot in Forest Hills Cemetery and reported to Caroline that the plantings looked healthy. The European year was important as a time of emotional adjustment for the Turner family — the relations of father, mother, and daughter continued always to be loving and supportive. There is no evidence to show that in the months abroad Turner did more than observe Europe and Europeans. Although the Turners later thought of spending Fred's first Harvard sabbatical in Europe, World War I intervened. One of the most influential interpreters of American uniqueness, Turner was never again to ponder at first hand the contrasts between the old world and the new.

In Madison the Turners slipped easily back into the everyday life of the university community — their close relationships with their Frances Street neighbors and other friends. Turner and Van Hise were members of a dining club of faculty members who met for a meal and talk at intervals and who referred to themselves as "the Apostles." While

Turner was abroad, Van Hise suggested that Haskins be invited to join the group, knowing that Turner would be pleased. The Turners were on the guest list at major university functions and at the entertainment of visiting dignitaries as a matter of course. In February 1903 Belle La Follette invited the Turners to the legislative reception in a note asking Mae to help in making the guests welcome. The Turners almost invariably entertained visiting historians and often asked them to stay in their home.

Now Turner was reaching his forties. With a past history of "nerves" and breakdown, fighting hay fever every summer, Caroline was considered the less robust member of the couple. Each summer Turner tried to arrange their living arrangements to protect her from the worst part of the midwestern hay fever season. In 1902 an opportunity to lecture in Colorado allowed the family to investigate a mountain climate and for Turner to test the trout fishing near Wagon Wheel Gap. Although subject to what he called "catarrhal colds," Turner had suffered no major illness since the meningitis of his undergraduate years. Still, friends noted that he looked less than well in early 1903, and in mid-May he entered St. Luke's Hospital in Chicago to have a grumbling appendix removed. Recuperating two weeks later, he thanked Dorothy for her note and the Madison clovers that she had sent to him. He complimented her on her "pen*girl*ship" and told her that he was required "to lie in bed and eat toast and eggs and drink chocolate through a glass tube and be washed and fed little tablets." He imagined that "it is a good deal like being a rag doll."[29] The summer of 1903 was one of recuperation, in part spent at Hancock Point, Maine, where the Slaughters summered.

When Turner assumed control of the University of Wisconsin School of History in 1901, other administrative changes were also under way on the campus. Full bearded and patriarchal in appearance, Charles Kendall Adams had studied in Germany and was credited with introducing the seminary system and vitalizing historical studies at the University of Michigan, where he had taught before becoming the president of Cornell University. After resigning that post, he had intended to devote the remainder of his life to writing and editorial work but found the presidency of the University of Wisconsin too attractive to refuse. Adams apparently never developed a close relationship with Turner.[30] But the president was highly successful in obtaining appropriations to expand the university's physical plant. Most impressive was the striking building designed to house the State

Historical Society of Wisconsin and the University Library, although Thwaites deserved much credit for this accomplishment as well.

Adams belonged to an older generation than Turner and Haskins. Although he boasted of the high quality of Wisconsin's history department, he was perhaps never completely at ease with its aggressive professionalism. Years earlier, Adams had not sought to involve Turner in a major way in the preparation of *Johnson's Encyclopedia*, and, in writing a high school history text, he collaborated with Trent rather than with the head of his own history department. Adams did not, one suspects, support as rapid a development of graduate studies at Wisconsin as Turner and Haskins wished, and they feared that the progress of practical studies such as agriculture and commerce indicated excessive commitment to the materialistic side of higher education.

Adams believed strongly in the benefits of athletics, even to the point of trying to persuade the father of a muscular young student that it was in the son's best interests if he were permitted to play football. Adams congratulated the members of the team after victory and consoled them in defeat. During the late 1890s Turner was already becoming convinced that intercollegiate athletic competition disrupted university life. When the faculty resolved that students with inadequate grades should be barred from intercollegiate competition, Adams failed to submit the recommendation to the regents. Under pressure from a regent subsequently, Adams allowed a notorious slacker to play in a contest with Northwestern University's team. In a tumultuous meeting in which the secretary of the faculty reproached the president for failing to bring the faculty action before the regents, Turner "in a voice vibrant with emotion, but under perfect control, expressed the feeling of the faculty."[31] Reputedly Adams concluded that he had been at fault and cherished no grudge against Turner. When President Harper sought to lure Turner to the University of Chicago, Adams's reaction was both professionally effective and personally warm.

But while Turner was deciding to remain in Madison, Adams was failing severely in health. Restorative sojourns at Hot Springs, Virginia, and Battle Creek, Michigan, and a leave spent abroad failed to restore him; he insisted that the regents accept his resignation in early 1902. During his illness, Adams had depended on Dean Edward A. Birge to administer the institution. Birge had been dean of Letters and Sciences since the early 1890s, but during these years the position was more akin to that of later registrars than to the powerful office of later generations. Birge read the Latin poets in the original for relaxation, was a limnologist of national stature, and was an impeccable administrator. Honest and austere, he inspired respect rather than love. Now Birge became acting president.

The regents, it was believed, preferred to select an outsider as president, and several fitting that description were considered, particularly President Benjamin I. Wheeler, of the University of California, who was not interested. Of local men, Birge was an obvious possibility, but some faculty members faulted his qualities of leadership or found in him an unsympathetic personality. While president, Adams had spoken admiringly of Van Hise—his honesty, his good judgment, his growing national reputation in the increasingly sophisticated science of geology. Other faculty members had high regard for him. He was Turner's neighbor, fellow dining club member, and his informal instructor in physiography. Although some considered Turner himself to be an eligible candidate, he disavowed any such interest and backed Van Hise, somewhat to the latter's initial dismay.

Turner assumed leadership of the Van Hise supporters on the faculty. By 1902 Turner had been associated with the university as student and staff member for more than twenty years. Friends and students were scattered through the state. His family heritage of politics and reporting had given him a sure sense of how things were accomplished in both state government and the university. As head of a school in the latter community he enjoyed stature and influence. Van Hise could not have found a better manager.

We do not know the intimate details of the campaign for Van Hise. But we know that Turner lobbied the regents in behalf of the candidate and that Regent James C. Kirwin was receptive to the information Turner provided him. He must have read Turner's comparative evaluation of Birge and Dr. Henry Prichett, a candidate from outside the immediate academic community, with keen interest. Birge's support in the faculty, Turner suggested, was in part one of sympathy because of his previous exertions on the university's behalf. "I have myself," he wrote, "the highest respect for Dr. Birge's ability to handle the *details* of university internal machinery, and for him personally. But he is peculiarly qualified to hold things together, rather than to construct; his ability is in conservative *ad interim*, rather than leadership on the march. . . . it is a different task to guard the ship at the moorings from the task of holding the helm, directing the course, and filling all hands with confidence, in the voyage of the ship at sea." As in the Bascom presidency, Prichett's appointment, Turner feared, might make the university a "football between the opposing camps of the temperance people and the liberal element." He evaded Kerwin's request for a head count of faculty supporters of Van Hise, maintaining, "More . . . active members of the faculty favor Van Hise on his merits than any other single candidate."[32]

Charles Van Hise became the new president of the University of Wisconsin. Notwithstanding Turner's activity, this outcome may have most reflected the fact that Governor La Follette favored appointment of his former classmate, Van Hise, and that regents whom La Follette had appointed were now a force on the board.

Through Turner's remaining years at Wisconsin he enjoyed the close friendship of the university president, and Van Hise valued Turner as confidant and advisor. Van Hise sought as well, however, to make best use of Birge's talents, the latter remaining as dean of Letters and Sciences. Turner and Birge were an interesting contrast: the historian—forthcoming, articulate, with genial laugh, a Unitarian in sympathy, though not in serious practice; the scientist—reserved and somewhat intimidating, a lifelong and conscientious Congregationalist. Turner was a dedicated fisherman. Birge studied the living communities of the local lakes but proclaimed that he had no "particular use for fish, either in the way of sport or food." Turner liked to generalize and interpret, often on the basis of incomplete evidence. Birge was the meticulous scientist painfully reconstructing the web of marine life. Van Hise understood that both were making great contributions to the university. Of the president, however, Birge later maintained, "Turner was his main adviser in the faculty until Turner went to Harvard in 1910. Then Van Hise turned to me."[33]

7   Dimensions

*"The possibilities for building up here in the Middle West
a great national center for historical instruction
are unsurpassed"*

During the Wisconsin years Turner was teacher and investigator but
also administrator, program builder, publicist, campus politician, and
emerging power in the history discipline. The growth of the university
and the creation of the School of History allowed Turner to design a
program reflecting his conception of what academic historians should
do. The most important decisions of the director of an academic
program involve the hiring and retention of faculty. The university's
commitment to Turner ensured junior appointments in both American
and European history. For the first of these positions, Turner recommended the hiring of Carl Russell Fish, who completed his doctoral
dissertation "Political Patronage in the United States" at Harvard in
1900. Fish was still in his early twenties when he arrived in Madison—
so youthful in appearance that he was often taken for an undergraduate. Harvard thought well of Fish; he radiated the luster of eastern
polish and had command, it was said, of six languages. As an undergraduate he had studied at Brown University under Jameson, who
strongly recommended him. Urged by Adams to broaden the scope of
his hiring activity, and with the advice of Haskins, Turner also engaged
a young Yale Ph.D., Asa C. Tilton, to bolster the European program.
Tilton remained in the department for only a few years, moving to the
staff of the Historical Society. In 1901–2, George C. Sellery joined the
department as an instructor. Sellery had impressed Turner when he
was a member of Turner's class at the University of Chicago during
1899–1900. Like Haskins, Sellery had prepared a doctoral dissertation
in American history, but he was to spend his career in the European
field. Like Fish, Sellery remained at Wisconsin, serving ultimately as
dean of Letters and Sciences.

Turner hoped to make the Wisconsin program the leading center of
historical studies beyond the Alleghenies. From 1890 onward he and
Haskins occupied adjacent offices in University Hall, lived under the
same roof for much of the time, and shared their thoughts and dreams.
Pleasure at his friend's success mingled with disappointment in

Turner's mind when Haskins accepted a position at Harvard University in December 1901. Haskins had not published a great deal while at Wisconsin, but he visited European universities and archives and laid the foundations of a scholarly career during which he became America's leading medievalist, a founder of the Medieval Academy, and, like Turner, a president of the American Historical Association. Haskins and Turner remained close friends during the remainder of their lives, and their professional careers continued to be closely intertwined, as we shall see.

To replace Haskins, Turner recommended the appointment of Dana C. Munro, of the University of Pennsylvania. Munro was an excellent choice. Trained in Germany and at the University of Pennsylvania, and an experienced teacher, Munro quickly assumed the responsibilities of leadership in the European field. He was a talented administrator who directed the summer school at Wisconsin for a number of years in addition to fulfilling his teaching duties. By this time he had selected the crusades as his particular research interest in medieval history, and he was recognized as their foremost American student by the time of his death. He never completed his magnum opus on the subject, but Munro was a successful author of articles and textbooks. He too was highly active in the historical profession, becoming president of the AHA as well as president of the Medieval Academy. Like both Turner and Haskins, however, he spent the ripest years of his career in the Ivy League.

In effect, Turner's decision to reject the offer from the University of Chicago meant that Orin G. Libby would not be retained in the Wisconsin history program. It was an outcome that prompts us to consider the relations between professors and their graduate students and junior staff members during the 1890s when history's professional culture was being shaped. Turner sometimes referred to the *comitatus* of the graduate director. What precisely did he mean? Graduate students learn most when doing research in their director's area of greatest knowledge. But who is to benefit from the information that they unearth? Some of Turner's graduate students of the 1890s gladly accepted the idea that they might be providing data for works by their mentor. But young scholars are also expected at this stage of training to be laying a foundation of research for their own professional advancement. Ideally the processes of graduate instruction work to the mutual benefit of student and supervisor. This being the situation, should we question the way in which Turner directed two of his graduate students of the 1890s?

One of the cases—that of George H. Alden—relates to the degree of separation appropriate between the research of major advisor and student. Alden began a study of the establishment of new states in the federal union in Albert B. Hart's seminary at Harvard University and was apparently awarded a fellowship at the University of Wisconsin at the conclusion of academic year 1894–95. In early June 1895 Jameson invited Turner to contribute to the first issue of the *American Historical Review*, and he responded immediately, offering to prepare an article entitled "State Making in the West, 1772–1789," which Jameson wished in hand by the end of the summer.[1] During the year 1895–96 Alden completed a dissertation on "New Governments West of the Alleghanies before 1780" under Turner's direction, defending it successfully in 1896.

Turner was much concerned during the mid-1890s with marking out his turf and in the summer of 1895 told Haskins that a recent statement of the importance of the West by Wilson made it important for him to "get out a new article."[2] Turner prepared his contribution to the *American Historical Review* before Alden did much of his work upon a dissertation that overlapped Turner's selected topic to a considerable degree. But with Alden's Harvard record before him, had Turner moved to preempt the field with a publication on a subject already addressed by a student accepted for admission to graduate work under his direction? Or given the fact of Turner's publication, did he allow Alden to develop a topic on which his own work provided more guidance for the student than appropriate? The dissertation was published under Turner's editorship in a Wisconsin bulletin series, and Alden cherished the most friendly of feelings toward his director in later years. In the preface to his dissertation, he thanked Turner "more than . . . all others" for his assistance in preparing his study.[3] Hart's growing respect for Turner was unaffected.

Turner's relations with Libby were more extended and complex. After obtaining a normal school diploma and teaching high school for several years, Libby entered the University of Wisconsin as a junior in 1890 and continued his studies in the graduate program. He presented his master's thesis, "The Erie Canal as a State Enterprise," in 1893. He so impressed Turner with his research on the geographical distribution of the vote on the federal constitution as to lead the latter to propose that Libby and another Wisconsin graduate student be invited to present papers at the Chicago meeting of the AHA in 1893. This failing approval, Turner again recommended Libby even at cost of his own spot. When Libby completed his second year as departmental fellow, Turner appointed him to instructor rank, and he stayed at this level from 1895 to 1902. Libby's duties mainly involved teaching lower-level classes in Ancient history.

Among other aspects of the Erie Canal's history, Libby examined the geographical distribution of the vote on John C. Calhoun's proposal to provide federal assistance for its construction. In his doctoral research he analyzed the distribution of the voting for delegates to the state conventions called to ratify the Constitution of 1787. In this connection, he prepared an elaborate map showing the areas of federal, antifederal, and mixed sentiment recorded at the county level or in minor political subdivisions. He explained these voting patterns by relating them to the "physiographic, social, and economic" character- istics of the various regions or subregions of the nation.[4] Libby was apparently the first American historian to map congressional roll calls and electoral data for analytical purposes.

After continuing research, Libby presented an able plea for the intensive study of roll calls in the Congress of the United States at the meeting of the AHA in 1896. By mapping the votes of the representa- tives and senators in Congress and relating them to sectional charac- teristics, he explained, the investigator could identify the motivation of political behavior. The speeches of legislators then became "a valuable commentary and supplement, nothing more. This method enables one to discover the physiographic areas that become in time economic and political sections. . . . It reveals the action of steady forces through a long series of years, localized in such a way that they can be studied to advantage. It is . . . the laboratory method of the botanist, the chemist, and the geologist applied to human action, and it is offered merely as enabling us to use a store of unworked material for the better solution of the politico-economic problems of our national life."[5] Libby announced that he was working on a study of voting patterns in the United States Congress that he had thus far carried from the beginnings of the republic to the early 1840s. The types of maps and general method of analysis that Libby pioneered using have provided the empirical basis for many subsequent analyses of American politics, particularly its sectional manifestations.

In March 1894 Turner prepared a recommendation for Libby. The latter's dissertation, he asserted, "applies a new method to American history and opens the way for rewriting much of that history." He also affirmed, "I have never found a student more devoted to his work, and more acute in following out a historical lead, than Mr. Libby." In "appearance" Libby was "prepossessing . . . full of earnestness and vigor."[6] Turner's editorial introduction to Libby's dissertation in the *Economics, Political Science and History Series* of the university's *Bulletin* struck a different note. It was, he wrote, "one of a series of studies carried on in my seminary in American history, with the design of contributing to an understanding of the relations between the political history of the United States, and the physiographic, social, and economic conditions underlying this history." He showed how Libby's findings fit within his own interpretation of American development and quoted a passage in which Richard Hildreth used "economic divisions to explain political action, in a limited period" in his *History of the United States*.[7] He did not refer to the uniqueness of Libby's method nor its revisionary nature. Turner distributed copies of Libby's dissertation as advertising for the Wisconsin program, including one that he sent to Achille Loria.

Although not devoid of error, Libby's dissertation was a more important substantive and methodological contribution to American historiography than Turner's own thesis. It has served as the starting point for much interesting analysis by other historians. Turner had suggested the importance of sectional interplay in American politics in his *Aegis* article of 1892 and had incorporated it in the Chicago paper of 1893, although emphasizing it less than the concept of the frontier. He had also noted the importance of sectionalism in the description of his course in economic and social history of 1892–93.[8] Emphasis on sectionalism is at least implicit in Turner's paper "The West as a Field for Historical Study" presented in 1896. The Herbart edition of the frontier essay showed further development of his ideas about the development of sections and their relation to the physiography of the United States. But Turner never published any research during the 1890s in which he utilized the methods of mapping sectional manifestation advocated and used by Libby. Then and for some years thereafter, Turner focused his research activity on the diplomatic history of the West during the early national period.

Libby left an intimate record of his years at the University of Wisconsin from the mid-1890s to the end of the century in letters to his friend, later fiancée and wife, Eva Cory. They show a young man scarred by economic privation, debt, and personal sorrow, limited by a parochial midwestern upbringing, stiff-necked and puritanical, and somewhat naive. He was extremely hard-working, in love with history, ambitious, and hoping to round out his education with a year of study and travel in Europe. Libby had studied ornithology beyond the limits of the amateur, and his willingness to share his knowledge won him friends in the university community. But his letters offer a contrasting view of Turner compared to that recorded by other Wisconsin graduate students of the 1890s.

Libby explained to Cory in April 1896 that he had "opened up some very valuable fields of work in American history which will give me position and reputation for life if I can once get my discoveries fairly known to the experts and two or three chapters written or published."[9] He believed that Turner had plotted to appropriate some of his research. Thenceforth Libby saw himself engaged in a silent war with the head of the history program. It is a painful story. Libby sought to announce his activity by giving a paper at the AHA meeting in 1896 and believed that Turner was trying to thwart his efforts to appear on the program. He gave his paper and was rightly disappointed in the small amount of attention it received. Turner did not attend the meeting, although contributing a paper.

Restricted mainly in his teaching to the introductory survey course in ancient history, Libby worked under the supervision of Haskins, with whom his relations were cordial. But increasingly he was determined to specialize in American history and particularly in the kind of sectional analysis that he had begun in his master's and doctoral studies. Year by year he hoped for substantial raises and did not receive them. He interpreted an invitation from Ely to assist in the revision of one of the latter's books as an indication that the director of the school would ensure his advancement, but after giving Ely considerable assistance, he was disappointed. When President Adams reacted enthusiastically to one of his papers, Libby hoped for aid from that source but to no avail. In 1898–99, however, Libby was allowed to offer a course in "American Sectionalism," described as "A study of the geographical distribution of political parties with especial reference to votes in Congress and in state legislature[s]."[10] An adequate number of students enrolled, and he was delighted when a number of them elected to write their senior theses under his direction. They were, he believed, doing better work than those working with Turner, and indeed some of the work of his students was published.

Libby told himself at times that a record of successful publication would influence campus opinion in his behalf and force Turner to improve his salary and recommend his promotion to assistant professor. During the late 1890s Turner was trying to write a textbook, and thus, thought Libby, his own concern with research would be the more obvious. At one point Turner suggested that he would like to use some of Libby's maps to illustrate his text, assuring Libby that he would give him credit. Libby evaded the request, and one of his faculty friends jibed that Libby should hold out for cash rather than credit.

As early as the end of academic year 1896–97 Libby reported that his position had become "more and more uncomfortable," and thereafter his hopes rose and fell, his evidence of professional accomplishment blunted by repeated rebuffs when new budgets were approved. His superior, he believed, was a mere politician, bright but unscrupulous, who wished him gone because of his interest and accomplishments in a field that Turner wished to be his alone. Libby considered other positions, but the thought of leaving the Madison libraries deterred him, or, in one case, the expectation that he must conduct chapel services in his new position. Initially Libby had desired advancement so that he could make his much desired trip to Europe and study with Ratzel. By late 1898 this objective was superseded by his need for an income sufficient to allow him to marry Eva Cory. In late January 1899 he confronted Turner and requested that he be promoted to assistant professor and that his salary be raised by several hundred dollars to fifteen hundred dollars. He summarized Turner's response for Cory:

He said my line of investigation was too much like his for us both to stay in the department. That I never could be more than an instructor unless I would teach and work in another line. If I would do that I could have $1500 and chance of a steady rise. You can imagine my fix. To see the wished for prize attached to such hard conditions. Of course in the end I had to refuse because I am pledged to carry out the line of work I have begun. It is too late to change—it is what I am fitted for and nothing else. It was dastardly of him to ask me to leave my work for pay and do what I am not fitted to do. Yet the temptation to accept was stronger than he knew because it meant our settling down at once.[11]

Libby received a raise of one hundred dollars that spring although he had hoped for considerably more.

He faced more temptation during the late spring of that year. An eastern scholar who was committed to teaching history in the Wisconsin summer session withdrew, and Turner offered an appointment to Libby. He refused because he was planning to spend the summer in research in eastern libraries. Libby spent two weeks in late June helping the victims of a tornado at New Richmond, Wisconsin, and then journeyed east on a research trip. As a member of a family that had provided a participant in John Brown's expedition against Harper's Ferry, he agreed, while in Washington, D.C., to help disinter the bones of those in Brown's party who had died at Harper's Ferry and to accompany them to a new resting place in New York. But he spent the rest of the summer working feverishly in eastern research repositories and returned as eager as ever to advance both his career and his personal life.

In his last years at Wisconsin Libby believed that Haskins was particularly helpful, assuring Libby that he would be retained until a satisfactory alternative position could be found. Haskins offered to assist him in the search, at one point intimating that there might be a place for him at Stanford University. When Turner accepted the University of Wisconsin's response to the Chicago offer and was named director of the School of History, Libby concluded that any chance of staying was gone. Although his heart went out to Caroline Turner in the loss of her children, he was so alienated from Turner that he confessed he could feel little sympathy for him.

After an initial refusal, Libby was allowed to teach summer school in the summer of 1900, and he and Cory were married. In the spring of 1902, Turner, without consulting Libby, strongly recommended him for an assistant professorship at the University of North Dakota. He only ventured to submit his name, he explained, because Libby desired "to secure more general work and in different lines from the work which is open to him here." Given "the detailed organization of our courses," he continued, "the work is very much specialized, and the opportunity for promotion . . . very slow." Libby's instructional work at Wisconsin, wrote Turner, had been "of the highest kind." He was sending along some of his young colleague's publications to show "his ability in investigation."[12] Libby reluctantly accepted the position at the University of North Dakota and informed Turner of his resignation in the curtest of terms. Turner's acknowledgment was also short, although he expressed hope that Libby would "enjoy" his new position and assured him that he would "have our good wishes for your success" and that we "have the highest appreciation of the work which you have done here."[13]

A year after Libby left Madison, Turner assessed his abilities for Andrew C. McLaughlin, then planning the history program of the Bureau of Historical Research of the Carnegie Institution. Turner strongly supported the publication of a historical atlas of the United States that would include "a map of the sectional grouping of political parties in local and national elections" as shown in the monographs by Libby, G. D. Luetscher, T. C. Smith, and Ulrich B. Phillips. He had suggested the studies to these men, he explained, and they "repre-sent[ed] the method of interpreting political action which we make very prominent here." Turner suggested that Libby was the right person to "take up this grouping of political parties." He was a "very thorough, careful worker" but should be controlled by an editor because of "a tendency to go off on tangents." He cautioned McLaughlin still further, "I should not be so ready to favor his appointment in a position in which commentary upon the work was the fundamental thing; but, for persistence and accurate collection of material and mapping it, I doubt if you could find a better man. Moreover, I think he has already done more in this line than any other single investigator." Despite "limita-tions" of the method, Turner believed that such a series of maps would be "a decidedly important contribution, not only to the history of American political parties, but also to the general science of Sociology, and the relations between the social and political features" of America.[14]

Libby had prided himself on an appearance of equanimity, and he apparently did not quarrel with Turner. The latter may never have understood the depth of Libby's unhappiness. Nor can we be sure how the relationship should be interpreted or the degree to which either or both were at fault. Graduate students and junior faculty members sometimes read too much into the actions of superiors and suspect malign intent where none exists. Although initially acknowledging Libby's work to be of major importance, Turner also saw Libby as brilliantly "following a lead" that he had provided. Libby viewed himself as developing new methods and producing new findings for which he should receive primary credit. The ambitious Turner saw Libby as evidence of the quality of a history program that he was developing and for which he sought national eminence. The ambitious Libby perceived Turner as unsupportive, even parasitic.

Libby never produced another monograph as important as his doctoral dissertation, but he was not the type of scholar who writes an outstanding dissertation on a subject recommended by an advisor and subsides thereafter into mental torpor. He produced other works of scholarly value and more than any other person shaped the historiography of his adopted state from his position in its university's history department and as secretary and editor of the North Dakota Historical Society.

Perhaps Libby was too stubborn and introverted to accept the guidance necessary to develop fully the foundation of research that he laid during the 1890s. Despite his talents, Libby probably was lacking in polish and in those "urbane" qualities of intellect that Turner admired When Turner first attended an AHA meeting, he made numerous useful professional contacts. Libby, however, in 1896, apparently delivered his paper and abruptly departed. We cannot know the degree to which Turner sought to help Libby to realize his professional promise. If Turner failed in trying to provide guidance and support for Libby, it was the profession's misfortune. If he did not attempt to do so, Libby was to some degree a sacrifice to Turner's broader ambitions for himself and the Wisconsin departmental program. On the other hand, the resources at Turner's disposal were limited—his growing vision of an American history program that stressed sectional analysis was best served by the appointment of a specialist in southern history rather than continuance of Libby's appointment. While Libby was deciding whether to hang on at Madison in hopes of a better alternative to the University of North Dakota, Turner was trying to locate Ulrich B. Phillips, who, he hoped, would be able to develop studies in southern history at Madison.

During the early fall of 1902 Turner prepared a report on the work of the School of History for Acting President Birge. It was an enthusiastic description of accomplishment and future promise, although also emphasizing the need for additional institutional support. Cynics might view the founding of the school as primarily a means of keeping Turner and Haskins at the University of Wisconsin. Turner, however, affirmed that it had been established "to provide for increased efficiency in the work in history for undergraduates, to provide for the proper utilization and development of the resources of the historical libraries in Madison, to afford historical training for the various social sciences, and to promote graduate study and investigation in history."[15] The emphasis on relations with the social sciences and graduate study were significant. They reflected Turner's personal inclinations.

Turner pointed out that from the fall semester of 1900–1901 to that of 1902–3 the enrollment in history had grown from 603 students to 822; the enrollment of 62 graduate students at the first date had risen to 90 in the second. Such leading historians as Moses Coit Tyler, H. Morse Stephens, Alfred B. Hart, Max Farrand, and Thwaites had presented lecture series or taught summer courses during this period. James H. Robinson was to appear in the coming year. Thus Wisconsin students were stimulated by "the eminent scholars of the country" and the "University and its historical resources . . . made better known among our sister institutions." No less impressive testimony of the program's growing reputation than its increasing enrollment was the varied background of the graduate students and history major seniors.

Staff changes and modification of courses had "enabled a reconstruction of the work of the School." Introductory courses now covered the full year rather than a semester as before. The historians had divided the large classes in English and medieval history into "small quiz sections thus bringing instructor and student into closer acquaintance." Instructors now provided "more effective specialization" and the "heads of departments" could give "increased attention . . . to advanced instruction and research." The publication record of the department was satisfactory. Staff members had contributed "a considerable number of papers" to "the leading periodicals." The director was "preparing several books" and his colleagues had recently published substantial works or had volumes in press. Four doctoral dissertations were to be published during the coming year, and twenty seniors were writing history theses.

Turner believed that the school should also be interested in the teaching of history in the public schools. Faculty members had been an "important influence" in a recent conference on the teaching of history convened by the National Educational Association. Haskins had served on the AHA's Committee of Seven on the status of history teaching in the schools. His successor, Munro, had worked actively with history teachers in his former appointment. Turner had been in frequent contact with school teachers in "reference to methods of history teaching." Historians had assisted the work of the Free Library Commission in developing history syllabi and reading lists for library use.

The school's greatest need, Turner explained, involved improvement of the university library collections in European history. Students must study in this area increasingly, if they were to bring adequate knowledge to bear on the problems they would face as citizens in the future. In this respect, the needs of the Schools of Economics and Political Science and of Commerce paralleled those of history. The history program had "hardly entered the field of Oriental history," and here library resources were extremely deficient. More funds should be expended to purchase duplicate copies of books under heavy use in the larger courses.

Moving from specifics to the general, Turner explained that the school had a great opportunity to attract students from the West and the South. "Already we are pioneers in the work of offering courses in western history," he wrote, and work was beginning in the history of the South. Its reputation in the West was already "gratifying," but

> increased efforts should be made to acquaint the Universities of the South and West with our opportunities and to secure in larger measure the attendance of their graduates upon this university. The resulting advantages to the state in the wider extension of the field of professional activity to our own graduates is an additional reason for attention to this subject. In conclusion it is submitted that the work of the School is only fairly begun, but that the possibilities for building up here in the Middle West a great national center for historical instruction are unsurpassed. If with our existing resources we allow our rivals to outstrip us, by a lack of energy and continued development, we shall let pass a golden opportunity not likely to be again presented.[16]

Phillips figured importantly in Turner's plans to develop sectional analysis in the Wisconsin department. This young southerner first studied at the graduate level under one of Turner's seminar mates at Johns Hopkins, John H. T. McPherson, who brought the Wisconsinite's work to the attention of his students at the University of Georgia. Phillips scraped together the funds to enroll in Turner's seminar and lecture course in the University of Chicago summer session in 1898. Then and thereafter, Turner encouraged Phillips in his research on the politics of states rights in Georgia and in the use of voting maps. Under the direction of William A. Dunning, at Columbia University, Phillips expanded his master's thesis into a dissertation that won the Winsor

Prize of the AHA. With Libby's resignation a possibility, Turner queried Dunning and McPherson about Phillips.

McPherson had known Phillips as student and history tutor and thought him well grounded in history, "extremely ambitious, energetic, hard-working and willing. . . . gentlemanly and agreeable" with "all the charm of cultivation." But also, noted McPherson, there was in the young man "an inordinate self-esteem, a constant tendency to self-assertion, with a lack of delicacy, — tact, — modesty, — judgment."[17] Turner was not deterred. Uncertain of his prospects in Georgia, Phillips gladly accepted the Wisconsin offer. Despite an enthusiasm for the history of the South that rivalled Turner's earlier commitment to the West, Phillips considered himself unprepared when Turner suggested that he organize a course on that topic. He gladly accepted the assignment, however. Fish provided northeastern balance by offering "The History of New England" in academic year 1902–3, and Phillips's course entered the curriculum in the following year. When considered in conjunction with Turner's offerings in western history, these courses provided a unique emphasis upon sectional analysis and gave Turner added reason for placing his department among the nation's leading history programs.

Turner apparently did not conduct widespread and meticulous searches for personnel. The leading centers of graduate training in history were few in number, and his involvement in the activities of the AHA and other professional connections brought him into personal contact with men and women from most of them. Information also spread through the pervasive Hopkins network of graduates. This relationship was decisive in the appointment of Fish. In addition, Turner knew both Phillips and Sellery as students in his classes at Chicago. However casual his methods, Turner succeeded in assembling an excellent staff. Munro's career was to be distinguished, and Phillips' impact on southern history more lasting than even that of his teacher, Dunning. If hardly of first rank among the profession's scholars, Fish and Sellery were men of high competence.

As an institution, the Wisconsin School of History was short lived. President Adams had encountered problems in adjusting the relations between colleges and schools, and in President Van Hise's orderly mind the proliferation of schools complicated channels of administrative communication. The creation of a School of Commerce had particularly caused concern among some members of the faculty. As director of the School of Economics and Political Science, Ely was

especially jealous of his prerogatives. On the other hand, absorption of
the schools within the College of Letters and Sciences would strengthen
that entity in its relations with faculties such as those in law and
agriculture.

Soon after his selection as president, Van Hise moved to rationalize
the situation. The politics of the transition are unclear, but, in retrospect, Munro believed that Van Hise had assured Turner that nothing
of consequence would be lost in the transition from school to department. A document approved by the faculty of the College of Letters
and Science provided that five schools, including history, were to be
discontinued; assigned various courses to appropriate departments;
noted that there was to be no change in the scope of the history
program nor that of several others; and added that the duties of a senior
professor of a department should be those of "a chairman of a
committee of the professors of a department" and that there was to be
"no modification in salaries . . . arrangements for assistance, lectures,
library allowances, or publications . . . assigned salaries or scholarships; or in any other privileges which the various organizations have
heretofore had as schools." So ended the School of History at the
University of Wisconsin. Turner continued to direct the history
program energetically and enthusiastically. In these years Turner
showed himself capable of both curricular innovation and the dis-
cerning choice of personnel, although first Haskins, and later Munro,
also made major contributions to the early development of the discipline of history at Wisconsin.[18]

Meanwhile, Turner was active in the national profession. Just five
years after completing his graduate work, he was elected to the Executive Council of the AHA. He served there until 1899 and during this
period was selected as a member of the association's Historical Manuscript's Commission, overseeing the organization's most important
activity, aside from the annual meeting and its relation to the *Review*.
The Hopkins connection was important in these developments, given
Adams's position as secretary of the association and Jameson's role as
first chairman of its Manuscript Commission. Turner's geographical
location was also an important factor. The association leadership
recognized the importance of sectional balance in the councils of the
organization, and Turner was not only a Hopkinsized westerner but

one who spoke eloquently on behalf of his section. To these considerations one must add the attractive qualities of his personality.

When Turner rejected Harper's handsome offer, the latter turned instead to Jameson, then still at Brown University. So little did Chicago's resilient president resent Turner's refusal that he invited him to introduce Jameson when the latter's new colleagues formally welcomed him to their ranks. On migrating westward, Jameson surrendered editorial control of the *American Historical Review* to McLaughlin, then head of the department at the University of Michigan. Born in the same year as Turner and trained at Michigan, McLaughlin served on the council of the AHA with Turner in the 1890s. Since McLaughlin solicited material from Turner and was supportive of his students, Turner found him no less satisfactory an editor than had been Jameson. As the Carnegie Institution laid plans for work in various scholarly disciplines, Jameson, McLaughlin, and Adams served as a committee to propose a program in history. Early in 1903 McLaughlin became director of the Bureau of Historical Research of the Carnegie Institution in Washington. He soon tired of his duties in Washington, however, and, in effect, switched positions with Jameson, who assumed control of the Carnegie history program and picked up his old duties as editor of the *Review*.

Turner returned to the AHA Executive Council in 1901, serving until 1904. In that year he was chairman of the nominating committee that recommended Jameson for the position of second vice-president, an appointment signifying nomination for the presidency in two years hence. Turner played minor roles in the affairs of the AHA during the next several years, but in 1907 he became second vice-president and then successively first vice-president and, at the December, 1909 meeting, its president for the following year.

While Turner shared so fully in the governance of the AHA, the association was consolidating its position as the institutional voice of the academic history discipline. In the first years of the new century AHA leaders particularly discussed projects that would strengthen the profession. Among these was the idea of a historical school or institute, under the auspices of the association, which might support a variety of historical programs and with which graduate students and scholars researching in Washington might affiliate. Jameson later maintained that Turner had first outlined this proposal in conversation with him and others on the Turner porch. Now, however, wrote Turner to Jameson in late 1901, "Mr. Carnegie's ten million dollar bowling-ball has rather knocked down the historical ten pins that we set up for the school at Washington." But he believed that if the funds of the Carnegie Foundation were to be "used exclusively for graduate study and investigation it will stimulate higher education most powerfully, and ought" he thought, "to receive the warmest support of all institutions."[19]

Jameson's committee on the future role of the Carnegie Institution in history referred its draft report to Turner, and he responded at length. He saw in the Carnegie initiative a golden opportunity for obtaining funds that would allow historians to collect materials and finance travel essential to their research. These monies could be used to support the publication of historical source materials to a degree currently beyond the resources of the AHA's Historical Manuscripts Commission. He believed also that a school of historical studies recommended in the report was too modest in scope, visualizing instead a Washington headquarters for visiting research scholars and their students. He also supported the idea of developing a project for the publication of an atlas of American history including maps depicting party votes in subdivisions below the state level. He knew from the experience of Libby that "work of this sort . . . needs subsidy" because such maps were "somewhat expensive."[20]

Later in the year, as plans for the Carnegie Institution's Bureau of Historical Research continued to develop, Turner urged that the bureau should do "something besides collect and classify the material in the various archives." He would feel, he wrote, that "we had only gone half way unless we secure provision for a band of investigators, each with his comitatus of graduate student investigators, at Washington." Such an arrangement would stimulate historical studies in the United States and offer the historian the kind of research opportunity that the Geological Survey offered to geologists.[21] Expressing delight in 1903 that McLaughlin was to head the bureau, Turner noted that his only reservation about the recommendations of the advisory committee was its moderation.

Shortly after writing this letter, Turner inquired of McLaughlin about the possibility that a proposed program of research assistantships might cover the worthy young Wisconsin instructor, Dr. Ulrich B. Phillips, a man of "distinct promise as an investigator." He wondered whether perhaps his own work in diplomatic history might be worthy of support. McLaughlin responded that the future was still unclear. "Of course," he wrote, "I cannot promise that the Carnegie Institution will do everything that men like yourself and Jameson will suggest, but I am very desirous of having your continual assistance and cooperation."[22] Phillips soon received funding from the Carnegie Institution. Linked as they were in the councils of the AHA and its various scholarly activities and in their common interest in the developing program of the Carnegie Institution, Jameson, McLaughlin, and Turner traded lecturing invitations through these early years of the twentieth century.

Meanwhile, the officers of the AHA discussed other plans for enhancing the history discipline. Indefatigable planner and promoter Albert B. Hart proposed that the association should republish historical works that would find a broad readership. Turner was not enthusiastic, believing rather that the organization should promote "scholarship and investigation" rather than "popular wants." He was, he told Jameson, "more concerned about the large mass of unpublished manuscripts in Washington and elsewhere."[23] More useful, he believed, was the association's endorsement of a project to publish original narratives that the members of the AHA Council approved, selecting Jameson as the general editor of the series.

Winning Turner's hesitant support was another proposal from Hart, "much less a scientific contribution than might be hoped"—the monograph series that became *The American Nation: A History*.[24] In the end, that scholarly entrepreneur did not persuade the AHA to provide an advisory committee to assist in the project. But Turner and Thwaites were the leading members of a committee that the State Historical Society of Wisconsin established for this purpose.

Clearly, Turner participated actively in these exciting historical plans and projects of the early twentieth century. His advice was widely sought and highly valued, and some of the new ideas or departures within the AHA or the Carnegie Bureau grew out of the give-and-take of discussions in which he participated. The historical school or institute in Washington, D.C., which he considered "vastly more necessary than any school at Rome," did not materialize immediately, although a pale shadow of such an agency emerged before his retirement.[25] The atlas of historical geography appeared in 1932, the year of Turner's death. Administration of these, or other disciplinary projects, did not attract him. He disavowed any interest in replacing McLaughlin at the Carnegie Institution's Bureau of Historical Research. Turner excelled as an advice giver rather than as an executive.

Turner enjoyed the informal fellowship associated with work in professional meetings and associations. Such activity gave him opportunities to have meals with Haskins and other friends and swap gossip and good conversation. Free evenings at such meetings provided opportunities to go to concerts or to the opera as when Haskins and Turner attended a presentation of *Die Walküre*. Yet despite the social pleasures and the intellectual and professional benefits involved, activity in the councils of the discipline also carried costs. In the fall of 1902 Turner confided to Jameson that he could not afford to attend both the AHA Council meeting in November and the annual meeting in December. He recalled reimbursement in the past for travel on AHA business, but Jameson informed him that this had been provided in his capacity as a member of the Manuscripts Commission. Why, Turner wondered, was it necessary to have council meetings prior to the convention? The situation was quite different for those who lived on the east coast. "The effect of it," he wrote, "is either to limit membership in the Council to men of considerable means, or to throw a disproportionate control into the hands of the seaboard members," perhaps "a good thing, but . . . a little unfortunate for those of us who live beyond the Alleghanies."[26] In deference to such views, the council liberalized its reimbursement policy, and this action contributed later to a lively chapter in the history of the AHA and in the lives of both Turner and Jameson.

Members of later generations of American historians have thought of Turner as a scholar who produced an important interpretation of American history in his early career and then fell short of his scholarly promise and own ambitions. There is truth in such a view, but it understates the eventual number of Turner's publications and the breadth of his professional contributions.

During the years between the creation of the Wisconsin School of History and his departure in 1910 for Harvard University, Turner maintained an impressive level of professional activity, including the publication of a substantial volume of work. He contributed frequently to the *American Historical Review* or to the *Annual Report* of the AHA, edited a large volume of documents for the latter's Historical Manuscript Commission, prepared an important volume for the *American Nation: A History*, contributed to the publications of the Mississippi Valley Historical Association, the State Historical Society of Wisconsin, and the Minnesota Historical Society, placed several articles in the *Atlantic Monthly* and pieces in the *International Monthly*, the *World's Work*, and the *American Monthly Review of Reviews*, and prepared a number of short essays on various American immigrant groups for the *Chicago Record Herald*. It is true that a good number of these publications were not documented in scholarly fashion.

In 1901 the *Record-Herald* planned the publication of a series of short articles on the subject of American immigration. Turner contributed double-column pieces on Italian, French and Canadian, and Jewish immigration, and two little essays on German immigrants, as well as an account of the historical pattern of migration to the United States. These pieces were hack work, elementary surveys, but they revealed some of Turner's social ideas and qualify the critics who later maintained that he ignored the immigrant contribution. They also place Turner among the progressive intellectuals who deplored the character of the "new" immigration from southern and eastern Europe. Conceding some useful contributions, he continued, "It is obvious that the replacement of the German and English immigration by southern Italians, Poles, Russian Jews and Slovaks is a loss to the social organism of the United States." He would not, he wrote,

> discuss the various evils arising from this change in the quality of our immigrants. The lowering of the standard of comfort, the immigrants' competition which is counteracting the upward tendency of wages, the sweatshop system, the congestion of foreigners in localities in our great cities, where they become the troops of the local boss; the increase in crime and pauperism attributable to the poorer elements . . . and the anarchistic elements which are found among them—all these . . . are presented by this transformation of our immigration.[27]

Turner lumped Jewish immigrants in this general indictment and also considered them separately. He did not reveal the initial repulsion toward "Jewry" that he experienced during his first trip to Boston, and he described major aspects of Jewish migration to the United States with relative objectivity. However, he wrote, "They [the Jews] have made New York City a great reservoir for the pipe lines that run to the misery pools of Europe." He dwelt in some detail upon New York's sweatshops and the danger that clothing made by workers suffering from tuberculosis and other diseases constituted to the public health.

He repeated the racial stereotypes of Jews current among educated Americans of the time: "The Russian and Polish Jews are alert, thrifty to disgracefulness, keen to find a way upward. They have the traits of their race. Their ability to drive a bargain amounts to genius. They are nimble-minded, lucid and accurate in thought, quick to apprehension and generally devout followers of the Jewish law. But . . . the Jewish conscience has not emerged unscathed from the ghetto. . . . He has learned by . . . the discipline of oppression how to adapt himself to resist extinction by the Christians."

Turner believed that the American environment would allow the Jewish immigrants to improve their condition, although their religious leaders might impede the process. He noted that Jews had become eminent in the United States and held "important positions in all American universities." Some had reached the United States Congress. "That [the Jewish race] has yet a still more important part to play in American life cannot be doubted," he wrote. Although we find condescension here, we do not find overt anti-Semitism—indeed Turner maintained in his essay that the United States was relatively free from anti-Semitism. But neither here nor elsewhere did Turner display sensitivity to the immigrant side of intercultural processes.[28]

Turner contributed a solid survey of the development of the Midwest to the *International Monthly* in 1901 and published a short survey of education in the Midwest in the *World's Work* two years later. In the latter article he outlined the midwestern educational system and noted that the student numbers and expenditures almost equalled those of the East. There was, he maintained, "no more striking illustration of the democracy of the West than" that provided "by its educational system." He concluded with a ringing endorsement of the state university: "Here, if anywhere, is found a body capable of mediating between contending forces and of educating all classes into respect for law and order in the promotion of the higher interests of the commonwealth."[29] Turner provided a further illustration of his thinking of these years in the Phi Beta Kappa address that he delivered at Northwestern University in 1902 and published as "Contributions of the West to American Democracy" in the *Atlantic Monthly*. Turner began this essay by contending that previous writers had neglected the "underlying factors of historical development" in discussing democracy. Democracies, he argued, differed, and political institutions changed in the face of "underlying conditions and forces." "The forces that ultimately create and modify organs of political action" could be identified by examining the "social and economic tendencies of the state." In the United States "such profound economic and social transformation" was under way as to suggest that the nature of democratic institutions in the country might be affected.[30]

Turner pointed to four major changes that together "constitute[d] a revolution": the exhaustion of free lands; the "concentration of capital in . . . fundamental industries"; "expansion of the United States politically and commercially into lands beyond the seas"; and the tendency of political parties "to divide on issues that involve the question of Socialism." To understand the possible effects of these great changes, one must, he argued, "examine the conditions that have produced our democratic institutions." Thence Turner sketched the importance of the western or frontier regions in the development of American democratic institutions and ideology, using Thomas Jefferson, Andrew Jackson, and Abraham Lincoln to symbolize phases in the process. "The last chapter" involved American democracy's "conquest over the vast spaces of the new West" where in the arid lands, the "old individual pioneer methods" no longer sufficed, and cooperative activity in water use and "capital beyond the reach of the small farmer" were essential. "The old democratic admiration for the self-made man, its old deference to the rights of competitive individual development, together with the stupendous natural resources that opened to the conquest of the keenest and the strongest, gave such conditions of mobility as enabled the development of the large corporate industries" now marking the West.[31]

Now, maintained Turner, "the problem of the United States is not to create democracy, but to conserve democratic institutions and ideals. In the later period of its development, Western democracy has been gaining experience in the problem of social control. It has steadily enlarged the sphere of its action and the instruments for its perpetuation." Its system of public education had created a "larger single body of intelligent plain people" than anywhere in the world. The Democratic, Populist and Republican political parties all supported "greater social control and the conservation of the old democratic ideals." It was unclear, he thought, whether the new industrial leaders were "a menace to democratic institutions, or the most efficient factor for adjusting democratic control to the new conditions."[32] Whatever the outcome "of the rush of this huge industrial modern United States to its place among the nations of the earth," affirmed Turner, "the formation of its Western democracy will always remain one of the wonderful chapters in the history of the human race." In conclusion, he exhorted, "Let us see to it that the ideals of the pioneer in his log cabin shall enlarge into the spiritual life of a democracy where civic power shall dominate and utilize individual achievement for the common good."[33]

While Turner was refining his basic theories and using them to explain contemporary political issues in the periodical press, he was also concerned with more scholarly publications. As he had pointed out in his study of western state-making, the frontiersmen beyond the Alleghenies were establishing their settlements in a region still coveted by the English, French, and Spanish. The Draper manuscripts in the Historical Society included documents revealing the western policies of the rival powers and the efforts of their agents to find sympathizers among the American settlers. Given the efforts of the AHA Manuscripts Commission to edit and publish important manuscripts and documents and Turner's membership in that body, it is not surprising that he extended his research into the diplomatic history of the Mississippi Valley during the later years of the eighteenth century and edited a series of relevant documentary materials. From 1896 through 1905 Turner published eight documentary contributions of this sort, ranging in length from several pages to more than one hundred.

Turner edited correspondence between George Rogers Clark and Thomas Jefferson and between Clark and Edmond Genêt, documents relative to Clark's successful expedition against Kaskaskia in 1777–78, the correspondence of Michel A. Mangourit concerning Genêt's plan for attacking the Floridas, French documents relating to Louisiana, transcripts from the English Public Record Office relative to England's American policies of the early 1790s, and a collection of papers from American, French, and British sources relating to Senator William Blount's unsuccessful effort to direct a filibustering expedition against the Spanish Floridas. In this work Turner drew upon the holdings of the Wisconsin Historical Society and also used copyists to transcribe documents from British, French, and American official archives.

Turner's greatest editorial contribution for the Manuscripts Commission was his work on the *Correspondence of the French Ministers to the United States, 1791–1797,* a fat volume of more than eleven hundred pages. Worthington C. Ford and his brother Paul L. Ford had directed the copying of these materials in the French Archives du Ministere des Affaires Etrangeres and later presented them to the New

York Public Library. With the approval of the commission and the consent of the director of the New York Public Library, Turner edited the collection, adding supplementary documents.

As an editor, Turner provided introductory statements and notes that set the documents in historical context and directed those interested to other relevant collections. Although he included few of the wide-ranging or meaty notes typical of later major documentary projects, Turner's editing projects enriched contemporary scholarly analysis of the diplomacy relating to the Mississippi Valley and the American West. They also provided the foundation for scholarly presentations and articles in the *American Historical Review*, the *Atlantic Monthly*, and the *American Monthly Review of Reviews*, clarifying details and emphasizing the importance of the West as a factor in American foreign relations during the early national period. In 1904 Turner announced that he was finished with diplomatic history. It is perhaps ironic that he had spent so much effort in contributing to this field of American history. He always maintained that one of his major goals lay in moving western history beyond consideration of its diplomatic aspects. But the work amplified aspects of his research, advertised his contributions to the profession, and strengthened his relations with important figures in the profession, most notably Jameson.

During the early years of the century Turner continued to review books for scholarly publications. Since he seldom stated his views on the role of the historian, his review of Alexander Brown's study of *English Politics in Early Virginia History* is of particular interest. Although complimenting Brown because he had "transferred the center of gravity of early Virginia history from Pocahontas to the London company," as well as for other contributions, he criticized the author for writing from "the point of view" of the "patriot party" in its contest with the "court party." "Nothing is more dangerous to judicious and discriminating historical work," wrote Turner, "than to enlist on the side of a party." Later he asked, "Why should the case not be examined with cool-headed historical criticism free from 'viewpoints,' of any sort?"[34] In "The Significance of History" Turner had acknowledged "that each man is conditioned by the age in which he lives," that "no historian can say the ultimate word,"[35] but nonetheless exhorted the historian to search for truth. In reviewing Brown's work he seemed more optimistic about the possibility that the historian might achieve objectivity; at least Turner disavowed specific commitments—his act of faith lay in adherence to scientific method.

Written in 1903, Turner's last major review in the field of history appraised Woodrow Wilson's *History of the American People*. According to Merrill H. Crissey, Turner later told him that Wilson's reaction to this review convinced him that he should cease reviewing. It was, however, neither carping nor vicious. Turner began by contrasting Wilson's five small volumes with J. R. Green's survey of English history, noting the Englishman's emphasis on "the deeper undercurrents of economic and social change," whereas Wilson was particularly "a critic of politics, more at home in characterizing political leaders and the trend of events." Wilson's style was "often brilliant"; he especially tried to produce an "artistic literary form" rather than emphasizing "investigative results." Wilson's history was one of "interpretation." Turner did not agree that Wilson unduly sacrificed facts to style but suggested that "the stream of narrative too frequently runs like a rivulet between the illustrations." The latter frequently revealed "irrelevancy." But Turner commended Wilson on his "perspective and proportion." Whatever the criticisms, no other author had "in similar compass" produced "so sustained and vital a view of the whole first cycle of American history that rounded itself out with the nation's completion of the conquest of the west, and its step overseas into colonial empire." Although Turner concluded with a list of "errors of fact," he believed there were no more of these than was "common to first editions." Evaluating Wilson's interpretation of southern development, Turner suggested that he had insufficiently appreciated the degree of material and ideological change that occurred in the antebellum South.[36]

Crissey's account had its parallel in a story that Turner told to his former student Paul L. Ford. Having described James Schouler's multivolume history of the United States as "essentially commonplace," he was struck by remorse when he later met that sweet elderly gentleman at an AHA convention. Chronology weakens this incident as explanation of Turner's withdrawal from reviewing. He had probably met Schouler several years before he reviewed his history in 1896, and he continued to review books for quite some years thereafter. There are problems with Crissey's story as well. Wilson visited Madison in the spring of 1903 and described a most enjoyable visit with Turner. Wilson's book would almost certainly have entered the discussion but there was no contemporary hint that it was the focus of discord. If there was a drifting apart thereafter it was probably because Wilson's career traced a very different path than that of Turner. In an interview during his last few years, Wilson expressed the warmest of feelings for Turner.

Turner's critique of Wilson's book was not his last review. As we shall see, he published a review article of books by the geographers Albert P. Brigham and Ellen C. Semple. In 1906 he published a minor notice of Hiram Chittenden's study of early steamboat navigation on the Missouri River and a four-page review essay, "The Western Course of Empire," discussing volumes in Thwaites's series of western travel narratives, *Early Western Travels*. Fewer than thirty lines in length, the first of these pieces little more than summarized the aspects of western history covered in the book. In a few additional lines Turner challenged the picture of the relations between fur trader and Indian, provided by Chittenden's central character, as "somewhat idealized." Citing evidence of less happy aspects of Indian relations than those described, he ended enigmatically "however, the Indian at his best is a comparative statement after all."[37]

Thwaites had been his friend and ally for some twenty years when Turner reviewed a selection of narratives from *Early Western Travels*, one of Thwaites's most important editorial projects. Turner described his favorites in the collection, set them within the framework of western history, and lauded the importance of the project. The little essay is a restrained puff. So, six years later, was his review of the history of Wisconsin's Supreme Court by its chief justice, John B. Winslow.[38]

The interval between 1903 and 1906 perhaps reflects Turner's concentrated labors under the editorial whip of Hart, rather than any revulsion from the role of reviewer. But the Wilson review was Turner's last serious exercise in the art within his discipline. Wilson's reaction to the review of 1903 may have been sufficiently lukewarm that it alerted Turner—admittedly sensitive to political nuance—that bad reviews might erode cherished relationships. In part reviewing had been a means of spreading his ideas through the craft. By 1903 these were well known; he had firmly established himself within the profession. But up to and through the Wilson critique, Turner's reviews also demonstrated his keen critical sense, his ability to place historical contributions within a broad perspective, and his conception of the role of the historian. He was never unfair, but, as we have noted, was a keen critic, sometimes quibbling on matters of detail. His last reviewing efforts dealt with the work of writers outside the history guild or were favors for friends. It is fair to say that he did not adulterate the professional's tea with the milk of friendship until his review of *Early Western Travels*, and in this case the transgression was a minor one.

8　*American Nation*

*"I am quite ready, so long as I remain here, to turn from
the conduct of large graduate classes to the work of a few
and to my own investigations"*

After he recovered from his appendix operation in 1903, Turner's health improved, despite colds and the occasional "bilious attack." But he smoked so devotedly that family members expressed concern. As a result of his liking for good food and appropriate accompaniment, he had lost his youthful slenderness. During the early years of the decade he played tennis and golf and did some cycling, but fishing remained his great love along with the tramping and paddling associated with it. He would always believe that the outdoors was the best restorative of both body and soul.

There were to be no more babies after the return from Italy, and the bonds between Caroline, Dorothy, and Fred were extraordinarily strong. Dorothy had become a lively, outgoing teenager, and Turner tolerantly bore her struggles in Latin and geometry classes. Their ties outside the immediate family continued to remind the Turners of life's uncertainty. Mae's younger sister, Tirzah, was a charming and vivacious student at Wisconsin during Turner's early years of teaching. She died suddenly in 1901, leaving a desolate young husband.

Turner was devoted to his younger sister, Ellen Breese, "Breesie," during her years at home and as a student at the university during the early 1890s. After marrying a young industrial engineer, she lived with her husband in the Chicago area, and her home became a regular visiting place when the Turners were in Chicago. Turner's relations with his younger brother, Rockwell Lafayette Turner, were less close. Will Turner did not share his brother's interests. Neither Andrew Jackson Turner nor Fred seem to have completely understood Will, who was a railroad employee in Portage for much of his life. Politically, he was much more conservative than his brother, and Fred had reservations about Will's financial judgment. Turner, however, was hardly in a position to criticize his brother's views on money management. The note and mortgage on 629 Frances Street stood undiminished through the early years of the century.

Max Farrand became Turner's friend during these years. Farrand completed his undergraduate course at Princeton in 1892 and proceeded

Dorothy Kinsley Turner, about 1900. Reprinted with permission of the State Historical Society of Wisconsin, Madison, Wisconsin. (X3)908.

to graduate work both there and abroad. Captivated by Turner's frontier essay, he focused his doctoral research at Princeton on the American territorial system. Farrand took his Ph.D. in 1896 and began his teaching career that year at Wesleyan University. Apparently he and Turner first met at the AHA meeting in Cleveland in 1897. Thus began a strong and lasting relationship based on Farrand's admiration for Turner and his ideas and the fervent enthusiasm of both men for trout fishing. Although complementary in personality, they were not always on the same wavelength. Turner once responded to the gift of a humorous work from Farrand by confessing that he did not understand it, but, as the sick man remarked of the gift of brandied peaches that he could not eat, he appreciated the spirit in which it was sent. Farrand conducted a seminar in the Wisconsin summer session of 1902 and gave an extended course of lectures in the Wisconsin history department during the spring semester 1906. In a letter thanking Caroline for her hospitality, Farrand pictured a happy domestic circle— Turner contentedly seated in a Morris chair beside the fireplace, Caroline settling herself after attending to some domestic task, and Dorothy tramping through, perhaps accompanied by a youthful friend or admirer. Many years later Dorothy reminisced about evenings when Turner would read favorite poetry—that of Rudyard Kipling particularly lingered in her mind—to her and her mother.

The Wisconsin catalogues of the early twentieth century show a well-balanced offering of courses, including one on the methods of teaching history in schools, designed particularly for school teachers. Turner collaborated with Haskins and later with Munro in teaching it. Although reactions to Turner's performance as an undergraduate teacher were mixed, he continued to enthrall some students at that level. Selig Perlman recalled that in his year in Turner's class in western history, he and a little band of other professing socialists would coalesce at the foot of University Hill and proceed to class while excitedly speculating on the content of Turner's forthcoming lecture. In those days Turner's history was radical history. But Turner's particular interest lay in the American history graduate program. Here, the work of his students continued to enthuse him, although after 1903 none at Wisconsin won the Winsor Prize. Still the promoter and builder, he sought to increase the numbers in the American program, responding in friendly and detailed fashion to inquiries from prospective candidates. For example, a graduate student at the University of Nebraska, L. E. Aylesworth, explained that he hoped for a career in teaching history at the college level and asked for advice on the selection of a topic for his master's thesis that might be extended into doctoral study. Turner's typewritten response carried to a fifth page. He touched first upon the importance of students moving to new academic environments for graduate work. Aylesworth had expressed interest in the history of the territorial system, and Turner urged that he not allow Farrand's study of territorial enabling acts to deter him from developing a topic dealing with the territorial system.

Turner described to Aylesworth the "excellent" opportunities in the "field of immigration," suggesting travel in Europe to determine the causes underlying emigration of a particular group and examination of its later history in the United States. He outlined opportunities in the study of land policy, including administration of public lands and the effect of the railroad on western settlement. There were, he wrote, numerous opportunities in the study of political parties at the state or national level with regard to geographic distribution and social and economic factors. Or such analysis could be applied to the period of a presidential administration.

Aylesworth, Turner suggested, might prefer a topic that brought him "in touch with larger national problems" rather than a Nebraska subject. If he wished to work in Nebraska history, Turner recommended a study of "socialistic or Populistic sentiment," tracing it to its roots in population groups and classes and examining its manifestations in legislative and judicial decisions. "In other words," he would study "the socialistic tendencies of the United States as expressed in an agricultural population under the form of Populism" and "treat[ing] the subject as a special study of the large western forces in the interior of the country." Aylesworth, concluded Turner, should not hesitate to write him again.[1] This was not a unique exchange for Turner. In the role of graduate student advisor, as in his career generally, he was an inveterate but sensible advice giver.

By 1905 Turner was fretting that the history department was receiving too little financial assistance to attract as many promising candidates as desirable. In that spring he protested to Van Hise that the current system of awards did not "promote the growth of graduate work in departments whose resources and equipment result in exceptionally strong applications." In the recent competition there had been fourteen applicants in American history, including current fellowship holders and instructors in other institutions, as well as an outstanding young scholar from Radcliffe College, and others of somewhat "less reputation." He warned the president that it would be "impossible to compete on equal terms with rival institutions unless more than the assigned fellowship is at our disposal." The faculty, he reminded Van Hise, was not willing to assign appointments from the fellowship pool to departments or programs like history, which were guaranteed one such award. History had also been forced to ignore the candidacies of outstanding seniors. He was himself alleviating the situation somewhat by "agreeing to pay for the services of Mr. Buck . . . for next year" to assist "on some private work."

Turner suggested to the president that additional fellowships be assigned where there was "exceptional demand," and additional fellowships and scholarships created, or perhaps additional assistantships, exempt from tuition, should be assigned to departments with large classes and many applicants for graduate study. He was not complaining, he assured the president, merely presenting facts. "The *best* men" would not pay to study in a new program "when old and established centers will reward their superior ability by fellowships and scholarships." "Personally," he asserted, "I am quite ready, so long as I remain here, to turn from the conduct of large graduate classes to the work of a few and to my own investigations. Such an outcome would be entirely congenial to me."[2]

Historians at the University of Wisconsin have never considered the resources available for the support of graduate students to be adequate. Van Hise responded, rather unkindly, that fellowships should be allocated on the basis of quality rather than according to the numbers of applications per department. He wondered whether the historians received special favor in the rival departments that Turner mentioned. But he ended on a mollifying note. The situation was indeed unsatisfactory, and he planned to discuss it with Dean Birge. Given their friendship, the exchange between Turner and Van Hise is an interesting one. Turner was not completely satisfied, and in the phrasing "so long as I remain here" he introduced the possibility that he might not remain at Wisconsin.

Turner's dissatisfaction with the university administration also extended to its regulation of undergraduate social life. As elsewhere, the student body at the University of Wisconsin was sometimes disorderly. Freshmen refused to accept hazing rituals as prerogatives of the members of the sophomore class. Faculty efforts to control the practices produced ill feeling. Periodically students waged guerilla warfare against the Madison police. Football fever raged, and tumultuous celebrations followed in the wake of great victories. Turner became increasingly unsympathetic to hijinks that distracted undergraduates from their studies. He had criticized President Adams for coddling athletes. Nor did he believe that Van Hise was adequately firm in dealing with unruly students. After episodes of student rowdiness in the spring of 1904 Turner wrote to Caroline that Van Hise was

reaping the harvest of a long period of concessions to students, and especially of petting and glorifying the athletes. They have the idea that the University is for the students—& interpret this to mean that faculty &c are there to do their wishes. I mean the disturbing element has this idea. The general body of students is sound, but lacks somewhat in esprit de corps in such matters. . . . I fear that Van hasn't fully appreciated the need of having the "whiphand." He follows Adams & Birge in the process of conciliation & presents too much. They need law more than conciliation. But it is the vice of the day—there is a general failure to understand that the 'fear of the Lord' is the beginning of wisdom—

I speak as a man of the elder, cave-dwelling generation. I am glad
that you also are a 'cave-dweller.'[3]

In fact Van Hise and Birge were reasonably successful in coping with
student disorder, creating and coopting a student council that worked
to alleviate the situation. Athletics proved to be more of a problem.
During these years Alonzo Stagg, Fielding H. Yost, and other coaches
were laying the foundations of the modern collegiate game of football.
Training tables emerged, and football players were becoming campus
heroes. Alumni looked far and wide for outstanding players, and the
tramp athlete flourished. It appeared to Turner and other faculty
members that enfevered alumni and students thought of little else
during the midwestern fall but the coming struggle on the weekend.

As early as 1903 Van Hise began to discuss the athletics problem
with other presidents from the midwestern universities. Turner's
Frances Street neighbor, Slichter, was involved as a faculty representative in interuniversity discussions of athletic matters. Reformers argued
that supervision of athletics, recruiting practices, academic eligibility
rules, the length of the season, the professionalization of coaching,
ticket pricing, and the handling of athletic revenues required additional supervision. Van Hise arranged a reorganization of the athletic
association at Wisconsin, but the football season of 1905 so concerned
faculty members that they recommended appointment of a committee
to review the state of athletics in the university and to recommend
changes in policy. Turner, Munro, and Slichter served on this committee, which recognized that the problems extended beyond the bounds
of any one university. Its members requested Van Hise to ask James
B. Angell, president of the University of Michigan, to convene a
conference of delegates from the Intercollegiate League of the Upper
Mississippi Valley. In mid-January 1906 Turner attended this conference as Wisconsin representative. His instructions from the faculty
were to recommend that the meeting formally condemn the excesses
of collegiate football and suggest that intercollegiate games be suspended for two years so that "rational, moral, and normal relations
between athletics and intellectual activities may develop in each
institution."[4]

Shortly after returning from the conference, Turner spoke on the
problems of intercollegiate athletics at an alumni banquet. Everyone,
he said, recognized that athletics is an important part of university life.
"The only question is how to keep the system clean and in right

relation to the purpose of the university." In the mid-nineteenth century, he explained, athletics had been little emphasized. Now the situation was greatly changed. Where it was once proper to worry about the health of "pale and ascetic students in their cloisters," there was currently "fierce college rivalry," professional coaches, and "experts, fighting for victory on the football field." Increasingly the average student took his exercise "vicariously," at best in an organized cheering section. Turner sketched the delirium of athletics in major schools—recruiting, the "hide and seek" of professor and tramp athlete, the glorification of the football hero. "Human values" were "put in wrong perspective," the university's "fundamental purpose" ignored, "college ideals . . . distorted, while the high schools imitate and exaggerate the evils of the situation."

No wonder, said Turner, that the Wisconsin faculty had called for a "breathing space." Faculty members had never intended to ignore the wishes of alumni and students, but "leadership and final responsibility belongs to the faculty." At their recent conference, representatives of the "big nine," for the most part "experienced chairmen of athletic committees" all believed that "it is not . . . a question between modifying the game and leaving it alone. It is a choice between suspending the game as an intercollegiate sport or cutting away its evils." The Wisconsin faculty, he continued, was "fighting to sustain the higher mission of the university, determined that it shall not fall behind the moral sentiment of the community, that it shall not forget its obligation to the taxpayers of the state of Wisconsin."

The faculty, concluded Turner, had not considered abolishing intercollegiate athletics and understood the exhilaration of collegiate rivalries, "but the brutality of the game must go, mercenary professionalism, immorality, deceit, and corruption of student sentiment must go, and, in their place, must come a game that students can play, a game kept subordinate to the intellectual life . . . a game that leaves no slimy trail . . . no stain on the fair name of our alma mater." Students and alumni must not make the faculty alone keep football "free from taint and . . . within the bounds of moderation. They will cut it out, root and branch, if the forces of demoralization continue to vitiate the university atmosphere."[5]

Veterans of academic committee campaigns can imagine the many hours that Turner spent in talking about the athletics problem to colleagues, students, and alumni and in communication with like-minded faculty elsewhere. The conference convened by President

Angell prepared a long list of reforms that the delegates carried back to their campuses. Should they be rejected, the report recommended that a two-year suspension of intercollegiate football be implemented. As the situation developed, there was no moratorium. But under intense and sometimes angry pressure from some alumni and students— an effigy, presumably of Turner, was hung on Frances Street—Madison faculty members failed to support the full slate of suggestions. Farrand interpreted newspaper reports as indicating that Turner and the other reformers had been defeated. Turner, however, explained that they had in essence been successful. The football season was to be shortened by several weeks and other aspects of intercollegiate athletics purified.

Suspicion of faculty intent lingered among students and alumni, and during the fall of 1907 alumni and students became increasingly suspicious of the faculty's attitude concerning intercollegiate athletics. In early December it was Turner who submitted to the faculty a set of resolutions that disavowed any intention of abolishing intercollegiate athletics and affirmed support of the existing rules while at the same time reiterating opposition to "harmful practices and excesses." He then headed a faculty committee that worked with alumni and students to restore mutual confidence. Thus for several years the problems of intercollegiate athletics distracted Turner.

Meanwhile, Turner's professional reputation continued to rise. He had become a popular speaker in academic circles, sought both as a historian with an important message for his discipline and as a "name" for ceremonial occasions. Turner taught at Harvard during the spring semester of 1904, replacing Edward Channing, who was on leave. During that spring he spoke at the dedication of the John Carter Brown Library at Brown University. Both in 1903–4 and the following academic year, Turner delivered a series of lectures in the history department at the University of Michigan. His local reputation was perhaps at its highest in the years immediately following the selection of Van Hise as president. June 1904 brought the fiftieth anniversary of the University of Wisconsin's first commencement, and a "Jubilee" celebrated the occasion. Recently returned from his teaching stint at Harvard, Turner gave the "Address on Behalf of the University Faculty," and made it primarily a salute to the new president.

The Lake Mendota waterfront at the University of Wisconsin about 1904. Turner's home was adjacent to the lake on Frances Street, two blocks beyond the towered gymnasium building at the right of this picture. Reprinted with permission of the State Historical Society of Wisconsin, Madison, Wisconsin. (X3)50973.

University (later Bascon) Hill circa 1904. Turner regularly strode up this hill during his many years as student and faculty member at the University of Wisconsin. Reprinted with permission of the State Historical Society of Wisconsin, Madison, Wisconsin. (X3)50976.

As summer began in 1904, the three Turners journeyed west to Berkeley, where Turner taught in the University of California summer session. Then followed a delightful expedition with Farrand to a fishing camp, Glen Alpine, near Lake Tahoe. Fred and Max spent most of their days fishing while Mae and Dorothy stayed behind at the camp. A communal campfire in the evening produced fish tales aplenty. A side trip of a few days took the party still deeper into the mountains. The Turners returned to Berkeley for the summer session of 1906, stopping for a couple of days to view the wonders of the Grand Canyon on their way. Descending part way into this great chasm, Turner and his mule "pivoted amid sheer precipices that went down to the beginnings of things!" and, one morning, he "saw the world made at sunrise." But he was appalled that the authorities were replacing the names of scenic spots with those of "incongruous Indian tribes." The practice created "false ideas of Indian history and location," he wrote to Van Hise. He was particularly aroused by the pending action that would change Grandview Point to Pai-Ute Point, thus recognizing "the most degraded [sic] & disgusting and lo down aggregation of grass-hopper eating savages that disgrace the West."[6] He besought Van Hise to use his influence to have the policy reversed. Throughout his career Turner called repeatedly for study of American Indian policy. Emerging as an authority on that subject, Annie H. Abel told Turner that she had always believed that he knew more about her subject than any other historian in the country. She was probably correct in this impression, but Turner did not have a sympathetic understanding of tribal cultures.

Although the earthquake of 1906 had left life in the bay area much disorganized, the Turners again spent an enjoyable summer in California. Turner accompanied Berkeley president David S. Jordan on a visit to see Luther Burbank's horticultural marvels, participated in the "Jinks" of the Bohemian Club, and ended the summer with some weeks of fishing at Glen Alpine. From one of the California summers a photograph survived, showing Fred, Dorothy, and pack animal on a Sierra trail.[7] Turner wears slouch hat, neckerchief, and old clothes, but the urban dweller's sleeve garters glint in the western sun.

Ending his summer of 1904 in Berkeley, Turner entrained for St. Louis, leaving Caroline and Dorothy to return to the Midwest some days later. At various stops he mailed notes to Mae, advising her of educational vistas that Dorothy should note on their way east. He also provided details of his own trip and his impressions of countryside and fellow travelers, including an intriguing French couple—monsieur

Turner in his middle years on a Wisconsin lake. He is
seated in the stern. Reprinted with permission of the
State Historical Society of Wisconsin, Madison,
Wisconsin. (X3)934.

sporting the red rosette of the legion of honor in his lapel and madame
manipulating a capacious purse. The messages reveal Turner's inquisi-
tive and distractable nature; they do not report progress in completing
his paper "Problems in American History," which he delivered a few
days later before the congress of historians at the Universal Exposition
in St. Louis. The small but select audience included the distinguished
German historian, Karl Lamprecht and J. B. Bury from Cambridge
University, leaders in the reshaping of their fields of history.

Turner briefly noted the differences between the major tasks of
American and "Old World" historians. "Our problems with respect to
material are . . . not primarily those of the technique of verification
and criticism of scanty documents," he argued, "but are chiefly those
of garnering the scattered material, printed and written . . . rendering
available for historical workers the sources for understanding our

development." "What is the special significance of American history?" asked Turner. Its "peculiar importance," he suggested, was the opportunity that it gave "for understanding the process of social development." Then came a capsule description of the development of "a vast continent, originally a wilderness, at first very sparsely occupied by primitive peoples." His summary phrases must have been familiar to many of his hearers: adjustment of old institutions, creation of "new ideas of life and new ethnic and social types," "successive stages of economic, political and social development," and progression from the primitive to "highly organized civilization." In America, he added, "the factor of time . . . is insignificant when compared with the factors of space and social evolution." Loria was introduced and the stages of evolutionary social development compared to the rock strata mapped by geologists. But the simile, cautioned Turner, disregarded the repetitive nature of social development—processes still present in the "northern areas of prairies and plains in Canada."[8]

Turner again called Henry Adams to witness in emphasizing the United States as a unique field for the study of the development of democratic institutions. The major tasks of American historians, Turner maintained, were "not those of the narrative of events or of the personality of leaders" but those dealing with "the formation and expansion of the American people, the composition of the population, their institutions, their economic life, and their fundamental assumptions—what we may call the American spirit—and the relation of these to the different periods and conditions of American history."[9]

Within this great assignment historians confronted "a multitude of subordinate problems." For example, they would have to confront "the fact that the vast spaces over which this forming people have spread are themselves a complex of physiographic sections." "Impressed by the artificial political boundary lines of states," or such broad divisions as North and South, scholars had overlooked the "several natural, economic, and social sections that are fundamental in American historical development." "The American physical map may be regarded as a map of potential nations and empires, each to be conquered and colonized, each to rise through stages of development, each to achieve a certain social and industrial unity, each to possess certain fundamental assumptions, certain psychological traits, and each to interact with the others" in forming the United States. Explaining this process was the American historian's task.[10]

Physiographers had identified natural provinces and had recognized their importance, Turner noted, as had sociologists. But here was a great task for the historian to trace the development of these "natural, social, and economic divisions in the United States"—their colonization by various "stocks" and migration streams, "their economic evolution, their peculiar psychological traits, the leaders which they produced, their party history, their relations with other sections."[11] Turner illustrated the opportunities in this approach with particular reference to New England and the South.

Turner also outlined a number of general topics "as yet very imperfectly studied"—"the development of national character," or, in different phrasing, "a natural history of the American spirit," and a political history that would "penetrate beneath the surface of the proceedings of national conventions to the study of the evolution of the organs of party action and of those underlying social and economic influences in the states and sections which explain party action." Thus far the "agrarian history" and the land system of the United States had been "inadequately treated." The study of immigration beckoned the researcher, as did relations with the American Indian, the history of American law and religion, further development of labor history, the growing political power of the common people, and comparative study of settlement in other lands.[12]

If regions had been inadequately studied, historians had also failed to examine sufficiently various periods of American history. Eighteenth-century colonial history had been primarily examined "from its military aspect." The accompanying "transformations in . . . economic, political, and social institutions" required investigation. Lacking also were adequate accounts of America subsequent to the Reconstruction era. Perhaps "the first problem of all," Turner concluded, "is . . . how to apportion the field of American history itself among the social sciences." Few now considered history as merely "the history of past politics." Rather, "dominant" opinion held that history was "the study designed to enable a people to understand itself, by understanding its origins and development in all the main departments of human life." Such an approach required the "cooperation" of "many sciences and methods hitherto but little used by the American historian. Data drawn from studies of literature and art, politics, economics, sociology, psychology, biology, and physiography, all must be used. The method of the statistician . . . is absolutely essential." Lack of interdisciplinary cooperation had left "great fields . . . neglected", over-lapping grounds . . . uncultivated," "too many problems . . . studied with inadequate apparatus, and without due regard to their complexity." Physicists, chemists, and mathematicians had made great achievements by combining to attack problems of natural science. The "history of social development" required the use of "all of the apparatus needed" if "illuminating contributions" were to be made.[13]

Completed in true Turnerian fashion at nine-thirty on the morning of its presentation, the St. Louis paper was a "think piece." To one who reads Turner's work systematically, the social theory involved is all familiar. The research agenda that Turner outlined here was the strongest statement of needed investigation that he ever made. The paper also contained Turner's best definition of sectional processes to date and even included a call for the writing of intellectual history. His emphasis on the importance of studying sectionalism rather than frontier processes was important, although the scholar who followed Turner's prescriptions would certainly not ignore the latter. Neither thereafter would Turner, but his major interest henceforth lay in the phenomenon of sectionalism and its manifestations in American history. Critics suggest that Turner flubbed a great opportunity to proclaim a new progressive history that would adequately catch the spirit and needs of the age. Certainly he did not proclaim unalloyed belief in continuing progress or present a formula that would enable America to retain its unique democratic heritage. The element in his message that he saw as an integral part of America's future history was sectional interplay. That prediction or act of faith was indeed to be validated. The specifics of his research agenda were sound recommendations, followed by legions of researchers. Turner himself believed his St. Louis remarks sufficiently important that he placed them first in the collection of essays on sectionalism that he was assembling at the time of his death.

Turner ended his second term on the AHA Executive Council in 1904 and in that year chaired the nominating committee that proposed Jameson as second vice-president, the first step to the presidency. He was a member of the committee on bibliography thereafter, and at the annual meeting of 1907 he himself began progression through the vice-presidencies to the presidency. Turner and Thwaites hoped to entice the association to hold its annual meeting in Madison. They were not initially successful, but when the association met in Chicago in 1904, they invited their fellows of the Nucleus to visit Madison. Some, including A. Lawrence Lowell, William A. Dunning, Andrew C. McLaughlin, and Worthington C. Ford declined the invitation, but Archibald C. Coolidge, Charles Hull, Alfred L. P. Dennis, H. Morse Stephens, and Haskins journeyed to Madison for their annual dinner. They dined royally at the Thwaites residence—quaffed abundant champagne, enjoyed humorous place cards that Farrand had contributed, and had a fine time. Turner, somewhat befuddled, departed for home in the overcoat belonging to Dennis of the University of Chicago, an oversight rectified by railroad express.

In 1905 Jameson replaced McLaughlin at the Carnegie Institution. How, he asked Turner in October of that year, should the publications of the bureau be arranged in series? He visualized three of them, he explained—one involving "reports on archives or on other bodies or classes of material"; another "of lists, inventories, bibliographies, handbooks, atlases, or works of reference"; and a third of "books containing the text of historical documents." Turner suggested that the first two categories might well be combined and also inquired about the status of the American historical atlas, in which he was particularly interested. Jameson responded that he had kept this project in mind from the very first stage of Carnegie planning. In the previous year he had presented McLaughlin with a proposal to develop a plan for the work under the hands of Turner "and other experts," but his predecessor had not obtained approval for it. But Turner could rest assured that he would not discard the idea.[14]

Turner's efforts to produce the manuscript of a textbook during the late 1890s were unsuccessful, in part, perhaps, because of the stress of bereavement. But he still hoped during the early years of the century that he could produce manuscripts of book length. During 1901 he was negotiating with the publishing house of Houghton Mifflin. An earlier commitment to write a book for this firm, to be entitled "The Retreat of the Frontier," had as yet come to nothing, but Turner outlined plans for a short biography of George Rogers Clark in its Riverside Biography series. He would, he explained, describe the "characteristics of life in the 'Old West,'" the scene of Clark's boyhood, and sketch the Kentucky

and western background of his "brilliant military expedition into the
Illinois country." He planned to contrast this service with Clark's later
career of international intrigue, which "admirably illustrate[d] the
western radical separatist elements and their filibustering tendencies."[15]
Although he assembled a considerable cache of research notes for this
project and once pledged that he would complete it during the summer
of 1903, Turner agreed after several years to leave the field open to his
friend Thwaites. In the summer of 1902 he told Woodrow Wilson that
he was looking forward to the appearance of the latter's history of
the United States and commented ruefully, "As for me, I should be
delighted if I could get out any book with or without artistic embellishment; but I seem to be rather under water with university engagements most of the time."[16] Despite such frustration, Turner's pen was
not completely idle during this period of his career, as his contributions to diplomatic history show.

In these years also Albert Bushnell Hart set the stage for one of
Turner's major achievements, the completion of a volume in *The
American Nation: A History*. Hart was one of the leading academic
entrepreneurs of his generation. A prolific author, editor, and mus-
tachioed Harvard institution, he served as president of both the AHA
and the American Political Science Association. The planning and
editing of *The American Nation* in twenty-eight volumes was one of
his greatest achievements. When enlisting a distinguished corps of
authors, Hart decided that Turner must contribute. He explained to
Thwaites that Turner had described his writing commitments to him,
but Hart shrewdly understood that none of them would be finished
soon. "The brotherhood," wrote Hart virtuously to Thwaites, "has the
right sooner than that to call from him some rounded piece of work.
We need the results of Turner's studies . . . before it would be physi-
cally possible for him to prepare a large and extended work."[17] Hart
informed Turner that he had teased his peers too long with exciting
essays, edited documents, and enthusiastic verbal accounts of his
discoveries; now he must produce a book, and to what more distinguished company could he aspire? Although Turner reported to
Jameson in early 1902 that he was "praying not to be led into temptation," he capitulated, agreeing to produce a manuscript describing
American development during the 1820s.[18]

On a larger scale, preparation of *Rise of the New West, 1819–1829*,
duplicated a pattern that typified many of Turner's shorter efforts.
Initially he rummaged enthusiastically for information in the intervals

between other obligations, but composition was postponed until deadline loomed close. In this case there was much to divert Turner's attention. His growling appendix, operation, and extended recuperation complicated his schedule in 1903, when he was still ostensibly trying to come to grips with Clark and advance a volume on the frontier. His electioneering activities on behalf of Van Hise and the later negotiations that converted schools to departments in the university further convoluted his life. During the spring semester 1904 he taught at Harvard, replacing Channing, who was on leave. There were other lecturing engagements. These were also the years when he tried to put intercollegiate athletics in its proper place.

In preparing the manuscript of *Rise of the New West*, Turner, however, made a sustained effort unequaled during his later career, and focusing both his energies and those of his seminar members on the project. In late 1904 Hart informed Turner that the first wave of five books in the American Nation Series had appeared and that the next group was scheduled for the upcoming spring. Turner's volume was to be in the third wave, and Hart requested that he choose the portrait of a public man for the frontispiece and indicate the information to appear on the book's maps. Turner's reaction was apparently one of dismay at his situation. As the year 1905 began, he confided to Farrand:

> As my uncompleted books—*unwritten* would be more to the point!—loom up before my imaginative vision, I grow more & more covetous of the freedom from University work needed to bring them about and I am impressed by the idea that a man ought to have either the wealth of [James Ford] Rhodes or Henry Adams (with their pluck in sticking to their job) or University connection for only a part of the year, to enable visits to the various libraries and for writing. This breaks up the home life badly however, and I "guess" the best thing a man can do is to quit pipe dreams and go to work on that salvation of all needy professors, a kindergarten history in words of one syllable, phonetically spelled! I am certain that this is the only way whereby the profession can be saved financially.[19]

In the spring of 1905 Hart was turning the screw, and missives—sometimes letters and sometimes telegrams—flew thick and fast from Cambridge to Madison during the ensuing year. Hart was determined to send the book to the printer in the spring of 1906, and Turner set himself to the task of writing during the summer and fall of 1905. Observing Turner at work in these months, Phillips concluded that his chief found writing to be agony, and Turner admitted as much to one of his students, confessing that he was forced at times to alternate spells of writing at his study desk with frequent cigarette breaks and nervous pacing around the house on Frances Street.

By August Hart had some of the manuscript in hand. The first three chapters surveyed economic and social patterns within the nation's sections and related them to the political impulses of their residents. They "open a new vista," Hart exulted, and did successfully what McMaster had failed to do. The sketches of personalities, he believed, were "very graphic and very important." Although the manuscript was long overdue, Hart assured Turner that his chapters promised a book, "so meaty so judicious and so enlightening" that the waiting was well worth it.[20] After reading through chapter 8, Hart assured Turner that "no volume which has so far gone through my hands will do more to set in people's minds right notions of how things actually came about." Although he had "long known [Turner's] power of taking a particular problem, or question, or tendency, and throwing it up in broad relief," this was the first time in which he had seen "a larger subject grow under your pen." It was now late summer and Turner was pleading for a break, and Hart agreed that a rest might speed the writing process.[21]

On December 7 Turner wrote to his "dearest girruls," then visiting in Chicago, that he had completed the rough draft of his final chapter. "Ecco! Selah! Voila! Whoopla!"[22] When it was in the post, he might well, he assured them, drink the champagne surviving from the visit of the Nucleus Club. But Hart did not release his author. He believed that the narrative chapters, describing the flow of national politics during the years between 1819 and 1828, needed "careful review" to eliminate repetition and "to bring things into a little more consecutive order." Nor did the chapters on the Missouri Compromise and the Monroe Doctrine throw "into relief the immensely vital questions with which they are concerned." They reminded him of a neighborhood child's criticism of a little girl: "'She turns her toes in and she hasn't a bit of sparkle.'" Nonetheless, Hart predicted that "this piece of work will enhance the large reputation which you enjoy for scholarship and for insight. It is a suggestive, revealing kind of book."[23] Hart regretted that work on the book was in part responsible for keeping Turner away from the good times at the AHA meeting that year, but the loss, he believed, would be overbalanced by his joy when the last page proof was approved.

There were to be yet several months of revisions, proofreading, preparation of bibliography, review of maps, and other last-minute details before *Rise of the New West* could appear in print. Hart found the number of Turner's corrections on the galleys excessive and hoped that he would not change the page proofs. Turner, in turn, considered Hart's proposed editorial introduction inadequate. Hart quipped that it might have been easier had he written the book and Turner the editorial introduction. But finally it was done.

When Farrand commiserated with his friend about his trials under Hart's hand, Turner expressed admiration for his editor as well as gratitude. Although the fish might be sucker rather than trout, Hart had steadfastly brought it to net and at least made it look like a trout. "Still," Turner continued, "I really think Hart has helped me to make the book better, everything considered, and I think it only just to say this, in spite of my kicks, —and I rather like the little fish after all." He had, he hoped, "given in some respects a logical and occasionally a new interpretation to my decade."[24] Adding to the pleasure of achievement was the fifteen hundred dollars that he received from Harper and Brothers in return for his labors a sum swelled by an additional few hundred dollars because Jameson published chapters from the book in the *American Historical Review*, at a time when the journal was still paying for solicited papers. Frederic L. Paxson would later joke that the book might never have been completed had not the house on Frances Street desperately needed a new furnace. It was upon that improvement that Turner spent the payment from his publisher. But none can doubt that professional considerations were his primary motivation.

The dissertation and the collection of frontier essays aside, *Rise of the New West, 1819–1829* was the only book-length study that Turner published during his lifetime. In writing it, Turner explained, he had "kept before [himself] the importance of regarding American development as the outcome of economic and social as well as political forces." His "principal purpose," he continued, had been "to make plain the attitude and influence of New England, the middle region, the south, and the west, and of the public men who reflected the changing conditions of those sections in the period under consideration."[25]

Turner began the book with a short chapter entitled "Nationalism and Sectionalism, 1815–1830," in which he outlined the major trends of the period, identified the social forces then in play, and explained the book's organization. He noted the growing sense of nationalism that followed the War of 1812, the country's enhanced presence in the Caribbean, the recognition of the Latin American republics, and the enunciation of the Monroe Doctrine. Industrial America too was changing as the transportation network was "revolutionized," the factory system took hold, and cotton culture swept into the lower South. From the older sections, particularly in the South, as well as from Kentucky and Tennessee, a "flood of colonists" was flowing into the Mississippi Valley where "forests were falling . . . cities were developing . . . and new commonwealths were seeking outlets for their surplus and rising to industrial and political power." It was "this vast development of the internal resources of the United States, the Rise of the New West,' that gives the tone to the period."[26]

But this great economic transformation, Turner argued, inspired reaction in the form of protests against loose construction in both Congress and the Supreme Court decisions of John Marshall but "more significantly in the tendency of the separate geographical divisions of the country to follow their own interests and to make combinations with one another on this basis." "Sectionalism," explained Turner, "had been fundamental in American history before the period. . . . The vast physiographic provinces of the country formed the basis for the development of natural economic and social areas, comparable in their size, industrial resources, and spirit, to nations of the Old World. In [this] period these sections underwent striking transformations and engaged, under new conditions, in the old struggle for power." Political leaders must accommodate to the changing conditions within their sections and "if they would achieve a national career . . . make effective combinations with other sections." Under the "superficial calm of the 'Era of Good Feelings' . . . there were arising new issues, new party formations, and some of the most profound changes in the history of American evolution."[27] Turner quoted Henry Clay, John Quincy Adams, and John C. Calhoun to show that the leading politicians of the period understood the situation.

As Turner explained, the characteristics of the period dictated the organization of the book. He first surveyed the various sections of the country and the major interests within them. He used the "conventional division, into New England, middle region, south, and west," although aware, he explained, that internal subdivisions within the sections were also of great importance. But the larger divisions revealed "fundamental and contrasted interests and types of life," and "in the rivalries of their leaders these sectional differences found political expression." He admitted, however, that a sectional survey could not "fully exhibit one profound change"—the "formation of the self-conscious American democracy, strongest in the west and middle region, but running across all sections and tending to divide the people on the lines of social classes."[28]

After devoting chapters to discussion of the older regions, Turner next allocated four chapters to description of the development of the West, showing how the impact of the depression of 1819 stimulated discontent and led to a reassertion of state powers. He then wove the interplay of sectional interests into a discussion of major national developments and legislation through the 1820s. Turner ended his narrative with a discussion of Calhoun's "Exposition" of the doctrine of nullification in 1828. This statement was the "culmination of the process of transformation" examined in the book. Sectional alignments had hardened, and the people of the middle states "and those of the growing west were rallying around the man who personified their passion for democracy and nationalism, the fiery Jackson." His final sentence ran, "and on the frontier of the northwest, the young Lincoln sank his axe deep in the opposing forest."[29] The book contained a dozen maps, including ones depicting the spread of population, the distribution of congressional voting on key national legislative issues, and others charting the vote in the electoral college and the federal House of Representatives in the presidential contest of 1824 and 1825.

Rise of the New West, 1819–1829 represented a very important step in Turner's professional development. Here he laid out ideas that he was developing during the 1890s, setting them within the perspective of national history. As in his earlier writings, politicians spoke as sectional representatives, not because they were colorful characters, scoundrels, or involved in dramatic events. Nor did they represent virtue or evil, or God's will. This is a history essentially of mediation — the national government provided a stage where the spokespeople of the interests and "social forces" of the sections bargained the nation's future, particularly over the issues of tariffs, internal improvements, and slavery. The book contains striking passages and phrases—some carried through from earlier writings—but Turner could not sustain the rhetorical force of 1893 through a monograph of this length. The prose is mostly clear, workaday exposition; his efforts to enliven or embellish are sometimes florid. "Kentucky," he wrote, "ardent in its spirit, not ashamed of a strain of sporting blood, fond of the horse-race, partial to its whiskey, ready to 'bluff' in politics as in poker, but sensitive to honor, was the true home of Henry Clay."[30] As always in his discussion of American democratic ideals, Turner displayed an unfortunate tendency to mix evidence with simple assertion.

Rise of the New West, volume 14 of *The American Nation*, skillfully harvested the work of the first generation of academic institutional scholars and melded it with the documents of national and state governments, the contributions of local historians, antiquarians, biographers, and the scribblings of generations of travellers who tried to describe Americans at work and play. It was the most successful effort yet among American historians to break from narrative and presidential history, substituting an integrative analytical approach that related social and economic development and politics. It was a sharp contrast to those "shimmering pages" of Parkman that once had so impressed Turner. But Turner's prose compelled interest and conveyed a richer understanding of historical events than did that of most narrative historians.

The volume was also an intellectual milestone in Turner's development. Although he deprecated it as perhaps a sucker rather than a trout, he was justly proud of the book. Its preparation may have confirmed his growing belief that sectionalism was a more important and interesting phenomenon than the frontier process. The latter explained much about Americans and their institutions, particularly westerners, but to study sectional interplay was to study the nation as whole. And it was a key to the ongoing present and the future. His study, thought Turner, stamped its author as a historian of the nation and not a mere "leggins and breech clout" scholar or regionalist. Turner was disappointed by some of the early reviews of *Rise of the New West*, but Van Hise judged them to be highly supportive. He had, he wrote to Turner, "absolute confidence that your delay in undertaking large enterprises will not prevent your giving to the world the best and ripest fruit of your living appreciation of the great forces which have moulded the nation."[31]

Extracting a monograph from Turner proved to be a unique achievement—a deed, Hart boasted, fit for inclusion in his epitaph. The Harvard rumor that he motivated Turner by sending him collect telegrams was an exaggeration, but Hart's stream of editorial admonition was staggering. He was also Turner's friend and a professional eminence whose good will Turner highly valued. Breaking faith with Hart would have damaged Turner's reputation far more than failure to meet the deadline of a commercial publisher—a breed assumed ever ready to victimize academic authors. Failing in this assignment would also have shown Turner to be somehow less in ability than his many peers, also numbered among the authors of *The American Nation: A History*.

Early in 1905, as we have seen, Turner sadly referred to his "uncompleted books" in a letter to Farrand. This was a time of high frustration on that score. Turner even consulted Walter Hines Page about the possibility of exchanging academia for the life of the professional writer. As the year progressed and he faced the brutal necessities of meeting Hart's demands, his old friends at Holt and Company renewed their demands and blandishments. Knowing that Turner acknowledged the prior right of Ginn and Company to the grammar school text, Bristol explained that he and his colleagues assumed he was working on that manuscript. But could not it and the secondary school volume be developed at the same time by using a collaborator? Turner suggested that a feeler be extended to Farrand, but that wise gentleman was not to be ensnared. Bristol proposed that the matter should be taken up with Ginn and Company. When that firm proved willing to defer its claim on Turner, Holt and Company sweetened terms and suggested an immediate advance on the secondary school text. Turner promised to begin work on that project in the fall and in October sent this note to Bristol: "Two years from date I promise to pay Henry Holt & Co five hundred dollars for value received without interest. This note is given to protect an advance of five hundred dollars on royalties for a high school history which I have contracted to write for the said publishers." Turner's communication sealed an agreement that he regretted many times in years to come.[32]

The Wisconsin capitol sits on a slight eminence in the middle of the isthmus between lakes Mendota and Monona. From here State Street runs for approximately a mile westward to the more imposing heights of what, in Turner's time, was University Hill. This adjacency has both blessed and cursed the university. University spokespeople have found it easy to approach state officers and legislators, and the latter have benefited from the advice or service of faculty experts. But the processes of higher education have always been the subject of intense scrutiny from legislators, who realize that criticism of so important an institution can give them press coverage to a degree unrivaled by that derived from other legislative activity.

In early 1906 state senator George Wylie presided over a legislative inquiry on the subject of faculty teaching loads and remuneration from outside activities. Turner provided testimony. When the Madison *Democrat* reported him to have said that he received no royalties from textbooks, Turner decided to amplify his position in a lengthy letter to Wylie. For some years, he explained, he had had outstanding contracts with publishers, committing him to write a high school and a college textbook in American history. He had postponed preparation of these books to work on "*un*remunerative investigations in which I was interested." To placate increasingly "impatient" publishers, he had agreed to accept an advance on royalties and work on these assignments during the spring semester of 1906—months when he was entitled to a leave of absence under university practice because he had taught two summer sessions previously without remuneration.

Turner explained that the preparation of textbooks by faculty members benefited the university and the public. The author must consider his material in the light of pedagogical needs, which made him a better teacher. In writing a textbook that incorporated the latest knowledge in the field, the scholar was keeping learning on that subject "fresh and vital." "An able and ambitious man," wrote Turner, could "hardly be expected to serve universities if . . . limited in his income to salaries usually paid." During the last ten years he had "refused at least two publishers a year" who had "suggested remunerative royalties which were expected to aggregate more annually" than his current salary. He had also rejected the suggestion that he should abandon teaching and enter into an arrangement in which a publisher would provide him with advance royalties considerably greater than his present income. Thus far he had preferred to stay within the university setting. Institutions of higher learning should have places for men with ambitions such as his.

Little of the "really important historical *writing*" in the United States, he explained, was the work of men "*connected with universities.*" "To be a productive scholar in history, and to produce *a large work*, it has been necessary *not* to be connected with a university." This tended to "limit the historians to men of private fortune." Turner's course, he wrote, had left him "badly in debt. I have never been able to live on my salary, and this has not been due to an extravagant life." "Some of the most important universities of the country" had tried to entice him into their faculties by offering higher salaries than his remuneration at Wisconsin, but he had preferred to stay in Madison. One such institution was currently in informal contact with him, proposing to raise his salary and also to approve a yearly leave of absence for several months, allowing him "to carry on investigations in other libraries."

Turner concluded his letter to Wylie by discussing the advantages and disadvantages of requiring senior scholars to assume a heavier load of elementary teaching.

> Certain men in every great university . . . have developed their science to such a point that they are more useful in training juniors and seniors and graduates than in dealing with elementary students. It is an old adage that it is poor policy to use a razor to cut grindstones. To use the man who by training has brought his chisel to the point where he can do delicate, artistic, and creative work, in the rough-hammered stonework of foundations, is poor economy. On the other hand, he may well give some work to elementary students for inspiration and suggestion.

The use of such men for instruction at the lower levels would be too expensive to be practical. It must be recognized "that a university needs two types of men in its faculty: the investigator, who meets undergraduates in his classes, but whose main service is investigation; and the teacher, who keeps his teaching vital by investigation, but whose main work is with undergraduates." Requiring the creative investigators to carry heavier teaching loads would force them to go elsewhere, and hiring men of lesser renown to replace them would have unfortunate consequences in both teaching and university reputation. If instructors must forego "outside interests," they must be paid more. Involvement beyond the campus kept men from becoming "closet scholars" and vitalized their approach and thinking. "Perhaps," Turner suggested, "the main difference between the traditional college professor, supposed to be impractical, visionary, and out of touch with the world," and today's scholar lay "in just this tendency of the modern professor to mix up with the life of his fellows and to do his share of the work of the world while he does his teaching and research."[33]

Turner's letter to Wylie was frankly elitist; there were planets and moons in his firmament—artists who sculpted delicate and imaginative work and others who wielded sledges in the elementary undergraduate quarry. Division of teaching and research to this day produces envy, acrimony, and charges of unfairness in remuneration within faculties as well as complaints from students in the elementary levels that they are denied access to the best faculty minds. Turner saw himself as a creative investigator, a member of academia's upper class, but he was troubled by his failure to benefit financially to a greater extent from his position of leadership in the profession. That frustration stimulated his continuing efforts to improve his position so that he could produce the scholarly works he and others expected of him.

Turner's experience in writing *Rise of the New West* may have led him to be more realistic in evaluating his capacity for writing extended studies. In the years immediately following the book's publication, he told correspondents that he was focusing his major efforts on completing his contracted texts. But he also explained that he saw the need for a major study dealing with the development of the various sections and their relation to American development in the years between 1830 and 1850. This would be his major research project for the future and would lead him to focus intently on the nature of American sectionalism and the evidence and methods that might be used to illuminate it. This line of research would, Turner hoped, produce the "great book" that he had not yet written. However, the contracted texts and the great project may have worked at cross purposes within Turner's mind. Time spent in researching the patterns of nineteenth-century sectionalism was time unspent in writing the long-due texts, and frustration at his delinquency as text writer disrupted concentration on the great research project. And there were always departmental, professional, family, or recreational activities to distract Turner. At about the time of his exchange with Wylie, Farrand wrote to him, "It seems to be an impossibility for you to keep your hands off things in the University and in your department."[34] The semester that Turner explained to Wylie was to be dedicated to textbook writing failed to produce a book manuscript. And the "great book" of Turner's imaginings and hopes would be the ever-present challenge and also the millstone of his later career.

The institution courting Turner when he wrote to Wylie was Stanford University. His rejection of President's Harper's offer did not end speculation that he would move if the terms were right. After Herbert Baxter Adams died in 1901, President Ira Remsen of The Johns Hopkins University inquired whether Turner would consider a call to Baltimore. Turner quickly disclaimed any interest in moving. The family was still adjusting to its tragic losses and, if Frances Street held sad memories, the Madison community also symbolized supportive friends. Turner's professional future at Madison was bright, and Hopkins leadership in the social sciences was fading. A potential colleague in Baltimore was reputedly a difficult personality. Renewed urging from friends on the Baltimore faculty a year or so later failed to persuade him to change his mind.

Other university executives in search of leadership in history also looked longingly toward Madison, and in general Turner paid little heed. The case was different when two rising institutions on the West Coast expressed interest in him. The University of California and Stanford University had energetic and persuasive presidents in Benjamin I. Wheeler and David S. Jordan. In each case the history department included close friends of Turner who were eager to make him their colleague—H. Morse Stephens at Berkeley, and Farrand in Palo Alto.

The Turner family first sampled the California environment when Turner taught summer school at the University of California in 1904. The Turners believed that the severe hay fever attacks that Caroline endured in Madison made her vulnerable to other illnesses. She was pleased to find herself free of hay fever while in California. Turner loved the magnificent scenery of the mountain and coastal regions and the exciting opportunities there for the fisherman. He was also impressed by the happy futures that Wheeler and Jordan predicted for their institutions and the congeniality of their western historians. He was, however, aware of the deficiencies of the Stanford University library. This problem would be less acute at Berkeley.

By fall 1904 Farrand was urging President Jordan to build Stanford's library collections rapidly, not only for the general welfare of the institution, but because such action would help to attract Turner. The two friends had fished together that summer, and Farrand apparently had urged the Turner family to consider westward migration. He also charmed Caroline with his thoughtfulness on behalf of the women in their camping party. The intelligence that McLaughlin was not enjoying his work for the Carnegie Institution was rippling through the channels of the history profession, and Turner was mentioned as a successor. In late December Farrand wrote to Turner and urged him "to take no irrevocable step without giving me a fair show."[35] Prior to this exchange Stephens had written from Berkeley to tell Turner that President Wheeler believed that he already had an offer in hand from Stanford. He urged Turner to delay decision until he could talk with him at the meeting of the AHA in Chicago in late December. Stephens assured Turner that Wheeler could "duplicate" the Stanford offer and wished Turner to be able to make a fair comparison between the two institutions.[36] So Turner entered the year 1905 with two attractive California suitors in train and in June told Haskins that he planned to write him "of some of my problems on which I wish your advice, for I shall probably have to settle some important questions for the future in the next few months at most."[37]

Once more Turner was in the enviable but stressful situation of comparing the pros and cons of his position at Wisconsin with what he might find elsewhere. Farrand and Jordan were more aggressive than the Berkeley men at this time, and, like Wilson and Harper before them, they found in Turner a man who was adept in the art of advancing one foot while withdrawing the other. There was Stanford's weak library and Wisconsin's strong one to be considered, as well as Caroline's hay fever, Turner's salary, his privilege of taking a semester off at full pay in return for teaching two summer sessions, the secretary available for "personal as well as official use," and other Madison amenities. But he had a family for which he must provide, his house was mortgaged, and he was indebted against his insurance to the amount of several thousand dollars. However, he assured Farrand, "the fascination of California is still strong. I am not sure but that I have done my work for Wisconsin." Possibly, he continued, it was unnecessary to decide at this point—perhaps the whole matter might be postponed for a couple of years.[38]

By mid-December 1905 both parties appeared willing to let matters drift for the time being, although in early 1906 President Jordan expressed interest in soon seeking the approval of his trustees. Turner had informed Van Hise of Stanford's interest, and the latter tried to make Turner's position more attractive by having the regents allow his friend to teach one semester yearly and use the second for research and writing, with the understanding that he could pursue the latter activities away from Madison. Interest in Turner at Stanford remained keen through the winter of 1906—specifics were discussed when Jordan visited Madison in March. Then an earthquake destroyed most of Stanford's campus buildings. Jordan wrote to Turner, asking him "to let our matter rest in abeyance. . . . I cannot at least for the coming year make any additions to the faculty. It is my hope, however, that the time will come when you can be with us."[39] Turner, the environmental theorist, had received a practical demonstration of the impact of environment upon the designs of human beings.

The Stanford negotiations worked to Turner's advantage in Madison. Van Hise's efforts were successful, and the day before Jordan wrote his apologetic letter, the regents instructed their secretary to inform Turner of their approval of the resolution:

> in order that Professor Turner may advantageously carry on the very important investigations in history upon which he has been engaged for many years, and put the results of the same into form for publication, that he be relieved from instructional work for one semester in each year, or such part thereof as may be necessary to that end, with the understanding that so far as advisable, he may carry on his investigations at other places than Madison.[40]

Actually, Van Hise had obtained approval of this formula in the appropriate subcommittee of the regents in January and told Turner to take his time in considering it. Turner explained later to Farrand that the passage of the resolution on the day before the earthquake determined his decision to stay at Wisconsin. But why in the negotiations with Stanford University did Turner keep Farrand in suspense for several months after he understood what the regents proposed to do? Apparently he feared that Van Hise, friend and confidant, as well as university president, might accept an invitation to direct the Smithsonian Institution. The regents, however, lightened the president's administrative burdens, and Turner served in the "astonishingly unsuitable" role of toastmaster at a banquet celebrating Van Hise's decision not to seek the Washington post. He had, Turner confessed to Farrand, no more qualifications for his assignment as master of ceremonies than had Farrand "to run a prayer meeting."[41]

With Stanford repulsed, or so Van Hise hoped, Turner had exposed himself once more to temptation by returning to Berkeley for another stint in the summer sessions of the University of California in 1906. He had been "in a mood for moving" during that year, he told Farrand early in the next year. But with the regents' commitment in hand and Van Hise still ruling University Hill, Turner still failed to put the possibility of migration from his mind. "I am not vain enough to want to keep myself in your eye permanently with reference to a Stanford appointment," he assured his friend but then continued, "on the other hand I find the nomadic arrangement of mine not easy to carry out. Mrs. Turner came home this fall, and hay fever took possession of her and stayed until far into November leaving her far from well. Now we shall have to shut up our house, lose our cook (!) and go away from Madison from February 15 to May 15, to avoid wasting my leave by demands on me here, and also to avoid the trying spring for my wife. Then again in August we must take up the march once more, and Mrs. Turner cannot safely return until mid November."

Settling at Stanford University would, thought Turner, alleviate Caroline's hay fever problem, although they were as yet uncertain as to the effect of California's winter months. They had hoped to spend a month of Turner's research leave there during the spring semester of 1907 to test the climate and explore the library facilities, but this had proven infeasible. On the other hand, wrote Turner, Wisconsin had been "very liberal" in approving his research "arrangements," and he was "conscious of the great advantage I get from a seminary of graduate students who bring home to me the spoils of the rich library day after day." He should "try the situation out [at Stanford] for a month or so." How long, he wondered, could "the question remain in its present state?"[42] In response, Farrand reiterated Stanford's interest in Turner and suggested that Turner's research arrangement in Madison could be duplicated in Palo Alto. By this time also, Turner's most important personal ties had been severed in Wisconsin. In 1905 members of the business community of Portage closed their doors on the afternoon of Andrew Jackson Turner's funeral, and Mary Hanford Turner died in the following year.

In 1907 Turner tested his new freedom to undertake research off campus during the school year by spending much of the spring semester in Washington. Arriving there at the beginning of March, the Turners established themselves at the Marlborough Hotel in a suite of rooms recently vacated by a western congressman. Herbert Putnam, the librarian of Congress, put an alcove and other facilities at Turner's disposal, and here he dug into the Van Buren, Jackson, and Polk manuscripts, as well as the newspapers of the 1830s and 1840s, the years that he planned to cover in the "big book" to come. At times also he drafted sections of the history of the United States which Holt and Company was so eagerly awaiting. He usually took lunch at the Round Table in the library where Putnam presided, and Turner chatted with scholarly civil servants, local faculty, and visiting celebrities. He met Gifford Pinchot and twice chatted with Lord Bryce, whom he urged to attend the meeting of the AHA in Madison in the forthcoming December. He listened while locals criticized the "Roosevelt cult," but Madison remained much on his mind. Van Hise asked him to go New York to address the Wisconsin alumni there, and there was frequent interchange of letters with department members in Madison. Before the semester was over Turner was back in Madison participating in the graduate examinations and other departmental business.

During the first half dozen years of the twentieth century, Turner's professional activity and accomplishments were considerable. He had published articles in respected magazines and scholarly publications. As both author and editor he had made a significant contribution to American diplomatic history. He had published a monograph, notable in organization, conceptual approach, and method. He had fleshed out the disciplinary agenda that he had begun to build in the early 1890s. Conversely, he had also agreed to write a small family of books, and yet only Hart, uniquely talented and placed, persuaded him to fulfill his commitments. In fact, Turner's optimistic aspirations and the realities of his position and work habits did not match. He was a highly distractable man who loved to play the advisor and oracle—in letters to prospective graduate students and his professional peers, in conversations with students and colleagues, in endless committees and meetings. While trying to build a preeminent history department, he involved himself in broader issues of policy in the university. He was active in the discipline's leading association and in planning the profession's future. He was interested in the teaching of history in the public schools. Visiting scholars found in him a genial host. He loved to rummage in the library on fact-finding expeditions, at the expense of time spent at his desk writing. He was a member of numerous university or community groups or clubs and was committed to substantial vacations. There was also family tragedy and sickness to disrupt routines and contemplation of research. Nevertheless, Turner remained committed to his objectives of writing books—both texts and research monographs. Successful completion of *Rise of the New West* gave him new hope that he was capable of doing so. It was, he would prove, an unrealistic conception. In sober moments Turner perhaps realized the fact. But when doubts possessed him he blamed the Madison environment and thought of becoming a professional writer or moving to a more congenial environment.

Meanwhile, the Wisconsin department continued to grow and prosper. When it became possible to make a middle-level appointment in European history in 1905, Turner and Munro selected Alfred L. P. Dennis from the history department at the University of Chicago. It was Dennis who in 1901 had obtained the writing assignment for Turner in which he prepared sketches of immigrant groups for the *Chicago Record Herald*. Primarily a specialist in British history, Dennis also was much interested in relationships between European and far eastern nations. Fish and Sellery were proving to be outstanding teachers of undergraduates, and Sellery also displayed talent as an administrator. Phillips's work indicated that he might become an outstanding research scholar. Other major schools sought to lure these men away, and Turner urged promotions and salary improvement as a means of keeping them.

Although student fellows and scholars came and went, as fellows and scholars do, other changes in personnel in the history department were few during the mid years of the twentieth century's first decade. Tilton, however, withdrew from the department to take charge of the public documents collection in the Historical Society. Another instructor was found to replace him. Through the 1890s Turner had, in effect, given Haskins an equal voice in departmental decision making. So was it also after Munro replaced Haskins. Munro had a talent for administration and acted as chairman while Turner served as a visiting professor at Harvard University during the spring semester 1904. Munro also administered the summer school for a time. With the arrival of Dennis, the senior partnership became a triumvirate, and Dennis served as departmental chairman beginning in the spring semester 1907. Turner's commitment henceforth was ostensibly to be to teaching, research, and the needs of the American history program. But at Wisconsin his restless mind refused to recognize such restrictive boundaries.

Once back in Madison in 1907 Turner urged Van Hise that a salaried editor for the university bulletins be established and later inquired whether "a good deal of the work now done by committees in *term* time might not be handled by administrative chairmen, or deans, with consultation and some mode of publicity where important issues arose, and advice was proper." The new faculty club house he believed, however, would somewhat ameliorate the "irritation" of "too much formal debate in committee rooms." Van Hise professed willingness to have Turner work out and present a plan to the faculty "looking toward greater administrative efficiency" but was skeptical about its reception. The faculty had become "red haired" at a recent suggestion that a director be appointed to administer a program, preferring a committee instead, and in addition tended to interfere in the work of committees and second-guess their recommendations.[43] Despite such expressions of interest in the welfare of the university, Turner was becoming increasingly frustrated by the demands of his situation, and his discomfort with his surroundings and his place within them would climax during the next several years.

9   Departure

*"So my quarter century of work at Wisconsin closes up
and what is writ is writ"*

The years 1907 through 1910 were a time of domestic tranquility for
the Turners. There were no deaths within the immediate family circle,
and relations with their faculty friends remained close. In the late
summer of 1907 Turner arranged a family canoeing vacation at
Temagami in northern Ontario where Van Hise hoped to rendezvous
briefly with him. The expedition was a mixed success. Both Turner
and Dorothy became ill, and the youngest member of the family so
severely that she was carried across the portages on the return to base.
Undeterred, the Turners arranged to spend a month of the following
summer canoeing and fishing with Charles and Janet Van Hise and
their daughter, Hilda, to the west and north of Lake Superior in
Canada. In preparation Turner bought a new canoe and a Remington
"Special" rifle with three hundred rounds of ammunition. He recorded
details of fish caught and moose and bears sighted on this outing in a
long and happy letter to Farrand. Caroline's memories were less happy.
As the expedition neared its end she was suffering from a cold, and she
had sprained her arm in trying to cast flies; the campsite was malodorous. She wished, she recorded, that she was safely at home. That fall,
Turner began suffering abdominal discomfort and learned that he must
wear a truss to alleviate the problem. He grimly contemplated—so he
said—a future in harness.

In Madison, Caroline continued to be an exemplary hostess. Taste-
ful flower arrangements invariably greeted her dinner guests, and the
picnic expeditions that she loved were as carefully organized as an
African safari. The long-continued efforts of Turner, Thwaites, and
Munro to bring the AHA to Madison for its annual meeting were
finally successful in 1907. The organization held its meeting there in
December. Dennis served as program chairman, and the Turners
entertained a formidable number of history notables during the course
of the meeting at reception, luncheon, or dinner. During one of the
functions the Turner range rebelled, and Caroline won plaudits for the
pluck that she showed in improvising and successfully feeding her
guests.

All too conscious of his unfulfilled writing commitments, Turner became increasingly content to see others perform departmental administrative tasks. Under the arrangement of 1906 he took semesters of research leave in the following two years. But when not teaching, he kept in close touch with developments in the department. While in Washington during the spring semester 1907, he exchanged frequent letters with Dennis, the acting chairman, and Fish, making it clear that he expected his views on the proper distribution of graduate awards to be honored. Since Turner's opinions on such matters were changeable and Fish was somewhat at odds with Dennis, the young Americanist spent a frustrating semester. Dennis continued to serve as chairman, but Turner felt obligated to remain in the teaching cadre during the spring semester of 1909 because of the resignation of Phillips and leave granted to Fish.

Turner made few changes in organizing his seminar instruction after 1900 other than usually having his classes work together on subjects focused within the same presidential administration. Emphasis continued to be on the search for information and the evaluation of its reliability, rather than on the philosophical problems of writing history. Homer C. Hockett described Turner's teaching method during the new century:

> The topic was the same for the whole group . . . and each student was assigned or chose a phase of it which could be studied from source material. What the appropriate material was, each student was supposed to know, or to know how to find out and how to handle. . . . Reports were read and criticized by the group — not very acutely. Sometimes they were written, sometimes given from notes. Turner's theory seemed to be that one learned to use the tools by cutting one's fingers with them rather than by formal instruction. Lack of training in critical method is what I am most conscious of as I look back.[1]

During 1904–5 the members of Turner's seminar investigated the nullification movement of the early national period, and one student remembered "search[ing] the documents and old newspapers for every thought which contributed to Nullification." Another of Turner's later students, Jane I. Newell, recalled the seminar experience as one in which she found no "definite concrete information or neat, satisfying theories about this or that," but instead spent her time accumulating facts, "becoming acquainted with books . . . finding out where information was *not*" and learning to suspend "judgment when evidence was lacking."[2]

Another of Turner's students, Edgar F. Robinson, completed his master's degree in 1910 and later recalled that "somehow at Wisconsin concrete and imagination were well mixed." Somehow too Turner impressed his stronger students with the excitement of academic life and inspired emulation. "Once in my freshman year I saw—one evening—" wrote Robinson, "you and Professor Fish and Munro— walking down *or* up—State Street at a break-neck speed—toward the square about 5.45. Whether you were making the post-office before closing or merely taking a joint constitutional after seminar—I do not know—but I like to remember it—as one of the first impressions of a world I so much desired. I miss that '*movement*' here."[3]

Between the time that Turner assumed the role of director of the Wisconsin School of History and the end of academic year 1909–10, thirty-two graduate students completed the master's program in American history and thirteen successfully defended doctoral dissertations. During this period Turner and his colleagues increasingly chose to accept creditable bachelors' theses in lieu of a master's essay. However, most of the students electing this option had developed topics of particular interest to Turner. Those writing theses studied social and economic factors in local Wisconsin development, the impact of southwestern Indians on international relations in the mid-1790s, French minister Pierre Auguste Adet's mission to the United States, abolition petitions in Congress, politics in the press during the Monroe and Adams administrations, and antebellum northern sentiment on black suffrage. Others examined Vermont during the American Revolution, Alabama during the 1820s, the early history of Oregon, Stephen A. Douglas and popular sovereignty, literary leadership in New York and New England, early internal improvements in New England, land legislation in Georgia, the Populist Party, Tennessee politics during the Jackson era, and political groupings in the Twenty-second Congress. Turner handled the major share of the direction of these studies, and during his great confrontation with the rising West, he focused course and seminar work particularly on the issues that he was treating in the book.

Among the doctoral students at Wisconsin after 1900, Louise P. Kellogg studied the colonial charter, Carl Becker examined political parties in New York during the Revolutionary era, Amelia C. Ford investigated colonial precedents for the national land system, and Robert C. Clark wrote about colonial Texas. But most of the dissertations dealt with nineteenth-century America. Among the students examining aspects of institutional political history, Charles McCarthy analyzed the Anti-Masonic Party. John L. Conger investigated the South Carolina nullifiers, Joseph Schafer described the acquisition of Oregon, Royal B. Way studied the issue of internal improvements during the Monroe and John Q. Adams administrations, Charles H. Ambler dealt with sectionalism in antebellum Virginia, and Melvin J. White defended a study of the secession movement, 1847–52. Reflecting Turner's interest in western economic development, William V. Pooley studied the settlement of Illinois, 1830–48, and William J. Trimble examined the activity of the miners in the western inland empire of the late nineteenth century.

The Wisconsin history professors, particularly Turner, were also members of doctoral committees within the disciplines of economics and political science as well as directing the occasional student of sociology or literature. At least twenty-nine doctoral candidates in such disciplines prepared one or more history fields during Turner's Wisconsin tenure. Thus Turner was involved in the development of Benjamin H. Hibbard's study of the development of agriculture in Dane County and in the preparation of other studies that became standard references in institutional economic history.

Turner's influence as a graduate director extended beyond the circle of Wisconsin degree holders. Herbert E. Bolton studied for the bachelor's degree in Madison during the mid 1890s and enrolled for a year of graduate work there before moving to the University of Pennsylvania for the doctorate, but he sought advice recurrently from Turner in the years when he emerged as the acknowledged authority on the southwestern borderlands. Arthur C. Boggess also completed his doctoral study of early Illinois settlement at the University of Pennsylvania, but he had begun to develop the topic as a bachelor's thesis at Wisconsin. Master's candidates who studied under Turner did outstanding work elsewhere. Clarence E. Carter, for example, won the Winsor Prize of the AHA in 1908, honorable mention going to the Wisconsin entrant, Charles H. Ambler. Edgar E. Robinson and other members of Turner's seminar at Wisconsin never completed the Ph.D. but enjoyed productive careers in the profession nevertheless. Young historians responded to Turner's message and charm when he lectured at the University of Chicago, Harvard, Berkeley, the University of Michigan, and elsewhere.

The work of Pooley, Trimble, Schafer, and others showed Turner's continuing interest in topics that examined social, economic, and diplomatic aspects of western expansion. But his graduate advisees at the University of Wisconsin in general developed research topics that focused on politics and political sectionalism rather than engaging in the studies of frontier development that he had called for in the famous essay. At the president's request, Turner wrote in mid-June 1908 to Van Hise about the successes of his graduate students. In detail he listed those who had won the Winsor Prize with dissertations prepared at Wisconsin and other prize winners who had studied with him elsewhere or who had won the award after leaving Madison for further training. He noted that one of the winners of the Herbert Baxter Adams Prize in European history had developed his field of research originally in bachelor's and master's essays at Wisconsin. He could not take all of the credit for such achievements, he wrote, for these had been investigators of natural ability, and they had benefited from the tutelage of Haskins and others in the department. But he believed that these young scholars reflected the "special intellectual interests . . . a certain attitude toward . . . problems . . . [an] attention to research," and the availability of library resources at the University of Wisconsin. He quoted Albion W. Small, who had referred to historical study at Wisconsin as "the most distinctly American school of history which has developed in the United States," where "Professor Turner . . . has . . . been studying American history in terms of the interests which have contended with each other for political and industrial power."

If there was a "Wisconsin idea," continued Turner, another "line of interest" was also included in it, "the Western movement of American society and its effects upon the nation." This was "more generally recognized as our contribution than the study of opposing sectional interests *per se* or the emphasis upon economic and social interpretation." But in a draft of this letter he had described the direction of his seminar from the late 1890s as "the study of economic and social interpretation of our development in limited periods." And in ending this letter to Van Hise, Turner also noted his role in preparing a bevy of bright young economists who were making a distinguished mark in their field as well as many lawyers and teachers who were helping to shape the development of Wisconsin and the nation.[4]

Observers stationed elsewhere in academia recognized the implications of Turner's work at Wisconsin. Jesse Macy, of Grinnell College, reacted to one of Turner's book reviews, emphasizing the need of a history of American political parties and asserted that he knew "no one so well equipped to produce such a history" as Turner. "The work already done at Madison makes it peculiarly fitting that the standard history of our Party System should come from that institution. . . . In some way out of the work done by yourself and Mr. Libby and many others of your students there should come a thorough history of the great organs of mediation between the American citizen and his government."[5]

Turner's students developed quantitative mapping techniques and analysis in American historical research that were genuinely innovative. Turner's initial contribution to such methods lay in his recognition of their value and the encouragement that he gave to students to apply them. He did not himself do such research in his early years at Wisconsin. Libby demonstrated the usefulness of mapping both electoral and legislative roll call data and other students aided in the task of discovering the contemporary boundaries of local political districts during the early national period, as well as correlative social and economic information. This was a historical exercise of some magnitude. As we have seen, Turner was an early and enthusiastic proponent of the historical atlas project at the Carnegie Institution.

Interpretation of the maps and data was a fascinating challenge. During the 1950s a new generation of quantitative political historians began to analyze the roots of political action and were impressed by the effect that religious affiliations apparently had upon political behavior. They would have been astonished to read a letter from Anson E. Morse to Turner in early 1904. Morse had been pursuing research in Madison and sent maps to Turner showing Federalist voting patterns in Massachusetts and Connecticut. Included in his analysis was an effort to test the hypothesis that the presence of Congregational ministers predicted federalist majorities and that of Episcopalians and dissenting ministers reflected the dominance of democratic republicans. Morse reported that his predictive test was not uniformly successful, although it "work[ed] out better in western Massachusetts."[6]

While Turner was writing *Rise of the New West, 1819–1929*, a promising young graduate student, Solon J. Buck, served as his assistant in preparing two national electoral maps of 1824 and 1825 and a number exhibiting voting within the House of Representatives on key issues of the period. Buck explained his procedures for determining constituency boundaries in a communication to Edgar E. Robinson, who applied them in studying the United States Congress of the early 1830s, and so the expertise of the Turner group grew. By at least the time that he completed his contribution to the *American Nation*, Turner was highly committed to analysis of electoral maps in his own research. In 1907, in a presentation to the members of the American Sociological Association, he used maps of party county pluralities in arguing for the continuance of political sectionalism in the United States.

These were exciting years. Graduate student after student was demonstrating that Turner had introduced them to highly productive fields of research. Their work, in turn, enhanced his understanding of American history. He offered to summarize the research being done under his direction when John M. Vincent invited him to visit the Hopkins graduate seminary in 1907. Studies of settlement in the western states, he explained to a correspondent, allowed one "to better understand the evolution of institutions, the formation of society, and the resultant political attitude" in "great sections of the country." He was becoming "more and more convinced that any scientific history of society, political parties, industrial development, etc., must depend to a large extent upon the basal study of the movement of population into the western environment."[7] Charles H. Ambler's study of sectionalism in Virginia, he informed the Macmillan Company, was "an interesting example of the newer mode of historical approach to the political and institutional aspects of our development by interpretation of the underlying social, economic, and geographical factors."[8] Only those who in some sense have seen research in their seminars vitalize and change their discipline's stock of knowledge can fully savor the exhilaration that Turner must have found in his "workshop" during the first decade of the twentieth century.

Whatever the meaning of the Libby chapter in Turner's life, his amiable and supportive relations with a number of graduate students developed into lifelong friendships. This was particularly the case with Carl Becker. Although Becker enrolled in the Wisconsin graduate program after receiving the baccalaureate degree, he did not complete the requirements of the master's degree there. Turner helped him to obtain aid at Columbia University for further study and later supported him in his search for other positions. After Becker had settled into a teaching post at the University of Kansas, he decided to complete the doctoral requirements at Wisconsin rather than at Columbia. Turner willingly sketched out the rather elastic requirements he was expected to meet, but, at least as far as their correspondence reveals, he seems to have provided Becker with very little advice or direction in the preparation of the dissertation. Becker defended his "History of Political Parties in New York Province, 1760–1776" in 1907.

"I like your thesis exceedingly," wrote Turner to Becker. After he had absorbed the full implications of Becker's argument, he told him that it would "go far to make clearer the importance of the class struggle" in revolutionary New York. He feared that Jameson's plans to write "the social history of the Revolution" would never be completed and predicted that "the next work [in American history] is to be the investigation of the general subject of social development of the U.S. in *all* periods. Not only the revolutionary parties must be reconsidered, but all party history, and issues with reference to this neglected topic."[9] The interchange is a revealing one, illustrating the way in which the work of graduate students might trigger the absorptive, generalizing, and interpretive side of Turner's mind. But initially Becker's dissertation may have given Turner momentary pause. He told Farrand, in "develop[ing] the relation of democratization, party alignment . . . to the Revolution in New York, [h]e thinks the social reorganization as important in many ways as the fight for self government." He continued, "I guess he is right. But his thesis is too full of detail I fear for the public."[10]

In his 1903 contribution to the *Atlantic Monthly* Turner had himself identified within the colonies during the Revolutionary era an internal struggle that pitted the democratic pioneers of the back country against the propertied interests of older regions, continuing at the same time the contest with the mother country was being waged. But Becker's dual revolution—simultaneous contests over the issues of "home rule," as contrasted with "who should rule at home," was not that of his advisor. In the student's account, urban workers and mechanics provided the radical thrust. Becker was significantly revising his teacher's position, but his argument may have led Turner to refer to the conflict of eastern labor with capitalist forces in the two major addresses that he gave during 1910.[11]

Turner supported Becker resolutely through the early years of his career. The latter was critical of the university administration at the University of Kansas, and his colleagues questioned his teaching abilities. Turner counseled, "Do not cut your Kansas bridges until you have something else." He should, Turner suggested, maintain good relations with colleagues and students. Administrative policies would change in the long run. In the meantime he should not associate with malcontents: "The best policy is to *boost* hard and make yourself indispensable by your helpfulness—Then if something better is open you can choose." Cheerfulness was the best strategy. But, explained Turner, he did not "advocate any time serving, or stifling of freedom of action or debate, or boldness of faculty policy." He concluded, "what hurts is the tendency of groups to be discontented in whispers, or to fight as though they didn't realize the difficulties of the administration. . . . helpfulness is what wins, and frank sympathetic criticism, with reasons, in personal talks with the persons criticized."[12] Some years later Turner's support helped place Becker upon the editorial board of the *American Historical Review* and in the history department of Cornell University. Becker became the only member of Turner's Wisconsin group of Ph.D.'s to be a president of the AHA.

Turner did not support his students indiscriminately. Scion of the western county seat elite, Turner emphasized appropriate appearance and behavior. Able young westerners who lacked in social graces were not supported for initial positions in institutions where in Turner's mind polished manners were important. Abilities also must match the institution. When an ambitious young scholar who had struggled in finishing his exams and dissertation suggested that he was interested in a vacancy at the University of Michigan, Turner informed him that he was not right for that position, explaining that he would support him for positions at smaller institutions instead.

The career lines of the Wisconsin history graduate students can be briefly summarized. The University of Wisconsin retained Paul S. Reinsch on its faculty, and Becker and William V. Pooley spent most of their careers at Cornell and Northwestern universities. Turner's male Wisconsin Ph.D.'s in general, however, pursued their profession in state universities then of the second rank—Texas, West Virginia, Oregon, North Dakota University, North Dakota Agricultural College, Tulane—or small midwestern colleges. Others among his students taught in such institutions without completing the Ph.D. Turner noted in 1908 that the history departments at Washington, Oregon, and Stanford, particularly, were "either Wisconsin colonies or . . . saturated with 'the Wisconsin idea.'"[13]

Among the women who completed Ph.D.'s under Turner's direction, Kate Everest Levi mixed social work, secondary school, and college

teaching in her career as well as service in the manuscript department
of the Historical Society. Kellogg unsuccessfully sought employment
in teaching institutions, losing out in the contest for a position in one
western state university, in part because her hearing was believed
insufficiently acute for one who must supervise a ladies' hall. She
settled into historical editing and research at the Historical Society
and capped her career by serving as president of the Mississippi Valley
Historical Association. Amelia Ford taught in a woman's college in
Milwaukee, and Anna Reed also taught at the college level in a career
that mixed teaching and government service.

These women obtained four of the eighteen doctorates granted in
American history during Turner's years at Wisconsin. Others worked
in graduate work in American history above the master's level at
Wisconsin during this era and used that training as the basis for work
in higher education or government service. At least two of Turner's
female students at Wisconsin completed their doctorates in the
program after his departure. Of these, Turner's seminar student of the
early 1890s, Florence P. Robinson, served Beloit College long and
faithfully but was never allowed to teach history there. She completed
her doctorate at Wisconsin during Turner's first year of retirement and
later left a bequest to the university for the support of a chair in
American history in the history department in memory of her father
and of friend Martha Edwards. A Turner student, Edwards completed
her advanced degree in 1916, and labored eventually in the extension
program at the University of Wisconsin. The chair, Robinson specified,
was to be filled by a woman scholar, equal in status in all respects to
other members of the department.

As a student at Stanford University, Lois Kimball Mathews greatly
impressed Turner's friend Farrand. From Stanford she moved for
further study to Radcliffe College. She spent the summer session of
1905 at the University of Wisconsin to benefit from contact with
Turner. Her developing interest in the spread of New England settlement and institutions so deeply impressed him that he offered her a
teaching assistantship to continue her studies at Wisconsin. She,
however, succumbed to the pleas of her Radcliffe teachers and accepted
aid there, allowing her to become that institution's first Ph.D. in
history. Reporting to Turner on a successful but traumatic passage
through the general examination, she also communicated Professor
Channing's evaluation of Turner's work: "Turner and I are the only
men in the country who really know the whole of American history.

Others know it in spots but we've got it all the way."[14] Turner was convinced that Mathews would be an ideal dean of women at Wisconsin, and, due largely to his influence with Van Hise, so she later became. Would Turner have been equally enthusiastic about the appointment of Mathews to a full-time teaching appointment in a major department? We cannot know, because she herself expressed preference for a position that combined teaching and administration.

Turner understood that women could make significant contributions to scholarship. He spoke admiringly of Lucy Salmon, Vassar's leading historian of this era, and was highly impressed by Ellen C. Semple in the field of geography. But in describing his offer of an assistantship to Mathews he admitted that, "as a rule," he was "disposed to give preference, other things being equal, to a man."[15] To Farrand he wrote, "If she only would give bond not to get married I should find it easier to give the fellowship,—and harder to reconcile with my sense of the fitness of things!"[16] But successful women applicants for aid were not unusual at the University of Wisconsin. Although the four Ph.D.'s garnered by women advisees of Turner during the Wisconsin years may appear a small number, few, if any, American history programs of the time produced more. Turner, however, was no fiery apostle of a new era when women would be accepted on scholarly merit alone in graduate programs and also be considered for teaching positions of every description in American academia.

Turner's ambivalence on the place of women in the history profession perhaps reflects a larger anomaly in the attitude of turn-of-the-century academic progressives on social issues. Turner considered himself a progressive in politics. Within academia he was willing to crusade against the evils of athletics. But so little did he appreciate the problems of black Americans that he believed the fifteenth amendment, as passed, to have been a mistake. Never aggressively anti-Semitic and convinced indeed, as he argued in his newspaper columns on Jewish immigration, that anti-Semitism was much less a problem in America than in Europe, he still exclaimed in anger that a matron intent on hiring away the Turner cook was a member of "the tribe of Israel."[17]

At the University of Wisconsin Turner was deeply involved in his teaching with students and faculty in economics and political science. As he pressed his research and developed his ideas following the great

proclamation of 1893, he became increasingly conscious of the usefulness of the ideas of geographers, and he, himself, ventured to outline
a sociological approach to American history in an address. In his book
reviews, as we have seen, he made it clear that social scientists had
their shortcomings, but he continued to observe developments in the
social sciences with interest. When he addressed historians at the
Historical Congress of the Universal Exposition in 1904, Turner urged
them to use the literature of related fields. Interaction with an old
Hopkins friend, sociologist Albion W. Small, at the Congress led him
to write that there should be more sociology in history and more history in sociology. Still, the disciplinary missions differed in his eyes,
and he never proclaimed himself to be a social scientist. Many
historians since have exhibited a similar strange reluctance to admit
their commitment to the ideas and methods of social science.

During the early years of the twentieth century, sociologists and
economists were debating the proper definition of social science and
the obligations of its practitioners. Turner read papers on such matters
by Small, Robert F. Hoxie, an economist, Franklin H. Giddings, and
others. He marked key passages, as was his custom, by underlining
with black, blue, or red ink, drawing lines in the margin, or sketching
little hands with pointing fingers. In apparent approbation, Turner
underlined Hoxie's statement that "a social science is an examination
and interpretation of human experience as such from some distinctive
human standpoint, aspect, or interest; or it is an attempt to describe
and explain or interpret human experience as it is ranged about and
related to some one special interest which is for the time being
regarded as the end of human experience and in a sense outside it."[18]

Turner's argument that history provided preparation for citizenship
accords with the practical objectives of many social scientists of the
time. He never proclaimed himself in search of broad and immutable
laws of history, but his commitment to stage theories of social development and other evolutionary analogies placed him in the camp of
the social scientist. His general theories of frontier influence and
sectional interaction were more compelling generalizations about
American life and development than many advanced in related disciplines. If social science can rest upon generalizations about society
that hold true over extended periods of time within particular nations
or cultures, Turner deserves to be considered a social scientist.

From 1905 onward Turner's interdisciplinary interests became more
obvious. At a joint session of the AHA and the American Economics

Association in December 1906, Edwin F. Gay presented a paper discussing the stage theories of the German historical school of economics. Haskins vainly attempted to persuade Turner to join the panel to discuss the American case. Although he refused, Turner was sufficiently interested to request a copy of Gay's paper. Gay responded by outlining his remarks and sketching his conclusion that stage theories did not adequately catch the variety of historical phenomena nor the breadth of secular change in economic institutions. Billington has argued that this exchange stimulated Turner to think more deeply about frontier stages and sequences and to reject his earlier commitment to stage theory. He did not make a public disavowal of past positions, however.

Turner continued to be particularly interested in the ideas of geographers. In 1905 he reviewed Albert P. Brigham's *Geographic Influences in American History* and Ellen C. Semple's *American History and Its Geographic Conditions* in the *Journal of Geography*.[19] He complimented Semple and Brigham for not making "the mistake of trying to state a law of historical development in terms of physical conditions." Though possessing "admirable features," both books were "in the nature of introductory and popular treatises." In conclusion Turner stated his own position:

> The United States is a collection of physiographic provinces comparable in areas, and in resources, to countries, and even to empires, of Europe. Across these potential nations . . . the stream of American settlement flowed. Each great province received these tides of population, adjusted them in successive eras to successive revelations of the resources and physiographic influences of the province. Each bred its own society, produced its leaders, and interacted upon its neighbors. When the American historian shall unfold the combined influences of geography acting upon western expansion and shaping society to the resources of these vast provinces, and of the ethnographic and social groupings, in explaining American development we shall come nearer to an understanding of the meaning of the nation's history.[20]

Turner arranged and chaired a conference on the relation of geography and history at the AHA Meeting of 1907, inviting Semple to give a paper that she entitled "Geographical Location as a Factor in History." Perhaps in an effort to improve relations with Libby, he asked his former student to appear on the panel also. The latter spoke on "Physiography as a Factor in Community Life," drawing particularly upon Indian occupation of North Dakota for illustration. Ulrich B. Phillips provided an example of political cartographic analysis. Using a map of the southern states that showed presidential voting in 1848 and one recording "the local preponderance of whites and negroes in the population according to the census of 1850," he showed "a significant relation between the two" sets of data.[21] In chairing the session Turner emphasized the usefulness of studying the "relations between geography and history" in a country that "affords one of the most important fields, if not the most important, for the study of the interactions between man and his environment." As reporter he also noted George L. Burr's reservations about Semple's effort to show that physiography determined economic and social outcomes. Burr maintained that no historical "outcome [could] be inferred from a single factor alone," and cautioned, "when to nature is imputed what is planned and achieved by man, the sufferer from the fallacy is history."[22]

The American Sociological Association met in Madison at the same time, and at its meeting Turner delivered a paper entitled "Is Sectionalism Dying Away?", the first of many that he was to deliver on aspects of American sectionalism. He questioned Secretary of State Elihu Root's contention that national life was "crystallizing about national centers." The assertion of state sovereignty, Turner countered, had been the weapon of sectionalism, a force that antedated American nationalism and still survived. In identifying sectionalism, Turner proposed to "recognize as tests . . . all of those methods by which a given area resists national uniformity . . . opposition in public opinion on the part of a considerable area, . . . formal protest . . . combining its votes in Congress and in presidential elections; and also those manifestations of economic and social separateness involved in the existence in a given region of a set of fundamental assumptions, a mental and emotional attitude which segregates the section" from others.[23]

He continued, "Geographical conditions and the stocks from which the people sprang are the most fundamental factors in shaping sectionalism. Of these the geographical influence is peculiarly important in forming a society like that of the United States, for it includes in its influence those factors of economic interests, as well as environmental conditions, that affect the psychology of a people." After describing American physiographic provinces and zones of settlement, Turner used maps of presidential voting in Ohio, Indiana, and Illinois and in the nation at large to illustrate sectional expressions of political opinion. In discussing the Ohio Valley states he concluded, "So deeply seated is political habit that, in election after election, almost the same party sections are seen in all these states. On the whole, the explanation for this grouping would appear to be that the different stocks followed their different habits; and that psychological tendencies, rather than the physiographic fact of prairie against forest, determined sectional alignment. But the physical conditions determined the location of the stocks, and they continue to exert an influence." Turner admitted that there were nonconforming subsections within the larger regions and that recurring majorities were often small. Party affiliation, however, Turner believed, masked sectional commitments to some degree.[24]

Concluding, Turner threw off "the historical mantle, in order to venture upon the role of prophet" and suggested that

> as the nation reaches a more stable equilibrium, a more settled state of society, with denser populations pressing upon the means of existence, with this population no longer migratory, the influence of the diverse physiographic provinces which make up the nation will become more marked. They will exercise sectionalizing influences, tending to mould society to their separate conditions, in spite of all the countervailing tendencies toward national uniformity. . . . Congressional legislation will be shaped by compromises and combinations, which will in effect be treaties between rival sections, and the real federal aspect of our government will lie, not in the relation of state and nation, but in the relation of section and nation.[25]

Here Turner linked the concept of the section with his idea of closed space.

The discussion of Turner's paper in the sociology panel was lively, and approval mixed with dissent. Frank W. Blackmar, Turner's seminar colleague at Johns Hopkins some twenty years earlier, believed that Turner had failed "from a sociological standpoint to give an adequate solution of the question as a present-day problem," having insufficiently emphasized the influence of "transportation and commerce, and . . . unified economic interests" upon the development or decline of sectionalism. He argued that the kind of sectionalism reflected in congressional balancing of interests would never die out, but that which was "born of prejudice and local pride" would fade in the faces of "more complete processes of socialization."[26] Other listeners, including Phillips, suggested minor qualifications of Turner's paper but in general praised it.

Turner's statements of 1907 reveal ambivalence. Quite rightly he argued that sectionalism reflected both adjustments to physiography and cultural antecedents. He would, we suspect, have liked to proclaim the natural environment the more important of the two streams of influence. But caution prevailed. Nor in retrospect had he reason to feel that his ideas were treated with utter scorn. However, there was criticism, and he took Burr's position particularly as a challenge. Responding to a supportive Claude H. Van Tyne, Turner wrote, "The maps certainly require some explanation by those who would ignore the influence of geography; but I suppose Professor Burr would say that *Democracy* was a 'position.' I haven't quite gotten sure of what I think myself in the degree of control by geographic factors. I am sure that there is a geographical side of social development &c that needs fuller study."[27]

The Madison sessions sparked sufficient interest to justify another "Conference on the Relations of Geography to History" at the meeting of the AHA in 1908. Turner's former student, Charles H. Ambler, related physiography to the "beginnings" of the American revolution in Virginia, and John S. Bassett, a Johns Hopkins alumnus, contributed a paper entitled "The Influence of Coast Line and Rivers on North Carolina."[28] In the discussion Turner emphasized "the necessity of analyzing the various divisions of America in order to see of what economic sections they are composed." He also urged the importance of thinking in terms of economic areas rather than of States. Again Burr was present to warn "of the danger that lay in regarding geography as anything more than one factor in human development." At a conference session on research in southern history two days later, Turner pointed out that southern historians had "been neglectful of" that section's "social, religious, and industrial history." They had a "duty," he said, to develop this field, "turning from the study of theories to the study of facts."[29]

In his great proclamation Turner had called, among other things, for a comparative treatment of frontiers. Although he never fulfilled his own prescription, he had, by this time, prepared papers or articles upon the evolution of the Ohio Valley, the Middle West, and the Populist fringe of the Middle West. These were distillations of scholarly research for audiences whose members were less specialized in interest than those found at the meetings of the major scholarly associations. When Thwaites invited him to speak to the members of the State Historical Society of Wisconsin in 1908, Turner drew upon research which he had done while developing a study of the the Old West before the turn of the century—a book that had never materialized. The next year he spoke on "The Significance of the Mississippi Valley in American History" before the fledgling Mississippi Valley Historical Association. The first of these papers dealt with the piedmont frontier during the century prior to the American Revolution and was one of Turner's finest scholarly studies. Almost eighty pages in length and well documented, it was a masterful survey of settlement. His summary of the results of expansion in this region during the eighteenth century provided much specific evidence in support of his argument that institutions were becoming increasingly democratic as the frontier moved westward into this region.

In 1908 Turner confessed to Becker, "I have always tried to make my historical stones kill a whole flock of birds—though in my own case I am not sure that I didn't sometimes miss the flock!"[30] He drew also upon his fund of historical information for addresses that he was invited to give at academic ceremonials—convocations, Phi Beta Kappa inductions, and the like. Although containing factual descriptions of settlement processes and development, these were also interpretive paeans to the American spirit, reflecting, he believed, frontier "ideals." The analytical tone of Turner's more serious scholarship is never completely lost in these essays, but again we find some of the word pictures, the soaring periods, the emotion-stirring quotations of which Turner the young orator was an apt master. Although differing from his more scholarly pieces in their general tone as well as in their lack of documentation, most of these laudations of the American character and experience ultimately came to rest in academic publications. In 1910 Turner delivered such a presentation, entitled "Pioneer Ideals and the State University," at the June convocation of Indiana University.

"Ideals" he told his hearers, were "assets in . . . civilization as real and important as per capita wealth or industrial skill," and America "was formed under pioneer ideals." These, Turner maintained, were those of conquest, of discovery, and of "personal development, free from social and governmental constraint," that is, individualism. But equally with the latter ideal, Americans had cherished democracy, hardly conscious amid the wealth of American resources that the two might be in conflict. But now, in the early twentieth century, they faced "the practical exhaustion of the supply of cheap arable public lands open to the poor man, and the coincident development of labor unions." Although the American Revolution had given a great impetus to democracy—here he injected Becker's idea of a dual revolution— "the strength of democratic movements [had] chiefly lain in the regions of the pioneer." But as settlers pressed westward in ever greater numbers after the passage of the homestead law, the greater need for capital and heavier dependence upon transportation "profoundly modified pioneer ideals." The exactions of capital and carrier and the Greenback and Granger responses marked a change in western ideals; the "pioneer democrat" had come to "regard legislation as a an instrument of social construction," and in the conditions of today "the pioneer of the arid regions must be both a capitalist and the protégé of the government."[31]

He continued, "In almost exact ratio to the diminution of the supply of unpossessed resources, combinations of capital have increased in magnitude and in efficiency of conquest. The solitary backwoodsman wielding his ax at the edge of a measureless forest is replaced by companies capitalized at millions." No longer did the nation enjoy a "safety valve of abundant resources open to him who would take. Classes are becoming alarmingly distinct." He added that "an inharmonious group of reformers are sounding the warning that American democratic ideals and society are menaced and already invaded," and outcomes would be decided, Turner predicted, in the Middle West where Americans had come closest to achieving a "self-determining, self-restrained, intelligent democracy."[32]

This historical survey concluded, Turner addressed "the relation of the University to pioneer ideals and to the changing conditions of American democracy." The state universities formed the upper level in great systems of public education that sank "deep shafts through the social strata to find the gold of real ability in the underlying rock of the masses." In this significant era, the state universities must produce educated leaders, not only industrialists, "by furnishing well-fitted legislators, public leaders and teachers, by graduating successive armies of enlightened citizens accustomed to deal dispassionately with the problems of modern life, able to think for themselves, governed not by ignorance, by prejudices or by impulse, but by knowledge and reason and high-mindedness, the State Universities will safeguard democracy."

The university must "summon ability of all kinds to joyous and earnest effort for the welfare and the spiritual enrichment of society." America must exact a commitment of "supreme allegiance and devotion to the commonweal" from the "constructive business geniuses who owe their rise to the freedom of pioneer democracy." The state universities and their graduates, he believed, were the most appropriate agents to foster this "outcome" and temper "the asperities" of the attendant "conflicts."[33]

In describing American ideals in this address, Turner was very much the rhetorician, sweeping and forceful in generalization, marshaling arresting figures of speech, and poetic even to the point of quoting Kipling's poem "The Explorer." He more freely conceded the lawless and exploitive nature of frontier development here than in most of his essays, but Turner was not apologizing. Given their institutional circumstances Turner found it reasonable that the frontiersmen broke land laws, took justice into their own hands, and practiced exploitive agriculture. Much of his presentation—as in other essays of the same type—was undocumented assertion. The American Revolution, he admitted, fostered democracy but was less significant in this respect than the frontier regions. He did not present compelling evidence in support of this judgment. In his mind the frontier was the dominant influence; he found it unnecessary to explain why he believed this to be true.

In this speech Turner implicitly provided his vision of the academic's role. When he wrote of citizens "governed not by ignorance, by prejudice or by impulse, but by knowledge and reason and high-mindedness," can we doubt that he visualized himself as one who passed on knowledge and nurtured reason and high-mindedness? This address has also been identified as a major illustration of Turner's search for a new formula that would ensure the continuance of American democracy now that the free lands were in effect exhausted. Turner did believe that their exhaustion represented a major challenge to Americans and their policy makers. Undeclared social scientist that he was, he forecast elements of the future in this address, but as we know, he also visualized a more complex American future shaped in major part by the processes of sectional bargaining. Perhaps his description of the development of American ideals does reveal a fond enthusiasm and some nostalgia for frontier times past. But as a good progressive, he faced the future unafraid.

In terms of Turner's publishing commitments, the final years of the century's first decade were ones of frustration. During the spring semester 1907 he had found the attractions of the manuscript and newspaper collections of the Library of Congress much more engaging than the task of writing his textbooks for Holt and Company. Returned to Madison, he was resolved to work off his these obligations, but his attention was diverted by invitations to speak and by the affairs of the department and the university. The beginning of Turner's second semester of research leave in 1908 found him deeply involved in one of Jameson's projects on behalf of the profession in general.

However they might discount Theodore Roosevelt's practice of their craft, and he deride academics, professional historians had a friend in the White House during Roosevelt's presidency, and the astute Jameson cultivated sympathetic ears in high places. Perhaps during Turner's sojourn in Washington in 1907, Jameson and Turner discussed the heterogeneous array of documentary source materials issuing from the Government Printing Office, ranging from volumes in the *Official Records of the War of the Rebellion* to the *Calendar of the Jefferson Papers*. If so, they would have noted that these materials left important aspects of the American experience untouched. Jameson discussed the problem with Roosevelt, who agreed that if American history were to be "help[ed] forward . . . with a maximum of economy and efficiency, such publication ought to be based on a well-considered plan, to the framing of which we should apply the best historical intelligence the country affords."[34]

With the president's approval, the members of the AHA appointed a preliminary commission in December 1907, under Jameson as chairman, to develop a plan for furthering documentary publication in American history. Joining Jameson on this body were Charles Francis Adams, Charles M. Andrews, William A. Dunning, Worthington C. Ford, Albert B. Hart, Captain Alfred T. Mahan, Andrew C. McLaughlin, and Turner. The scanty resources of the association, however, suggested that the activities of the commission must be a bootstrap operation. The president solved this problem by requesting his Committee on Department Methods to use unexpended funds by adding consideration of historical documentary publications to their duties and to recruit a subcommittee of experts that would "frame a preliminary plan which" would "represent the deliberate judgment of the best historical experts" and "serve to guide subsequent governmental work of this kind into the best channels." Now the members of the association's commission became a subunit of the Committee on Department Methods. Ford replaced Jameson as its chair, the latter assuming the position of secretary. Turner was present when President Roosevelt received the committee in June 1908 and heard him boast that in developing the arrangement, "I had my way."[35]

Turner and Ford worked as a subcommittee to consider the needs in American economic and social history, and Turner prepared that section of the report. He solicited opinions from scholars working on the economic history project, which was subsidized by the Carnegie Institution at that time, and from other informed individuals. He put considerable effort into fulfilling this assignment, but his elaborate report was compressed into some five pages in the committee's final statement.

As usual when giving advice, Turner mingled common sense and vision in his recommendations, sketching ideal principles for pursuing the work but also suggesting activity that should be given immediate attention. Those assembling documents should not adopt overly restrictive rules as to source, character, or chronology. Heading his list of desirable areas of coverage were geography as revealed in documents of exploration and railroad surveys. There was no subject, he continued, more fundamental in American history than that of the public lands, and agriculture also sadly lacked documentation. Census publications, he believed, made the situation concerning manufactures less pressing, but labor and industrial organizations, transportation, and the post office would provide great opportunities for useful publication. Among subjects relating to population and social organization he believed that there was particular need for extending the coverage of Indians in the *American State Papers* and that documents should be collected concerning the "negro and the actual economic workings of the institution of slavery."[36] Turner's contribution to the report was both sensible and far-sighted.

In January 1909 Gifford Pinchot and his co-chair of the Committee on Department Methods submitted the formal report of their "Assistant Committee on the Documentary Historical Publications of the United States Government" to the president. But in the end the committee's suggestions were not followed, and Turner's textbook had advanced but little.

The year 1908 also found Turner enthusiastically concentrating upon the period 1865–1907. American development, particularly in the West, had proceeded so rapidly in these years, he believed, that historians had dealt inadequately with the mass of source materials available. The information that he dug out was to be grist for his texts, for his lectures in western history, and also for an article in the next edition of the *Encyclopaedia Britannica*. And again his busy spade work proved to be far more fun than writing.

Although his own writing moved slowly, he was keenly aware that others, including Farrand, were making great progress. As early as 1903 his friend had asked Turner whether he would be poaching if he prepared an article on manifestations of western sectional attitudes in the federal constitutional convention. "Even if I had the ambition to monopolize the subject," Turner had responded, "it would be absurd to keep any scholar from the sources found in Madison's reports!" But Turner also informed him that he would himself be providing "incidental treatment of this subject" in a book that he hoped to complete that year, a volume never to be published.[37]

In 1907 Farrand was nearing the end of documentary work on the framing of the federal constitution and again asked for guidance in avoiding encroachment in the Turner preserve. Turner declared the field open but noted that he had touched upon aspects of Farrand's tentative interest "incidentally in one or two places." Two years later "delimitation of spheres" was again at issue. Turner assured Farrand that he would "shout *bon voyage* to whatever trip you make in the historical ocean" but refused to bound his own domain: "I am not sure enough of my own future plans to mark out my course yet. My craft goes tramping about so many ports that I feel unable to chart out a sailing route, as a well ordered ocean liner ought." But he hoped, he wrote, "to cover (some time) the period from Adams to Rhodes." He would not focus on the Mexican War, but "there is much development of American society between 1840 and 1850 which I do hanker after as a field of work, and which I must do to supplement my studies of the western movement." He did not "dream of being a trust magnate" but was "too uncertain of [his] own wishes or future interests to decide on any definite limitation now." He continued, "until my studies go farther I can't be sure that it would be wise for me to eliminate any period into which I may need to go in the development of my bent."[38]

From this communication Farrand might have concluded that his friend regarded most of the first half of the nineteenth century in the

United States as well as the westward movement to be his proprietary colonies. Turner may have believed that Farrand was only the frankest of numerous scholars eager to exploit his province before he could prove his claim. Frustration generated by his inability to achieve objectives that friends seemed quick to accomplish contributed to Turner's growing disaffection at the University of Wisconsin.

Turner displayed no interest when one of the trustees of Amherst College inquired about his availability in May 1907. The Stanford matter rested after the earthquake although President Jordan and his historians still hoped to bring him there. Evidence of Turner's high stature in the history profession continued to mount. Requests to speak came in such numbers that he was obliged to refuse some of them. The University of Illinois bestowed an honorary degree upon him, and his feet were now set on the vice-presidential path to the presidency of the AHA. But all was not well in Madison. Under Governor La Follette's successor, James O. Davidson, the composition of the board of regents was changing. Its members now showed a disconcerting tendency to emphasize practical studies at the expense of general education and to encroach upon the prerogatives of university administrators and faculty. The spring convocation meeting of the regents in 1908 brought to a boil the simmering differences between board members and the faculty of letters and sciences and directly involved Turner and Ely.

A special regent's committee on the state of the university registered disapproval of the arrangement under which Ely was paid four thousand dollars and provided with an additional nine hundred to pay a secretary. "In order to keep good faith," however, committee members recommended that the arrangement be continued, but "only" during the coming fiscal year. They further doubted the wisdom of the arrangement with Ely and Turner "by which, while they receive full salary, they are excused from instructional work in the University for one semester in each year." This should be discontinued "at as early a date as may be consistent with good faith on the part of the Board." Other recommendations criticized the fact that departments of letters and sciences had obtained almost all of the fellowship and scholarships during the current year and recommended that teaching ability be given more weight when appointments and promotions were under consideration. The faculty rules should be amended by inclusion of a provision that specifically noted the faculty member's right to appeal decisions to the regents.

The board modified some of the special committee's recommendations and deferred consideration of others. The resolutions relating to Turner and Ely were not to be acted upon, but they were, of course, part of the records of the regents' deliberations. Van Hise arranged an evening meeting between leading faculty members and the regents where views were exchanged. In suggesting in this forum that regents were going beyond proper bounds, Turner engaged in a sharp exchange with some of the board members. At least one regent believed, however, that some advances in understanding were achieved between the two groups. Before concluding their June meeting, the regents agreed that their chairman should select a committee to confer with one appointed by the faculty. However, they had also extended the life of the Committee on the State of the University, the motion for continuance reflecting the belief that some members of the College of Letters and Sciences were "not giving the proper time and attention to instructorial work."[39]

Although Van Hise believed that he had successfully quelled the troublesome regents, he asked Turner to prepare a letter describing his teaching. In twenty-six pages of response, the latter listed the impressive number of winners of the Winsor Prize who had studied with him at some point in their training and mentioned other successful historians and social scientists who had been members of his classes or seminary. He noted also that many of the former students of his colleagues and himself were now prominent in law and politics and helping to shape "the political ideals, and information of the Middle West." The "spirit of research" that Turner had helped to inculcate— "though it [had] lessened the number of [his] books"—had "as much importance for the welfare of the state and the nation," he maintained, "as research in the Colleges of Agriculture, Engineering, Law or Medicine."[40] Later he prepared a summary of his own research for the use of Van Hise. When the Turner and Van Hise families vacationed together, north of Lake Superior during the summer of 1908, we can be sure that Van and Fred discussed more than fishing and the geologic structure of the Precambrian Shield. Van Hise well knew Turner's stature in the historical profession, and fresh evidence that he could bring to the attention of the regents also came to hand.

In 1908 Farrand accepted Yale University's invitation to join its history department, thus removing the best fly fisherman from the Stanford history program and one of Turner's strongest friends and supporters. Department head Ephraim D. Adams assured Turner that he was no less eager to bring Turner to the West Coast and continued his pleas to this effect during the summer of 1908. This interest was apparently put to good use by Van Hise, and in October Adams wrote philosophically that Turner's decision to stay at Wisconsin had not surprised him. "I am glad to know at least," he continued, "the re-opening of the plan was of some assistance at Wisconsin, in settling an uncertain situation there."[41]

But neither in Turner's mind nor those of some regents were matters settled. There were to be no personal references to Turner and Ely in the minutes of the regents at their next several meetings. But the Committee on the State of the University lived on and in April 1909 presented a slate of recommendations that, among others, suggested abolition of assured scholarships and fellowships to particular departments and colleges and changes in student grant application and faculty appointment procedures. Committee members also recommended that the faculty be requested to produce recommendations for a more efficient system of faculty government and that student convocations be held monthly. By the June meeting some of these proposals had been modified, but, given other regent activity, there were still grounds for believing that the attitude of the regents had not changed materially.

Although Van Hise maintained that he could successfully educate the board, Turner's dissatisfaction persisted. And again the Golden West beckoned. This time, Turner's proposed refuge was the University of California, Berkeley, where President Benjamin I. Wheeler and his leading historian, H. Morse Stephens, were as eager to capture Turner as had been Farrand and Jordan. In August 1909 Stephens placed the matter within the context of institutional development. It would be a "wrench" for Turner to leave Wisconsin, he knew, but

it would be the best way of supporting . . . the promotion of the graduate study of history. Hopkins kindled, Harvard followed and Wisconsin took up the great cause in the history field in the West. Now a change comes. The Wisconsin regents jib and you are made to feel uncomfortable. The best thing to wake up these jibbers would be for you to strengthen the hands of the believers in graduate work by going elsewhere. How better could you support Van Hise? How better could you emphasize your position?[42]

Two days after Stephens thus linked the future of graduate studies in history with Turner's destiny, Wheeler wrote to him at his vacation resort in northern Wisconsin offering him a position in the Berkeley history department. Turner agreed to meet with Wheeler as the latter passed through Chicago in mid-September and found himself confronting a problem in protocol. He believed that he had been appointed the university's delegate to the installation of A. Lawrence Lowell as president of the Harvard Corporation in early October 1909, where Turner was to be awarded an honorary degree. But would it be proper for him to represent the University of Wisconsin if he had already accepted Wheeler's invitation to join the Berkeley faculty? Van Hise saw no difficulty in that eventuality but begged him to delay his response to Wheeler. Finding the latter willing, Turner postponed an immediate decision but cautioned Van Hise, "I do not see that any real change can be effected in my problem and I do not mean to leave by this delay any implication that I am seeking to have alterations in my position; and especially I hope you will not seek from the regents any arrangement for me that would be an embarrassment to you or that would arouse the expectation that I was awaiting changed conditions in my relations in order to remain."[43]

Learning that Turner was seriously considering an offer from Berkeley, Haskins at Harvard also asked him to delay acceptance. Turner had long interacted with the Harvard historians in the councils of the AHA, with Hart in his editorial function, and in many a pleasant social setting. His teaching at Harvard some years earlier had given general satisfaction. Hart considered *Rise of the New West* to be an outstanding contribution to American history as well as a monument to his own powers. The impish Edward Channing equated only Turner with himself in ability to see American history in the whole. Archibald C. Coolidge, chairman of the history department, and Lowell, also held Turner in high esteem; Dean Haskins of the Graduate School was his devoted friend and champion. There had been earlier discussion among the Harvard historians of the possibility of bringing Turner there; the honorary degree was testimony of their esteem.

There was no specific vacancy in the ranks of the Harvard historians, nor was it initially clear where funds to support an appointment might be obtained, but Coolidge quickly moved to justify the appointment and propose a means of funding it. Although Hart and Channing were "good," he wrote to Lowell, there had been a decline in the numbers of American history graduate students at Harvard. Turner, on the other hand, was drawing large numbers into his seminar "from everywhere." Although "no younger man in American history" had "so far really distinguished himself," Turner was "a very strong man, perhaps the strongest professor in American history in the United States outside of Harvard." It was unfortunate that he had "founded a school rather than produced much himself," but much of his writing was "brilliant." And Coolidge knew that he wanted to write more. At Wisconsin he had been much involved in "all sorts of things"; in the quiet of Harvard he could write more. Coolidge urged also that Turner's appointment would demonstrate Harvard's interest in the West, please the university's western alumni, and draw graduate students from the region. If Turner moved to California he would not wish to come back. It was "now or never" and "no time to lose." As to Turner's salary, Coolidge was himself prepared to put up five thousand dollars per annum for five years, provided that he was relieved of a less important obligation to the college.[44] Lowell acquiesced in the plan.

Turner arrived for the convocation ceremonies in the morning of October 5, 1909, and later that day conferred with Lowell, who informed him that funds were available and that his teaching obligations would be the same as at Wisconsin if he accepted the position. Stephens, from Berkeley, was also in attendance at the convocation and aware of Harvard's efforts. After a "big luncheon," Turner talked to him for several hours and reported to Caroline that the Californian "really wants me for more pioneering—the joy of building up a department in a new land." But he wrote, "I have drunk pretty deeply of this wine for twenty five or so years and if I did feel this call I believe Van Hise could make the argument with more force." Stephens's health was uncertain and a turn for the worse could place Turner back in departmental administration. "So," he concluded, "if the details are satisfactory—and if the votes of the various governing bodies are made for ratifying Lowell's plans . . . I expect to accept here."[45]

A day later, Turner told Caroline that he had not yet "given an official reply" but that he had informed Van Hise and Haskins of his intentions. "Poor Morse," he wrote, was "badly cut up. And it hurts me, too." His mind had been "fully settled" on Berkeley, but "pioneering again" would likely produce "no solid results." Van Hise also attended the Harvard convocation. He had feared that success by the University of California would be a harbinger of other raids from state universities, but was "reconciled to Harvard." When it was time, Turner explained, he would "simply resign. . . . I shall air no grievances—but I shall not deny that if the course of the regents had been different I should have stayed." He added, somewhat wistfully:

> So my quarter century of work at Wisconsin closes up and what is writ is writ. I don't for a moment think it hasn't been worthwhile, and I hope for future crops where Allen settled, and I helped widen the clearing. They have been rich years—in experience of all the things the world offers; and you have been at my side through it all, and we shall push on together to see the stars (revider le stelle) again, knowing that the only really [sic] joy is in the effort to fulfill what is best in us. It isn't easy to know what is best. But I have tried to choose deliberately. I know that you will think what is done is best. I hope out of my heart it will be best for you.[46]

And so the Wisconsin years were to end. In mid-November Turner formally accepted Harvard's offer and sent a brief letter of resignation to Van Hise, thanking him for "the encouragement . . . always given me and my work" and expressing hope that the "regents and the State may cordially support" him in his "wise and farsighted" policies.[47]

Turner's resignation climaxed a series of incidents in which members of the Wisconsin faculty believed that the regents had interfered in the internal affairs of the university, forced resignations, altered tenure and salary status without faculty advice, rejected recommendations for promotion, established direct communications with individual faculty, exercised selective approval of departmental budgets, interfered with curricular content, threatened academic freedom, inquired into individual work loads, and sought to deemphasize research in the College of Letters and Sciences. In December 1909 the conference committee of the regents met with a faculty committee to discuss the disaffection on campus. There faculty members suggested that Turner's resignation had capped a "growing feeling of unhappiness and dissatisfaction." One regent denied that the board had taken action against Turner; they had discussed his case, said the regent, because students had complained that they were unable to enroll in his class. If true to fact, this response was disingenuous, as the board's minutes reveal. Another maintained that Turner had "virtually made a threat that the Regents should know their place" in the meeting of faculty and regents at Van Hise's home in the spring of 1908. But a faculty member maintained that regent responses to Turner must have seemed "almost equivalent to a request to resign."[48]

To Farrand, Turner explained that he had "practically decided to accept" Berkeley's call when, to his surprise, "Harvard people" asked him to delay the decision. It had seemed to him that "California meant more exploring in new fields and constructing historical clearings and cabins, and that I really ought to settle long enough to raise a crop. . . . with my long residence and relations to Wisconsin, I did not see how I could do this here." He could have remained at Wisconsin without change in his position, perhaps even at a higher salary, but his "case seemed to be part of a general problem." He could best serve the university by resigning. The regents, he expected, would be "particularly hospitable" to his successor, having learned "that too many cooks spoil some broths, anyway."[49]

What was Turner actually telling Farrand in this letter? Harvard displaced Berkeley as refuge because California symbolized starting over, whereas on the banks of the Charles River Turner could produce those "unwritten books" in a less demanding environment than that in Madison. By leaving Wisconsin, he was also emphasizing to the regents that they should support graduate research in letters and sciences and interfere less in the internal affairs of the university. Turner's friends and students found these to be admirable motives. But thought of moving had been recurrently in Turner's mind for years, and the irritating behavior of Wisconsin regents and legislators was not new. He had completed a well-received book, but once removed from Hart's editorial discipline, he was again floundering in his efforts to advance his writing projects.

In confronting his situation at Wisconsin in these years, Turner was unrealistic. He had transferred the departmental chairmanship to his colleagues but still allowed himself to become absorbed in the details of faculty and departmental affairs. He complained that the graduate program at Wisconsin was hampered because of inadequate provisions for fellowships, although growth would increase his own obligations. In the summer of his great decision he spent six weeks "paddling, fishing and tramping the trails about Trout Lake" in northern Wisconsin.[50] To those who have tramped these trails and paddled these waters, six weeks appears to be more time than enough to trigger restoration. Turner blamed the local distractions for his inability to make satisfactory progress in his writing, and the professional and social life of a senior faculty member in a state university situated in a state capital could indeed divert the divertable. Yet eminent colleagues produced works in quantity. Turner found it easier to blame his circumstances than to diagnose his lack of self-discipline.

In the continued contemplation of leaving that had gone on in Turner's mind since the mid-1890s, the shock or fright at imagining himself elsewhere had apparently vanished. He also perhaps believed that his leadership in the Madison faculty was not universally respected. His position on athletic reform had generated opposition. In 1908 he allowed his name to be advanced for the presidency of the University Club, taking the position that it should not dispense alcoholic beverages, and he was defeated. He knew that his colleagues Munro and Dennis had been displeased when he had successfully pushed for the promotion of Fish in 1908 without fully consulting them.

If the local attractions had dwindled in their power to hold, Cambridge offered strong inducements to move. Harvard was a well-endowed university, and if the research resources in Turner's field of study fell short of those in Madison, the Harvard administrators assured him of their willingness to meet his needs. His best friend was at Harvard University in a position of honor and power. His friendships with Harvard's other historians had grown steadily since his report of years earlier to Caroline that he "like[d] them exceedingly." Whether in his old mode of calculation or because he could not resist demonstrating his abilities and his qualities of good fellowship, he had, in effect, courted the Harvard scholars for years. Harvard University also had a superior retirement system linked to the Carnegie Foundation's system of retirement allowances for college teachers. Included were pensions for widows of teachers with substantial service prior to death. Given Turner's demonstrated inability to accumulate assets, the Harvard arrangements were attractive.

None, considering Turner's departure carefully, can dismiss it as having been forced simply by a set of bumbling regents, although their actions of 1908 and 1909 added a final straw. He had seriously considered moving before the regents had begun the current round of encroachments. In Wisconsin the education of these officers has been long, painful, and subject to recurrent setbacks. But the incidents of 1908 and thereafter were no more frightening than earlier regent or legislative activity. Turner, however, had reached the stage—neither rational nor calculated and experienced by many a departing professor—where it was simply easiest to say, "I'll go!" Although the regents were not completely to blame for Turner's departure, they had questioned the terms of his appointment. At some later date Turner noted on one of the letters involving his departure that a regent had urged him to surrender his research appointment in return for higher salary, an arrangement that he refused to consider. Here too he suggested that some regents might have resented his role in securing the university presidency for Van Hise.

Turner's loss was part of an unfortunate institutional pattern at the University of Wisconsin. When Haskins left the university, it lost a future president of the AHA. In Turner's departure, the president of the organization was lost. Other Wisconsin history professors ultimately became presidents of the association, but only one, aside from Turner, was at Wisconsin when named to the office.

In a letter to Van Hise of late December 1909, Turner summarized the details of the various arrangements under which he had worked at the University of Wisconsin, apparently in an effort to arm Van Hise fully when he and the faculty laid the various reasons for faculty distress before the regents. In all, he noted, he had obtained less leave at Wisconsin than he might have expected if employed at an institution where sabbatical leaves were the rule and where it was understood that no particular research commitment was involved in return. In other correspondence he informed Van Hise and Dean Birge that in order to leave his area in good order, he did not propose to take leave during the spring semester of 1910 but would work half time in the program, trading credit already earned by working a term of summer session without pay for the other half of his salary.

Turner's students and friends affirmed their respect and support in a great outpouring of sentiment. Noting that the Harvard announcement merely stated that the Fellows had appointed Turner in the apparent belief that acceptance was assumed, Carl Becker "wish[ed] someone would surprise those Fellows once by refusing" but wished him the best of everything. "Wisconsin without Turner," remarked another, "will seem strangely like the elimination of the Prince of Denmark from a celebrated play by Mr. Shakespeare."[51]

Of Turner's students, Becker received the fullest explanation for his teacher's decision. Neither "ambition nor . . . avarice" had dictated his actions, he explained. "But there was a general question of the place of research in the College of Letters and Science involved—hours of teaching of the men, in general, were under fire; attempts at individual regent administration were made; regent attacks in public upon the relation of the University to the school system were being made; and a strong tendency was showing itself to increase the technical side of our work against the cultural"—worrisome developments. Turner found himself "in a position where I could not concentrate my attention upon my work, and where it seemed to me that I could not fight successfully from a position of a specially favored man in research for the right of research and for faculty administration as compared with regent internal administration of educational problems." He had not been aware of all of the implications of his action, he told Becker, but believed that he could "see beneficial results in clearing the air already." There seemed "a good chance both to keep the University out of an open political fight and out of the disasters that the regents' tendencies were leading to." "No man's coming or going" would permanently affect Wisconsin's position as a leading center of historical research. He himself had built upon Allen's work, and Haskins "was as much (or more) responsible for the establishment of Wisconsin's history position" as he was. Munro, Dennis, Fish, Sellery, and the specialist in ancient history, William L. Westerman, had all done "great work for the University—a work in which I had a *share* only." Western history would continue, and he, Turner, remain a loyal alumnus of the University of Wisconsin.[52]

In a less detailed explanation to Matthew B. Hammond, Turner sounded some of the same strains—his "going was not because of ambition or of desire for a higher salary, but because of . . . certain conditions, here, . . . I could do my best work by going; and incidentally do some good to the institution by creating a consideration of some of the problems essential to its future."[53] In describing Turner's great decision, the word "incidentally" has been sometimes disregarded— like those of most academic professionals in similar situations, Turner's action was not an exercise in self-sacrifice. Despite his disavowal of ambition and his effort to place his decision within the context of university policies, it was made in furtherance of his own professional objectives and his family commitments. But the realistic and highly focused young man of the late 1880s was no more—now he had misread his circumstance. If he was finding it difficult to reap the harvest of scholarship that he desired, the reasons lay mainly within Fred Turner and not in the actions of the Wisconsin regents nor in the demands of his Wisconsin constituency.

As Turner's residence in Madison drew to a close, he was feted and dined to a surfeit. One former student, James A. James, collected a harvest of testimonial letters from other students, and the letters, along with a handsome tea service, were presented to the Turners at an emotional dinner hosted by Fish. The resident graduate students lightened the affair considerably when they presented Turner with a map designed to illustrate his educational influence by showing the current locations of former students—their equivalent of the famous cartography used by Herbert B. Adams to portray the colonial system of his program at John Hopkins. His pockets bulging with protruding maps, Turner was depicted as pursuing an axe-wielding pioneer across the top of his chart, the latter hard on the heels of a trapper and his long-barrelled rifle. The testimonial letters of 1910 delighted Turner, although he joked that many provided "evidence that excellent historical students can produce very deceptive history."[54] With a wealth of detail his students explained how they had benefited from their studies with him. He responded to each in letters that touched felicitously upon their contributions to history. The letters also emphasized to Turner the magnitude of his decision. But "please," he exclaimed to Becker, "do not think of me . . . as really dead or buried to the West (sometimes as I have read my mail, I have felt more like a ghost caught indecently in pillaging his bodily representative's obituary notices)."[55]

Turner worked the summer session at Wisconsin in 1910, attending to the final details of packing and business arrangements after Caroline and Dorothy had departed. Although Farrand had been the first choice of Turner and his colleagues, Frederic L. Paxson was his successor, a younger man whom Turner had long regarded with approval. A fine scholar and also a man of good judgment, in Turner's view, Paxson purchased Turner's house as well as taking his position. On August 5 Turner reported to Caroline, "The last lecture is lectured, the last seminary held, the last examination . . . this afternoon." In a gesture of respect, Fola La Follette and Zona Gale attended his final lecture. After a few more days of working on his article for the *Encyclopaedia Britannica*, he expected to "skip for Cambridge." As sole human occupant of 629 Francis Street, he had visited with a mouse every half hour for a time during the previous night but finally "willed him to Paxson, and went to sleep." These final days had their frantic hours as Turner supervised the loading of the family furniture and other goods in a railroad car. During the last few years the Turners had enjoyed a player piano purchased on credit. Although he had earlier given Turner permission to ship the instrument, the merchant became anxious at the last moment lest Turner fail to meet the final payments. An irate historian "told him what [he] thought of him," made arrangements to pay off the final installments in a lump sum, and told Caroline that the music man had "a yellow streak and suspects others of the same."

There were during the last weeks various surprise parties, including a departmental one hosted by Thwaites, at which Selle: ; made a speech and Turner was presented with a "beautiful Zeis binocular." He met several regents at the club and, although they were polite, Turner was "frigid and brief." Reporting the encounter to Caroline, he remarked "although only the regents now remain to give me a dinner and a present, they haven't yet done so, and I fear the worst."[56] Late in the process of leave-taking, Turner's graduate students, Edgar E. Robinson and August C. Krey, called upon him to say farewell. As they stammered their goodbyes, Turner broke into tears. By late August he had arrived in Cambridge.

10   Eminence

"It's a comfort to know also that the youngsters can make books if the old man can't"

Writing from Cambridge to a former colleague at the University of Wisconsin in early October 1910, Turner reported the family established at 175 Brattle Street, "an old colonial mansion," rented for a year from a "fortunate colleague," Roger B. Merriman. Here amid the "evidences of luxury" gathered by his landlord, they would "pick out the quiet spot where we can install such fragments of our own furniture as survived the journey." The house would, he believed, also "make a pleasant background for the future of that kind of plain living and healthy pessimism which characterize the lot of the average of us here."[1]

After leaving Madison, Turner had finished his "beastly article" for *Encyclopaedia Britannica* in Cambridge. Then he enjoyed a "delightful three weeks of outing" in the vicinity of the Rangley Lakes in Maine where he and his companions explored mountain trails and tote roads, and he reveled in the "fun of trout fishing." At Harvard his work had begun "pleasantly," he told Jastrow with about eighty students enrolled in his undergraduate lecture course. Most of them were "New England boys," their names symbolic of "eastern conservatism" but "engaging young rascals" even so. "To guide them over western trails," would be, he foresaw, "an interesting experience." There were also in the class "many western fellows . . . from sons of Seattle sewer contractors to those of railroad magnates and bank presidents." In this letter to Jastrow, Turner included a cryptic "*net* (i.e. men)" after the word *eighty*, thus noting his departure from undergraduate coeducation and perhaps recording an uncharacteristic jibe at women students.[2]

A semester later Turner again described his students. Westerners were abundant among them, chiefly from the Ohio Valley. "Men of large means—the 'Mt. Auburn youth'" had soon left "in sadness rather than anger" on learning that "salvation lay through the library." Such men, he mourned, were "mighty promising stuff if one could set fire to their purposes," but "extra-legal activities" were too diverting and students feared the label of "greasy grinds." His students' topical reports were better than their examination papers; the men did almost all of the assignments by themselves. Numerous football players "took [their] medicine like men, and got good grades."[3]

Turner's migration to Cambridge took him from perhaps the leading state-supported university in the United States to the institution whose admirers considered it to be the country's one "truly national" center of higher learning. A commitment to Unitarianism was of long standing here; Turner need not fear the alumni on that score. Indeed, when Harvard abandoned compulsory chapel a generation earlier, wags could jest that even God had been subsumed within President Charles W. Eliot's cherished system of elective courses. Turner found a different student body here than in Madison—somewhat smaller but more diverse, drawn indeed from the nation, although dominated by Massachusetts and New England youths. Heirs to great wealth were present, as indicated by Turner's comment to Jastrow about the residents of the gilded ghetto of expensive apartments on Mt. Auburn street, but there were also impoverished scholarship students. By this time the proportion of private school graduates had fallen to less than half of incoming classes. Although a full-scale coeducational commitment was lacking in the Harvard classrooms, Radcliffe College used Harvard professors in its program.

Turner was not entering a quiet intellectual oasis. Lowell, the formidable new president, worshipped the best in scholarship and in education generally. Change, he maintained, was a basic tradition at Harvard University. Eliot's system of electives had long impressed him as inadequate in conception and result. Under Lowell's leadership came concentration and distribution requirements, tutors, a reading period, general exams, and a divisional arrangement of departments. A continuous process of construction changed the physical face of the Yard and particularly its immediate surroundings during Lowell's presidency. New student housing, lecturing, laboratory, and museum facilities all appeared. With the building of a strategic dam at the time of Turner's arrival, the malodorous and shifting waterfront along the Charles River was eliminated and the result embraced in Harvard's development. When Turner arrived, Lowell considered Harvard's collection of books to be magnificent but the physical condition of the library to be deplorable. In 1913 the cornerstone of the Widener Library was set in place, and the building itself opened in 1915, thereafter to be Turner's headquarters on campus.

In his inaugural address President Eliot had remarked that "the poverty of scholars is of inestimable worth in this money-getting nation."[4] Himself a man of considerable wealth who had already donated a building to Harvard and who would make further gifts to the institution, Lowell was not convinced of the wisdom of this precept. But he was no spendthrift either. Although in line or slightly in advance of those paid in other leading eastern institutions, Harvard salaries were not princely when the cost of living in Cambridge or Boston was taken into consideration. After he had settled his accounts in Madison and calculated the costs of the move to the east, Turner estimated that after twenty years of academic labor he was only a few hundred dollars ahead, although he probably did not take his household goods and personal library into consideration. Unless he could increase his income from lecturing and royalties, his Harvard salary of five thousand dollars per annum—although handsome in its time—did not promise rapid improvement in the financial status of the Turner family.

Turner was president of the AHA during 1910, and in late December its annual meeting took place in Indianapolis. Although lacking "distinguished architecture" and "impressive 'sights,'" Indianapolis, wrote the association's secretary, was a "pleasant and hospitable city." Turner also found the meeting "pleasant.... Wisconsin men ... present in force, and ... a good dinner." Describing the president's address, the secretary noted that Turner "dealt, as only a devoted and accomplished student of western history could do, with the new light cast on our whole history by the extraordinary developments of the last 20 years, and with the new duties which this imposes on the historian."[5]

Turner initially intended to use the phrase "American ideals" in the title of his address, reiterating the theme of his Indiana address and several other recent speeches. Instead, he entitled it "Social Forces in American History." The essay was Turner's last formal effort to address the broader problems of the historian. He began by telling his audience that the last twenty years had seen a "revolution in the social and economic structure of the country" fully comparable to those of the Revolutionary and Civil War eras. In "less than a generation" since the Superintendent of the Census had declared that a "frontier line ... could no longer be described.... the age of free competition of individuals for the unpossessed resources of the nation is nearing its end." Another chapter of national history was closing; America's age of colonization was ending—it was "the conclusion to the annals of . . . pioneer democracy." It had been, he told his listeners, a "wonderful chapter, this final rush of American energy upon the remaining wilderness."[6]

As at Indiana University six months earlier, Turner documented the major economic and social changes taking place—the growth of industry and railroads, the flow of immigration that had greatly changed the demographic composition of the country, and the failure of agriculture and population to expand commensurately with industrial growth. With the "Far West" colonized, explained Turner, it was natural that America was expanding abroad to become "an imperial republic with dependencies and protectorates—admittedly a new world-power." This, in turn, had brought the "need of constitutional readjustment."[7]

The impact of structural change in America upon "American society and domestic policy" had resulted, argued Turner, in "palpable evidences of the invasion of the old pioneer order." "The pressure of great numbers of immigrants of alien nationality and of lower standards of life" had "unfavorably affected . . . the sympathy of the employers with labor." As the supply of free lands neared exhaustion, "capital and labor entered upon a new era":

> Colossal private fortunes have arisen. . . . Labor on the other hand has shown an increasing self-consciousness, is combining and increasing its demands. . . . the old pioneer individualism is disappearing, while the forces of social combination are manifesting themselves as never before. The self-made man has become in popular speech, the coal baron, the steel king, the oil king . . . the monarch of trusts. The world has never before seen such huge fortunes exercising combined control over the economic life of a people, and such luxury as has come out of the individualistic pioneer democracy of America in the course of competitive evolution.

The magnates did not believe that they had repudiated American values, but rather that they exemplified a republic in which individuals had the "freedom to compete for the natural resources of the nation." The West, on the other hand, was now leading in demanding government intervention to control the activities of such interests for the broader benefit of society.[8]

From the pioneer era, argued Turner, Americans had derived two fundamental ideals. One was belief in "individual freedom to compete

unrestrictedly for the resources of a continent—the squatter ideal. . . .
The other was the ideal of a democracy—'government of the people, by
the people and for the people.'" The abundance of free lands shaped
American democracy but also provided the opportunity for individuals
and interests to accumulate vast resources. Time had shown that these
two ideals "had elements of mutual hostility" and threatened to
destroy democratic institutions. America, he continued, "finds itself
engaged in the task of readjusting its old ideals to new conditions and
is turning increasingly to government to preserve its traditional
democracy." Progressive reforms, Turner suggested, were offered as
"substitutes for that former safeguard of democracy, the disappearing
free lands. They are the sequence to the extinction of the frontier." As
these developments were occurring, noted Turner, sectionalism was
both persisting and developing.[9]

In identifying "even a portion of the significant features of our recent
history," it had been necessary, Turner explained, to consider a
"complex of forces." He had touched upon "geography, industrial
growth, politics, and government." But "with these," he continued, "the
changing social composition, the inherited beliefs and habitual attitude of the masses of the people, the psychology of the nation and of
the separate sections, as well as of the leaders" and their creative
powers, must be considered as well also as "moral tendencies and . . .
ideals." "All are related parts of the same subject and can no more be
properly understood in isolation than the movement as a whole can be
understood by neglecting some of these important factors, or by the
use of a single method of investigation," he noted. Then came the
kernel hypothesis of his address: "American history is chiefly concerned with social forces, shaping and reshaping under the conditions
of a nation changing as it adjusts to its environment. And this environment progressively reveals new aspects of itself, exerts new influences,
and calls out new social organs and functions."[10]

Turner explained that he had summarized major developments in
recent history because it had "seemed fitting" to note the significance
of "American development since the passing of the frontier" and also
"because in the observation of present conditions we may find
assistance in our study of the past."

Turner then considered the role of the historian by referring to

the familiar doctrine that each age studies its history anew and
with interests determined by the spirit of the time. Each age finds

it necessary to reconsider at least some portion of the past, from points of view furnished by new conditions which reveal the influence and significance of forces not adequately known by the historians of the previous generation. Unquestionably each investigator and writer is influenced by the times in which he lives and while this fact exposes the historian to a bias, at the same time it affords him new instruments and new insight for dealing with his subject.

So the "present and the recent past" were important objects of study "for themselves but also as the source of new hypotheses, new lines of inquiry, new criteria of the perspective of the remoter past. And, moreover, a just public opinion and a statesmanlike treatment of present problems demand that they be seen in their historical relations in order that history may hold the lamp for conservative reform."[11]

"Seen from the vantage-ground of present developments what new light falls upon past events!" exclaimed Turner. He illustrated the point by noting the fatefulness of George Washington's activities at Fort Duquesne, the ultimate importance of "political parties and reform agitations," considered minor in their time, and particularly the clash of capitalist and "democratic pioneer." The latter—a thread in American history since the colonial era—had in recent times shown itself to be of tremendous importance and revealed strikingly in the current "insurgent movement." This recital, Turner explained, did not express his "present judgment" but illustrated the fact that "present events" gave "a new significance to [the] contests of radical democracy and conservative interests . . . rather a continuing expression of deep-seated forces than fragmentary and sporadic curios for the historical museum." "Similar" reconsideration of the history of the public lands and American agriculture would yield "return[s] far beyond those offered by the formal treatment of the subject in most of our histor-ies."[12] "Rework[ing] our history from the new points of view afforded by the present" revealed, for example, that slavery and the problem of the freed Negro were only "one of the interests in the time."[13]

In conclusion, Turner discussed the ways in which the historian should conduct investigation of the "social forces in American life" and the connection of such activity to "the relations and the goals of history." Here came a mild "dig" at the Adams tradition. He was not privileged, he said, to "bend the bow of Ulysses," to introduce "the laws of thermodynamics and to seek to find the key of historical development or of historical degradation." His would be a "lesser task." Historians, he suggested, could find guidance among the scientists. Here "new conquests have been especially achieved by the combination of old sciences." The new geologist uses "chemistry, physics, mathematics, and even botany and zoology," approaching his research, moreover, without *a priori* conception as to the relative importance of components. He had "abandoned the single hypothesis for the multiple hypothesis. He creates a whole family of possible explanations of a given problem and thus avoids the warping influence of partiality for a simple theory."[14]

Next came a series of warnings. In history, specialists endangered themselves if they failed "to recognize that the factors in human society are varied and complex." Those who believed that the historian must simply "tell the thing exactly as it was" should realize that "the fact . . . is itself a part of the changing currents, the complex and interacting influences of the time, deriving its significance as a fact from its relations to the deeper-seated movements of the age, movement so gradual that often only the passing years can reveal the truth about the fact and its right to a place on the historian's page."[15] Turner warned against generalizing on the basis of *a priori* reasoning and then using history merely as a source of corroborative evidence, as, he suggested, some economists did.

However, "the economist, the political scientist, the psychologist, the sociologist, the geographer, the student of literature, of art, of religion," all had "contributions to make to the equipment of the historian" in materials, tools, points of view, hypotheses, and suggested relationships. In all disciplines workers should guard against an excessively narrow view. "The historian must so far familiarize himself with the work, and equip himself with the training of his sister-subjects that he can at least avail himself of their results and in some reasonable degree master the essential tools of their trade." Those in "the sister-studies must likewise familiarize themselves and their students with the work and the methods of the historians, and cooperate in the difficult task."[16]

This approach, concluded Turner, was important "not so much" because it might give the historian the "key to history" or reveal "its ultimate laws." Rather it was the historian's duty

to see in American society with its vast spaces, its sections equal to European nations, its geographic influences, its brief period of development, its variety of nationalities and races, its extra-ordinary industrial growth under the conditions of freedom, its institutions, culture, ideals, social psychology, and even its religions forming and changing almost under his eyes, one of the richest fields ever offered for the preliminary recognition and study of the forces that operate and interplay in the making of society.[17]

As a distillation of wisdom gained during the course of his professional career, it is not surprising that Turner's presidential address covered much old ground. It also lacked the tautness, logical organization, and rhetorical force of the essay of 1893. As in 1893, Turner immediately introduced the frontier thesis and the concept of free land. But now he was concerned with the new chapter of American history that began, he argued, during the 1890s, and with relating the structural changes occurring thereafter in American society and economy to his frontier theory. Turner merely reaffirmed his views on sectionalism in terms similar to those used in his St. Louis and Madison papers of 1904 and 1907. The concept of closed space in a new era, however, became, in effect, a central theme in his presidential report.

The young Turner of 1893 had combined various related concepts from the social theory of the day in his presentation—germ theory, evolutionary development of institutions, behavioral survivals, environmental adaptation, stage theory, and illustrative types of personality. In 1893 he found "much truth" in Loria's contention that "America has the key to . . . the course of universal history" Though muted, much of Turner's theoretical conception of social change of the early 1890s was still in place in 1910—environment, evolutionary process, organic differentiation—although he no longer talked of institutional germs. But whereas the young Turner had made the frontier environment the basic mechanism of change, he now sketched a more embracing theory of American development. American history he now saw as shaped by the interaction of multiple social forces within a nation changing in adjustment to its environment—a context that "progressively reveals new aspects of itself, exerts new influences, and calls out new social organs and functions." The historian's prime obligation of 1893 had been search for the "key" to the understanding of social development. Now the historian should equip himself not to discover "the key to history" or identify "ultimate laws," but to engage in "the preliminary recognition and study of the forces that operate and interplay in the making of society."[18]

During Turner's first two decades of teaching, leading sociologists made much use of the concept of social forces. Agreement as to appropriate definition, however, was difficult to achieve, and by the 1920s many sociologists preferred to find the wellsprings of motivation within the individual. Did Turner mean that each of the various subjects listed in his concluding paragraph constituted a social force? We do not know. In 1893 Turner's enthusiastic adoption of the word *frontier* contributed immeasurably in the creation of an academic masterpiece. His decision to use the term *social force* a generation later was less fortunate. The concept was by now challenged dogma, and if he had been imprecise in defining the meaning of *frontier* in 1893, he made even less effort to define *social force* other than by giving a diverse list of the conditions or formative elements that in changing concert shaped American development.

In 1893 Turner hinted at the importance of cooperating with representatives of other disciplines. In 1907 he expressed strong commitment to the idea and endorsed it more fully in his address of 1910. Study of the past would be most effective if collaborative. Turner's call for the use of the multiple hypothesis method has drawn the criticism that he did not accurately describe the "method of multiple working hypotheses" outlined by his former colleague Thomas C. Chamberlin.[19] His failure here lay not in his description of the method but his later tendency to refer sometimes to it as that of the multiple hypothesis. In so doing he introduced a term that hints at the emerging statistical method of multiple correlation, which provides measures of the relative importance of various causal factors to an outcome under study. In Peter Novick's analysis of the conflicts among American historians between advocates of objectivity and relativism in the writing of history, he refers to the specification and testing of competing hypotheses as "quixotic . . . absurd and impossible." If the historian is sensible—Chamberlin used the word "rational"—in his method of application, this procedure can, however, constitute a beneficial stage in research. Turner's various references to it, however, do not indicate that he understood or advocated the concept of multiple correlation, as understood by statisticians. Nor for that matter did Turner demonstrate in published work that he had himself applied Chamberlin's suggested method.[20] In his endorsement of multiple working hypotheses and in his use of the concept of social forces, Turner was fuzzy in his thinking. But his willingness to cross disciplinary boundaries gave his message an interest, an aura of adventure, and an added legitimacy that some younger scholars found attractive.

For Turner in 1910 the role of the historian had changed little from his conceptions of the early 1890s, but there were some differences. The historian in a new generation must still rewrite the pages of history, although now perhaps not completely. Then, however, Turner had emphasized the fact that new sources would have revealed different aspects of the past; now he stressed that new institutional developments required the rewriting of history by showing that hitherto little-regarded processes had been of greater significance than earlier understood. Placing these in proper perspective was essential if history was to "hold the lamp for conservative reform," a different but related obligation in the training for citizenship that Turner saw as the history teacher's great mandate in 1891. In "The Significance of History" Turner had argued primarily that study of the past allowed us to understand the present. Now his emphasis on the factual history of the last two decades also emphasized his belief in the importance of studying recent history, an advanced position among historians in 1910.

In 1891 Turner quoted von Ranke's rubric, to "tell things as they really were" but noted that the German historian's "history was primarily past politics." Admitting that "man is conditioned by the age in which he lives and must perforce write with limitations and prepossessions," he endorsed Droysen's conception of history as a "striving" and a "consecration" to the "truth and the light." Now, in December 1910, Turner qualified von Ranke's phrase in greater detail. Novick flatly denies that Turner was a relativist in his approach to history. As we have seen, Turner in 1891 expressed reservations about the scope of von Ranke's approach but not his ideal of a scientific history. He distinguished between objective history, dealing with "the events themselves," and subjective history, concerned with the historian's interpretation of these events. He noted the difficulties of the historian's task in evaluating evidence, providing "just selection, emphasis, perspective." "The historian," he wrote, "must have a passion for truth above that of any party or idea." But each had "limitations and prepossessions" because he was "conditioned" by his age; none would say the "ultimate word."[21]

In 1910 Turner again acknowledged that generations rewrite their histories but now perhaps only in part. Again he agreed that "the times in which he lives" influences the historian. But they also gave him "new instruments and new insight." Now he specifically questioned the "effort to tell the thing exactly as it was." But not, as the committed relativist would argue, on the grounds that the preconceptions, interests, and intentions of the historian so colored the analysis that the distinction between objective and subjective could not be made. In both years Turner thought in terms of historical understanding that improved as new sources opened and as the passage of time provided clearer perspective. In his view of history, as of the world, Turner was a progressive. He had not relaxed his early views that history was to be a rigorous scientific search for truth, pursued in a spirit of non-partisan inquiry, and that one could separate the objective from the subjective in historical analysis, given a particular level of access to sources and tools. He still believed that historical research could provide the basis for enlightened social policy.

Turner recognized the problems that relativists found so endangering to the historical enterprise, but his response was a more optimistic one. His student Becker, however, had expressed doubt in the *Atlantic Monthly* in the year of the presidential address that the objective and the subjective could be separated. Turner perhaps agreed with Becker's assertion that historical synthesis could only be "true relatively to the needs of the age which fashioned it." Explaining the problems of writing social history to sociologists several years later, Becker approvingly quoted the section of Turner's presidential address in which he argued recent history's usefulness in suggesting new hypotheses for understanding the past and the historian's obligation to revise history so that it might "hold the lamp for conservative reform."[22] Although Turner was not a relativist as this position was later defined, there was much in his approach that a historian of that persuasion found congenial.

Turner's scientism of 1910 was somewhat more restrained than that of the 1890s. Where once he had talked boldly of keys to understanding American development—even identifying physiography in that respect—and quoted Henry Adams with apparent approbation, he now ventured a mild joke about the laws of thermodynamics. But he applauded the scientific methodology of multiple hypotheses and called for the use of the methods and ideas of related disciplines. Although he introduced the concept of sectionalism in his presidential address, he did not discuss the interdisciplinary methodology involved in sectional analysis. He borrowed the concept of social forces from social science but left unclear the methodological details of his proposed master agenda—the documentation of social forces.

If there was much that his students and his professional colleagues found familiar in his presidential address, there were also emphases that some later critics ignored. Neither Turner's America nor his West ended in 1893. He understood that the twentieth-century West differed from the Middle West with which he was so much concerned in his own writings. And—perhaps Becker's research was much in his mind—he was no longer prepared to write as in 1896 of the "nonexistence of classes," now identifying class conflict as a significant element in the American experience.[23]

On the final evening of the Indianapolis meeting, the historians gathered to hear James Harvey Robinson present a paper, "The Relation of History to the Newer Sciences of Mankind." Leading advocate of the emergent "New History," Robinson urged his hearers to incorporate the new findings in anthropology, comparative religions, paleoethnology, and social and animal psychology into their work. George L. Burr was there to warn Robinson's listeners that the social sciences were not history and to predict that when "biology and anthropology have explained for us all they can, when the social sciences shall have accounted for every survival, every instinct, every imitation, there will still remain for history a field broad enough and noble enough for any study, and woe betide the social sciences themselves if we forget it."[24] Given his stress on the use of related disciplines, belief in the integration of recent history in the curriculum, and his concern that history be placed at the service of policy makers, Turner had as much right to consider himself a "new" historian as did Robinson. In years to come, he would privately say so but also discourage any effort of friends to claim that Turner was first in the field.

At the Indianapolis meeting Guy Stanton Ford and other former students had prepared a *festschrift* in Turner's behalf. This expression of respect particularly touched Turner. Only four of the contributors— Joseph Schafer, Becker, Charles H. Ambler, and Paul S. Reinsch—had as yet completed doctoral dissertations under Turner's direction, but Lois K. Mathews, James A. James, Homer C. Hockett, Ulrich B. Phillips, and William S. Robertson had studied with him, and Harvard would grant Solon J. Buck the doctorate in 1911. The chapters well reflected Turner's interests. The contributions of Hockett, Buck, Ambler and Phillips emphasized nineteenth-century party history;

James dealt with the era of the 1770s and Schafer with Oregon diplomacy. Robertson and Reinsch touched upon Latin American relations, a topic that Turner had confronted in *Rise of the New West*. In discussing congregationalism in the region west of the Mississippi, Mathews drew attention to Turner's broader interests in social history. Becker's effort to catch the historical essence of Kansas—a "'state of mind,' a religion, and a philosophy in one" is still one of the most charmingly thoughtful contributions to the history of the American states.[25]

The Turner festschrift began a tradition of students preparing such volumes to honor AHA presidents. Turner reported himself "as pleased as a grandfather with a new 'grand baby'" and sent thanks and a photograph of himself to the young authors. The collection, he told another of his students, was "a great pleasure to me, and a matter of pride." But there was a note of chagrin in his reaction as well. "My students will now relieve me of the odium of not writing more and I am inclined to take to the chimney corner and watch them grow; but not just yet," he confided to Hockett. He commented wryly to Robinson, "It is a comfort to know also that the youngsters can make books if the old man can't." Hockett assured him that all the works of the students would be as nothing in comparison to the word from the master when it came, and it must come. Thus the pressure upon Turner to publish books mounted.[26]

After spending a year in Merriman's residence, the Turners rented a nearby house, 153 Brattle Street, for a few years, and for part of 1912–13 they shared this property with Charles Haskins and his bride, Claire—the "B and G" as Turner referred to them. Investigation of the local real estate market convinced Turner that they could lease a satisfactory dwelling more reasonably than purchase or build one. He and Caroline moved in 1914 to 7 Phillips Place, where they remained tenants for the remainder of their residence in Cambridge.

In 1910 the Turners holidayed in Maine, and that state was to be their favorite summer refuge thereafter, although they also enjoyed visiting the Pacific Coast or mountain states. They became members of a little colony of congenial folk at Hancock Point, including the Slaughters and the Haskins. Turner's love affair with the outdoors continued; he joined a fishing club in Boston and found new pleasures in the woods and waters of the Northeast and in the far West. Although the banks of the Charles River did not convey the sense of continuity with a wilderness past that he had found on the Madison lakes, that stream still provided pleasant—"dreamy" according to Dorothy—canoeing.

Dorothy Turner had entered the University of Wisconsin in 1908, completing her sophomore year in 1910 and then departing to the east with her parents in that same year. She did not continue her college education in the East, preferring to concentrate on the social and cultural opportunities of Cambridge and Boston. She corresponded with close friends in Madison and returned to Madison for extended visits. She had become a charming and vivacious young woman and never lost her early skill in the art of managing a doting father. She was a dog lover, and Turner described her young Airedale, Rummy, as "homely beyond the dreams of those who carved grotesques on Medieaval Cathedrals, and yet with intelligence and affection that really make his awkward activity endurable." Boarded while the Turners were away in the summer of 1912, Rummy was not a Haskins favorite, and Turner tried to delay his return home while the "B and G" were in occupancy. Apparently he failed, and Rummy gained a reputation for greeting ladies with an enthusiasm that embarrassed the Turners. In Dorothy's absence, Rummy pledged allegiance but not obedience to Turner, vocalizing at will and once boarding a street car with him, despite Turner's commands. The conductor ejected the unwelcome passenger.[27]

By 1913 Dorothy had formed an attachment to an attractive young man, John Main, a descendant of one of Madison's oldest families. In a letter, Turner invited him to vacation in September 1913 on Lake Kennabago with the family and described the fishing opportunities there in detail. Included was a list of White-tipped Montreals, Parmachenee Belles, and other flies that he might wish to bring along, as well as a short disquisition on appropriate rods. Although a novice fisherman, John proved his mettle and, after returning to Madison, wrote to request Dorothy's hand. The parents counseled delay, but, undeterred, the young people planned their marriage. Turner acquiesced handsomely, noting only as an "outstanding limitation" the fact that John didn't "know how to fish with a fly."[28] As Dorothy's marriage approached, Turner wondered if the marriage could endure Rummy's presence.

As the spring semester ended in 1914, Turner supervised the last stages of moving from the second Brattle Street residence and then journeyed with Caroline to Madison, where Dorothy married John Main on June 3. From there he and Caroline crossed the continent to Seattle, where he dashed off a "confounded commencement address" for the convocation exercises of the University of Washington, delivering it to an audience of some twenty-five hundred.[29] After giving a series of lectures in the University of Washington history department and relaxing with Edmond S. Meany and other friends, Turner and Caroline journeyed to Eugene, Oregon. Here Joseph Schafer had arranged a lecturing assignment in the summer session of the University of Oregon. In Eugene, Turner again enjoyed the outdoors, writing to Dorothy in mid-July of a fishing trip up the McKenzie river. Though the mountain trail had been "hard" and he had broken two tips on his "Leonard rod," it was all "good fun." Later that summer the Turners rendezvoused with Dorothy and John for a camping and fishing expedition in the Bitterroot Mountains. This ended prematurely when Caroline became ill, but it had been a "wonderful summer," Turner reported to Farrand in October.[30]

Cambridge had its hay fever season, and Turner was determined that Caroline should avoid that irritating affliction if possible. Typically, therefore, he preceded her to Cambridge at the end of their summer vacations. He hated to return to the city, sometimes making a makeshift sleeping room of canvas on the porch in preference to a stuffy bedroom. As outdoorsman Turner was genteel—a man who used guides and packmen in his more elaborate sorties and whose nose for compass north or the correct trail sometimes erred—but he found nature rehabilitating. The late winter and early spring of 1915 was a particularly trying time. In Madison, Dorothy lost her first baby, and their old friends, the Slaughters, saw a second daughter, Trudion, also waste away with a mysterious illness. Alone in Cambridge while Caroline ministered to Dorothy, and beset by his classes, Turner took his fishing rod into Boston for repair, and after buying some trout flies and a book on dry fly fishing, "the woods and the river and the mountains and lakes all came back like a healing vision."[31]

Turner had hardly recovered from a painful abscess of the inner ear and a debilitating attack of erysipelas in the spring of 1915, when he and Caroline left for the west Coast. Their destination was California, where Turner participated in a history program that Stephens had organized at Berkeley in conjunction with the Panama-Pacific International Exposition at San Francisco and the California summer meeting of the AHA. On their way west they once again visited the

Grand Canyon and found San Diego's Panama California Exposition to be "a perfect gem." At Berkeley, Turner delivered six lectures dealing with aspects of American expansion and sectionalism. Of these the last two dealt with developments in the Pacific Coast region and the last phase of the westward movement, again demonstrating that he was not ignorant of American development on the Pacific Rim.

At Berkeley, Stephens had also enlisted Jameson and others among Turner's circle of professional friends in the summer program to their mutual pleasure. The organizers of the AHA program had scattered the sessions in a variety of interesting locations, including the Pacific Exposition grounds—"a splendid dream of form and color," thought Turner—and both the Berkeley and Stanford University campuses. Including receptions hosted by the William Crockers and Mrs. Hearst, the social gatherings "made a sum total of social pleasure" reported the association secretary, "which can hardly have been equaled at any previous meeting, and which certainly could never be paralleled at any meeting held in the east in December." Stephens serving as patron, Turner frolicked sedately on a weekend with the members of the Bohemian Club, in whose grove he found so many "witty and clever and noted people . . . that a mere historian feels as little as the tarweed beside the redwood trees," and, more importantly from his standpoint, that summer he again fished the waters of the Sierra Nevada.[32]

Joined by the Slaughters, the Turners camped under Sierra Club auspices for two weeks in Yosemite National Park. With pack train support, they invaded the Tuolumne meadows, and Turner climbed to "the top of Cloud's Rest on his own legs." Turner's zest on this expedition was only slightly dampened when a rattlesnake tried to appropriate Caroline's clothes while she was bathing, and the campers feared that other such creatures might invade their sleeping bags. But there were poignant moments in that summer, because it was the first for the Slaughters since Trudion's death. In this respect, the Turners would have been understanding indeed. During that summer the Turners also found time to enjoy the seashore at Carmel. They concluded a successful visit to the West with a fishing expedition to Glen Alpine.[33]

Once back in Cambridge, Turner focused his energies on his family, his teaching, his research, his broader professional commitments, and recreation. He seems to have been little involved in institutional politics or the broader spectrum of college or university committees that had taken so much of his time at the University of Wisconsin. He became a member of the Administrative Board of the Graduate School of Arts and Sciences in the year in which he began teaching at Harvard but did not resume that obligation after his sabbatical leave in 1917. He was never a member of any of the other standing committees or boards listed in the Harvard *Catalogue.* He continued to be an avid armchair analyst of contemporary politics as it played out in the daily press. But, unlike his Harvard colleague Hart, he did not mix in practical politics. Shortly after the move to Cambridge, he described his classroom stance on political issues: "I am determined not to get so interested actively that I shall not be able to tell my story without prejudice or the reasonable apprehension of bias on my part by the class."[34]

Family tradition held that Turner had cast his first ballot for a Democratic candidate, much to his father's dismay. But his political views are best described as progressive. He had qualified as a Massachusetts voter in early fall 1912 by reading a paragraph from the Massachusetts Constitution, demonstrating that he could write his name, and showing that he had paid his one dollar of poll tax. He had sometimes applauded La Follette in Wisconsin state politics, but now an old friend, Woodrow Wilson, was in the field as a Democratic candidate for the presidency. Taft he rejected out of hand, and he faulted Theodore Roosevelt's lack of interest in tariff reform, his support from Wall Street, and disingenuous aspects of the Square Deal program. The personal tie with Wilson might have determined Turner's commitment in any event. But he did plan, he told Dorothy, to support the Massachusetts Progressives at the state level.

For twenty years, as leader of the history program at Wisconsin, Turner sought eminence and in great degree succeeded in his quest. Now in his first few years as a member of the history faculty of Harvard University, he could enjoy that eminence and, incidentally, confirm his right to it. He found much to enjoy as he developed his work in Cambridge. He forged new friendships with graduate students and members of the Cambridge and Boston intellectual circles, and he maintained the relationships with that circle of professional peers formed during the 1890s and early 1900s. Other scholars expressed their respect. He found congenial spirits with whom to dine on a regular basis—at the Shop Club in Cambridge, where he ate well and listened to faculty colleagues discuss their research, and the Thursday Club in Boston. He now had local affiliation in the Colonial Society of Massachusetts, the American Antiquarian Society, and the Massachusetts Historical Society. The Colonial Society—which accepted only descendants of colonial New Englanders—welcomed him into its resident ranks so enthusiastically that he became its president in 1914. None of these associations, however, provided the sense of belonging, nor symbolic memories comparable to those known in the limestone and marble building at the junction of Park and State Streets in Madison.

Although he enjoyed mimicking local pronunciation, "Caaambridge" life flowed at higher intellectual voltage than had that in Madison, and Turner could report lunch or dinner with such dignitaries as William H. Taft, Theodore Roosevelt, Lord Bryce, and James Ford Rhodes. At a dinner hosted by Rhodes, Turner essayed a witty speech and reported success, while vowing never to venture into that métier again. But Harvard University was not the University of Wisconsin, where Turner had the ear of the president as did no other faculty member and where this fact, as well as his scholarly and political abilities, won him special deference. Accepted as a fine teacher and as a genial personality, he seems never to have surmounted the hedge of reservations, that barrier of "smug satisfaction"—in a friend's phrasing—that committed Harvardians erected around themselves. He does not seem to have penetrated the inner circles of power at Harvard. Where once he had led and protected, now he was himself protected, we suspect, by the powerful Haskins. And we infer that Turner's teaching at Harvard gave him less satisfaction than had been the case at Wisconsin, where he had believed his "workshop" was truly extending the boundaries of historical scholarship in the United States and recognized in the profession as so doing.

Turner joined a group of exceptionally talented scholars in the Harvard University history department. Ephraim Emerton, Archibald C. Coolidge, Haskins, and others outside the field of American history enjoyed high reputations in their fields. By the time of Turner's arrival, Albert B. Hart and Edward Channing, each in his own way, had achieved notable reputations in building the program in American history. "Short, and rotund," smooth-shaven, gruff in demeanor, if not at heart, "his lectures . . . charged with irony and wit . . . ever a foe to tradition, myth, and historical humbug,"[35] Channing was by this time almost obsessive in his dedication of time and attention to the great multivolume survey of American history that he had begun years earlier. Hart was a man of different style. A sturdy chin growth topped by a flaring mustachio contributed to his imposing presence, whether striding into an introductory class attended by dutiful assistants, holding forth at his entrepreneurial best in the councils of the AHA, or instructing a political conference or convention. Hart was named to the presidency of both the AHA and the American Political Science Association, and after the administration of courses in government were separated in 1911 from those in history, he concentrated mainly on his work in political science.

Although Channing had developed a considerable range of course offerings in American history, Turner found himself in a less comprehensive program than he had developed at the University of Wisconsin. He admitted to McLaughlin in early 1915 that he felt a "general American history man" might be more useful in the Harvard program than a specialist in western American history. In actuality Turner became the backbone of the American curriculum as Channing was increasingly granted half-year leaves to labor on his "big book." In early 1917 Turner reported that he was the only full-time Americanist in the department and, although Harvard moved to fill the half year vacated by Channing's arrangement, the American program was still smaller than on Turner's arrival. He noted wistfully that "other large universities have three or more American history men, as Chicago 3 or 4, Wisconsin, 3 and one half, and I think Yale."[36]

Turner had left a large program, where his wish was a command, for a position in which he was carrying a major part of the student undergraduate load in American history and was only one of a half-dozen major departmental figures. As a newcomer and westerner in the Yard and in New England, he was perhaps least highly regarded of them all. Whereas in Madison Turner saw his university president frequently and the Turners and Van Hises camped together, Turner now learned of President Lowell's decisions through intermediaries. His Harvard colleague and director of the library, Coolidge, was a courtly gentleman and supportive, but it is doubtful that he took seriously Turner's efforts to explain the way things were done in the library of the State Historical Society of Wisconsin.

Despite his assurance to Caroline that his teaching commitment would be essentially the same as at Wisconsin, Turner did not benefit from the kind of arrangement during his early years in Cambridge that had, in theory, allowed him to alternate semesters of teaching and research at Wisconsin. Compensating somewhat for the difference, Harvard had a sabbatical system, but it was not until 1916 that Turner was eligible to seek this relief from teaching. Although he expanded his undergraduate offering to include the second half of an American history survey, "History 17. The History of the West" remained his staple undergraduate offering. In 1911 he published a *List of References in History 17* for the use of the students in this course and revised it periodically thereafter. This guide charted the organization of his lectures and was much used by his students and other teachers in developing similar courses.

Critics of the western history courses that became common in the curricula of American colleges and universities have emphasized that many instructors concluded their lectures with treatment of the 1890s despite the fact that there was much later settlement and initial exploitation of natural resources in the American West. During the early Cambridge years Turner gave heavy coverage to the colonial frontiers, breaking the course for semester's end at about 1850. But he did not end his course on the history of the West with the decade of the 1890s. Of the fifty-two reading units in the *List of References* of 1913, the last five dealt with the West after 1900—"The New West, 1900–1910," "Combinations and the Development of the West," "Conservation and the West," "The Progressives," and "Contemporaneous Western Ideals." In the edition of 1922 Turner and Frederick Merk added a section entitled "The West in the World War and Reconstruction." If many instructors misrepresented western history by implying that it ended in the 1890s, Turner did not. The morning paper each day brought him a new installment of source material to modify or supplement his understanding of American development and the West's relation to it.

At Wisconsin Turner's primary commitment to the graduate program was unabashed. There eighteen students completed the doctorate under his direction, and many others studied with him at the graduate level. At Harvard he enhanced his reputation as a stimulating and supportive advisor, but most of those who completed their work under his immediate direction defended their dissertations during the last five years of his tenure. Solon J. Buck, his former graduate student at Wisconsin, completed his famous study of the Grangers at Harvard in 1911. In 1914 George M. Stephenson defended his study of federal land policy between 1840 and 1862, and in the following year Kenneth W. Colegrove brought his study of state instruction of members of the federal Congress to a close. His former student at both Wisconsin and Harvard, Raynor G. Wellington, published *The Political and Sectional Influence of the Public Lands, 1828–1842* in 1914 but did not complete doctoral requirements at either institution. The studies directed by Turner in his early years at Harvard University clearly reflected the major focus of the doctoral work he had guided at Wisconsin, emphasizing sectional aspects of American politics during the nineteenth century.

Graduate students at Harvard University found conferences with Turner highly inspirational. His enthusiasm was contagious, his grasp of bibliography comprehensive and sure, and his manner supportive. His letters of advice were helpful. For example, writing to Reginald F. Arragon in the summer of 1916, he discussed the problems involved in selecting a subject for a doctoral dissertation. He preferred the student to "find his own subject," he told Arragon, but also believed it wise for the young scholar to discuss the matter with "an older man." Although the latter might not actually suggest a specific topic, he might start the student "on a train of thought" leading to the "thing he wants." This had happened in Turner's case, he recalled, when he had been set to investigating the "common fields of the old French towns in the State," a project that had in turn developed into a study of the fur trade. Library resources too must be considered. He saw considerable opportunity for research on the "settlement of the states of the Great Plains and the Rocky Mountains," but much of this investigation would have to be done on the ground in the "records, newspapers, and . . . general historical collections" of the state historical societies. Then Turner suggested an impressive list of possible topics to Arragon, many of which were to find their historians in coming years.[37]

Turner was adept at suggesting to advanced students how refractory sources could be managed, and when necessary he provided sympathetic understanding. Colegrove found it difficult to develop a coherent narrative. Turner assured his dejected student that "there is always a time when a man is disappointed in his thesis, or any other work, if it's worthwhile. That time is often the darkest hour before the dawn!" Turner advised him to "stand far enough off from your material to see it in *general* and you may find that there are changes, period by period, that indicate that not only the material of instruction changes but also the spirit and form of the instruction idea, and that this is due to changing composition and spirit of the American people and of the particular sections involved." In ending, he rallied Colegrove's slumping spirit: "I have hopes! Let me hear from you and see you when you are ready." The letter melded understanding, sound advice, and an affirmation of faith. The letter also, it is true, was dated three months after Colegrove sent his communication to Turner, that missive having become part of a "mass of mail" that accumulated while Turner was in camp.[38]

Arthur Buffinton illustrated another side of graduate direction. Buffinton had his first conference with Turner shortly after the latter arrived in Cambridge. By 1912 this student had begun a long-continuing correspondence with Turner about the progress of his dissertation. Working fitfully on his research and producing some fine articles along the way, Buffinton seemed incapable of completing his doctoral thesis. Over the years, Turner urged him on and suggested various strategies to bring the work to completion. Ultimately it was, but not until after Turner's retirement. Turner, however,—according to Farrand—only demonstrated such patience when he detected real promise in the student. He understood that some in the flock were geese rather than swans. Nor did he accede to every request for a recommendation from job-seeking former students.

Turner also retained his interest in his Wisconsin students. He regarded Edgar E. Robinson as one of the most promising during his last years in Madison. The doctorate uncompleted, Robinson continued to investigate congressional voting blocs during Turner's early years at Harvard when the latter's own interest in empirical research methods was most keen. Turner advised him elaborately on the response that he should give to another student who had expressed interest in working on the same dissertation topic. Teacher and former student discussed the possibility of Robinson coming to Harvard for further work, but the latter was never able to do so. In this case the outcome was happy. Robinson established himself solidly within the Stanford University history department and earned a national reputation as a political historian without benefit of the doctoral union card. Homer C. Hockett had been a stalwart in the Wisconsin seminar, as well as serving as Turner's assistant. As Hockett began his teaching career in a major state university, Turner admonished him, "I know how hard it is for a man to produce. But don't yield to the temptation of doing your duty as a teacher *solely*. Your growth and the *stimulation* of your teaching depends in part on your continuing to investigate and publish."[39]

Some of Turner's graduate students at Wisconsin believed that he did not spend great amounts of time in preparing his undergraduate lectures. He may have given more care to his lecture preparation within the Harvard setting. Perhaps because of this fact, perhaps because his physical resilience was diminishing, undergraduate teaching seemed to exact a heavier toll on him in Cambridge. His large class, he explained to Caroline in early March 1915, required "a good deal of expenditure of nervous energy." A few weeks later he reported that lectures "keep me running pretty rapidly"[40]

Although in these years he directed fewer graduate students in the last stages of preparing dissertations than had been the case at Madison, dissertations at Harvard had to be approved by three readers, and Turner served on the reading committees of candidates directed by other faculty members. After some years, impatience at such duties showed in his letters to Caroline. When Colegrove promised that he would soon deliver a "bulky thesis," Turner termed doctoral dissertations a "rather trying literature." Later, with two in hand, he ruefully noted that he was "booked for a long sentence."[41]

Most modern scholars would consider that they had labored productively if they had produced the number of publications in a decade that Turner did during the first ten years of the twentieth century. In his mind it was not enough, interacting as he was with the leaders of the profession, and having, as special friends, such relentless scholars as Farrand and Haskins. In accepting the call to Cambridge, he viewed Harvard as a refuge where he could harvest the fruits of years of preparation. But Turner did not reap the anticipated crop. Although his brain did not atrophy while he was at Harvard, he published less in these years. Aside from his presidential address to the AHA, Turner's publications in his first few years at Harvard were bibliographical or encyclopedia contributions. During the 1890s Hart and Channing prepared a guide to American history, which the teachers of the developing history profession found indispensable. Now Turner joined them in preparing the *Guide to the Study and Teaching of American History* of 1912, a publication destined to bring a meager trickle of income into the Turner coffers. In preparing the new edition of the guide, Turner was responsible for providing bibliography relating to the West and to recent American history.

After mild haggling designed to double his honorarium, Turner prepared the article in the eleventh edition of the *Encyclopaedia*

Britannica that covered the history of the United States from 1865 to 1910. Written amid the distractions involved in moving to Cambridge and appearing in 1911 as a much more elaborate contribution than the encyclopedia editors had initially requested, this exercise in writing contemporary American history allowed him to interpret the economic, social, and political trends under way around him. Turner outlined a changing America in terms similar to those in his presidential address to the AHA. But here, brief discussions of the economic and social forces changing America appear between longer passages tracing the elections of presidents and the major legislation, court decisions, and foreign policy developments of their administrations. Thus he combined discussion of long run trends with a presidential synthesis.

Turner's antiseptic account did not suggest particular sympathy for the problems of southern poor whites or freedmen, concern about American imperialism, the plight of the Indians, discrimination against immigrant groups, or the concentration of resources in the hands of large corporations. On the other hand, he presented the emergence of reform movements and the efforts of state and federal governments as understandable reactions to the more disconcerting aspects of industrialization. Perhaps Turner's lack of passion about social issues reflects the homogenized encyclopedia format in which he was forced to work. But this characteristic of his article also reflects his early commitment to impartiality, a position that he always maintained in theory, although sometimes departing from it in practice, as we shall later see. When he sketched the "forces" at work in the transformation of modern America, Turner did not use the word *frontier* or portray the 1890s as a great breaking point in American history. The influence of sectionalism in shaping national policy outcomes, however, was a recurrent theme in this article.

Turner also prepared pieces on the American frontier, sectionalism, and the "West as a Factor in American Politics" for the *Cyclopedia of American Government*, edited by Hart and McLaughlin. His article on the frontier summarized ideas long since developed; the pieces relating to sectionalism presented his current thinking on a subject about which he would continue to ponder during the remainder of his career.

Apart from his encyclopedia articles and his work on reference guides, Turner's new publications during the second decade of the twentieth century totaled but half a dozen—addresses or essays all. No book appeared until the publication in 1920 of thirteen previously published essays now brought together in *The Frontier in American History*. Of these, only four were published as late in Turner's career as 1910. His first decade at Harvard was one of unrealized expectations, when achievement and pleasure were well mixed with disappointment.

In 1913 Turner found the task of preparing a memorial address for Reuben Gold Thwaites to be uniquely painful. Thwaites had thought highly of the young Turner, even suggesting that they establish a newspaper on the southwestern frontier and help shape the country there. Some eight years Turner's senior, this brilliant, energetic, and outgoing man proved a firm friend and supporter during Turner's graduate student years and while he was building the Wisconsin history program. After completion of the Historical Society's building the history department had its offices there. The two men rapidly emerged as mutually supportive leaders in the AHA and were members of the Nucleus. They shared commitments to Unitarianism, to canoeing, camping and cycling, and above all to history.

Speaking on October 23, 1913, Turner soberly and gracefully eulogized his friend. He recalled that Thwaites had "opened a seminary room to the advanced students in American history, with full access to the stacks—an unheard of liberality among non-university libraries at that time." In his skillful administration of the society, Thwaites had played a major role in creating "one of America's greatest historical workshops."[42] He had done "a man's work, and left an indelible impress not only on this Historical Society and the State of Wisconsin, but upon the historical activities of the nation." He had been a "great historical editor and modernizer, the builder of a new type of state historical society."[43]

Thwaites's career and that of Turner had their parallels—the older man bringing the Historical Society into a new era of professionalism and scholarly productivity and the younger doing the same for the Wisconsin history program. The memorial service may have suggested to Turner that his career too might be moving to its inevitable conclusion.

Two of Turner's presentations in these years of his first decade at Harvard show him at his scholarly best. Addressing a joint meeting of the two national associations of geographers in 1914, Turner spoke on the subject of "Geographical Influences in American Political History." He began his paper with concise and contrasting definitions of the terms *frontier* and *section*, "two of the most fundamental factors in American history. The frontier is a moving section, or rather a form of society, determined by the reactions between the wilderness and the edge of expanding settlement; the section is the outcome of the deeper-seated geographical conditions interacting with the stock which settled the region."[44]

The lengthy abstract of this paper contains the only extended discussion of Turner's methods of mapping election returns and congressional roll calls. He noted some shortcomings in the methods he had developed. In analyzing "political sectionalism" in the United States, the investigator must remember that, in contrasting the North and the South or the East and the West, interior divisions within these sections must also be subjected to "further analysis." In using the votes of congressmen to ascertain the opinion of the residents of their districts, it must also be understood, cautioned Turner, that representatives were not always in accord with the voters whom they represented and that gerrymandering and the differing sizes of congressional districts might also make the researcher's maps somewhat misleading reflections of local sentiment. In order to detect local concentrations of particular types of voters, Turner preferred maps that showed voting at the county level or smaller electoral units. "The final refinement of such mapping" he wrote, "would be by election precincts, which would be a much more satisfactory mode of exhibiting the relations of voting to soils, resources, position, population, etc."[45] This last step, he admitted, had not yet been taken.

Turner conceded that these methods of mapping obscured the presence of divergent minorities and, in merely recording voting pluralities, might conceal very considerable changes in local political sentiment and behavior. Nor could they adequately reflect the ambiguities, compromises, and inconsistencies that were involved in building and maintaining political parties, thus perhaps serving better as indications of specific political behavior than of political opinion. In *Scribner's Statistical Atlas* electoral maps depicted the outcome of the election of 1880 in terms of the party percentages of votes cast. This method, Turner noted, was more precise than the pluralities depicted in the maps and slides that he used to illustrate his lectures. He maintained, however, that his "coarser reconnaissance system" showed "the more durable and pronounced political areas," even if failing to show "areas of transition and of political instability" as clearly as did maps based on party voting percentages. "The limitations noted in theory are not so important in practice as they might seem," he argued.[46]

Turner used his maps as the basis for a discussion of the political character of particular geographical areas. He concluded that in the United States "there are areas influenced or controlled by geological factors, wherein capitalistic considerations are strongest, and that such areas tend to be Whig and, later, Republican." But "social or psychological considerations sometimes reverse[d] the result." "The problem," he suggested, "resembles that of a complex geological area and demands the use of the multiple hypothesis." Still, "the main thesis, that there is a geography of American politics and that the relation between geography and political history becomes clearer the farther the method of investigation is refined, seems established. The facts demand combined investigation by geographer and historian." In a footnote Turner explained that Orin G. Libby had "begun" the series of "studies of political geography" that had been thereafter continued in his seminar. Other seminal and illustrative publications listed in the note included works by Albion W. Small and Franklin H. Giddings.[47]

For a generation Turner's seminar had been the leading history workshop in the United States where sectional processes in American history were analyzed. On his arrival at Harvard he was eagerly pursuing all types of maps that might reveal sectional differences within the United States. Turner and his students were not simplistic geographical determinists in their electoral and roll call analysis. They recognized the importance of cultural baggage and suspected that religious affiliations might have something to do with political behavior. Perhaps they underemphasized the significance of class, but after he accepted Becker's dissertation at least, Turner conceded that this factor must be considered in evaluating political outcomes. Still, the mapping methods fell short of the more exact measures of political behavior and causal inference that scholars of the 1950s and thereafter utilized. During Turner's most fertile years scholars in even the most empirical social science were not yet using statistical correlation and regression techniques in electoral analysis nor clustering methods and indices of cohesion and likeness for the analysis of legislative behavior. But the methods of political map analysis developed in Turner's seminar had a major impact upon the nature of American political history in his time.

Turner's presentation of 1914 impressed geographers, and he gladly accepted membership in the Association of American Geographers. The address culminated twenty years in which he had been intensely interested in American sectionalism and the methods by which it might be studied. The topic would be his primary concern for the remainder of his life. He constructed a series of maps depicting sectional voting patterns on cheesecloth backing and at appropriate times in his courses suspended the maps by large safety pins along one wall of his classroom. Small outline maps on which he or students had recorded senate voting on political issues in both the nineteenth and twentieth centuries are scattered through the Turner papers at the Huntington Library. But in analytical method Turner had by 1914 reached an outer boundary. He realized that voters and legislators voted as members of parties as well as regional representatives and might be influenced by other considerations as well. But he did not attempt to measure the relative strength of the various factors affecting electoral or legislative behavior. Even in his era, simple quantitative tests would have been possible.

After outlining the progress of various frontiers across the continent in his essay of 1893, Turner wrote that "it would be a work worth the historian's labors to mark these various frontiers and in detail compare one with another."[48] He never completed this task himself. But a few years after moving to Cambridge, he prepared a presidential address for the Colonial Society of Massachusetts on a frontier theme. Entitled "The First Official Frontier of the Massachusetts Bay," this essay considered the years extending from the mid-seventeenth to approximately the mid-eighteenth centuries. As a newcomer in the Harvard and Boston communities, Turner was on his mettle, and the published paper is one of the most heavily documented of his publications.

Harking back once more to the passage from the *Census Bulletin* of 1890 that reported the disappearance of a frontier line, Turner noted that the General Court of Massachusetts had in 1690 designated the location of the colony's frontier, making provision for its defense. In the years between these two actions, said Turner, "westward expansion was the most important single process in American history." The term *frontier town* had come into use by at least the 1660s, and the unique characteristics and role of such towns in the colony were recognized earlier. When the eighteenth century opened, Massachusetts was designating frontier towns that settlers were not to abandon, and Turner identified "an officially designated frontier line for New England."[49] He outlined the impact of the society in its vicinity upon the laws and the social practices of Massachusetts, giving particular attention to the problems of frontier defense and the distribution of land.

"This early prototype," he concluded, displayed "many of the traits of later frontiers." It bordered Indian country and advanced into it, encouraged "militant qualities," affected "psychology . . . morals . . . institutions," and, requiring defensive measures, stimulated "consolidation." Following the fur traders, "eastern men of property" and "democratic pioneers" combined to settle the frontier areas. Sometimes the process generated antagonism. The East tried to control frontier development, but "wilderness conditions" and the memory of past "contentions" worked to emphasize "individualistic and democratic tendencies." Freedom from "customary usages" and the guidance of a longer-settled clergy also encouraged innovating tendencies. Some eastern leaders deprecated the impact of the West on "pillars of society" and believed that its opportunities for investment might corrupt. "The frontier," said Cotton Mather, was "the Wrong side of the Hedge."[50] Turner's audience must have glowed in self-satisfaction when his concluding passages extolled the great contributions that New England had made to settling a West that eventually extended far beyond its colonial frontier.

Turner's description of the Massachusetts Bay colony's frontier is smoothly written and abounds in colorful quotations. At first glance one might assume that Turner had done no more than present new evidence in support of his ideas of 1893. There are, however, subtle differences. In 1914 Turner emphasized that frontier settlement might move in a variety of directions given the nature of the physiography and not necessarily flow from east to west. He maintained that there was a "common sequence of frontier types (fur trader, cattle-raising pioneer, small primitive farmer, and the farmer engaged in intensive varied agriculture to produce a surplus for export)" but that "these stages succeeded rapidly and intermingled." Thus did he qualify but also retain the stage model of westward development that he had described in 1893. In 1893 the frontier process of land-taking and settlement had "explain[ed] American development." Now, he argued, "in the two hundred years between [the] official attempt to locate the Massachusetts frontier line, and the official announcement of the ending of the national frontier line, westward expansion was the most important single process in American history." Thus he admitted that other "processes" had helped to shape American development, although these were less important than the frontier.[51]

Turner addressed the members of the Colonial Society in April 1914. In June he was the commencement speaker at the University of

Washington, where he spoke upon "The West and American Ideals," his former student Edmond S. Meany beaming from the university president's chair. Perhaps if Turner had not been ill that spring, he would have exerted greater effort in preparing this talk, but perhaps not. Planning to devote his time on the transcontinental train to preparation, he allowed the scenery and other passengers to divert him. He arrived in Seattle with script still unfinished. As delivered, the speech was another paean to western ideals, a reprise of material in his speeches of the last five years on that subject. He contrasted recent developments in the United States with those in a nation dominated by the westward movement. Again he described the ideals that he believed the westering processes had engendered, explained the role of the university in a nation where free lands no longer existed, and concluded that there would be a "new era . . . if schools and universities can only widen the intellectual horizon of the people, help to lay the foundations of a better industrial life, show them new goals for endeavor, inspire them with more varied and higher ideals." His last words echoed the lines from Tennyson's poem "Ulysses," "Come my friends, / 'Tis not too late to seek a newer world."[52]

If Turner approached the stage of cliché in presenting his ideas, if he sailed far from the mooring of fact, if he oversimplified, if his figures were sometimes strained, there were hundreds of commencement addresses being delivered in the same June that were far worse. The address contains Turner's most memorable phrasing of the origin of American democracy, "born of no theorist's dream; it was not carried in the *Sarah Constant* to Virginia, nor in the *Mayflower* to Plymouth. It came out of the American forest, and it gained new strength each time it touched a new frontier." It showed a Turner still incorporating evidence into his argument, quoting Godkin for the only time in his various essays on the frontier.[53]

Noting that "legislation is taking the place of the free lands as the means of preserving the ideal of democracy," a process that was "endangering the other pioneer ideal of creative and competitive individualism," Turner was hopeful about the future and decided in his social priorities: "It would be a grave misfortune if [Americans] so rich in experience, in self-confidence and aspiration, in creative genius, should turn to some Old World discipline of socialism or plutocracy, or despotic rule, whether by class or by dictator. Nor shall we be driven to these alternatives. Our ancient hopes, our courageous faith, our underlying good humor and love of fair play will triumph in the end.

There will be give and take in all directions." Leadership in these processes would most "likely" come from "men trained in the Universities."[54] Speaking less than fifty years after Americans had ended a civil war in which the give-and-take had involved the deaths of more than half a million men, Turner was both optimistic and naive, and yet as prophet he was to be more right than wrong.

Turner was less than satisfied with his performance, but reported to Haskins that because the audience included half a dozen vocal babies, his "prophetic Jeremiads didn't stir up the animals as they should have done if they had been heard. Always take along a supply of babies when you preach. They are as good as an accident policy." Now in relaxation he felt "about as the fellow does who relaxes in the electric chair after the first adequate shock is applied."[55] His Seattle address marked the beginning of a fallow period in Turner's publication history. His only publications during the next two years were short committee reports, summarizing activity on behalf of the AHA.

11 Eminence Challenged

"The master politician of the ring"

In describing the attractions of Madison during his early career, Turner always emphasized the rich collections of the State Historical Society of Wisconsin. The Harvard University to which Turner moved was in the process of building magnificent library collections, but its western holdings did not equal those in Madison. This deficiency would not handicap Turner to the degree that one might assume. He was now committed to understanding American development in the whole through the lens of sectional interaction, as well as through investigation of a particular region. And to his great joy, he found a benefactress waiting, poised to help in improving Harvard's resources in western history.

Alice (Elsie) Forbes Perkins Hooper was the daughter of Charles Elliot Perkins, president of the Chicago, Burlington and Quincy Railroad Company. Perkins had extended this railroad system across central and western America, making it one of the great carriers of the nation. The Perkins family always regarded Burlington, Iowa, as their true home, but Perkins also established a residence in Boston, and his duties allowed him to take family members into the mountain West and California for extended periods. Bright and vivacious, Elsie Perkins grew into young womanhood loving the West but also enjoying entree into the higher social circles of New England. In 1895, when she was in her late twenties, Elsie married William Hooper, a proper New Englander and widower twelve years her senior, who was auditor of the Calumet and Hecla Mining Company at the time. Later he became treasurer of the Boston Elevated Railway Company. In 1910 Alice Perkins Hooper and her husband were living at Elsinaes, an impressive residence in Manchester, Massachusetts.

Alice Hooper described herself as a woman of "creative spirit and a wild unbridled imagination," and she cultivated wide, if somewhat eccentric, interests.[1] A photograph of Hooper, taken during her middle years, shows a substantial woman clothed in loose garments, with determined chin, wide mouth, and generous nose. Large eyes gaze commandingly from under heavy eyebrows obscured by the brim of a hat reminiscent of a shallow, inverted flower pot. When she first met Turner, Hooper suffered from recurrent ill health and used a crutch in getting about. But she refused to resign from the world and, although inclined to gush a bit, was a woman worthy of admiration.

Hooper was not the archetypical predatory hostess interested primarily in attracting "names" to her table. If she had been born in the right place and time her drawing room might accurately have been termed a *salon* because she presided over what she called a "precious little society of friends."[2] But she was too much the social activist to be dismissed as a mere salon keeper. She was deeply interested in charitable causes, including the Arbella Club of Manchester that she founded and subsidized in order "to teach girls who have limited horizons how to lead useful happy lives."[3]

By early 1910 Hooper had begun to consider the possibility of assisting Harvard University in the purchase of books in the history of the American West as a memorial to her father, who, as president of a great land grant railroad, had been deeply involved in western settlement. When she broached this idea to Harvard officers, they encouraged her and suggested that Turner, the incoming member of the history department, would be much interested, and a fruitful source of advice. At the end of September 1910 she dropped a line to Turner, explaining that one of her cousins was unable to accept her invitation to dine in a small party with President Taft and his wife, and she invited Turner in his stead. "I dare say you [and the President] are old friends," she wrote.[4]

Hooper's plans miscarried, and instead Turner joined her for lunch in early October. This was to be a very successful meeting. Turner met Mr. Hooper—"Willie" or the "Squire"—as well, perhaps, as members of the small pack of Scotties that also resided at Elsinaes. In an afternoon drive through blazing fall foliage in the Hooper limousine, Turner and Hooper discussed her plans for giving western history materials to the Harvard Library. Turner promised to advise her further after additional thought and investigation of Harvard's holdings. The visit to Elsinaes was to be the first of many, and the correspondence and friendship begun at this time continued until Turner's death.

A week after Turner's visit Hooper wrote to her "Dear New Friend" assuring him that he was "welcome to join" the friendship circle and explaining that she did not wish to be part of a joint effort. "I don't *want* others to contribute. I want to build a little memorial to do good, and I want you to be the guide and the chief cook of the whole proceeding. My invitation applies not alone for business but for you when you want a walk or a drive or a whiff of the sea at our 'Farm in Patagonia.'" The Hoopers, Alice informed him, would like to see him again, even if he had not "reached any conclusions about the books." He had, she continued, "a permit—forever and ever" to visit them in their "peaceful exile."[5]

In response, Turner gracefully apologized for his delay in writing— "a high tide of duties and hospitalities ha[d] rolled over" him after his journey to Manchester. He then got down to business. He had "looked over the alcoves where the western histories are chiefly located" and was "pleased to find the foundations better than I expected." Turner assured Hooper that Harvard "would gratefully accept a contribution annually along the lines of our conversation, and that one thousand dollars would be an outside annual amount for such book purchases." He summarized the plan as he understood it at the time: "a fund for Western history as a memorial" to Charles Perkins in the amount of about one thousand dollars for an undetermined number of years, "its purposes to include the collection of books and other sources for the study of western history and the promotion of research in Western history." After planting a few more seeds for thought—traveling grants for graduate students and allowances for publication—that Hooper might consider if she wished to expand her activity, Turner informed her that he was sending her "some books and pamphlets . . . in which I have tried to set down some western ideas." One of these, he noted, was a first edition of the *Frontier*, published "when the appreciation of the western influence was new."[6]

So began the friendship between Alice Hooper and Turner. As the institutional relationship developed and the personal exchange deepened into respect and affection, he became in correspondence, "Historicus" or other more personal substitutes, and she "Dear Lady" or even "Contessa." A surprising aspect of Turner's letter of mid-October 1910 is the implication that he had not investigated the library stacks when considering the Harvard invitation—evidence, one assumes, of the depth of his disenchantment with the situation at Wisconsin in 1909 and his lack of realism in confronting it.

To Turner initially, Hooper must have appeared a godsend, who, in satisfying her own commitment to family and heritage, was willing to meet some of the needs of western history at Harvard. As such she should be tactfully nurtured—an exercise in which Turner was highly skilled. He called her "friendship" his "new honorary degree" and told her that it had brought him "happiness."[7] But very rapidly he found much more than a donor in this enthusiastic lady. In Hooper's mind and experience, the West and East were inextricably merged, but never in a way that discounted the western experience. She was not intimidated by eminent public men, by captains of industry, or by members of Harvard's power elite. Knowing her was a comforting experience to a man from Portage and Madison who had based his scholarly reputation on the argument that the West was equally or more important than the East in the building of America and who constantly encountered men who viewed his ideas with polite skepticism. Through Hooper's door as well, Turner entered a very different world than that of the county seatocracy in which he had been reared or Madison's mingling of gown, town, and government. Now he glimpsed the family life and social contacts of those railroad and industrial leaders who had revolutionized the economic life of the West during his early years. Mingling admiration and flattery, Turner described her as a "marvelous center of radiant energy, which draws into its vortex bodies light and bodies heavy—socialists, Progressives, ex-Presidents, Taffy-eaters, Women Reformers, Society B——r Fl——s, and Railroad Presidents . . . straws and pearls, dust and diamonds, all go whirling around that red room's central point." He hastened to explain that *"dust"* was involved only in the "spiritual sense," referring to "such as FJT."[8]

On her part, Hooper found in Turner a source of sound and enthusiastic advice on the historical materials that she wished to gather in memory of her father. She also discovered a renowned and charming intellectual who lacked the arrogance of many eastern academics and who did not put her down because she took up his time, nor because she was a woman and not a scholar. Very early in their acquaintance they realized that they shared reservations about unadulterated New Englandism. In every respect Hooper found Turner to be a worthy companion in her western "crusade." After several years she was to tell him, "You and all you stand for are a great asset in my garden of friends and . . . you have no idea of how much I appreciate your taking the time to come to me."[9]

In November 1910 Hooper formally addressed the President and Fellows of Harvard College, offering a contribution in the sum of $1,000 annually for the purposes that she had discussed with Turner. A bookplate honoring Charles Elliot Perkins was to be placed in all books bought with such monies. The President and Fellows were pleased to accept the gift, although perhaps wishing it larger and less parochial in objective. Mrs. Hooper and Turner set themselves energetically to the task of spending her money, she consulting well-placed friends and he colleagues and librarians as to the possibility of obtaining historical materials dealing with the westward movement. Given Hooper's background, they particularly sought railroad records initially, but Turner's vision also embraced western newspapers and other relevant sources. As the hunt developed, so did Hooper's enthusiasm and, as hoped, her generosity began to exceed the annual $1,000 gift. In 1911 she donated a $300 fellowship to Harvard to support a graduate student working in western history.

Meanwhile, Edgar H. Wells, secretary of the Harvard Alumni Association and a good friend of Hooper, suggested to her that the work of collection could be aided by creating a commission on western History composed of dignitaries with Harvard connections whose names would impress prospective donors. Receiving her willing assent, Wells organized the Harvard Commission on Western History with the help of Turner and Coolidge, Harvard's historian-librarian. Justified to the President and Fellows as an agency designed to build "a large collection on the history and development of the West," the commission was approved by those worthies in early 1912. Their action, Wells informed Hooper, constituted a "distinct epoch at Harvard all due . . . to your farsighted imagination, energy, and generosity."[10]

Wells regarded the commission as a means of strengthening Harvard's research resources in an important field of study but also as providing an opportunity to bind Harvard's western alumni more closely to their alma mater. Turner explained the objectives of the commission in articles in the *Harvard Alumni Bulletin* and the *Harvard Graduates' Magazine* and distributed reprints to western friends and acquaintances, accompanying them with personal messages of explanation. The commission's function, as he described it, would be to seek "newspaper files, maps, pamphlets, letters, journals, account books, business records, trade magazines, reports of chambers of commerce or agricultural societies, church and school records" and other materials bearing upon western economic and social development.[11]

Turner understood that some western scholars and archivists might consider the efforts of the commission to be piratical. He therefore emphasized that the western progression of the frontier was a national phenomenon that could be studied appropriately in Harvard University. To Stephens at Berkeley, for example, he wrote, "Our aim is to build up *in the East* an adequate center for the study of the West as a whole." Never could the collection rival Berkeley's "collections for Pacific slope history," nor would Harvard wish "material to which your institution has a superior claim," but Harvard should accept materials that might otherwise be lost: "[W]e wish to cooperate, — drawing from duplicates and extra material in Western libraries ... and adding interstate and interregional material which may legitimately come to us."[12]

The plans for the commission involved appointment of an archivist to administer the collecting program and relieve the commissioners of much of the burden of correspondence, thus far borne by Hooper, Turner, and the secretary of the commission, Wells. Hooper agreed to increase her annual contribution to support such an employee. Accepting the recommendation of one of the western commissioners and despite doubts on the part of both Turner and Hooper, the commission engaged Archer B. Hulbert. Then teaching at Marietta College and author of works on the development of western America, Hulbert had little advanced training in history. This deficiency he hoped to remedy by participating in the Harvard doctoral program while serving the commission.

At first Hulbert showed great promise. He searched energetically for materials for the Perkins Collection in Ohio and suggested plans for similar activity in other western states and northern New England. But he was much too eager to use his appointment as a step toward obtaining an instructorial position at Harvard, and he persisted in efforts to change the terms of an agreement under which he would have established residence at Harvard for an extended period. Wells called on Turner to extricate the commission from the relationship in the summer of 1914. Hulbert did, however, make some contribution to the development of Harvard's collection of western books and manuscripts.

Meanwhile, commission members had achieved a great coup by obtaining a magnificent collection of books and pamphlets relating to the development of the Church of Latter-Day Saints from a resident of Salt Lake City, Eli H. Peirce. Brought to the attention of the commission by a Harvard librarian who noted its advertisement by a midwestern bookstore, this collection inspired the commissioners to conduct an energetic and somewhat devious campaign. This involved backtracking through two agent book stores in an effort to bypass them and save commission costs. The commissioners pursued much of the preliminary investigation while still uncertain as to whether they could find the required purchase funds. Originally the amount, believed to be about five thousand dollars, stood far in excess of what Hooper might be expected to give, and initially she disclaimed interest in a collection of Mormon materials. But good soldier that she was, she recanted.

The commission's agent, David Heald, journeyed to Salt Lake City in great haste lest a purchase option expire and the Church of Latter-Day Saints acquire this historical treasure. Once there, he bypassed the commission's initial Utah contact and engaged in a nerve-wracking negotiation with Peirce. Soon the pending transaction attracted unfavorable local attention. After first agreeing to negotiate directly with the commission, Peirce decided that he must honor his original agreement to give a commission to the local bookstore that had been his agent in the beginning. Heald agreed reluctantly to provide some of this sum and eventually supervised the shipment of several thousand books and pamphlets to Cambridge. Turner and other members of the commission celebrated at a small dinner marked by the quality of the food and the amount of libation involved. Although the expenses of "operation Mormon" totalled some $7,000, the Harvard authorities contributed $1,000 and the sale of duplicates reduced Hooper's contribution to about $4,000. Harvard now, Turner assured her, was unrivaled as a center for the study of Mormonism's beginnings.

Turner assessed Hulbert's contribution to the Perkins Collection for Hooper in a long letter to "My dear Mrs. Clio," written in the second half of 1914. Although the relationship had not worked out well, Hulbert had, Turner maintained, obtained some useful materials, and the publicity that he had generated would continue to bear fruit. He was perhaps generous in this evaluation, but Turner always remained on friendly terms with Hulbert. In the meantime, continued success "would be immensely facilitated by having a man devoted to that work primarily such as Secretaries of Historical Societies are for the western states." He hoped that she would not object to his "springing the proposal if the right person happens along."[13] That individual appeared in Thomas P. Martin, who entered Turner's seminar in the fall of 1914. A bright young Texan, Martin had received his initial training at Stanford University and followed it with a year of work at Berkeley under the direction of Turner's former student, Bolton. In June 1915 Hooper began to provide funds to support Martin as a part-time assistant in the work of the commission as well as to pay for a secretary for Turner.

Diligent, systematic, ambitious, and self-reliant, Martin was an excellent choice for the job. He immediately began a wide search for historical materials. He contacted the families of early New England traders to the Pacific Coast region, with gratifying results, and successfully broadened the search for railroad records begun by Turner and Hooper. Keeping his hand in the game, Turner courted Oswald G. Villard to the point where he surrendered the papers of his father, Henry Villard, of the Northern Pacific Railroad. The enthusiasm of commission members even briefly infected Harvard's president, Lowell, who wrote a number of letters soliciting family manuscripts from friends or acquaintances.

Harvard's collecting activity in the West, however, faced obstacles. Hooper viewed her father as a benefactor of the West. She was proud that he had reimbursed the creditors of a failed bank of which he was a director in Lincoln, Nebraska, during the 1890s, sacrificing much of his personal fortune. Many westerners, however, viewed railroad executives of the western systems differently, considering their wealth wrung unfairly from hard-pressed western producers and consumers. Some western archivists and scholars were infuriated that such a fortune should finance the study of western history at Harvard and whisk the records of western enterprise into the Harvard Yard. In a draft letter to Clarence S. Paine, secretary of the Nebraska Historical Society, Hooper informed him that she could not contribute to his organization: "I gave [the money] to Harvard College because Harvard College [as] the oldest deserved to be the mecca for young men and because New England men and New England money in a large measure have contributed to make western America and because I am a firm believer that we of the west when we can should get as near the older civilization as possible and learn from it an indescribable something it can pass on to us and in our turn bring to Harvard the breeziness and the independence of thought and the optimism bred in the western bone."[14] Turner tactfully complimented her on the letter but suggested that Paine might not understand her position. Even when bred in the bone, optimism is not bankable.

Turner understood that the Harvard commission might stir western animosity. Martin reported hostility in the lobbies at the annual meeting of the AHA in 1915, voiced particularly by Milo M. Quaife, Thwaites's successor at the State Historical Society of Wisconsin. Turner wrote firmly to Quaife affirming the commission's good intent, but even members of western Harvard alumni clubs reacted angrily to efforts to use their groups in behalf of the collecting program, western loyalties prevailing over those to alma mater. Nor did President Lowell ever regard the commission as a major Harvard enterprise or worthy of being part of the institution's larger fundraising efforts.

"No more pioneering," Turner had said in rejecting Berkeley for Harvard. But at Harvard he found himself devoting time to tasks and socializing in behalf of building library collections, obligations that he had not assumed at Wisconsin and probably would not have fulfilled at Berkeley either. Alice Hooper, however, inspired Turner's innate need to instruct, to give advice, to sparkle in personal communication. In her he found a patroness whom he thoroughly enjoyed—their friendship ripened and continued past the demise of the commission. Because her interest in arts and letters and current events was broad rather than deep, she contributed little to Turner's intellectual development, but she was, in a sense, a historical source, a window through which Turner derived enhanced understanding of both New England and its upper class. And her engagement in life, despite her rheumatic problems and various illnesses, was inspirational. "That woman who sits in her chair in the house day after day has more real contact with the world than any other person I know," confided Turner to Caroline.[15] She did not, however, inspire him to complete his great work.

The years between Turner's arrival in Cambridge and the outbreak of World War I found Turner firmly established as a leader in the history profession. He was acknowledged to be the creator of a school of American history. He was a former president of the AHA, a continuing power in its councils—one of the most powerful, some believed. He was a member of the small band of arbiters on the editorial board of the *American Historical Review* whose collective decisions meant the difference between national recognition and mere local or regional reputation. His suggestions usually carried great weight with the program chairman of the AHA, and he freely gave them. When Henry E. Bourne filled that office for the Cincinnati meeting in 1916, he asked for "a little advice" on papers dealing with the westward movement in the Ohio valley. Turner responded with a letter of six typewritten pages and four days later sent a second installment.[16] Program chairmen thought it a coup to include him among those giving papers. Turner's reputation had also spread into the realms of other disciplines, particularly the field of geography. History departments sought his services as a guest lecturer, and when the University of Chicago celebrated the twenty-fifth year of its graduate program, the faculty selected Turner to speak on behalf of the history discipline.

Turner had achieved the secret fantasy of many an academic when, ostensibly, he showed a board of regents the consequences of their blundering interference by resigning. From the mid-1890s onward, presidents and influential faculty members at other institutions used their most persuasive wiles to convince him that he should join their faculties. In the eyes of many, Turner attained the pinnacle of the profession by moving to Harvard University. His major objective, he explained, was to find that fertile and prepared field where he could harvest his matured crop of research. There was, he said, to be no more gazing at the horizon "where the strange roads go down." Few university presidents or departments could now afford to place out a welcome mat for a scholar so well placed and so advanced in years. But on a few occasions after moving to Cambridge, Turner did scan the skyline.

After the death of Thwaites, Van Hise inquired whether Turner would be interested in becoming secretary of the Historical Society, suggesting that an equivalent to his Harvard salary could be arranged by a university contribution, in return, perhaps, for teaching a course. In the society he might devolve some of the administration on others. Visiting in the West at the time, Caroline and Dorothy heard rumors that Turner might be invited back to Madison. As in the move to Harvard, Turner made up his mind without benefit of family consultation. Paxson was chair of the society committee searching for a new executive officer. Turner told Caroline that a letter from a member of the group indicated that an offer would come if he encouraged his western friends. But he continued, "I couldn't be happy trying to do that work; and couldn't do it well; and couldn't afford it financially."[17]

A week later Turner told Caroline that he had informed Van Hise that even a joint appointment in which he was relieved of much of the administrative work in the society would still involve "so much legislative and administrative responsibility that I can continue my lecturing as now with more prospect of writing." This decision, he feared, "will disappoint you and I have said it with some reluctance." Only Fish had told him that the members of the history department would find such an arrangement agreeable, and it would be "awkward" for Paxson. In the society, the lessened status of the administrator would make it more difficult to find someone of quality. The history department might lose funds desired for other purposes, and the arrangement would be one "imposed . . . from the outside." He could not see how the *"details"* of a satisfactory arrangement could be worked out. Yet he had not said no with finality, concluding, "At least I have put the case where if they go on they will do it at their own risk."[18]

As on previous occasions the intimations of interest from another institution were not secreted within the Turner family. Rumor of yearnings beyond the Alleghenies leaked into the press. Hooper enlivened the telephone wires, and Turner discussed the situation with some colleagues. "Men have been very kind here in their expressions of concern," Turner noted.[19] As the Wisconsin scenario played out, a more attractive possibility emerged. James W. Thompson wrote to Turner in mid-December 1913 to inquire whether he could be interested in joining the faculty of the University of Chicago. Responding, Turner wrote that he appreciated Thompson's interest but thought "it probable that I shall spend the remainder of my academic days here." That, however, was "not an absolute certainty." He was, he explained, fifty two years of age and "a little raw in the harness. The time remaining for my writing is growing short." The "possibility of acceptance" on his part would be "small."[20] Turner thus left the door ajar for further negotiations.

Soon, McLaughlin, the Chicago history department chair, took up the subject. "The question of your coming here . . . interests me tremendously," he wrote. His department was well staffed in American history, and there was no search underway to fill a specific vacancy, but to have Turner as a colleague would be "a source of immense gratification." He visualized an appointment in which Turner would teach a seminar and give a lecture course to graduate students, obligating him in all to four classroom hours per week. No administrative work would be required of him, although he would be expected, of course, to handle the direction and reading of his students' theses. Much of the thesis direction, however, would take place in the seminar. At this point McLaughlin had no authority to negotiate with Turner but, wrote he, "I am hopeful & I am crazy to have you here." He wished to "kindle the fires of enthusiasm & make soup." He would be delighted to lug the wood for Turner's "meal," he added, and urged him to send him the "products" of further rumination.[21]

"Feeling frisky again" after having had a painful carbuncle "chopped into submission," Turner soon responded. Teaching graduate students rather than underclassmen, "'standing with *reluctant* feet where the brook and river meet'" was indeed attractive as were "other elements" in the proposed arrangement. The suggestion that McLaughlin would "'make soup'" while Turner "'enjoyed the meal'" was "inconceivable," but the "*idea* of cooking & eating *together*" had "strong appeal." He had always "liked" the members of the department at Chicago. He could not, however, "state terms" that would lead him to join them. "I'm not perfectly sure," he continued, "that I'm so useful here as I should be in the West; and I sometimes have doubts whether a general American history man isn't needed here more than a Western history specialist." But Harvard authorities did not apparently agree, and to encourage an offer seemed unwarranted, "particularly since my personal relations are pleasant and I have no grievances." He was most grateful for the interest in Chicago, but if approached formally he would feel obligated to "go to the bottom of Harvard's feelings." He admitted that he had already discussed the matter with Merriman, his chairman, and Haskins on a "*hypothetical* basis entirely, not official," making it "perfectly clear" that he was merely acting on the basis of a "purely personal inquiry of a friend." "As a result," he "must decide . . . on the basis of my own attitude, rather than of what I conceive to be Harvard's problems!" After this enigmatic remark he closed his letter by assuring McLaughlin that he had not "shown" his letter to "any one, nor discussed it."[22]

McLaughlin did not lose interest. At the beginning of June 1914 he suggested that they meet when Turner passed through Chicago on his way west to the University of Washington and summer teaching in the West. But he noted that Chicago would not be able to provide a salary above five thousand dollars per annum. Already Turner had been given the opportunity to raise his income beyond that figure by teaching at Radcliffe College. The negotiations with Chicago petered out. We cannot precisely estimate the degree to which the efforts of Van Hise and the Chicago men helped Turner to enhance his position at Harvard, but rumors of piratical intent and "hypothetical" offers work wonders in academia, and these surely did Turner no harm. The interchange with McLaughlin and his colleagues was Turner's last serious professional flirtation.

On December 30, 1915, Claude H. Van Tyne rose in the largest business meeting ever assembled at an annual meeting of the AHA and moved, "*Resolved*, That the attacks made during the last year upon the character and motives of certain prominent and honorable members of this association meet with our entire disapproval, and that we hereby express our full confidence in the men whose motives and conduct have been thus impugned."[23] The audience shouted its approval. One of the association members in whom the meeting voted confidence on that day in Washington, D.C., was Turner. The resolution and vote were parts of a sequence of events that had begun several years earlier, although elements in the situation could be traced to the 1890s when the members of the founding generation of professional academic historians were emerging.

In 1895 twenty-six individuals "interested in history" agreed to found the *American Historical Review*, created a board of editors, empowered it to hire a managing editor, and pledged themselves as guarantors to make good on deficits for a period of three years. When the journal was still not self-sustaining at the end of the guarantee period, the editors sought subsidy from the AHA in return for providing copies of the *Review* to all of its members. After a preliminary arrangement to this end, the parties agreed in 1898 that the aid should be set at two dollars per member and that the association would have the right to fill vacancies on the editorial board. When the Carnegie Institution established its Bureau (later Department) of Historical Research in 1903 it was agreed that its first director, McLaughlin, would continue his duties as managing editor of the *Review*. In effect this arrangement provided an additional subsidy for the publication and allowed it to pay contributors. The editors did not assume that this process of institutional entwinement infringed upon their control of the journal's budget or constituted association ownership of the periodical.

By the early years of Turner's tenure at Harvard it was clear that there had been great continuity in the board of editors, numbering six members plus the managing editor. Jameson had held the latter office since the *Review*'s beginning, with the exception of the several years in which McLaughlin had served while organizing the Bureau of Historical Research. Although John B. McMaster and Harry P. Judson had withdrawn from the board after some years, other members had accepted reappointment at the conclusion of their initial terms of six years. When Turner joined the board in 1909, four of his colleagues had begun their service in 1898 or earlier.

The editors of these years who served on the council of the AHA typically ascended to the presidency of the organization. Of the original seven members of the editorial board, only one did not attain that post, and every new appointee, through and well beyond Turner's presidency, headed the association. Residents of the hinterlands could note also that most of the editors were faculty members at major northeastern schools. The leaders of the generation of professional historians that emerged during the 1890s not only moved into the discipline's positions of leadership, but once within the magic circle, they tended to remain there. Their contributions, of course, had helped to make their positions seats of prestige and power.

Turner's rapid rise in the historical profession was aided in part by the sense of other western scholars that he spoke for a region whose importance was not fully recognized in the older areas of the country. His departure for Harvard seemed to provide evidence to western scholars that higher education in the Northeast was superior in its resources to that of their region. Southerners too believed themselves misunderstood and undervalued. The Johns Hopkins University had trained a generation of southern and western scholars in history and the social sciences and had enhanced their sense of regional self-worth. William A. Dunning's famous seminar at Columbia University fostered regional pride among the young southerners who returned from it to southern history posts. During the years of the early twentieth century southerners and westerners examined the programs of the AHA and the pages of the *American Historical Review* and concluded that southern and western topics and faculty members were inadequately represented. A sense of regional deprivation climaxed in acrimonious bickering within the AHA during the years 1913 through 1916; this was the context of Van Tyne's motion of 1915.

In 1913 the association held its annual meeting in Charleston, a fitting setting for southerners who might wish to complain about its administration. In the business meeting, Dunbar Rowland, of the Mississippi Department of Archives and History, protested against the present system of electing officers. The constitution of the AHA specified election by ballot and did not include the appointment of committees among the duties of the council. It was customary, however, for the council to appoint a nominating committee to propose a slate of nominees at the business meeting. Usually this was approved by a vote calling upon the secretary to cast a unanimous ballot in favor of those proposed. Not until 1912 was the nominating committee appointed a year in advance. Even so, the composition of the slate was unpublicized until the meeting began. Maintaining that he expressed sentiments that were increasingly shared within the membership, Rowland denounced the nominating process as both undemocratic and unconstitutional.

Rowland found efforts to defend the nominating procedures in Charleston unconvincing and promptly carried his criticisms into the columns of the *Nation*. There he concluded his description of current practices by charging that the AHA was "suffering from a dangerous disease," too serious to be cured by "homeopathic treatment. It is a case for the knife." "The modest, earnest, scholarly men who sustain the Association," he predicted, would not "submit further to arbitrary and unconstitutional methods in the administration of the affairs of one of the greatest associations of scholars in the world."[24]

In response, members of the association explained that past nominating committees had encountered great difficulty in obtaining suggestions for their slates. They maintained that a simple balloting procedure might allow small and unrepresentative caucuses to dominate the election process. Jameson questioned Rowland's charge of unconstitutional procedures and reminded him that his "vehement speech" at Charleston had elicited little support at the time. Moreover, the business meeting had instructed the new nominating committee to report on "the whole procedure of nominations," as well as producing a slate of nominees.[25]

Jameson's secretarial account of the association's annual meeting appeared in the April 1914 issue of the *Review*. In its concluding pages he tried to answer Rowland's charges of oligarchic control. The association had prospered. Placing a premium on experience in the selection of officers would best facilitate the scholarly tasks that it had assumed. On the other hand, frequent rotation of places of honor could also be defended. He believed, he wrote, "that if the business meetings can be so conducted as to allow ample time for explaining what the Council has done and the reasons, contentment will prevail, and a system not widely divergent from the present will continue to be maintained."[26]

John H. Latané, of The Johns Hopkins University, joined Rowland as a critic of the council in the columns of the *Nation*. He contrasted the procedures of the AHA with those of the American Political Science Association. Setting aside those positions involving administrative labor, Latané argued that there were "fourteen positions of honor, with little work attached, to be filled each year" in the AHA and seventeen in the national organization of political scientists. In the history organization thirteen of the fourteen current holders of such office had also served during the previous year. Among the political scientists only six of the seventeen had also served during the previous year. The political scientists, he maintained, shared "the honors" of the association with "the younger men who have demonstrated their ability to do good work . . . enlisting their aid and counsel." What explained the contrast? He suggested several possible answers. These included the "purely selfish one of reserving the honors for a select group of older men" or an effort "to guard zealously the interests of the Association against the radical views of the rising generation of historians," or perhaps current practice showed "that the present group of office-holders believe[d] that they enjoy[ed] a monopoly of the brains and talents of the Association."[27]

Rowland incorporated material from the *Nation* into a pamphlet, *The Government of the American Historical Association*, adding a summary of thirteen ways in which "unconstitutional control of the Association ha[d] been brought about." Many of these involved the appointment of committees by the executive council, an unconstitutional function, as was that body's appointment of new members of the editorial board of the *Review*. Among other charges, Rowland listed the practice of council members serving on "the most conspicuous and important committees," transformation of the council's annual meeting in New York City into an expensive social function, centralization of "the executive duties of the Association in the Department of Historical Research of the Carnegie Institution of Washington," establishment of "an unwise and undemocratic succession in the offices of president and vice-president," and failure to have "every act of the Council . . . confirmed by the Association." Rowland also drew attention to the close relations between the council of the association and the editorial board of the *American Historical Review*. Historians and scholars, he warned, were "not different from other men; if they are allowed too great latitude . . . they become too ambitious, unmindful of others, and forget the restraints which should be and always are thrown around the exercise of authority."[28]

Rowland's compilation bore the date December 1, 1914. He had designed it for circulation prior to the annual meeting of the AHA in Chicago at the end of that month and in preparation for continuing his campaign in the business meeting there. At its meeting in November the council had already sought to outflank the rebels by agreeing, apparently on Turner's suggestion, to recommend to the association that a committee of nine should "consider the constitution, organization, and procedure of the association, with instructions to report at the annual meeting of 1915" and also to review the relationship between the organization and the *Review*.[29]

But how was this committee to be selected? The business meeting agreed that the nominating committee, chaired by Charles Hull, would prepare a slate. Only three members of that committee of five being present, Turner's former student, Guy S. Ford, successfully moved that Rowland and Turner be added to that nucleus, making a committee of five for the purpose of recommending members of the committee of nine. Thus Turner not only joined Hull, long a friendly associate, but found himself serving with Lois Kimball Mathews, his former student and protégée.

When Hull presented the committee's work to the adjourned business meeting of the AHA on the last day of the convention, he explained that he and his colleagues had sought "a reasonable diversity of residence and historical interest." They had understood also that the matters to be considered by the committee of nine had evolved over the course of twenty-five years. To ensure proper understanding of the situation, Hull and his colleagues had included three former presidents in their list, William A. Dunning, Andrew C. McLaughlin, and James Ford Rhodes. But "mindful also that the report . . . [might] well influence the procedure of the association for years to come," younger scholars were also suggested. Both Turner's friend Farrand and his former junior colleague at Wisconsin, Winfred T. Root, were to be members of the committee of nine.[30]

At the AHA meeting in December 1914 the board of editors of the *Review* also took defensive measures, sending a letter to the executive council over the signature of its secretary, Turner, in which its members expressed willingness to have the six-year term of service shortened to three years. But if the leaders of the AHA believed that they had silenced criticism by placing the complaints of the reformers in the hands of the committee of nine, they were sadly wrong.

As a member of the committee of five, Rowland suggested the names of various members of the committee of investigation but believed that little would come of its deliberations, given the group's composition. Both he and Latané continued criticisms of AHA leaders and procedures. The two were joined in public censure of the AHA by Frederic Bancroft, former librarian of the United States Department of State and now an independent scholar and journalist living in Washington. Bancroft had been elected to the AHA Council in 1913 and sought to become the voice of reform within that body. He also had ties to the *Nation* that perhaps account for the welcome that this periodical extended to critics of the association. At this time also, according to the AHA treasurer, the finances of the association were less healthy than in previous years. Bancroft endeavored to meld the charge of undemocratic practices, the relations between *Review* and association, and financial issues in a slashing denunciation of an inner ring, whose members hogged positions of honor and drained the exchequers of both organization and journal in their own behalf.

Bancroft put the case for reform before local and visiting scholars in Washington and corresponded with likely rebels in the academic provinces. In January 1915 he launched an investigation of the payments made to council members for travel expenses. Concerned about the current deficit of the association and apparently somewhat sympathetic to the rebels, association treasurer Clarence W. Bowen provided Bancroft with this information. He also refused to pay the travel expenses of members of the committee of nine.

George L. Burr, Cornell University's librarian and medievalist, was treasurer of the editorial board, and in early March Bancroft asked him for a listing of all payments to editorial board members during the previous three years. This request produced much interchange between Burr and the members of the board, including managing editor Jameson. The executive council had not created the editorial board when the *Review* was established, and Burr and Jameson doubted the right of an individual member of the council to investigate its internal affairs. However, board members expressed willingness to cooperate and offered to show Bancroft the current account book at Jameson's office. This was not exactly what Bancroft had requested, and there ensued a lengthy exchange of letters in which he became increasingly recriminatory, even abusive, implying that Burr was stalling in response to his requests. Bancroft broadened his demands to include examination of the editorial board's accounts from its inception. This involved further delay, as the records were scattered. During this period Turner counseled his colleagues to be cooperative in providing Bancroft with information, to treat "the matter objectively with neither profession of friendship nor enmity, and to continue to offer such information as may be in our power, with reasonable consideration of our own convenience in the matter of time and mode of reply."[31]

In early summer 1915 the three leading rebels released a pamphlet, *Why the American Historical Association Needs Thorough Reorganization.* In their introduction, Bancroft, Latané, and Rowland asked if this organization was to "be allowed to continue as virtually the private property of a few who, only after nearly a score of years, pass on their claims to their favorites"? Terms such as "oligarchy," "big-university trust," and "old guard" had been on many lips for some years now, they said. When the present situation was denounced on the floor of the business meeting in Charleston, the "spokesman of the 'old guard,'" obviously Jameson, had "denied all charges" and implied lack of appreciation and personal prejudice on the part of critics.[32]

The rebels then moved to specifics. They suggested that the current financial stringency faced by the association was linked to the practice of reimbursing the members of the executive council and the editorial board for their expenses in attending the meetings of those bodies. Men with "comfortable incomes" should not, they suggested, expect such assistance when younger scholars would have served for the honor of the appointment. Moreover, some of the travel was unnecessary. They saw little need for program chairmen to attend council meetings, for example, and paying the cost of a council luncheon was sheer extravagance.

After "insistent and repeated requests," the reformers had obtained access to the financial data of the editorial board. Together with information from the association treasurer, the material allowed them to establish the reimbursements for expenses received by board members. These, ran the inference, suggested cupidity and extravagance. The board also held more meetings than was necessary, they alleged. They attacked Jameson's ill-advised suggestion that the editors owned the *Review* and pointed to the affiliations of the board members to a small number of "great institutions—Carnegie Institution, Harvard, Yale, Pennsylvania, Columbia, Cornell, and Chicago" universities. True, Wisconsin briefly had a voice, and that was a sad story: "When it dawned on a certain Harvard member of the board [Hart] that he was outstaying the proprieties, he withdrew and secured the election of a professor in Wisconsin University. This was considered most chivalrous. Only lately has it become known, except to a few, that the new member had already accepted a call to Harvard!"[33]

Moreover, alleged the critics, the individuals who served both on the board and the council composed a "ring" whose members controlled the offices of the association and accepted a "joy-ride" by having the *Review* pay their traveling expenses. During the last year, the chairman of the nominating committee had been a "subordinate" of one member of the ring and had been a colleague of both members of that group who were to be "advanced" through the vice-presidential sequence within the association. In selecting the committee of nine, the nominating committee had been "steadied by the addition of the master politician of the ring" and one reformer to form a group that "could be trusted to choose the committee." The reformers ensured that Turner would be recognized as the "master politician" by inserting, as an aside, the identifying information that "the first year he was a member of the board [he] charged the *Review* $54.00 for his trip to Indianapolis to deliver his own presidential address." They noted that the committee of nine had chosen as chairman "one who had long been a chief and beneficiary of the inner circle [McLaughlin], enjoyed the anomalous arrangement between Carnegie Institution and the *Review*, and is largely responsible for the practices, irregularities and self-seekings against which the reform movement is directed." He, they charged, had drawn at least $1,716.84 in expense money from association enterprises through the years.[34]

Bancroft attached excerpts from his correspondence with Burr, omitting the latter's temperate responses. In his letters to Burr, Bancroft particularly denounced the board's practice of holding meetings both in November and at the association's annual meeting in December. Board members believed the practice necessary because the second meeting allowed consideration of papers presented at the annual meeting for possible publication in the *Review* as well as deliberation on actions of the council and association at that time. Bancroft, however, believed that such papers could more reasonably be considered after their authors had "recast to suit the *Review*." Rather, he alleged, "It has been those 'other deliberations,' most of all making 'slates' year after year and putting them through, that made meetings 'necessary' where the Council met in November and where the Association met in December."[35]

Bancroft wrote the greater part of the pamphlet, and his tone was accusatory and often sarcastic. He used no names, but Jameson, whom he called the "dean," was easily identifiable. Turner was both the short-lived editorial board member from Wisconsin and the "master

politician" who had used the *Review* to pay his expenses to Indianapolis when president. McLaughlin was the great boodler who assumed
the chairmanship of the committee of nine.

The pamphlet concluded with "Some Proposed Reforms," over
Latané's signature. The editors must "renounce the claim of editorial
ownership" of the *Review*, and the "mysterious relation" linking it to
the Carnegie Institution must be publicly clarified. The ex-presidents
of the AHA should not enjoy life membership on the council. The
practice by which individuals rose through the two vice-presidencies
to become president of the association should be terminated. In effect
it had "given to the ring the backing of three aspirants for the presidency." "The Council," continued Latané, "should elect and dominate
the editorial board, and the board should aid and direct the managing-
editor." Dual service had furthered "boss-and-ring rule," which had
been the "direct or indirect cause of most of the unfortunate conditions
in the Association."[36]

Finally, Latané proposed that a finance committee of the association
should approve the payment of all expenses and the treasurer publish
detailed statements of disbursements. Latané predicted that the committee of nine would do little to realize these reforms "for the leading
idea in its organization was to prevent or check reform." He urged the
members of the association to approve a plan at the next annual
meeting that would "end the evils long complained of in vain."[37] In the
face of such criticism, the board of editors prepared a historical statement describing the origins of the *Review* and its relation to the
association and its publisher. This document reached the association
members during late 1915.

Turner initially advised his colleagues on the editorial board to
cooperate with the critics, but his own patience was soon tested. The
pamphleteering rebels specifically identified him as a malefactor. But
even before their revelations became public, Bancroft, having successfully badgered Burr into disclosing the financial records of the editorial
board, had turned his attention to Turner as the secretary of the
editorial board.

As we have seen, Stephens and the Berkeley history department
arranged a special summer session at the University of California in
conjunction with the Panama-Pacific Exposition and the AHA meeting
during the summer of 1915. Jameson, Turner, and other major figures
in the AHA served in Berkeley's summer program. The leading rebels
interpreted this arrangement as a payoff to ringleaders for supporting

Stephens for the presidency of the AHA. In the late spring of 1915 Bancroft sought information from Turner about the relations between the *Review* and the Carnegie Institution, but he did not press Turner for additional information until after his return to Cambridge in the fall. Then he demanded copies of the publishing contracts negotiated by the board in the past, a list of the original incorporators and guarantors of the *Review*, and the opportunity to consult the minutes of the board and to make such excerpts as he desired. Acting with a deliberation that infuriated Bancroft, Turner had the contracts sent to Evarts B. Greene, secretary of the council of the AHA, and distributed by him to all its members. Turner rejected for the time being Bancroft's other requests, telling him that he would place them before the board at its meeting in Thanksgiving week. There his colleagues voted to make such material available only on the request of the AHA Council.

When the AHA Council met at the end of the November, its members listened to an "extended report" from the editorial board. A council member moved that the body should "receive, accept, and approve the report . . . and . . . express its full confidence in the efficient and unselfish manner in which the board of editors have conducted the affairs of the Review since its foundation." But Bancroft led in proposing revised wording that deleted the word *approved*, required that the report be printed for distribution within the association, and instructed the secretary to provide him with a typescript "as soon as possible." The revised resolution was approved, with Latané's colleague John M. Vincent qualifying his vote but "reserving differences of opinion on matters of policy" and some others, including Bancroft, Jameson, and Turner abstaining.[38]

Meanwhile, there had been further discussion of the issues in the columns of the *Nation*. Ulrich B. Phillips had been Turner's disciple and later his protégé and colleague. But as a new member of the association council he published letters in the *Nation* supporting most of Latané's proposed reforms and chiding the editorial board for lack of openness. Other members of the profession wrote to give encouragement to the leading rebels. Bancroft's indignation mounted. As the association's annual meeting of 1915 approached, he prepared another denunciatory pamphlet and sought to rally support for the impending battle at the Washington meeting in late December.

Jameson marveled at the way in which Bancroft's campaign had progressed from civil and rational requests for information during early 1915 to the feverishly suspicious and belligerent behavior of year's end. Although Burr and Turner smarted under Bancroft's lash, and some believed that the campaign was in part designed to deny Burr the presidency of the AHA, they and their colleagues on the editorial board also suspected that the rebels had the downfall of Jameson as their major objective. But the emphasis of the rebels on personalities alienated many scholars who were otherwise sympathetic to the belief that power had become too concentrated in the association, that historians of the outback had less access to the columns of the *Review* than was fair, or that changes in fiscal policies were needed.

The leaders of the association viewed with trepidation the approach of the annual meeting at Washington in late December 1915. As never before, members flocked into the business meeting, as many as five hundred perhaps. They heard Edward P. Cheyney, now chairman of the editorial board, deliver an eloquent defense of the editorial board of the *Review* and Jameson convincingly defend its course as well. When the latter took his seat, Van Tyne presented his mixed resolution of support for the board and condemnation of the tactics of its critics.

Although he complained to Turner about time expended thanklessly, McLaughlin had labored as chairman of the committee of nine to produce a fruitful outcome. That group placed various constitutional amendments and alterations of the by-laws before the AHA business meeting. The constitutional provisions included increasing the number of elected council members from six to eight, terminating the voting rights of former presidents on the council at the end of three years, and specifically granting to the council the right to create committees. The association in its annual meeting would now be able to instruct the council to terminate or initiate activities. The by-laws specified the manner of appointing the nominating committee and balloting procedures that allowed consideration of candidates in addition to those proposed by the committee. Now council members could collect travel expenses for one meeting only and were not to include those involved in attending the annual convention. Provisions as to scheduling and committee reports were designed to insure ample time for discussion in the business meeting, particularly concerning new organizational initiatives.

The assembly deferred final action on many of the recommendations of the committee of nine to the next annual meeting, but it was resolved that the association should assume full ownership and control of the *Review*. The relations with the Carnegie Institution and the journal's publisher were to be maintained. A committee of association officers would work out the details of these relations and report their recommendations to the next annual meeting. As generally expected, the members of the AHA present at the annual meeting of 1916 approved the committee's major recommendations of the previous year.

Called to the bedside of his younger brother Will, seriously ill in Portage, Turner did not attend the AHA meeting in December 1915. Letters from friends and fellow officers of the editorial board and the association assured him that he and his fellows had been fully vindicated. Jameson pictured Bancroft and Rowland as repudiated by the membership of the association, the latter pitifully unaware of the extent to which the rebels had failed. Writing to Turner, McLaughlin had earlier exclaimed, "Oh lackaday what tempest in a thimble, made by these ragged-headed politicians, with brains in their feet."[39] Certainly the association members resoundingly repudiated the smear tactics and focus on personalities to which the critics had resorted. Yet in accepting the recommendations of the committee of nine in 1915 and 1916, the association democratized its procedures and policies to some degree, improved its fiscal practices, and clarified the anomalous status of the *Review*.

With the withdrawal of McLaughlin, Turner, and Burr from the editorial board, the duplication of its membership within the upper reaches of the association council was diminished. Insofar as the rebellion was an attack upon Jameson, or an effort to discredit McLaughlin, Turner, Burr, and other members of the editorial board, it failed. Although the *Review* became incontestably the property of the association, the transfer was made without immediate alteration of the six-year term for editors or other significant change in the board's internal practices. Describing the meeting in the columns of the *Nation* soon afterwards, Sidney B. Fay proclaimed the editors to be vindicated and the suggested changes in procedures as due to the efforts of the committee of nine. To this Latané took exception, writing in response that Fay's account inadequately conveyed the extent of the reforms and suggesting that Jameson's prestige had been severely damaged. In addition, wrote Latané, the old guard had abandoned their intention of naming a member of the editorial board, Cheyney, to the second vice-presidency, thus placing him in the line of presidential succession. Instead, the nominating committee had selected a man acceptable to the reformers. This communication, wrote the editor of the *Nation*, would end its coverage of the controversy.

There had been a considerable concentration of power in an association whose members in the years of this quasi-rebellion numbered almost three thousand. Scholars who had emerged in leadership positions during the 1890s had held fast to controlling positions in the AHA, and the tendency for members to link place on the editorial board with place in the association council suggested that some yearned unduly for power. Some of the fault here surely belonged to Jameson. Somewhat arbitrary and impatient in manner, he liked to hold onto advisors whose judgment he had come to trust. "You are not only one of the most friendly of counsellors, but one of the wisest," he wrote to Turner on one occasion.[40] Those under attack did not recognize the irony in the controversy. Turner and his friends had replaced older leaders, and now a new generation of ambitious men were chafing for greater recognition at their expense. For Turner the irony ran deeper. He had won initial place and fame as a scholarly spokesperson for the West but was denounced as a member of an eastern establishment. A student of sectionalism, he had not realized how potent a force regional jealousies might be within a learned society.

Turner and his colleagues considered themselves to be public-spirited gentlemen who had sacrificed much in time and labor for the welfare of the profession. They were shocked to be accused of hoggishness and crass motives, and they reacted with indignation. In his report of AHA Council activities at the annual meeting of 1915, its secretary found it "unfortunate" that some had not followed the custom of discussing the affairs of the *Review* "with frankness and yet with that mutual courtesy which ought to prevail among gentlemen who are also members of a great scientific organization."[41]

McLaughlin and Burr resigned from the editorial board without completing their current terms, and Turner announced that he would not return at the expiration of his term. He also informed friends that he would stop attending council meetings. During the controversy he was a voice of moderation, initially counseling compliance with Bancroft's demands for information. He advised colleagues to refrain from jousting with Bancroft in the columns of the *Nation*. When he became a target of that gentleman's demands, however, he was not completely cooperative, passing responsibility to the board and the council. He was a proponent of preemptive action, recommending that ownership of the *Review* be vested in the association, and he favored reducing the term of service of editorial board members from six to three years. He played a major role in selecting the committee of nine.

However, when offered the opportunity to join that group in place of
John B. McMaster, he declined. Absent from the association meeting
of 1915, perhaps he was relieved that he must allow friends to defend
his name.

For Turner the controversy was both distracting and enervating. He
always counseled his students that rational discourse produced the
right results. Participation in a mud-slinging battle was not his style.
Aside from what he considered the gross unfairness of the criticism,
Turner found additional reason for discomfiture. Although he clearly
enjoyed contact with some of his graduate students more than others,
he regarded them all as friends. Friends who were gentlemen did not
betray friends. And now some of Turner's graduate students had given
comfort to the enemies or even consorted with them.

Although rejecting the charges of personal turpitude leveled against
the AHA leaders, Turner's former student and colleague Phillips had
criticized AHA leaders and been less than fully supportive as a
member of the council. The case of Charles H. Ambler was even more
painful. Ambler had been one of Turner's last few doctoral candidates
at Wisconsin and a strong contender for the Winsor Prize. Once he was
in the field, Ambler stayed in frequent touch but showed some
tendency to grouse. Turner chided him for misunderstanding his
motives in leaving Wisconsin and for being too aggressive in trying to
improve his own position in the profession. But Ambler expressed
strong commitment to Turner and was one of the contributors to the
festschrift. To his dismay Turner learned that Ambler had been a
confidant of Bancroft and Latané and as a "class leader" had sought to
rally other Virginia historians in the reform cause.

There was an embarrassing exchange of correspondence between
Ambler and Turner during early 1916 in which the former student
tried to explain his actions. Admitting he had agreed that some reform
of practice was in order in the AHA and that he had sounded out
colleagues in other institutions about the matter, he had not, he
asserted, ever joined Bancroft and Latané in personal denunciations,
and he had certainly never meant to criticize Turner. Nor had he
agreed with the extreme position at which the leading rebels had
arrived by December 1915 and had broken with them before the
association's annual meeting.

Jameson had shown Turner a letter, sent by Ambler to a professional
colleague in the upper south, that seemed to demonstrate a commitment to Bancroft beyond what Ambler admitted. Turner's response to

Ambler's efforts at reconciliation, therefore, was crushing. "Analysis," he wrote, "would bring out a difference of standards as to what is involved in the matter of an attack upon the honor of one who is called a friend and a difference of opinion as to what were pertinent facts in the history of the episode. You would not understand. Let us therefore not continue the correspondence."[42] Frustrating to Turner also must have been Ambler's contention that Bancroft had claimed at least six other Turner students among his supporters in the "war on the ring" and that he, Ambler, had copies of letters from various Turner students denouncing the practices of the association as well from various leaders in the profession.

The rebellion in the AHA did not involve Turner in additional labor to the extent experienced by McLaughlin and Jameson, but it required additional correspondence and much thought about editorial and council strategy and practice. To this was added the anger, worry, and frustration generated by what he considered to be Bancroft's unjust and malicious personal attacks and by the failure of former students to remain loyal. To a man of distractable temperament like Turner, the events of 1914–15 within the association must have compounded his inability to concentrate upon research and writing. Although his dis-illusionment with association activities in these years could in theory have freed additional time for his writing, such was not the case.

12   Shadows

*"I realize that I am over the top and not likely to be fit
for the things I wanted to do"*

Again and again in the publications of Turner's first twenty years as
professional historian, he contrasted the development of the United
States and Europe, at times explicitly, at others by inference. As early
as 1899 he pointed out that the physiographic provinces of the American continent were equivalent in size and differentiation to European
nations. The outbreak and early course of World War I led Turner to
consider further the divergent developments of Europe and America.
Early in 1916 he lectured at Trinity College in Durham, North
Carolina, posing the question of why, given the continental dimensions and its centuries of development, the United States had not
become another Europe. "Space, and time, and the freshness of youth,"
he explained, had "permitted this nation to grow up remote from the
tyranny of Old World customs and traditions; permitted us to bind our
sections together with gentle ties of party organization, with outlets
for sectional ideals and interests, sectional feeling and sectional energy
under the forms of party agreements between sections, party rivalries,
and peaceful voting."

Although he held that no generation should be bound utterly by the
decisions of its predecessors, Turner, at this point, believed that the
United States should not enter World War I. Despite recent developments, it did not follow, he warned, "that we should be carried into
that maelstrom, and particularly not on European terms." Washington's warnings against entangling alliances were still valid and gaining
"new force from the awful tragedy which meets our gaze whenever we
look across the Atlantic."[1]

In the late winter he analyzed the politics of the situation for John
Main. He agreed with Senator La Follette that if "stand pat" Republicans rode the horse of patriotism into power, "we should have a riot
of tariff, extravagant purchases from private ammunition plants, and
all the rest of the plundering." Turner also believed, as did La Follette,
that standpat Republicans would use a strong program of preparedness
as "a pretext for neglecting social reforms and internal development on
the right lines." But he deplored the fact that La Follette's course had

convinced Germany that the nation would not support President Wilson's policy. "Such a catering to the German vote will bring upon the nation a train of woes, a division into nationalistic groups, Irish, Jewish, Slavic, Italian, as well as German, that will transfer the determination of American policy to . . . the Old World, and leave us a helpless hulk . . . upon the high seas of international relations." He also believed that the senator was encouraging disastrous divisions in the country. "American hopes of affecting the civilization of the World and of escaping the fate of Europe rests upon *two* things: 1 furnishing a superior type of civilization; and 2 developing the pride and unity of nationality that will enable us to hold our own people together as Americans, rather than as transplanted Germans, Irish, etc. and therefore, to enable us to resist the grave danger of being absorbed into the European state-system" and compelled to take orders from abroad. Turner was, he said, "appalled at the few people who are thinking in purely *American* terms."

Party politics, Turner maintained, should not be allowed to govern the situation. He was being forced, he wrote, to try to explain the middle-western point of view to easterners whose sympathies lay primarily with the Allies. He was sure that the country would not follow the lead of the Middle West if its politicians, in fear of giving undue profits to munitions makers or in seeking to defer to the German vote, allowed other nations to set our foreign policy.[2] Some weeks later Turner wrote to Wisconsin senator Paul O. Husting, urging a firm stance in foreign affairs, in relations both with Europe and Mexico.

When the semester ended in spring 1916, the Turners journeyed to Madison, where they were reunited with Dorothy. Fred spent a month in research at the Historical Society library, preparing a series of lectures on the Middle West for delivery at Western Reserve University in the fall. When Madison sweltered in searing heat, they fled to northern Wisconsin. From there they traveled to Montana, and they spent an enjoyable four weeks in Glacier National Park and its vicinity. Here a guide, Roy Priest, took them on a ten-day packing expedition to the forks of the Big Badger River. Reared, so he claimed, by a genuine mountain man, Priest led them to such trout fishing as Turner had never before seen. Happily suffering falls and duckings, he was "snowed in and frozen up" and had a glorious time.[3]

On his return Turner began his sabbatical year 1916–17 by spending another month preparing for his lectures at Western Reserve University.

Jameson had invited him to serve as a research associate at the Carnegie Institution from November through April 1917. There his duties involved advising Jameson concerning the programs and policies of the historical department and reporting to the department staff on his own research and its implications. The position, Turner told Caroline, involved "nominal duties" and was "supposed to be primarily for the purpose of giving a man a chance to write, and giving Jameson good company & general advice!"[4] Caroline later noted that the Turners had once hoped to spend the sabbatical year in Europe but that the war led them to abandon the idea, suggesting perhaps that Turner's writing at this point ranked less high in his priorities than is sometimes suggested.

Meanwhile, the Harvard Commission on Western History was promising a useful contribution to Harvard's research resources in western history. Joining the commission as a half-time assistant in mid-1915, Thomas P. Martin displayed impressive aptitude for the duties of collector and archivist. Now Turner and other commission members envisioned greater activity. At their instigation the participants in the annual meeting of the Associated Harvard Clubs in 1915 resolved that these clubs should organize committees on western history to cooperate with the commission's efforts. This initiative seemed to promise great things when an energetic Chicagoan, Frederick W. Burlingham, became president of the organization in 1916 and threw his support to the cause of collecting. Martin quickly developed a considerable correspondence with likely donors and conducted a successful collecting campaign in Vermont during the fall of 1916. In this seedbed of western migration he concentrated on rural towns and portrayed himself initially as a scholar in search of research materials, rather than as a manuscript collector. Other institutions recognized Martin's abilities, and Alice Hooper soon found herself investing in them more heavily. In reality her resources were limited, but other donors appeared to be a possibility. Unfortunately, the war was increasingly diverting the interests of Americans from the plans and problems of higher education.

In mid-fall 1916 the Turners took up residence in the Brighton Hotel in Washington, D.C. They spent Thanksgiving, however, in Cambridge, and Turner broke away from the capital in December to attend the annual meeting of the AHA in Cincinnati. Here he attended the reception given by Charles Taft, who, Turner noted admiringly, had not housed his "wonderful selection of paintings" in a separate gallery but allowed the family to live among them "gracefully."[5] He was pleased that the association members unanimously approved the recommendations of the committee of nine that had been deferred for action until the meeting in 1916. So also were accepted the arrangements for vesting the ownership of the *American Historical Review* in the organization and for improving the association's fiscal procedures.

During these months sympathy for the Allies was rising within the nation and antagonism to the German cause intensifying. Turner closely followed the development of government policy. During the summer of 1916 the nation's major railroad brotherhoods threatened to strike for an eight-hour work day. The famous Burlington strike of 1888 seared in her memory, Hooper advocated a stern response from the government. Turner, however, approved Wilson's more restrained program of arbitration followed by partial concessions and the establishment of a commission to investigate the impact of the shorter day on railroad operating costs. He admitted, however, that "the men carried out the barest sort of a hold up."[6]

With American declarations of neutral rights ignored and unrestricted submarine warfare in effect, Turner by February 1917 had become convinced that the Germans had "done their d——st to make us fight them." He was now willing to accept this outcome. He was not "naturally a fighting man," he told Hooper, but "it is time to assert ourselves or bear the stigma of servitude." He suspected that England had somewhat "fostered this German readiness to violate neutral rights."[7] As spring began, he lamented that neither "the newspapers, [nor] the small talk around the Cosmos Club and the Library" of Congress allowed him to "get . . . into any kernel of the situation," if indeed there "*is* any kernel."

Turner contrasted the way in which Roosevelt would have handled the situation with Wilson's course. The latter's cautious foreign policy, he believed, reflected a desire to stay in step with public opinion. But, thought Turner, "only a small minority now would refuse adhesion to an aggressive reply to German arrogance." He was fearful that Wilson might too long delay decisive action. "Only by using this great national stress to strengthen our sinews and harden our tissues and learn our national lesson," he wrote, "shall we hereafter play an independent part in the world's affairs."[8]

The situation in Europe was "most perplexing." What was to be the effect of the Russian revolution? Would "idealistic visionary discussions of constitutional doctrine, and divergence of class interests," contribute to a "temporary weakening of efficiency?" What of Ireland and German socialism? What would be the outcome of the "retreat on the Western front?" He was heartened, however, by Wilson's successful efforts to avoid a railroad strike. The cooperation of the railroad workers and the Supreme Court's validation of congressional legislation dealing with this crisis revealed that the country was not devoid of patriotism, and Congress had demonstrated that it could "act in the national interest." But Congress, he continued, "gives me the *creeps.* . . . no man's patriotism is safe who sees Congress at close range. There are practically no *first class* men in it, and it is a painful thing to watch." But then—wryly—"any of the godly company of Cambridge" might, in past times, have well made the same complaint. Still, he detected "a spirit of sacrifice for national ends rising"— something that was sorely needed, he told Hooper, "a substitute for religion!"[9]

At his best a reluctant scholarly writer, Turner found it "hard to write [his] historical stint" while resident in Washington during these stirring times. When the president and the Congress led the country into the war at the beginning of April 1917, he reacted with patriotic fervor. Harvard University pledged its resources in support of the national government, prompting Turner to write to Lowell and volunteer his services. The latter responded encouragingly, suggesting that Turner might be contacted directly by the government. Such a commitment, he explained to Dorothy, would not involve military service, but he might "be able to run errands, or do clerical work," and if located in Washington, he would "at least be in the *heat* of the fray." An opportunity to provide service might not materialize, however, and the "most patriotic thing a man can do now is to plant potatoes and do his best to keep his wife and children from becoming a charge on the community."[10]

Meanwhile Jameson invited historians from major American universities to meet at the offices of the AHA to discuss the contributions that they might make in behalf of the nation. Turner attended the meeting. The participants organized a National Board for Historical Service to serve as an adjunct of the Committee on Public Information. Chaired initially by James T. Shotwell, of Columbia University, the board planned to place historical scholarship at the service of both the

national government and the general public and to ensure also that
materials documenting American participation in the war were adequately preserved.

The board or its designates produced *The President's War Message
and the Facts Behind It* and various other publications. Some were
factually oriented, as in the case of a war dictionary, and others
addressed more generally major issues raised by the European struggle.
Less potentially controversial were the board's efforts to encourage
archives, historical agencies, and libraries to save a full documentary
record of the war and to ensure the preservation of federal war records.
Turner's name appeared on the stationery of the board, and he sent
letters explaining its purposes to various friends and acquaintances,
as well as identifying individuals who might undertake particular
assignments.

During the fall of 1917 Sidney M. Mezes, president of the City
College of New York and brother-in-law of President Wilson's advisor,
Col. Edward M. House, was organizing the scholarly investigation
known as "the Inquiry." This body was to prepare the factual foundation for American participation in the peace conference when that
event occurred. Shotwell was also involved in this activity, and when
the executive committee of the National Board for Historical Service
met in November 1917, he requested that it cooperate in the work of
the Inquiry. The group organized an advisory committee consisting of
Turner, William E. Dodd, of the University of Chicago, and William
A. Dunning, of Columbia University.

From the very beginning of his professional career, Turner understood that the historian's background and circumstances might affect
his comprehension of past events and that their meaning to researchers
would change through time. He also believed it was possible to prepare
an account of past developments that would be judged a "best" account
according to the standards of historical research and the sources
available at the time. He had long believed that the historian should
assist the policy maker and that knowledge of the past should inform
the citizen's engagement with current issues. The historians's role
visualized by the members of the National Board, however, might or
might not accord with such premises. Although determined that their
efforts would not ultimately embarrass them, Turner and his colleagues, we suspect, were ingenuous in supposing that the historian's
arm of the Committee on Public Information could serve both the
cause of the allies and Clio without conflict.

In the spring of 1917 Farrand wrote to Waldo G. Leland, secretary of the board and the AHA, expressing concern about the activity that board members were planning. Turner explained his position to Farrand at length in early May 1917. "Both in the matter of public opinion and national policy in respect to the war, and in regard to the American interests and principles respecting conditions on which peace may be made, American historians ought to have useful contri butions to make," he maintained. England, for example, had justifiably often suffered ill repute in the United States, but Americans should consider that nation more positively in this instance. In the debates to come some would falsify "the facts of history." "If the historians, including *local* teachers . . . cannot be helpful in the formation of correct thinking on such topics, who can?" he asked.[11]

He and his colleagues, Turner assured Farrand, were not trying to establish a "professed repository of historical orthodoxy," had no interest in "warping of history to serve a special end," and were not trying to establish a "historical machine with its governing levers here." Rather, the board was to be a "center of information" about war-related subjects on which the public was misinformed or might well be. Its members planned to identify individuals qualified to speak or write about such matters and encourage them to do so, as well as providing those in need of information with the names of historians well qualified to provide it. Broader policy issues involving the Allies and the terms of the peace should also be addressed. On such matters the board might sponsor conferences or otherwise promote public interchange of ideas.

Turner could think, he wrote, of many important questions that needed public discussion—how much sacrifice was justifiable in defense of American ideas as viewed in the perspective of the nation's past, for example? Should not the terms of peace accord with the "ideals of democracy"? Was it not useful to examine the history of such values? Would it not be worthwhile to trace "our own federal and sectional evolution in an area equal to all Europe . . . with reference to its bearings upon Europe's problems"? And "what were the historic ideals that are worth dying for?" Such questions, he told Farrand, "were in part at least historical . . . not to be answered alone by flag raising and cheers, but by examination and illustration." Whatever historians in general might think of the board's activity, some individuals would try to use history to "affect opinion and action. Such history as is used . . . should be real history, the search for the truth, the truth in its full significance and in relation to its times."[12]

Turner sent a more general letter to former students and other historians explaining the board's plans. He urged recipients to interest their graduate students in the study of war issues and their relation to American ideals in order to make the findings available at the community level. Professors should also encourage their students to investigate the "problems which will be the pivot of politics and legislation during their lives." Turner and his colleagues encouraged their correspondents to lay their ideas on such matters before the board, as well as suggesting specific contributions that they might make to the board's work and inviting others to enroll in the work.[13]

Turner left Washington in late spring 1917. Before his departure he informed his colleagues on the board that he must withdraw from active participation. He agreed to play an advisory role, however, and continued to serve on the board, and later, on its link with the Inquiry, until the board's dissolution in 1919. Had all gone well on his return to Cambridge, he might have been more active in the board's work than was to be the case. But the hernia problem that had become evident in his later years at Wisconsin became acute. Entering the Stillman Infirmary, he underwent surgery and spent some weeks in recuperation.

Despite his earlier misgivings, Farrand was delighted in May 1917 when he received "an astonishing, but most attractive proposition to do a short volume for this internal propaganda committee or whatever it may be." He explained to Turner that he had deferred the writing of a survey of United States history on the grounds that it might scoop Turner by incorporating ideas that were rightfully his. The current proposal, however, he understood, had originated with Turner, who now believed that he could not himself prepare such a work. Farrand asked assurance that his understanding was correct. Receiving it, although in equivocal language, Farrand wrote *The Development of the United States: From Colonies to a World Power*, a short interpretation of American development, dedicated "To the Allies: In the Hope of a Better Understanding."

Haskins and others among Turner's Harvard colleagues and professional friends worked on projects promoted by the board or as part of the Inquiry. Channing, however, carried his skepticism of American involvement abroad to the point of reminding the members of his undergraduate class that Robert Todd Lincoln had served his country in the Civil War by remaining enrolled at Harvard during most of the conflict. Turner found Channing to be unsympathetic to the activities of the board. Turner himself did not prepare any history material on behalf of the board, nor apparently did he serve on any of its many subordinate committees. Evarts B. Greene was chairman of the board for an extended period, heading a committee as well that advised secondary school teachers on appropriate course materials. In August 1918 he wrote to express his regret that Turner had been unwell but still hoped that he would provide a short article for the *History Teachers Magazine*. Greene assured Turner that he had found his advice on various matters to be helpful and looked forward to receiving more suggestions from him.

In part the state of Turner's health explains his failure to enter the scholar's war more completely, but the designs of Harvard colleagues also were involved. Writing to Turner in early spring 1917, Haskins asked him, "How is the book coming on?" but softened the impact by relaying the comment of a Harvard undergraduate who maintained that he had learned more from Turner than from any of his other history teachers. The student explained that "Turner gives all his time to us, instead of spending it writing books and articles like the others!"[14] Peer pressure came from elsewhere. In late June President Lowell invited Turner to deliver the prestigious Lowell Institute Lectures during the coming winter. The series, Lowell suggested, should consist of six or eight lectures; he hoped that Turner had "something in . . . mind that [he] would like to write down."[15] Turner understood that beneath this Cambridgean blandness there ran another message, "Move ahead with the great work!" He also knew that the invitation was an honor and an effort to be helpful, and he hoped that the deadline involved in the preparation of the lectures would spur his work.

By early July 1917 Turner was back at the house on Phillips Place and looking after himself since Caroline had departed to be with Dorothy, who was expecting a baby. He found the energy to spend a day with the Hoopers where he found the "Contessa . . . all fired up about canning and preserving the nation." As for himself, he wrote Caroline, not being "needed to save the country in the government 'service,'" it was best that he should "try to do my regular job and support my family!" Lowell had astutely suggested to Turner that his lectures should deal with the whole country rather than the West. This would mean much work that summer but would "help out toward the Book." Contemplating his notes, Turner reported that "condensation and arrangement" would be required. Instead of joining Caroline, he believed that, for the time being, he should work upon the lectures insofar as his "good for nothing head and pen" would allow. He was not able to "steam ahead full speed," although he was "getting stronger and fitter every day."[16]

Meanwhile, Turner carefully watched events in Europe and Washington. He viewed the behavior of Wilson's former rivals for the presidency with scorn. "They are thinking more of putting him in a hole for the glory of congress and their particular advantage, than they are of winning the war." He continued, "It hurts to see how the minorities can harm and selfish & small leaders *mis*lead." But the "unrest and revolt" in Europe was also disquieting. The war might even end there in social revolution. Germany might emerge as the dominant world power. "Better to fight, and if necessary go down fighting," than endure such an outcome: "that destiny intends that such a ruling class as the German government shall permanently dominate Europe and America isn't conceivable." But he believed, he said, "in the obscure outcomes of historical change, rather than in what seems obvious and certain."[17]

Turner remained in Cambridge during July 1917, roughing out the lines of the Lowell lectures. He found time for luncheon and a swim at Nantucket Beach with his former graduate student Colegrove, saw something of Haskins and other Cambridgeans, and noted that the draft numbers of Tom Martin of the commission and "Sammy" [Samuel E.] Morison were "well up in the list." Although he could not find his calling cards, nor the "shampoo sprinkling shower hose," he assured Caroline that he loved her "just the same."[18]

The heat, his physical condition, and occasional social encounters slowed Turner's progress with the lectures, but he provided the series coordinator with working titles for eight lectures on July 31. He planned to begin with a survey of national developments between 1830 and 1850, followed by four lectures dealing with the major regions of the country. Then would come a lecture on Jacksonian Democracy and sectional rivalries and another dealing with the expanding sections, 1840–50. His final lecture was to survey the United States in the mid-nineteenth century. Although less elaborate, the organization of the Lowell Lectures of 1918 roughly outlined the long-awaited great work when it was finally published after Turner's death.

After traveling to Madison to admire his grandson, Jackson Turner Main, Turner spent much of September at Hancock Point. To Dorothy he lamented that he had broken his rod and hung up his leaders and been reduced to planning for his fall classes. He had signed a contract with the ever-hopeful Holt and Company for the publication of the Lowell Lectures. He would sooner, he maintained, have been doing "some fighting," grandfathers not being useful "for much else." The government refusing to concede even that, it must be "the chimney corner and a book and a pen." He planned to precede Caroline to Cambridge where he might "invent a saw dust pancake and ragweed syrup," thus bringing him "fame as a man who deserves well of his country." Caroline joined him in early October, bringing two cocker spaniel pups. These allowed Turner to apply his practical talents in building kennel and run, serving as canine valet and maid and striving to produce appropriate names. Turner's classes that fall were "small," he reported, "but good stuff."[19]

Turner found developments in Europe and the home front particularly vexing at the time. Aroused by the outspoken opposition to conscription voiced by psychologist J. McKeen Cattell, Columbia University's Board of Trustees dismissed him from its faculty. Protesting this breach of academic freedom, Charles A. Beard, chairman of the Columbia University department of political science, resigned. Although he had "never liked" Cattell, Turner deplored Columbia's action. "The way to make radical revolutionaries," he told Hooper, "is to shut off men who do not think conventionally, from the ordinary avenues of expression." Nor, said he, "had be been able to agree with Beard," but he had been most unfairly attacked in the press. On the national scene he was disgusted with the behavior of Robert La Follette—"so filled with class hatred that he can't see patriotically." Columbia's president, Nicholas Murray Butler, also was at fault; he was "using aroused national feeling to put out of business those who differ with him on social and political reorganization."[20]

Although he must have understood that delivery of the Lowell Lectures would strain his physical resources, Turner agreed to teach "an additional half course at Radcliffe" in the second half of the academic year 1917–18. It would "help out and assist in reducing the cost of living," he explained to Caroline. The decision further illustrates Turner's unrealistic optimism about his own capacity for work and his penchant for making decisions without consulting Caroline.[21] Dorothy sought to entice the Turners to Madison for the Christmas season of 1917, but Turner explained in early December that he must work during the vacation period. Typically, his paper "The Significance of the North Central States in the Middle of the Nineteenth Century," to be delivered at the meeting of the AHA in Philadelphia at the end of December, was still unprepared, and there too he would have to attend a meeting of the Board for Historical Service. "Since I got into these duties I cannot respectably back out," he confessed. His remaining time Turner intended to devote to preparation of the Lowell Lectures.[22]

During these weeks Turner also acknowledged receipt of Edgar E. Robinson's recent book, *The Foreign Policy of Woodrow Wilson, 1913–1917,*[23] a publication perhaps instigated by the National Board. The book was "well done," and Turner agreed "that there has been more consistency, a firmer basis of underlying principle, in the President's foreign policy than has been generally recognized." But he also found the book more supportive of Wilson's course than was perhaps justified. Because "history likes to find consistent evolution," Robinson's portrayal might well stand. But Turner believed that Wilson had "exhibited not a little of the changing sentiment and veering winds of opinion that have appeared in the people of the United States in these years, and that there is more opportunism and somewhat less consistency" in his course than Robinson depicted. Turner suspected also that Wilson's Mexican policy had "encourage[d] both Mexico and Germany to disregard our interests and discount our power and our determination." Nor, thought Turner, had Wilson been sufficiently forthright in dealing with the "foreign stocks," failing to rally them opportunely behind "American rights and principles" in the face of challenge. Wilson, thought Turner, had "left too long a period for the hyphenated Americans to conceive the situation as one between England and Germany alone; and he did not convince the aggressors that we meant what we said, by preparations to back our words contemporaneous with the call to the people."[24]

By late January 1918 Turner was in the midst of the exam period and still "cudgelling [his] poor brains to work out a set of Lowell lectures for a month from now." Boston, he reported, had almost exhausted its coal, and rationing simplified menus remarkably. The Turners might be imagined as "gnawing our ear of unshelled corn in a corner . . . eating . . . rye bread with a wry face . . . barely existing on barley bread" and contemplating "saw dust and board for [their] frugal board." But they were, he assured Dorothy, "cheerful." Harvard's transition to wartime status was now well advanced—the buildings and other facilities serving the Student Army Training Corps and other military programs. Earl De Moe, the son of Turner's sister, Breese, was one of "three or four thousand radio lads" who ate in Memorial Hall and marched in strength "to the stadium."[25] Some colleagues were now temporarily in the civil service or preoccupied with government advisory obligations. The needs of the Red Cross, the YMCA, and the armed forces had thinned the ranks of the junior faculty and graduate students. When late February arrived and Turner began his delivery of the Lowell Lectures, they were noted in the press but created little stir in wartime Cambridge and Boston.

Delivering the lectures and attending to his other faculty duties left Turner in a state of exhaustion that he compounded by delivering the dedication address at the opening of the new building of the Minnesota Historical Society on May 11, 1918. Buck, secretary of the society, and his other students and friends in Minneapolis listened with pleasure to Turner's speech, "Middle Western Pioneer Democracy." He himself heard unpleasant news that sprang from medical specialists. The bursting of small blood vessels in one eye, he learned, was warning of more serious ruptures, should he overtax himself. He was told that he was suffering from high blood pressure and hardening of the arteries.

The Slaughters were working with the Red Cross in Italy, and the Turners rented their cottage at Hancock Point for the full summer of 1918, inviting Dorothy and Jackson to vacation with them. Here on June 18 Turner took a "morning dip . . . defying the diagnostician" and found it "great." "Nothing like cold salt water to put youth back, and give you optimistic views of life," he wrote.[26] It was a summer of picnics on the beach and other family outings, as well as fishing expeditions, work around the cottage, and conversations between grandfather Puff Puff and his articulate, if unintelligible, grandson. Turner's physical condition improved, but the packs of research notes that he had brought to the Point remained largely untouched. Not surprisingly, Turner did not provide his publisher with a manuscript draft of the Lowell Lectures, suitable for publication, within a year of delivery, as the contract had specified.

Dorothy returned to Wisconsin believing that her father was in good health and "looking fine and lazy." But he admitted to his son-in-law John that his recovery "after a summer of enforced idleness" was only partial. The medical specialists had warned him that "hard mental work may not be possible much longer." Given these facts and John's

Turner with his grandson, future historian Jackson Turner Main, on the steps to the beach at the Slaughters' summer home at Hancock Point, Maine, in 1918. Reprinted with permission of the State Historical Society of Wisconsin, Madison, Wisconsin. (X3)1363.

uncertain draft status, he thought it best to inform him of his financial situation. His current annual income, he explained, amounted to some $6,500—$5,500 from Harvard, $700 from Radcliffe under an arrangement that was renewed annually, and some $300 to $500 from the family investments in Liberty Bonds and stocks.

Turner saw little prospect of early returns from an investment of some years earlier in Brazilian iron lands that he had made on the advice of Van Hise. He was also indebted to Henry Holt and Company for an advance in the amount of $500 and minor "obligations" to Ginn and Company that would be liquidated as the Hart, Channing, and Turner *Guide* continued to sell. A life insurance policy was substantial in terms of the monetary values of the day. Should he retire in the near future, his income would fall to less than half its present amount under the current practices of Harvard University and the Carnegie Foundation's retirement program for university personnel. Despite his uncertainties, Turner scrawled a postscript. If some type of war service was offered to him, he would, "seriously consider any such proposition if my University work seems to promise as little of value to the war as it may under new regulations."[27]

Turner struck a different note for Hooper in early October. He had been "rather worthless" during most of the summer, he told her. Despite a partial "come back," he had an "explosive eye which becomes a carbuncle every time I put any strain on myself." Still, "so far we have been well, and are taking a daily precautionary two hours in the open, paddling on the Charles or walking. It's all in the lap of the Gods, and I shall not speak to the Devil until I meet him, as a Nova Scotia guide of mine was accustomed to say when I foresaw trouble on one of my canoe trips."[28] He unburdened himself in a letter to Slaughter a few days later. He had begun the summer as "a good bit of a wreck" and despite some recovery had not been able "to write as . . . planned." He explained the diagnostician's sentence and added, "I realize that I am over the top and not likely to be fit for the things I wanted to do. I don't like it, but hope I will not make too much of a mess of the remainder of the descent. Lord, how I envy you, doing something worth while!"

By this time Turner had largely accepted the popular propagandistic view of the Germans. In their retreat from the Hindenburg line they were showing a "hellish spirit." Their actions would force America to condone "devastation of German towns and wholesale slaughter of German people." Perhaps, however, the German people would over-throw their leadership. If they lacked the virtue to do this, "the war of Light and Darkness must go on until Day or Night and chaos hold the heights." But he rejoiced in the patriotism—the "liberty bond buying and enthusiasm" that had flamed in the American West. He foresaw problems ahead for both Wilson and the allies, but in America, he believed, the war had mitigated class conflicts, and ethnic differences had merged into one loyalty "to the American ideal."[29]

Turner's grandson, Jackson, celebrated his first birthday on August 6, 1918, and in mid-November Dorothy sent a photograph taken on that occasion to his grandfather. Turner hailed it as a birthday "worth celebrating," occurring so close to the Armistice. This year, they should hope, would begin "a long peace and the reign of what the President calls *just* liberty." And, he continued, "may American ideals of 'live and let live' prevail over the rule of *Macht*." However, Turner was concerned about the future in Russia and Germany and in America as well, where "extremists of the Red Flag and of *extermination* of the enemy" worried him. He was gratified that the La Follette forces had suffered a setback in Wisconsin but predicted—"more's the pity"— that "'Bob'" would hold "a dangerous power in the on-coming Senate, and . . . be courted again."[30]

An event in Madison that fall plunged Turner into profound sorrow. In mid-November President Van Hise entered a Madison hospital to undergo a minor operation and died of postoperative infection shortly after the medical procedure. Turner's capacity for forging enduring friendships was remarkably strong, and Van Hise had been his instructor in geology, faculty colleague, campus ally, neighbor and camping companion, dining club fellow, confidant, and ultimately, protector. Edward A. Birge, dean and one-time rival for Van Hise's ear, invited Turner to give the key memorial address. None had known Van Hise so intimately, he said. Turner refused, pleading ill health but explaining also to Dorothy, "I feel his death so strongly that it would have been very hard . . . even if I had been fit otherwise." Turner had occasionally been mildly critical of Van Hise's policies but lauded him as an advocate of beneficent natural resource policy and an administrator whose resilience fully matched Wisconsin legislators at their most cussed. Van Hise had been more than a scholar, said Turner, "he was a man as well."[31]

The death of Van Hise again aroused speculation that Turner might return to Madison. Birge had replaced Van Hise on an interim basis but might not be continued in the post of president. In the following May Turner's brother-in-law informed him that his name had been mentioned favorably in deliberations of the alumni committee charged with making recommendations for the presidency. From Texas, former student Frederic Duncalf mentioned that he had heard a rumor that Turner would become Wisconsin president. Although he respected both Harvard and "teaching and investigation," Duncalf "almost wish[ed]" that Turner would assume the post. Recent developments in the university left something to be desired—"the history department has certainly lost its prestige, and the library is too good for that to be permitted."[32] Meanwhile, Milo M. Quaife had responded to criticism by surrendering his position as superintendent of the Wisconsin Historical Society. That organization was seeking a new administrator. Again Dorothy heard her father's name mentioned, but he dismissed the rumor. I "haven't the faintest desire to administer anything," he told her.[33]

The war turned Harvard into "a military camp." By the fall of 1918 Turner's seminar had disappeared, and his upper division classes had withered to almost nothing—"three or four men only—and a handful of Radcliffe women." Haskins was offering a course on war aims to the young men of the Student Army Training Corps, and Turner agreed to hold "Haskins' hat" and lead discussion sections. He read the blue books and graded the map exercises of some seventy such students each week. Some through "wit or dullness" located Bohemia in France, and others placed Moscow in Italy. "A pie of some 150 papers a week is rather plump," he wrote to Hooper, but he would not feel "content if he had no finger in" it. "The naivete of the youth, and their idealism" was "compensation." He was pleased to find that his students believed the idealistic acts of the victors in the forthcoming peace conference would contrast sharply with the self-interested behavior at the Congress of Vienna. If Wilsonian in that outlook, he admitted wryly, they would probably vote for Henry Cabot Lodge, given the opportunity. That worthy's initials, he reminded Hooper, stood for "high cost of living." At the recent election he had cast his "first un-modified democratic ticket."[34]

By late December 1918 Turner could report to Dorothy that the Student Army Training Corps had been disbanded and with it his job as teaching assistant. To Robinson he wrote that the corps had been "hardly a success—too much kitchen police and too little time for real study." "Conquest" had contended all too successfully with "Culture" for the student's attention. More emphasis on one or the other might have been advisable, he thought. But "youth is captivating even when it strains at the leash and longs for the trenches," he continued, and some of the students had revealed unsuspected capacities. Turner did not believe that he and his colleagues should return to the old curriculum. He hoped that a cooperatively taught course might be developed, linking "recent history and the present issues," giving "reality and interest to history and government," and putting the "present issues in a more comprehensible form."[35]

In January 1919 Turner was greeting returnees from France and American training camps. He reported that he was "so busy talking to them between classes that [he had] gotten behind [his] time card!"[36] Happily this year found him somewhat restored in health. The Turners spent the summer of 1919 at Hancock Point. Dorothy and Jackson were with them again, and they enjoyed a peaceful summer in the "coolness and beauty of the Maine Coast." A two-week fishing expedition to the Roach Pond region of Maine provided "the real vacation of the summer." "I was born to live in old clothes and a log cabin and be called 'Fred' by the native neighbors," he told Hooper. Hancock Point was attracting more visitors than previously, and the Turners were obliged to change their rented quarters three times during the season. Caroline increasingly wished for a place that she "could call *home*." Real estate values in Cambridge were too high for this objective to be realized there, and she much liked the third of their dwellings that summer. Now she used a small inheritance to purchase the "Moorings," next door to the Slaughters' house and close to Haskins's cottage. But again the research notes were little touched. Turner was not, he reported, "able to do any mental work—not having the necessary machine to do it with!"[37]

That fall, however, Turner assumed a new teaching obligation. The Harvard historians developed a curricular offering for seniors entitled "The History of Liberty." Beginning in academic year 1919–20 Turner contributed lectures in this course dealing with American aspects of the subject from the colonial era, characterized by an expanding frontier, to the modern period, in which liberty must be viewed from very different perspectives. Turner's willingness to participate in the course was not surprising. Liberty was at the heart of his conception of the frontier and of American democracy and ideals. Participation allowed him to rethink such matters. Although contemporaries might think of Turner's Wisconsin school of history primarily in terms of institutional economic, social, and political history, he had long also stressed the importance of ideas. His lectures on the history of liberty were an exercise in intellectual history. But were they also perhaps an additional excuse for not buckling down to "the book"?

Turner, however, considered another invitation to participate in innovative teaching to be too distractive. He had known James H. Robinson since the 1890s. He had also come to know Charles A. Beard, although Turner always believed that Beard overemphasized the importance of class differences in early American development. As both Robinson and Beard labored during 1919 to launch the New School for Social Research in New York, they invited Turner to assist in the development of its program by giving a course of lectures during the following year. Robinson indeed suggested that "perhaps a slight obligation may rest on you to aid us," but this Turner declined to do, apparently pleading the state of his health.[38]

Despite Turner's understanding that he might have few years remaining in which he could muster the physical strength and mental clarity necessary for productive scholarship, he remained a committed advice giver. With the war ended, he suspected that reestablishing the European political system might be akin to nailing "currant jelly to a barn wall." But his consideration of the differences between the European and American experiences allowed him, he believed, to identify the elements essential to a lasting peace in Europe. He prepared a memorandum on the subject for Wilson, heading it "International Political Parties in a Durable League of Nations." Haskins, serving in the American Commission to Negotiate Peace, laid it before the inner circle of the American delegation in mid-December 1918.

In his first paragraph Turner described the document as "an *abstract of suggestions* (derived from the study of the history of American sectionalism and the geography of American political parties) upon the bearing of American experience on the problems of a League of Nations." There too he summarized his conclusion "that in such a League there should be a Legislative body, with substantial, but at first limited, functions, as well as a Court, or Council of Nations, and particularly that the *operation of international political parties in connection with such a Legislature* would promote the permanence of the League." The American section, Turner argued, was an *"imperfect image of a nation in the European sense,"* and the history of American development and sectional interaction provided clues to ways in which a peaceful postwar Europe might be ensured. Despite great sectional diversity, the United States had survived with but one great political crisis. Turner found the explanation for this success in the American political system where *"national political parties ran across all sections,* [and] *evoked intersectional or nonsectional party loyalty."* If the peace settlement provided an international system in which political parties emerged that extended across the national boundaries of Europe, a more peaceful future might be ensured. The common peoples of Europe at least, he believed, were ready to accept the example of America.[39]

In preparing this memorandum, Turner was fulfilling the conception of the historian's role that he had identified in his presidential address to the AHA—that of the scholar "hold[ing] the lamp for conservative reform." Later he explained to Hooper that he had "advocated a legislative organization, representative of people rather than of departments of foreign relations, to consult and advise on the deeper problems, and to legislate on some problems of a restricted nature, pointing out that by adopting the method of diplomatic negotiation the old order and its old hands in the diplomatic game would return, with the old results."[40] Central to Turner's formula lay his understanding of American political development—the dynamic interaction of political parties would brake disruptive nationalist [sectional] impulses and create, as in America, a political system more stable than that characterized by the national rivalries, power politics, and formal diplomacy of prewar Europe.

Turner and Haskins argued at length the merits of the proposed League of Nations. Haskins was more critical of Wilson and the idea of the league than was Turner, who viewed the European situation and the Senate debates over ratification during the fall of 1919 with frustration. Americans, he believed, had "overestimated Europe's capacity to learn from its dreadful lesson," and Europeans overestimated "the durability and unselfishness of the flame of idealism that for a time burned out the dross and allowed us a vision of a nobler order."

Senator Henry Cabot Lodge, Turner wrote, was "little and spiteful and plays great issues as pawns in a game for the satisfaction of his own wounded vanity." He and his senate allies had framed the reservations concerning American league membership "to kill, not to remedy imperfections in the league plan." Turner admitted American aversion to militarism, the hope that we could once more "keep out" of Europe's affairs, the "tendency to let well enough alone," the antagonisms of American ethnic groups, and the leaderless state of the Democratic Party. But writing in late November 1919, he was sure that many Americans supported the league and believed "in an America that is constructive and capable of leadership instead of an America that fears 'innovation' and is timid in the presence of new conditions, and distrustful of its power among other nations in council." There was "love of fair play" and "dislike of the Senate" at work. He did not want the United States to accept mandated territories; it "needn't become European in order to play a reasonable part in the League." Turner still believed that the league could only operate successfully by acquiring legislative responsibilities and acting "not as a diplomatic congress of chess playing representatives of the old conceptions of balance of power, and diplomatic cleverness, and diplomatic traditions, but as voicing whatever internationalism there is among the various countries." He would not be surprised, he admitted, to see "the treaty lost, so far as the league goes." And so, in effect, it was.[41]

Turner later admitted that his scheme of international organization was "no doubt unworkable." To readers familiar with the development of the European Union, it appears less fanciful than it would have seemed in Turner's time. Turner never learned whether Wilson read the memorandum. The president was, Turner admitted, a man of "large *intellect*" but not, like Lincoln, a statesman of "large nature." Wilson had "thought himself the bearer of a great idea," but in fencing with the "champions of different nations" he had allowed the "bearer to become too prominent."[42]

Sitting on the porch at 629 Frances Street one evening early in the twentieth century with Jameson, Haskins, and perhaps others, Turner sketched a plan for developing a history institute or center in Washington. Here advanced graduate students from American centers of graduate training could affiliate while researching in the nation's capital. In full development the center would maintain an advisory staff or accommodate senior professors with *comitati* of graduate students. Although the Carnegie Institution considered the idea of a center for advanced research in history in developing its initial history program, it did not materialize at that time.

In 1916 Carnegie staff members informed Turner that Robert M. McElroy, a Princeton University scholar, was promoting a similar idea. Jameson urged Turner to attend a meeting of scholars at Columbia University to discuss the idea. He did so but was not actively involved in the processes that resulted in the organization of the University Center for Research in Washington in 1921, largely through the efforts of the AHA and the American Political Science Association. Turner had visualized an agency that included a residential center, but such a facility was deemed to be too expensive. In effect, the University Center for Research was to be a mentoring service provided by Washington-based scholars for both domestic and foreign graduate researchers doing research in the Washington area. It illustrated a minor aspect of a trend toward increased sophistication of professional organization among scholars and their associations that became evident in the immediate postwar years. The American Council on Education, the National Research Council, the American Council of Learned Societies, and the Social Science Research Council all emerged as important components in the system of American higher education at about this time.

Arranging leave from Yale to plan the new Commonwealth Fund's future course, Farrand sought Turner's advice on his assignment in a letter of February 12, 1919. He also wondered whether his friend could fill in for him at New Haven on a weekly basis during his absence. Replying immediately, Turner explained that he had found his weekly visits to Chicago during the late 1890s extremely taxing when he was "fuller of steam" than now. Yale would do better, he thought, to line up a younger person like Edgar E. Robinson, whom he praised highly. Farrand's assignment for the Commonwealth Fund interested Turner greatly, and he responded at length with both specific and general suggestions.

Turner explained to Farrand that the growing practice of wealthy individuals endowing foundations "*outside* of the Universities" was a further development of the "pioneer principle of association" and might have "significance in American life and cultural tendencies." Even though such foundations had thus far concentrated upon medical and scientific research and social problems, Turner believed that there lay open "a field of activity in keeping alive and extending among the— shall we say? *Bourgeoisie*, the best ideals of our pioneer era—and helping to keep a knowledge of the America of the past clear while we adjust it to new conditions." There was a place, he continued, for "a laboratory on American civilization, its processes, and tendencies, [where] the things of the spirit could also find a place." Why not as a man of "executive gifts," steer "several millions $ horsepower" in that direction? Turner admitted that it would be easy to waste "energy" on "visionaries or academic dreamers in easy chairs." Distributing funds in the humanities to "really important and useful work" was more difficult than in science, but, he wrote, "*the creation of an attitude of mind toward the problems of American society and toward what America means, in its past,* as well as in its present and future, is as important as the problem of applying philanthropic gifts . . . directly to *particular* scientific or even social activities."

Turner submitted several pages of detailed suggestions on "types of subjects for study," methods of procedure, and the scholars who might play a part in the work of an "Endowment for Research on American History and Social Policy." The latter's program was to be one of "scientific examination—not propagandist." There should, Turner wrote, be studies of leaders, and American society should be studied in both its historic and contemporary dimensions. The latter would involve studies at state, regional, and national levels. Class formation and competition should be investigated, as well as the "natural history of political parties," including their geographic, economic, stock, and class sources of support. American industries should be examined, as well as "American ideas, as expressed in literature." Special topics worthy of consideration included American agrarian development, the factory system, mining, a variety of topics relating to the American population, immigration, interstate migration, Americanization, and various ethnic and racial groups including both Indians and blacks. Education in broad perspective should be examined, as well as religion in its institutional aspects rather than as systems of theology, and "general agencies for social activity."[43]

Researchers in various regions and programmatic emphases should be brought together periodically for discussion of their work in progress, Turner continued. The results of research sponsored or encouraged by the foundation should be disseminated not only in the scholarly community but through the general population as well, using community and interest group gatherings as forums. The research of historians should be coordinated with that of economists, sociologists, and political scientists.

No one reading Turner's letter to Farrand in its entirety can seriously argue that his approach to American history emphasized only frontier and sectional processes, or that American history in his view ended with the 1890s. The agenda he had prepared was sweeping in its coverage, although a modern social historian would note significant omissions, issues relating to gender for example. Nor can we be sure that Turner clearly understood how this broad program of research would yield the results that he hoped might come from it. Nor was he unique at the time in proposing activity of this kind. Albion W. Small and others had also outlined ambitious programs of social research. But few, if any, within the history discipline could have spontaneously dashed off so visionary a letter as the one Turner sent to Farrand.

At a less elevated level, Turner responded to a call for assistance from those searching for a secretary at the State Historical Society of Wisconsin. He had, he told, Dorothy, "recommended half a dozen nice young men."[44] Among them was Joseph Schafer, one of his first advanced students and an energetic member of the faculty at the University of Oregon. Schafer won the position and would direct the Midwest's leading historical society through the following decades of prosperity and depression.

Even the arrival of a reprint could stimulate a lengthy response from Turner if it struck the right chord. When a young New York scholar,

Dixon Ryan Fox, sent him a copy of his article dealing with politics in early-nineteenth century New York, Turner thanked him, noting that it bore upon his "own studies." Then at length Turner summarized his current "vacation amusement," analyzing national voting maps of political majorities by counties during the years 1844–56 and comparing the patterns revealed there with those found in the results of later elections. He found class factors and voting to be related—a linkage stressed by Fox in his work—but Turner's maps also showed that region shaped voting results. With references to appropriate sources, Turner analyzed the factors that apparently influenced voters in their decisions to support either the Whig or Democratic party. He believed that Fox's use of newspapers and his understanding of their relation to the politics of the day was sound—though caution was advisable—and the data relating to city residence and voting were "convincing." "Whig slogans of opposition to executive interference" had been more effective than "frank statements of class interests," he believed. "Under *strain*" "idealistic issues" might prevail. "Men will vote at times from patriotic, or religious, or moral motives against their personal interests," he reminded Fox. He confessed in closing, "When I started I meant to write but a page or two!"[45] Fox was amazed that Turner would spend such time and effort in responding to an unknown instructor.

At war's end, traffic in Harvard's history department picked up as more serious and traveled students resumed their studies and were joined by newcomers in the history programs. Once more graduate students began to consult with Turner about their research, to forward reports on archival findings, and to send him drafts of papers or thesis chapters. In October Turner's student Lewis D. Stilwell described his summer of research on migration out of Vermont during the mid-nineteenth century. From London, subsequently, Reginald Arragon reported on his investigations of the Panama Congress of 1826 at the Public Record Office. He had made notable progress, he confided, thanks to the fact that his wife was helping him take notes. Meanwhile, the persevering Buffinton touched base with his mentor a few times. Undergraduates felt free to correspond with Turner as well. In mid-summer of 1919 a bright young undergraduate student from Omaha named Merle E. Curti wrote to tell him that he was having a copy of an article dealing with the cultural frontier of North Dakota sent to him and informing him that he wanted to do a thesis on a Mormon subject in History 17a. Turner would be happy to learn, he was sure, that "Mr. Merk's work in the summer school" had been to everyone's liking.[46]

Former students likewise kept Turner abreast of their professional progress. Among them in 1919 was his former student Martha Edwards, of Lake Erie College, who in May sent him a paper on religious forces in American politics that was a beginning on the larger study of religious factors in presidential elections that he had suggested she undertake. In the fall she reported that she was completing her study of Indian missions during the Jacksonian period and apologized for taking his time. It was, however, "the penalty" he had "to pay for inoculating students with the virus for research."[47] Edwards had completed her doctorate at the University of Wisconsin in 1916, and her letters illustrated the kind of continuing influence that Turner exerted upon some students whose graduate study was completed under the direction of others.

During the fall of 1916 the Harvard Commission on Western History seemed to promise a productive future. As its archivist, Martin was building a creditable foundation of achievement. Efforts to enlist the Harvard Alumni Clubs in its service appeared to be enjoying success. The funding of the commission was inadequate, however, to produce the results that its members, particularly Turner and Hooper, desired. During the spring of 1917 Turner's conciliatory nature ran afoul of financial reality. Quaife and other western historical society directors had engaged a scholar to calendar western historical documents in the files of government departments in Washington. Pressed for funds, they urged Turner to bring the commission into the project. Remembering the western criticisms of Harvard's collecting program, Turner urged his colleagues to agree to using commission funds in this way. Archibald Coolidge condemned this suggestion; Harvard, he wrote, had no obligation to this shaky enterprise and the end product promised to be no more than "pleasant and mildly useful." Dependent on Hooper and the occasional contribution from other sources, the commission should use its funds in the ways envisioned by its patroness. He anticipated, he said, "crushing rejoinders . . . and withering scorn" in Turner's response but received a plaintive missive in which Turner deplored the fact that Harvard would neither provide institutional support for the commission nor give it free rein in fund-raising.[48]

The incident illustrated both the bootstrap nature of the commission's activity and Turner's occasional propensity to push beyond the limits of reality in practical matters.

Meanwhile, the energetic Martin was seeking to develop leads and contacts in numerous directions and was in need of secretarial assistance beyond the amounts that Coolidge could bootleg to him from the resources of the Harvard library. Pressed to distraction by the demands of his position, Martin's patience snapped on one occasion, and he was rude to one of the commission's most enthusiastic supporters. Turner calmed the waters, but collecting activity was soon threatened from another source. Martin was eligible for service under the military draft, and his number indicated an early call to the colors. He joined the Red Cross in September 1917 and soon went overseas. The war also diverted the attention of Turner and Hooper and other leading members of the commission.

With the war at end and Martin interested in resuming his studies at Harvard, Turner hoped to restore the commission to its earlier level of activity. His hopes were dashed. Martin could be reestablished in the commission only through an endowment capable of producing five or six thousand dollars per year or an equivalent flow of income. Hooper's resources were not unlimited, and she had contributed more in support of the collecting program than she had first planned. She had hoped that the commission would also assist in developing greater understanding between Harvard and its western alumni and that Harvard in return would wholeheartedly support the collecting initiative. Encouraged at first by President Lowell's attitude, she came to realize that he did not share her conceptions of the commission nor have any interest in supporting its program with Harvard funds. She explained also that wartime taxes and contributions had diminished her ability to contribute—perhaps only five hundred dollars per annum would now be possible, although later she was prepared to double the sum. In 1919 William Hooper suffered a serious heart attack, shifting her attention to domestic life.

Could Harvard alumni, perhaps, find the funds necessary to maintain a successful program under Martin's direction? Harvard University launched a major endowment drive at this time, but the commission was not visualized as a beneficiary. In spring 1919 the commission once again tried to rally the alumni clubs to the cause. Even Channing wrote a letter in support of the collecting program, and the commission's needs were presented at the meeting of the clubs that June. But the attempt failed because western alumni preferred to keep western materials in the West or desired that their resources be used in other ways.

Through 1919 Turner, Hooper, and other members of the commission discussed its future. They wished to see it survive and prosper, but their prognosis became increasingly gloomy. The funding problem was intractable, and Turner began to question Martin's suitability as archivist. "The jealousy of western men" concerning the loss of "manuscripts or rarities" would be a continuing problem. Although he closed the letter "with goodest wishes," Turner told Hooper in early 1920, "I am convinced that we shall not get far without an assured income rather than year by year uncertainties." As commission member and Harvard librarian, Coolidge brought the issue to a head in correspondence with Lowell; succor was not to be found in the president's office. Hooper was philosophical, "Unless the Powers that Be see the possibilities in our crusade—for the University—it is utterly futile to try to make them. It is just one of those ventures that didn't jell and the graceful thing to do is to plume ourselves a little on having tried to make the University a bigger place with a wider horizon."[49]

The Harvard Commission on Western History enjoyed its greatest success between 1913 and 1917. Through its efforts more than a thousand books were added to the Harvard Library collections and a considerable amount of important manuscript materials as well, most notably the papers of Villard. Although Hooper and Turner had hoped for greater success, they had assisted the Harvard Library in becoming a major center for the study of the history of western America. As for Turner himself, he had found his involvement in the affairs of the commission to be educational. The man whom Turner liked to call "Sammy" Morison later wrote, "There is no art, science, or experience that cannot be turned to the service of Clio."[50] In campaigning with Alice Perkins Hooper, Turner came to understand much better the strengths and foibles of Harvard, New England, and even of the Midwest. But the papers of the commission also reveal that its activity was a time-consuming distraction for Turner, an additional diversion for a man too easily diverted.

13 Rebound

"I seem to have pulled through the reviewers' fire
from Boston to Portland"

After 1914 the pressures of work and profession, social obligations, flagging health, vacationing, and evasive mental stratagems all perhaps contributed to the difficulty that Turner experienced in trying to write. But the comments or inquiries of former students, colleagues, and friends kept the subject of publication much in his mind. At the annual meeting of the AHA in December 1917 Turner listened to Dunning discuss "A Generation of American Historiography" and heard him praise Theodore Roosevelt and others for calling attention to the history of the West. Dunning further remarked, "For the perpetuation of the spirit and method of these writers in the twentieth century, it is unnecessary to mention to this audience how potent has been the influence, and how disproportionately scanty, alas! the historiographic output of our own Turner."[1] Was Dunning's jibe to be considered as payback for Turner's career-long insistence that slavery and racism were secondary issues in American development, an outgrowth of differences in personality between the two historians, or perhaps a product of institutional rivalry? Whatever the cause, the sally struck home.

In January 1919 Guy Emerson, an admiring New York banker, began to correspond with Turner. The latter sent him reprints, and Emerson inquired whether Turner was going to bring his ideas together in book form. In April Jameson wrote to Turner inviting him to contribute to the *Review* the paper "The Significance of the North Central States in the Middle of the Nineteenth Century" that he had delivered at the annual meeting of the AHA in 1917. Aside from his presidential address, noted Jameson, Turner had not published in the *Review* for thirteen years—a "rather shocking state of things." Turner responded that he was in better health but trying to develop longer publications. Jameson gave him leave to ignore his "importunate solicitations" but assured him that he still coveted the paper and must have it "if it can be had without any damage to you."[2]

In mid-summer Haskins forwarded a passage from a letter received from Emerson in which the banker suggested that Turner was capable of producing "some unusually fine books, if he could only be induced to take the time from his academic work to prepare them." Being absent from the country, wrote Haskins slyly, and out of "touch with the rapid progress you have been making on this book . . . I could not assure him of its immediate appearance. Doubtless a little encouragement of this sort is all that is needed to finish it up this summer!" He understood, Haskins continued, that Holt was "issuing an edition of your complete works." He hoped that "revision of these is not going to take too much time and thought from the other job."[3]

Turner had long hoped to publish a collection of his essays on the frontier. Reacting to the unfavorable diagnosis from his doctors and aware that he might not be able to deliver a manuscript based on the Lowell Lectures, he discussed this alternative with Henry Holt and Company. The firm approved. Turner did not plan to revise the essays or provide extensive editorial background for them. To Bristol, of Holt and Company, he argued that "to use them as materials for a new structure" would be confusing. As they stood, they had a "certain value in the history of self-consciousness of Americans at successive years, in our reactions between changing conditions and older ideals and conceptions." He himself had been "an indicator of these things" and so the articles were historical artifacts. They were also evidence of the influence that he had exerted upon the profession. Revision would "lose" him "the right to my evidence of pioneering, and be open to the intimation of moulding them to others' work." To Guy S. Ford he also explained that major revision into "a consistent whole," or pulling the essays together into a general account, would have been a slow process, requiring him to discard much material.[4] All too conscious that others had expected more from him, Turner realized that the unrevised collection would be the quickest means toward providing a work of substance.

In his preface to *The Frontier in American History* Turner rationalized the book's format in terms similar to those given to Ford and to his publisher. The essays might "have some historical significance as contemporaneous attempts of a student of American history, at successive transitions in our development during the past quarter century to interpret the relations of the present to the past." Turner did not make it easy for the reader to follow the transitions either in America or in his interpretive thought. The great proclamation of 1893 appears as the first chapter of the book, and his Minneapolis address of 1918 provides the final chapter. The essays between do not follow chronological order of publication. To the original texts he added only the preface, two pages in length, and brief notes identifying the original place and date of publication. He explained as well that he had corrected a few "slips in the text" and omitted occasional "duplication of language."[5]

Of the thirteen essays in *The Frontier in American History* Turner had written and presented all but three before the end of 1910. Only his Minnesota address of 1918 reflected his thinking at a date close to the publication of the volume. As such it is worth attention. The historical society's building, said Turner, was being dedicated in a time of war, and this was fitting because Americans were fighting in behalf of "historic ideals." They were at war "that the history of the United States . . . filled with the promises of a better world, may not become the lost and tragic story of a futile dream." America's great material contributions were "born of the love of Democracy." The "plain lives and homely annals" of the midwestern pioneers to be studied in the society's new home were

> part of the story of the building of a better system of social justice under freedom, a broader, and . . . more enduring foundation for the welfare and progress under individual liberty of the common man, an example of federation, of peaceful adjustments by compromise and concession under a self-governing Republic, where sections replace nations over a Union as large as Europe, where party discussions take the place of warring countries, where the *Pax Americana* furnishes an example for a better world."[6]

A state historical society, Turner explained, was a "Book of Judgment wherein is made up the record of a people and its leaders." He then briefly sketched midwestern development, describing the three great streams of "stock" that occupied and developed it—the interior southerners, the New England element, and the immigrants. The southerners were committed to "backwoods democracy . . . based upon equality of opportunity" while "resent[ing] the conception that opportunity under competition should result in the hopeless inequality, or rule of class." If individualists, the frontiersmen showed "capacity for extra-legal voluntary associations." They were "responsive to leadership" and emotional in both their religion and democracy. The Yankees brought "the habit of community life," built cities, and created markets. But "the winds of the prairies swept away almost at once a mass of old habits and prepossessions." Immigrants from the old world also contributed. Despite "slowness of assimilation . . . and a certain persistence of inherited *morale*," the melding of the three was "the creation of a new type . . . neither the sum of all its elements, nor a complete fusion in a melting pot. They were American pioneers, not outlying fragments of New England, of Germany, or of Norway."[7]

Society in the Middle West was mobile, one of cross-fertilization, but also with emergent sectional attitudes. Egalitarian, it had intellectual aspirations as well, had developed a unique educational system, adapted to regional ideals and needs. "The goal of the Middle West" was "the welfare of the average man." The pioneers had not always given "disciplined devotion" to the governments they had themselves "created and operated." But as the Civil War had shown, they could commit themselves nobly to a great common cause. They exemplified the kind of governmental discipline that "proceeds from free choice, in the conviction that restraint of individual or class interests is necessary for the common good." Turner contrasted these attitudes with "Prussian discipline, the discipline of a harsh machine-like, logical organization, based on . . . military autocracy." Here ranged "the discipline of Thor, the War God, against the discipline of the White Christ."[8]

It had been necessary to temper the "individual unrestraint" of pioneer democracy. Americans had learned that the trained specialist "has a place in government . . . whether as umpire between contending interests or as the efficient instrument in the hands of democracy." With "the era of free land" ended, the "perpetuity of the republic" required that selecting "the fit and capable for office" was as "important as the extension of popular control. When we lost our free lands and our isolation from the Old World, we lost our immunity from the results of mistakes, of waste, of inefficiency, and of inexperience in our government." Now Americans were recognizing that government service could be a greater claim to distinction than business triumphs. Now too Turner saw in the patriotic efforts of voluntary organizations a reaffirmation of the "pioneer principle of association that was expressed in the 'house raising.'"[9]

Turner concluded with a restatement of "the heritage of pioneer experience." It was, he said, a "passionate belief that a democracy was possible," in which "the individual [had] a part to play in free society . . . which trusted in the common man, in his tolerance, his ability to adjust differences with good humor, and to work out an American type from the contributions of all nations"—a type that he would defend and for which "he would make sacrifices, even the temporary sacrifice of individual freedom and his life, lest that freedom be lost forever."[10]

In preparing his Minnesota address Turner wrote with much of his old eloquence. The speech was not devoid of factual evidence. He illustrated the tendency toward voluntary association by listing "the log rolling, the house-raising, the husking bee, the apple paring, and the squatter's association . . . the camp meeting, the mining camp, the vigilantes, the cattle-raisers' associations, the 'gentlemen's agreements'" as "a few" illustrations. He noted novel features in the new midwestern state constitutions of the 1840s and 1850s to show midwestern democracy at work. He included an apt passage from the observations of Harriet Martineau and cited de Tocqueville as authority. But there was much here that was pure assertion and evocative oratory. For instance, his opening echoed the stirring passage from Walt Whitman's poem "Thou Mother with Thy Equal Brood" that begins "Sail, Sail thy best, ship of Democracy."[11]

Turner's brief discussion of an America without free lands, revealed his continuing commitment to the idea that their role had been central in American development until the turn of the century. The address was also an endorsement of the basics of progressive reform. The trained expert must enter government, "organs of government" be specialized, an umpired economy prevail, public service, philanthropy, and voluntarism be honored. But the common man should not be allowed to perish—he was the exemplar of pioneer democracy; his legacy should remain and be enhanced, for it was unique and worthy of defending at all costs. Although Turner always maintained that the historian should be objective, his comparison of the Prussian and American systems demonstrated the difficulty he found in adhering to that ideal. If momentarily shrill in denunciation of the followers of Thor, his was a rousing and withal an optimistic message. As usual in such celebratory presentations Turner's basic ideas were familiar ones. Nowhere, however, did he use the word *frontier* in the address.

After *The Frontier in American History* appeared in October 1920, Turner eagerly scanned the reviews sent to him by a clipping service. To Hooper he announced jubilantly, "So far I seem to have pulled through the reviewers' fire from Boston to Portland, Ore., from labor papers to Transcript, from Nation to the Methodist church organ of the Pacific Northwest, and from the Atlantic Monthly to the country newspaper, with nothing but 'them kind words.'" Although lamenting that "the sales will not bring me in postage stamps for correspondence," he reported some weeks later that his book was "reviewed in the most flattering way" in newspapers and periodicals "from the Pacific Coast as well as the Atlantic." The recipients of gift copies responded appreciatively, and Turner was touched by Becker's letter of acknowledgement: "Whatever I have written in American history shows the influence of ideas which are expressed in these essays and addresses; and in my last book . . . I have appropriated your interpretations without scruple, without fear also, without reproach I hope, and certainly without research. . . . It was you more than any one, you and Haskins, who shunted me into the scholar's life."[12]

During early February 1921 Beard dampened Turner's spirits by publishing a critical review in the *New Republic*. To Turner's free land and westward expansion as significant factors in American development, Beard wished to add slavery, labor, and capitalism. He denied that Americanization proceeded more rapidly on the frontier than elsewhere. Beard suggested also that the social and political conflicts that Turner interpreted as outgrowths of the westward movement were actually "economic group conflicts," and Turner had ignored those between capitalists and organized labor. Dorothy was distressed at such criticism of her father's work, but Turner explained to "Dear Fighting Peggy" that Beard was "an ex-Columbia professor, radical in tendency," who wished to project the current importance of "the struggle of capital and labor" backward to an era when that aspect of American life was less important.[13]

Turner wrote a letter of remonstrance to Beard that has not been preserved. He had challenged "some points of his criticisms which didn't seem to me sound," he told Hooper. Though disavowing competence in the matter, that loyal ally found the review in the *New Republic* "not convincing." She remembered that on their single meeting she had found Beard to have a "gosling-ostrich look to him." Would Beard have been less critical had Turner agreed to lecture at the New School? Probably not, since Beard's criticisms were consistent with his views on American development generally, and he was not known to bear grudges on small grounds. In response to Turner's letter, he was polite but qualified his criticisms only in minor respects.[14]

As reviews in the scholarly journals followed those in newspapers and popular periodicals, Turner could feel pleased at his decision to publish the frontier essays. There were some criticisms. Clarence W. Alvord noted in the *Mississippi Valley Historical Review* that the frontier sequences outlined by Turner did not hold true for all parts of the country, and Allen Johnson told the readers of the *American Historical Review* that the collection would have been improved if Turner had provided a precise definition of *democracy*. But these reviewers were also generous in praise, and other reputable scholars treated Turner's book with equal respect.[15]

Lacking the myriad publications of a colleague like Hart, or the accumulating volumes of a megaserial like that of Channing, Turner was anxious that his somewhat different contribution to history be recognized. He eagerly recorded acknowledgments of his work. In 1918 he had been delighted to find that Farrand's interpretive survey of American history described a "new history" that took "other than political and military events into consideration" and upon which Turner had exercised "the greatest influence . . . through his classes and in his writings." To Hooper he reported that James Ford Rhodes had mentioned him appreciatively in the current volume of his account of post–Civil War America.[16] Turner was gratified that William E. Dodd noted his influence upon Woodrow Wilson in his biography of the president and affirmed that the Wisconsinite had "influenced the writing of [American] history more than any other man of his generation."[17]

In mid-1920 Guy Emerson sent a copy of his new book, *The New Frontier*, to Turner. He had, he explained, tried to develop the modern implications of the frontier tradition, and he fulsomely acknowledged Turner's scholarship. Turner sent to Emerson a copy of the paper "Greater New England in the Middle of the Nineteenth Century" that he had presented before the American Antiquarian Society in 1919, and Emerson responded gratefully, commenting upon "the great loss to the historical work not only of America but of the world if you were to fail to complete this history which Holts' want you to do." Turner instructed the Harvard Coop to send copies of both the Dodd and Emerson books to Hooper, writing, "in each of which (by judicious use of the index), you will find that I'm quite a fellow after all, and that the 'pioneer' is coming to his own in American political writing!"[18]

Support came from elsewhere as well. Mathematician and amateur historian Archibald Henderson referred flatteringly in his *Conquest of the Old Southwest* to Turner's contributions to American history and dedicated the volume to him in gratitude for friendly counsel. At the AHA meeting of 1920 Turner hailed Professor D. S. Muzzey's paper on the Puritan contribution not only for its quality, but also because it included several references to his own work. Although he professed embarrassment at frequent complimentary references from participants at the Mississippi Valley Historical Association's dinner during the AHA meeting in 1920, they deeply pleased him. And he was delighted to discover that Dutch historian Johan Huizinga had cited some of his essays "in a very gratifying spirit of approval."[19] In all of this one senses not conceit so much as self-justification mingled with naive pleasure in being well regarded.

Turner was startled in 1919 when Dodd told him that he had, for a time, believed it was Wilson who first perceived the significance of the frontier in American development and that Turner had followed Wilson's lead. Although the timing of a contribution by Wilson in the *Forum* during 1893, as well as his book of that year, *Division and Reunion, 1829–1889*, suggested this possibility, Wilson assured Dodd that he had obtained his understanding of the importance of the frontier from Turner. "All I ever wrote on the subject came from him. No, it was in no sense a discovery of mine," he told Dodd.[20] Turner responded to Dodd in a lengthy letter in which he praised Wilson and described the stimulation that he had derived from their relations at Johns Hopkins, as well as his commitment to Wilson as political figure. He also outlined the development of his own understanding of the frontier. Professor William F. Allen had sparked Turner's original interest in institutional adaption to changing circumstances in his lectures on the institutions and society of the Middle Ages. Turner developed his ideas on the subject further in his thesis on the Wisconsin fur trade, and Wilson's enthusiastic reaction to his seminar report on the subject at Johns Hopkins had greatly encouraged him.

Turner recalled that Adams had spurred him on his own bent when he remarked that members of his seminar would be turning henceforth to topics in European history, having exhausted the opportunities in "local institutional history in the United States." Then Turner had formulated his basic ideas in the *Aegis* article of 1892 and had developed them further in the Chicago paper of 1893. Turner had sent copies of the *Aegis* piece to members of the Hopkins circle, including Wilson, and had read the draft of the Chicago paper to him while he visited Madison in late July and prior to the appearance of the latter's article in the *Forum*. As for Wilson's direct influence upon him, wrote

Turner to Dodd, he had suggested using the first word in the phrase
"hither edge of free land." Dodd responded to Turner's letter suppor-
tively and at some point Turner placed his letters in a separate folder,
along with a copy of his *Aegis* article of 1892, enclosing an explanatory
note as to their content and suggesting in it—the modesty is perhaps
overdone—that Dodd possibly overstated the Turner influence upon
Wilson. The latter, on the other hand, had helped Turner in turning
a phrase but provided "none of the ideas; merely helped me to an
apt word."[21]

Turner's exchange with Dodd began the development of an authorized version of the origins of the frontier hypothesis. Turner continued
its development in correspondence with Constance Lindsay Skinner,
who had reviewed *The Frontier in American History* most suppor-
tively in the *New York Evening Post*. She did complain mildly that
Turner had given insufficient credit to the Scotch Irish and Scottish
Highlanders for their contributions to American individualism and
democracy. This reaction led Turner to initiate a friendly correspondence with Skinner. He was delighted to learn that she had been raised
at a Canadian fur trading post. In 1922 she asked Turner for information about himself to be used in editing an anthology in which his
most famous essay was to be included. He replied at length, providing
biographical details and sketching the development of his ideas and
teaching career. He described his influence upon other scholars and
discussed the environmental and intellectual influences that played
upon him as a youth and a developing scholar.

Turner's account of the origins of his ideas for Skinner's benefit
expanded upon what he had told Dodd, but without mention of
Wilson. "The Significance of the Frontier" was, he wrote, "a programme,
and in some degree a protest against eastern neglect, at the time, of
institutional study of the West, and against western antiquarian spirit
in dealing with their own history." Turner did not mention other
writers who had emphasized the importance of frontier influences.
Examining American economic and social development and the
advance of the frontier, he told Skinner:

> I saw at once, that the frontier passed into successive and varied
> regions, and that new sections evolved in the relations between
> these geographic regions, and the kinds of people and society
> which entered them and adjusted to the environment; and that
> these sections interplayed with each other and reacted on the old

East and on the nation, in economic life, political forms and legislation, and in social results and ideals as expressed in education, literature, religion, etc. In short, the national spirit, — Uncle Sam's psychology, — was a complex, due to a federation of Sections. Behind the apparent state and nation type of federation lay the federation of sections, explaining manifestations of so-called State sovereignty, which are, more deeply manifestations of sectional differences."[22]

This understanding of sectional processes, he continued, he had suggested in his article in the *Aegis* and in the edition of the essay of 1893 that the Herbart Society published in 1899. Turner treated sectional processes to some degree in his article of 1892 but not in the sophisticated fashion of 1922. By 1899 he had more fully incorporated the physiographic side of the argument into his analysis, and here too he first proclaimed that "the great physiographic provinces which have been won by civilization are economically and socially comparable to nations of the old world."[23] Even so, in 1899 Turner could not have written so neat a statement of the workings of sectionalism as that of 1922. Turner had not grasped the major elements of his later sectional theory "at once."

In both the explanations to Dodd and to Skinner there were unwarranted implications of virgin birth. Turner's assertion that Herbert Baxter Adams had declared opportunities for research in American institutional history to be exhausted is suspect, as we have seen in discussion of Turner's early career. In his letters to Professor Allen Turner had criticized the lack of attention given to the West in the Hopkins program but had admitted that some students there were working on western subjects. Advising Albert Shaw in 1883, Adams had stressed the importance of institutional and economic history and had assured him that scholars would "gain more by striking Northwest and Southwest than by hanging around Plymouth Rock." Writing more generally of opportunities for study in American local life during 1889, Adams had proclaimed that there was "left historical territory enough for student immigration throughout the next hundred years."[24] His reaction to the *Aegis* article had been enthusiastic. Turner began that article with a story similar to the one that he told Skinner but in which a Wisconsin state legislator played doubting Thomas. Would Turner have had the cheek to attribute the comment to a Wisconsin state legislator in the first paragraph of the *Aegis* article and then send a copy to Adams if his teacher had really made the same point? Or perhaps Adams had said something of the sort in banter; he was a master in motivating graduate students, and professors from New England were not all devoid of humor. In that case, Turner might have been nervy enough to tweak back. That two prominent people should have made the same observation to Turner within the space of several years does test credulity.

In writing to Skinner, Turner did not refer to the numerous references to the significance of free lands and unique frontier institutions and traits to which he had been exposed. Nor did Turner inform her that while he was developing his early theory of sectionalism, one of his doctoral candidates was doing intensive research along similar lines. Nor is there mention here of an ambitious young graduate student searching for a domain comparable to that of Parkman and determined to place his claim stakes around it. Passing years simplify and distort recollection; for this Turner cannot be blamed, but the subject's ability to revise his own history is something that the biographer should never forget.

Although less active in the AHA during the 1920s than a decade earlier, Turner still was involved in its affairs. He agreed to give two short addresses at its 1920 meeting. He discussed scholarly opportunities for research in Washington, D.C., in a panel chaired by Jameson and spoke informally at the dinner of the Mississippi Valley Historical Association. Organized on the assumption that it would be an intimate gathering, that event attracted more than two hundred historians. Although he cut his remarks short in deference to Channing's presidential address, Turner believed that they had been well received.

Turner declined an invitation to speak at the AHA meeting in 1921, but a year later he discussed research opportunities at the dinner meeting of the fledgling Agricultural History Society. He disavowed any intimate knowledge of farming, not knowing "a rutabaga from a pumpkin." He had accepted the invitation, he explained, because some of his former students at Wisconsin were now employed in the United States Department of Agriculture and were leaders in the new organization.[25] Turner perhaps gained his knowledge of contemporary agriculture by spending a few boyhood days on farms near Portage during the harvest season, overnighting at farm homes while on fishing expeditions, and gazing over rural road fences. He knew a great deal, however, about agriculture's contribution to the development of the United States. In the research agenda that he laid before his students and the historical profession, he particularly emphasized the importance of investigating subjects in agricultural history. For two generations at least, scholars developed research topics that Turner identified in his talk to the members of the Agricultural History Society.

At that same AHA meeting, Turner enjoyed hearing Haskins deliver his presidential address and also "talked with a group," assembled for breakfast by Farrand, on the subject of intellectual history.[26] In developing this interest, he anticipated the future content of the history curriculum, as in his earlier advocacy of social and economic history. It was no sudden conversion. He had called for the study of ideas in his presidential address and was involved in the Harvard department's "History of Liberty" course, a pioneering offering in intellectual history in American history departments.

Under the procedural revisions of 1915–16, Turner's voting rights as an ex-president in the AHA Council had vanished, and despite his great professional influence, he was no longer at the center of the association's councils. He felt no deprivation at this change of status. But he was associated with one very important professional initiative of the 1920s. In 1919–20 the American Council of Learned Societies (ACLS) emerged as an important coordinating influence for the humanistic disciplines, and during its early years Turner represented the American Antiquarian Society at its meetings. At the first of these Turner proposed that a dictionary of national biography be included among the projects of the ACLS. The council then named a committee to develop a proposal to that end, including Jameson, Turner, and others. Funding seemed to present an almost insurmountable barrier to the realization of the committee's goal, but so persuasive were Turner and his colleagues that the owner of the *New York Times* ultimately agreed to underwrite the project. The *Dictionary of American Biography* was not the creation of Turner alone. Leaders in the AHA discussed many ideas for the advancement of the profession from the 1890s onward. Hart had espoused a project similar in concept to that of the *Dictionary*. Jameson, indefatigable organizer and facilitator, pushed the committee's work on the project forward. Haskins was an early president of the ACLS, but Turner proposed the project and supported it strongly thereafter.

In the spring of 1920 Caroline departed for the west where a new baby was expected. In mid-May Turner reacted to dispatches from Madison by assuring Dorothy that he was delighted by "the dimples, the brown hair . . . the successful dairy . . . and the whole little Betsy." His grandson generously proposed that Grandmother "Lailie" should take Betsy back to Cambridge with her. Turner did not withdraw from society in Caroline's absence. He went fishing with a "nice lot of men," who "sang in chorus very well indeed, told good stories, recited like professionals & were a really gifted bunch." On his return from the fishing trip, he entertained his student from Oklahoma, Edward E. Dale, and his wife, by taking them to dinner. They returned to Phillips Place to discuss the effect of Oklahoma winds on feminine nerves and other interesting western subjects. The couple "quite cheered me up!" he informed Caroline.[27]

In ensuing letters Turner told of listening to Hooper read passages from the novel that she had in hand and of entertaining Dale and an Osage lecturer from the Chautauqua circuit. This gentleman had been—so he said—captured by Kiowas as a child, experienced the Battle of the Washita and knew Custer, Buffalo Bill, advocate of Indian education Gen. Richard H. Pratt, and the hallucinogenic properties of the mescal button. A week later Turner found the empty house depressing and attended a performance of *Hamlet* at the Opera House. Thereafter he tried to look up Haskins and subsequently made another social call, before calming the dogs, bored to the point of fighting in Caroline's absence.

A few days later the Dales invited him to dinner, serving him sausages and biscuits, prepared by Dale "a la camp." Afterwards he took them to the Pops concert. Other social engagements followed, including dinner with the Merks, whom he considered to be "very interesting Wisconsin people," and where he "quite lost [his] heart" to Mrs. Merk. After noting a club dinner and a dinner invitation from Haskins at that writing on May 22, Turner reported that he would be "dining out from now until your return, which helps some on the high cost of living."[28] Although Turner affirmed that he did not like an active social life, he was no recluse. Some committed scholars might have taken advantage of their wives' absence to bury themselves in their research and writing. Turner liked to eat in company and found an empty house oppressive.

After acquiring the Moorings, the Turners spent longer periods of the spring and summer at Hancock Point and were usually joined during the early 1920s by Dorothy and the children. In March 1921 Turner acknowledged himself *"eager* to see" the westerners and "have the sea air about us." So eager indeed for the Maine coast was he that he had, the day before, walked the beach at "City Point" and "visited the aquarium to get a look at a real trout again." The residents were, he discovered, "quite engaging, but rather slow," and the bellowing of hungry seals had sent him in search of an "oyster cocktail."[29] In that year Turner and Caroline arrived at Hancock Point in May. In mid-June he returned to Boston, scribbling a note to Caroline while on the train, asking that she forward his shaving brush and ointment and commenting on industrialized Haverhill—"once a perfectly good 'frontier town,' just look at the d——d thing." From Boston it was westward again to Chicago, an overnight stay with sister Breese, and on to Madison where he was to be awarded an honorary degree at commencement.

Madison, Turner reported, "look[ed] natural but grown up more," now served by "yellow and black & white taxis." He stayed with the Slaughters, next door to his old home, now occupied by a sorority. Turner found the *"costumes* of the girls" bathing and sunning on the Mendota shore, the "most startling revelations I've ever seen," adding that "bare legs . . . bare arms . . . bosoms" made "it clear that Wisconsin needs a mother and father not to mention the policeman." An eastern city would not tolerate such "revelations of what one cheerfully hopes is primitive innocence, and paradise regained." Awakening at the Slaughters', he saw at every window of their old home "bare arms, and curl papers of the rising houris of the harem." "Like enough," he philosophized, "all these things that shock the puritan eyes are really not all they seem to symbolize; but I'm glad I've no daughter here in college."[30] So, having met the jazz age at the University of Wisconsin, Turner accepted his LL.D., visited with old friends, and then accompanied Dorothy and the grandchildren to Hancock Point.

Through the early 1920s Turner watched the unfolding of a postwar world with interest and anxiety. Although he had reservations about Wilson's policies, he defended him against the sterner criticisms of Haskins. In January 1920 he heard his friend lecture on territorial readjustments in Europe and found him more sympathetic to the administration than he had expected. Discussion of her father and the nature of leadership with Hooper led Turner to analyze the role of government in America in a letter to her. Despite their achievements, the actions of business leaders like Edward H. Harriman had persuaded Americans that some government intervention in the economy was required. Should England and Canada nationalize their economies, there would be a demand for like action in the United States. However, he explained, "our brief experience and the form in which the demand is made on a class basis will not at present appeal to the 'average American'—if there is such a person. But the forces behind the demand are powerful forces."[31]

While Caroline was in Wisconsin, Turner tried to identify the major presidential candidates for her: Leonard Wood, Hiram Johnson, Frank O. Lowden, and William G. McAdoo were all possibilities, he believed. But he predicted that the parties would be "much broken up by cross currents of organized labor, organized farmers, organized Germans and a disorganized nation." If inflation and labor problems continued, perhaps even Herbert Hoover might emerge as a viable candidate. Late June found him "disgusted with the Republican convention, as a Democrat has a right to be; and am hoping the Dems. will really get religion and find a Moses." Entrenched at Hancock Point in mid-summer 1920, he found "time to say disrespectful things about the Unholy Alliance of the senators who guide the Republican party." Back in Cambridge, he saw Lodge, Harding, and Hiram Johnson in action and intoned, "'let us not talk of them, but look and pass.'"[32] He wrote to Dorothy that he would vote for Cox.

On the eve of the national election he painted a discouraging picture of American politics for his daughter. The country needed "a leader as well as the World a League." Such a leader should know his course and not "back-track." This description, he believed, did not fit Warren Harding. Moreover, Harding's "creators and councillors" were of the "discredited type" whose activities had led to the "Roosevelt revolt." Penrose was "corrupt, cynical and materialistic," and Lodge was a "vain aristocrat, whose self-esteem was wounded when Wilson didn't let him do it all." He had harsh words for Knox and Taft, as well as Johnson and Borah, who would not accept the League of Nations if it "came at the hands of an Archangel." Complicating the picture were radicals who wanted to "punish the administration" and foment a "new revolution." Divisive ethnic groups—Irish, Greeks, Italians, Poles, Germans,—

were advancing their own selfish agendas, "pro-Frenchmen who wanted the Rhine, English enthusiasts who want us to pay the British debt," and so on. How, asked Turner, could a man who "doesn't know how to drive or where he is going" manage such a "run-away drove?" Whom could Harding ask for help? "If I were a Republican I'd pray for defeat under the circumstances," concluded Turner.

Still, he admitted that "the good Lord, or something, has saved the United States from quite as feeble presidents as Harding . . . and may help him out likewise." He expected that Harding would be elected. Although Cox had waged an "able campaign," "the mass of Americans will vote as they have in the past on habit." It was, he believed, "an era of exhaustion and reaction after a mighty effort."[33] Turner's letter to Dorothy reveals his perceptive understanding of the mechanics of American electoral politics. Parties were important in mobilizing voters, but crosscurrents of economic, regional, ethnic, and ideological beliefs also affected their decisions, as well as feelings of patriotism, frustration, or other personal sentiments, the charisma of leaders, and the voting habits of the electorate.

Turner continued to believe that the concept of the League of Nations was flawed but regretted the failure of the United States to participate more fully in it. He was deeply moved by Wilson's breakdown and sent Hooper a copy of the account that Dodd had written of his interview with the bedridden president at the time of the AHA meeting in 1920. When the Armament Conference convened at Washington in late 1921, Turner intently followed the proceedings. "The diplomat and the expert, tied to the old rules of the 'game,' the old cynicism and suspicion, will be the ruination of such conferences," he told Hooper midway through the proceedings. Alas, the "golden hour" for an appropriate postwar settlement had passed when Senator Lodge substituted "(Republican partisanship) for the chance to work while things were plastic, for a better world," nor had Wilson been "free from obstinacy."[34]

A few days after the delegations of the various world powers adjourned in early February 1922, Turner assessed the conference's work hopefully. If the Japanese kept faith, he had "great hopes of the results" and "agree[d] with Harding and Hughes that it rested on the only basis which can sustain a worth-while World—namely mutual understanding and good will and 'give' as well as 'take'—the old pioneer custom of the neighborly 'house raising.'" But Harding was asking a great deal of "self-restraint and forgiveness" when he asked the

Democrats in the Congress to support the conference agreements, much as Wilson had pled that shunning the league would "'break the heart of the World.'" Although Harding did not recognize the fact, he was, suggested Turner, apologizing to Wilson for the earlier course of the Republicans.[35]

Although Turner worried about American foreign policy, he was delighted as a "student of the interplay of sections" by the emergence of the "farmers' bloc" in the Congress and its use of the balance of power to alter Republican agricultural policy. Here was further proof of the importance of sectionalism in American politics. He reported himself "highly elated—over my *diagnosis* primarily rather than over the fate of the patient!" The triumph of "this combination of South and Middle West, though a "party minority," was "really startling." "A new national center of gravity" was emerging, he believed, although in part it was "an old alignment," even recalling "the days of the Federalist defeat, the Hartford Convention, etc." The "votes and the press comments on the successive stages of the contest" had "perfectly demonstrated" his "theory of the persistence and importance of sectional groupings in congressional votes."[36]

The off-year election of 1922 reduced Republican strength in the Congress. Writing to Dorothy, Turner expressed some satisfaction that La Follette had been "saved from the wreck." The G.O.P. might still have a future, provided, thought Turner, that he did not quarrel with Borah and Johnson.[37] Turner told Hooper that he was reconciled to the fact that Lodge had narrowly escaped defeat but believed that he "must have had the shock of his life." He regretted, however, that Senator Albert Beveridge had failed to be reelected. This senator had given promise of helping to provide sorely needed leadership. The "rapid oscillations of public sentiment" reminded Turner of Victor Hugo's loose cannon. He was less sympathetic to La Follette, explaining that his huge majority was due to the fact that he had lacked effective opposition in the Wisconsin race. Turner hoped that Senator Irvine L. Lenroot, Wisconsin's junior senator, would become the leader of the Senate Republicans, perhaps forcing La Follette into a third party and "incurring the odium" of disrupting the Republican Party. "I am myself," he wrote, "a liberal and not in sympathy with the ultra-conservatives; but La Follette's type doesn't appeal to me, especially with his war time sins on his head. Yet the radical reaction is strong and may strengthen his hand." The tendency of the midwestern states to show similar voting trends in the election of 1920 provided

Turner, he believed, with another "interesting gloss" on his theory of sections.[38]

In December 1922 Turner judged that "the World never seemed 'madder' than at present" and seemed "to be plunging into a European Niagara, not without its effect on us." He was not uniformly critical, however, of the Republican leadership, sympathizing with the reluctance of Secretary Hughes and Senator Borah to forgive the European war debts. We should require assurance that the act would not inspire a further "military and imperialistic drunk with the proceeds!" Still, the European nations seemed inclined to that course anyway. "Few of us," he admitted, "realized how deep seated the European malady was. Perhaps our entry into the League would have alleviated the matter; but perhaps we might merely have caught the pest, or found ourself a cordially hated nurse or doctor by the whole body of invalids!"[39]

As a collection of essays, *The Frontier in American History* was not "the book" for which Turner's former students, colleagues, and professional friends had so long waited. On this score the Harvard authorities had again tried to be helpful. In late April 1920 William S. Ferguson, chairman of the history department, informed him that President Lowell had suggested that he might be relieved from teaching during the second half of academic year 1920–21 to prepare his Lowell Lectures for publication. The Radcliffe salary would be lost for that period, but that could be borne, given recent improvement in his Harvard stipend. He would be expected to participate in doctoral examinations, but aside from that, he told Caroline, "the requirement is *merely*(!) a book." Ferguson had added that the "arrangement might possibly be renewed, *à la* Channing." Turner had understood that Lowell wished to provide faculty members with time for their writing but had believed that Channing's arrangement would prevent support in his own case. His leave was granted "in order to complete one or more books in American history."[40]

Would illness, however, foil Turner's hopes? The doctors were continuing to monitor his ailments. He experienced minor illnesses and had had a mole removed from his lip, but these did not predict disaster as in 1918. A conservative regime of work with ample exercise and diversion might postpone the meeting with the "Devil" indefinitely; the work in progress might be completed. During the summer of 1920

Turner on the beach at Hancock Point with a canoe named "Mumps." Reprinted with permission of the State Historical Society of Wisconsin, Madison, Wisconsin. (X3)909.

Turner corrected the page proofs of *The Frontier in American History* and read some thesis draft. He did little with the Lowell Lectures. He explained to Hooper, "It's strange how busy one can be on a vacation, when you are errand boy, grandfather, picnicker-in-chief, canoeman, carpenter, tent dweller, and in the intervals proof-reader and belated critic of theses!" Later he catalogued his summer distractions: a baby's smile, a small boy who wished him to dig clams, a trout, sunsets over the Maine mountains as viewed from the veranda of the Moorings, and withal "a seeming inability to lift a pen."[41]

Perhaps this was the summer that provided Dorothy with one of her favorite stories about her father. He had access to an automobile and was determined to learn to drive it. While Dorothy was supervising young Jack at play near the Moorings, her father came chugging down the road. He waved heartily and the car followed the direction of his arm, careening through the fringe of vegetation between road and yard. "Whoa, whoa!" shouted Turner, stabbing frantically for the brake while Dorothy rushed to scoop young Jack from her father's path. The car wheezed to a stop, and Jack was saved for the history profession. The Hancock Point summers of the early and mid-1920s allowed Turner to enjoy grandfathering to the full. Clever with the pencil, Turner drew pictures for the children and once composed a poem for young Jack, which began, "Said the Mermaid to the Main" and relayed the pleas of the resident seal, clams, and other Point personages for Jack to return to Maine.

The spring semester of 1921 was to be Turner's for writing, and he hoped that a productive summer thereafter would see the task completed. He took his leave and made progress, but not without self-doubts. Midway through that term he analyzed Turner the writer for Lincoln MacVeagh, of Henry Holt and Company. His "strength," he explained, lay "in interpretation, correlation, elucidation of large tendencies to bring out new points of view and in giving a new setting." He doubted his competence to write *condensed* narrative." He was not "a good saga-man." But, as he worked, he might find "power coming" to him "in these respects." Turner cautioned MacVeagh that he wrote "most effectively . . . under full steam"; he "must write passionately if [he was to] do it well." He could not maintain a pace of "so many hundred words a day" over an extended period. He cautioned that past attempts to "really *push* ahead" had placed him in the hospital. Given the state of his health, he must be moderate in his efforts, lest he suffer a "blow up of the type of Mr. Wilson's." If able to apply half of the year to his writing for the next several years, with an adequate stenographer, he could, he believed, complete his task. Absolute relief from teaching would make the end still more certain because, he said, "I can't teach and write at the same time." This reflected both "temperament" [*sic*] and physical condition. If an earlier retirement had been possible he would, wrote Turner, "have been in better repute with Henry Holt & Co. as a Keeper of Promises."[42]

Despite such second thoughts, Turner was in good enough spirits during the spring of 1921 to envision timely completion of the Lowell Lectures manuscript. He discussed the format of the new book with MacVeagh, hoping that it would be more attractive in appearance than the frontier collection. But when the Holt representative once more painted a picture of an academic world in desperate need of the survey text that only Turner could write, the latter sent a reimbursement of part of the advance against royalties that he had received so many years before. This the Holt officers refused to accept, offering to cancel the obligation. Meanwhile Turner had reached the point of depositing

Picnicking with friends in Maine during the 1920s. Caroline is at the extreme right. Reprinted with permission of the State Historical Society of Wisconsin, Madison, Wisconsin. (X3)46051.

with the publisher a series of maps to be used in the more specialized book, and there had been discussion of the appropriate length and title.

When the Turners departed for Hancock Point in the spring of 1921, they carried with them a "big lot of notes," but Turner made little use of them. In early fall, however, he was heartened by the news that royalties from *The Frontier in American History* had wiped out his note with Holt and Company. Harvard again exempted him from teaching in the spring semester, and as he completed his grading in February 1922, he anticipated the imminent day when he would "put on the invisible mantle, hunt up my invisible Oriental carpet and go into the realms of writing . . . if the Lord permits." By May he was laboring on the book in Cambridge and finding the going rough with Caroline already established at Hancock Point. He was now using a stenographer. A first hour's trial "was an awful mess," and he saw that he had "his work cut out" for him. The typist was good, and he wished "my stuff . . . farther advanced toward dictation." Two weeks later he confessed, "Dictation is hard for me, and I am rather discouraged to find how much there is to do before the book can be said to be ready."

A few days later Turner met with President Lowell to seek permission to take his next sabbatical as a half year during the second term 1922–23. Both men were ill at ease, Lowell perhaps the more so,

Turner reported, but the president approved the request. June found Turner in the very depths of discouragement as he wrote about his progress to Caroline. The context is unclear, but one sentence runs, "If I bring up another big lot of notes and take them back again as last year, I might as well confess failure and go out." At this point the page is torn away.[43]

A secretary assisted Turner for a time at Hancock Point that summer, her activity watched with great curiosity by young Jack. Turner was optimistic enough to tell MacVeagh that he hoped to place the book manuscript of "Sections and the Nation, the United States, 1830–1850" in the publisher's hands by November. In his forthcoming sabbatical, he would take up the long-delayed text concerning which MacVeagh had pictured a "long felt need and rich reward." Turner hoped also that he might be able to do something further in contrasting the development of American sections and European nations. In mid-August he reported that the work was "still very much in the rough." He sketched his routine of those days: "I go fishing about once a week, much to the disgust of my stenographer and I bring home very few trout — to the equal disgust of my family; but I get well inoculated by mosquitoes and black-flies, midges and moose-flies, well wet by wading in the stream and fishing in the rain, and sunburnt in the intervals when the clouds roll by."[44] In mid-August he confessed to MacVeagh that his dictation had produced far more pages than he had planned to allot to the section under preparation. He promised to apply the hydraulic press. But then the engines of Harvard labored to life, and Holt and Company did not receive a manuscript in November. Turner had, however, made substantial progress that summer.

Mid-February 1923 found Turner reporting that, once his examination books were read, "Then to my book! I feel like writing and hope we shall keep well." Some weeks later he was safely on sabbatical and "living in 1846 with Dave Wilmot's 'Proviso,'" the "'world' . . . a mess . . . the 'flesh' . . . picking up" and the "'Devil'" not to be mentioned.[45] The officers at Holt and Company were now encouraging Turner to let his manuscript develop as it would — to curtail revision and move ahead. "What we want, is the book as you feel it *ought* to be written," wrote MacVeagh.[46] In early May, Turner sent two chapters to the publisher. Inquiring about the possibility of more in early summer, MacVeagh learned that Turner had been quite ill. But by typing up Turner's draft in their offices, the publishers managed to extract chapter 3 and much of chapter 4 by the end of October. Now, however,

Turner was caught up in a final year of teaching in which he carried the undergraduate hours that he had borne prior to 1920 and also offered a new course, "History of the United States, 1880–1920," for graduate students and advanced undergraduates during the spring semester 1924. Then came a summer session assignment at Utah State, preparation for the transfer of goods and persons to Madison and Hancock Point, and a fall lecture series in Cambridge. Although in December 1924 he warned his publisher to expect another chapter in the near future, it apparently never arrived.

Some may wish to view Turner's years between 1920 and his retirement in 1924 as ones of tragic anticlimax. Since at least 1908 he had proclaimed his major professional objective to be preparation of a book that would extend his analysis of the development of the United States through the years 1830–50. By 1917 the Harvard authorities were trying to help him in producing "the book," and after 1920 they adjusted his teaching schedule to that end. Yet the book did not appear. His health was suspect, but he suffered no major illness or breakdown. He did, however, fear collapse if he pushed too hard, and he allotted himself time for physical exercise and mental diversions, longer periods perhaps than modern medicine suggests were necessary. It was a pattern carried over from his younger days when he was recovering from meningitis. And he was distractable, incapable of the single-mindedness that his colleague Channing was displaying in producing successive volumes. That persevering scholar was devoting even his Sundays to work on his *History of the United States*. Turner in these years wasted no substance of time or intellect in reviewing books or writing for encyclopedias. He could not restrain himself, however, from preparing a couple of time-consuming pieces that did not bear directly on the contents of "the book."

During the war period Turner had continued to detect sectional processes at work in national politics. Avidly scanning newspapers, he found politicians expressing sectional sentiments and noted that federal representatives and senators aligned themselves particularly with colleagues from nearby states in voting on war issues. The sections of the country differed on indicators varying from the distribution of automobiles in the population to the proportion of males unfit for national service. Turner observed the tendency in Washington to resort to regional organizations in developing war programs and in mobilizing the national system of transportation. Living in New England, Turner was impressed by the growing tendency of the northeastern states to react similarly to economic and social challenges and to cooperate with their neighbors. As we have seen, he was especially pleased by the emergence of the Farm Bloc in the United States Congress as a bipartisan regional manifestation of concern over the agricultural problems of the Middle West and the South.

Convinced that sectionalism was becoming increasingly important in American affairs, Turner was stimulated by the politics of the early Harding presidency and by the readjustments in national boundaries abroad into giving a number of presentations on the current mani festations of sectionalism, illustrated by appropriate lantern slides. In early May 1922 he told academic audiences in Ann Arbor and Chicago that "there is no more enduring, no more influential force in our history than the formation and interplay of different regions of the United States." The draft of these talks contains an effort by Turner to identify different manifestations of sectionalism, six in all.

Turner first described a form of sectionalism fueled by hatred and a sense of injustice that carried self-determination to the point of secession and civil war. In less extreme form sectional sentiment could result in the organization of "purely sectional political parties." Alternatively, parties might remain national in scope but be dominated by a sectional wing, and this development in turn produce a sectional revolt leading to the defection of party members to the opposition or to the formation of a third party. Usually sectionalism was revealed in milder form in the legislative process by dissent from the party line in preliminary votes, or amendments, and by the offering of alternative planks for party platforms in political conventions. These gestures once made, sectionalists typically then yielded to party discipline. Underlying these political manifestations, Turner explained, was a sectionalism of material interests, often mobilized in the form of voluntary associations. Finally, noted Turner, there was a "sectionalism of culture" in the United States. Teachers had their regional associations, popular speech had its regional variants, and the works of literary figures showed a "special regional quality." Indeed, he continued, "our American literature is not a single thing. It is a contrapuntal song of many sections."

During this same period Turner prepared an article on sectionalism that he submitted to the *Atlantic Monthly*. When the piece was rejected summarily, he turned to the *Yale Review* which published it in the fall of 1922. Bringing the article into final shape cost him some of the summer of 1922. True, the central theme of his projected book was sectionalism, but his analysis of its nineteenth-century aspects benefited little from the enthusiastic labor that he put into the development and publication of this article. It was, however, a well-argued statement and notable for a ringing conclusion in which Turner proclaimed his faith in the American spirit, American ideals, and the future of the American system of government:

> We are members of one body, though it is a varied body. It is inconceivable that we should follow the evil path of Europe and place our reliance upon triumphant force. We shall not become cynical, and convinced that sections, like European nations, must dominate their neighbors and strike first and hardest. However profound the economic changes, we shall not give up our American ideals and our hopes for man, which had their origin in our own pioneering experience, in favor of any mechanical solution offered by doctrinaires educated in Old World grievances. Rather, we shall find strength to build from our past a nobler structure, in which each section will find its place as a fit room in a worthy house. We shall courageously maintain the American system expressed by nation-wide parties, acting under sectional and class compromises. We shall continue to present to our sister continent of Europe the underlying ideas of America as a better way of solving difficulties. We shall point to the *Pax Americana*, and seek the path of peace on earth to men of good will.[47]

When preparing for publication the collection of Turner's essays on the sectional theme, his friends used the article of 1922 as the concluding chapter. As a result, this passage seems to stand as his last words on the subject. It was a tribute to America, the exceptional, mingling an optimistic understanding of American democracy and promise, a conviction of unique virtue, and endorsement of governance by a party system that effected compromise between sections and classes—in sum a model for the world. If Turner's tribute to America was unrealistic and old-fashioned in its fervor—a dream hopelessly out of step with the cynicism of the 1920s and, as good history, debatable—it reflected the yearnings of a decent, thoughtful, and learned man.

Turner was again diverted when he put considerable effort into preparing an address marking the thirty-fifth anniversary of the founding
of Clark University in early February 1924. He had devoted much of
his AHA presidential address to describing the changes that occurred
in the United States since 1890, and he had essayed a similar task
when he helped mark the twenty-fifth anniversary of the University of
Chicago Graduate School in 1915. His talk at Worcester, Massachusetts, drew to some degree on these antecedents, but he devoted much
effort to assembling details of alterations that had occurred in the
years intervening between the founding of Clark University and the
early 1920s.

Turner described changes in the area of American settlement and
development as a Pacific power, the transformation in the composition
of the American people, the marvelous technological development,
and the advances in chemistry, physics, and geographical knowledge.
He outlined the impact of such developments upon the industries and
workers of America and on the nation's rise as a great naval power.
There had been changes as well, he explained, in our arts and ideals.
The concentrations of power based on America's abundance of natural
resources had changed our views of the role of government and
inspired a progressive response to the excesses of business. Thence,
he moved to supportive evaluations of Theodore Roosevelt and Woodrow Wilson. Although Wilson had not succeeded in his international
objectives, Turner hoped that "the vision of a world adjusting its
problems by negotiation and by judicial determination in some common organ of decision, [would] not pass away." Should it do so there
would be another "catastrophe to civilization," more terrible than
the last because of the contributions of science to warfare and because "the shrinking earth is bringing all mankind into a common
destiny."[48]

In this address Turner introduced an old concern in modern guise.
In the frontier essay he had introduced the concept of closed space.
During the early 1920s he was following the writings of scholars from
a number of disciplines who were contributing to an alarmist revival
of Malthusianism. Some were pointing out that the occupation of the
world's better agricultural lands, coupled with surging population,
promised food shortages in the near future. Others forecast acute

scarcity of important minerals in a matter of decades. "Truly," said Turner, "a shrinking earth! An earth compelled by irresistible forces to exercise restraint, to associate, agree, and adjust, or to commit suicide." In conclusion, he expressed doubt that catastrophe was as imminent as predicted, but he continued,

> I do not doubt the trend, and to me who have spent much of my life in the study of the movement of peoples into the vacant spaces of the United States, it is a dramatic outcome of a process that began with the first wanderings of the cave man. But I prefer to believe that man is greater than the dangers that menace him; that education and science are powerful forces to change these tendencies and to produce a rational solution of the problems of life on the shrinking planet. I place my trust in the mind of man seeking solutions by intellectual toil rather than by drift and habit, bold to find new ways of adjustment, and strong in the leadership that spreads new ideas among the common people of the world; committed to faith in peace on earth, and ready to use the means of preserving it.[49]

Turner's papers of the early 1920s show a mind still deeply engaged in both the contemporary world and the domain of scholarship. Although undocumented, these essays rested upon much searching of the contemporary press and publications in several fields of research. Despite disquieting challenges facing America, Turner's message was one of restrained optimism. Educated man would find a way, and American formulas prevail. We can scoff that Turner misread facts and ignored others, but he continued to do his homework. He jokingly called his celebratory disquisitions jeremiads, and some historians have interpreted them seriously as such—lamentations for a simpler and happier age, warnings of disaster ahead. But speeches like his commencement address at the University of Washington and his presentation at Brown University almost a decade later were too dispassionate in their offering of evidence and too hopeful of the future to be considered genuine jeremiads. Were his addresses and talks of the early 1920s important enough, however, to justify taking time from preparation of "the book"? He convinced himself that they were.

By the early 1920s Turner had reached the point in his career where even his teaching at the graduate level was more a distraction from his writing than a source of new ideas, useful evidence, and stimulation. When Ferguson informed him in 1920 that he was to be freed of teaching obligations during half of the following year, the conversation foretold a basic change in Turner's teaching obligations. Frederick Merk completed the Ph.D. that year, and the Harvard department added him to its teaching faculty. With the coming year Merk taught the second half of the "History of the West" course and shared responsibility for graduate direction in that area with Turner. Although he continued to lecture in the course "History of Liberty" for a time, Turner's undergraduate teaching responsibilities now focused primarily on the West and were restricted to one annual semester for several years.

The testimony of students who knew Turner during his Harvard years suggests that he displayed less spontaneous sparkle and humor as an undergraduate teacher than had been the case at Wisconsin. In neither setting was he ever a spellbinder. One found him "controversial rather than oratorical in delivery," his lectures "carefully prepared" but with a "certain air of informality." He was "always dignified and restrained giving the impression of strength and knowledge," but with a "genuine modesty" as well, reported Avery Craven, who also emphasized that the general course in American history that Turner offered for some years at Harvard was as high in quality as was the "History of the West." Other students particularly remembered his frequent recourse to sources and the massive slide collection and maps that he had developed to illustrate the details of American development. He was a firm believer in term papers and map assignments. Until the end of Turner's career he drew relatively large numbers into his class on the West, in part, Merle Curti believed, because of the personal interest he displayed in students, often engaging them in conversations about their backgrounds and the role of their families in the American story.[50]

Turner introduced the course entitled "History of the West" to the American college curriculum. He had long since set its basic structure when he moved to Harvard, giving heavy coverage to the colonial frontiers and breaking at the end of the first semester at about 1850. As we have seen, he published *List of References in History 17: History of the West* in 1911, expanding and revising it periodically thereafter. There were fifty-two reading units in the edition of 1915, the last five dealing with the West after 1900—"The New West, 1900–1910," "Combinations and the Development of the West," "Conservation and the West," "The Progressives," and "Contemporaneous Western Ideals." In the edition of 1922 Turner and Merk added a section on "The West in the World War and Reconstruction." As revision of the guide followed revision, the text lengthened, reflecting the growing interest in western history and also the increase in the number of publications by Turner's students.

The course notes of several students from Turner's final teaching years have been preserved, including those of John M. Gaus. Destined for distinction in political science, Gaus enrolled in Turner's western history lecture course for the spring semester of 1920. His class notes reveal Turner's approach to the second half of the course during the last year prior to the changes in his teaching status of the early 1920s. After discussing the extension of transportation facilities westward from the Appalachians and the territorial system, Turner turned his attention to the trans-Mississippi West. His lectures melded economic, diplomatic, and political history. He did not disregard social institutions and the role of ideas—idealism, in his words—but these were less emphasized. Addressing the twentieth century, he still used the basic concepts of frontier, section, and closing space to give broader meaning to his material. Gaus recorded descriptive statistics only occasionally, but Turner's slides probably provided such data. If Turner often emphasized colorful incidents or told anecdotes, Gaus did not record them. As teacher, Turner was basically a question asker or a proposer of hypotheses, although he introduced illustrative individuals and used telling aphorisms. "The logic of events does not assume a logic of purpose," noted Gaus on one occasion.

Critics have correctly argued that Turner's interpretation of the westward movement revealed blind spots and lack of sensitivity, particularly faulting his treatment of ethnicity, gender, and class. Although he did not ignore the indigenous population, Turner's use of the phrase "Indian barrier" in his lists of references is cited as revealing the one-sidedness of his approach. But on 29 March, noted Gaus, Turner included an evaluation of American Indian policy and introduced the concept of conquest—a term much used by a later generation of specialists in western history:

The spread of population [scribbled Gaus] is fundamental in explaining the Mexican War—rather than any conspiracy of slave holders and using diplomacy to get more territory. Previous spread had been into unoccupied areas—unorganized by civilized people, not expansion by conquest. But we had conquered the Indians. Was this just? Failure to use resources will submit people to subordination of a superior type which *does*. An inevitable process. But a better way could have been found for dealing with [the] Indians than was found.

Later Turner referred to the occupation of the Black Hills as a "betrayal" of the Sioux. So we find a mingling in Turner of Spencerian inevitability, acknowledgment of injustice, and regret at past policies, but hardly moral outrage.[51] Although well aware of it, he apparently did not dip deeply into anthropological and ethnographic literature. In discussing the American pioneer he recognized the importance of culture—"the cake of custom"—but he never used it as a perspective in dealing with the Native American, nor for that matter, in describing the interaction of the Hispanic population and white settlers.

Even though Turner had numerous women in his classes and seminar at Wisconsin and taught the female students of Radcliffe, Kit Carson's mother is the only woman to be mentioned in the frontier essay. Turner did not much improve his record during the spring of 1920. While describing the background of the Grange, Turner, however, pictured the farmer as "isolated and ignorant. Wife still worse off. Only an occasional religious meeting—no normal social functions," the children "lured" away by "city growth and urban improvements." He noted that women were full-fledged members of the Patrons of Husbandry and played important ceremonial roles in the order, but he ignored the female orators of the Populist movement. Although the *Reference List* of 1922 shows that Turner was somewhat interested in the family's role in the westward movement, the gender issues and matters of domestic economy that our generation has made an integral part of social history did not appear in his lectures, nor, to be fair, in those of contemporaries.[52]

And what of class and its influence? Turner sketched at length the great changes that occurred in the American economy during the late nineteenth and early twentieth centuries and the West's part in them—the spread of settlement, changes in transportation and marketing, the impact of western minerals, the denuded pineries, the growth of great corporations and combinations. Increased agricultural production and deflation put the West and its farmers at a disadvantage.

The latter constituted a "class in a *region*." The passage of the Granger laws, Gaus learned, meant that "individualistic competition and fear of govt [had] now [been] deserted by the farmer. *A turning point in the history of American development*. But a system of socialism was not sought."[53]

The recently settled West constituted a new section and joined the South in a free silver group, but the northeastern wing of the Republican party overwhelmed the midwestern presidents, and "bloody shirt" rhetoric was diverting as well. Building a great industrial empire in the West was a "new type of pioneering—a pioneering of capital and organization by men of imagination." James J. Hill was "a type of the new western man." "The capitalist, wrote Gaus, "was applying the principle of the squatter, but at the very time when such individualism [was becoming] a new thing because of disappearance of land." Where once the squatter farmer had ruled, now "combinations of industry and capital were predominant," and large stockmen dominated the range country by organizing associations. The basic principle, Turner explained, was that of the old farmer's protective associations and mining camp vigilance committees, but this was a "squatter sovereignty by business interests."[54]

The Populists, Turner told his class, represented a stage in the "advance of industrialism." William Jennings Bryan was thoroughly a "frontier type," whose family had followed the frontier. His denunciation of eastern America's "cross of gold" in 1896 was a "remarkable effort" destined to "stand in history as a landmark." In concluding lectures Turner emphasized the concentration of control over natural resources, the Progressive reaction that this produced, and the enhanced role of government visualized by Theodore Roosevelt and Gifford Pinchot. Where squatter individualism had once prevailed, now government paternalism worked to provide "new functions due to western needs." Although there were "some areas yet to be developed in the West . . . [it would] be under conditions unlike the Old West. It will," forecast Turner, "be through government or corporations— possibly through tenantry or peasantry. The Old West will remain a disembodied idea."[55]

In his last lecture Turner explained that the concentration of control in natural resources and other industries made political discontent "natural in our time." "Revolting political movements pass one into another—Bryanism, Insurgency—Progressivism." Gaus summarized Turner's conclusions as the lecture and semester ended:

> The frontier [was] important—settlement pressing forward into
> the wilderness—a new type developing different from Europe—
> opposite to every thing Prussian.
> The movement had ended by 1900. With it had gone on the
> formation of provinces or sections. Each show signs of persist-
> ence—The U. S. in terms of sections—Danger in intolerance. We
> must realize the composite quality of our life. Made up of pieces
> of Europe. Study the house raising of [the] West.[56]

And thus Turner sent his students forth in that spring of postwar
America, admonishing them to take heed of the cooperation and
democratic behavior that he believed the frontier cabin raising had
exemplified—principles that he had hoped to see established as well in
the world that Woodrow Wilson sought to shape.

At Harvard Turner continued much the same method of graduate
direction that he had developed in Wisconsin. The students in seminar
worked within a time period or on a topic that he specified. In Cambridge Turner focused these subjects on the period of the proposed
great book, 1830–50. Each member of the seminar served as the group's
authority on the subtopic they had chosen. They were responsible for
a report in which they presented their specialized research contribution and one in which they correlated their findings with the broader
history of the subject under study. Graduate students might also
register with Turner while developing individual research, and he was
generous in giving them conference time. In this relationship, thought
Curti, he was "immensely stimulating and informing . . . really at his
very best—better certainly than in . . . lectures, better even than in the
seminars." Such sessions were "priceless conferences," recorded a
student of this era, which led students to "'bubble over' with enthusiasm for him, for American history, and for scholarship in general."[57]
Both his Harvard and his Wisconsin graduate students remembered
that Turner created the impression that he and they were comrades
together in research rather than judge and judged.

Merk worked under Turner's direction as a graduate student during
the years 1916–18 and was thereafter his departmental colleague, collaborator in the area of western history, and successor. When Becker's
chapter on Turner in *American Masters of Social Science* appeared in

1927, Merk found the sketch of Turner as teacher during the 1890s a "vivid picture of my beloved teacher" and "enjoyed it so much" that he "read it over twice in succession." Twenty-plus years had intervened between Becker's experiences as Turner student and those of Merk, but the latter found Becker's portrait "precisely the picture I would have drawn if I had the pen of a Becker." The "outstanding impression" that Merk carried from Turner's classes, he explained, was of his "suggestiveness." He had discussed this reaction once with seminar colleagues and one of them affirmed that he found Turner's methods of instructing graduate students much superior to those of another Harvard professor with whom he had studied. Another companion, Colin B. Goodykoontz, lapsed into "cowboy sententiousness [quite] foreign to him. 'Turner is as full of ideas as a dog is of fleas.'" In Turner's course on the West there would, recalled Merk, be a "sentence or two [spoken] with particular impressiveness, with that 'lifted flash of the eye,'" described by Becker, and he, Merk, would copy it with special care and later explore its implications to his great "profit." "I used to glory in the thought," he told Turner, "that I was in a kind of secret communion with you, that you were giving out something that only a few were privileged to see; and this spurred me on."[58]

From the mid-teens of the century Turner's personal correspondence reveals a growing understanding that there were costs involved in the direction of graduate students as well as benefits. Now he wrote that dissertations were a somewhat "trying" literature. As a new instructor at Beloit College in the fall of 1921, Curti described for his teacher the many demands on his time. In American higher education, Turner explained, there was inadequate recognition of the value of "leisure in the production of scholars." He had come upon a "poor little spring" in the Maine woods that summer that was filling up. Passing by again several hours later, he noticed that a wild cat had drunk it dry. Young instructors were given too little time to refill their springs. Later the college teacher would teach fewer hours, but by that time "vitality is somewhat diminished," committees, administration, and "other wild cats" now demand attention. "Then there are the personal conferences which take more out of the spring than is sometimes realized, for the graduates are expert *drinkers* and they are not satisfied with anything less than *fresh* water." In recompense there was at "this stage . . . stimulation . . . renewal . . . and information" in such exchanges and college youths provided a constant "inspiration and . . .

challenge" to their instructors.[59] Turner's analysis of cost and benefit would have been less measured twenty years earlier.

Writing to Hockett while in retirement, Turner reiterated that American colleges and universities exposed their faculty unduly to "the exactions of the class room." But in his case this had "not been so much a check upon writing as have been the number of graduate students who have needed personal guidance in so many and so different fields that I have had to scatter my research."[60] This is a remarkable statement of self-justification, given the format of Turner's seminars, bearing as they did at Harvard on the years to be covered by "the book" And given also the bibliographical legwork that seminars involved for participants, which unquestionably benefited Turner as well as the young investigators.

After Turner had been at Harvard University for some time, a graduate student must do more than demonstrate academic competence in his courses and write a good general exam if he were to have Turner for a thesis adviser. In 1918, for example, he informed Ferguson that although Mr. —— had written a "surprisingly good general examination" and was "quiet, gentlemanly" and might "under some other direction . . . blossom into a real Ph.D.," he had dissuaded him from attempting a dissertation under his direction because of his seminar performance.[61] Yet it is true that he gave freely of himself to many graduate students and that his letters to them during his last half dozen years at Harvard are as rich and supportive as the communications of earlier years.

Turner also continued to surrender to incidental diversions. He played hooky for half a day with Colegrove to go swimming. When Dale, uninvited, penetrated the fastness of Hancock Point, Turner gladly gave him time and hospitality. Dale later told of the frequent visits that Turner paid to him and his wife during the Dales' final year at Harvard. Turner was not, however, of the type who in later faculty generations would make a habit of drinking with their graduate students in a convenient tavern on Friday afternoons. In late January 1923, when word of Turner's decision to take early retirement had begun to circulate at Harvard University, Curti sent him a letter of appreciation, telling him "you are the only one whom I have idealized and for whom I have been constantly forced to widen and enrich my ideal. Quite aside from the intellectual side, your kindness, your sympathy, strength and lovableness have given me something I cannot even try to measure. And it is because I know I am merely one of a great number that I write."[62] Apparently on the very same day, Turner gracefully responded. He was "thankful when any of my students see me as I ought to be rather than as I am." He had enjoyed his "compan[ion]ship in history" with Curti, and he believed in his student's future in the discipline, even though he "did not display the critical spirit important in that field when you estimate your instructor."[63] And so the Turner personality, his willingness to know young people as human beings as well as students, did reach beyond the bounds of professional obligation, but the basis of the relationships was the study of history.

14   Retirement

"No longer a teacher, but I hope, a writer"

Writing in 1921 to MacVeagh, Turner described two arrangements that might allow him to complete his book. He might, he said, take half-year leaves over a period of several years, or he might retire at an earlier age than was customary. As he tried the first alternative without great success, he more and more seriously considered the second. In November 1922 he told Dorothy that he hoped to have completed "plans for retirement," including the location of their retirement home, by the end of the academic year.[1] Turner thought much about these matters during the next few months, considering the cost of living under various arrangements in different places. At this point his regular annual salary at Harvard was eight thousand dollars, an amount increased somewhat by teaching at Radcliffe, small sums from publishers, and interest on a few small investments. He estimated that he would receive little more than half of his current income in retirement. The cost of living in Cambridge was much too high, he believed, to allow the Turners to continue to live there.

In mid-May of 1923 Turner told Dorothy that his retirement had been announced to take effect in September 1924. At that point he would become "Professor Emeritus." And "so" he wrote, "after another year, I am no longer a teacher, but I hope, a writer." At this point the retirement destination of the Turners was still undecided. Turner hated the thought of giving up the cottage at Hancock Point and toyed with the possibility of finding a "very moderate apartment," perhaps in Madison, and subletting the Moorings for part of the year "to pay travel." Retirement, Turner confided, would be "a good deal like starting life over as a pioneer on a new clearing. It will be hard on your mother, and I am afraid we can't give ourselves much lee-way! But at best it is only anticipating what would happen three or four years later, at not much more income when I would not be so likely to have a head for writing—which is a question even now! At any rate retirement doesn't mean a Morris chair to me—not even a tent and a fly which would be preferable."[2] By late September 1923 Turner was in Cambridge preparing "to begin the last lap of . . . university lecturing." As he came down from Hancock Point "the woods were aflame with autumn coloring . . . a sign," he wrote, "that another year has turned the corner. At least we have the memory of a happy summer."[3]

In late November Turner replied to a letter from Edgar E. Robinson. He had listened on the previous evening to a visiting professor from France give his impressions of life in the Harvard Yard: "Professors and students running to classes, incredible number of hours of class work, and yet publication beyond that of French professors!" Still, said the Frenchman, he would "not like to be an American professor." This position, wrote Turner, "fitted . . . my mood" as retirement neared. "If it gives me opportunity (and if my strength may be sufficient . . .) for writing I shall die happy; and if it doesn't I shall at least not die in the class room, an act for which I have always had a dislike—too spectacular, even if it isn't 'messy.'" His book, he added, "goes very slowly through the high seas of University activities." He wished for emancipation. "I am very glad and very proud to have had some thirty-eight years of teaching and contact with the men who are now doing things in history, and I am fond of my students; but the time has come when I must yield to the temptation to take my bowl and sit under the tree and I hope to have fountain pens and blank paper, as well as the necessary rice for my family." His diminished income would require some lecturing, however, for he was not "sufficiently near Karma to ignore family ties."[4]

The Turners did not decide upon a retirement residence until the school year 1923–24 was well advanced. John Main was a realtor and able to give advice about housing in Madison, and Dorothy provided estimates of other costs her parents might encounter there. The opportunity to be close to her and her growing family drew the Turners westward as well. Finally, resolution replaced consideration—the Turners would return to Wisconsin. As late as March 1924 they assumed that they could only afford a well-located apartment where they would live during the winter and the transitional periods of spring and late fall. They planned to continue summering at Hancock Point. Turner dreaded the constrictions of an apartment, so, with relief, they accepted Dorothy's timely suggestion that they build a small house beside the new home the Mains were planning in west Madison. Dorothy and John volunteered to assist in the details of purchasing the lot and to supervise the construction. The Turner cottage was to be modeled on that of Nantuckett fishermen, and ground was broken in spring 1924. Now, said Turner, he and Caroline, were to become "more or less nomadic—ornithological on eastern and western migration lines."[5]

Some later suggested that Turner's great accumulation of data and his understanding of the complexity of history prevented him from completing a book based on the Lowell Lectures during the early 1920s, thus forcing an early retirement. During his many years as seminar director and scholar, Turner had indeed gathered a vast store of information. To the end of the Harvard years, he continued to read a wide range of periodicals and American history generally. Electoral and roll call voting analysis in the precomputer age challenged the researcher to prolong research almost indefinitely. Complicating matters also was Turner's conviction that history was not just the study of politics or economic development but also embraced social and intellectual processes. Thus completion of "the book" might seem a staggering task, made all the more intimidating and difficult because Turner believed that it would be judged as his life's major work—a test of the worth of the research agenda that he so vigorously had advertised. How much easier, then, it must have been to allow distractions to creep in during his leaves of the early 1920s, to break from his study to chase down some tantalizing lead or minor detail, or to be diverted by recreational reading. But also, as an essayist who produced best while writing at white heat for short periods of time, Turner was trying to prepare a major manuscript during an extended period of steady effort—something that he had never before been able to do—except during the short period of time when, younger and more resilient, he produced a less elaborate study under Hart's editorial whip.

Turner's desire to finish "the book" was uppermost in his mind when he decided to retire. Had enjoyment of life been his primary concern, he could have drifted along easily at Harvard for several more years. Harvard Yard has not been devoid of denizens who "toil not, neither do they spin"—at least not much. Turner's relations in the Harvard department were no less satisfactory than in earlier years. His best friend, Haskins, was solidly established in the Harvard hierarchy. Turner had found other members of the faculty to be both friendly and cooperative. Channing, rumor had it, was an exception. Many in the history profession had heard that this prickly gentleman had waved a pamphlet before his assembled seminar and proclaimed that all of Turner's ideas lay within its pages, returning it to his desk drawer so quickly that none was able to add it to his or her reading list. Conversing with Edward E. Dale, Channing dismissed Turner as a "dear fellow, but he has no idea of the value of time. He has never written any big books." In 1924 Arthur M. Schlesinger hesitated to accept Harvard's offer of a permanent position because of "reports . . . his testy Yankee colleague Channing had made life so miserable for this son of a newer and rawer part of the United States that he had ever since regretted leaving Wisconsin."[6]

But when consulted, Turner denied the truth of this story. He was sometimes the target of "digs" from Channing. But reputedly Turner held his own in repartee. When Channing suggested that Turner would accomplish more if he used a stenographer, Turner retorted that he lacked the means since he had never written a textbook—implying that his colleague had stooped to produce a potboiler. Turner also liked to josh and even scored off Henry Adams in his presidential address to the AHA.

Turner and Channing had differences of opinion, although their full nature is unclear. The two colleagues read the American past differently, and there were differences in personal style. The New Englander's self-centered commitment to finishing his great history could also be viewed as lack of cooperation in maintaining the departmental program. Channing criticized one of the earlier doctoral dissertations that Turner supervised at Harvard. He was also critical of the activities of the National Board for Historical Service. When Channing provided a letter endorsing the efforts of the Harvard Commission on Western History to raise an endowment, Turner commented that his colleague had now progressed sufficiently far in his writing that the commission's efforts might be helpful to him. And when Turner arranged his sabbatical for the second half of academic year 1922–23, he told Caroline that he would "insist on not attending to the doctoral theses and examinations" during that period. After noting the financial disadvantages of the arrangement he continued, "Anyway I can let E. C. do the doctoral arranging that half," a suggestion, perhaps, that he had felt himself exploited in this respect by "E. C." in the past. As word of his announced retirement circulated through the Harvard community, Turner reported to Caroline that "Channing has just called to express his grief and explain his superior method of keeping young and fit—he really seems sorry at our leaving and sends his regards to you."[7] There is a wry twist in these lines but nothing to indicate more than rueful awareness of his colleague's eccentricities.

When Channing died in early 1931, C. L. Haskell, a former student of both men and a member of the editorial staff of the *Kansas City*

Star, unfavorably contrasted Channing's contributions with those of Turner. The latter told Dorothy that he did not wish publicly to endorse any such position. "We had many differences of opinion and points of view," he wrote, "but he was a friend in spite of all; and I think he was a much more important historian than the editor seems to indicate." Writing to Hooper, he expressed pleasure that Channing had so nearly reached his goal in writing the great history and described him as "a very interesting personality of a New England type."[8] They had, he explained to Merk, "quite unlike conceptions of the trend of American history" and Turner had been "radically critical of much of his position and his selection and emphasis of material" in the fourth volume of Channing's *History*. But he "appreciated the scholarship of the man and his New England point of view." He confided to Merk that he believed Channing was coming increasingly to acknowledge the West "as he grew older."[9] Neither this exchange nor the preceding evidence suggests a conflict of personality so unpleasant that it led Turner to leave the Harvard department prematurely.

With the spring of 1924 came formal recognition that Turner was leaving. In mid-April the students of his last seminar announced that they were organizing an "appropriate observance of this event, which may be said to mark the closing of an epoch in American historiography." They made known that they planned to present a portrait of Turner for the university to display in the History Seminar Room of Widener Memorial Library and that they also hoped to establish a "fund in his honor" to "promote the further investigation of American History along the trail blazed by him."[10]

On May 24 thirty-three faculty colleagues, students past and present, and other friends feted him at a formal dinner at the Harvard Club in Boston. Walls in the banquet room were hung with caricatures of the maps that Turner used in his course, including one that traced the western migration of the Plymouth Rock chicken, males colored in blue and females in red—"'all others' in green." Everything contributed, wrote Turner to Hooper, to "a jolly time—a real wake with the corpse participating." A former colleague gave him a particularly notable memento of retirement, a large cartoon in colored chalks. From the caption "WESTWARD THE COURSE OF EMPIRE," a red line of arrows terminates on the hip of a hobby horse bearing the brand, "HIST.17." Astride the horse, a buckskinned Turner shades eyes that seek the western horizon. Beyond the horseman, a wagon train of prairie schooners toils west carrying lantern slides and innumerable

In 1924, late in his career at Harvard University, Turner stands outside his residence on Phillips Place, Cambridge. Reprinted with permission of the State Historical Society of Wisconsin, Madison, Wisconsin. (X3)19251.

maps across plains, dotted with preemption stakes, toward the mountains and passes leading to San Francisco and other destinations of the far West. Buffalos, coyotes, rattlesnakes, and mountain goats view the procession in wonderment. A compass symbol pointed west rather than north and Turner's left ear was labeled "THE FRONT EAR IN AMERICAN HISTORIOGRAPHY."[11]

Farrand and Haskins flanked Turner at the banquet table of the Harvard Club. Since Turner had demurred at the student's wish to commission an oil portrait of him, Alexander James, the artist son of William James, was enlisted to prepare a crayon portrait that the students presented to the history department. Merk read testimonial letters from former students unable to attend. In Madison during the summer of 1910, Fola La Follette and Zona Gale had attended Turner's last lecture. Seated opposite Harvard economics professor and former Wisconsin student Jesse Bullock at the dinner in the Harvard Club was Robert R. La Follette, a member of the final seminar. So was the spirit of Wisconsin Progressivism invoked in this farewell also.

Archibald C. Coolidge had been department chairman on Turner's arrival and, as university librarian, his ally in building research holdings in western history at Harvard. Forced to miss the testimonial dinner, Coolidge wrote a graciously touching letter to Turner. President Lowell entertained the Turners at dinner, as did others of the Harvard community. During these last hectic weeks Turner gave a farewell talk to the graduate History Club where he offered a "flippant account" of the youthful experiences that kindled his interest in western history and his experiences in graduate school.

The festivities over, in the first days of June Turner boarded the train for Madison, unfortunately carrying the wrong key for his valise. Reunited with Dorothy and her family, he viewed the building site on Van Hise Street and signed a contract with a builder for the erection of the retirement cottage. A few days more and he was on his way to teach in the summer session at Utah State Agricultural College.

Caroline did not accompany Turner to Logan in the summer of 1924, and the solitary trip west must have given him opportunity to reflect on the years that had taken him from Portage to the Harvard Yard and thence into retirement. He had accomplished much, but if Turner did review his career in memory during that trip to the West in mid-1924, he perhaps thought most of his contributions in graduate teaching. Shortly after retiring, Turner urged Becker, "Please . . . do not drop me down to posterity as a teacher (by intention at least!). . . . I was interested in history and the companionship of men like yourself."[12]

Undue speculation on this text is unwarranted—he was also willing to make women his comrades in historical exploration. One can, however, speculate that in his words of advice to young scholars he did find an outlet for the fathering instinct that was blighted by the death of his son. And sometimes in interaction with students or former students he ventured beyond the professional to the personal dimension. When Edgar Robinson wrote in 1923 to assure Turner that he had opened a new world to him, the latter replied that such assurance was the teacher's "compensation"—that "he is custodian of the keyes [sic], and truth to say, he gets credit for much that is merely the accident of his being *concierge* for the moment. Yet I value most deeply the expression of your regard for my over-estimated part in the education of E. E. R., and I like you a lot."[13] The alliance of Turner and his students produced a great body of American history and a living legacy of workers in the profession subsequent to his retirement. Although Turner apparently directed more doctoral candidates at Wisconsin than at Harvard, the members of the Cambridge group were impressive. In numbers, westerners and southerners dominated—a fact that

Turner's colleagues welcomed for its leavening effect in the Harvard University graduate program in history.

When instructors of graduate students move from one institution to another, a few of their advisees may move with them, but it takes some years to build up another covey of fledglings. Raynor G. Wellington studied with Turner at both Wisconsin and Harvard, publishing the research that he had begun under Turner's direction but never fulfilling the formal requirements of the doctoral degree. Turner's Wisconsin student Solon J. Buck finished his graduate work under Turner's direction at Harvard in 1911. Thereafter only George M. Stephenson (1914) and Kenneth W. Colegrove (1915) completed dissertations under Turner's direction until in 1920 Frederick Merk defended his economic history of Wisconsin during the Civil War era. During the next several years, however, there was a great harvest of doctoral research in Turner's areas of specialization at Harvard.

Turner's interest in sectional and state politics was reflected among his Harvard Ph.D.'s in Buck's work on the Grangers, Stephenson's study of the politics of the public lands, Colegrove's thesis on the state instruction process, Merk's monograph on Civil War Wisconsin, Thomas P. Abernethy's study of early Alabama, Arthur B. Darling's examination of Jacksonian Democracy in Massachusetts, and William G. Bean's investigation of antebellum party transformation in Massachusetts. Others prepared monographs in social and economic history, including Colin B. Goodykoontz's study of home missions, Edward E. Dale's investigation of the range cattle industry in Oklahoma, James B. Hedges's examination of Henry Villard's impact on the transportation system of the Pacific Northwest, and Marcus L. Hansen's survey of immigration to the United States from central Europe. Turner's earlier interest in relationships with Hispanic America bore fruit in Frederick B. Arragon's dissertation on the Panama Congress of 1826 and Arthur P. Whitaker's study of the Old Southwest during the 1780s. At Radcliffe College, Turner's advisee Hannah G. Roach prepared her dissertation on the manifestations of sectionalism in the Congress from 1865 to 1890, and Grace Lee Nute investigated the history of American foreign commerce between 1825 and 1850. Many among this group of young scholars were destined for distinguished careers. Paxson sometimes scoffed that Turner had produced few outstanding Ph.D.'s, but when his Harvard graduates of the 1920s had made their mark, that judgment was surely proved false.

Counting doctorates completed does not do full justice to Turner's impact in graduate teaching. Some of his Madison and Cambridge students finished their studies after his departure. Hockett illustrated this pattern at Wisconsin, as did Curti, who completed his work under the direction of Schlesinger at Harvard. Buffinton, whom Turner was urging to finish his dissertation long before American entry into World War I, finally succeeded in the fall of 1924. Turner approved his draft but apparently did not attend the defense. "You will do yourself more justice I suspect if you prepare and go through that performance without friendly visitors on the side line," wrote Turner. But he advised him on preparation. He should widen his "general knowledge of the period you submit. . . . with the aid of recent general & special books on the field." He should be prepared for questions about the works of relevant statesmen, be ready to compare the positions of modern authorities—Van Tyne and McIlwaine, for example. He should "know something about the 'monographists' and 'standard' historians of the period, and . . . biographers even if you haven't read them all." And "above all come to the examination rested and courageous . . . rather than worn out by cramming and worry."[14]

Sketching his contributions to western history for Constance Lindsay Skinner in 1922, Turner wrote that "now something like half the states have such a college course, and many of the leading universities, east and west, include it in their curriculum. A considerable portion of the instructors were trained in my seminary."[15] Turner's influence in encouraging the study of the American West was indeed potent. Financial considerations drew some students with Wisconsin or Harvard credits elsewhere for the doctorate, but they remained committed to western history. Some became influential professionals without completing the doctorate. Many in addition succumbed to his influence merely by sitting in on his lecture course or listening to his public lectures. Other scholars—Farrand for example—accepted his major ideas, and they found their way rapidly into textbooks in American history and government.[15]

So, as Turner journeyed westward in spring 1924, he could look back upon an academic career that had its full share of achievements and rewarding relationships. Although not boastful, he had a strong sense of his own worth, and notes scattered through his papers suggest that he expected a biographer to record his contributions at some future time. He was never a diarist, except of the pocket appointment book variety, nor did he speak of writing an autobiography. Yet investigators have noted his propensity for affixing his name to folders and other papers, indicating perhaps a strong sense of self-worth. Photographs of Turner survive in considerable number, reinforcing this impression. He was not, however, a man who dwelt excessively in his thinking upon the past. His major concern in the spring and summer of his retirement year was fixed forward upon the life he hoped to have as independent scholar and writer.

Seeking to enrich the program of the Utah Agricultural College by developing a "National Summer School" there, President Elmer G. Peterson asked Turner to present a course of lectures during the 1924 summer session. The financial costs of retirement were much on his mind, and here too was an opportunity to explore another part of the Mountain West. Turner accepted Peterson's invitation after bargaining an improvement in salary and working out an agreement that required him to teach the first three weeks of the session only, with Merk instructing in the second three. Receptive as ever to new experiences, Turner greatly enjoyed his weeks in Logan and wrote enthusiastically to Caroline about his impressions. He was driven to the university from Salt Lake City "over concrete roads that put Massachusetts state roads to shame[,] past little Mormon villages, like New England towns with tabernacles in the center . . . into valleys flanked by smiling green fields, running into browns and grays and blues and silvery snow filled gulches, golden rocks, and misty curtains of haze which made it all dream-like and exquisite."[16]

Soon after arriving in Logan, Turner walked in the "wonderful mountain walled valley last night and marvelled. The song of running irrigation rivulets, the smell of the lush green meadows, the miles of concrete walks, bridges, aqueducts, everything trim and garnished. It was a contrast to Cambridge & to Madison." Turner hit it off with his Mormon hosts and they with him. He attended a quarterly meeting of the church, where "the singing and organ beat anything I ever heard from a church in the east. The faces were really fine old spiritual faces in most of the congregation."[17]

Turner joined an excursion up Logan Canyon where he viewed a giant, gnarled juniper that his fellow member of the summer staff, Professor Henry C. Cowles, of Chicago, estimated to be perhaps five

Turner and distinguished ecologist Henry C. Cowles share the shelter of an ancient juniper tree near Logan, Utah, in 1924. Reprinted with permission of the State Historical Society of Wisconsin, Madison, Wisconsin. (X3)1362.

thousand years of age. He spoke briefly to the local Kiwanis and "warbled with the best of them" in their lunchtime sing, sending Caroline the words to "No Place Like Dear Old Cache to Me," which began

This Valley fair that we call Cache,
So beautiful to see,
Made rich by nature's living fount,
Is very dear to me.[18]

He was taken to visit a water fowl nesting grounds and to Bear Lake. Meanwhile, he tried his luck with the trout in Logan Canyon and found the water so fast that he had difficulty in retaining those that he hooked. The only sour note in these weeks sounded when he visited a former student in the Salt Lake City region, and his wallet was stolen. Summing up, he told Caroline, "I have made more of an impression than my lectures deserved and everybody is very kind. I am a Mormon in everything but *revelation*. Polygamy is over so don't be alarmed—But honestly it is a most lovable, sincere, sound, clean population and I love them."[19]

During the course of Turner's stay President Peterson invited him to return to the program during the following summer. He deferred a decision until he could talk it over with Caroline and learn the impact that the income would have upon his retirement benefits. Leaving Utah in early July, Turner spent the Fourth in Madison, where he found their "house . . . roofed, nearly all shingled . . . quite cunning," roomier than he had expected, and ready for their household goods in September.[20] Here too he found an accumulation of bills—construction was again proving to be more expensive than predicted. From Madison Turner journeyed to Boston and thence to join Caroline at Hancock Point.

As always, Turner had written to Caroline frequently while en route, and a letter from the Berkshires included suggestions for the name of the cottage at 2214 Van Hise Street, Madison. Listing nautical names beginning with the Anchorage and ending with the Strand, he explained that *Fisherman's Luck* should probably be discarded, meaning as it did, a "wet seat, and a hungry gut." Perhaps, he suggested, names more in keeping with Wisconsin would be appropriate—the Scrub Oak, or the Squatter's Claim, and, among others, the Chimney Corner that, in the end, was the Turners' choice. During the second week of September Turner shipped household goods and books from Boston to Madison. Other books went to Hancock Point. During these months also he made the final financial maneuvers that allowed him to pay off the Madison building contractor. These arrangements involved cashing in his life insurance with the exception of five thousand dollars.

Although the Turners considered selling the Moorings, they retained this well-loved seaside retreat. Nor did Turner say final good-bye to Harvard in September 1924. He had been invited to give a series of lectures on American sectionalism at the Dowse Institute in early November. He arrived from Maine to deliver them, after a flurry of last-minute lecture preparation, complicated by an unseasonable spell of cold weather. A struggle with frozen pipes had encouraged an attack of laryngitis, so his lectures became an exercise in survival. Between lectures, coughing disrupted his sleep. Friends and former students entertained him, but the socializing made his recuperation more difficult. Intervals were spent in packing the last books and other items from his Harvard study. Scheduled to give his final lecture on the evening of November 15, he was that morning completely without voice. A friendly waitress dosed him with egg white and lemon, and, in one of his favorite expressions, he "pulled through," despite "exhibitions" of barking. Now exhausted, Turner was free to travel west. He had told Curti, "At my time of life a man cannot afford to take such care of himself that he prolongs a vegetable existence instead of finishing his task. . . . Wish me *results* rather than length of life!"[21]

As in his last days at Wisconsin, Turner hoped at the time of his retirement that changed circumstances would allow him to complete major writing commitments. His optimism on that score was, however, tempered in doubts expressed to Curti and Robinson and in admission that he would have to accept some lecturing engagements or do some writing for publications that paid their authors. Invitations to lecture or to undertake teaching assignments began to arrive well before Turner surrendered his study at Harvard. Now superintendent of the State Historical Society of Wisconsin, Schafer invited him to address that organization's meeting in the coming October. Turner demurred—the Turners would not yet have arrived in Madison, and he must also deliver the Dowse Lectures that fall. Besides, he wrote, he liked to offer " a bright idea" to the society members, and he doubted that he had one.[22] But when Schafer offered to change the society's meeting to January 1925, Turner yielded. He also agreed to give a series of lectures that spring of 1925 at the University of Wisconsin and consented, as well, to a lecture swing in Illinois, where he would speak at Knox College, Milliken University, and the University of Illinois.

With the happy memories of his first sojourn in Logan in mind, as well as his reduced income, Turner consented to return there in the summer of 1925. When neither Merk nor Robinson could share the assignment, Turner bargained a handsome salary to teach a full six-week course. These assignments were easily rationalized because they all would deal with sectionalism and therefore contribute to the development of "the book."

There was much about the Chimney Corner at 2214 Van Hise Street to delight the Turners as they settled into retirement. Grandchildren lived next door to excite their affection and interest, although their grandfather admitted that noise sometimes rose beyond tolerance. Old Madison friendships were renewed, and the fisherman's cottage — described also by Turner as a bungalow and more facetiously as a shanty — was, he attested to Merk, "very cosy and compact . . . It is like living in a ship's cabin."[23] If more room was required in the future, dormer windows might be expanded outward to create two more rooms, but the little house soon proved that it could accept as many as ten dinner guests without undue strain. Turner is said to have used a hand sprayer to apply salt water to the cottage to give its shingled exterior an authentic Nantucket sheen.

Madison, Turner told Merk, had "*outgrown* its old beauty." Situated as they were "in the suburb," he confided, "it hardly seems as if we were in the Madison I knew, at all." But their location was "quiet and rural and 'folksy,'" and it was pleasant to be close to Dorothy and her family.[24] Houses were still rising in the neighborhood, and they feared that a new high school might be located very close to them. In that same year of 1924 a new assistant director of the Forest Products Laboratory purchased the house at 2222 Van Hise. Thus, Aldo Leopold, the advocate-to-be of a new environmental ethics and champion of the preservation of wilderness areas, and Turner, the history profession's greatest environmental theorist, would live for parts of several years within a hundred yards of each other in west Madison.

The Turners fed the birds and were rewarded with a grateful assembly, this effort fostered in part because sister Breese had purchased the lot behind them, and it was still in a state of nature. But winter 1924–25 recalled the aspects of the Madison environment that Turner had most disliked. Years earlier his doctor had informed him that only a change of climate would end the catarrhal colds that he suffered in the Madison winter. Relocation in Madison began inauspiciously in November 1924 when his doctor sent him to bed with a recurrence of the bronchial cold that had plagued his Dowse lectures. Hardly had he regained his feet when he was struck down with intestinal flu. On Paxson's motion, the Board of Curators of the Historical Society had created the position of Fellow of the Society, named Turner its first occupant, and instructed Schafer to put an office and other assistance at his disposal. Not until mid-December and still recuperating did Turner settle fully into his study on the third floor of the society. Apparently also through Paxson's agency, he was invited to join the X Club, one of the informal faculty dining groups so common in that era.

Early March 1925 found Turner suffering a recurrence of the "grippe." He recovered sufficiently to embark on his lecturing trip to Illinois. This was a wearing experience, but one made enjoyable by the renewal of old friendships. At Knox College, John L. Conger, Turner's Wisconsin Ph.D. of 1907, had returned after wartime service. In Champaign there was Laurence M. Larson, for whom he had written many supportive placement letters during the early century. There too was Avery Craven, who had been in his seminar at Harvard before completing the doctorate at Chicago. Turner concluded that he had been too formal in his lectures at Knox College but was more pleased with his performance thereafter. In Decatur he found a mixed audience of school teachers, students, and departmental faculty, "a little like my Mormons in intellectual appetite."[25] At the University of Illinois Turner survived a grueling schedule. There were lectures before "very mixed" audiences, from "able professors in many fields down to flappers!" They had increased in numbers, lecture by lecture, he noted. In addition, he talked to groups of graduate students and the Harvard alumni, lunched with the department, survived other social activity, and was driven across prairies that he found "flat & monotonous," a landscape that he did not believe himself capable of standing "for more than a week!"[26]

Returned to Madison, Turner unpacked the lantern slides that he used to illustrate his presentations on sectionalism and delivered his lecture series at the university. Here his message seems to have been less appreciated than in times past, his audience dwindling lecture by lecture. Shortly thereafter, both he and Caroline checked into the hospital to have their tonsils removed—their response to the Madison winters. Caroline's surgery went well, but Fred was less fortunate. Seeping sutures twice forced a return to the operating room and the unpleasant experience of being restitched without benefit of anesthetic. Not until mid-May could Turner return to the Chimney Corner, to recoup strength, and to prepare for his stint at Utah State College. The lecturing commitments, he explained to Hooper, had been made to defray living costs before he received word in late winter of 1925 that Harvard had awarded him a grant of twenty-five hundred dollars from its Milton Fund designed to further faculty research. The terms of this grant specified that it was made in order to allow Turner to finish a history of the United States from 1830 to 1850.

In late spring of 1925 Caroline accompanied Turner to Utah, where they enjoyed two weeks in the Zion and Bryce Canyon National Parks before spending an enjoyable six weeks in Logan. Caroline, Turner reported to Dorothy, won the affection of all Logan—dogs, small children, and adults. Turner fished, with less success than he had hoped—he "guess[ed] its time to take up golf & ornithology"—picnicked with Caroline and friends up Logan Canyon and ventured on a fishing expedition into southern Utah with a Logan colleague. "I wish you could see the beauty of the valley," he told his daughter, "the Mts—the evening lights & shades & sunset colors. . . . We are in love with Utah—but not with Utah to the exclusion of Madison, Wisconsin USA—or Hancock Point."[27] By mid-summer they had exchanged the beauties of the mountain west for those of coastal Maine.

Enjoyable though the sojourn in Utah was, the teaching combined with the altitude of northeastern Utah had taxed Turner's heart. Once more the doctor advised a regime of cautious moderation. But Turner reported to Hooper in late December 1925 that "the book goes along, slowly but surely."[28] By this time, however, the Turners were fighting colds, and he was girding to deliver a paper on "Geographic Sectionalism in American History" to the annual meeting of the Association of American Geographers, convening that year in Madison. In the meantime he had found the *Yale Review* willing to accept his article "The Children of the Pioneers" and committed himself to an article entitled "The West—1876 and 1926: Its Progress in a Half-Century" to be delivered to *World's Work* during the coming year. He had also agreed to speak on Lincoln and sectionalism before the Illinois Historical Association in mid-winter, but before he could fulfill that obligation the Turners had decided they must flee the northern climate. They spent much of the late winter in Louisiana and Texas.

Turner had departed from Harvard, but his former students continued to seek his advice and his support. These Turner continued to give, a more congenial use of his time, perhaps, than buckling to the sifting and winnowing of notes involved in writing chapters of "the book." There was Curti to be consoled because Professor Schlesinger believed his dissertation topic, "Young America," was not shaping into a satisfactory dissertation and had urged him to develop a study of the peace movement instead. Later Curti could be praised for a fine showing on the exam over his special field and on acceptance of the new dissertation. Goodykoontz was safely placed at the University of Colorado, but his plans for study overseas required discussion. Turner urged him to publish his study of the home missionary movement soon. Thomas P. Abernethy and Arthur P. Whitaker—"my southerners" as Turner referred to them—were not yet satisfactorily established in the profession. Turner supported them in their quests for better positions, discussed their research, and thanked them for the assistance that they gave him in his own work. He was particularly enthusiastic about Marcus L. Hansen's developing study of nineteenth-century immigration to the United States and aided his successful search for teaching positions and research grants.

Less well advanced in his graduate work than the others, Fulmer Mood sought Turner's advice on the potential of a dissertation dealing with frontier promotional literature. Disavowing any desire to usurp the rights of Mood's instructors at Harvard, Turner suggested a number of ways in which the subject might be fruitfully developed. Mood should not, however, throw too wide a loop nor devote an excessive period of time to preparing a dissertation. He should remember also, warned Turner, that "the literary aspect of American history" was not yet "fully recognized as a field for new work." He would meet "conservative inertia" in presenting a study "on the history of ideas as expressed in literature."[29] Given this and the other exchanges, Turner had some justification in referring to himself as a reference bureau in a letter to Merk.

Although he was no longer active in the affairs of the AHA or the foundations concerned with historical research, Turner's advice was still sought on historical activities. During the mid-1920s Buck kept him informed of the efforts of the AHA to raise an endowment in support of its programs. Merk assumed the place that some years earlier would have been Turner's in efforts to develop a large comparative study of pioneer belts under the sponsorship of the Social Science Research Council. Turner successfully evaded an invitation to attend a summer meeting of the planning committee. But the project gave Merk much to correspond with Turner about. Curti and Becker were frequent correspondents in these years, particularly when they were preparing their respective chapters on Turner and his work for *Masters of the Social Sciences* and *Methods in Social Science.* Former students of the Wisconsin years, Duncalf, Hockett, and Meany, kept in touch. Turner sent copies of his article from the *World's Work* to former students and friends, and they responded with warm praise.

In spring 1925 Turner addressed the members of the State Historical Society of Wisconsin on the subject of sectionalism in general, and early in January 1926 he discussed geographic sectionalism at the annual meeting of the Association of American Geographers. The

papers soon appeared in the periodicals of those societies and were
Turner's last broad statements on the subject of sectionalism prior to
his final word in the first chapter of *The United States: 1830–1850:
The Nation and Its Sections*, published after his death. Increasing
pressure of population upon resources, Turner believed, was now
enhancing awareness of sectional differences.

Turner told the geographers that the study of regional geography
would in the future attract in the United states—"at least the same
degree of attention . . . as in Europe." Again he argued that the American
section was analogous to the European nation and that sectional interaction resembled the international relations among the European
countries, "but these phenomena have been concealed by the disproportionate attention to federal legislation, to state legislation, and to
political parties, without digging beneath the surface." Although he
referred to the "interesting geography of party preponderance," he did
not focus his paper primarily upon it, as in his presentation before the
geographers in 1914. He had closed then with a plea for collaboration
between geographer and historian, and in 1926 he expanded the plea,
proposing that geographers, statisticians, politicians, economists,
bankers, railroad experts, "business men in general; the historians; the
students of literature and of society" should cooperate "to make a more
adequate survey of what are actually the natural regions in human
geography, as shown by human action."[30]

Turner's papers on the subject of sectionalism during the 1920s were
not mere repetitions of those of earlier years. In the interim he had
further developed the parallel between the continental sectionalism of
North America and the international relations within Europe. He had
continued to amass supportive evidence derived from government
documents, newspapers, contemporary journals, pronouncements by
American statesmen, politicians, and observers, as well as from
scholarly authorities like Josiah Royce. Now, in documenting the
"persistence of the sectionalism of the West . . . against the East,"
Turner added the "Farmers' *Bloc*, and the La Follete movement" to the
"antimonopolists, the Grangers, the Populists, the Insurgents, the
Progressives."[31] By 1926 he had incorporated the Colorado River
Compact and the debates over the feasibility of the St. Lawrence River
seaway into his presentations. During the 1920s both he and some of
his students and former students continued to map and to analyze
electoral returns and the patterns revealed in congressional voting.
Although Libby had demonstrated the utility of map analysis in

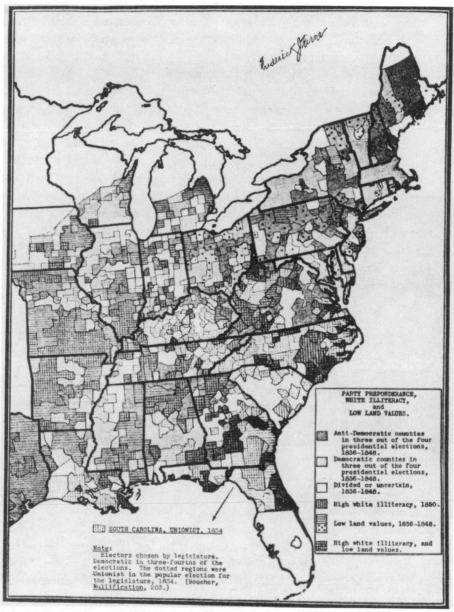

This map, prepared by Turner, shows his cartographic analysis at its most ingenious but also reveals the complexity involved when several variables are depicted on the same map. Reprinted with permission of the estate of Dorothy Parker Main.

Turner's seminar of the early 1890s, Turner had carried it well beyond the intitial stage. His maps showing regional party predominance and his technique of combining two or more variables on the same map were ingenious applications of the mapmaker's art.

There is in the years after 1914 a broadening of Turner's conception of the various ways in which sectionalism might manifest itself—in art, literature, and architecture. And significantly also, Turner had refined in his mind during these years the relationship between sectionalism and the national political parties. The latter mitigated and harnessed sectionalism by facilitating the agreements and compromises involved in major federal legislation. But "party voting has more often broken down than maintained itself, on fundamental issues," he argued.[32] Although prepared to acknowledge the importance of class relations as an influence in politics by the time of his presidential address, Turner never consistently accorded it a significance equal to that of sectionalism.

In mid-1926 Turner published "The Children of the Pioneers" in the *Yale Review* and the "The West—1876 and 1926: Its Progress in a Half-Century" in *World's Work*. In comparing the trans-Mississippi West of 1876 with that of fifty years later for the readers of the latter periodical, Turner sketched the growth of political organization in the region, the changes in its population and the attendant migration, the transformation in the extractive industries built upon western natural resources, and the growth of western transportation facilities and manufacturing. Once a field "of colonization and . . . eastern investment and industrial development," the West was now "assuming aspects and developing ambitions like the East."[33] Turner sketched the important role of the West in the political development of the nation in these years and concluded his survey with mention of its impressive cultural progress. In conclusion he admitted that some western characteristics had moderated through time but maintained that the "West's old initiative, its love of innovation, its old idealism and optimism, its old love of bigness, even its old boastfulness, are still here." Indeed, he forecast, "It may yet make new contributions to America, by its union of democratic faith and innovation with a conservative subconsciousness."[34]

Turner had presented sketches of American economic and social development on previous occasions, but he introduced a good many new facts in his article in *World's Work*. His theory of American development and the changing political scene were familiar, however. His contribution to the *Yale Review* was somewhat fresher. Turner had long been intrigued by Cotton Mather's declaration that the residents of the new settlements had "got unto the *Wrong side of the Hedge*" and the contention of later New Englanders that western migrants ran the danger of slipping into a condition of barbarism.[35] In his leisure time he had gathered evidence from biographical sources, newspapers, and the periodical press that enabled him, he believed, to evaluate the charge that the West was a region impoverished in matters intellectual and forced to depend on "families who remained in the East" for leadership in "scholarship . . . creative business . . . enlightened politics . . . [and] finer social organization."[36]

Examining the North Central states primarily, Turner presented long lists of eminent Americans who had been born or reared in the West and who had achieved eminence in their fields of business, education, or the arts, including himself among the historians. Admitting that such a compilation might "appear as tiresome as a catalogue of ships in Homer," Turner maintained that it was "the only way" to "effectively set forth the part played in recent American civilization by distinguished children of the Middle Western pioneers" and "would seem to prove" that they were not "intellectually stunted by . . . transplantation of the parents into the wilderness." In the behavior and achievement of such men—and women (listed in one paragraph)— Turner saw the western traits of personality that he had so often praised, especially an "interest in the common man." In conclusion, however, he warned the grandchildren of the pioneers that they must not seek to "standardize" all to the measure of that common man, nor regard universities as "social mirrors" rather than "levers," and must not exile . . . the dissenter from majority opinion." In doing so they would "be false to the spirit of the pioneer."[37]

Turner's papers and articles of 1925 and 1926 proved that there was life after Harvard. He published more in his early retirement than he had for many years past. The four essays of these years ultimately formed a substantial part of his collected essays, *The Significance of Sections in American History*, but they contributed little to progress on "the book." Turner rationalized the diversion as necessary to supplement his diminished income. At least and at last he was the writer he had visualized when deciding to retire. Remembering his brave talk of not so many months before, however, his friends deplored this activity—once more Turner was himself delaying the magnum opus.

By early March 1926 the Turners had returned from the South and were enjoying the fire in their grate, as well as old friends. Turner was at work on his article for *World's Work*. He had hired a stenographer, he reported, "a widow of maturity and of a perfectly safe angularity."[38] He and Caroline left for the Maine coast in mid-May, and Turner hoped to see Hooper and other friends enroute. Unfortunately, he suffered a disturbance of the inner ear during the trip east. His sense of balance much impaired, he entered the Stillman Infirmary immediately on arrival in Cambridge. He had been suffering hearing loss for some time; although hypertension was assumed to be responsible for attacks of dizziness, his symptoms appear also to be consistent with those associated with Ménière's Syndrome. While Turner was in the hospital, Hooper deluged him with flowers and culinary delectables, and at the end of May he reported that he was "slowly getting control of my steering gear and the ear is not so musical as it was."[39]

During the second week of July Turner wrote from the Moorings at Hancock Point that he was still wobbly but hoped soon to be able to get down to work. His symptoms, however, lingered, and he found it difficult to move his research and writing forward during the second half of 1926. The thermometer hovered at minus fifteen degrees in Madison during mid-December of that year, promising another testing winter. His doctor advised flight to a milder climate, so Turner tentatively planned a southern expedition that would allow him to visit areas of the South that he had never seen and that he must describe in a chapter of "the book." The Turners, however, changed their plans, departing in January for New Orleans, whence they proceeded after a couple of weeks into the Southwest. There, Turner told Buck, he hoped it would be hot enough that "I can heat up my ear and get into shape by the warming-pan route, for writing—which has not been practicable for the past months."[40]

15   San Marino

*"The more I sample the Library, the more I am astonished
and delighted at its riches in many fields"*

On their trip to the Southwest in the winter of 1927 the Turners
traveled from New Orleans to San Antonio and from there across New
Mexico into Arizona to Tucson. While in Arizona they visited the
Roosevelt Dam, enjoying the "hair-raising hairpin curves" of the
Apache Trail. Turner's boyhood friend, Jim Cole, had participated as a
young army officer in the pursuit of Geronimo over this same route.
Their driver, Turner reported to Dorothy, was an ex-cowboy and
mountain man who had ridden the southwestern ranges, "made and
lost a fortune in cattle," and was of "the real sort." For Hooper, Turner
pictured the contrast between cacti, "snow-dusted" mountain "crests,"
"Apache 'hogans,' Mexican 'dobes,' and Mormon houses," with "belching"
copper smelters. As always, Turner enjoyed the local "types," read the
local newspapers closely, and tried to understand the regional "mood."
He and Caroline seemed, he told Hooper, to be "ships of the desert — a
nomadic couple — with no definite oasis for a stop. This air and eleva-
tion agrees with me perfectly," he continued, "but I dislike to send my
Ms. into the ranch regions in the desert, which I should have to do if
I tried to work here."[1]

Caroline had numerous relatives in the Los Angeles area, and this
was the Turners' next stop after leaving Tucson. By late February they
were occupying a little bungalow in Claremont, enjoying a profusion
of blooming flowers and bird life, palms, and other vegetation. They
visited with Archer B. Hulbert and his wife, whom they "ran across,"
as well as other old friends, and absorbed the sights and visual
contrasts of this interesting land. Turner had brought a "trunk of notes"
with him, but other attractions prevailed. "The temptation of the open
road is strong," he wrote, jokingly. "I am convinced that I do not belong
to civilization, but to desert and mountain, the uninhabited sea shores,
and life among the wild creatures — barring rattle snakes and Gila
monsters."[2]

During the next few weeks Turner's future prospects improved
marvelously. Some years earlier Henry E. Huntington had decided to
place his magnificent library, art collection, and botanical garden in

San Marino at the service of the public. He selected an impressive board of trustees, and in the mid-1920s they invited Farrand, then directing the programs of the Commonwealth Fund, to evaluate the Huntington resources and to suggest plans for effectively mobilizing them. In his report Farrand suggested that they be used as the foundation of a research center devoted to the study of the development of Anglo-American civilization. His recommendation so impressed the Huntington trustees that they invited him to become the first director of research at the Huntington Library and Museum.

As a collector in the fields of history and literature, Huntington had been primarily interested in rare books and manuscripts, but he had not hesitated to buy complete libraries in accumulating such treasures. The result was a collection rich in rarities and emphasizing early modern English and colonial American history and literature as well as materials relating to the American West. Huntington's holdings, however, lacked the more common books, periodicals, and reference tools the research scholar also needed. In early 1927, while Farrand was in the East concluding his service with the Commonwealth Fund, he learned that the Turners expected to be in Pasadena during the late winter and early spring visiting Carl C. Thomas, a former Wisconsin colleague, and his wife as well as other friends and relatives. Thomas was now a faculty member at the California Institute of Technology. In late February Farrand wrote to George E. Hale, a distinguished scientist at Cal Tech and member of the Huntington Board of Trustees, enthusiastically recommending that Turner should be invited, while in Pasadena, to conduct a preliminary survey of the Huntington Library collections and review the plans for their development.

Turner's advice, Farrand suggested, would be highly beneficial. He was not sufficiently robust to justify offering him a position on the permanent staff, but if he could be persuaded to accept a later appointment as a research associate, his continuing counsel would be invaluable, and his scholarly reputation would highlight the Huntington Library's attraction for distinguished scholars. Farrand sent a personal note of invitation to Turner that he asked Hale to forward to him if he found it satisfactory. Turner was delighted by Farrand's proposal and Hale's invitation to spend time in the Huntington Library evaluating its resources. The Turners delayed their return to Madison for a month while Turner investigated the collections.

Turner was not long in southern California before members of the faculty of Pomona Colleague and the California Institute of Technology suggested the possibility of developing an institutional tie with him. Invigorated by the southern California environment, he was tempted by the prospect of spending substantial periods in the Los Angeles area. As the initial arrangement with the Huntington Library was perfected, it included the possibility of continuing the assignment during the following fall and winter. Now a new vision of retirement unfolded, one in which the Turners spent substantial amounts of time in the salubrious California climate and in which Turner thereby improved his retirement income.

After a week of investigation in the Huntington history holdings, Turner wrote to tell Farrand, "the more I sample the Library, the more I am astonished and delighted at its riches in many fields." At this point, however, he was uncertain whether he should return as a research associate during the coming year. What duties would be expected of him? Would he be expected to spend most of his time in "exploring the Library," or required to set aside his own work—"to complete which I am under obligation"—in order to pursue research in the holdings of the Huntington Library? If so, he would be unwise to agree to the arrangement. Here flashed Turner's old bargaining style. Others might represent a better investment of Huntington funds than he, *but* despite this "I need both California and income! and . . . I rate companionship with you even more highly than you do with me."[3] Still, he needed a more definite statement of his duties and must consider whether his health could sustain his obligations to the library.

As Turner's stay at the Huntington Library lengthened, he reported to Hooper that he and Caroline "were strongly inclined to spend our winters at least in Southern California hereafter, whether for 'a consideration' or not. It's no use being next to our daughter and the family, if you are laid up with colds, and the fight against the climate. . . . At 65 I found that the mere matter of resisting the cold was absorbing about all of my energy." They would continue to summer in Maine for the time being, he thought. But that spring in California, he confided, had "been a real rebirth of enthusiasm to me." There were some negative considerations—his health was improved but far from robust, his ear was "permanently more or less out of commission." He had not "accomplished much writing," but he had "hopes of doing more because of the change of climate and the cheering up that my experience and reception have wrought." He reported he had found "almost more of the New England and the best of the Middle

Turner in 1927 at the doors of the Henry E. Huntington Library, San Marino, California. Reprinted with permission of the Huntington Library.

West that I knew in my youth out here now than in those regions themselves after the deluge of immigration." He had enjoyed meeting a succession of eminent visitors at the Huntington Library. But given its distances and dependence on the auto, southern California was an expensive society—"a rich man's land, without the urban industrial-ism," but it was not "materialistic." Southern Californians had gathered in "thousands on thousands" for Easter sunrise services, and "art and music, as well as science and literature, [were] a part of their love, not merely of their condescension."[4]

Farrand banished Turner's doubts about returning to the Hunting-ton Library. After summering at Hancock Point, he and Caroline took up residence in Pasadena in the fall of 1927. His duties as research associate resembled those that he had discharged while at the Carnegie Institution—reacting to the situation and making his observations known to the director. Giving advice was still second nature to Turner. In October 1927 he submitted a lengthy memorandum to Farrand, noting the deficiencies of the library for his own work. The collections lacked standard sets of the memoirs and writings of American statesmen and runs of historical periodicals. He found the coverage of American regions beyond the West to be deficient; there was no serial set of United States legislative documents, and books of reference were missing. Turner concluded, "All this implies no failure on my part to recognize, appreciate, and be grateful for myself and for the profession, of the wonderful riches now in the library. The nuggets are mined; what is needed is the machinery and the material for treating this gold, for minting it, and for acquisitions in the ore fields essential to our work, but where the initial cost is low."[5] In the previous March Turner had feared he would not be able to work productively on his own research in the library for more than a year because of the gaps in the collections. But as he came to know the resources of the library better, as Farrand strengthened its holdings, and as the other resources of the immediate area became clear, this caveat was discarded. His appoint-ment endured until the end of his life.

It is not too fanciful to suggest that Turner's friends conspired during the last fifteen years of his life to help him bring "the book" to completion and to see him reap the full fruits of his career. That activity began when President Lowell invited him to give the Lowell Lectures and extended through various grants of assistance from Cambridge sources during his last years of teaching and early retire-ment. Now Farrand tried to provide a situation that would give Turner the best possible chance of bringing his work to completion. Friend-ship was involved in this gesture, but Farrand also realized his own intellectual indebtedness to Turner and was convinced that he had made an unrivaled contribution to American history. Nor did the benefit from the Huntington appointment run only toward Turner. Turner's knowledge of bibliography and library practices was wisdom that Farrand needed at the time. Turner's advice reinforced Farrand's recommendations to the trustees of the Huntington Library. His presence at the library gave it immediate legitimacy and stature.

As he settled into his appointment at the Huntington Library, Turner optimistically envisioned years of productive scholarship ahead. Not only would he complete "the book," but he might, he hoped, complete a series of additional studies. He admitted that this might be an unduly optimistic prediction of what his health might allow. But in early November 1927 he reported to Hooper that he had been "pretty steadily 'on the job'" since the Turners had arrived in Pasadena some weeks earlier. He was putting in working days from 9:00 A.M. to 4:30 P.M. daily, lunching on a sandwich and fruit with Farrand in his "Gothic Hall Office" where they discussed "Library matters." Farrand was determined that this would be the usual extent of his obligations.[6]

The Turners rented 23 Oak Knoll Gardens in Pasadena and began to enjoy modest local excursions and social occasions, including lunch at the home of the Hales. On another occasion they dined at the "Patio," from where they could see the Indian supers clustered at the Community Theater as the drama *Red Wing* was performed. How strange, thought Turner, to be sitting at dinner in California, within eyesight of the performance of a play whose setting centered on Fort Winnebago, so closely adjacent to Portage. Ominously, however, other distractions appeared. Although admitting to Hooper that he found public presentations "a strain," he agreed to speak at a Harvard Club luncheon in Los Angeles, participate in the Pasadena Lecture Course, and address the Pasadena Librarian's Club. A more encouraging development occurred when Merrill H. Crissey, Turner's one-time secretary at Wisconsin, left the business world to serve him at the Huntington Library. Marvelously efficient and devoted, Crissey was the last major player to join "the conspiracy of the book" before Turner's death. His effective and solicitous encouragement contributed much to the progress of the manuscript during Turner's California years. Aiding the cause also was the fact that Turner began to decline invitations to lecture at local colleges and refused to prepare material for the next edition of the *Encyclopaedia Britannica*.

On New Year's Day 1928 Turner reported himself well but missing the Madison members of the family. He knew, however, that Dorothy preferred "a live dad on the Pacific Coast, to an invalid in the Middle West!" At this point he was working every day to provide copy for Crissey who was "efficient, but very driving."[7] Late January 1928 found Turner still in acceptable health, although Caroline, after an enjoyable fall, had proven that colds might afflict even Californians. Turner was dieting—"vegetables, fruit, milk, and lima bean bread, with three full glasses of orange juice daily." They were delighted that a new granddaughter had arrived safely in Madison, and Turner insisted on contributing to the wages of an additional maid to ease Dorothy's burden. Their future residence was still uncertain, Turner reported, since his current arrangement was limited to six months, terminating in May 1928. He told the Mains that in his own opinion the library's money would be better spent on "men more suited to its present needs."[8] Farrand and the Huntington Trustees, however, believed that Turner's arrangement should be extended for as long as he could use its facilities.

The Turners lived pleasantly in Pasadena during the winter of 1928. As in Madison, Turner fed the local wildlife and here attracted a motley crew of orioles, sparrows, wrens, finches, blackbirds, mockingbirds, and blue jays. The San Gabriel mountains were crowned with white, and in Pasadena and San Marino the palms, oaks, and lesser trees, shrubbery, and flower beds made a pleasing landscape. At the Huntington Library a botanical wonderland surrounded a library far richer in resources than Turner had at first believed.

Early October 1928 found Fred and Caroline safely returned to Pasadena from Hancock Point. Turner discovered Crissey at work in a new office on the second floor of the Huntington Library, somewhat quieter, he believed, than his earlier quarters there. In general the library was "as delightful a workshop as before." He continued to observe national politics closely and broke his commitment of many years to the Democratic Party in presidential politics by casting an absentee ballot in Maine for Herbert Hoover. The latter had a "directorial mind," judged Turner, but would "Congress and the [party] organization take orders?" If so he could "do much good." But was he too "timid" to oppose "those who are more experienced in *politics?*" In that case he might meet disaster on "Scilla instead of Charybdis."[9]

The newspapers of these months reported that Thomas C. Chamberlin had died, the fourth of the University of Wisconsin's presidents to die since Turner had been a student there—which made him feel "quite all" his "sixty seven years." He had liked Chamberlin, he told Dorothy, and always found him "responsive." This judgment contrasted somewhat with the reports that he had given to Caroline and to Woodrow Wilson when the young Turner was scrabbling for a foothold at the University of Wisconsin. Nor did he mention that it was from Chamberlin he had borrowed the concept of the "multiple hypothesis."[10] The Christmas season of 1928 passed pleasantly. Caroline decorated a small Christmas tree, and they burned orange and live oakwood in the grate. It was hardly necessary, Turner thought, given the climate, but he didn't "know how people live without an open wood fire!" Outside, the birds were in attendance, and a new kitten gave them company inside. Friends took them on local sight-seeing expeditions, and on one of these Caroline tried to pick some fragrant drying plants—"withered old weeds," Turner called them. A forest guard informed her that taking such liberties with nature was contrary to California law.[11]

Turner's rather derisive account of this encounter between Caroline and the forest officer reveals an ambivalence in his thinking about nature and human occupancy. To the last he retained his love of eye-filling natural landscapes and the sights and sounds of forest, stream, lake, or ocean. He was whimsically regretful when a path that he helped to cut in the Sierra became a much-travelled route. He doubted, he said, that the dryads and wood nymphs would forgive him. He wrote admiringly of Van Hise's book on the conservation of natural resources and viewed Progressive regulatory legislation as appropriate response to the success of private enterprise in seizing control of America's natural resources. We do not find in his letters or writings sharp condemnation of exploitive practice—the excesses of hydraulic mining in California, overgrazing, or the wasteful cutting of the pineries of the Great Lakes. In his presidential address to the AHA, he referred to the "final rush of American energy upon the remaining wilderness" as a "wonderful chapter" in American history. Although natural settings served him as restorative, he appears to have been more sympathetic to the Progressive ideal of wise and efficient use of resources found in the thought of Gifford Pinchot and Van Hise than to John Muir's commitment to pure wilderness. He crossed paths with both Henry C. Cowles and Aldo Leopold, but there is no suggestion that he sensed the stature they would eventually be accorded in the realms of ecology and environmentalism. He camped with members of the Sierra Club, but government enlisted in the cause of "weeds" was too much. He followed what was to him a sensible middle course.

The Pacific Coast Branch of the AHA met in late December 1928 in Claremont, and Turner attended in company with John M. Vincent, a longtime faculty member at Johns Hopkins University. It would be his last AHA meeting. Edgar E. Robinson and his wife dined with the Turners a few days later, and they watched the Rose Bowl Parade from Farrand's home. All seemed to be going well. By this time the Turners were committed to California. In January 1929 they conveyed the Chimney Corner to Dorothy but looked forward still to summers at The Moorings.

When Turner took up residence at the Huntington Library, he had apparently not extended the completed portion of the manuscript of "the book" much beyond the point he had reached in 1924. Some other sections were outlined or in rough draft. The sum total represented an amazingly scanty harvest, given his various lecture series on the subject of sectionalism, the research leaves and sabbaticals, and the summers ostensibly devoted to the manuscript from 1917 onward. The Huntington setting stimulated a period of creative activity. With Crissey—"who, like Oliver Twist, demands more!"—as production manager, the manuscript grew.[12] Turner added several more chapters to those already finished. But then progress slowed. Turner showed a frustrating tendency to return to text once thought completed, to revise or to incorporate new facts or insights, and to explore in the Huntington's enticing collections. As his friend Farrand reported, "Hardly a day and never a week passed but he would excitedly and delightedly report upon discoveries he had made. A reference was to be added here, a sentence must be changed there. Some new material was important enough to modify a conclusion already reached or to demand consideration in the chapters still unfinished. 'The book' had reverted to the pioneer stage."[13]

If Turner's health had held stable, Farrand and Crissey might perhaps have gently bullied Turner into completing "the book" within a reasonably short time, although Farrand later doubted that possibility. But in February 1929 Turner's weakening constitution again betrayed him. Hot in pursuit of new leads, he suffered an attack of vertigo at the Huntington Library. He saved himself from falling by seizing a portable sign that announced "no admission to visitors," and a "very kind lady" joined him in a "war dance" around it until he had reestablished his balance.[14] The doctor prescribed bed rest until his blood pressure dropped, and after ten days of that regime a chastened Turner tried to develop a more restricted working routine.

Turner's energies were flagging, and it became clear that hypertension was not the source of all of his problems. In April 1929 his Pasadena doctors informed him that he was suffering from "bladder retention"; the "toxic effect" was affecting his "system," and a two-part operation was necessary. He informed Hooper that he would not be coming east that year, although he hoped that he would not "go West" either. Do not, he told her, let the "prospect before me give you concern. It's all a part of life's game and the stake is worth it."[15] In early May he wrote to Dorothy from a wheelchair in the hospital garden, reporting satisfactory progress in recovering from the first surgical procedure. Barring a setback, he would be able "to play the cutup" in another week or two. Turner survived the second operation also and by the end of the month reported from his wheel chair that he was "smoking again like an incinerator as well as irrigating like a desert rancheo."[16]

Despite the lingering effects of the operations, Turner spent the latter part of the summer of 1929 at Hancock Point. There his medical problems, now diagnosed mainly as heart disease, continued, and on doctor's advice he returned to California, so unwell that he did not visit Hooper in passing through Boston. Back in Pasadena, recovery was discouragingly slow. In early November his hand was so "wobbly" that he must dictate his letters. Several weeks later he reported that he was unable to dictate "for more than an hour a day, and that from a couch." Still there was improvement, and he and Crissey made some progress on "the book." He retained enough interest in Hooper's previous benefactions in western history to advise her that she should leave her gifts in the university library rather than transferring them to the Harvard Business School in which she had become interested at his urging.[17] Given Turner's commitment to tobacco and the methods of treating cardiovascular conditions at the time, it is not surprising that in February 1930 he suffered a mild heart attack. At some point in this progression, Farrand believed that there was a mild stroke. The prognosis in 1930 was grim. A fatal incident might come at any time.

By this time Turner's doctor believed that the stress of traveling to Hancock Point might be greater than Turner could withstand. Farrand urged Dorothy to convince her father that he should not make the trip in 1930, and she in turn expressed interest in visiting California. The Turners rented a house at La Jolla, California, from June through

September, and Dorothy and the children joined them during part of the summer. Before leaving for La Jolla, Turner prepared memoranda for Farrand in which he suggested ways of dealing with various topics in "the book" if it was unfinished at his death. He directed as well that the dedication be to Max Farrand. This grim preparation proved unnecessary, but after his return to Pasadena an attack of phlebitis forced him to bed. Plagued by his rebelling cardiovascular system, he struggled ahead—going to the Huntington for partial days when his health allowed it, dictating drafts to Crissey, and correcting them both there and in bed at home.

The ebbing of his physical strength frustrated Turner. It slowed his writing, and he was embarrassed because he believed that he was not providing an adequate *quid pro quo* in return for his stipend from the Huntington Library. As his physical problems mounted, he proposed that the $5,000 per annum be reduced to $3,000, but Farrand reassured him that his association was worth a great deal to the library even if he was completely unable to work. The library paid him at the rate of $4,000 per annum in his last years. Even so, money was a worry, and in an effort to save on rental payments the Turners considered buying the small bungalow at 23 Oak Knoll Gardens in which they had lived for most of their stay in Pasadena.

During the 1920s Turner remained concerned that his scholarly contributions be understood and respected. Beard had challenged his view of American development, but Turner was convinced that Beard placed undue emphasis on the role of labor and capital in the earlier centuries of that process and was, in effect, an economic determinist. Beard and Turner kept their exchange on a polite level of scholarly discourse, and others reaffirmed Turner's contributions, some in most laudatory terms. In the discussions of American historiography that they published during this decade, Schlesinger and Harry E. Barnes credited him with giving "a new direction . . . to American historical research." They acknowledged the importance of his emphasis on economic factors, and Barnes judged that he had "introduced more vitality and realism into the study of American history than any other American historian of this or any earlier generation."[18]

There was, however, some dissent. In 1925 Schlesinger and Merk drew Turner's attention to an article, "The Shibboleth of the Frontier," which appeared in the May 1925 issue of the *Historical Outlook*, a periodical for school teachers. The author, John C. Almack, a Stanford University professor, attacked the central place accorded the frontier in explanations of American history and character during the previous thirty years. "Frontier theory," he maintained, "appears to be nothing more than a diluted form of Marxian determinism." Its environmental aspects, its Puritan commitment to the idea that "hardships promote . . . well being," and its emphasis on the sectional aspects of politics were all suspect, thought Almack. The ideas advanced by Turner and his followers could only be accepted or rejected by comparative analysis as yet not attempted. Almack believed that evidence failed to show that frontier areas were forward-looking, citing their educational backwardness and lawless nature.[19]

Responding to Schlesinger before he had read Almack's essay, Turner expressed surprise that his ideas had not been more criticized in the past. He was willing to believe that Almack had created a "man of straw," although regretting that this graduate of a teacher's college had not understood his ideas more fully. Perhaps, he mused, "attempts to minimize the frontier theme" reflected "the pessimistic reaction against the old America that have [sic] followed the World War—the reaction against pioneer ideals," the tendency to "write in terms of European experience, and of the class struggle incident to industrialism."[20]

Turner was more frank in writing to Merk. Although Almack had pummeled a straw man, he, Turner, did not "quite enjoy being fashioned into that kind of a scarecrow for exhibit to teachers who haven't read what I really wrote." He took to heart, he told Merk, the "fact that I could have written any thing capable of such distortion in a reader's mind." Concerned with the "influence of regional geography" as he was, Turner wondered rather nastily whether Almack's Ozark origins might explain his problems in understanding the famous essay, or perhaps his normal school background was to blame. "Of course," Turner conceded, "the Frontier paper is open to criticism and would have received it anyway. It is no credo, sacrosanct, unalterable. But the job could have been better done! The idea that I was attributing all that was good in American civilization to the Frontier and the backwoods-man in his cabin and that a statistical demonstration that education and ability existed in the east was needed by a Stanford man gives me pain as it shows how ineffective my mode of statement must be. I am glad I have turned the west over to you!"[21]

Few immediately echoed Almack. Perhaps Turner's most prestigious critic of the 1920s among historians, aside from Beard, was Allen Johnson. His little book, *The Historian and Historical Evidence* (1926), denounced the methods of electoral map analysis found in studies of American sectionalism without, however, mentioning Turner by name. "The general theory," wrote Johnson, "assumes that well-defined physiographic areas will tend to produce distinct sets of economic interests, which, in the long run will find expression in policy." Although an "engaging theory," it involved a "subtle fallacy." The "tabulator" noted "only the majority vote of a district and then . . . recorded the vote in Congress of the representative chosen by that majority."[22] But of the two hundred thousand voters in an electoral subdivision, as many as ninety-nine thousand might have voted against the individual elected. Why, asked Johnson, had not physiographic and related factors influenced the votes of the minority no less than the preferences of those supporting the winning candidate? Turner seems not to have responded to Johnson's reservations. Had he done so, he would probably have pointed out that he was aware of other factors that influenced individual behavior in addition to sectionalism. These included ethnic attachments, migratory status, and religious and party ties. He was aware also that behavioral stimuli may affect individuals in different ways. Johnson later denied that he had intended to include Turner in his indictment, but his criticism bore directly upon methods that Turner had both advocated and used.

Such reservations paled in contrast with the supportive endorsements that Turner received in his retirement years. Two of his most cherished students, Becker and Curti, produced accounts of his work that recounted his achievements, explained his scholarly contributions exhaustively, provided a compelling portrait of Turner the teacher, and also incorporated Turner's own version of the development of his ideas. In the mid-1920s sociologist Howard W. Odum invited Becker to prepare the chapter on Turner in a volume of biographical sketches designed to show the emergence of the social sciences as scholarly disciplines in the United States. Becker asked Turner for his blessing as well as for biographical information. He also inquired whether Turner would like to read the manuscript before he sent it to Odum. Turner gladly approved Becker's participation in Odum's project but responded that monitoring it would be inappropriate. He willingly cooperated, however, in providing information.

For Becker's benefit Turner in 1925 described his publications and influence on the writings of others, his approach to teaching, the origins of the frontier thesis, and his Portage background. Becker must not, Turner told him, portray him as a dedicated teacher. Rather he was "enamoured" of history, "saw how much remained to be done on it, by stressing the economic and social aspects of it and the geographic aspects of it." This led him to realize that "aside from narrative history, and annexation-of-territory history the *West*—the land beyond the Alleghanies, was almost virgin soil, and that the *frontier process* began with the coast; and that the South also—indeed all the *sections*— needed re-study objectively." Nor had institutional history been adequately studied in America.[23]

Turner had realized that the task of reassessment required the labors of more than one individual. "*That*, with a genuine liking for my graduate students, and for advanced men of the undergraduates, led me to a desire to interest men in my subject to urge them to 'carry on.' I sensed (because I had no conscious theory or plan in the matter) the fact that a rubber stamp of my own on these men would crush out their initiative. That too harsh criticism would produce inhibition also." He had therefore "*tried most of all not to be a teacher*, and . . . was blessed with an historical progeny of which I am proud—(C. L. B. among the large stars!) They were my friends and colleagues." He liked the analogy of the teacher as radiator. But it was "love of original research," the spirit captured by Kipling in his poem "The Explorer," that inspired his students, he believed. He had been merely "the keeper of the keys . . . received from Allen, and a man with an explorer's instinct, who had enough common sense to keep out of the way of you men who were willing to blaze trails of your own." Of course he had intervened when seminarians "got lost, or soldiered." In closing this letter Turner summed his position, "I had no interest in the 'shooting' of the 'young idea.'" Love of history and the joy of working with like-minded young scholars had inspired him, he maintained.[24]

Turner told Becker at some length how the frontier thesis came to be. As in his response to Skinner, he suggested that Allen's ways of looking at the institutional history of Europe had led him to approach American history from a similar perspective. This time he gave Herbert Baxter Adams some credit in this respect as well. Again he recalled Adams's pronouncement that the American book of institutional history should now be closed. "The frontier was pretty much a *reaction* from that due to my indignation," he wrote. The environment at Johns Hopkins was "friendly to new ideas," and Wilson as well as members of Adams's seminary had stimulated him and "challenged" his "originality." Adams, Turner maintained, had contributed "absolutely nothing" in Turner's development of his doctoral thesis or ideas about the frontier. Nor had anyone else, unless perhaps it had been Gannett's maps and the interpretive commentary in *Scribner's Atlas* and the authors of some of the guidebooks that Turner quoted in his essay. Adams's contribution to Turner's development lay in his "sympathetic expectation [of] good things. He encouraged me."[25]

Turner told Becker that he was uncertain as to the degree to which his frontier thesis grew out of his doctoral dissertation. His account of the background of that study is somewhat confused. In Turner's junior year, he explained, Allen had set him to work on a paper relating to French land tenure in Portage. As he wrestled with the unpromising topic, he had been rescued by old Mr. Draper, the builder of the State Historical Society of Wisconsin, who had showed him a collection of papers and ledgers relating to the activities of the French fur traders along the Fox and Wisconsin rivers. Turner had then written a paper that when expanded became his dissertation. "Thus," he explained, "while a Junior, I did the thesis, which in substance, I later turned in for my doctoral dissertation. It was my own idea—by accident." Here Turner seemed to equate his study of the Grignon Tract with the master's thesis that he wrote during his years of graduate study at Wisconsin. As published, Turner's study of the Grignon Tract had merely traced the land titles of the tract adjacent to the portage. On returning to the university in 1885 he had told his father that he would like to write the history of the traders. Thus his undergraduate assignment gave him the idea for a thesis but not its "substance." Turner also speculated about the "unconscious influence" upon him of the Portage environment with its fur trading heritage and elements of frontier process unfolding before his youthful eyes.[26] Then too, he mused, he was perhaps affected by the pioneering urge that had run, generation after generation, in the blood of the Turners and his mother's family, the Hanfords. Turner believed also that his father's experiences as editor and politician helped him to understand that the appearance of events often belied their underlying histories.

Becker had been assigned the task of placing Turner's work within the perspective of the social sciences. To the delight of most readers since, however, he devoted almost half of his essay to describing Turner the young teacher through the eyes of the rural Iowa lad, Carl

Becker. That youngster was led into the study of history by a fascinating teacher with blazing blue eyes, a marvelous voice, and a unique capacity for persuading students of ability that they were his comrades in a most important pursuit—the search for historical truth. Becker concluded that his mentor's transcendent impact upon students lay in his "lively and irrepressible intellectual curiosity; a refreshing freedom from personal preoccupations and didactic motives; [and] a quite unusual ability to look out upon the wide world in a humane friendly way, in a fresh and strictly independent way, with a vision unobscured by academic inhibitions." Turner could not be typed; he was "just himself, a fresh and original mind that goes its own way, careless of the proprieties, inquiring into everybody's business . . . forever the inquirer, the questioner, the explorer."[27]

Turner's personality and style established, Becker analyzed his intellectual contribution, devoting one of the four sections of his essay to the frontier and sectional theses and a final one to his teacher's contribution to the history discipline and social science. Becker queried one aspect of Turner's thinking—gently pointing out his ambivalence in dealing with the possible impact of an industrializing America on the ideas and democracy derived from the frontier experience. Although in his celebratory addresses Turner seemed to "regret" or even "forget" the implications of environmental change, wrote Becker, his message was clear: "American institutions and ideals are the result of a primitive, and therefore surely a passing stage of social evolution."[28] Here his student pushed Turner to a position that the latter never fully accepted. Although always willing to agree that society did evolve, Turner never abandoned the concept of institutional "survivals," nor his hope that other evolving elements in American social processes would preserve the best of the past.

Much of the final section of Becker's chapter responded to those who deplored Turner's failure to produce a "great work." Turner's kind of history was not, Becker explained, "well adapted to quantity production." He did not write "straight narrative" history; rather it was "descriptive, explicative, expository," summarizing a wealth of data and impressive research in small compass. Attempts to combine a "synthesis of social forces" with description of the "evolution of society" must inevitably limit an author's production. "Turner's fame," Becker concluded, "must rest, not upon the massed bulk of books published, but upon the virtue and vitality of the ideas he has freely scattered about." But even so, his great influence within his generation rested upon more than "his published work," for the man himself was more than that, as his students particularly knew: "Some indelible impression . . . some virtue communicated to us from the alert intelligence and the fine integrity of a high-minded gentleman, still shapes our lives and gives added substance to our work."[29]

Curti was the last of those who sought during the 1920s to have Turner describe his formative years in history. A bright young midwesterner of Swiss extraction, Curti was an undergraduate in Turner's classes at Harvard and chose to work under his direction there as a graduate student. The two forged close ties of friendship, and Curti continued to seek Turner's support and advice after the latter's retirement. In 1928 Curti was a junior faculty member at Smith College and was surprised when his senior colleague, Sidney B. Fay, invited him to prepare an essay on Turner's methods of research for inclusion in a volume to be sponsored by the Social Science Research Council on the research methods of the social sciences. Turner was the only American historian whose work was to be discussed.

Curti found the assignment intimidating and all the more so when he learned that two senior scholars had refused it because of other commitments. But Fay was persuasive. It was midsummer, and, with the end of September set as deadline for the article, Fay believed that he would be unable to find another author. Curti explained the circumstances to Turner and asked for his help—for "suggestions, cautions." Turner willingly obliged at length by letter and also entertained Curti at the Moorings for several days during his preparation of "Analysis 23: The Section and the Frontier in American History: The Methodological Concepts of Frederick Jackson Turner."[30]

When Curti confessed that he found it difficult to describe the Turner "methodology," Turner comforted him. "I shouldn't know what to say myself. If I have one I don't know what it is!" He explained that he had never formulated "a philosophy of history, or of historical research, or of pedagogy." After noting a few methodological elements in his approach, including his commitment to the use of "the Multiple Hypothesis," he suggested "perhaps at bottom the belief that all the social sciences were one, and related to physical science, has influenced my work. The need of dealing with economic, political and social (in the largest sense, including Literature, Art, Religion etc.) fields has shaped my conception of historical research." Turner then proceeded in this letter to provide Curti with the "suggestions" that he had requested.[31]

In discussing the formative influences that played upon him, Turner again paid homage to Professor Allen, crediting him with having anticipated the use of the seminar method and with encouraging him, Turner, to do *"creative* research rather than to memorize narrative history in the fashion then prevalent." Because his own early contributions had been in western history, he told Curti, his work in that field had been given "undue emphasis." Actually, his approach had been much broader—he had viewed the West as "a *process* rather than a fixed geographical region" and had conceived of "the 'frontier' . . . as the 'thin red line' that recorded the *dynamic* element in American history up to recent times." Given this perspective, said Turner, "it became clear to me almost from the beginning that the advance of settlement required a study of the Atlantic coast sections and an understanding of their make up—their people, institutions and ideas; and an understanding of the geographic provinces into which they moved—the new environments and conditions which modified these colonists as well as the contributions which the colonists made." This larger conception of American development, this emphasis on physiography, demography, and interest in changing "literature, art, religions, ideals" led Turner, he believed, "into a conception of American history which differed from that of my contemporaries." Examination of the college and university catalogue offerings in history of the "later eighties" would allow one to judge the differences in his approach from that of others, "whether good or bad." The approach to western history at that time, he argued, was "largely antiquarian or of the romantic narrative type."

To Curti, Turner emphasized the relatively small amount of formal instruction in American history that he had received as a student. This made for problems in his early teaching, but it was also an advantage because his approach was not molded by other instructors. In developing command of American history, he had tried year by year in his own teaching to emphasize successive eras of the American experience. He had emphasized class reports based on original sources, and in discussing them he had served "as listener, correlator, and interpreter," relating the various presentations to the "conventional histories" so that the members of the class would see themselves "as engaged in creative work." His method was "Socratic," and he downplayed his own role while emphasizing both "wide reading in standard histories" and "independent study of the subject." But he discouraged "too cocky or scornful an attitude toward the men who had built before." Turner left specific choice of topic to the students, he explained, and as a result they had become specialists in many fields. He catalogued the names of those who had worked in railroad history, in the history of agriculture, in diplomatic history, in public land policy, and in immigration history. Perhaps he had stimulated such scholars, he admitted, "but much was due to 'salutary neglect' and to an attitude of hopeful expectation." He preferred to defer "severe criticism until the student had acquired some confidence in himself."

Turner's interest, he explained, had focused on the reaction of leading individuals to the shaping force of the social and political environments, rather than in idiosyncratic behavior. His students had perhaps believed that he too much emphasized detailed research, but such stress "was designed to cultivate critical thoroughness, and to furnish a safe basis for elimination and for reaching conclusions." Turner had found that using county and congressional district maps was helpful in analyzing geographical and regional relationships in American politics. "This method," he wrote, "came out of my seminary, with the start by Libby" in his dissertation.

In conclusion, Turner suggested that his methodology had been "largely unconscious," based on his "search beyond the skyline for new truth" and on his willingness to do whatever "immediate need and resources permitted." As in his interchange with Becker, he speculated that his early education in the political realities of Portage and his training as a reporter had taught him that many factors might be involved in a particular circumstance. "Pedagogy" had been of much less interest to him, he wrote, than "the subject which I was studying with the aid of student companions." These he had not tried to shape in his "own special mould." He had been a "porter at the gate, rather than a drill seargent." Finally, Turner referred Curti to a number of authors whose discussions of his work might be informative and to former students whose observations might also be helpful.

"How generously you give," responded Curti in a highly complimentary but politely probing letter designed to elicit still more information. Was not his application of the "multiple hypothesis idea" a "very great methodological contribution?" Was Schlesinger not correct in suggesting that Turner was the first "to perceive the importance of economic influences in American history"? Was he not in the vanguard of the "new history"? Was Beard not being "a little unfair" in contending that Turner placed too much emphasis on "free lands and the frontier" and too little noted the "conflicts between organized labor and capital?" Was not Turner's "emphasis on sectionalism. . . . a very significant contribution"? What had geographers like Ratzel and Shaler contributed to his thinking, or perhaps Josiah Royce?

Curti sought to draw out Turner about his recognition of intellectual history, his use of statistics, his mapping methods and criticism of them by Samuel Eliot Morison and Allen Johnson. How had the idea of mapping electoral, social, and economic data occurred to Turner? Should Curti not make some reference to Turner's work in diplomatic history? Was he correct in believing that Turner had never tried "to say just *how* much environment, or just *how* much social inheritance explained things?" Had Turner been correct in deprecating Harry Elmer Barnes's estimate of his importance? He, Curti, believed not. Would Turner care to elaborate on his earlier remarks about the ultimate need of discarding detail?[32] Curti's skillful combination of praise and query elicited another long report from Turner.

Turner preferred, he told Curti, that the latter would not identify priorities among scholars in the adoption of methods or emphases. "Do not create enemies for me by creating jealous rivalries and criticism." As for Beard, Turner agreed with Curti but did not believe "it necessary to deal with him by name." Turner did not dispute Curti's evaluation of the importance of sectionalism as he had developed the concept but noted that he had developed his ideas still further in his papers of 1925 and of 1926. He did not remember that he had learned anything from the geographers Ratzel or Shaler or from Royce's ideas on cultural sectionalism.

Turner was also vague about the origins of the map analysis in his seminar and in his own work. Libby had been the first seminar member to produce analytical maps in the course of his research, but "how far the idea of mapping came from Libby, I can't say." He noted that the *Scribner's Atlas* of 1885 had included maps showing electoral returns and that Giddings had referred to them in a contemporary article. He had "forgotten" the details. His own contribution in this area, he believed, "was to knit together the cultural and economic mapping with the political," to emphasize "the relations of political mapping to physical geography and cultural and economic data more generally than would be indicated in such paper's as Libby's." He had, he added, done "a good deal of editing of Libby's paper" and contributed a quotation from Hildreth's *History of the United States* in his editorial introduction to the published version.

Turner identified a number of additional scholars whom he had perhaps encouraged to pursue sectional analysis or to follow his lead in diplomatic history. He cautioned against the assumption that such writers had merely "worked out my ideas." Responding to Curti's interest in the problem of eliminating data, Turner explained, "no historian . . . can be really and absolutely free from the personal equation. But to preach the importance of reaching conclusions on relative importance of facts, and the need of dealing with relations, the causal element and with results, is the only way to avoid mere dumping of brick and mortar for another's use." In final admonition, Turner told Curti that "comparisons are odious," as well as difficult, unless the writer knew all parties involved. As to his relation to the New History, Turner remembered that he had delivered his presidential address on social forces at the same meeting of the AHA where Robinson delivered a paper "propounding some of his 'new history.'" Even so, he urged, "Don't claim so much for me that you start a row!"[33]

Curti continued to probe in still a third letter of August 1928, assuring Turner that he would not "start a row" and that he would "try to write of you as you would want to be written about." He sought to draw out Turner on the degree to which he had emphasized "sheer accidents or the results of personality" in the shaping of historical events, as opposed to tendencies, mass movements, and the like. Had not some of Turner's contemporaries differed from him by refusing to speculate on the implications that past developments might have for the present? What was to be the future of pioneer ideals? Was Becker correct in suggesting inconsistency in Turner's stress upon the importance of such values in a world fated to become increasingly industrial in character? Or had Turner merely been expressing a provisional hypothesis about the direction of future developments? In such tentativeness, Curti told Turner, he found his work conforming "to the best canons of science." He ended on a personal note—whether or not it was proper to introduce "hopes and faith" in a discussion of methodology, it had been Turner's "faith and hope and belief in what America stood for that gave to me a sense of value in living."[34]

Turner replied immediately. "His studies," he told Curti, had persuaded him that "much of what was regarded as 'sheer accident,' 'fortuitous circumstances,' and 'personality' was really dependent upon preparatory conditions, deep-laid tendencies released by the special circumstances or man." However, a Lincoln or a Roosevelt might well shape "the events of a limited era." But he could not "see that history is either the 'lengthened shadow of the great man,' or the result of economic determination in which the leader doesn't count." Continuing to play to Curti's lead, Turner acknowledged the very considerable influence of the Rankeans in his early days but noted that even then some took exception to their tenets—and their reservations still held in his opinion. Environments, both social and economic, changed through time, Turner agreed. He hoped, however, that "inherited ideals persist long after the environmental influence has changed." The past was indeed the historian's "legitimate field." But the present did sometimes illuminate the significance of past developments, and, he concluded, "if I didn't believe that history helps us understand the present I should not have the interest in it which I have."[35]

In describing Turner's contributions to social science for the volume *Methods in Social Science: A Case Book*, Curti produced a lucid essay summarizing Turner's approach to history and his conception of the United States as a unique laboratory in which to examine social evolution. Turner believed, explained Curti, that "the chief purpose of history is to aid in understanding the process by which interacting forces have made society." Curti noted the influence of the natural sciences upon Turner's work, including his commitment to the "method of multiple hypotheses." He also understood that historical research must differ somewhat from that in the natural sciences.[36]

Turner had not sought, Curti explained, to "determine the ultimate laws of history" but attempted "to establish tendencies and to understand mass movements and processes in America." Even his concepts of frontier and section were merely "keys to . . . understanding of the process by which man and his environment in America have reacted on each other." Curti described Turner's early commitment to the introduction of economic and social factors in historical analysis and his use of physiographic analysis and mapping techniques. Summarizing Turner's major ideas, Curti skillfully refuted the major criticisms that had thus far emerged, and he also emphasized the number of Turner's productive students and the varied nature of their fields. Within the historical profession, concluded Curti, Turner's influence— through "his writing, his teaching, and his personality"—had been "almost immeasurable."[37]

No historian could have placed his reputation in the hands of more skillful and solicitous executors than Becker and Curti. Their essays were brilliant examples of historiographic analysis and shaped Turner's later image within the profession to a considerable degree. Theirs was a brilliant rear-guard action in defense of a beloved mentor. Nor did they intentionally distort the truth, but each in his separate way persuasively used the information that Turner provided them. And so far as Turner had forgotten the details of some forty years past, omitted relevant facts, or unintentionally misrepresented past events, Becker and Curti worked from a flawed record. Nor were they about to hurt the feelings of their revered teacher and benefactor by unduly emphasizing the chinks in his armor.

Turner was delighted with Becker's and Curti's essays and brought them to the attention of Dorothy and Hooper and other correspondents. He was pleased also when he read an article in the *Century Magazine* on the proper relations of student and teacher in university education by Harold Laski, the brilliant English scholar. Drawing upon his experience as a faculty member at Harvard, Laski included Turner in a small group of "the greatest university teachers." Laski listed continuing research, a fresh mind, and the cultivation of students as friends as the three "great obligations of the teacher." Laski did not include publication among his criteria, and in this respect he again referred to Turner. "Some of the greatest scholars of the last half-century, Lord Acton, for instance, and F. J. Turner, published comparatively little; but their knowledge was so wide and deep, their power, born of that knowledge, to ask creative questions so fundamental, that they were able to fertilize all other work in their generation by reason of it."[38]

Other developments in his retirement years pleased Turner and sustained his sense of self-worth. Two of his former students, Willard and Goodykoontz, arranged a symposium on the history of the trans-Mississippi West to be held at the University of Colorado in June 1929. They broached their plans to him at an early date and invited him to appear on the program. He preferred, he told them, to play the role of advisor and friendly presence. Although his health did not allow him to attend, the general character of the program and references to his work in various of the papers were gratifying. From Wisconsin in early 1931 Schafer informed him that the new governor, Philip La Follette, had quoted the frontier essay in the opening sentence of his inaugural address. Although he had not always agreed with the new governor's father or senator brother, Turner deemed it an honor to be mentioned. He would not, however, he told Schafer, endorse any of the substitutes that "clashing groups" proposed as replacements for the beneficence of the frontier: "I don't want to be anybody's patron saint! Can't fill the bill!"[39]

At a more personal level, as we have seen, the *Kansas City Star* proclaimed Turner the winner in his long, if friendly contest with Channing. More significantly, in that year Turner's student Kellogg, as president of the Mississippi Valley Historical Association, presided over an annual meeting program that featured a "survey . . . of the frontier thesis." Paxson, John D. Hicks, and Buck discussed a Turner hypothesis "set forth . . . so cogently," said Buck, " that as yet no one [had] been able to add very much to it, or to detract from it."[40] In sum, the panelists called for research that would further elaborate Turner's ideas. Convention participants of that year sent a congratulatory telegram to Turner. Early in the following year he had the pleasure of reading the presidential address given to the AHA by Becker.

Of all the related fields at which Turner cocked an inquiring eye, it was in geography that he felt most at home. He was a member of the major organization and read the leading periodicals of that discipline. But his paper at the meeting of the Association of American Geographers in 1926 did not inspire the enthusiasm that had greeted his presentation of 1914. Interest in political phenomena was not dead among geographers, but no individual had emerged in the field to exploit and publicize the electoral geography that so fascinated Turner through most of his career. Although Carl Sauer worked this area of research in his early career, he became increasingly critical of studies that emphasized environmental influences in explaining human behavior. When Willard and Goodykoontz invited him to participate in the symposium on the history of the trans-Mississippi West that they organized, Sauer's address was in part an attack on Turner's ideas.

Discussing "Historical Geography and the Western Frontier," Sauer found two "principal difficulties" in the environmentalist approach. First, "one particular causal relationship is to be studied without such means of eliminating or controlling other causal factors as exist in laboratory experiments." Second, "there is no limitation whatsoever as to data studied. . . . Environmental influences in settlement, in political campaigns, in judicial decisions, in the causes of wars and the strategy of campaigns are all equally good demonstrations of the all-conditioning environment." Sauer would, one assumes, hold Turner guilty on both counts. The study of *culture morphology*, which Sauer advocated, was, in his mind, quite different. In this approach "the thing to be understood," he wrote, "is still the earth's surface, but it is the surface as modified by human occupation and utilization." Turner is nowhere mentioned in this presentation, but Sauer stated flatly,

> The eternal pluralism of history asserts itself on the American frontier: there was no single type of frontier, nor was there a uniform series of stages. The nature of the cultural succession that was initiated in any frontier area was determined by the physical character of the country, by the civilization that was brought in, and by the moment of history that was involved. The frontier has been in fact a series of secondary culture hearths, of differing origin and composition, which there began their individual evolution. In some cases this evolution has been convergent, but it has not been such so much in terms of the compulsion of a physical environment, or of an inherent tendency toward similar development inherent in cultures, but rather because of the will to unity that has come from a growing common political consciousness radiating from the older sections of the country.[41]

Obviously, Sauer believed that he was rejecting much of the Turner message of 1893. (At a considerably later date he also accused Turner specifically of making "an unfortunate error when he accepted an ancient, deductive view that human progress advances through an identical series of stages.")[42]

Turner apparently never responded to Sauer's manifesto. He did, however, react to the treatment of his work by Isaiah Bowman, a geographer, whose eminence during the 1920s and 1930s far surpassed that of Sauer. Bowman had invited Turner to give his paper of 1914 to an audience of geographers and nominated him for membership in the Association of American Geographers. Their relations continued to be cordial. In one of his major publications Bowman drew specifically upon Turner's article in the *Yale Review* of 1922, emphasizing the significance of the passing of the free lands era. He also accepted the historian's explanation of the way in which sectional influences shaped American politics. Reared in rural frontier America, Bowman conceived the idea of studying contemporary pioneer life while a young employee of the United States Geological Survey in 1905. In 1925, as a power in his discipline and in American social science generally, he submitted a proposal for the comparative scientific study of frontier belts to the National Research Council, and from thence it moved for consideration to the Social Science Research Council. That body named Turner to represent it on a joint advisory committee representing the two councils. He, however, apparently arranged that Merk serve in his stead.

As the project developed, Bowman aroused Turner by publishing an article maintaining that historians of the American frontier had misled their readers by suggesting that the frontier had ended in 1890. When Bowman sent him a gift copy of the frontier belt project's introductory volume, *The Pioneer Fringe*, Turner noted that Bowman had repeated the criticism Turner noticed as well that the only specific acknowledgement of his publications in the volume was a citation of "The Children of the Pioneers," used to document the argument that life need not retrograde to barbarism in new settlements. Turner wrote politely to Bowman in mid-December 1931. When writing his paper of 1893, he explained, he understood that the disappearance of the frontier *line* did not end the frontier process. "Doubtless," he wrote, "it was an inadvertence on my part to have used the sentence at the end of the article: 'And now the frontier has gone.'" His major purpose in the paper had been "to suggest that . . . continuous progress of the nation into vast areas of unoccupied land had been more fundamental in the shaping of our history than historians had as a rule perceived." The idea was not so much new as neglected. He had tried to make the point that the end of the frontier line did symbolize "the end of a real chapter in our history" and continued to believe that the 1890s represented a turning point in American history although frontier regions still existed. Nor did he hold that the "frontier phenomena [was] the one key to American history" but simply "a key and a neglected one." "Frontier conditions" in Bowman's pioneer belts, he suggested, should be regarded as illustrations of "survival" and not comparable in their results to the impact of the great free-land frontier of earlier days. Turner assured Bowman that he had found "pleasure and profit" in the book and listed some ways in which such studies might be profitably extended.[43]

Bowman assured Turner that he had leveled his spear at historians who used the term *frontier* "in an uncritical sense," rather than at Turner, whose "own use of it was amply safeguarded." He assured him that "like so many other students of American history and geography I feel that you are the pioneer in pioneer studies" and suggested that

Turner might wish to review his book for the *American Historical Review* or the *New York Times*. Turner declined, pleading that he had long since ceased reviewing and also that he had been confined to his bed during some months "during most of the day" and forced to dictate "therefrom."[44] That Turner took the time under these circumstances to defend himself surely reflects the solicitude with which he viewed his intellectual estate.

Bowman continued to cherish some reservations about Turner's contributions. A few months later he termed the historian's death a "severe loss" to both American geography and American history, for Turner represented a "rare combination of historical originality with geographical insight." But he also typified the "historian who rests his case on documents and general impressions rather than a scientist who goes out for to see." Turner, Bowman believed, had done too little fieldwork. As to differences in approach between the two scholars, Bowman considered his own views concerning frontier influence not so much "contrary as *variant*" to those of Turner.[45]

The historical atlas that had been conceived so many years earlier at the Carnegie Institution, and that Turner had so strongly supported, finally appeared in 1932 as the *Atlas of the Historical Geography of the United States*. Geographer John K. Wright emphasized its utility in a published note that began with a supportive reference to Turner's emphasis on the continuing prevalence of political sectionalism in American history. Wright presented maps of presidential voting, congressional tariff votes, and the densities of slave and colored populations in illustration. In the same presidential year Wright also published a note on American voting habits, using two maps that summarized aspects of presidential voting between 1876 and 1928 and showed the persistence of patterns of voting behavior. Again he paid his respects to Turner, concluding, "It is largely to Turner's inspiration that studies of 'the adjustment of politics to natural features' owe their origin."[46] Unfortunately, Turner died before he could enjoy Wright's supportive little articles.

Despite some dissent, Turner's reputation stood high during his final years of teaching and most of his retirement. He was shocked, therefore, when he read an article, "American Democracy and the Frontier," in the winter number of the *Yale Review* of 1931 to which

Merk had altered him. The essay's author, Benjamin F. Wright, Jr., was an instructor in Harvard's department of government. His academic credentials had survived the baleful scrutiny of a respected Harvard department, and he had won access to the pages of a respected periodical in which Turner had published two major articles within the last decade. No teacher's college fugitive from the Ozarks here! Wright flatly challenged the assertion that the West had made original contributions to the development of democratic government in the United States. He also criticized Turner's tendency to think primarily in terms of the Middle West, his propensity to write as though the frontier hypothesis had been fully proven, and his disregard of other major sources of American democracy.

After reading Wright's article, Turner told Merk that Wright had not realized that his concern was with "the *American* character of American democracy as compared with that of Europe." The coastal men who shaped American democratic institutions had been influenced by developments in the interior. He believed that there was much evidence to show that western influences played a part in the liberalization of colonial governments. He had developed such evidence in his lectures and in his own investigations to a greater extent than he had in print. Data existed, he believed, that would render Wright "less confident" of his position, had he "considered it fully." "A whole lot of rather able men had been misled," if Wright was indeed correct. Given his health, he explained, he "must not turn aside from my present work . . . to deal with the views of Mr. Wright." He did not know, he continued, "how important Mr. Wright is."[47]

What Turner could not know was that Wright symbolized the tendencies of a younger generation to test and challenge his work. Wright's article was the first in a series of critiques and attacks on Turner's frontier theory that extended into the 1950s and elicited impassioned rebuttal from some of his former students and followers. Turner's inference that young Dr. Wright was unimportant, although understandable, carried the scent of arrogance. Later in the same year, as we have seen, Turner found the energy to respond to the eminent scholar Bowman. In a sense, Turner's explanation was unanswerable. Indeed, it was the differences that made for contrast between American democracy and that found elsewhere. But that defense was also a truism, and if unanswerable, not fully convincing. It is doubtful, however, that a prompt response to Wright along the lines followed in Turner's letter to Merk would have lessened the assaults that were to come.

As we have seen, Turner corrected to some degree the argument of the frontier hypothesis in later writings or at least in his thinking. He had initially argued that the frontier process explained American development. He later retreated to term it the most important element in that process. His wording was sufficiently unclear as to suggest that frontier processes ended in the 1890s. He later explained that he had meant only that the census frontier line had disappeared, and his own course in the history of the West sailed bravely into the twentieth century. He had seemed to equate the West with his own Middle West, but the Herbart edition of the essay of 1893 and his presidential address made it clear he understood that the arid west would be settled in quite different fashion. He had embraced stage theory, but by at least the early years of the new century he modified this concept, noting the possibility of differing sequences in different places and their intermingling one with the other. He had maintained in the beginning that the frontier had changed American character and fostered a unique democracy. He stood firm on these assertions, but his affirmation in response to Wright's challenge was so couched as to be true, if only one minor element of democracy in the United States could be attributed to frontier influences.

Turner had not, however, completely corrected the weakness of his original conceptualization. He did not systematically test or prove his work. He scattered intriguing bits of supportive evidence through his writing, but his analysis was impressionistic at best, his use of evidence highly repetitive. Particularly in the commemorative addresses, assertion ruled. His endorsement of Loria's promise that study of America would lay bare the laws of social development was as unfulfilled in 1932 as in 1893. Turner approvingly noted the achievements of the Progressives in ameliorating the ill effects of industrial change. Although reformers in their way, members of that generation, including Turner, did disregard various political and social evils of the time. Turner showed little concern for the plight of exploited minorities or other grim aspects of life in the West and has been faulted for such omissions. As historian he sought detachment; critics have viewed his attitude as one of blandness.

There is some irony in the fact that the frontier was not Turner's primary interest through much of his career. But his failing health inspired him to collect the frontier essays, and the defense of his publications was to be largely based on that foundation, although Curti's contribution of 1931 was much more broadly conceived. None can doubt that the frontier thesis was influential. It provided a comforting legitimacy for legions of scholars who found that it easily subsumed their institutional studies of developing America. The frontier essays captivated and excited generations of scholars, but they did not reveal Turner as practicing craftsman nearly so well as did his contributions on sectionalism.

16   Ending

"Tell Max I'm sorry that I haven't finished my book"

By 1931 Turner's flagging energies were committed almost solely to survival and to finishing "the book," although he was also planning to publish a collection of his essays on the subject of sectionalism as a companion to *The Frontier in American History*. The articles on sectionalism, he believed, were equal to, if not more important than, the frontier essays. The work with Crissey inched along slowly, but author and secretary made progress; when the first issue of the *Huntington Library Bulletin* appeared in that year, it carried Turner's essay "New England, 1830–1850," which would ultimately be chapter 3 of "the book." Now the Turners enjoyed little social life, and Turner was less often seen around the Huntington Library, although spending several hours there during days when he was able. He husbanded his energies for the manuscript, and Caroline expended hers in seeing to his welfare.

Turner's fragile health was mirrored during 1931 in the frequent appointments with his doctors recorded in his pocket diary. Dorothy and her youngest daughter visited at Oak Knoll Gardens for several weeks during the spring. Spending part of the summer at Hancock Point was out of the question, but the Turners vacationed for some weeks during the late summer on the California coast at Carmel, as Turner said, "a beautiful place to sit and consider America. If only the Huntington and Bancroft Libraries were here!"[1] By the second half of the year the notation "bad night" was appearing periodically in his pocket diary. In early November Turner's condition turned for the worse when phlebitis developed in one of his legs, and he was forced to bed. From there for several months he continued to dictate material to Crissey and to correct manuscripts. And, as before, he rallied. By mid-winter he was well enough to go to the library for parts of days. There, in early March, Mark A. DeWolfe Howe visited him in his study. Although Turner was resting on a sofa, there was still "the bright intentness" of eye, "the ruddy smiling countenance," his conversation marked by "infectious merriment and quiet laughter." He still impressed one as "vivid, alert, keenly interested in human beings and

The Moorings in 1996. Turner's retreat in Hancock Point, Maine, remains in the possession of his descendants. Photograph by author, August 1996.

Turner loved to watch from the veranda of the Moorings as the sun set behind Mount Desert and the other highlands across the water of the inlet. Photograph by author, August 1996.

their thought," displaying no undue pride in his accomplishments nor any concern that they were about to end.[2]

On March 14, 1932, Turner was again at the library in the morning, and those who saw him reported that he was in good spirits. After attending to correspondence and matters of research, he returned home. After lunch Mae went for a walk and returned to find him in pain. She immediately summoned Turner's doctor, who ministered to his patient and gave an optimistic prognosis. But Turner was convinced that this was to be a fatal incident. Caroline reassured him, but he died within a few hours. One of his last messages was, "Tell Max I'm sorry that I haven't finished my book." A Unitarian minister conducted a simple funeral service at Farrand's residence on the following Saturday. Avery Craven, then in residence at the Huntington Library, wrote a moving appreciation of his former teacher that Farrand read to the group. Turner's ashes were returned to Madison to rest beside his children in Forest Hills Cemetery. Before the funeral Farrand wrote to Schlesinger to report the circumstances of Turner's death, asking him to inform Haskins, then fighting Parkinson's disease, and other friends. Turner's book, he wrote, was almost complete except for a final chapter, but he did not "believe that ever would have been done." Turner had been "happy and contented, and . . . accomplished a good deal" while at the Huntington. Thus his passing, said Farrand, although "a shock," was a cause for "rejoicing rather than mourning."[3]

During his last years Turner well understood that he might not live to see his work completed. He drafted tentative instructions that were to serve as guides in completing "the book" and in bringing the essays on sectionalism together. He wished his great accumulation of professional correspondence, lecture drafts, research notes, reprints, clippings, and maps to be placed at the service of scholars and donated these materials for that purpose to the Huntington Library.

Farrand was as faithful in fulfilling Turner's wishes as he had been during his friend's life. Assisted by Craven, he did an initial sorting of Turner's papers. Turner had not systematically retained copies of the many letters that he had written to students and professional correspondents. Within weeks of Turner's death Farrand circularized to as many of his students as he could identify to inquire whether they would deposit copies of the letters from their teacher that they

possessed. Their responses immeasurably enriched Turner's correspondence files at the Huntington Library. Due also to Farrand's tactful
advice, the Turner family added family correspondence to the library
collection. Hooper contributed the twenty-plus years of letters that she
had received from "Historicus," accepting Farrand's assurance that he
and the Huntington Library would be more appropriate custodians
than Sam Morison and the Harvard Library.

Farrand was also determined that both of Turner's book projects
would be brought to successful conclusion. Craven assisted in
providing editorial supervision while Crissey continued as combined
researcher and secretary. Before the former returned to his appointment at the University of Chicago in the fall of 1932, the two had
corrected the galley proofs of *The Significance of Sections in American
History*, and Craven had set the manuscript for *The United States,
1830–1850: The Nation and Its Sections* in order and drafted an introduction for it. Henry Holt and Company had never reaped the great
harvest that its officers had hoped Turner's college history would yield
but had profited both in prestige and sales from *The Frontier in
American History*. As we have seen, the firm had labored hard to
extract a manuscript on the nation and its sections from Turner during
his last years at Harvard. Farrand found its men still interested and
cooperative. The collection of essays on American sections appeared
in late 1932. The publisher moved more slowly with the larger manuscript, not bringing it to market until 1935.

In 1933 the Pulitzer Prize Committee declared *The Significance of
Sections in American History* to be its selection in American history
for 1932. Farrand had written a strong brief in behalf of the book, but
others believed that they played an important role in obtaining this
honor for Turner. Turner's brother-in-law, Arthur Chapin, was living
in Washington at the same address as a distinguished member of the
committee, Robert L. O'Brien. Chapin was convinced that his vigorous
lobbying on behalf of Turner's book affected the outcome. Another
member of the committee, Mark A. DeWolfe Howe, maintained that
he also had urged the book's merits upon his colleagues. Other
scenarios have been suggested. Farrand was somewhat amused by
these claimstakers. He was glad that Turner received the recognition
but even more pleased that Caroline Turner's limited resources would
be enhanced by the $2,000 prize. If the various stories suggest a lack
of system and rigor in the awarding of the Pulitzer Prize, identification
of the other major contender of the year in history allays concern. It

was a volume in Mark Sullivan's *Our Times*, a respectable book, but in retrospect one that has proved a far less important contribution to American history than Turner's essays on sectionalism.

Turner's death and the publication of his collected essays on sectionalism further encouraged the general evaluation of his work, reflected in the Becker and Curti essays, Wright's article, and the symposium at the Mississippi Valley Historical Association in 1931. It had been Turner's successor at Wisconsin, Paxson, who produced the first major western history survey, a *History of the American Frontier, 1763–1893*, tapping the college text market that Holt and Company had hoped to exploit with Turner's text and winning a Pulitzer Prize in the process. At the annual meeting of the AHA in 1932 Paxson delivered the lead paper in a session devoted to Turner and his work, using the title, "A Generation of the Frontier Hypothesis: 1893–1932." It was a thoughtful presentation. Turner had died, said Paxson, before presenting his results, but he had "with modesty . . . point[ed] a way." "His hypothesis. . . . has not been proved, and it cannot be," said Paxson. American historians should "consider whether" it was "still plausible enough" for another generation to use it as "chart."[4]

Curti, Paxson noted, had suggested that Turner's emphasis on sectional processes had perhaps been as important as the frontier concept "in leading to a reinterpretation of American history." Paxson quoted the passage approvingly and then moved to a consideration of the more famous hypothesis. He found little to fault in Turner's factual description of the westward movement—the sequences of economic types and so on. Given the sources, "any competent historian" would produce a similar account. But in his "analysis of consequences" Turner had ceased to be "mere historian, becoming social philosopher on a large scale." Here Turner's hypothesis rested upon "less certain ground."[5]

For Turner, Paxson suggested, the significance of the frontier lay in its relation to "composite race and Americanization, democracy, social re-creation in the light of frontier experience, and nationality." If these had been "derived" from the frontier experience, as Turner believed, then his thesis still stood; if not, qualification was in order, even to the point of discarding the concept. Paxson believed that Turner had been perhaps too optimistic about the forces leading to Americanization because "newer aliens seem to have classified on horizontal social strata." In that case, "re-examination" was in order. The frontier had contributed to the development of democracy in America, thought Paxson, but we could only know "how definitive was this share" when we knew "enough to measure the other share that came from the realization of the aspirations of the workers in industrial society." Paxson agreed that the frontier had given Americans the opportunity — territory by territory, new state by new state — to re-create their institutions with beneficial results. Turner had been correct also when he argued for the importance of the frontier in shaping American nationality. Although Turner's term *consolidating agent* needed amplification, Paxson agreed completely with his argument that we "must study" the "economic and social consolidation of the country" if we are to understand "why we are today one nation, rather than a collection of isolated states."[6]

Paxson concluded that Turner's frontier hypothesis, "when . . . used as its framer framed it . . . is as useful a guide as it ever was." The facts yielded by subsequent research "fit comfortably into the matrix that he prepared for them, or they carry on the analysis farther than he pushed it." "The weakness of the straggling attacks upon his hypothesis" could perhaps be explained, said Paxson, "by the inherent weakness of the case against it."[7]

Some of Turner's students viewed Paxson's endorsement of the frontier thesis as an inadequate summary of their teacher's professional contributions. In justice to Paxson, his critique was not intended to fulfill that function, and he probably believed that Curti's essay of the previous year did so quite adequately. Phillips prepared a paper on Turner's "traits and contributions" for the same session at the AHA meeting in 1932, and, among his other former students, Kellogg, Robinson, and Nute published memorial notes that mingled fond personal reminiscence with a recording of Turner's achievements. For the benefit of the profession they recalled "his dancing eye, his vibrant mellow voice, his ringing laugh, his eager questions and ready comments," his habit of taking notes in seminar, the stimulation of a research conference with him, and the alternating brilliance and disorganization of his undergraduate lectures.[8]

Meanwhile, the publication of *The Significance of Sections in American History* brought Turner's scattered essays on sectionalism together for the benefit of the history profession. The dates of the initial appearances of these essays spanned even more of Turner's professional career than had his collection of essays on the frontier; their publication followed closely upon Turner's death. These circumstances prompted reviewers to place the book in the perspective of Turner's career in general. To a considerable extent they forecast the controversies that would center upon Turner's work through the coming generations. Several established historians of the West or Midwest, Paxson, Frank H. Hodder, Jonas Viles, and George M. McBride, factually and respectfully summarized the contents of the collection. He was the "historian's historian," wrote Paxson, and had changed the course of American historiography.[9] "His theory made a greater impression upon the teaching and writing of American history than any other single idea and it put the West permanently upon the map," suggested Hodder, who particularly approved some of the essays of the 1920s.[10] Viles noted Turner's change in focus during his career from frontier to section and suggested that his essays on sectionalism of 1922 and 1925 went "far toward meeting the current reaction against the emphasis on the frontier hypothesis." He hailed the final essay, "Sections and Nation," as "a distinct contribution toward the technique of research" on sectional processes.[11] McBride believed that by emphasizing American sectionalism, Turner had "turned a large part of American historical interpretation into a fresh channel."[12]

Overall, reservations filed by the members of this group were minor, some dealing with the organization of the book. However, Hodder noted that some now believed that the frontier thesis had been overworked and that Turner's theory of sections was "based too exclusively upon economic interest." Turner's diplomatic history, he added, was in some respects outdated. Hodder also embarrassed the meticulous Crissey by pointing out that a line of type was misplaced.

In addition, three of Turner's former students published reviews of *Sections*. To a Pennsylvania regional publication Buck contributed a substantial review that was impressively descriptive and judicious. Although he maintained that Turner's contributions to the interpretation of American history were "generally recognized as more influential than those of any other single individual," he too noted revision in the field of diplomatic history and suggested that Turner had paid less attention to the formation and influence of classes than was warranted.[13] Stephenson catalogued Turner's many achievements, noted his gift for "brilliant generalization and succinct characterization," his "marvelous power of analysis" combined with "'journalistic punch,'" and marveled that a scholar who had "tumbled from its throne a dynasty of historians" should have been "the object of a chorus of praise with scarcely a single discordant note. Alone among American historians he founded a school that bears his name."[14]

The third of the former student reviewers, Curti, sharpened supportive judgments he had made initially in his essay of 1931 on Turner's methodology. "If anything," he argued, sectional processes were "even more important in Turner's thinking" than those relating to the frontier. Turner's cartographic analysis had allowed him to make "brilliant generalizations" about the relations between sections. He was "a pioneer in advocating a *rapprochement* of history" and related disciplines and had "also invented and effectively used a sharp and objective technique for studying interrelations between physical geography and the political and cultural responses which it evoked."[15] However, Curti too suggested that Turner had investigated class conflicts within sections less fully than was desirable, but he was convinced that Turner would have welcomed such analysis.

During the 1930s some of Turner's students charged that his most severe critics tended to be young, eastern-trained scholars. This was not uniformly the case among the reviewers of *Sections*. New York–born and Columbia-trained Michael Kraus asserted that Turner "overemphasized the influence of the frontier," but also maintained that his work was "a much needed corrective to the traditional New England view" of American history. His writing and teaching had, "like the gust of a fresh wind," blown aside "many of the cobwebs of our history," his "infectious enthusiasm" had inspired "many a youthful student." The great number of authors who followed his lead testified to his influence. "The memory of his personality, as well as his writings," formed "a cherished heritage.[16]

Others of eastern connection were less supportive. "Young" Benjamin F. Wright, Jr., used his review to continue his critique of Turner's work. Conceding that Turner had revealed "genius" in identifying the importance in understanding American history of "two obvious, and neglected, factors," frontier and section, Wright asserted that Turner's formula needed "evaluation lest continued uncritical acceptance be succeeded by equally uncritical attack." Although at one point Wright termed Turner's scholarship to be of "highest quality," he devoted his extended review to challenging Turner on myriad fronts. The latter had "turned the study of America inward," resulting in "excessive emphasis upon intra-American, or rather intra-United States, history." He had fostered "scholarly . . . splendid isolation" even though "European influences had been continuously effective in the United States." "A very large proportion of the principles of American democracy were importations" and had been fostered in "the older regions of the East." Turner's essays on sectionalism maintained the same point of view as his earlier collection dealing with the frontier. Again, his concepts required clarification and further analysis and were, moreover, repetitive in their content.

Wright noted that the concept of the geographical section had not been new with Turner but conceded that he had provided a useful corrective to the writings of historians who were unduly preoccupied with American states. But Turner had, suggested Wright, perhaps overstressed physiographic factors while "unduly" minimizing "ethnic and cultural influences." He had moreover dealt insufficiently with the internal complexities of the American sections. He had also been excessively preoccupied with the Middle West, and his "curious essay" on the achievements of the children of the pioneers both mislabeled some midwesterners as pioneers and disregarded the scions of the pioneers outside Turner's favorite region.[17]

Wright devoted his final page and a half to close questioning of Turner's contention that western conditions had encouraged the democratization of American political institutions. Turner had not provided compelling evidence on this score. Had not western constitutions been copied largely from those in older states? Had not Tennessee retained a property qualification for suffrage long after most other states? Was Turner's claim that western regions uniformly had sought more equitable representation really correct? Had not residents of such an area in Kentucky tried to discriminate against urban populations? Was Turner's symbolic figure of democracy, Andrew Jackson, really democratic in outlook, and had he not also drawn great support from eastern as well as western groups? If western regions had been nationalistic in outlet on occasion, had they not also often demonstrated particularism? Although valuable, the formula of 1893 was "so inadequate as to be definitely misleading" unless subjected to further analysis and placed in the perspective of "other factors of a quite different character."[18]

A number of reviewers of *Sections* suggested that Turner had devoted too little attention to the development and interaction of

FREDERICK JACKSON TURNER: Strange Roads Going Down

social classes. Columbia University's Louis M. Hacker brought a Marxian perspective to this line of argument. Turner, he maintained, had not proven his thesis but "continually reiterated" it. Hacker found "amazing errors" in Turner's work and stigmatized the great body of research that he had inspired as "quite worthless." He and his followers were the "fabricators of a tradition . . . not only fictitious but also to a very large extent positively harmful." Turner had ignored the growth of "monopolistic capitalism" and impending imperialism. The free lands engendered not a "unique 'American spirit,'" but rather the agricultural base needed for the international transfers that helped build a "native industrial enterprise." In addition, the presence of the frontier helped "to explain the failure of American labor to preserve a continuous revolutionary tradition." By draining off "the most spirited elements" from "the eastern working and lower middle-class populations," it had prevented class lines from becoming "fixed."[19]

The retrospective evaluation of Turner and his work begun in the memorial notices and the reviews of *The Significance of Sections in American History* was to continue for generations. Scholars emerged who expanded upon the reservations expressed particularly in the reviews by Wright and Hacker. But Turner's followers and students were quick to defend their old teacher, none more so than Schafer at the State Historical Society of Wisconsin. During the 1930s he published a number of appreciations of Turner and, at one point, hoped to write his biography. In mid-1934 he delivered a paper, "Turner's America," before the Madison Literary Society, an organization that had once numbered Turner among its members. A panel composed of university faculty members supplemented his remarks. Curtis P. Nettels noted the degree to which the remedial social and economic programs of the early 1930s had been based on the assumption that new government initiatives must be substituted for the effect of the frontier upon American development. George C. Sellery explained that the profundity of Turner's investigations did not allow him to amass a great volume of publication. Turner's old rival, dean, and later university president, Birge, volunteered that few historians were ever able "to reinterpret the history of a great nation!" But Turner had possessed the "spark of genius" that allowed him to do so.[20] These comments in the summer of 1934 did not end the encomiums from Turner colleagues and students. Craven, Dale, August C. Krey, and Fulmer Mood added their recollections and evaluations of the master to those already on record. Curti made the final contribution to such testimony in 1987.

Having worked on the manuscripts of both *The Significance of Sections in American History* and *The United States, 1830–1850: The Nation and Its Sections* in their last stages, Craven was convinced that the latter would be viewed as a much greater contribution than the Pulitzer Prize–winning study of American sectionalism. Deeply researched, painstakingly documented, judicious in tone, Turner's last work was indeed a very fine book, but the outcome predicted by Craven was not to be. In organization the book followed the model of his earlier study of the 1820s. Description and analysis of the various American sections in the earlier chapters was followed by chapters in which Turner traced the play of sectional influences in national affairs during the presidencies of his hero, Andrew Jackson, who "represented the dominant forces of his time," and his successors. But death prevented Turner from completing the final chapters and giving the manuscript its final polishing. These circumstances perhaps affected the profession's acceptance of the book. And despite its impressive scholarship, breadth, and insightful passages, the book did not convey a sense of new departures. Turner and his followers had worked the vein too long. Reviewers once again acknowledged Turner's impact upon the profession, but they also repeated the criticisms that had been expressed in some of the reviews of the collection of essays on sectionalism and that were being further developed by iconoclastic younger historians. Of the latter, Hacker produced a shrill review in the *New Republic*, calling Turner a "non-economic historian" who did not understand "the productive system" and its attendant "class relations and hostilities." He charged that Turner's approach failed utterly in explaining the Civil War, termed the "interaction of sectional life" a "pet fancy," and dismissed his methods as "blunted tools."[21]

Reviewing a reprinting of *The United States, 1830–1850* some fifteen years after the publication of the original draft, Mood noted with regret that no reviewer had conscientiously tried to analyze the degree to which the book advanced the state of knowledge beyond that attained by the authors of the other major surveys of the same era that were in wide use during the early twentieth century. Nor did reviewers make much of the fact that the first chapter represented Turner's last and most sophisticated contribution to the methods and theories of sectional analysis. In this respect he had moved from the conventional groupings of colonies and states used by his teacher Allen through the adoption of Powell's physiography, the development of cartographic analysis, the reconciliation of the concepts of section and frontier (a section that moved), and the development of the analogy of American section and European nation. He had enunciated the relation of section to political party and to class division, specified subsections or regions within the larger sections, and accumulated many data showing sectional interplay at work in the history of the nation. That the frontier and the processes it involved were important factors in American life cannot be doubted, but exactly how and how much they contributed has never been established. Sectionalism was much more easily documented, both in literary sources and through systematic mapping analysis, and hence has been an extremely useful investigative concept, particularly at the middle range of research. Turner was correct in believing in its significance, although at times he perhaps overestimated its importance.

Thanks to Farrand, Crissey, and Craven, "the book" finally was placed in the hands of American historians. *The Nation and Its Sections* stands symbol for the greatest mystery in its author's career. Why could he not himself finish it? As we follow Turner through the years from 1917 onward we share his frustration in not producing "the book." We find in him no social radical, it is true, but a devoted husband and father, an intelligent and responsible man, rich in knowledge, possessed of a saving sense of humor, deeply committed to the scholarly and professional values that he and other members of his generation particularly had implanted in American academia. Perhaps during the early years of his career he had allowed ambition to taint his relations with one student and subordinate. He never was one to encourage mediocrity, and he may have overvalued the polished manner. Early professional success and family tragedy may have dulled the edge of his ambition, but the verdict of his students in general was highly positive. If accomplishment merits reward, Turner deserved to complete his task. But as we share Turner's frustration, we develop a moiety of our own. Why could the man not so order his life as to crown it with this final achievement?

Other Harvard professors, facing similar demands on their time, produced important books, including Channing and Turner's most intimate friend, Haskins. Nor can we blame Harvard University. If Turner's original role in the Cambridge program was hardly to his liking, and if Channing placed more of the "joe" work of the graduate program on his shoulders than was quite fair, it paid him a salary that was handsome in the academy of the time and, unlike many American institutions of higher learning, provided him with the benefits of a sabbatical program. President Lowell tried to help by inviting him to give the Lowell Institute Lectures of 1918. For several years after 1920 he was relieved of undergraduate teaching for half of the academic year and was given a grant to assist in completing his book even after retirement. Should not this assistance have allowed Turner to produce the great work?

Turner thought about these matters. In his own explanations, implicitly or explicitly, he emphasized his health problems. He believed that his style of production—short bursts of creativity at white heat, which when extended in the past had brought him down with assorted ills—required daily diversion as well as recreational periods in natural surroundings. By 1921 Turner had accepted the idea that he could not teach and write at the same time. To these considerations he added the argument that the breadth of his disciplinary interests and the diversity of the graduate work pursued under his direction had required him to put much time into learning about areas that did not contribute directly to his own writing.

Turner's health was indeed failing by the end of World War I. Perhaps it was too late to change his domestic lifestyle. Although he disliked large social events, Turner was a social creature who enjoyed the gatherings of the Shop and Thursday clubs, liked to lunch or dine with congenial colleagues or friends, and continued to do so even when Caroline was in the West or at Hancock Point. The efforts that the Turners made to counter Caroline's hay fever produced a home life that was more than normally disrupted by comings and goings and eating out while new domestics were sought. Caroline liked fine clothes, set a good table, and was never long without hired help until Fred's retirement. He, on the other hand, did not stint on the purchase of books and planned vacation forays that were more elaborate than necessary for the mere maintenance of health. Although there is no evidence that Turner begrudged any aspect of his domestic life, he did once remark on the disruptions caused by Madison's hay fever season. But did this lifestyle require Turner to spend excessive time in writing articles and in lecturing for pay at the expense of major projects? Since the number of his articles was not great and since both they and the public lectures were related directly to his research and to the enhancement of his professional reputation, the answer would seem to be "no."

But we find in Turner's behavior in these years also a refusal to focus his scholarly attention solely on his major objective. He had long since given up reviewing books and refused to join editorial advisory boards after leaving the board of the *American Historical Review*. Although his publications failed after 1918 to match in number those of the first decade of the century, he apparently spent considerable time in searching for data, thinking, and giving presentations about the contemporary manifestations of sectionalism that he brought together in his article in the *Yale Review* as well as eagerly following the publications of the neo-Malthusians, whom he mentioned in his address at Clark University.

As in his last days at Wisconsin Turner hoped at the time of his retirement that changed circumstances would allow him to complete the magnum opus. His optimism on that score was, however, tempered in doubts expressed to Curti and Robinson and in acknowledgment that he would have to accept some lecturing engagements or write for the periodical press. We find here the same lack of realism that characterized his approach to writing throughout his career. Or is there a less happy explanation? Was Turner, despite his solid achievements as disciplinary statesman and beloved teacher and academic advisor, in part a charming confidence man? Did he spin captivating ideas without any intention of laying a major work before the judgment of his peers? Or was he essentially an honest man with a marvelous ability to deceive himself as to the future and his own capacities?

Turner's correspondence with Holt and Company representatives reveals the embarrassment that he suffered during the many years while the advance against royalties of 1905 was unredeemed. This was not the reaction of a confidence man. So we return to the various explanations that Turner and his followers suggested—research accumulation to the point of stasis, a paralyzing awareness of the range of factors to be considered in his analytical type of history, his sense that he must humor his constitution with breaks, exercise, and diversion. Or did the failure reveal a restless curiosity and distractibility that enticed him along diverting but time-wasting research trails or into recreational reading or family genealogy? Or did it perhaps reflect pleasing but time-consuming interaction with students or inability to write in anything but fevered bursts?

Some would probe still more deeply, suggesting that Turner's writing block reflected suppressed feelings of guilt at his displacement of William Francis Allen as head of the history program at the

University of Wisconsin. He had indeed regarded Allen as his intellectual father, and he had to that time never experienced the death of one so closely linked to him. Both Allen and Turner had expected the young man to replace the older at some point, and Turner's grief at his teacher's passing was deep. But he had already had difficulty in completing an extended study, as three years of work on a relatively short master's thesis showed. Although he undoubtedly hoped to succeed Allen, Turner had no wish that this would take place immediately. At the other extreme of less likely explanations, one may blame Harvard University, the institution that took Turner from a rewarding, if somewhat troubled, environment and placed him in a setting to which he never completely adjusted. Turner's last decade at Wisconsin was far more productive in scholarship than his first ten years at Harvard, but even before he left Madison, he was deeply frustrated at his failure to advance major projects. So it remains best, perhaps, to leave Caroline with the last word. She put it simply—he could not "buckle down." In a letter to Farrand, she mused, "perhaps he is more beloved just because of his qualities which prevented his buckling down to work."[22]

Despite the critics, Turner's scholarly legacy was great—of American historians only Francis Parkman and Henry Adams left an imprint upon American history comparable to that of Turner, and theirs were less varied than his. Most notably in Turner's case, there was his advocacy of the basic ideas of frontier, section, and closed space, involving as well attendant corollaries such as the idea that the frontier had been a social safety valve and that an expansive foreign policy was to be expected in latter-day America. Utilizing these ideas, he had developed a college lecture course that served as the model for many other such curricular offerings. In the year of Turner's death, substantially more than half of the leading history programs in the country provided a course similar to Turner's "History of the West" for their students.

Turner's contemporaries credited him with changing the nature of American history, emphasizing as he did the importance of economic and social factors in American development. He popularized the use of empirical methods of analysis and encouraged the incorporation of methods and findings from related disciplines. Never much interested in the philosophical issues involved in writing history, Turner made

the analytical essay as important in American history as the traditional narrative form. He developed and publicized a research agenda
designed to amplify and test his theses and to fill a great void in
historical knowledge about America's historical development. He was
a major force in emphasizing the American aspects of national development rather than the continuities derived from the European
heritage. Scholars in related disciplines incorporated his ideas in their
writings.

In his classes Turner trained a body of dedicated students who
joined the members of a broader following in cherishing and enlarging
their inheritance. At the University of Wisconsin he led in building
one of the major centers of advanced history instruction in the United
States. Within the discipline of history he forged ties of understanding,
cooperation, and friendship with other leading historians, and together
they enunciated the values and built institutional structures that
persisted in the profession for generations. He was revered in these
circles both as one who had vision and one who gave good advice. He
was, for example, a leading advocate of both the *Atlas of the Historical
Geography of the United States* and the *Dictionary of American
Biography*. To read Frederick Jackson Turner's correspondence, to
trace his daily routines, and to try and rethink his thoughts is to relive
much of our own experience as historians. His was the generation that
established modern academic history—its place in the academy, the
sense of its practitioners that graduate instruction and research are
more important than undergraduate teaching, and the understanding
that job offers power the academic escalator.

It is correct to attribute such contributions to Turner, but in his
approach to history he was also expressing tendencies of the time.
Others would not have expressed them in quite the same way, but the
approach of American historians would have changed during the
twenty-five years between 1885 and 1910 had the young man decided
to become a frontier newspaper man or, like his brother, worked on the
railroad. Turner played a major role in establishing western history
within the academy, but his impact there also should be placed in
perspective. In 1988 John R. Wunder identified seventy-eight deceased
writers who had made major contributions to the history of the West.
Sixty-two of the seventy-eight were academic historians; the remaining
fifth were journalists, creative writers, lawyers, a gold rush merchant,
and so on. The academic historians studied in twenty different
graduate schools, ten claiming degrees from Wisconsin and six from

Harvard. The graduate schools of the University of Pennsylvania and Chicago each prepared five scholars and the University of California at Berkeley was represented by four graduates. Others took their training in schools scattered from Oxford, England, to Palo Alto, California. Although Wisconsin and Harvard produced sixteen of the academic western specialists, more than a quarter of the total, Turner was the final doctoral advisor of only five of the sixteen—two at Wisconsin and three at Harvard.[23]

In 1941 Samuel Eliot Morison, once a member of Turner's seminar, wrote in mingled praise and deprecation:

> Turner's thesis served a very useful purpose. It stimulated study and interest in American history, served to differentiate our history from that of other lands, removed the inferiority-complex of the West and made that section proudly conscious of her immediate past, struck at the intellectual complacency of New England, and the romanticism of the South—and, not least, gave to hundreds of young westerners topics for books they could integrate with their environment.[24]

This Olympian judgment said much but also left much unsaid.

At its most elemental level western history was the foundation on which a charismatic young scholar rose to eminence in a growing and professionalizing academic discipline. At the institutional level, the history of the West was also a weapon in a contest for regional educational hegemony that reflected the booming, developmental aspirations of western educators. Emphasis on the history of the West at the University of Wisconsin represented in part an effort to capitalize on local assets in a race with the University of Chicago for midwestern educational leadership. In regional terms, academic history of the West demonstrated that the region beyond the Appalachians also had a proud history and was an integral and important part of the American experience, a fit subject for the historian's labor.

It was Turner's genius and luck that he was able to meld basic facts of western development with long-held ideas of western uniqueness and with the scientific theories and popular concerns of the day in a rhetorical statement that became one of the most powerful explanations of American development and character. Although the western history course in important elements preceded the statement of the thesis, that statement in turn provided a conceptual core that other history courses lacked. To study western history was to understand American growth, institutions, and values. Spread in hundreds of classrooms, the message could also be used by specialists elsewhere in the discipline—diplomatic history for example, or as a baseline in the study of national cultures—and could be useful to the psychologist or to Aldo Leopold advocating the retention of wilderness. Absorbed within American culture, it could reinforce the American sense of uniqueness and accomplishment, strengthening our very nationalism.

At a less rarified level the history of the West gave generations of college students the best and, often, only introduction to their region and locality in college history courses. Here they learned how the Indians were dispossessed in their area, how the land was distributed to their ancestors, how their local and state governments came to be, and how this contrasted with experience in other regions. Explicitly or implicitly, depending on the instructor and the time, the survey course in western history was a record of American aspirations, dreams, and myths. It was for many an unmatched exercise in self-identification.

It was significant also that Turner's model of American development was interdisciplinary. Graduate students at Johns Hopkins absorbed large amounts of political economy. Turner in 1892 and 1893 was a faculty member of the School of Economics, Political Science, and History at the University of Wisconsin. The influence of other disciplines are apparent in his early publications. One of the most interesting aspects of western studies is the fact that interaction with other disciplines recurrently leads to change in the content of western history.

In his later years Turner expressed surprise that his major ideas had been accepted with so little controversy. By the time of his death, criticism or rejection of both the frontier and sectional themes had become apparent in some quarters, and points of challenge were suggested in memorial statements and in reviews of *The Significance of Sections in American History*. The controversies would rage for generations and indeed still continue. They were the subject of a full-length book by Wilbur R. Jacobs in 1994 and will reward still further study. As we have seen, critics denied that frontier processes greatly enhanced the development of democratic institutions in America and criticized Turner's alleged tendency to think primarily in terms of the

Middle West and to write as though the frontier hypothesis had been fully proven. Others criticized Turner for failing to provide clear definition of terms, for taking positions that were inherently contradictory, for ignoring sources of institutions and personality traits other than the frontier, for the scantiness of his supportive evidence, and for the amount of repetition in his essays. He had, said others, ignored America as Europe's frontier.

Turner's contention that the frontier had served as a social safety valve in the United States resulting in the alleviation of labor unrest came under heavy attack. Other aspects of Turner's social theory were sadly dated, charged critics. Marxists and members of other persuasions criticized Turner's lack of emphasis upon class conflict. George W. Pierson focused the criticism to some extent by conducting a survey of scholarly opinion about the frontier thesis that he reported upon in late 1941. Scholars began to search for the sources of Turner's ideas and their suggestions and their findings, implicitly or explicitly, impeached Turner's originality. It became common for critics to argue that Turner had emphasized the differences between the American experience and other national histories at the expense of more important continuities.

Publishing a critique of the ideas of major Progressive historians in the late 1960s, Richard Hofstadter deplored Turner's "blandness," his failure to react to "such aspects of Western development as riotous land speculation, vigilantism, the ruthless despoiling of the continent, the arrogance of American expansionism, the pathetic tale of the Indians, anti-Mexican and anti-Chinese nativism."[25] Hofstadter also criticized Turner for his failure to read the work of major social critics of his era and react to them. During the 1970s social historians became increasingly concerned with groups hitherto neglected in both national and western history—women, Hispanic Americans, and other social minorities. Turner's history, they noted, had been written from the point of view of the male Anglo Saxon. Although Turner had acknowledged the concept of culture, he had failed to use it to further his understanding of other groups. Turner had asserted that a chapter in American history closed during the 1890s, and many of his followers had ceased consideration of western history with the 1890s. By the late 1980s members of a new generation of western historians were in revolt against the conventional dogma despite modifications that had been made in it.

Turner's followers did not retire ignominiously from the field in the face of the critics of the 1930s and beyond. They reaffirmed their faith in his major contentions and rejected the criticisms as wrong or exaggerated. If there were seeming contradictions in his work, Turner's America was a society of contradictions, and if he found grounds in the evidence of a "drift toward 'democracy and nationalism,'" that did not mean that he was unaware of countervailing influences. Some went so far as to maintain that only those who had heard Turner expound his ideas in person could fully appreciate them. Farrand informed Caroline of the critical articles that Pierson was publishing about Turner's ideas and explained that he had told Pierson that "on the major thesis, he (Pierson) was everlastingly wrong, for he didn't know what he was talking about."[26] No uncritical admirer, James C. Malin called Turner a creative genius, acknowledged the difficulties that innovators have in finding appropriate wording, noted that "many of his contradictions [represented] accurate historical reporting of contradictory behavior of men" and dismissed much of the criticism of Turner's "use of . . . terms and definitions" as "mere hairsplitting verbalism."[27]

Additional factual research in these years appeared to support Turner's theses, although some studies also suggested the reverse. Various scholars in the 1950s and 1960s—Stanley Elkins, Eric McKitrick, David Potter, Merle Curti, and this writer—pointed out that contemporary social theory suggested that the frontier experience might well have had some of the effects argued by Turner. Scholars in American studies focused on the West as continuing symbol and myth in American culture, thus providing a more satisfactory explanation of the long-term effects of the frontier experience than Turner's concept of "survivals." Although the major outlines of Turner's argument relative to frontier influence might appear to stand unchanged throughout his career, he did, as we have seen, make subtle changes and concessions in his presentation. As historian he carried his own research and teaching into the twentieth century, and careful reading of his writings and research in his papers shows that he both understood the differences between frontier processes in the high plains and beyond and in the Midwest. He also acknowledged the importance of class conflict in American history, as Beard was later to admit. However, he considered it to be far less important prior to the end of the nineteenth century than did Beard. On various occasions Turner identified other important elements, including urbanization and the presence of minorities, that the American historian must consider, as well as the workings of frontier and section. Taking these facts into consideration, his biographer, Billington, argued in 1973, "To summarize his views on the frontier process is to recognize that they would be accepted by most historians today."[28] Although it lost its place in many departmental curricula, particularly in institutions located east of the Mississippi River, the western history or frontier course survived into the late twentieth century, in part because textbook writers made various concessions to its critics.

By the late 1980s proponents of a "new western history" were asserting the inadequacy of the work of historians who merely brought a revamped Turner to an interpretation of western development. Their critique appeared particularly in the collection entitled *Trails: Toward a New Western History*. Turner, wrote its editors, had bequeathed the profession "what many historians regard as an interpretive straitjacket." Among the authors, Donald Worster argued that Turner merely recited the "agrarian myth," and Worster echoed Hoftstadter's judgment that he had failed "to see the shameful side of the westward movement." He wanted, wrote Worster, "to leave out" "those unsmiling aspects" of western history. He had obscured the fact that the West was the site of the painful creation of a "multiracial, cosmopolitan" society and "in the forefront of America's endless economic revolution." But now "truth is breaking in." For "the old 'frontier school,'" wrote Worster, the West was a "simple democratic place." But the "frank" new western historians were revealing that the "West has in fact been a scene of intense struggles over power and hierarchy, not only between the races but also between classes, genders, and other groups within white society." The Turnerians had "offer[ed] cover for the powers that be" and "fail[ed] to see themselves as critical intellectuals." Turner's history was a "celebration of 'my people,'" by a historian playing "the subservient role of cheerleader or defender." Although indebted to the work of their predecessors the new western historians were "ready to perform a very different role in society."[29]

Patricia N. Limerick conceded that Turner had noted the federal government's "vast paternal enterprises of reclamation in the desert" and the revealed "dangers of modern American industrial tendencies" in the Rocky Mountain West. He had urged historians to study the present as well as the past. But the critics of the 1930s and 1940s thoroughly discredited the "Old Western History" based on Turner's work, Limerick believed. Unfortunately, misguided scholars had created a "Restored Old Western History," postponing the possibility of developing "more inclusive models for the teaching and writing of western history."

"The old frontier model relentlessly trivialized the West," maintained Limerick, and "worked against a recognition of the American West as . . . a region of significance with a serious history." Thinking themselves "rigorously neutral, without ideology or bias," its practitioners "placed their sympathies with English-speaking male pioneers and then called that point of view objectivity." In addition, Turner and his followers had ignored major characteristics of the western experience beyond the Midwest—aridity, the continuing presence of Indian peoples, the Hispanic population element, Asian immigration and other Pacific Rim phenomena, unique problems relating to the public domain, undemocratic aspects of government, and twentieth-century developments. "Old Western Historians" told a tale of "progress" and "improvement," ignoring the "roads of western development [that] led directly to failure and to injury." Limerick concluded, "The most fundamental mission of the New Western History is to widen the range and increase the vitality of the search for meaning in the western past. . . . That mission has been accomplished."[30]

Another new western historian, Richard White, associated Turner with the best of the "the Old Western History" and noted that the environment "was central to [his] explanations of the history of the West." But Turner's frontier separated nature and culture, and his subjects were always intent on establishing a new society in the West. Turner posited a "western type" of resident, but, argued White, the diversity of peoples in the West gave the lie to any such type. New western historians, he explained, "look initially at three things . . . the contesting groups . . . their perceptions of the land and their ambitions for it . . . the structures of power that shape the contest." The West of the new western historians is defined by "historically derived relationships . . . not preordained qualities of the land itself or the qualities of any single set of occupants."[31]

Other contributors to *Trails* argued that the frontier concept must be discarded as a key to understanding western history, deploring a definition that described the frontier as the meeting place of savagery and civilization. The West should be viewed, wrote one, "as a cultural crossroads rather than a geographic freeway" and women's role given full treatment at that intersection. For Michael P. Malone, Turner provided "the conceptual lodestone of . . . frontier/western historiography," but he was a historian of the frontier rather than the West. Malone argued for a "new [multifaceted] regional paradigm" in which "the enduring impact of both Turner's frontier and Webb's aridity must be taken into account." But Turner's paradigm was "timeworn [and] "also the fundamental cause of the mischievous treatment of frontier and West—as if the terms were synonymous." To William G. Robbins "the old verities" of Turner's "grand thesis" seemed "quaint and mythical." His was "an argument that fit the prevailing *mentalité* of the patriarchal, Anglo-Saxon–dominated world of the early twentieth century" and made the American frontier "a powerful environmental determinant . . . little influenced by outside forces . . . in shaping human inhabitants to accord with its own requirements." It was a model that was stridently positivist and exceptionalist in emphasis. "It ha[d] been a hard fall," wrote Brian Dippie, "from the heady days when Turner held a chair at Harvard and frontiering defined national history."[32]

In 1987, even as new western historians criticized the Turnerian heritage, William Cronon, a historian sometimes classified among them, found vitality and usefulness in Turner's ideas, while also finding the need for restatement and elaboration. That reformulation would be in accord with Turner's approach—the need to explain different regional outcomes, to enhance our understanding of developing systems of social relations, to learn how differing definitions of regional environment have emerged, how differing visions of optimal use of those environments have interacted, how resources have "shaped" "class consciousness and republican government," and, in broadest sum, how "nature and humanity transform each other." He concluded that we continue to follow Turner's example in "ignoring the walls between disciplines, in his faith that history must in large measure be the story of ordinary people, in his emphasis on the importance of regional environments to our understanding the course of American history." Turner, Cronon concluded, fashioned a "rhetorical framework" that gave "American history its central and most persistent story." In 1991 Cronon wrote that although he was willing to "safely declare the frontier thesis dead, or at least so badly flawed that any new formulation must be built on an entirely redesigned foundation. . . . Whether one speaks of studying comparative frontiers, or colonization, or invasion, or even the legacy of conquest, one proposes to study process rather than region, and the best of Turner's approach will still be very much alive."[33]

Although "new political historians" and electoral geographers of the years from 1955 to 1980 viewed the sectional analysis of Turner and his followers as respectable if dated in quantitative method, Billington was much less impressed by the usefulness of Turner's ideas on sectionalism than by the frontier concept. In the same publication in which Cronon updated his position, however, Michael C. Steiner argued strongly that Turner's sectional thesis provided an important means of understanding American development both in the frontier and postfrontier eras. The sectional thesis actually "anticipated many trends that are revitalizing the field" of western history, wrote Steiner—"an emphasis upon the West as a distinct 'place undergoing conquest'; a concern for common people 'who stayed behind' and inhabited the land; and an interest in a distinctive western 'sense of identity' and an emerging 'cultural voice.'" "At the very least," wrote Steiner, "we should acknowledge Turner's importance as 'a remote ancestor' to contemporary regional studies." Subsequently, he would further elaborate the importance of Turner's ideas about sectionalism. In 1984, political scientist Richard F. Bensel devoted a substantial monograph to arguing that sectionalism was a major force in determining the nature of modern American political development. Scholars were now writing of core, hinterland, and periphery but still emphasizing regional differences. Other scholars seeking to develop the history of American myth, or to limn out the contours of American republican thought, or to describe the evolution of politico-history, also found it necessary to confront Turner.[34]

Scholars who had invested intellectual capital in the Turnerian heritage were not always dispassionate in their responses to the critical onslaught of the New Western Historians. They were, said some defenders of the Turnerian standard, misanthropic spawn of the troubled 1960s. Their leaders had been corrupted by the teachings of Paul de Man and other advocates of deconstruction. And it was true that amid their legitimate criticisms of the state of western history, the new westerners sometimes showed ignorance or misunderstanding of what Turner had actually believed and the contributions that the intervening generations had made.

By the 1990s few American historians could recall the themes or emphases in Channing's multivolume history of the United States or the major works of Turner's other leading contemporaries. The index of *Trails: Toward a New Western History* listed forty references to discussion of new western history. In comparison, there were thirty-five entries for "Frederick Jackson Turner," thirty-one under "Turnerian history," twenty-eight for the heading "myth in Turnerian history," and one under "Turner bashing." Turner, his students, and their work had not been forgotten.

Many have quoted or paraphrased the sentence from Turner's 1891 article on the significance of history, slightly modified in 1910, "Each age writes the history of the past anew with reference to the conditions uppermost in its own time."[35] By that dictum Turner's work should have been discarded, but his resilience suggests that we sometimes read the rule too restrictively. Succeeding generations will quite properly ask new questions of the past. That does not mean that all of the old questions were wrong or cease to have interest.

For Turner's ideas to have survived—at least in many of their elements—beyond his own generation, there needed to be some fundamental substance, or truth, or continuing myth in them that later scholars and Americans continued to accept. Of course, the cynic may suggest that the frontier thesis lived because historians have not been rigorous thinkers and critics. True enough, alas, but insufficient explanation, I believe. Interest in Turner's ideas has continued because he dealt with issues that were of great and continuing concern. For example: Are we as Americans different in character and institutions from citizens of other nations, and in what respects, and why? Was indeed America in the midst of a great sea change as Turner alleged, and if so, what did this mean for subsequent generations? What determines a nation's relations with other polities? How do communities grow, and with what effect upon the participants? How do individuals interact with their natural and social environments? What factors shape economic, social, and political development? How should a nation manage its heritage of natural resources? Why and how do people migrate? What are the processes, benefits, and costs of cultural mingling? In the American case these are not merely theoretical queries—they involved a great human migration and massive impact upon the natural resources of a continent initially, and they still challenge us for answers. Turner spoke to these fundamental questions in such a way that others have been able to use his ideas as starting points, way stations, or rejected formulas in their own efforts to read the meaning of the American past. If we drop our sights to the policy level in the United States, we can quote Limerick, who wrote, "In the second half of the twentieth century, every major issue from 'frontier' history reappeared in the courts or in Congress."[36] As the issues have remained, so has the relevance of studying their background.

There were also personal and institutional factors involved in the resilience of Turner's ideas and reputation. Former students and admirers provided a spirited defense of the frontier legacy during the first generation of criticism subsequent to Turner's death—a defense couched in intellectual terms but fueled as well by the affectionate personal regard with which many viewed him, and by the allure of romance and myth. Dale wrote, "So long as young hearts shall beat a little faster at the recital of the exploits and adventures of the trappers, argonauts, and cowboys . . . or so long as men and women thrill to the story of the pioneers driving their covered wagons out into the sunset . . . just so long will it be remembered that Turner first taught us the significance of these things."[37] Such affirmation was remarkably prolonged. And, in turn, some of the students of Turner's students, or other scholars, took up the cause.

The task of Turner's defenders was made easier because the one-time tutor in oratory used the wiles of the rhetorician in presenting his argument. The task was made easier as well, one suspects, by the imprecisions of definition, the pregnant asides, and the statements of qualification that Turner scattered through his work, as well because of the subtle amplifications and revisions that he inserted in his argument through time. There was a plasticity in Turner's presentation that allowed scholars to use it as the basis for fresh starts. Much of the supportive literature of the years from 1945 to 1975 was based on redefinition of Turner's positions.

In part, Turner's genius lay in his ability to articulate the feelings and needs of his generation. If, during the 1890s, Turner thought in imperial terms even to the point of quoting the poet of imperialism, Rudyard Kipling, to his classes, many Americans of the time were also prepared to quaff that heady brew. (There is, of course, no proof that he regarded his suggestion in the essay of 1893 that Americans might now extend their control beyond the continental borders as a prescription for national policy that he himself favored.) If he argued the importance of midwestern development in American history, midwesterners could but agree. If he believed that recent material development in the United States constituted a "wonderful chapter" in the country's history, his fellow believers in progress could happily assent. If he reaffirmed a story of western influence that was part myth as well as part reality, it was one already accepted by a large constituency. But there was more to his success than this. He stated his message in such a way as to make it acceptable within the academic world. And

significantly, if much of the message was indeed dated, an expression
of the times, Turner also focused—as we have suggested—on themes
that, though reinterpreted, remained relevant in the future. In the
wake of the controversies of the 1980s and early 1990s understanding
of these facts has spread, and in 1995 one leading new westerner could
publish an article in the *American Historical Review* under the lead
title, "Turnerians All."[38]

As Turner admitted, albeit with reluctance, valid criticism could be
made of the frontier hypothesis. His essay of 1893 advanced a thesis,
or, better stated, a set of hypotheses. He noted supporting evidence,
but it was not conclusive. Nor did he thereafter set himself systematically to prove the validity of his argument. He scattered intriguing
bits of proof through his writing, but his analysis was impressionistic
at best and his use of evidence highly repetitive. His model of proof
was sadly underspecified. And sometimes he wrote as though the
frontier thesis or elements of it had long since been graven in stone.
Particularly in the commemorative addresses, assertion ruled. He was
imprecise in definition, using words loosely; his frontier was sometimes boundary, sometimes region, and sometimes process. There
were elements of contradiction in his argument that he did not take
the trouble to resolve—in print at least.

In 1893 Turner had in effect challenged historians to lay bare the
laws of social development. Neither he nor the members of his profession had gone far in responding. Turner professed to be interested in
explaining American evolution in broadest terms, but he really
focused on two or three major elements of that development. He
repeatedly endorsed the technique of multiple hypotheses—actually
misnaming it sometimes—without himself using it. He believed that
interaction between humans and their environment shaped human
behavior and thought, but physiographic influences dominated his
treatment of environment. His conception of space as being made up
of wilderness, zone of frontier processes, and civilization was a highly
restricted view of the interaction of man, woman, and the natural
world—all the more circumscribed because he viewed frontier processes primarily from the standpoint of a particular congeries of male
participants. Much of the context of social and scientific theory in
which he originally presented his ideas—organic evolution, stage

theory, survivals, social forces—was in disrepute by the time of his death. Although he rightly prided himself on the introduction of economic and social dimensions into American history, his social history lacked the rich texture that later social historians provided. Although Turner urged investigation of literature, art, and the history of ideas, little of this appears in his own work. He used the word *culture*, or synonyms for it, but failed to exploit its analytical implications. Turner's correspondence shows that he acknowledged the power of individuals to influence history, but in his writings he reified social forces. Individuals, when introduced, were usually prototypical figures. Generation by generation, critics identified missing elements in Turner's approach—substantive evidence, comparative analysis, other causal elements, the presence and activity of particular social and ethnic groups, and indignation at the waste of human and natural resources and other shameful aspects of western development. But the vitality—the continuing "truth"—inherent in Turner's ideas and their match with American values and expectations insured that his work remained interesting.

It is ironic that historians have focused particularly on Turner's understanding of the frontier, because it was not his primary interest through much of his career. He used the word *frontier* only in passing in his presidential address to the AHA. But his uncertain health led him to collect the frontier essays, and later defenders of his contributions concentrated upon their frontier element. As practicing craftsman, as teacher of advanced students, Turner was most impressive in his analysis of sectionalism as a national phenomenon. Although in other respects he gave full measure, he failed in one dimension to measure up to those obligations that he and his peers believed scholars should fulfill. He did not in his lifetime produce the "big book," as his contemporaries defined it. But, in sum, he served his profession magnificently, and he provided an explanation of American development and character that was not to be matched in popularity during his lifetime or later. In retrospect, we detect flaws as well as grandeur in that contribution, but it was *Turner's* achievement, and in justification of it he might have answered in the words of one of his favorite poets, "Anybody might have found it, but—His Whisper came to Me!"[39]

Appendix
Turner Correspondence
Box References

GENERAL CORRESPONDENCE
(HEHT Boxes 1–63)

Box 1: 1879–94
Box 2: 1895–99
Box 3: 1900–02
Box 4: 1903–04
Box 5: 1905
Box 6: 1906 (Jan.–March)
Box 7: 1907 (April–Dec.)
Box 8: 1907 (Jan.–March)
Box 9: 1907 (April–June)
Box 9A: 1907 (July–Dec.)
Box 10: 1908 (Jan.–April)
Box 11: 1908 (May–Dec.)
Box 12: 1909 (Jan.–Sept.)
Box 13: 1909 (Oct.–Dec.)
Box 14: 1910 (Jan.–May)
Box 15: 1910 (June–Dec.)
Box 16: 1911 (Jan.–Dec.)
Box 17: 1912 (Jan.–May)
Box 18: 1912 (June–Dec.)
Box 19: 1913 (Jan.–May)
Box 20: 1913 (June–Oct.
Box 20A: 1913 (Nov.–Dec.)
Box 21: 1914 (Jan.–July)
Box 22: 1914 (Aug.–Dec.)
Box 23: 1915 (Jan.–Feb.)
Box 24: 1915 (March–May)
Box 25: 1915 (June–Dec.)
Box 26: 1916 (Jan.–Dec.)
Box 27: 1917 (Jan.–Dec.)
Box 28: 1918 (Jan.–Dec.)

Box 29: 1919 (Jan.–Dec.)
Box 30: 1920 (Jan.–Dec.)
Box 31: 1921 and 1922
Box 32: 1923 (Jan.–Dec.)
Box 33: 1924 (Jan.–Dec.)
Box 34: 1925 (Jan.–June)
Box 34A: 1925 (July–Dec.)
Box 35: 1926 (Jan.–June)
Box 35A: 1926 (July–Dec.)
Box 36: 1927 (Jan.–June)
Box 37: 1927 (July–Dec.)
Box 38: 1928 (Jan.–March)
Box 39: 1928 (April–Aug.)
Box 40: 1928 (Sept.–Dec.)
Box 41: 1929 (Jan.–April)
Box 42: 1929 (May–Dec.)
Box 43: 1930 (Jan.–Feb.)
Box 44: 1930 (March–June)
Box 44A: 1930 (July–Dec.)
Box 45: 1931 (Jan.–June)
Box 46: 1931 (July–Dec.)
Box 47: 1932 (Jan.–March)
Box 48: 1932 (April–June 10)
Box 49: 1932 (June 11–Dec.)
Box 50: 1933 (Jan.–April)
Box 50A: 1933 (May–Dec.)
Box 51: 1934 (Jan.–Dec.)
Box 52: 1935–63
Box 53: 1907–33
Box 54: 1877–99
Box 55: 1900–10
Box 56: 1911–26

Box 57: 1927–55
Box 58: Photographs
Box 59: Ephemera (1880–1928)
Box 60: Ephemera (1929–47)
          Fragmentary letters
          Newspaper clippings
Box 61: Business papers,
          receipts, etc.
Box 62: Pocket diary pages
          Scrapbook kept by
          Turner
          Genealogical data
          Miscellaneous sketches
Box 63: Correspondence to and
          from Henry Holt
          and Co.

FAMILY CORRESPONDENCE
(HEHTF Boxes A–K)

Box A: 1862–1887 (May)
Box B: 1887 (June–Dec.)
Box C: 1888 (Jan.–Sept.)
Box D: 1888 (Oct.)–1889 (July)
Box E: 1889 (Aug.)–1893
Box F: 1894–1904
Box G: 1905–10
Box H: 1911–13
Box I: 1914–21
Box J: 1922–26
Box K: 1927–39

TURNER-HOOPER
CORRESPONDENCE
(HEHTH Boxes 1–8)

TU–H Box 1: 1910–12
TU–H Box 2: 1913–14
TU–H Box 3: 1915–17 (June)
TU–H Box 4: 1917 (July)–1919
TU–H Box 5: 1920–24
TU–H Box 6: 1925–26
TU H Box 7: 1927–29
TU–H Box 8: 1930–44

Notes

Chapter 1

1. Mary O. Turner to her sister, Martha, 22 January 1862, Frederick Jackson Turner Papers, Henry E. Huntington Library. The writing of this letter was extended over several weeks. Hereafter I shall use the abbreviation HEHT to identify the location of letters or letter copies in the manuscript boxes containing general correspondence relating to Turner's career. Letters in the Turner Family correspondence, a subpart of the larger collection, will be designated by HEHTF and in the Turner-Hooper correspondence by HEHTH. Collection box numbers can be identified through reference to the appendix but will be identified in the notes for special items.

2. Butterfield, *History of Columbia County*, 2: 538, 930–31; Berthrong, "Andrew J. Turner, 'Work Horse' of the Republican Party," 77–86.

3. Frederick Jackson Turner, "Genealogical Notes," HEHT, Box 62.

4. *United States Census, Columbia County, Wisconsin* (Population Schedules, Microfilm, 1870, 1880).

5. Originals or copies of the autobiographical letters are found in the Turner Papers. Ray A. Billington made most of these letters more conveniently available by reprinting them in *The Genesis of the Frontier Thesis: A Study in Historical Creativity*. See Frederick J. Turner to Constance Lindsay Skinner, 15 March 1922, 205–16; Turner to Carl L. Becker, 16 December 1925, 234–44; Turner to Merle E. Curti, 8 August 1928, 257–65, HEHT. Turner covered much of the same early ground with some variation in his letter to Alice F. B. Hooper, 13 February 1921, HEHTH. Most of the letters between Turner and Hooper later cited are also to be found in Billington, *Dear Lady: The Letters of Frederick Jackson Turner and Alice Forbes Perkins Hooper*. See 323–27.

6. Mermin, *The Fox-Wisconsin Rivers Improvement*. The best account of the early development of Columbia County and Portage is provided by Butterfield, *Columbia County*. Two volumes give an

excellent introduction to Wisconsin history during Turner's years in
Portage: Nesbit and Thompson, *Wisconsin: A History*; and Current,
History of Wisconsin, Volume II: The Civil War Era: 1848–1873.

7. Butterfield, *Columbia County*, 2:588.

8. Ibid., 599.

9. See note 5, above.

10. Butterfield, *Columbia County*, 2:643.

11. Turner to Caroline Mae Sherwood, 20 May 1888,
HEHTF.

12. Turner to Dorothy Turner Main, 12 December 1917,
HEHTF.

13. Andrew Jackson Turner, in Butterfield, *Columbia
County*, 538.

14. Turner to Caroline, 15 June 1887, HEHTF.

15. In his later years Andrew Jackson Turner used some of
this material as the basis of a small book. See Andrew Jackson Turner, *The
Family Tree of Columbia County, Wisconsin*. Joseph Schafer believed that
Turner wrote much of the 1880 Columbia County history, edited by
Butterfield. See Mood and Edwards, "Frederick Jackson Turner's 'History
of the Grignon Tract,'" 113, n. 3.

16. Turner clipped the *Wisconsin State Register*'s account
of the graduation published on 6 July 1878 and pasted it in his "Scrapbook,"
Box 55, HEHT. The text is reprinted in Carpenter, *The Eloquence of
Frederick Jackson Turner*, 117–20.

17. Carpenter, *Eloquence*, 117–18.

18. Ibid., 118–19.

19. Ibid., 119–20.

20. Andrew Jackson Turner to Fred Turner, 21 August 1878,
HEHTF.

21. Ibid.; Jones, "Miles Talcott Alverson," in *A History of
Columbia County, Wisconsin* 2:575–76.

22. University of Wisconsin Transcript, "Classical," Fred
Jackson Turner.

23. Turner, "Scrapbook"; Carpenter, *Eloquence of Frederick
Jackson Turner*, 15–16.

24. Carpenter, *Eloquence of Frederick Jackson Turner*. This
author was not the first to speculate about the rhetorical elements in
Turner's work. See Berquist, "The Rhetorical Heritage of Frederick
Jackson Turner," 23–32.

25. Turner, "Commonplace Book," Vol. III, HEHT. The list ends with 1883; Turner probably prepared it at the conclusion of his junior year. The pages in "The Commonplace Book" are not numbered.

26. Turner "Scrapbook," columns from the *Portage Republican*, dated 13, 14, 15 February 1882.

27. Mood, "Frederick Jackson Turner and the Milwaukee *Sentinel*, 1884," 21–28, discusses Turner's relationship with *The Badger*.

28. Turner, "Eulogy of David B. Frankenburger" in Carpenter, *Eloquence of Frederick Jackson Turner*, 132.

29. David B. Frankenburger, "Memoir of William Francis Allen," in Allen, *Essays and Monographs*, 13.

30. Hall, ed., *Methods of Teaching History*; Vincent, et al., *Herbert Baxter Adams—Tributes*, 40.

31. Turner to Caroline, 12 December 1886, HEHTF.

32. Frankenburger, "Memoir," 17.

33. W. F. Allen Notebook, "History of Civilization," a course lecture outline, currently in Andrew Jackson Turner and Frederick Jackson Turner Papers, Box 3, State Historical Society of Wisconsin, Manuscript Collections. The handwriting is not that of Turner, and on the cover "W. F. Allen" is faintly printed. Since Turner took over Allen's courses for the remainder of the academic year after the latter's death, it is reasonable to assume that this was Allen's course outline book.

34. Turner Notebook, "Ancient Institutions," Turner Papers, Box 3, State Historical Society of Wisconsin; Allen, *Essays and Monographs*, 215–30 (quoted passage appears on p. 224). This essay was reprinted from Wisconsin Academy of Sciences, Arts, and Letters, *Transactions* 6 (1886).

35. Allen, *Essays and Monographs*, 344–50, 92–111, reprinted from *Nation* 26 (10 January 1878); Allen, "The Place of the Northwest," 3:331–48 (quoted passages appear on pp. 347, 348).

36. Carpenter, *Eloquence*, 121, 122, 123–24.

37. Ibid., 125–26. The text refers to "logwood," but Turner surely used "lopwood," denoting discarded material.

38. Turner's description of Draper is in Turner to Caroline Mae Sherwood, 16 October 1887, HEHTF; Turner, "History of the 'Grignon Tract.'" Mood and Edwards prepared a short introduction for a reprinting of this little history, "Frederick Jackson Turner's 'History of the Grignon Tract on the Portage of the Fox and Wisconsin Rivers,'" *Agricultural History* 17 (April 1943): 113–20. Admitting the "modest"

nature of the contribution, Mood and Edwards explained, "the earliest works of men of genius will never lack for interest" (114).

39. The "Class Book of the Class of 1884" contains a history of the class and sketches of the graduates of that year, handwritten and organized alphabetically on unnumbered pages. Joseph Schafer quoted the class prophecy in "The Author of the 'Frontier Hypothesis,'" *Wisconsin Magazine of History* 15 (September 1931): 89.

CHAPTER 2

1. In the following paragraphs I depend particularly upon Fulmer Mood, "Frederick Jackson Turner and the Milwaukee *Sentinel*, 1884," 21–28, and "Frederick Jackson Turner and the Chicago *Inter-Ocean*, 1885," 188–94, 210–18.

2. Mood, "Turner and the Milwaukee *Sentinel*," 25. The description is from Turner to Caroline Mae Sherwood, 23 May 1888, HEHTF. Merle Curti and Vernon Carstensen examined the warfare between the University of Wisconsin Regents and President Bascom in *The University of Wisconsin: A History 1848–1925*, 1:246–74.

3. Mood, "Turner and the Milwaukee *Sentinel*," 27.

4. Martin, *The Life and Thought of Isaiah Bowman*, 121.

5. Turner to Caroline Mae Sherwood, undated but no doubt from January 1887. The salutation, "My Little Sunbeam," is one of many that Turner used. Andrew Jackson Turner to Frederick J. Turner ("My Dear Fritz"), 6 February 1887, HEHTF.

6. Turner to Caroline, 11 September, fall (undated), 28 August 1887, HEHTF.

7. Turner to Caroline, 27 June 1886, HEHTF.

8. Turner to Andrew Jackson Turner, 27 June 1887, Turner to Ellen B. Turner, 30 June 1887, HEHTF.

9. Turner to Mary O. Turner, 30 June 1887, Andrew Jackson Turner to Turner, 3 July 1887, Turner to Caroline, 18 August 1887, HEHTF.

10. Turner to Caroline, 24 August 1887, HEHTF.

11. Turner to Caroline [two letters of late August 1887], 5 September 1887, HEHTF.

12. Turner to Mary O. and Andrew Jackson Turner, 23 September 1885, HEHTF.

13. Turner to Caroline, 11 May 1887, HEHTF.

14. Turner to Caroline, 23 October, 15 June 1887, HEHTF.

15. Turner to Caroline, 11 May 1887, HEHTF.

16. Turner to Caroline, 5 September 1887 and fall 1887 [undated], HEHTF.

17. Turner to Caroline, 4, 11 September 1887, and 26 January 1889, HEHTF.

18. Turner to Caroline, 28 June, 18 August, 1887, HEHTF.

19. Turner to Caroline, 6 September, 23 October 1887, HEHTF.

20. Turner to Caroline, 11 December 1887, HEHTF.

21. Turner to Caroline, 2, 11 December 1887, HEHTF.

22. Turner to Caroline, 5, 10 March 1888, HEHTF.

23. Turner to Caroline, 25 March, 21 April, 2, 7 May 1888, HEHTF.

24. Turner to Caroline, 13 April 1888, HEHTF.

25. Turner's paper on the fur trade would be read before the Historical Society. Although he put it to various uses, Turner did not publish the paper on the Ordinance.

26. Turner to Caroline, 7 September 1888, HEHTF.

27. Turner to Caroline, 25 September 1888, HEHTF.

28. Herbert B. Adams, *The College of William and Mary*, U.S. Bureau of Education, Circulars of Information, no. I, 1887, 73–74, cited in Holt, ed., *Historical Scholarship*, 94, n. 1.

29. Vincent, et al., *Herbert B. Adams: Tributes*, 41–42, 45–46.

30. Turner to Caroline, 7, 12 October 1888, 18 April and April (?) 1889, HEHTF.

31. Turner to William F. Allen, 31 October 1888, Allen to Turner, 14 October 1888, HEHT.

32. Adams, "Special Methods of Historical Study, as Pursued at the Johns Hopkins University and Formerly Smith College," in Hall, ed., *Methods of Teaching History*, 124. This passage appears in the first edition, 1883, p. 160.

33. Turner to Frederick W. Moore, 14 September 1903. This letter was in response to an inquiry from Moore concerning the development of history teaching at Wisconsin and was kindly brought to my attention by Professor Paul H. Hardacre.

34. Turner to Allen, 31 October 1888, HEHT.

35. Turner to Caroline, 6 October 1888, HEHTF.

36. Turner to Allen, 14 March 1889, HEHT.

37. Gettleman, *The Johns Hopkins University Seminary of History and Politics*, 2:540.

38. Turner to Caroline, 27 December 1888, HEHTF.

39. John Franklin Jameson to John Jameson, 5 January 1889, in Donnan and Stock, eds., *An Historian's World*, 46.

40. Allen, "The Place of the Northwest in General History," 3:331–48; Turner to Allen, 31 December 1888, HEHT.

41. Turner to Caroline, 26 January, 13, 28 February, 6 March 1889, HEHTF; Turner to Allen, 14 March 1889, HEHT.

42. Turner, "Fur Trade," *Proceedings*, 52–98.

43. Francis Parkman to Frederick Jackson Turner, 2 May 1889, HEHT.

44. Turner to William Francis Allen, 31 December 1888, HEHT.

45. Turner to Caroline, 8, 21, 26 January 1889, HEHTF.

46. Turner to Caroline, 3, 22, 28 February 1889, HEHTF.

47. Turner to Caroline [undated, spring 1889], HEHTF.

48. Turner to Caroline, 21, 24 June 1889, HEHTF.

49. Allen, "Gradation and the Topical Method of Historical Study," in Hall, ed., *Methods of Teaching History*, 5.

50. Turner to Caroline, 13 August 1888, HEHTF.

51. Turner to William F. Allen, 31 October 1888, HEHT.

52. Turner to Caroline, undated letter in folder dated 19 April 1888, HEHTF.

53. Turner to Caroline, fragment *c.* 30 December 1888, 14 May 1889, HEHTF; Turner to William F. Allen, 31 December 1888, HEHT.

54. Turner to Caroline, 15 September 1889, HEHTF.

55. Turner to H. B. Adams, 10 December 1889, HEHT.

CHAPTER 3

1. Frederick J. Turner to Herbert Baxter Adams, 11 January 1890, in Holt, *Historical Scholarship in the United States, 1876–1901*, 123; Turner to Woodrow Wilson, 23 January 1890, HEHT. The Turner-Wilson correspondence is also available in Link, ed., *The Papers of Woodrow Wilson*, vols. 6, 8, 9, 10, 11.

2. Turner to Wilson, 23 January 1890, HEHT. Link reads the concluding words of this sentence as "for my official head!"

3. Turner to Wilson, 5 February 1890, HEHT.

4. Reuben G. Thwaites to Wilson, 23 December 1889, HEHT.

5. Turner to Wilson, 5 February 1890, HEHT.

6. Turner to Caroline Mae Sherwood, 8 September 1889, HEHTF.

7. University of Wisconsin, *Catalogue, 1891–92*, 98.

8. Ford, "Testimonials from Former Students," in Jacobs, *On Turner's Trail*, 272–73.

9. Becker, "Frederick Jackson Turner," in Odum, et al., *American Masters of Social Science*, 273–318 (quoted phrase, p. 276).

10. Matthew B. Hammond to Turner, 7 May 1910, HEHT, "Red Book." (The "Red Book" is a red-bound notebook in which are pasted the supportive letters written to Turner by former students when he left the University of Wisconsin.) Kellogg, "The Passing of a Great Teacher— Frederick Jackson Turner," 270.

11. James A. James to Herbert B. Adams, 8 April 1891, in Holt, ed., *Historical Scholarship*, 151.

12. University of Wisconsin, *Catalogue, 1891–92*, 86. For general background see Cook, "A History of Liberal Education at the University of Wisconsin, 1862–1918."

13. Turner to Richard T. Ely, 25 January 1892, Ely Papers, State Historical Society of Wisconsin, Madison; Charles H. Haskins to Ely, 25 January 1892, Ely Papers.

14. Turner to Ely, 8 February, 14 March 1892, Ely Papers.

15. Turner to Ely, 29 January 1892, Ely Papers.

16. Ibid.

17. Turner to Ely, 1 February 1892, Ely Papers.

18. Turner to Ely, 19 February 1892, Ely Papers.

19. Turner to Ely, 19, 28 February 1892, Ely Papers.

20. Ely to Turner, 13 February 1892, HEHT.

21. Thomas C. Chamberlin to Ely, 27 June 1892, Ely Papers.

22. Turner to Ely, 11 April 1892, Ely Papers.

23. This was the committee to which was referred the matter of the handbook of graduate study and the general question of the relation of the University of Wisconsin to graduate work. "Report," 11 February 1895, Ely Papers. Ely chaired this committee, and Turner was among its members.

24. Turner to Adams, 26 February 1892, HEHT; Ely, *Ground Under Our Feet*, 179.

25. Louise P. Kellogg, "Preface," in Turner, *The Early Writings of Frederick Jackson Turner*, v.

26. Turner, "Fur Trade," *Proceedings*, 53, 54, 62.

27. Turner, "Fur Trade," *Proceedings*, 92, 98.

28. Lucien Carr to Turner, 8 May 1889, HEHT; Turner to Caroline, 14 May 1889, HEHTF.

29. Turner, *The Character and Influence of the Indian Trade in Wisconsin*, 82, 84. For convenience I have used the reprinting edited by David H. Miller and William W. Savage, Jr. (Norman: University of Oklahoma Press, 1977). Note also the editors' thoughtful introduction.

30. Turner, "Fur Trade," *Proceedings*, 78.

31. Ibid., 61.

32. Turner, *Character and Influence of the Indian Trade*, 18, 84–85.

33. Ibid., 5. Here Turner introduces the "primitive/advanced" contrast but elsewhere repeats the dichotomy of the Wisconsin paper, contrasting savagery and civilization (Miller and Savage, eds., "Introduction," xviii–xx).

34. Turner, "Significance of History," *Early Writings*, 43, 45, 46, 47, 48.

35. Ibid., 49, 51, 52.

36. Ibid., 52–53.

37. Ibid., 53–55.

38. Ibid., 57.

39. Ibid., 64–65. The quoted passage is found in Adams, "Special Methods in Historical Study," 126–27. Turner interjected the first three words of the final sentence, after deleting several sentences including Adams's seeming endorsement of Freeman's dictum.

40. Ibid., 58, 63.

41. Ibid., 65–66, 67.

42. Ibid., 68.

43. Adams, "The Teaching of History," 247.

44. Turner, "American Colonization," draft paper, File Drawer 15, A, HEHT.

45. Turner, "Problems in American History," *Early Writings*, 71.

46. Ibid., 72.

47. Ibid., 73–74.

48. Ibid., 74, 76.

49. Ibid., 77.

50. Ibid., 78.

51. Ibid., 78–82.

52. Ibid., 82–83.

53. Turner, "Franklin in France," *Dial* 8 (May 1887): 7–10 and "Franklin the Peacemaker," *Dial* 9 (December 1888): 204–206, reviews of Edward E. Hale and Edward E. Hale, Jr., *Franklin In France* (1887, 1889); Turner, (unsigned) review of James R. Gilmore (Edmund Kirke), *John Sevier as a Commonwealth-Builder: A Sequel to the Rear-Guard of the Revolution* (1887), *Nation* (6 October 1887 [No. 1162]): 278.

54. Turner, "The Winning of the West," review of *The Winning of the West*, by Theodore Roosevelt, 2 vols. (1889), *Dial* 10 (August 1889): 71–73.

55. Turner, "The Journal of a Pennsylvania Senator," review of *Journal of William Maclay, U.S. Senator from Pennsylvania, 1789– 1791*, ed. by Edgar S. Maclay (1890), *Dial* 12 (July 1891): 78–81; Turner, "A New History of America," review of *History of the New World Called America*, by Edward John Payne, vol. 1 (1892), *Dial* 13 (December 1892): 389–91.

Chapter 4

1. Turner, "Significance of the Frontier," *Frontier in American History*, 1, 22, 37, 38.

2. Ibid., 1, 38.

3. Ibid., 11.

4. Ibid., 32, 37, 38.

5. Ibid., 1 (this author's italics), 3, 10.

6. Turner, "Problems," *Early Writings*, 72; Turner, "Significance of the Frontier," *Frontier*, 3.

7. Turner, "Problems," *Early Writings*, 72; Turner, "Significance of the Frontier," *Frontier*, 1.

8. Turner, "Significance of the Frontier," *Frontier*, 2; "Problems," *Early Writings*, 73.

9. Turner, "Problems," *Early Writings*, 76; Turner, "Significance of the Frontier," *Frontier*, 14–15.

10. Turner, "Problems," *Early Writings*, 83; Turner, "Significance of the Frontier," *Frontier*, 38. Italics added in this text.

11. Turner, "Significance of the Frontier," *Frontier*, 12, 20, 3.

12. Turner, "Problems," *Early Writings*, 77; Turner, "Significance of the Frontier," *Frontier*, 3, 10.

13. Turner, "Significance of the Frontier," *Frontier*, 11.

14. Ibid., 6, 18.

15. Turner, "American Colonization," File Drawer 15A, HEHT.

16. Turner, "Significance of the Frontier," *Frontier*, 3.

17. Charles Kendall Adams to W. W. Appleton, 17 July 1893 and to Charles C. Sonney, 21 October 1893, Charles Kendall Adams Papers.

18. Turner, "Significance of the Frontier," *Frontier*, 25, n. 42.

19. Nixon, "Precursors of Turner in the Interpretation of the American Frontier," 83–89.

20. J. Hector St. John de Crevecoeur, *Letters from an American Farmer*, 40, 42–43.

21. Dwight, *Travels in New England and New York*, 1:7.

22. Godkin, "Aristocratic Opinions of Democracy," *North American Review*, 209. According to Turner, this essay first came to his attention after Godkin republished it in a collection of his essays, *Problems of Modern Democracy*, 1–67. Andrew C. McLaughlin made reference to it in commenting on Turner's paper at the AHA meeting in 1896.

23. Ibid., 209, 212, 218, 222–23.

24. Ibid., 232.

25. George, *Progress and Poverty*, 389–90.

26. Baldwin, "The Centre of the Republic," 412.

27. Ibid., 413, 417.

28. Malin, in *Essays on Historiography*, p. 33, notes this passage.

29. Mood, "The Development of Frederick Jackson Turner as a Historical Thinker," 283–352.

30. The interdiction did not prevail completely. Henry Nash Smith cites Turner's "Commonplace Book" and other materials in the Turner Papers in *Virgin Land: The American West as Symbol and Myth*. See notes, pp. 294–97, 302, 303.

31. Loria, *Analisi della Proprieta Capitalista*; George, *Progress and Poverty*; Bagehot, *Physics and Politics*; Bryce, *The American Commonwealth*; Doyle, *English Colonies in America*; Payne, *History of the New World Called America*, vol. 1; Barrows, *The Indian's Side of the Indian Question*; W. Stull Holt, "Hegel, the Turner Hypothesis, and the Safety Valve Theory," 175–76.

32. Turner, "American Colonization," File Drawer 15, A, HEHT.

33. Benson, "Loria's Influence on American Economic Thought," in Benson, *Turner and Beard: American Historical Writing Reconsidered*, 33–34.

34. Billington, *Frederick Jackson Turner*, 124. Some pages are missing from the text of "American Colonization," but they appeared at a point in the manuscript where it would have been most unlikely for Turner to have mentioned the free lands of western America. Billington would describe Benson's theorizing as "ingenuous."

35. Francis A. Walker to Turner, 31 January 1894, John Fiske to Turner, 6 February 1894, Theodore Roosevelt to Turner, 10 February 1894, HEHT.

36. Strout, *The Pragmatic Revolt in American History*; Noble, *Historians Against History*; Noble, *The End of American History*; Hofstadter, *The Progressive Historians*, xii, 48, 73; Breisach, *American Progressive History*.

Chapter 5

1. William P. Trent to George P. Brett, 14 March 1896, HEHT. Copies of this and other Brett correspondence were obtained from the Macmillan Company Archives and added to the Huntington collections by Billington.

2. Slaughter, *Only the Past is Ours*, 111, 208.

3. Turner to Caroline M. Turner, 30 June 1898, HEHT.

4. Billington, *Frederick Jackson Turner*, 135–36; University of Wisconsin, *Catalogue, 1895–96*, 140.

5. University of Wisconsin, *Catalogue, 1891–92*, 98, *1892–93*, 62, *1893–94*, 72, *1895–96*, 140.

6. Turner, *Outline Studies in the History of the Northwest*; Turner to William F. Allen, 16 January, 14 March 1889, HEHT.

7. University of Wisconsin, *Catalogue, 1891–92*, 99, *1896–97*, 144.

8. Jacobs, *On Turner's Trail*, 273; Louise P. Kellogg to James A. James, undated letter, "Red Book," 1910, HEHT; Florence P. Robinson [to James A. James], undated letter [1910], "Red Book."

9. Jacobs, *On Turner's Trail*, 265.

10. Turner, "Problems in American History," *Sections*, 3.

11. Turner to Alfred B. Hart, 5 March 1897, HEHT.

12. Curti and Carstensen, *The University of Wisconsin, A History*, 1:525.

13. Ely, et al., "Report" of "The Committee to which was referred the matter of the hand-book of graduate study, and the general question of the relation of the University of Wisconsin to graduate work," 11 February 1895, Ely Papers.

14. Turner to J. Franklin Jameson, 1 August 1895, HEHT.

15. Turner, "Western State-Making in the Revolutionary Era," *Sections*, 86–88.

16. Ibid., 93, 133, 136, 138.

17. Turner, "The West as a Field for Historical Study," American Historical Association, *Report*, 1896, 282.

18. Ibid., 282–83.

19. Ibid., 283, 284.

20. Ibid., 285–86.

21. Ibid., 287.

22. Woodrow Wilson, "Remarks," American Historical Association, *Report*, 1896, 292, 294.

23. Nettels, *The Roots of American Civilization*, 678, n. 28.

24. Turner, "The Problem of the West," *Frontier*, 205–6.

25. Ibid., 210, 211.

26. Ibid., 219, 220–21.

27. Ibid., 221.

28. Turner, "Dominant Forces in Western Life," *Frontier*, 238, 239.

29. Ibid., 239, 240, 242.

30. Ibid., 236.

31. Hall, "Physical Geography and History," in Hall, ed., *Methods of Teaching History*, 224. This chapter carried through without change from the first (1883) edition.

32. Mood, "The Development of Frederick Jackson Turner as a Historical Thinker," 309.

33. Turner, *The Character and Influence of the Indian Trade*, 24, 22.

34. Turner's address to Chicago geographers, "Influence of Geography upon the Settlement of the United States," has the notation "Chi Geographic Society" written in the upper right-hand corner of the first

page. File Drawer 14, A, HEHT. It is quoted by Robert H. Block, "Frederick Jackson Turner and American Geography," *Annals of the Association of American Geographers* 70 (March 1980): 36–37.

35. Turner, "A Comparison of Differing Versions of 'The Significance of the Frontier,'" *Early Writings*, 275–92.

36. Ibid., 284, 289.

37. Ibid., 280.

38. Ibid., 284, 288, 291, 292.

39. Turner, "Roosevelt's Winning of the West," (unsigned) review of *The Winning of the West and the Southwest, from the Alleghanies to the Mississippi, 1769–1790*, by Theodore Roosevelt, 3 vols., 1895, *Nation* 60 (28 March 1895): 240–42.

40. Roosevelt to Turner, 2, 10, 26 April 1895, HEHT.

41. Turner, review of *Louisiana and the Northwest, 1791–1807*, by Theodore Roosevelt (1896), *American Historical Review* 2 (October 1896): 171–76.

42. Turner, "Crossing the Continent," review of *History of the Expedition under the Command of Lewis and Clark to the sources of the Missouri River, thence across the Rocky Mountains*, ed. by Elliott Coues (1893), *Dial* 16 (1 February 1894): 80–82.

43. Turner, "Francis Parkman and His Work," review of *Francis Parkman's Works* (1898), *Dial* 25 (16 December 1898): 451, 453, 452.

44. Turner, review of *Conquest of the Country Northwest of the River Ohio, 1778–1783, 1778–1783, and Life of Gen. George Rogers Clark*, by William Hayden English (1896), *American Historical Review* 2 (January 1897): 363–66.

45. Turner, review of *The Westward Movement. The Colonies and the Republic West of the Alleghanies, 1763–1789*, by Justin Winsor (1897), *American Historical Review* 3 (April 1898): 556–61.

46. Turner to Charles H. Haskins, 16 July 1895, HEHT.

47. Turner, review of *History of the United States from the Compromise of 1850*, by James Ford Rhodes, Vol. III: 1860–1862 (1895), *American Historical Review* 11 (March 1896): 167–70.

48. Turner, review of *The Growth of the American Nation*, by Harry P. Judson (1895), *American Historical Review* 1 (April 1896): 549–50.

49. Turner, "Recent Studies in American History," *Atlantic Monthly* 77 (June 1896): 837–44. This review essay discusses the following works: *Economic History of Virginia in the Seventeenth Century. An*

Inquiry into the Material Condition of the People, based upon Original and Contemporaneous Records, by Philip A. Bruce (In two volumes. New York: Macmillan & Co. 1896), pp. 837–39; *The Economic and Social History of New England, 1620–1789,* by William B. Weeden (In two volumes. Boston: Houghton, Mifflin & Co. 1890), p. 839; *History of the United States under the Constitution,* by James Schouler (In five volumes. New York: Dodd, Mead & Co. 1895), pp. 839–40; *A History of the People of the United States,* by John B. McMaster (Volume IV. New York: D. Appleton & Co. 1895), pp. 840–41; *Reconstruction during the Civil War in the United States of America,* by Eben G. Scott. (Boston: Houghton, Mifflin and Co. 1895), pp. 842–43. In this article Turner also commented (pp. 840–41) upon Volume 3 of James F. Rhodes's study, which he reviewed for the *American Historical Review.*

50. Turner, review of *A Student's History of the United States,* by Edward Channing (1898), *Educational Review* 18 (October 1899): 301–4.

51. Turner, "Recent Studies in American History," 839, 843.

52. Turner, review of *The American Revolution,* by George Otto Trevelyan, Part I, 1766–1776 (1899), *American Historical Review* 5 (October 1899): 141–44.

53. Turner, review of *A History of Political Parties in the United States,* by J. P. Gordy, Vol. I (1895), *Political Science Quarterly* 12 (March 1897): 163–64.

54. Turner, review of *The Middle Period, 1817–1858,* by John W. Burgess (1897), *Educational Review* 14 (November 1897): 390–95.

55. Turner, "Essay on History of U.S. by Von Holst, 189–," File Drawer 15, A, HEHT.

56. Turner, "Recent Studies," 837.

CHAPTER 6

1. Frederick J. Turner to George P. Brett, 28 March 1896, HEHT.

2. Brett to Turner, 4 April 1896, Turner note at bottom, Katie Stephens to Turner, 3 June 1897, HEHT.

3. J. S. Phillips to Turner, 9 October 1896, S.S. McClure to Turner, 19 October 1896, HEHT.

4. George H. Putnam to Turner, 27 March, 7 April, 25 September 1897, HEHT.

5. Brett to Turner, 18 September 1897, 8 October 1897, 3 November 1897, HEHT.

6. Henry Holt and Co. to Turner (Dear Sir), 16 February 1895, Henry Holt and Co. (Edward N. Bristol) to Turner, 26 October 1897, HEHT.

7. Turner, "Introduction to a College History of the United States," in Jacobs, *Frederick Jackson Turner's Legacy*, 191–92.

8. Andrew Jackson Turner to Turner, 18 March 1891, HEHT.

9. Turner to Woodrow Wilson, 8 November 1896, HEHT. The original of this letter and other Turner letters to Wilson are in the Wilson Papers, Library of Congress and are reproduced in Link, ed., *The Papers of Woodrow Wilson*.

10. Wilson to Turner, 15 November 1896, Turner to Wilson, 27 November 1896, HEHT.

11. Wilson to Turner, 30 November 1896, Turner to Wilson, 3 December 1896, HEHT. Ernest Lavisse and Charles Victor Langlois were distinguished professors at the Sorbonne. The latter coauthored a long-used manual on historical methods.

12. Turner to Wilson, 18, 27 December 1896, HEHT.

13. Wilson to Ellen Axson Wilson, 29 January 1897, *Papers of Woodrow Wilson*, 10:123; Wilson to Turner, 31 March 1897, HEHT.

14. Turner to Wilson, 3 April 1897, HEHT.

15. John B. McMaster to Turner, 12 April 1897, James H. Robinson to Turner, 12 April 1897, HEHT.

16. University of Wisconsin Board of Regents, Minutes, "E," 23 June 1897, University Archives, University of Wisconsin, Madison, Wisconsin.

17. Turner to Wilson, 12 March 1900, HEHT.

18. Turner to Caroline M. Turner, 23 February 1894, HEHTF.

19. Wilson to Turner, 4 April 1900, HEHT.

20. Charles R. Van Hise to Turner, 26 February 1900, HEHT.

21. Van Hise to Turner, 3, 14 March 1900, HEHT.

22. Turner to Charles H. Haskins, 12 March 1900, HEHT.

23. Haskins to Turner, 17 March 1900, HEHT; Charles Kendall Adams to Board of Regents, 16 March 1900, Regents' Papers, University Archives, University of Wisconsin, Madison.

24. Adams to Regents, 16 March 1900. It has been suggested that Ely was not enthusiastic about losing history from his school. It

would, in a sense, diminish his power, but he had affirmed his willingness to see this development when he came to Madison. Turner's letter to Haskins (3 March 1900) noted that they had not always approved of Ely's course, and Ely later reproached Turner for having opposed some of his ideas while a member of the School of Economics, Political Science, and History. Ely may, therefore, have had some reason for welcoming the new arrangement.

25. Turner to Haskins, 7 August 1900, HEHT.

26. Turner to Andrew Jackson Turner, 12 October 1900, Turner to family, 26 October 1900, HEHT.

27. Turner to Andrew Jackson Turner, 12 October 1900, HEHT.

28. Andrew Jackson Turner to Turner, 30 September 1900, HEHT.

29. Turner to Dorothy, 29 May 1903, HEHTF.

30. Turner to Wilson, 8 November 1896, HEHT.

31. Smith, *Charles Kendall Adams: A Life Sketch*, 69.

32. Turner to James C. Kerwin, 11 June 1902, HEHT. See also Kerwin to Turner, 10 June 1902.

33. Cook, "A History of Liberal Education at the University of Wisconsin, 1862–1918," 194.

CHAPTER 7

1. John F. Jameson to Turner, 7 June 1895, Turner to Jameson, 9 June 1895, HEHT.

2. Turner to Charles H. Haskins, 16 July 1895, HEHT.

3. Alden, *New Governments West of the Alleghanies before 1780*, iv.

4. Libby, *The Geographical Distribution of the Vote of the Thirteen States on the Federal Constitution*, 4.

5. Libby, "A Plea for the Study of Votes in Congress," 333–34.

6. Turner, Recommendation for Orin G. Libby, 27 March 1894, HEHT.

7. Turner, "Introduction," in Libby, *Geographical Distribution*, iii, v.

8. University of Wisconsin, *Catalogue, 1892–93*, 62.

9. Libby to Eva Cory, 19 April 1896, Libby Papers, University of North Dakota.

10. University of Wisconsin, *Catalogue, 1897–98*, 146.

11. Libby to Eva Cory, 6 June 1897, 31 January 1899, Libby Papers, University of North Dakota.

12. Turner to Pres. Webster Merrifield, 5 February 1902, Turner Papers, University of Wisconsin, Madison, Archives (hereafter, TPUWMA).

13. Libby to Turner, 2 May 1902, Turner to Libby, 6 May 1902, TPUWMA.

14. Turner to Andrew C. McLaughlin, 24 October 1903, TPUWMA.

15. Turner, Report of the University of Wisconsin, School of History to Acting President E. A. Birge, 4 October 1902, TPUWMA.

16. Turner, Report, 1902.

17. John H. T. McPherson to Turner, 12 May 1902, TPUWMA.

18. Faculty Document, Reorganization of Schools, TPUWMA.

19. Turner to John F. Jameson, 10 December 1901, TPUWMA.

20. Turner to Jameson, 29 April 1902, TPUWMA.

21. Turner to Jameson, 14 November 1902, TPUWMA.

22. Turner to McLaughlin, 23 March 1903, McLaughlin to Turner, 25 March 1903, TPUWMA.

23. Turner to Jameson, 10 December 1901, TPUWMA.

24. Turner to Jameson, 4 February 1902, TPUWMA.

25. Turner to Jameson, 1 November 1902, TPUWMA.

26. Ibid.

27. Turner, "The Stream of Immigration into the United States," *Chicago Record-Herald*, 25 September 1901. The series is bound in a cardboard binder in HEHT and is also found in the "Scrapbook," HEHT.

28. Turner, "Jewish Immigration," *Chicago Record-Herald*, 16 October 1901.

29. Turner, "The Democratic Education of the Middle West," 3754, 3759.

30. Turner, "Contributions of the West to American Democracy," *Frontier*, 243–44.

31. Ibid., 244, 245–46, 247, 257, 258.

32. Ibid., 266–67.

33. Ibid., 267, 268.

34. Turner, review of *English Politics in Early Virginia History*, by Alexander Brown (1901), *American Historical Review* 7 (October 1901): 160, 162.

35. Turner, "Significance of History," *Early Writings*, 55.

36. Turner, review of *A History of the American People*, by Woodrow Wilson (1902), *American Historical Review* 8 (July 1903): 762–65.

37. Turner, review of *History of Early Steamboat Navigation on the Missouri River*, by Hiram Martin Chittenden (1903), *American Historical Review* 11 (January 1906): 443–44; Turner, review of *The Western Course of Empire*, ed. by Reuben Gold Thwaites (1904–5), *Dial* 41 (1 July 1906): 6–10.

38. Turner, review of *The Story of a Great Court*, by John B. Winslow (1912), *American Historical Review* 17 (July 1912): 859–60.

CHAPTER 8

1. Turner to L. E. Aylesworth, 4 August 1902, TPUWMA.

2. Turner to Charles R. Van Hise, 11 May 1905, Van Hise Papers, University of Wisconsin, Madison, Archives.

3. Turner to Caroline M. Turner, 31 May 1904, HEHTF.

4. Curti and Carstensen, *The University of Wisconsin: A History, 1848–1925* 2:538.

5. Turner, "Athletics in University Life," speech at Alumni Banquet, 31 January 1906, typescript, TPUWMA.

6. Turner to Van Hise, 15 June 1906, Van Hise Papers, University of Wisconsin, Madison, Archives.

7. Turner to Van Hise, 3 August 1906, Van Hise Papers, University of Wisconsin, Madison, Archives.

8. Turner, "Problems," 3, 5, 6.

9. Ibid., 7, 8.

10. Ibid., 8, 9.

11. Ibid., 9, 10.

12. Ibid., 15–18.

13. Ibid., 19–21.

14. John F. [J. Franklin] Jameson to Turner, 17 October 1905, TPUWMA.

15. Turner to Houghton, Mifflin Company, 21 January 1901, TPUWMA.

16. Turner to Woodrow Wilson, 1 July 1902, HEHT.

17. Albert B. Hart to Reuben G. Thwaites, 8 February 1902, HEHT. Hart's contributions are described by Emerton and Morison, "History, 1838–1929," in *Development of Harvard University, 1869–1929*, 150–77. See also Baird, "Albert Bushnell Hart: The Rise of the Professional Historian," 129–74.

18. Turner to Jameson, 4 February 1902, TPUWMA.

19. Turner to Max Farrand, 3 January 1905, HEHT.

20. Hart to Turner, 23 August 1905, TPUWMA.

21. Hart to Turner, 28 August 1905, TPUWMA.

22. Turner to Caroline and Dorothy Turner, 7 December 1905, HEHTF.

23. Hart to Turner, 14 December 1905, TPUWMA.

24. Turner to Farrand, 29 December 1905, HEHT.

25. Turner, *Rise of the New West, 1819–1829*, xvii.

26. Ibid., 4–5.

27. Ibid., 6.

28. Ibid., 8–9.

29. Ibid., 330–32.

30. Ibid., 186.

31. Van Hise to Turner, 5 October 1906, TPUWMA.

32. Turner, note dated 20 October 1905, TPUWMA.

33. Turner to Sen. George Wylie, 22 February 1906, TPUWMA.

34. Farrand to Turner, 27 February 1906, HEHT.

35. Farrand to Turner, 24 February 1904, HEHT.

36. H. Morse Stephens to Turner, 13 December 1904, HEHT.

37. Turner to Charles H. Haskins, 19 June 1905, HEHT.

38. Turner to Farrand, 23 June 1905, HEHT.

39. David S. Jordan to Turner, 18 April 1906, TPUWMA.

40. E. F. Riley, Secretary, University of Wisconsin Board of Regents, to Turner, 20 April 1906, TPUWMA.

41. Turner to Farrand, 31 January 1907, HEHT.

42. Ibid.

43. Turner to Van Hise, 28 July 1907, Van Hise to Turner, 31 July 1907, TPUWMA.

CHAPTER 9

1. Jacobs, *On Turner's Trail*, 271.

2. Rosa M. Perdue to Turner, 23 April 1910, "Red Book"; Jane L. Newell to Turner, 6 June 1909, HEHT.

3. Edgar E. Robinson to Turner, 26 January 1913, HEHT.

4. Turner to Charles Van Hise, 19 June 1908, TPUWMA. The amended final draft is in the Van Hise Papers, also in the university archives.

5. Jesse Macy to Turner, 14 December 1903, TPUWMA.

6. A[nson] E. Morse to Turner, 19 February 1904, HEHT.

7. Turner to E. M. Violette, 18 January 1907, HEHT.

8. Turner to Macmillan Company, 19 January 1909, HEHT.

9. Turner to Carl L. Becker, 8 June 1907, 25 March 1909, HEHT.

10. Turner to Farrand, 21 March 1909, HEHT.

11. Klein, "Detachment and the Writing of American History," 123–24.

12. Turner to Becker, 13 April 1907, HEHT.

13. Turner to Van Hise, 19 June 1908. Draft, TPUWMA.

14. Lois K. Mathews to Turner, 9 March 1906, HEHT.

15. Turner to Charles H. Hull, 11 May 1905, HEHT.

16. Turner to Max Farrand, 14 April 1905, HEHT.

17. Turner to Caroline M. Turner, 14 May 1907, HEHTF.

18. Hoxie, "Sociology and the Other Social Sciences," 754.

19. Turner, "Geographical Interpretations of American History," *Journal of Geography* 4 (January 1905), 34–37.

20. Ibid., 37.

21. Turner, "Report of the Conference on the Relation of Geography and History," AHA, *Annual Report*, 1907, 47.

22. Turner, "Relation of Geography and History," 45–47.

23. Turner, "Is Sectionalism in America Dying Away?" *Sections*, 287, 288.

24. Ibid., 288–89, 297.

25. Ibid., 313–14.

26. "Discussion of the Paper by Professor Frederick J. Turner, 'Is Sectionalism in America Dying Away?'" *American Journal of Sociology* 13 (March 1908): 811, 812.

27. Turner to Claude H. Van Tyne, 25 April 1908, HEHT. George L. Burr had outlined his position on these matters in a paper

delivered on 19 October 1907, entitled "The Place of Geography in the Teaching of History," 1–13.

28. Edwin E. Sparks, "Report of the Conference on the Relations of Geography to History," AHA, *Report*, 1908, 57–61.

29. Sparks, *Report*, 1908, 61; Lyon G. Tyler, "Report of Conference on Research in Southern History," AHA, *Report*, 1908, 143.

30. Turner to Becker, 24 April 1908, HEHT.

31. Turner, "Pioneer Ideals and the State University," *Frontier*, 269, 271, 274, 276, 277, 279.

32. Ibid., 280, 281, 282.

33. Ibid., 282, 283, 285–86, 288, 289.

34. J. Franklin Jameson form letter to members, Commission on the Documentary Historical Publications of the United States Government, 1 February 1908, Turner Papers.

35. Jameson form letter, HEHT. Turner scribbled Roosevelt's boast in his pocket diary while in Washington for a meeting of the commission in June 1908.

36. Committee on Department Methods, *Report to the President: Documentary Historical Publications of the United States Government*, 27. A copy of Turner's more extended draft is in the Turner Papers.

37. Turner to Farrand, 17 October 1903, TPUWMA.

38. Turner to Farrand, 24 November 1907, 19 October 1909, HEHT.

39. University of Wisconsin Regents' Minutes, Vol. G, 199–201.

40. Turner to Van Hise, draft, 19 June 1908, Van Hise Papers.

41. Ephraim D. Adams to Turner, 19 October 1908, HEHT.

42. Henry M. Stephens to Turner, 15 August 1909, HEHT.

43. Turner to Van Hise, 19 September 1909, HEHT.

44. Archibald C. Coolidge to A. Lawrence Lowell, 28 September 1909, HEHT. Original in A. Lawrence Lowell Correspondence, Harvard University Archives.

45. Turner to Caroline, 6 October 1909, HEHTF.

46. Turner to Caroline, 7 October 1909, HEHTF.

47. Turner to Van Hise, 15 November 1909, Van Hise Papers.

48. Paul Reinsch, Minutes, Joint Meeting Conference Committees, Regents and Faculty, 10 December 1909, Regents' Papers.

49. Turner to Van Hise, 15 November 1909, Van Hise Papers. Turner to Farrand, 28 October 1909, HEHT.

50. Turner to Farrand, 19 October 1909, HEHT.

51. Becker to Turner, 21 November 1909, P. O. Ray to Turner, 27 November 1909, HEHT.

52. Turner to Becker, 5 December 1909, HEHT.

53. Turner to Mathew B. Hammond, 5 December 1909, HEHT.

54. Turner to James, A. James, 24 June 1910, HEHT.

55. Turner to Becker, 15 January 1910, HEHT.

56. Turner to Caroline, 5 August 1910, HEHTF.

CHAPTER 10

1. Frederick Jackson Turner to Joseph Jastrow, 5 October 1910, University of Wisconsin, Madison, Archives. Much about Turner's Harvard is described in Samuel E. Morison, ed., *The Development of Harvard University Since the Inauguration of President Eliot, 1869–1929* (Cambridge: Harvard University Press, 1930); Henry A. Yeomans, *Abbott Lawrence Lowell, 1856–1943* (Cambridge: Harvard University Press, 1948); Harold J. Coolidge and Robert H. Lord, *Archibald Cary Coolidge: Life and Letters* (Boston: Houghton, Mifflin Company, 1932); and Bernard Bailyn, Donald Fleming, Oscar Handlin, and Stephan Thernstrom, *Glimpses of the Harvard Past* (Cambridge: Harvard University Press, 1986).

2. Turner to Jastrow, 5 October 1910.

3. Turner to August C. Krey, 6 February 1911, HEHT.

4. Fleming, "Eliot's New Broom," in Bailyn, et al., *Glimpses of the Harvard Past*, 63.

5. Turner to Edgar E. Robinson, 7 January 1911; Waldo G. Leland, "Report of the Proceedings," in AHA, *Annual Report*, 1910, 25, 33.

6. Turner, "Social Forces in American History," 311–12.

7. Ibid., 315.

8. Ibid., 315–19.

9. Ibid., 320–21.

10. Ibid., 322–23.

11. Ibid., 323–24.

12. Ibid., 324, 325, 327, 328.

13. Ibid., 330.

14. Ibid., 330, 331.

15. Ibid., 331, 332.

16. Ibid., 333–34.

17. Ibid., 334.

18. Turner, "Significance of the Frontier," *Frontier*, 11; Turner, "Social Forces," *Frontier*, 323, 334.

19. Jacobs, "Turner's Methodology," 853–63.

20. Novick, *That Noble Dream*, 92.

21. Turner, "Significance of History," *Early Writings*, 51, 55, 67; Turner, "Social Forces," *Frontier*, 332.

22. Becker, "Detachment and the Writing of History," 28; Becker, "Some Aspects of the Influence of Social Problems and Ideas upon the Study and Writing of History," 667.

23. Turner, "West as a Field for Historical Study," AHA *Annual Report*, 1896, 282.

24. Leland, "Report of the Proceedings," AHA, *Annual Report*, 1910, 41.

25. Becker, "Kansas," in Guy S. Ford, ed., *Essays in American History Dedicated to Frederick Jackson Turner*, 86.

26. Turner to Homer C. Hockett, 3 January 1911, Turner to Edgar E. Robinson, 7 January 1911, HEHT.

27. Turner to Alice F. P. Hooper, 1 January 1912, HEHTH.

28. Turner to Dorothy Turner, 21 November 1913, HEHTF.

29. Turner to Charles H. Haskins, 18 June 1914, HEHT.

30. Turner to Max Farrand, 26 October 1914, HEHT.

31. Turner to Caroline M. Turner, 25 March 1915, HEHTF.

32. Leland, "The Meeting of the American Historical Association in California," AHA, *Annual Report*, 1915, 90; Turner to Hooper, 6 August 1915, HEHTH.

33. Turner to Farrand, 29 October 1915, HEHT. Turner to Hooper, 6 August 1915, HEHTH.

34. Turner to Robinson, 26 December 1911, HEHT.

35. Joyce, *Edward Channing and the Great Work*, 16, 24.

36. Turner to Hooper, 2 February 1917, HEHTH.

37. Turner to Reginald F. Arragon, 4 July 1916, HEHT.

38. Turner to Kenneth W. Colegrove, 5 January 1915, HEHT.

39. Turner to Hockett, 19 October 1910, HEHT.

40. Turner to Caroline, 4, 19 March 1915, HEHTF.

41. Turner to Caroline, 11, 30 March 1915, HEHTF.

42. Turner, "Reuben Gold Thwaites: A Memorial Address," in Carpenter, *The Eloquence of Frederick Jackson Turner*, 136–37.

43. Ibid., 133, 146.

44. Turner, "Geographical Influences in American Political History," *Sections*, 183.

45. Ibid., 184–85.

46. Ibid., 185–86.

47. Ibid., 191, 192, 186, n. 4.

48. Turner, "Significance of the Frontier," *Frontier*, 10.

49. Turner, "The First Official Frontier of the Massachusetts Bay," *Frontier*, 39, 43.

50. Ibid., 65.

51. Ibid., 39, 43–44; "Significance of the Frontier," *Frontier*, 1.

52. Turner, "The West and American Ideals," *Frontier*, 310.

53. Ibid., 293.

54. Ibid., 307.

55. Turner to Haskins, 18 June 1914, HEHT.

CHAPTER 11

1. Alice F. P. Hooper to Frederick Jackson Turner, 9 January 1916, HEHTH.

2. Hooper to Turner, October 1910, HEHTH.

3. Hooper to Turner, 25 January 1916, HEHTH.

4. Hooper to Turner, 30 September 1910, HEHTH.

5. Hooper to Turner, October, 1910, HEHTH.

6. Turner to Hooper, 13 October 1910, HEHTH.

7. Ibid.

8. Turner to Hooper, 7 March 1916, HEHTH.

9. Hooper to Turner, 13 October 1915, HEHTH.

10. Billington, *"Dear Lady"*, 25–26. Billington cites the Official Record of President and Fellows of Harvard College, 12 February 1912, and Edgar H. Wells to Hooper, 17 February 1912, Harvard Commission on Western History Papers.

11. Billington, *"Dear Lady"*, 27.

12. Turner to Henry M. Stephens, 25 April 1912, HEHT.

13. Turner to Hooper ("My dear Mrs. Clio"), undated, 1914, HEHTH.

14. Hooper to C. S. Paine, 1 March 1911, draft, HEHTH.

15. Turner to Caroline M. Turner, 1 March 1915, HEHTF.

16. Henry E. Bourne to Turner, 4 May 1916, Turner to Bourne, 7, 11 May 1916, HEHT.

17. Rudyard Kipling, "The Song of the Dead," *Rudyard Kipling's Verse, Definitive Edition* (Garden City: Doubleday and Company, 1940), 171–73; Turner to Caroline, 13 November 1913, HEHTF.

18. Turner to Caroline, 22 November 1913, HEHTF.

19. Ibid.

20. James W. Thompson to Turner, 18 December 1913, Turner to Thompson, 29 December 1913, HEHT.

21. Andrew C. McLaughlin to Turner, 3 January 1914, HEHT.

22. Turner to McLaughlin, 15 January 1914, HEHT.

23. Leland, "Minutes of the Annual Business Meeting," AHA, *Annual Report*, 1915, 51.

24. Rowland, in *The Government of the American Historical Association*, 8.

25. John F. Jameson to the Editor of *The Nation*, 5 February 1914, in Rowland, *Government of the American Historical Association*, 13–14 (quotes appear on 14).

26. Jameson, "The Meeting of the American Historical Association at Charleston and Columbia," *American Historical Review* 19 (April 1914): 490.

27. John H. Latané to the Editor of *The Nation*, 5 February 1914, in Rowland, *Government of the American Historical Association*, 14–16.

28. Rowland, "Statement," in *Government of the American Historical Association*, 17–20.

29. Evarts B. Greene, "Minutes of the Meeting of the Executive Council," 1914, 70–71. The council minutes do not show that Turner conceived this strategy, but his correspondence with McLaughlin suggests it.

30. Leland, "Minutes of the Adjourned Business Meeting," AHA, *Annual Report*, 1914, 54.

31. Turner to George L. Burr, 9 April 1915, HEHT, original in George Lincoln Burr Papers, Rare and Manuscript Collections, Carl A. Krock Library, Cornell University.

32. Bancroft, Latané, and Rowland, *Why the American Historical Association Needs Thorough Reorganization*, 2–4.

33. Ibid., 6, 8.

34. Ibid., 11.

35. Ibid., 14.

36. Ibid., 15–16.

37. Ibid., 16.

38. Greene, "Report of the Meeting of the Executive Council," 27 November 1915, AHA, *Annual Report*, 77–78.

39. McLaughlin to Turner, 22 October 1915, HEHT.

40. Jameson to Turner, 15 February 1916, HEHT.

41. Greene, "Report of the Meeting of the Executive Council," 29 December 1915, AHA, *Annual Report*, 66.

42. Charles H. Ambler to Turner, 16 January, 5 February, 1916, Turner to Ambler, 9 February 1916, HEHT.

CHAPTER 12

1. Turner, "Why Did Not the United States Become Another Europe," in Jacobs, ed., *Frederick Jackson Turner's Legacy*, 124–25, 140.

2. Turner to John Main, 31 March 1916, HEHTF.

3. Turner to Max Farrand, 13 October 1916, HEHT.

4. Turner to Caroline M. Turner, 20 March 1915, HEHTF.

5. Turner to Alice F. P. Hooper, 4 January 1917, HEHTH.

6. Turner to Hooper, 13 November 1916, HEHTH.

7. Turner to Hooper, 2 February 1917, HEHTH.

8. Turner to Hooper, 21 March 1917, HEHTH.

9. Ibid.

10. Turner to Dorothy Turner Main, 18 April 1917, HEHTF.

11. Turner to Farrand, 5 May 1917, HEHT.

12. Ibid.

13. Turner to Herbert E. Bolton, 11 May 1917, HEHT.

14. Charles H. Haskins to Turner, 23 March 1917, HEHT.

15. A. Lawrence Lowell to Turner, 26 June 1917, HEHT.

16. Turner to Caroline, 9 July 1917, HEHT.

17. Turner to Caroline, 24 July 1917, HEHT.

18. Turner to Caroline, 26, 29 July 1917, HEHT.

19. Turner to Dorothy, two letters September 1917 (no day of month), HEHTF; Turner to Hooper, 13 October 1917, HEHTH.

20. Turner to Hooper, 13 October 1917, HEHTH.

21. Turner to Caroline, 25 September 1917, HEHTF.

22. Turner to Dorothy, 12 December 1917, HEHTF.

23. Robinson and West, *The Foreign Policy of Woodrow Wilson, 1913– 1917*; Turner to Edgar E. Robinson, 19 January 1918, HEHT.

24. Turner to Robinson, 19 January 1918, HEHT.
25. Turner to Dorothy, 27 January 1918, HEHTF.
26. Turner to Hooper, 19 June 1918, HEHTH.
27. Turner to Main, 13 September 1918, HEHTF.
28. Turner to Hooper, 9 October 1918, HEHTH.
29. Turner to Moses L. Slaughter, 12 October 1918, HEHT.
30. Turner to Dorothy, 14 November 1918, HEHTF.
31. Turner to Dorothy, 22 December 1918, HEHTF; Turner to Robinson, 12 December 1918, HEHT.
32. Frederic Duncalf to Turner, 5 December 1919, HEHTF.
33. Turner to Dorothy, 4 January 1919, HEHTF.
34. Turner to Slaughter, 12 October 1918, HEHT; Turner to Hooper, 5 November 1918, HEHTH.
35. Turner to Robinson, 12 December 1918, HEHT.
36. Turner to Hooper, 23 January 1919, HEHTH.
37. Turner to Hooper, 9 October 1919, HEHTH.
38. James H. Robinson to Turner, 31 March 1919, HEHT.
39. Turner attributed the "currant jelly" simile to Theodore Roosevelt in Turner to Hooper, 13 November 1918, HEHTH; Turner, "International Political Parties in a Durable League of Nations," in Diamond, ed., "American Sectionalism and World Organization by Frederick Jackson Turner," *American Historical Review* 47 (April 1942): 545–51 (quoted passages, 547, 548, 549).
40. Turner, "Social Forces," *Frontier*, 324; Turner to Hooper, 6 May 1920, HEHTH.
41. Turner to Hooper, 23 November 1919, HEHTH.
42. Turner to Hooper, 6 May 1920, HEHTH.
43. Turner to Farrand, 13 February 1919, HEHT.
44. Turner to Dorothy, 4 January 1919, HEHTF.
45. Turner to Dixon R. Fox, 27 March 1919, HEHT.
46. Merle Curti to Turner, 10 August 1919, HEHT.
47. Martha Edwards to Turner, 24 May, 8 November 1919, HEHT.
48. Archibald C. Coolidge to Turner, 21 March 1917, Harvard Commission on Western History Papers, Harvard University Archives.
49. Turner to Hooper, 16 January 1920, Hooper to Turner, 4 May 1920, HEHTH.
50. Samuel E. Morison, "Edward Channing: A Memoir," 306.

CHAPTER 13

1. William A. Dunning, "A Generation of American Historiography," AHA, *Annual Report*, 1917, 352.

2. John F. Jameson to Turner, 14 April 1919, 20 May 1919, HEHT.

3. Charles H. Haskins to Turner, 19 July 1919, HEHT.

4. Turner to Edward N. Bristol, Henry Holt and Company, 24 April 1919, Turner to Guy S. Ford, 27 November 1920, HEHT.

5. Turner, *Frontier in American History*, v.

6. Turner, "Middle Western Pioneer Democracy," 335, 336, 338.

7 Turner, "Pioneer Democracy," *Frontier*, 340, 343, 344, 347, 348, 349.

8. Ibid., 355–56, 356–57.

9. Ibid., 357, 358.

10. Ibid., 358–59.

11. Ibid., 343, 336.

12. Turner to Alice F. P. Hooper, 20 January 1921, HEHTH; Turner to Dorothy Turner Main, 2 February 1921, HEHTF; Carl L. Becker to Turner, 20 October 1920, HEHT.

13. Charles A. Beard, "The Frontier in American History," *New Republic*, 16 February 1921, 349–50; Turner to Dorothy, 18 February 1921, HEHTF. See also Beard to Turner, 14 May 1921 and Beard to Merle E. Curti, 9 August 1928, HEHT. The latter letter is in the Turner Papers through the courtesy of Curti, and in it Beard credited Turner with "restoring the consideration of economic facts to historical writing in America," and with being a leader in putting history on a scientific plane and a scholar of "fine talents and unwearying industry."

14. Turner to Hooper, 13 February 1921; Hooper to Turner, St. Valentine's Day, 1921, HEHTH.

15. C. W. A. (Clarence W. Alvord), review of *The Frontier in American History, Mississippi Valley Historical Review*, 11 (March 1921): 403–7; Allen Johnson, review of *The Frontier in American History, American Historical Review* 26 (April 1921): 542–43.

16. Max Farrand, *The Development of the United States*, vii; Turner to Hooper, 23 November 1919, HEHTH.

17. Dodd, *Woodrow Wilson and His Work*, 28.

18. Guy Emerson to Turner, 23 June, 10 December 1920, HEHT; Turner to Hooper, 30 June 1920, HEHTH.

19. Turner to Hooper, 13 February 1921, HEHTH.

20. Dodd to Turner, 3 October 1919, HEHT.

21. Turner to Dodd, 7 October 1919, HEHT. Billington, *The Genesis of the Frontier Thesis*, pp. 181–201, has reprinted the Dodd-Turner correspondence and included both Turner's original draft of 7 October 1919 and the copy received by Dodd. The text of the explanatory note appears on pp. 200–201.

22. Turner to Constance L. Skinner, 15 March 1922, HEHT.

23. Turner, *Early Writings*, 280.

24. Herbert B. Adams to Albert Shaw, 21 April 1883, quoted in Graybar, *Albert Shaw of the Review of Reviews*, 24–25; Adams, "Special Methods of Historical Study," Hall, ed., *Methods of Teaching History*, 124.

25. Turner to Hooper, 16 November 1922, HEHTH.

26. Turner to Caroline M. Turner, 28 December 1922, HEHTF.

27. Turner to Dorothy, 13 May 1920; Turner to Caroline, 20, 22 April 1920, HEHTF.

28. Turner to Caroline, 22 May 1920, HEHTF.

29. Turner to Dorothy, 19 March 1921, HEHTF.

30. Turner to Caroline, [16?], [19?] June 1921, HEHTF.

31. Turner to Hooper, 26 February 1920, HEHTH.

32. Turner to Caroline, 28 April 1920, HEHTF; Turner to Hooper, 30 June, 29 July, 12 October 1920, HEHTH.

33. Turner to Dorothy, 30 October 1920, HEHTF.

34. Turner to Hooper, 31 December 1921, HEHTH.

35. Turner to Hooper, 10 February 1922, HEHTH.

36. Ibid.

37. Turner to Dorothy, 14 November 1922, HEHTF.

38. Turner to Hooper, 16 November 1922, HEHTH.

39. Turner to Hooper, 19 December 1922, HEHTH.

40. Turner to Caroline, 25 April, 4 May 1920, HEHTF.

41. Turner to Hooper, 29 July, 12 October 1920, HEHT.

42. Turner to Lincoln MacVeagh, Henry Holt and Co., 5 April 1921, HEHT.

43. Turner to Hooper, 10 February 1922, HEHTH; Turner to Caroline, 7, 20 May, (?) June 1922, HEHTF.

44. Turner to Hooper, 12 August 1922, HEHTH.

45. Turner to Dorothy, 14 February 1923, HEHTF; Turner to Hooper, 20 March 1923, HEHTH.

46. MacVeagh to Turner, 4 May 1923, HEHT.

47. Typescript, "The Significance of the Section in American History," with notation, "Ann Arbor, Mich. May 1, 1922, Chicago, Ill. May 2, 1922," Drawer 14, HEHT; Turner, "Sections and Nation," 339.

48. Turner, "Since the Foundation," *Sections*, 231–32.

49. Ibid., 234.

50. Avery Craven, Colin B. Goodykoontz, Merle Curti, in Jacobs, "Appendix B: Turner as a Teacher," *On Turner's Trail*, 275, 276, 257–59.

51. Gaus, "Notes," 29 March, 5 May 1920, Turner Papers.

52. Turner, "Significance of the Frontier," *Frontier*, 19; Gaus, "Notes," 14 May 1920; Turner and Merk, *List of References on the History of the West*, 7–12.

53. Gaus, "Notes," 14 May 1920, Turner Papers.

54. Ibid., 19, 24 May 1920.

55. Ibid., 26, 28 May, 2 June 1920.

56. Ibid., 2 June 1920.

57. Curti, in Jacobs, "Appendix B," *On Turner's Trail*, 259; Nute, "Frederick Jackson Turner," 161.

58. Merk to Turner, 4 July 1927, HEHT.

59. Turner to Curti, 12 October 1921, HEHT.

60. Turner to Homer C. Hockett, 21 January 1926, HEHT.

61. Turner to William S. Ferguson, 30 December 1918, HEHT.

62. Curti to Turner, 30 January 1923, HEHT.

63. Turner to Curti, 30 January 1923, HEHT.

CHAPTER 14

1. Turner to Dorothy Turner Main, 14 November 1922, HEHTF.

2. Turner to Dorothy, 14 May 1923, HEHTF.

3. Turner to Dorothy, 23 September 1923, HEHTF.

4. Turner to Edgar E. Robinson, 22 November 1923, HEHT.

5. Turner to Archer B. Hulbert, 23 May 1925, HEHT.

6. Dale, "Memories of Frederick Jackson Turner," 347; Schlesinger, *In Retrospect: The History of a Historian*, 79.

7. Turner to Caroline M. Turner, 24 May 1922, 29 May 1923, HEHTF.

8. Turner to Dorothy, 20 January 1931, HEHTF; Turner to Alice F. P. Hooper, 8 February 1931, HEHTH.

9. Turner to Frederick Merk, 26 March 1931, HEHT.

10. Circular letter from Frederick Jackson Turner Seminar of 1923–24 announcing retirement dinner, 17 April 1924; Seating Chart, "Turner Banquet, 24 May 1924," Turner Papers.

11. The cartoon original is in the Visual and Sound Archives, State Historical Society of Wisconsin; Turner to Hooper, 1 May [June] 1924, HEHTH.

12. Turner to Carl L. Becker, 23 November 1925, HEHT.

13. Turner to Edgar E. Robinson, 22 November 1923, HEHT.

14. Turner to Arthur H. Buffinton, 29 August 1924, HEHT.

15. Turner to Constance L. Skinner, 15 March 1922, HEHT. As noted elsewhere, however, Turner's claim, accurate as it was, is placed in perspective by the materials in Wunder, ed., *Historians of the Frontier.*

16. Turner to Caroline, 8 June 1924, HEHTF.

17. Turner to Caroline, 9 June 1924, HEHTF.

18. Turner to Caroline, 13 June 1924, HEHTF.

19. Turner to Caroline, 29 June 1924, HEHTF.

20. Turner to Caroline, 4 July 1924, HEHTF.

21. Turner to Caroline, 16 November 1924, HEHTF; Turner to Merle Curti, 30 January 1923, HEHT.

22. Turner to Joseph Schafer, 26 March 1924, HEHT.

23. Turner to Merk, 7 December 1924, HEHTF.

24. Ibid.

25. Turner to Caroline, 21 March 1925, HEHTF.

26. Ibid. See also 23 March 1925, HEHTF.

27. Turner to Dorothy, 27 June 1925, HEHTF.

28. Turner to Hooper, 23 December 1925, HEHTH.

29. Turner to Fulmer Mood, 1 May 1926, HEHT.

30. Turner, "Geographic Sectionalism in American History," *Sections*, 193, 203, 206.

31. Turner, "The Significance of the Section in American History," *Sections*, 25–26.

32. Turner, "The Significance of the Section," *Sections*, 40.

33. Turner, "The West—1876 and 1926," *Sections*, 245.

34. Ibid., 254–55.

35. Turner, "Significance of the Section," *Sections*, 25; "Massachusetts Bay," *Frontier*, 63–64.

36. Turner, "The Children of the Pioneers," *Sections*, 261.
37. Ibid., 283, 286.
38. Turner to Hooper, 8 March 1926, HEHTH.
39. Turner to Dorothy, 30 May 1926, HEHTF.
40. Turner to Solon J. Buck, 27 January 1927, HEHT.

CHAPTER 15

1. Turner to Dorothy Turner Main, 6 February 1927, HEHTF; Turner to Alice F. P. Hooper, 6 February 1927, HEHTH.
2. Turner to Dorothy, 24 February 1927, HEHTF.
3. Turner to Max Farrand, 19 March 1927, HEHT.
4. Turner to Hooper, 20 April 1927, HEHTH.
5. Turner to Farrand, 25 October 1927, HEHT.
6. Turner to Hooper, 3 November 1927, HEHTH.
7. Turner to Dorothy, 1 January 1928, HEHTF.
8. Turner to Dorothy and John Main, 21 January 1928, HEHTF.
9. Turner to Hooper, 27 December 1928, HEHTH.
10. Turner to Dorothy, 16 November 1928, HEHTF.
11. Turner to Dorothy, [late December] 1928, HEHTF.
12. Turner to Hooper, 21 January 1928, HEHTH.
13. Farrand, "Frederick Jackson Turner at the Huntington Library," 161.
14. Turner to Hooper, 8 March 1929, HEHTH.
15. Turner to Dorothy, 25 April 1929, HEHTF; Turner to Hooper, 19 April 1929, HEHTH.
16. Turner to Dorothy, 7, 28 May 1929, HEHTF.
17. Turner to Hooper, 2 November 1929, 4 January 1930, HEHTH; Turner to Winfred T. Root, 29 November 1929, HEHT.
18. Schlesinger, *New Viewpoints in American History*, 45–46, 70–71; Barnes, *The New History and the Social Studies*, 66–67.
19. Almack, "The Shibboleth of the Frontier," 197–202.
20. Turner to Schlesinger, 5 May 1925, HEHT.
21. Turner to Frederick Merk, 6 May 1925, HEHT.
22. Johnson, *The Historian and Historical Evidence*, 161–62.
23. Turner to Carl L. Becker, 23 November 1925, HEHT.
24. Ibid.

25. Turner to Becker, 16 December 1925, HEHT.

26. Ibid.

27. Becker, "Frederick Jackson Turner," in Odum, et al., *American Masters of Social Science*, 295, 316.

28. Ibid., 310.

29. Ibid., 311, 312, 313, 315, 317–18.

30. Merle Curti to Turner, 8 August 1928, HEHT; Curti, "Analysis 23: The Section and the Frontier in American History: The Methodological Concepts of Frederick Jackson Turner" in Stuart A. Rice, ed. *Methods in Social Science, a Case Book* (Chicago: University of Chicago Press, 1931), 353–67.

31. Turner to Curti, 8 August 1928, HEHT.

32. Curti to Turner, 13 August 1928, HEHT.

33. Turner to Curti, 15 August 1928, HEHT.

34. Curti to Turner, 25 August 1928, HEHT.

35. Turner to Curti, 27 August 1928, HEHT.

36. Curti, "The Section and the Frontier in American History," in Rice, *Methods*, 354, 357.

37. Curti, "The Section and the Frontier in American History," in Rice, *Methods*, 357, 354, 367.

38. Laski, "Teacher and Student: The Technique of University Education," 567, 574.

39. Turner to Joseph Schafer, 19 January 1931, HEHT.

40. John W. Oliver, "Twenty-Fourth Annual Meeting," 218–20.

41. Sauer, "Historical Geography and the Western Frontier," in Willard and Goodykoontz, eds., *The Trans-Mississippi West*, 270–71, 272, 283.

42. Sauer, "Foreword to Historical Geography," in *Land and Life*, 376–77.

43. Turner to Isaiah Bowman, 24 December 1931, HEHT.

44. Bowman to Turner, 5 January 1932, Turner to Bowman, 12 January 1932, HEHT.

45. Martin, *The Life and Thought of Isaiah Bowman*, 117–20.

46. Wright, "Sections and National Growth: *An Atlas of the Historical Geography of the United States*," 353–60; Wright, "Voting Habits in the United States: A Note on Two Maps," 666–72, 672.

47. Turner to Merk, 9 January 1931, HEHT.

CHAPTER 16

1. Robinson, "Frederick Jackson Turner," 260.

2. Howe, "Memoir of Frederick Jackson Turner," 501.

3. Max Farrand to Arthur Meier Schlesinger, 18 March 1932.

4. Paxson, "A Generation of the Frontier Hypothesis: 1893–1932," 35–37.

5. Ibid., 38, 43.

6. Ibid., 44–45, 46, 48, 51.

7. Ibid., 51.

8. Phillips, "The Traits and Contributions of Frederick Jackson Turner," 21–25, quote, p. 21. See also Kellogg, "The Passing of a Great Teacher, Frederick Jackson Turner," 270–72; Nute, "Frederick Jackson Turner," 159–161; and Robinson, "Frederick Jackson Turner," 259–61.

9. Paxson, review of *The Significance of Sections in American History*, 773–74.

10. Hodder, review of *Significance of Sections*, 174.

11. Viles, review of *Significance of Sections*, 579.

12. McBride, review of *Significance of Sections*, 452.

13. Buck, review of *Significance of Sections*, 205.

14. Stephenson, review of *Significance of Sections*, 316.

15. Curti, review of *Significance of Sections*, 265–66.

16. Kraus, review of *Significance of Sections*, 337.

17. Wright Jr., review of *Significance of Sections*, 630–34.

18. Ibid., 634.

19. Hacker, review of *Significance of Sections*, 108–10.

20. "Editorial Comment: A Literary Club Symposium," 96.

21. Hacker, "Frederick Jackson Turner: Non-Economic Historian," 108.

22. Caroline M. Turner to Max Farrand, 11 April 1943, HEHT. For a foray into psychological analysis see, Alan C. Beckman, "Hidden Themes in the Frontier Thesis: An Application of Psychoanalysis to Historiography," *Comparative Studies in Society and History* 8 (April 1966), 361–82. Robert T. Smith updates this approach in an unpublished paper, "Frederick Jackson Turner: Material Man in a Material World."

23. Wunder, ed., *Historians of the Frontier*.

24. Pierson, "American Historians and the Frontier Hypothesis in 1941," 41–42. A few minutes spent in consulting Mattison and Marion, *Frederick Jackson Turner: A Reference Guide*, shows that no

one can adequately summarize the criticism of Turner's ideas in a few pages. I have tried here to develop a few of its salient aspects and in part have followed my article, "Frederick Jackson Turner Reconsidered," 195–221.

25. Hofstadter, *The Progressive Historians*, 104, 106.

26. Farrand to Caroline, 20 January 1943, HEHT.

27. Malin, "The Turner-Mackinder Space Concept of History," *Essays on Historiography*, 12, 37.

28. Billington, *Frederick Jackson Turner*, 459.

29. Limerick, Milner, and Rankin, eds., *Trails: Toward a New Western History*, xi; Worster, "Beyond the Agrarian Myth," *Trails*, 10, 16, 18–19, 21–24.

30. Limerick, "The Trail to Santa Fe: The Unleashing of the Western Public Intellectual," and "What on Earth is the New Western History," *Trails*, 62, 63, 69–70, 67, 86, 88.

31. White, "Trashing the Trails," *Trails*, 27, 31, 37, 39.

32. Pascoe, "Western Women at the Cultural Crossroads," *Trails*, 44, 46; Malone, "The 'New Western History' An Assessment," and "Beyond the Last Frontier: Toward a New Approach to Western American History," *Trails*, 98, 102, 140; Robbins, "Laying Siege to Western History: The Emergence of New Paradigms," *Trails*, 184–86; Dippie, "American Wests: Historiographical Perspectives," *Trails*, 135.

33. Cronon, "Revisiting the Vanishing Frontier," 175–76; Cronon, "Turner's First Stand," 94. For a more recent statement, see Cronon, Miles, and Gitlin, "Becoming West: Toward a New Meaning for Western History," 3–27.

34. Steiner, "Frederick Jackson Turner and Western Regionalism," 124; Bensel, *Sectionalism and American Political Development, 1880–1980*. For Turner's placement within American republicanism, see Donald K. Pickens, "The Turner Thesis and Republicanism," 319–40, and, in social science, Ross, *The Origins of American Social Science*.

35. Limerick, *The Legacy of Conquest*, 31.

36. Turner, *Early Writings*, 52.

37. Dale, "Memories of Frederick Jackson Turner," 357.

38. Limerick, "Turnerians All: The Dream of a Helpful History in an Intelligible World," 697–716.

39. Kipling, "The Explorer," *Rudyard Kipling's Verse*, 104–7.

Selected Works by
Frederick Jackson Turner

BOOKS AND ARTICLES

"The Character and Influence of the Fur Trade in Wisconsin." *Proceedings of the Thirty-Sixth Annual Meeting of the State Historical Society of Wisconsin,* 52–98. Madison: Democrat Printing Co., 1889.

The Character and Influence of the Indian Trade in Wisconsin: A Study of the Trading Post as an Institution. Johns Hopkins University Studies in Historical and Political Science. Vol. 9, no. 11–12 (1891), 547–615. Reprint, edited by David H. Miller and William W. Savage, Jr. Norman: University of Oklahoma Press, 1977.

(editor) *Correspondence of the French Ministers to the United States, 1791–1797.* American Historical Association, *Annual Report,* 1903. Vol. 2 (*Seventh Report of Historical Manuscripts Commission*). Washington, D.C., 1904.

"The Democratic Education of the Middle West." *World's Work* 6 (August 1903): 3754–59.

The Early Writings of Frederick Jackson Turner with a List of All His Works Compiled by Everett E. Edwards and an Introduction by Fulmer Mood. Madison: State Historical Society of Wisconsin, 1938.

The Frontier in American History. New York: Henry Holt and Co., 1920.

"Geographical Interpretations of American History." *Journal of Geography* 4 (January 1905): 34–37.

"History of the 'Grignon Tract' on the Portage of the Fox and Wisconsin Rivers." *Wisconsin State Register* (Portage), 23 June 1883.

List of References on the History of the West. Cambridge: Harvard University Press, 1911, 1913, 1915, 1917, 1922. Some variation in titles. 1922 edition coauthored with Frederick Merk.

Outline Studies in the History of the Northwest. Chicago: C. H. Kerr and Company, 1888.

"Recent Studies in American History." *Atlantic Monthly* 77 (June 1896),
        837–44. (Specific works reviewed in this essay are listed
        under "Book Reviews," below.)
"Report of the Conference on the Relation of Geography and History."
        American Historical Association, *Annual Report*, 1907.
        Washington, D.C., 1908, 45–48.
Rise of the New West, 1819–1829. Vol. 14, *The American Nation: A
        History*, ed. Albert B. Hart. New York: Harpers and Brothers
        Publishers, 1906.
The Significance of Sections in American History. New York: Henry Holt
        and Co., 1932.
"Studies of American Immigration." XI, German Immigration in the
        Colonial Period; XII, German Immigration into the United
        States, 2; XIII, Italian Immigration to the United States; XIV,
        French and Canadian Immigration into the United States;
        XV, The Stream of Immigration into the United States; XVII,
        Jewish Immigration. *Chicago Record-Herald*, 28 August, 4
        September, 11 September, 18 September, 25 September, 16
        October 1901.
The United States, 1830–1850: The Nation and Its Sections. New York:
        Henry Holt and Co., 1935.

EDITED WRITINGS

Billington, Ray A., ed. *"Dear Lady": The Letters of Frederick Jackson
        Turner and Alice Forbes Perkins Hooper, 1910–1932*. San
        Marino: Henry E. Huntington Library, 1970.
————, ed. *The Genesis of the Frontier Thesis: A Study in Historical
        Creativity*. San Marino: Henry E. Huntington Library, 1971.
Carpenter, Ronald H. *The Eloquence of Frederick Jackson Turner*. San
        Marino: Henry E. Huntington Library, 1983.
Diamond, William, ed. "American Sectionalism and World Organization
        by Frederick Jackson Turner." (Originally titled by Turner
        "International Political Parties in a Durable League of
        Nations.") *American Historical Review* 47 (April 1942):
        545–51.
Donnan, Elizabeth, and Leo F. Stock, eds. *An Historian's World: Selec-
        tions from the Correspondence of John Franklin Jameson*.
        Philadelphia: American Philosophical Society, 1956.

Holt, W. Stull, ed. *Historical Scholarship in the United States, 1876–1901: As Revealed in the Correspondence of Herbert B. Adams.* Baltimore: Johns Hopkins Press, 1938.

Jacobs, Wilbur R., ed. *Frederick Jackson Turner's Legacy: Unpublished Writings in American History.* San Marino: Henry E. Huntington Library, 1965.

———. *The Historical World of Frederick Jackson Turner with Selections from His Correspondence.* New Haven: Yale University Press, 1968.

Kammen, Michael, ed. *"What is the Good of History?": Selected Letters of Carl L. Becker, 1900–1945.* Ithaca: Cornell University Press, 1973.

Link, Arthur S., ed. *The Papers of Woodrow Wilson.* Vols. 6, 8, 10, 11. Princeton: Princeton University Press, 1966–71.

Lokken, Roy, ed. "As One Historian to Another: Frederick Jackson Turner's Letters to Edmond S. Meany." *Pacific Northwest Quarterly* 44 (January 1953): 30–39.

Mood, Fulmer. "Little Known Fragments of Turner's Writings." *Wisconsin Magazine of History* 23 (March 1940): 128–41.

———. "Radisson and Groseilliers: A Newly Recovered Historical Essay by Frederick J. Turner." *Wisconsin Magazine of History* 33 (March 1950): 318–26.

———. "An Unfamiliar Essay by Frederick Jackson Turner." *Minnesota History* 18 (December 1937): 381–83.

Mood, Fulmer, and Everett E. Edwards. "Frederick Jackson Turner's 'History of the Grignon Tract on the Portage of the Fox and Wisconsin Rivers.'" *Agricultural History* 17 (April 1943): 113–20.

Morison, Elting E. *The Letters of Theodore Roosevelt.* Vols. 1, 6. Cambridge: Harvard University Press, 1951, 1952.

BOOK REVIEWS (LISTED ACCORDING TO AUTHOR AND WORK REVIEWED)

Brown, Alexander, *English Politics in Early Virginia History* (Boston: Houghton, Mifflin and Co., 1901). *American Historical Review* 7 (October 1901): 159–63.

Bruce, Philip A., *Economic History of Virginia in the Seventeenth Century. An Inquiry into the Material Condition of the People, Based upon Original and Contemporaneous Records*, 2 vols. (New York: Macmillan and Co., 1896).

"Recent Studies in American History," *Atlantic Monthly* 77 (June 1896).

Burgess, John W., *The Middle Period, 1817–1858* (New York: Charles Scribner's Sons, 1897). *Educational Review* 14 (November 1897): 390–99.

Channing, Edward, *A Student's History of the United States* (New York: The Macmillan Company, 1898). *Educational Review* 18 (October 1899): 301–4.

Chittenden, Hiram Martin, *History of Early Steamboat Navigation on the Missouri River: Life and Adventures of Joseph La Barge, Pioneer Navigator and Indian Trader, for Fifty Years Identified with the Commerce of the Missouri Valley*, 2 vols., American Explorer Series (New York: Francis P. Harper, 1903). *American Historical Review* 11 (January 1906): 443–44.

Coues, Elliott, ed., *History of the Expedition under the Command of Lewis and Clark to the Sources of the Missouri River, thence across the Rocky Mountains. . . .* , 4 vols, rev. ed. (New York: Francis P. Harper, 1893). *Dial* 16 (1 February 1894): 80–82.

English, William Hayden, *Conquest of the Country Northwest of the River Ohio, 1778–1783, and Life of Gen. George Rogers Clark*, 2 vols. (Indianapolis: Bowen-Merrill Co., 1896). *American Historical Review* 2 (January 1897): 363–66.

Gilmore, James R. (Edmund Kirke), *John Sevier as a Commonwealth-Builder: A Sequel to the Rear-Guard of the Revolution* (D. Appleton and Co., 1887). *Nation*, 6 October, 1887 (no. 1162), 278. (Unsigned.)

Gordy, John P. *A History of Political Parties in the United States*, vol. 1 (Athens, Ohio: Ohio Publishing Co., 1895). *Political Science Quarterly* 12 (March 1897): 163–64.

Hale, Edward E., and Edward E. Hale, Jr., *Franklin In France*, vol. 1, and *Franklin the Peacemaker*, vol. 2 (Boston: Roberts Brothers, 1887, 1889). *Dial* 8 (May 1887): 7–10; *Dial* 9 (December 1888): 204–6.

Judson, Harry P., *The Growth of the American Nation* (New York: The Chautaqua-Century Press, 1895). *American Historical Review* 1 (April 1896): 549–50.

Maclay, Edgar S., ed., *Journal of William Maclay, U.S. Senator from Pennsylvania, 1789–1791* (New York: D. Appleton and Co., 1890). *Dial* 12 (July 1891): 78–81.

McMaster, John B., *A History of the People of the United States*, vol. 4 (New York: D. Appleton and Co., 1895). "Recent Studies in American History," *Atlantic Monthly* 77 (June 1896).

Parkman, Francis, *Francis Parkman's Works*, 12 vols., rev. ed. (Boston: Little, Brown and Co., 1898). *Dial* 25 (16 December 1898): 451–53.

Payne, Edward John, *History of the New World Called America*, vol. 1 (New York: Macmillan and Co., 1892). *Dial* 13 (December 1892): 389–91.

Rhodes, James Ford, *History of the United States from the Compromise of 1850, 1860–1862*, vol. 3 (New York, Harper and Brothers, 1895). *American Historical Review* 11 (March 1896): 167–70. Also reviewed by Turner in "Recent Studies in American History," *Atlantic Monthly* 77 (June 1896).

Roosevelt, Theodore, *Louisiana and the Northwest, 1791–1807*, vol. 4, *The Winning of the West* (New York: G. P. Putnam's Sons, 1896). *American Historical Review* 2 (October 1896): 171–76.

———, *The Winning of the West*, 2 vols. (New York: G. P. Putnam's Sons, 1889). *Dial* 10 (August 1889): 71–73.

———, *The Winning of the West and the Southwest, from the Alleghanies to the Mississippi, 1769–1790*, 3 vols. (New York: G. P. Putnam's Sons, 1895). *Nation* 60 (28 March 1895): 240–42. (Unsigned.)

Schouler, James, *History of the United States under the Constitution*, 5 vols., rev. ed. (New York: Dodd, Mead and Co., 1895). "Recent Studies in American History," *Atlantic Monthly* 77 (June 1896).

Scott, Eben G., *Reconstruction during the Civil War in the United States of America* (Boston: Houghton, Mifflin and Co., 1895). "Recent Studies in American History," *Atlantic Monthly* 77 (June 1896).

Thwaites, Reuben Gold, ed., *Early Western Travels—1748–1846. A Series of Annotated Reprints. . . .*, vols. 5–20 (1904–5). *Dial* 41 (1 July 1906): 6–10 (under title *The Western Course of Empire*).

Trevelyan, George Otto, *The American Revolution . . . Part I, 1766–1776* (New York: Longmans Green and Co., 1899). *American Historical Review* 5 (October 1899): 141–44.

Weeden, William B., *The Economic and Social History of New England, 1620–1789* (Boston: Houghton, Mifflin and Co. 1890).

"Recent Studies in American History," *Atlantic Monthly* 77 (June 1896).

Wilson, Woodrow. *A History of the American People*, 5 vols. (New York: Harper and Brothers, 1902). *American Historical Review* 8 (July 1903): 762–65.

Winslow, John B. *The Story of a Great Court* (Chicago: T. H. Flood and Company, 1912). *American Historical Review* 17 (July 1912): 859–60.

Winsor, Justin, *The Westward Movement: The Colonies and the Republic West of the Alleghanies, 1763–1798* (Boston: Houghton, Mifflin and Co., 1897). *American Historical Review* 3 (April 1898): 556–61.

ENCYCLOPEDIA ENTRIES

"Frontier." *Johnson's Universal Cyclopaedia*. New York: A. J. Johnson, 1893–95, 606–7.

"Frontier in American Development." Vol. 2, *Cyclopedia of American Government*. New York: D. Appleton and Co., 1914, 61–64.

"The United States: History, 1865–1910." Vol. 23, *Encyclopaedia Britannica*. Cambridge: Cambridge University Press, 1911, 711–35.

"West as a Factor in American Politics." Vol. 3, *Cyclopedia of American Government*. New York: D. Appleton and Co., 1914, 688–75.

Selected Bibliography

The Turner Papers at the Henry E. Huntington Library provide the biographer with a voluminous collection of Frederick Jackson Turner's correspondence, lecture notes, drafts of addresses and papers, research and bibliographical notes, reprints, copies of articles by other authors, and maps. Many of his books, some annotated, are in the book collections of the library as well. Turner apparently did not save correspondence systematically before 1900. However, he preserved some incoming letters of particular interest or importance during the 1890s. With the creation of the School of History at the University of Wisconsin in 1900 and the emergence of departmental secretaries the situation changed, and copies of many Turner letters of the next ten years are found in the Turner Papers of the University of Wisconsin Archives and in the papers of the university president and the dean of liberal arts.

Turner seldom had a secretary during his fourteen years at Harvard University. During this period he sometimes retained handwritten drafts of letters and kept most of the professional and personal letters that he received. These materials returned to Madison with him on retirement, and he took them to California, along with a great hoard of teaching and research materials and much of his personal library, when he established himself at the Huntington Library in 1927. It was his wish that these materials should, on his death, be placed in the collections of the Huntington Library for the use of researchers. Aware that Turner had not kept copies of many letters to current and former graduate students, Max Farrand, director of research at the Huntington Library, sought copies of such communications from a considerable number of those who had studied under Turner after the latter's death. Most of them willingly complied.

Alice Forbes Perkins Hooper's interest in creating a memorial to her father at Harvard University in the form of books and manuscripts relating to western America was the basis of a friendship with Turner that generated a considerable and interesting correspondence covering the years from 1910 until his death. Hooper donated her friend's letters to the Huntington collection, so that his letters to her were joined with those she had sent to him. When separated, Turner and Caroline Mae Turner were faithful correspondents, and her susceptibility to hay fever led to more extended separations than are found in many marriages. Turner corresponded with his daughter Dorothy, as well, after her marriage to John Main in 1913. Caroline Turner and Dorothy Main ultimately contributed this family correspondence to the Huntington holdings, reserving the originals of only a small number of the more personal documents.

The Turner Papers were closed to researchers in general between 1946 and 1960. Two scholars, Ray A. Billington and Wilbur R. Jacobs, began biographical research in the papers almost immediately after the reopening, and their great contributions in writing about Turner and editing Turner letters and unpublished writings are recorded in the list of Turner's works and in this bibliography. They contributed substantially as well in broadening the range of correspondence in the Turner Papers by searching for Turner letters in the files of the State Historical Society of Wisconsin (SHSW), the University of Wisconsin (UWA), Harvard University, and in the surviving papers of Turner's professional contemporaries, and by adding copies of relevant materials to the Huntington collection. As a result, copies of Turner letters are found at the Huntington Library of which the originals are in the papers of Charles Kendall Adams (University of Wisconsin, Madison, Archives), William Francis Allen (Archives and Manuscripts, SHSW), Clarence W. Alvord (Illinois Historical Survey, University of Illinois), Frederic Bancroft (Columbia University Library), Carl Becker (Rare and Manuscript Collections, Carl A. Krock Library, Cornell University Archives), Edward A. Birge (SHSW and UWA), Herbert E. Bolton (Bancroft Library, University of California, Berkeley), George Lincoln Burr (Rare and Manuscript Collections, Carl A. Krock Library, Cornell University Archives), Richard T. Ely (Archives and Manuscripts, SHSW), Carl Russell Fish (Archives and Manuscripts, SHSW), Ginn and Company Papers (Ginn and Co., Boston), Charles H. Haskins (Firestone Library, Princeton University), Henry Holt and Co. Archives (Firestone Library, Princeton University), John F. Jameson (Mss Division, Library of Congress), August C. Krey (University Archives, University of Minnesota), Victor H. Lane (Michigan Historical Collections, University of Michigan), A. Lawrence Lowell (University Archives, Harvard University), Andrew C. McLaughlin (Department of Special Collections, Qniversity of Chicago Library), Macmillan Company (Macmillan Company Archives, New York), William F. Poole (Newberry

Library, Chicago), Dunbar Rowland (Mississippi Department of History and Archives, Jackson, Miss.), Joseph Schafer (Archives and Manuscripts, SHSW), Albion W. Small (Department of Special Collections, University of Chicago), Henry M. Stephens (Archives, University of California, Berkeley), Reuben Gold Thwaites (Archives and Manuscripts, SHSW), Charles Van Hise Papers (Manuscripts and Archives, SHSW), President Charles Van Hise Papers (University Archives, University of Wisconsin, Madison), and Claude H. Van Tyne (Clements Library, University of Michigan, Ann Arbor).

The Papers of the Harvard Commission on Western History are in the Harvard University Archives. These are filed alphabetically, and the Turner file particularly casts light on Turner's Harvard relationships that went beyond the activities of the commission.

In researching the Wisconsin sources, I placed major reliance in note-taking upon the collections in Madison, rather than upon the copies in the Huntington Library, and my source citations are to the copy location of which I made fullest use. Not all of the relevant materials in the Charles Kendall Adams Papers, the William Francis Allen Papers, the Richard T. Ely Papers, and other collections cited above at the State Historical Society of Wisconsin and the University of Wisconsin, Madison, are to be found in the Henry E. Huntington Library collections. This is particularly true of the Turner Papers in the University Archives, which in effect constitute most of the records of the University history department for the years 1900–1910. The much smaller collection of Turner Papers in the State Historical Society of Wisconsin also contains unique items. Although copies of most of Turner's letters to Charles Van Hise, available in the Madison collections, are in the Huntington collection, it is my impression that not all of his communications to Dean Edward A. Birge, currently available in the Files of the Deans, College of Letters and Science, University Archives, were copied for use in San Marino.

Orin G. Libby's papers are housed at both the North Dakota Historical Society, Bismarck, and at the Library at the University of North Dakota, Grand Forks. Billington reported that he found nothing of relevance at Bismarck and does not mention the collection in Grand Forks. I have used the latter, however, finding that it does contain material of interest, as my narrative suggests. I have also worked in the Burr Papers at Cornell University and am indebted to Rodney O. Davis for copying a number of useful items for me from the Edward Bancroft Papers in the Library of Knox College, Galesburg, Illinois.

MISCELLANEOUS PRIMARY SOURCES

American Historical Association. *Annual Report,* 1889–1925. Washington, D.C.

American Historical Association controversy, letters to the Editor of *The Nation:* Ulrich B. Phillips, 6 August 1915 (*Nation,* 16 September 1915, pp. 355–56); Frederic Bancroft, 5 September 1915 (*Nation,* 16 September 1915, pp. 356–57); John H. Latanć, 3 September 1915 (*Nation,* 16 September 1915, p. 357); Edward P. Cheyney, undated (*Nation,* 30 September 1915, p. 411); Albert Bushnell Hart, undated (*Nation,* 30 September 1915, pp. 411–13); Ulrich B. Phillips, 12 October 1915 (*Nation,* 21 October 1915, p. 495); Frederic L. Paxson, 10 October 1915 (*Nation,* 21 October 1915, p. 495); S. B. Fay, undated (*Nation,* 6 January 1916, pp. 22–23); John H. Latané, 12 January 1916 (*Nation,* 10 February 1916, pp. 170–71).

John M. Gaus. "Lecture Notes," February–June 1920. Filed with Turner Papers, University of Wisconsin, Madison Archives, rather than with the Gaus Papers, also held by this depositary.

Harvard University. *Catalogue, 1910–1924.*

"Minutes Book of the Class of 1884." University of Wisconsin Archives, Madison, Wisc.

Portage Presbyterian Church. "Session Minutes." Presbyterian Church Office, Portage, Wisc.

President's Committee on Department Methods. *Report to the President: Documentary Historical Publications of the United States Government.* (Washington, D.C., 11 January 1909).

United States Census, Columbia County, Wisconsin. Population Schedules, 1870, 1880. Microfilm.

University of Wisconsin. Board of Regents Papers. University of Wisconsin, Archives, Madison, Wisc.

University of Wisconsin. *Catalogue, 1877–1910.*

BOOKS

Abernethy, Thomas P. *From Frontier to Plantation in Tennessee: A Study in Frontier Democracy.* Chapel Hill: University of North Carolina Press, 1932.

Alden, George H. *New Governments West of the Alleghanies before 1780. (Introduction to a Study of the Organization and Admission of New States).* Bulletin of the University of Wisconsin, Historical Series, vol. 2, no. 1. Madison: University of Wisconsin, 1897.

Allen, William F. *Essays and Monographs.* Boston: George H. Ellis, 1890.

Appleby, Joyce, Lynn Hunt, and Margaret Jacob. *Telling the Truth about History.* New York: W. W. Norton and Company, 1994.

Ausubel, Herman. *Historians and Their Craft: A Study of the Presidential Addresses of the American Historical Association, 1884–1945.* New York: Columbia University Press, 1950.

Bagehot, Walter. *Physics and Politics: Thoughts on the Application of the Principles of 'Natural Selection' and 'Inheritance' to Political Society.* New York: D. Appleton and Company, 1879.

Bailyn, Bernard, Donald Fleming, Oscar Handlin, and Stephan Thernstrom. *Glimpses of the Harvard Past.* Cambridge: Harvard University Press, 1986.

Bancroft, Frederic, and John H. Latané. *Why the American Historical Association Needs Thorough Reorganization.* Part 2: Frederic Bancroft, *The Attempt to Seize the American Historical Review. Rejoinder to Professor Albert Bushnell Hart;* John H. Latané, *An Open Letter to Professor Andrew C. McLaughlin, Chairman of the Committee of Nine.* Washington, D.C.: National Capital Press, 1915.

Bancroft, Frederic, John H. Latané, and Dunbar Rowland. *Why the American Historical Association Needs Thorough Reorganization.* Washington, D.C.: National Capital Press, 1915.

Barnes, Harry E. *The New History and the Social Studies.* New York: Century Co., 1925.

Barnhart, John D. *Valley of Democracy: The Frontier versus the Plantation in the Ohio Valley, 1775–1818.* Bloomington: Indiana University Press, 1953.

Barrows, William. *The Indian's Side of the Indian Question.* Boston: D. Lothrop, 1887.

Bartlett, Richard A. *The New Country: A Social History of the American Frontier, 1776–1890.* New York: Oxford University Press, 1974.

Becker, Carl L. *Everyman His Own Historian: Essays on History and Politics.* New York: F. S. Crofts and Co., 1935.

————. *The History of Political Parties in the Province of New York, 1760–1776*. Madison: University of Wisconsin Press, 1960. Reprinted from the 1909 edition in the *Bulletin of the University of Wisconsin*, no. 286, Historical Series, vol. 2, no. 1.

Bennett, James D. *Frederick Jackson Turner*. Boston: Twayne Publishers, 1975.

Bensel, Richard F. *Sectionalism and American Political Development, 1880–1980*. Madison: University of Wisconsin Press, 1984.

Benson, Lee. *Turner and Beard: American Historical Writing Reconsidered*. Glencoe, Ill.: Free Press, 1960.

Billington, Ray A. *America's Frontier Heritage*. New York: Holt, Rinehart and Winston, 1966.

————. *Frederick Jackson Turner: Historian, Scholar, Teacher*. New York: Oxford University Press, 1973.

Bolton, Herbert E. *Spanish Borderlands: A Chronicle of Old Florida and the Southwest*. New Haven: Yale University Press, 1921.

Bowman, Isaiah. *The New World: Problems in Political Geography*. New York: World Book Company, 1924.

————. *The Pioneer Fringe*. New York: American Geographical Society, 1931.

Breisach, Ernst A. *American Progressive History: An Experiment in Modernization*. Chicago: University of Chicago Press, 1993.

Brigham, Albert P. *Geographic Influences in American History*. Boston: Ginn and Company, 1903.

Bryce, James. *The American Commonwealth*. 2 vols. New York: Macmillan and Co., 1888.

Burnette, Lawrence, Jr., ed. *Wisconsin Witness to Frederick Jackson Turner: A Collection of Essays on the Historian and the Thesis*. Madison: State Historical Society of Wisconsin, 1961.

Butterfield, C. W. *The History of Columbia County, Wisconsin*. 2 Vols. Chicago: Western Historical Company, 1880.

Cayton, Andrew R. L., and Peter S. Onuf. *The Midwest and the Nation: Rethinking the History of an American Region*. Bloomington: University of Indiana Press, 1990.

Chambers, John Whiteclay, II. *The Tyranny of Change: America in the Progressive Era, 1890–1920*. New York: St. Martin's Press, 1992.

Commons, John R. *Myself: The Autobiography of John R. Commons*. Madison: The University of Wisconsin Press, 1963.

Cook, John Frank. "A History of Liberal Education at the University of Wisconsin, 1862–1918." Ph.D. Dissertation, University of Wisconsin, Madison, 1970.

Coolidge, Harold J., and Robert J. Lord. *Archibald Cary Coolidge: Life and Letters*. Boston: Houghton, Mifflin Co., 1932.

Current, Richard N. *The History of Wisconsin, Volume II: The Civil War Era: 1848–1873*. Madison: State Historical Society of Wisconsin, 1976.

Curti, Merle, ed. *American Scholarship in the Twentieth Century*. Cambridge: Harvard University Press, 1953.

————. *The Making of an American Community: A Case Study of Democracy in a Frontier County*. Stanford: Stanford University Press, 1959.

Curti, Merle, and Vernon Carstensen. *The University of Wisconsin: A History 1848–1925*. 2 Vols. Madison: University of Wisconsin Press, 1949.

Dale, Edward E. *The Range Cattle Industry*. Norman: University of Oklahoma Press, 1930.

de Crevecoeur, J. Hector St. John. *Letters from an American Farmer*. London: Thomas Davies, 1782. Reprint, New York: E. P. Dutton, 1957.

Dillon, Merton L. *Ulrich Bonnell Phillips: Historian of the Old South*. Baton Rouge: Louisiana State University Press, 1985.

Dodd, William E. *Woodrow Wilson and His Work*. New York: Doubleday, Page and Company, 1920.

Doyle, John A. *English Colonies in America*. New York: Henry Holt and Co., 1887.

Droysen, Johann Gustave. *Outline of the Principles of History [Grundriss der Historik]*. Trans. E. Benjamin Andrews. New York: Howard Fertig, 1967.

Dwight, Timothy. *Travels in New England and New York*. Ed. Barbara M. Solomon and Patricia M. King. Cambridge: Harvard University Press, 1969.

Ely, Richard T. *Ground Under Our Feet: An Autobiography*. New York: Macmillan Company, 1938.

Farrand, Max. *The Development of the United States*. Boston: Houghton, Mifflin Company, 1918.

Ford, Guy S., ed. *Essays in American History Dedicated to Frederick Jackson Turner*. New York: Henry Holt and Company, 1910.

George, Henry. *Progress and Poverty: An Inquiry into the Cause of Industrial Depressions and of Increase of Want with Increase of Wealth: The Remedy.* Fiftieth Anniversary Edition. New York: Robert Schalkenbach Foundation, 1948.

Gettleman, Marvin E. *The Johns Hopkins University Seminary of History and Politics: The Records of an American Educational Institution, 1877–1912.* Vol 2. New York: Garland Publishing Inc., 1987.

Gibson, Arrell M. *The West in the Life of the Nation.* Lexington, Mass.: D. C. Heath and Company, 1976.

Godkin, Edwin L. *Problems of Modern Democracy: Political and Economic Essays.* New York: Charles Scribner's Sons, 1896.

Goetzmann, William H. *When the Eagle Screamed: The Romantic Horizon in American Diplomacy, 1800–1860.* New York: John Wiley and Sons, 1966.

Graybar, Lloyd J. *Albert Shaw of the Review of Reviews.* Lexington: University of Kentucky, 1974.

Gressley, Gene M., ed. *Old West/New West: Quo Vadis.* Worland, Wyo.: High Plains Publishing Co., 1994.

Grossman, James R., ed. *The Frontier in American Culture: Essays by Richard White and Patricia Nelson Limerick.* Berkeley: University of California Press, 1994.

Hafen, Leroy R., and Carl Coke Rister. *Western America: The Exploration, Settlement, and Development of the Region Beyond the Mississippi.* New York: Prentice-Hall, 1941.

Hall, G. Stanley, ed. *Methods of Teaching History.* Boston: D. C. Heath, 1883, 1884, 1889.

Hansen, Marcus Lee. *The Atlantic Migration: A History of the Continuing Settlement of the United States.* Cambridge: Harvard University Press, 1941.

Hawgood, John A. *America's Western Frontiers: The Story of the Explorers and Settlers Who Opened up the Trans-Mississippi West.* New York: Alfred A. Knopf, 1967.

Hesseltine, William B. *Pioneer's Mission: The Story of Lyman Copeland Draper.* Madison: State Historical Society of Wisconsin, 1954.

Hine, Robert V. *The American West: An Interpretive History.* Boston: Little, Brown, 1973.

Hockett, Homer C. *The Critical Method in Historical Research and Writing.* New York: Macmillan Company, 1955.

Hofstadter, Richard. *The Progressive Historians: Turner, Beard, Parrington*. New York: Alfred A. Knopf, 1969.

Hofstadter, Richard, and Seymour M. Lipset. *Turner and the Sociology of the Frontier*. New York: Basic Books, 1968.

Jacobs, Wilbur R. *On Turner's Trail: 100 Years of Writing Western History*. Lawrence: University Press of Kansas, 1994.

Jensen, Merrill, ed. *Regionalism in America*. Madison: University of Wisconsin Press, 1951.

Johnson, Allen. *The Historian and Historical Evidence*. Port Washington, N.Y.: Charles Scribner's Sons, 1926.

Joyce, David D. *Edward Channing and the Great Work*. The Hague: Martinus Nijhoff, 1974.

Libby, Orin G. *The Geographical Distribution of the Vote of the Thirteen States on the Federal Constitution, 1787–8. Bulletin of the University of Wisconsin*. Economics, Political Science, and History Series, vol. 1, no. 1, pp. 1–116. Madison: University of Wisconsin, 1894.

Limerick, Patricia N. *The Legacy of Conquest: The Unbroken Past of the American West*. New York: W. W, Norton and Co., 1987.

Limerick, Patricia N., Clyde A. Milner II, and Charles E. Rankin, eds. *Trails: Toward a New Western History*. Lawrence: University Press of Kansas, 1991.

Loria, Achille. *Analisi della Proprieta Capitalista*. Turin: Fratelli Bocca, 1889.

Malin, James C. *The Grassland of North America: Prolegomena to its History*. Lawrence, Kans.: James C. Malin, 1947.

———. *Essays on Historiography*. Lawrence, Kans.: James C. Malin, 1948.

Malone, Michael P. *Historians and the American West*. Lincoln: University of Nebraska Press, 1983.

Malone, Michael P., and Richard W. Etulain. *The American West: A Twentieth Century History*. Lincoln: University of Nebraska Press, 1989.

Martin, Geoffrey J. *The Life and Thought of Isaiah Bowman*. Hamden, Conn.: Archon Books, 1980.

Mattison, Vernon E., and William E. Marion. *Frederick Jackson Turner: A Reference Guide*. Boston: G. K. Hall and Co., 1985.

Merk, Frederick. *History of the Westward Movement*. New York: Alfred A. Knopf, 1978.

———. *The Oregon Question: Essays in Anglo-American Diplomacy and Politics*. Cambridge: Harvard University Press, 1967.

Mermin, Samuel. *The Fox-Wisconsin Rivers Improvement: An Historical Study in Legal Institutions and Political Economy.* Madison: Department of Law, University Extension, University of Wisconsin, 1968.

Nash, Gerald D. *The American West in the Twentieth Century: A Short History of an Urban Oasis.* Englewood Cliffs, N.J.: Prentice-Hall, 1973.

———. *Creating the West: Historical Interpretations, 1890–1990.* Albuquerque: University of New Mexico Press, 1990.

Nesbit, Robert C., and William F. Thompson. *Wisconsin: A History.* 2nd ed. Madison: University of Wisconsin Press, 1989.

Nettels, Curtis P. *The Roots of American Civilization.* New York: F. S. Crofts and Co., 1938.

Nichols, Roger L. *American Frontier and Western Issues: A Historiographical Review.* New York: Greenwood Press, 1986.

Noble, David W. *The End of American History: Democracy, Capitalism, and the Metaphor of Two Worlds in Anglo-American Historical Writing, 1880–1890.* Minneapolis: University of Minnesota Press, 1985.

———. *Historians Against History: The Frontier Thesis and the National Covenant in American Historical Writing since 1830.* Minneapolis: University of Minnesota Press, 1965.

Novick, Peter. *That Noble Dream: The "Objectivity Question" and the American Historical Profession.* New York: Cambridge University Press, 1988.

Paxson, Frederic. *History of the American Frontier, 1763–1893.* Boston: Houghton, Mifflin Company, 1924.

Payne, Edward John. *History of the New World Called America.* New York: Macmillan and Co., 1892.

Pomeroy, Earl. *The Pacific Slope: A History of California, Oregon, Washington, Idaho, Utah, and Nevada.* New York: Alfred A. Knopf, 1965.

Potter, David. *People of Plenty: Economic Abundance and American Character.* Chicago: University of Chicago Press, 1954.

Rader, Benjamin G. *The Academic Mind and Reform: The Influence of Richard T. Ely in American Life.* Lexington: University of Kentucky Press, 1966.

Riegel, Robert E. *America Moves West.* 2nd ed. New York: Henry Holt and Company, 1947.

Robinson, Edgar E., and Victor J. West. *The Foreign Policy of Woodrow Wilson, 1913–1917*. New York: Macmillan Co., 1917.

Ross, Dorothy. *The Origins of American Social Science*. Cambridge: Cambridge University Press, 1991.

Rowland, Dunbar. *The Government of the American Historical Association*. Jackson: Mississippi Department of Archives and History, 1914.

Sauer, Carl O. *Land and Life: A Selection from the Writings of Carl Orwin Sauer*. Ed. John Leighly. Berkeley: University of California Press, 1963.

Schlesinger, Arthur M. *In Retrospect: The History of a Historian*. New York: Harcourt, Brace and World, 1963.

———. *New Viewpoints in American History*. New York: Macmillan Company, 1922.

Semple, Ellen C. *American History and Its Geographic Conditions*. Boston: Houghton Mifflin Company, 1903.

Slaughter, Gertrude. *Only the Past is Ours: The Life Story of Gertrude Slaughter*. New York: Exposition Press, 1963.

Smith, Charles F. *Charles Kendall Adams: A Life Sketch*. Madison: University of Wisconsin, 1924.

Smith, Henry Nash. *Virgin Land: The American West as Symbol and Myth*. New York: Alfred A. Knopf, 1949.

Slotkin, Richard. *Regeneration Through Violence: The Mythology of the American Frontier, 1600–1800*. Middletown: Wesleyan University Press, 1973.

Snyder, Phil L., ed. *Detachment and the Writing of History: Essays and Letters of Carl L. Becker*. Ithaca: Cornell University Press, 1958.

Strout, Cushing. *The Pragmatic Revolt in American History: Carl Becker and Charles Beard*. New Haven: Yale University Press, 1958.

Toole, K. Ross, et al., eds. *Probing the American West: Papers from the Santa Fe Conference*. Santa Fe: Museum of New Mexico Press, 1962.

Truettner, William H., ed. *The West as America: Reinterpreting Images of the Frontier, 1820–1920*. Washington, D.C.: Smithsonian Institution Press, 1991.

Turner, Andrew Jackson. *The Family Tree of Columbia County, Wisconsin*. Portage: Wisconsin State Register Press, 1904.

Vincent, John M., et al. *Herbert Baxter Adams: Tributes of Friends.* Baltimore: Johns Hopkins Press, 1902.

Webb, Walter P. *The Great Plains.* Boston: Ginn and Company, 1931.

Whitaker, Arthur P. *The Spanish-American Frontier, 1783–1795: The Westward Movement and the Spanish Retreat in the Mississippi Valley.* Boston: Houghton Mifflin Company, 1927.

White, Richard. *"It's Your Misfortune and None of My Own": A New History of the American West.* Norman: University of Oklahoma Press, 1991.

Willard, James F., and Colin B. Goodykoontz, eds. *The Trans-Mississippi West: Papers Read at a Conference Held at the University of Colorado, June 18-June 21, 1929.* Boulder: University of Colorado, 1930.

Wrobel, David M. *The End of American Exceptionalism: Frontier Anxiety from the Old West to the New Deal.* Lawrence: University Press of Kansas, 1993.

Wunder, John R., ed. *Historians of the American Frontier: A Bio-Bibliographical Sourcebook.* New York: Greenwood Press, 1988.

Yeomans, Henry A. *Abbott Lawrence Lowell, 1856–1943.* Cambridge: Harvard University Press, 1948.

ARTICLES, CHAPTERS, AND REVIEWS

The periodical literature on Turner and his influence through 1982 is helpfully listed in Vernon E. Mattison and William E. Marion, *Frederick Jackson Turner: A Reference Guide* (see above). For the years thereafter see the bibliographical summaries of periodical literature in the *Journal of American History* and the references provided in the reference works and essay collections cited above. The following list notes contributions that I found particularly helpful.

Abbott, Carl. "Tracing the Trends in U.S. Regional History." *Perspectives* 28 (February 1990): 4–8.

Adams, Herbert B. "Special Methods of Historical Study, as Pursued at the Johns Hopkins University and Formerly Smith College." In *Methods of Teaching History,* 2nd ed., ed. G. Stanley Hall, 113–47. Boston: D.C. Heath, 1889.

———. "The Teaching of History." American Historical Association, *Annual Report,* 1896, vol. 1, 245–63. Washington, D.C.: 1897.

Allen, William F. "Gradation and the Topical Method of Historical Study." In *Methods of Teaching History*, 2nd ed., ed. G. Stanley Hall, pt. 3, 1–92. Boston: Ginn, Heath and Co. 1883.

———. "The Place of the Northwest in General History." American Historical Association, *Papers*, 1888, vol. 3, 331–48. New York: G. P. Putnam's Sons, 1889.

Almack, John C. "The Shibboleth of the Frontier." *Historical Outlook* 16 (May 1925): 197–202.

Alvord, Clarence W. (signed C.W.A.). "Review, *The Frontier in American History*." *Mississippi Valley Historical Review* 11 (March 1921): 403–7.

Baird, Carol F. "Albert Bushnell Hart: The Rise of the Professional Historian." In *Social Sciences at Harvard, 1860–1920: From Inculcation to the Open Mind*, ed. Paul Buck, 129–74. Cambridge: Harvard University Press, 1965.

Baldwin, James. "The Centre of the Republic." *Scribner's Magazine* 3 (April, May 1888): 409–19, 589–600.

Bassin, Mark. "Turner, Solov'ev and the 'Frontier Hypothesis': The Nationalist Signification of Open Spaces." *Journal of Modern History* 65 (September 1993): 473–51.

Becker, Carl L. "Detachment and the Writing of History." In *Detachment and the Writing of History: Essays and Letters of Carl L. Becker*, ed. Phil L. Snyder, 3–28. Ithaca: Cornell University Press, 1958.

———. "Frederick Jackson Turner." In *American Masters of Social Science: An Approach to the Study of the Social Sciences through a Neglected Field of Biography*, ed. Howard W. Odum, et al., 273–318. New York: Henry Holt and Company, 1927.

———. "Some Aspects of the Influence of Social Problems and Ideas upon the Study and Writing of History." *American Journal of Sociology* 18 (May 1913): 641–75.

Beckman, Alan C. "Hidden Themes in the Frontier Thesis: An Application of Psychoanalysis to Historiography." *Comparative Studies in Society and History* 8 (April 1966): 361–82.

Berkhofer, Robert F. "Space, Time, Culture and the New Frontier." *Agricultural History* 38 (January 1964): 21–30.

Berquist, Goodwin R., Jr. "The Rhetorical Heritage of Frederick Jackson Turner." *Transactions of the Wisconsin Academy of Sciences, Arts and Letters* 59 (1971): 23–32.

Berthrong, Donald J. "Andrew J. Turner, 'Work Horse' of the Republican Party." *Wisconsin Magazine of History* 38 (Winter 1954–55): 77–86.

Block, Robert H. "Frederick Jackson Turner and American Geography." *Annals of the Association of American Geographers* 70 (March 1980): 31–42.

Bogue, Allan G. "Frederick Jackson Turner Reconsidered." *History Teacher* 27 (February 1994): 195–221.

————. "The Iowa Claim Clubs: Symbol and Substance." *Mississippi Valley Historical Review* 45 (September 1958): 231–53.

————. "The Significance of the History of the American West." *Western Historical Quarterly* 25 (February 1992): 45–68.

————. "Social Theory and the Pioneer." *Agricultural History* 34 (January 1960): 21–34.

Boles, John B. "Turner, The Frontier, and the Study of Religion in America." *Journal of the Early Republic* 13 (Summer 1993): 205–30.

Bowman, Isaiah. "The Scientific Study of Settlement." *Geographical Review* 16 (October 1926): 647–53.

Brigham, Albert P. "Problems of Geographic Influence." *Science* (19 February 1915): 261–80.

Buck, Solon J. "Review, *The Significance of Sections in American History*." *Western Pennsylvania Historical Magazine* 16 (August 1933): 205.

Burr, George L. "The Place of Geography in the Teaching of History." New England History Teachers' Association, *Twenty-Second Meeting: Geography and History* 1–13. Boston: Ginn and Company, 1908.

Craven, Avery. "Frederick Jackson Turner." In *The Marcus W. Jernegan Essays in American Historiography*, ed. William T. Hutchinson, 252–70. Chicago: University of Chicago Press, 1937.

Cronon, William. "Revisiting the Vanishing Frontier: The Legacy of Frederick Jackson Turner." *Western Historical Quarterly* 18 (April 1987): 157–76.

————. "Turner's First Stand: The Significance of Significance in American History." In *Writing Western History: Essays on Major Western Historians*, ed. Richard Etulain, 73–101. Albuquerque: University of New Mexico Press, 1991.

Cronon, William, George Miles, and Jay Gitlin. "Becoming West: Toward a New Meaning for Western History." In *Under an Open*

Sky: Rethinking America's Western Past, 3–27. New York: W. W. Norton and Company, 1992.

Curti, Merle. "Review, *The Significance of Sections in American History.*" *American Journal of Sociology* 39 (September 1933): 265–66.

Dale, Edward E. "Memories of Frederick Jackson Turner." *Mississippi Valley Historical Review* 30 (December 1943): 339–58.

Davis. W. N., Jr. "Will the West Survive as a Field in American History? A Survey Report." *Mississippi Valley Historical Review* 50 (March 1954): 672–85.

Dippie, Brian. "American Wests: Historiographical Perspectives." In *Trails: Toward a New Western History*, ed. Patricia N. Limerick, Clyde A. Milner II, and Charles E. Rankin, 112–36. Lawrence: University Press of Kansas, 1991.

Dunning, William A. "A Generation of American Historiography." American Historical Association, *Annual Report*, 1917, 345–54. Washington, D.C., 1918.

"Editorial Comment: A Literary Club Symposium." *Wisconsin Magazine of History* 18 (September 1934): 85–97.

Elkins, Stanley, and Eric McKitrick. "A Meaning for Turner's Frontier: Part I: Democracy in the Old Northwest; Part II: The Southwest Frontier and New England." *Political Science Quarterly* 69 (September, December 1954): 321–53, 565–602.

Emerton, Ephraim, and Samuel E. Morison. "History, 1838–1929." In *Development of Harvard University, Since the Inauguration of President Eliot, 1869–1929*, ed. Samuel E. Morison, 150–77. Cambridge: Harvard University Press, 1930.

Faragher, John M. "The Frontier Trail: Rethinking Turner and Reimagining the American West." *American Historical Review* 98 (February 1993): 106–17.

————. "A Nation Thrown Back Upon Itself: Turner and the Frontier." *Culturefront* 2 (Summer 1993): 5–9, 75.

Farrand, Max. "Frederick Jackson Turner at the Huntington Library." *Huntington Library Bulletin* 3 (February 1933): 156–64.

Freund, Rudolph F. "Turner's Theory of Social Evolution." *Agricultural History* 19 (April 1945): 78–87.

Giddings, Franklin H. "The Nature and Conduct of Political Majorities." *Political Science Quarterly* 7 (March 1892): 116–32.

Godkin, Edwin L. "Aristocratic Opinions of Democracy." *North American Review* 206 (January 1865): 194–232.

Hacker, Louis M. "Frederick Jackson Turner: Non-Economic Historian."
    New Republic 83 (5 June 1935): 108.

————. "Review, *The Significance of Sections in American History.*"
    Nation 137 (26 July 1933): 108–10.

Hayes, Carlton J. H. "The American Frontier—Frontier of What?"
    American Historical Review 51 (January 1946): 199–216.

Hinton, Harwood P. "Frontier Speculation: A Study of the Walker Mining
    Districts." *Pacific Historical Review* 29 (August 1960): 245–55.

Hodder, Frank H. "Review, *The Significance of Sections in American
    History.*" *North Dakota Historical Quarterly* 7 (January/
    April 1933): 174–75.

Holt, W. Stull. "Historical Scholarship." In *American Scholarship in the
    Twentieth Century*, ed. Merle Curti, 83–110. Cambridge:
    Harvard University Press, 1953.

Holtgrieve, Donald G. "Frederick Jackson Turner as a Regionalist."
    Professional Geographer 26 (May 1974): 159–65.

Howe, Mark A. DeWolf. "Memoir of Frederick Jackson Turner." *Publica-
    tions of the Colonial Society of Massachusetts* 28 (April
    1933): 494–502.

Hoxie, Robert. "Sociology and the Other Social Sciences: A Rejoinder."
    American Journal of Sociology 12 (May 1907): 739–55.

Jacobs, Wilbur R. "Turner's Methodology: Multiple Working Hypotheses
    or Ruling Theory?" *Journal of American History* 54 (March
    1968): 853–63.

Jensen, Richard. "American Election Analysis: A Case History of Method-
    ological Innovation and Diffusion." In *Politics and the Social
    Sciences*, ed. Seymour M. Lipset, 226–43. New York: Oxford
    University Press, 1969.

————. "History and the Political Scientist." In *Politics and the Social
    Sciences*, ed. Seymour M. Lipset, 1–28. New York: Oxford
    University Press, 1969.

Johnson, Allen. "Review, *The Frontier in American History.*" *American
    Historical Review* 26 (April, 1921): 542–43.

Jones, J. E. "Miles Talcott Alverson." In *A History of Columbia County,
    Wisconsin: A Narrative Account of Its Historical Progress,
    Its People, and Its Principal Interests*. Chicago: Lewis Pub-
    lishing Company, 1914.

Kearns, Gerard. "Closed Space and Practical Practice: Frederick Jackson
    Turner and Halford MacKinder," (Environment and
    Planning D: *Society and Space*) 2, 1(1984): 23–34.

Kellogg, Louise P. "The Passing of a Great Teacher—Frederick Jackson Turner." *Historical Outlook* 23 (October 1932): 271–73.

Klein, Milton M. "Detachment and the Writing of American History: The Dilemma of Carl Becker." In *Perspectives on Early American History: Essays in Honor of Richard B. Morris*, ed. Alden T. Vaughan and George A. Billias, 120–66. New York: Harper and Row Publishers, 1973.

Kraus, Michael. "Review, *The Significance of Sections in American History*." *Historical Outlook* 24 (October 1933): 337.

Laski, Harold J. "Teacher and Student: The Technique of University Education." *Century Magazine* 117 (March 1929): 566–67.

Libby, Orin G. "A Plea for the Study of Votes in Congress." American Historical Association, *Annual Report*, 1896, vol. 1, 323–34. Washington, D.C.: 1897.

Limerick, Patricia N. "The Trail to Santa Fe: The Unleashing of the Western Public Intellectual." In *Trails: Toward a New Western History*, ed. Patricia N. Limerick, Clyde A. Milner II, and Charles E. Rankin, 59–77. Lawrence: University Press of Kansas, 1991.

———. "Turnerians All: The Dream of a Helpful History in an Intelligible World." *American Historical Review* 100 (June 1995): 697–716.

———. "What on Earth is the New Western History?" In *Trails: Toward a New Western History*, ed. Patricia N. Limerick, Clyde A. Milner II, and Charles E. Rankin, 81–88. Lawrence: University Press of Kansas, 1991.

Littlefield, Henry M. "Has the Safety Valve Come Back to Life?" *Agricultural History* 28 (January 1964): 47–49.

Lowell, A. Lawrence. "The Influence of Party upon Legislation in England and America." American Historical Association, *Annual Report*, vol. 1, 1901. Washington, D.C.: 1902.

Malin, James C. "The Turner-Mackinder Space Concept of History." *Essays on Historiography*, 1–44. Lawrence, Kans.: James C. Malin, 1946.

Malone, Michael P. "Beyond the Last Frontier: Toward a New Approach to Western American History." In *Trails: Toward a New Western History*, ed. Patricia N. Limerick, Clyde A. Milner II, and Charles E. Rankin, 139–60. Lawrence: University Press of Kansas, 1991.

———. "The 'New Western History': An Assessment." In *Trails: Toward a New Western History*, ed. Patricia N. Limerick, Clyde A.

Milner II, and Charles E. Rankin, 97–102. Lawrence: University Press of Kansas, 1991.

McBride, George M. "Review, *The Significance of Sections in American History.*" *Pacific Historical Review* 3, no. 4, (1933): 451–52.

Mood, Fulmer. "The Concept of the Frontier, 1871–1898: Comments on a Select List of Source Documents." *Agricultural History* 19 (January 1945): 24–30.

———. "The Development of Frederick Jackson Turner as a Historical Thinker." *Publications of the Colonial Society of Massachusetts: Transactions, 1937–1942* 34 (1943): 283–352.

———. "Frederick Jackson Turner and the Chicago *Inter-Ocean*, 1885." *Wisconsin Magazine of History* 35 (spring 1952): 188–94, 210–18.

———, "Frederick Jackson Turner and the Milwaukee *Sentinel*, 1884." *Wisconsin Magazine of History* 34 (fall 1950): 21–28.

———. "Notes on the History of the Word *Frontier*." *Agricultural History* 22 (April 1948): 78–83.

———. "The Origin, Evolution, and Application of the Sectional Concept, 1750–1900." In *Regionalism in America*, ed. Merrill Jensen, 5–98. Madison: University of Wisconsin Press, 1951.

———. "Review, *The United States: 1830–1850: The Nation and its Sections.*" *Wisconsin Magazine of History* 35 (Winter 1951): 149–50.

———. "Studies in the History of American Settled Areas and Frontier Lines: Settled Areas and Frontier Lines, 1625–1790." *Agricultural History* 26 (January 1952): 16–36.

———. "Turner's Formative Period." In *The Early Writings of Frederick Jackson Turner With a List of All His Works*, compiled by Everett E. Edwards, introduction by Fulmer Mood, 3–39. Madison: State Historical Society of Wisconsin, 1938.

Morison, Samuel E. "Edward Channing: A Memoir." In *By Land and by Sea: Essays and Addresses*, 299–329. New York: Alfred A. Knopf, 1953.

Nash, Gerald D. "One Hundred Years of Western History." *Journal of the West* 32 (January 1993): 3–4.

Nixon, Herman C. "Precursors of Turner in the Interpretation of the American Frontier." *South Atlantic Quarterly* 28 (January 1929): 83–89.

Nute, Grace L. "Frederick Jackson Turner." *Minnesota History* 13 (March 1932): 159–61.

Oliver, John W. "Twenty-Fourth Annual Meeting of the Mississippi Valley Historical Association." *Mississippi Valley Historical Review* 18 *(September 1931): 213–31.*

Pascoe, Peggy. "Western Women at the Cultural Crossroads." In *Trails: Toward a New Western History,* ed. Patricia N. Limerick, Clyde A. Milner II, and Charles E. Rankin, 40–58. Lawrence: University Press of Kansas, 1991.

Paxson, Frederic L. "A Generation of the Frontier Hypothesis: 1893–1932." *Pacific Historical Review* 2, no. 1 (1933): 34–51.

———. "Review, *The Significance of Sections in American History.*" *American Historical Review* 38 (July 1933): 773–74.

Phillips, Ulrich B. "The Traits and Contributions of Frederick Jackson Turner." *Agricultural History* 19 (January 1945): 21–23.

Pickens, Donald K. "The Turner Thesis and Republicanism: A Historiographical Commentary." *Pacific Historical Review* 61 (November 1992): 319–40.

Pierson, George W. "American Historians and the Frontier Hypothesis in 1941, " (I),(II). *Wisconsin Magazine of History* 26 (September, December 1942): 36–60, 170–85.

———. "The Frontier and American Institutions: A Criticism of the Turner Theory." *New England Quarterly* 15 (June 1942): 224–55.

Pomeroy, Earl. "Toward a Reorientation of Western History: Continuity and Environment." *Mississippi Valley Historical Review* 41 (March 1955): 579–600.

Ridge, Martin. "The American West: From Frontier to Region." *New Mexico Historical Review* 64 (April 1989): 125–41.

———. "Frederick Jackson Turner, 'The Significance of the Frontier in American History,' and the Gilded Age." *Hayes Historical Journal* 12 (fall 1992/winter 1993): 20–26.

———. "Introduction." *The Significance of the Frontier in American History,* by Frederick Jackson Turner, v–xiii. Silver Buckle Edition. Madison: State Historical Society of Wisconsin, 1984.

———. "A More Jealous Mistress: Frederick Jackson Turner as Book Reviewer." *Pacific Historical Review* 55 (February 1986): 49–63.

———. "Turner the Historian: A Long Shadow." *Journal of the Early Republic* 13 (summer 1993): 133–44.

Roach, Hannah G. "Sectionalism in Congress (1870–1890)." *American Political Science Review* 19 (August 1925). 500–526.

Robbins, William G. "Laying Siege to Western History: The Emergence of New Paradigms." In *Trails: Toward a New Western History*, ed. Patricia N. Limerick, Clyde A. Milner II, and Charles E. Rankin, 182–214. Lawrence: University Press of Kansas, 1991.

Robinson, Edgar E. "Frederick Jackson Turner." *North Dakota Historical Quarterly* 6, no. 4 (1933): 251–61.

Sauer, Carl O. "Historical Geography and the Western Frontier." In *The Trans-Mississippi West: Papers Read at a Conference Held at the University of Colorado, June 18–June 21, 1929*, ed. James F. Willard and Colin B. Goodykoontz, 267–89. Boulder: University of Colorado, 1930.

Schafer, Joseph. "The Author of the 'Frontier Hypothesis.'" *Wisconsin Magazine of History* 15 (September 1931): 86–103.

———. "Editorial Comment: Turner's America." *Wisconsin Magazine of History* 17 (June 1934): 447–65.

———. "Was the West a Safety Valve for Labor?" *Mississippi Valley Historical Review* 24 (December 1937): 299–314.

Shannon, Fred A. "A Post Mortem on the Labor-Safety-Valve Theory." *Agricultural History* 19 (January 1945): 31–37.

Steiner, Michael C. "Frederick Jackson Turner and Western Regionalism." In *Writing Western History: Essays on Major Western Historians*, ed. Richard Etulain, 103–35. Albuquerque: University of New Mexico Press, 1991.

———. "From Frontier to Region: Frederick Jackson Turner and the New Western History." *Pacific Historical Review* 64 (November 1995): 479–501.

Stephenson, George M. "Review, *The Significance of Sections in American History*." *Minnesota History* 14 (September 1933): 316–18.

Sparks, Edwin E. "Report of the Conference on the Relations of Geography to History." American Historical Association, *Report*, vol. 1, 1908, 57–61. Washington, D.C.: 1909.

Tyler, Lyon G. "Report of Conference on Research in Southern History." American Historical Association, *Report*, 1908, vol. 1, 131–43. Washington, D.C.: 1909.

Viles, Jonas. "Review, *The Significance of Sections in American History*." *Mississippi Valley Historical Review* 20 (March 1934): 579.

Von Nardroff, Ellen. "The American Frontier as Safety Valve: The Life, Death, Reincarnation, and Justification of a Theory." *Agricultural History* 36 (July 1962): 123–42.

White, Richard. "Trashing the Trails." In *Trails: Toward a New Western History*, ed. Patricia N. Limerick, Clyde A. Milner II, and Charles E. Rankin, 26–39. Lawrence: University Press of Kansas, 1991.

Williams, William A. "The Frontier Thesis: An American Foreign Policy." *Pacific Historical Review* 24 (November 1956): 379–95.

Wilson, Woodrow. "Remarks." American Historical Association, *Annual Report*, 1896, vol. 1, 292–96. Washington, D.C.: 1897.

Worster, Donald. "Beyond the Agrarian Myth." In *Trails: Toward a New Western History*, ed. Patricia N. Limerick, Clyde A. Milner II, and Charles E. Rankin, 3–25. Lawrence: University Press of Kansas, 1991.

Wright, Benjamin F., Jr. "American Democracy and the Frontier." *Yale Review* 22 (December 1930): 349–65.

———. "Review, *The Significance of Sections in American History*." *New England Quarterly* 6 (September 1933): 630–34.

Wright, John K. "Daniel Coit Gilman, Geographer and Historian." *Geographical Review* 51 (July 1961): 381–99.

———. "Sections and National Growth: *An Atlas of the Historical Geography of the United States*." *Geographical Review* 22 (July 1932): 353–60.

———. "Voting Habits in the United States: A Note on Two Maps." *Geographical Review* 22 (October 1932): 666–72.

Index

References to illustrations are in italic type.

Abel, Annie H., 202
Abernethy, Thomas P., 392, 400
Academic professionalism, 147
ACLS. *See* American Council of Learned Societies
Adams, Charles Francis, 162, 246
Adams, Charles Kendall, 71, 73, 91, 98, 99; athletics, promotion of, 164; and growth of University of Wisconsin, 127, 156, 163; illness, 164; Libby, Orin G., and, 172; Turner's evaluation of, 153; and Turner's negotiations with Chicago, 159, 164; and Wisconsin history department, 156, 164; Wisconsin's schools and colleges, relations between, 179
Adams, Ephraim D., 251
Adams, Henry, 129, 204, 266, 271
Adams, Herbert Baxter, 39, 44, 46, 47, 48, 50, 59, 67, 101, 145–46; and AHA, 180; geography, for history students, 135; graduate seminars, 46, 53, 356;

landholding systems, study of, 107; Turner's citing of, in 1893 paper, 99; and Turner's dissertation topic, 44, 45, 55, 358–59; and Turner's frontier hypothesis, 420; and Turner's "Problems in American History," 84, 91; Turner's relationship with, 72; and Turner's "The Significance of History," 79, 80, 81
Adams, John Quincy, 212
Adams, Mary Mathews, 120
"Address on Behalf of the University Faculty" (1904), 200
Adelbert University, 156
Adelphian Literary Society, 19, 26
Aegis, 82, 83, 171, 356, 357, 358
Agricultural history, 205, 230, 266, 359–60; gender issues in, 378
Agricultural History Society, 359–60
Agriculture, United States Department of, 137, 359
AHA. *See* American Historical Association
Alden, George H., 123, 169

Allen, William Francis, 21–24, 26, 54, 55; death of, 57; geography, history and, 134; Harvard reunion, 34; institutional history, 53, 77; "Place of the Northwest in General History, The," 48; survival concept, 114; Turner influenced by, 46, 106, 111, 356, 420, 421, 424, 450–51; and Turner's appointment to Johns Hopkins, 40, 42, 45; and Turner's book reviews, 37; and Turner's history instructorship, 38, 39; and Turner's master's thesis, 36; and Turner's Northwest history syllabus, 37; and Turner's professorship at Wisconsin, 50, 51, 52; Turner's substitution for, 31, 41
Almack, John C., 418
Alverson, Charley, 16
Alvord, Clarence W., 354–55
Ambler, Charles H., 230, 233, 242; and AHA controversy, 318–19; Turner's festschrift, contribution to, 272